Dictionary of
Business and
Economics

Dictionary of Business and Economics

Christine Ammer
Dean S. Ammer

THE FREE PRESS
A Division of Macmillan Publishing Co., Inc.
NEW YORK

Collier Macmillan Publishers
LONDON

The Free Press
A Division of Macmillan Publishing Co., Inc.
866 Third Avenue, New York, N.Y. 10022

Collier Macmillan Canada, Ltd.

Library of Congress Catalog Card Number: 76-41625

Printed in the United States of America

printing number
  2 3 4 5 6 7 8 9 10

Library of Congress Cataloging in Publication Data
Ammer, Christine.
   Dictionary of business and economics.
   Bibliography: p.
   1. Economics—Dictionaries.   2. Business—
Dictionaries.   I. Ammer, Dean S., joint author.
II. Title.
HB61.A53   330′.03   76-41625
ISBN 0-02-900590-6

For Karen, John, and David

The Authors

CHRISTINE AMMER (B.A., Swarthmore College) is a lexicographer with wide experience in writing and editing encyclopedias and other popular reference works. She is the author of *Musician's Handbook of Foreign Terms* (1971) and *Harper's Dictionary of Music* (1972).

DEAN S. AMMER (M.B.A., Ph.D., economics, New York University) is Research Professor and Director of the Bureau of Business and Economic Research at Northeastern University. For many years economics editor of *Purchasing* magazine, he has served as consultant to many corporations and frequently presents seminars and lectures to the business community in the United States and abroad. Author of *Materials Management,* 3d ed. (1974), *Production Management and Control* (1972), and *Purchasing and Materials Management in Health Care Institutions* (1975), and editor of *Readings and Cases in Economics* (1966), Professor Ammer has also published more than two hundred articles and monographs.

Preface

The entries in this dictionary cover an extraordinarily broad range, from economic theory of the past and present to its numerous applications in the world of business firms and consumers, from price and income theory to real estate, insurance, business law, and accounting, from public finance and labor economics to the world of the small investor. Biographies of the most important economists are included, but emphasis is on their ideas rather than their lives. Charts are used to cover material on relevant legislation—antitrust laws, labor laws, consumer-protection laws—as well as historical material, such as American tariff policies and strikes. Graphs and tables illustrate the basic statistical concepts used not only by academicians but by modern business managers.

Despite the breadth of coverage, every effort has been made to present material simply and clearly enough for the general reader as well as for the student of business management and/or economics. For this reason, comparatively difficult concepts, such as the theories of John Maynard Keynes, have been given more space than equally important but simpler ideas; the space allotted reflects only the practical considerations of adequate explanation.

The terms in the dictionary, whether they consist of one word or of several words, are listed in strict alphabetical order, letter by letter, up to the comma in case of inversion. When a numeral is part of a term, as in "M-1" or "W-2 form," the term is alphabetized as though the numeral were spelled out (M-one, W-two). Identical terms with different meanings are defined under a single heading in a series of numbered definitions. Terms mentioned in one entry but further explained in another, where the reader is advised to seek them out, are printed in large and small capital letters, as, for example, INDUSTRIAL REVOLUTION or INTEREST RATE.

We are deeply grateful to the many experts and friends who have answered questions and made invaluable suggestions, criticisms, and corrections. Among those who merit special thanks are Samuel Berman, Vice-President, Berman's Motor Express, Inc.; Dean W. Egly, Vice-President, Morgan Guaranty Trust Company; Michael G. Gero, Data Processing Manager, Sidney Farber Cancer Center; Earl W. Johnson, Bureau of Consumer Protection, Federal Trade Commission; Barry E. Loughrane, Managing Director, Gardner Advertising Company; Lamont L. Reese, U.S. Commodities Futures Trading Commission; S. James Rosenfeld, U.S. Securities and Exchange Commission; Dr. Paul N. Van de Water, Office of Income Security, Department of Health, Education, and Welfare; Professor Charles Dufton; Professor Carlo Gubellini; and Professor Edward R. Willett. This book has been vastly improved through their assistance; its errors and shortcomings are wholly our own responsibility.

Dictionary of Business and Economics

A

abandonment

1. In law, the relinquishment of property (personal or real) that one no longer wants, thereby waiving all rights to it. Since abandoned property is owned by no one, the first person to take possession of it acquires title to it. However, the party who claims such title must prove that the former owner intentionally relinquished his or her rights on a permanent basis. For a tenant's abandonment, see under LEASE.

2. In insurance, the practice of turning damaged property over to the insurer and claiming its full value. The property is then said to be "abandoned" to the insurer. Originating in marine insurance, where a ship piled up on shoals was sometimes abandoned to the marine underwriters, this practice is sometimes referred to in present-day property insurance policies (fire, automobile, etc.), which usually specify that the property in question may *not* be abandoned to the insurer.

3. In transportation, the refusal of a shipment by a consignee (the person authorized to accept a shipment) because of damage. Responsibility for the value of the goods then rests with the carrier.

ABC control   Also, *selective inventory control.* A system of inventory control in which every item carried in stock is assigned a rating of A, B, or C, according to its costliness, with the twofold aim of reducing capital investment in inventories and lessening the likelihood of running out of low-cost but important items needed for production. All items used in production, ranging from expensive machine parts to nuts and bolts, are listed in order of their cost for a given period (for example, the number of items used during one week multiplied by their unit cost). The most expensive items, constituting perhaps 10 per cent of the period's outlay,

are classed A; the next most expensive, comprising an additional 20 per cent of the period's expenditures, are classed B; all others are classed C. Since they represent a high investment, inventories of A items are kept as low as possible; inventories of B items are also kept low, but with a slightly greater safety margin against depletion; and inventories of C items are much larger and less closely controlled. In addition to reducing capital investment in stocks, the ABC system saves clerical costs (stock checking is reduced, since only A and B items require close control) and enables a company to take advantage of discounts for large-volume purchases of inexpensive supplies. However, large stocks of bulky C items (shipping containers, for example) can offset this gain somewhat by increasing storage costs.

ability-to-pay principle   The principle that tax assessments should be based on the taxpayer's ability to pay taxes, so that the rich pay more than the poor. This principle encompasses the idea of *horizontal equity*—that those with equal ability should be taxed equally—as well as that of *vertical equity* —different tax burdens for people with different abilities. Any PROGRESSIVE TAX, such as the U.S. Federal income tax and many state income and inheritance taxes, is based on ability to pay, being so designed that the wealthy pay higher taxes. Although in theory this principle is fairer than the imposition of a uniform tax rate on all income groups, in practice its fairness depends on how ability to pay is determined. One approach makes individual *income* the sole criterion, and some of its proponents also hold that since all taxes ultimately fall on the individual, individual income tax should be the only tax levied. Another approach considers *wealth* the measure of ability to pay. Still another approach

1

makes consumption, or expenditure, the criterion, making a *consumption tax* the only tariff and not taxing that portion of income that is saved. See also BENEFITS-RECEIVED PRINCIPLE.

absenteeism The absence of employees from work with more than normal frequency. On a large scale, it usually represents an expression of worker dissatisfaction and can be costly in terms of lowered output.

absentee ownership The ownership of capital, such as land or factories, by one or more persons living away from their property and employing others to manage and work it for them. Traditionally the absentee owner was a landlord who profited from the income of an estate or plantation. This practice, dating at least as far back as the Middle Ages, was still common in 19th-century Great Britain (notably in Ireland, where much land was owned by the English) and Russia, where many landowners preferred city life to their remote country estates. Since the absentee owner's interests generally differ from those of the local community, they often clash, at times violently. Whereas the owner seeks the largest possible profit from his holdings, the community tends to maintain that the revenues belong to those who live and work on the land. In Latin America, Africa, and other places with a long history of colonialism—itself a form of absentee ownership—such clashes still occur, though increasingly they are resolved through a peaceful government takeover of the property in question.

The role of the large-scale investor in an industrial enterprise resembles that of the absentee landlord's, and a similar conflict of interest may exist. Although here bloodshed or revolution are rare, the owner's remoteness may result in employee apathy, and his emphasis on pure profit may stifle growth and defer improvements and innovations. See also TECHNOSTRUCTURE.

absolute advantage See under ADVANTAGE.

absorption See FREIGHT ABSORPTION.

absorption costing In accounting, assigning all the fixed and variable costs of a business to the goods or services produced, without distinguishing between them. It is the opposite of *direct costing*, where direct, variable costs are distinguished from fixed costs and general expenses on the assumption that the former are a more valid basis for valuing output.

abstinence theory of interest Also, *agio theory of interest*. The idea that interest on savings is a reward for abstinence (that is, not spending). For example, the interest on a savings account is considered a reward for banking money instead of spending it on goods such as a new automobile. This theory, developed by BÖHM-BAWERK, SENIOR, and other 19th-century economists, assumes that people prefer to buy goods or services as soon as they can afford them and must therefore be induced to put off spending. Accordingly, it follows that the INTEREST RATE rather than the individual's income will determine how much he will save and how much he will spend. Though this idea may have some validity, in practice most decisions concerning spending or saving depend on a variety of factors, of which the interest rate is but one.

abstract of title A written document used to determine the ownership of a particular parcel of land. It summarizes the material portions of every DEED and other transaction that affect the title of that land, thus representing a history of its ownership. In the United States all abstracts of title are taken from the public records. An abstract is usually prepared by an attorney, a public official, or a firm specializing in this work.

accelerated depreciation Any method of calculating depreciation of a fixed asset whereby more depreciation is charged to the early years of its service life than to the later years. Most commonly used are the SUM-OF-DIGITS METHOD and the DECLINING-BALANCE METHOD. The chief advantage of accelerated depreciation lies in its ability to help a company recoup far more of its investment at an early stage, both because of smaller taxable income (since depreciation is tax-deductible) and through the availability of interest-free funds that would otherwise be used for tax payments. The total amount of taxes and of depreciation remains the same; only the time of payment changes.

accelerating premium See under WAGE INCENTIVE.

acceleration principle Also, *accelerator effect.* The idea that an increase in demand for consumer goods (food, clothing, furniture, etc.) produces a far greater increase in the demand for and production of capital goods (food-processing equipment, looms, lathes, etc.). For example, a 10 per cent increase in demand for television sets may result in a 100 per cent increase in equipment needed to manufacture the sets. Suppose that the standard demand for TV sets from a given factory has been 1,000 sets per year, and it has been filled by 500 "units" of capital equipment (factory space, machinery, etc.). Of the 500 units, 50 have had to be replaced every year (worn-out machine parts, depleted supplies, etc.). If demand for the sets now rises by 10 per cent to 1,100 per year, an additional 50 units of capital equipment will be needed to meet that demand (if 500 units produce 1,000 sets, 50 more units will produce an additional 100 sets). Thus, in addition to the 50 units already being replaced, another 50 will have to be acquired. In this way, a 10 per cent rise in demand for a consumer product has created a 100 per cent rise in demand for capital goods. Naturally, the accelerator effect operates only when the facility involved is already working at full capacity (that is, the most the factory can produce with present equipment is 1,000 sets per year), and when it uses capital goods that require regular replacement. If it is not working at full capacity, the factory obviously can produce more sets without additional equipment; if it need not replace some goods and equipment each year, the new demand may be absorbed during a year when little or nothing needs replacement.

Formulated by J. M. CLARK in 1917, the acceleration principle accounts for the frequent booms and recessions in the capital-goods industries. Only when consumer demand continues to rise at an ever faster rate does the demand for capital goods continue to increase. If, in the year after the initial rise in demand for TV sets, demand again rises by another 100 sets, to 1,200, only 5 additional units of capital will be required to meet demand (55 units to replace, plus 50 additional units needed). If demand remains constant (1,100 sets), the demand for capital goods will drop sharply, since only 55 units

would be needed (to replace 55 worn out or used up), as opposed to the 100 needed the previous year.

Acceptable Quality Level Also, *AQL.* In QUALITY CONTROL, the degree of deviation from a given standard that will be permitted. For example, an Acceptable Quality Level of .98 indicates that a buyer will accept a shipment of merchandise in which 2 per cent of the items do not meet the specifications set down in the purchase contract.

acceptance

1. Another name for BILL OF EXCHANGE.

2. *bankers' acceptance.* A common way of financing foreign trade when buyer and seller are unknown to each other, in which a bank accepts the obligation to pay the seller if the buyer defaults. For example, an American importer who wants to buy from a German exporter may take out a negotiable bank note from a U.S. bank that has well-established branches in Europe to cover the cost of the goods, usually for 90 days. The BILL OF EXCHANGE is presented to the bank, which stamps "accepted" on it (hence the name). The exporter presents the acceptance to its German bank and receives immediate payment, minus a discount for handling the paper. The German bank sends the acceptance, with shipping documents attached, to its correspondent bank in the United States, instructing it to take one of three actions: (1) hold the acceptance as an investment; (2) sell it to a third party through a dealer; (3) sell it back to the American bank that originally issued it. If the acceptance is resold to the issuing bank, that bank can either hold it until it comes due or sell it in the secondary market to a dealer or another bank. Bankers' acceptances are highly negotiable instruments freely traded in the MONEY MARKET. Moreover, many investors consider them to be as safe as deposits in the most reputable bank, and as a result their yield is close to the interest rate offered on large certificates of deposit by major American banks. Also, *banker's acceptance, bank acceptance.*

3. *trade acceptance.* See under BILL OF EXCHANGE.

4. In business law, the assent to the terms of an offer, required before a CONTRACT can be valid. It must be absolute and unconditional (otherwise, it is

4 / ACCEPTANCE BANK

not an acceptance but a *counteroffer*), may be tendered only by the person to whom the offer is directed, and must conform to any conditions concerning it that are set forth in the offer.

acceptance bank   Also, Brit., *accepting house*. An organization that specializes in accepting or guaranteeing domestic and foreign bills of exchange, more common in Europe than in the United States. Most modern acceptance banks have branched out into other activities as well and thus resemble a MERCHANT BANK.

acceptance sampling   In quality control, a process of sampling that forms the basis for accepting or rejecting a product. For example, an inspector might inspect 10 items from every lot of 200. From the number of defects found, the number of defects in the entire shipment can, by statistical inference, be estimated. See also ACCEPTABLE QUALITY LEVEL.

accession rate   Also, *hiring rate*. The number of employees added to the payroll during a given period, an important LEADING INDICATOR of future business conditions. A decrease in hiring may indicate a coming recession; an increase usually heralds the end of a recession. As business improves, companies initially tend to postpone hiring, in order to avoid future layoffs, but eventually they do begin to add personnel. Statistics on the accession rate of manufacturing establishments, expressed as a percentage of total employment, are compiled monthly by the U.S. Department of Labor.

access time   See under STORAGE, def. 1.

accident insurance   See HEALTH INSURANCE; LIABILITY INSURANCE; WORKMEN'S COMPENSATION.

accommodation endorsement   The endorsement of a note, bill, or other instrument of credit by one person to another, who is then able to obtain the loan. In effect, the endorser is accommodating the other person by lending his or her credit, and thus becomes a *guarantor* of the loan, agreeing to take on all or part of the responsibility for its repayment.

account
1. In accounting, a formal record of business transactions, expressed in terms of money and entered in a book called a *ledger*. It is nearly always arranged in terms of debits, entered on the left side, and credits, entered on the right, in order to provide a quick summary of the net result of all transactions. Obtaining this result simply involves adding up all the debits and all the credits, and subtracting one from the other to "secure the *balance*." The simplest kind of account is sometimes called a *T-account*, since its format resembles the letter T.

In recording the transactions of a business, a separate account is used for each ASSET (cash, notes receivable, inventory, etc.), each LIABILITY (notes payable, accounts payable, etc.), and each proprietorship or capital item (capital invested, money drawn for owner's wages, etc.) for which a separate record is required. Each account is given its own page or group of pages in the company ledger. Whether a transaction represents a credit or debit depends on the account it is entered in. For example, suppose Mary Smith invests $100,000 in her new drugstore. For the cash account of this business, the $100,000 represents a debit; for the Smith capital account, it represents a credit. (See also DOUBLE ENTRY.) The various accounts of assets and liabilities that are summarized to make up a firm's periodic BALANCE SHEET or FINANCIAL STATEMENT are called *real accounts* (or *balance-sheet accounts*), whereas those in the names of particular customers or suppliers and used to make up the firm's INCOME STATEMENT are called *nominal accounts*. The former are carried forward from one fiscal period to another, whereas the latter represent completed transactions for a particular period (usually an entire fiscal year). See also CONTRA ACCOUNT; OPEN ACCOUNT; SUSPENSE ACCOUNT.
2. *bank account*. Credit established under a particular name, usually by deposit, against which withdrawals may be made and which may or may not earn interest. The most common types of bank account are the CHECKING ACCOUNT, from which withdrawals may be made at any time, and the *time account*, on which due notice must be given before making a withdrawal. A *joint account* is opened in

the names of two or more persons jointly; in some instances, withdrawals must be signed by all the joint depositors, but more commonly withdrawals can be made by a single depositor alone. A *number account* is identified solely by a number instead of a name. Frequently held in Swiss banks, number accounts are used to conceal bank deposits, for tax evasion or other reasons.

3. In general business terminology, a particular client or customer. Thus, a given individual or firm is said to represent a brokerage account (business with a broker), advertising account, etc.

accountant A person trained in ACCOUNTING (def. 1), who may either be employed by a firm or work independently. See also CERTIFIED PUBLIC ACCOUNTANT; PUBLIC ACCOUNTANT.

account balance See *balance* under ACCOUNT, def. 1.

account executive In advertising, public relations, brokerage, investment counseling, and similar service industries, the person in direct contact with one or more of the firm's clients. The account executive passes on the client's ideas to others in the firm and presents the results of the firm's work to the client. See also REGISTERED REPRESENTATIVE.

accounting
1. The recording and summarizing of business transactions, and the interpretation of their effects on a business enterprise or other economic unit. Accounting embraces BOOKKEEPING, which involves primarily the recording of transactions, as well as auditing (see AUDIT), the design and installation of an accounting system, tax services, COST ACCOUNTING, and budgeting (the advance planning of business transactions).
2. A formal report of an economic unit's transactions during a given period, presented by an individual or firm charged with responsibility for the assets of that unit. Such accountings are generally required of agents who manage property for others, as well as executors of wills, trustees of property, guardians, etc.

accounting period A specific period of time for which an operating statement is normally prepared.

The most common such period is one month, but companies also may use 4 weeks, yearly quarters, 26 weeks, 48 weeks, 52 weeks, or any other time period of their choice. See also FISCAL YEAR.

accounts payable The amount owed by a business to its suppliers and other regular trading partners, who generally give customers anywhere from 10 to 90 days to pay for merchandise already shipped. Normally the classification of accounts payable is confined to the amounts owing for goods and services bought in everyday transactions and does not include long-term obligations. On the balance sheet, accounts payable are classed as current liabilities. See also ACCOUNTS RECEIVABLE; NOTES PAYABLE.

accounts receivable The amount owed to a business by its customers, who are customarily granted anywhere from 10 to 90 days to pay for merchandise already shipped. Normally the classification of accounts receivable is confined to debts incurred in everyday transactions and does not include accruals, deposits, or other long-term credit. On the balance sheet, accounts receivable are classed as current assets. However, they are not always automatically converted into cash since not every debtor pays his bills. Therefore, almost all companies deduct an allowance for bad debts from their receivables. See also ACCOUNTS PAYABLE; NOTES RECEIVABLE.

accounts receivable financing The use of money owed to a firm (see ACCOUNTS RECEIVABLE) to obtain funds for current operating expenses or other purposes. The accounts receivable either are used as collateral for a loan or are sold outright; the latter method is called *factoring*. Though accounts receivable financing may involve a relatively high rate of interest, it can be a convenience to small firms that have difficulty getting cheaper kinds of loan, as well as to any firms whose sales volume fluctuates considerably—seasonally or otherwise —since it enables them to increase or decrease borrowing accordingly.

accrual basis In accounting, a system of charging income and expenses to the period in which they are earned or incurred rather than to the period in which they are actually received or paid. Corporations almost always keep their books on an accrual basis to avoid a misleading INCOME STATEMENT. Individuals or very small firms, on the other hand, usually keep their books (and tax returns) on a cash basis because it greatly simplifies bookkeeping (see CASH BASIS).

accrued Describing earnings, sales, expenses, or other items of income or outlay that have been made or incurred but not yet received or paid. An *accrued dividend* is that part of a dividend earned since the last regular dividend payment but not yet paid out; similarly, *accrued interest* is the interest earned on a bond since the last regular payment (see also FLAT, def. 1). *Accrued income* is income earned during a particular accounting period but not actually received during that period (sales commissions, interest, rent, etc.); an *accrued liability* is one that has been incurred but not yet paid (wages, taxes, interest, etc.; see also LIABILITY, def. 1).

acid test See QUICK RATIO.

acquisition
   1. See under MERGER.
   2. *cost of acquisition.* A business's total cost of buying materials. It includes salaries and overhead in the purchasing department; expediting, receiving, and paying for the material; transportation between plants and within a plant; packaging; and miscellaneous associated expenses. The cost of acquisition must always be taken into account in determining an ECONOMIC ORDER QUANTITY.

acquittance A written acknowledgment that a debt or other financial obligation has been discharged, or paid in full.

acreage allotment See under AGRICULTURE, AID TO.

action In law, any proceeding instituted by one party against another. A *civil action* is one brought by a plaintiff against a defendant from whom he or she seeks redress; a *criminal action* is one brought by a government to punish or prevent an offense against public law or order. An action may begin

with the plaintiff filing an order with a court to issue a *writ of summons* to the sheriff, who in turn would inform the defendant to appear in court at a particular time. An action may also begin when the plaintiff files with a court a *complaint* stating the facts of the issue at hand; a copy of the complaint is then served on the defendant. Whatever the method, the defendant must be notified that an action is pending against him or her; this is called "serving with process," the "process" being the writ, summons, or notice. If the defendant does not respond to the process, the plaintiff usually wins the case by default. Most often, however, the defendant contests the suit, so the issue between the two parties must be formulated by the pleadings. The plaintiff must then file a written complaint (if this has not yet been done), to which the defendant must file an *answer*, either admitting or denying the facts of the complaint as stated by the plaintiff. In some instances the defendant may assert a *counterclaim* or *cross complaint* against the plaintiff. For example, if the plaintiff charges that the defendant did not pay for a TV set she purchased, the defendant might file a counterclaim that the plaintiff's truck damaged her driveway while delivering the set. If the questions raised by the pleadings are solely questions of law, the court will decide the case on the pleadings alone. For example, if the question hinges on whether or not a particular letter, admittedly written by the defendant, constituted an acceptance of the plaintiff's offer, the court may decide whether or not this letter did amount to a legal contract. On the other hand, if the defendant denies having written a letter that clearly would be a legal acceptance, the question is one not of law but of fact, and there must be a trial to determine the actual facts.

active market See HEAVY MARKET.

actuary
   1. A mathematician employed by an insurance company to calculate the premiums for different kinds of insurance on the basis of statistics and probability theory—that is, the calculated probable duration of a client's life, or the calculated probability of an accident, robbery, flood, or other relevant event. Actuaries are highly skilled mathematicians, with advanced training in logical analysis and prob-

lem-solving techniques. In the United States the Society of Actuaries has established standards of excellence through a series of examinations; it awards the degrees of associate and fellow to successful examinees.

2. A mathematician employed by a business firm to determine the probable life of its plant, machinery, and other assets, using methods similar to those of the insurance actuary (see def. 1).

additional extended coverage   See chart under PROPERTY INSURANCE (Fig. 69).

add-on contract   See INSTALLMENT BUYING.

adjuster   In insurance, a representative of the insurance company who determines the cause and amount of a loss and the company's liability. Adjusters may be salaried employees of the company or they may work independently, adjusting losses for whatever firm hires them. They also may work for an *adjustment bureau*, an organization owned and operated by an association of insurance firms who thereby pool their claim-adjustment work. In contrast to this kind of adjuster, who represents the insurer, is a *public adjuster*, who does the same work, but on behalf of the claimant.

adjusting entry   In accounting, an entry made to correct or offset an error, accrual, writeoff, deferment, etc.

administered price   Also, *managed price*. A price set by the seller but not totally under the seller's control. It is based on the seller's judgment both of demand for a product at various prices and of competitors' probable prices for the same or similar products, taking into account cost of production and the greatest possible profit. A seller may restrict its own output to keep prices high, yet it cannot charge too much lest customers turn to competitors. An administered price, which lies midway between a monopoly price and a free-market price, exists in a market characterized by IMPERFECT COMPETITION. In general, administered prices yield a profit higher than would accrue under pure competition but lower than with a monopoly. In practice, the range of administered prices is fairly broad. At one extreme, where suppliers are numerous,

prices come close to those under pure competition; at the other extreme, where producers are few, prices are virtually the same as with a monopoly (see OLIGOPOLY). The principal means of increasing profits (moving from the low end of the range to the high) involves reducing competition through advertising and product differentiation. The producer of a breakfast cereal, for example, must take into account the prices set by other cereal manufacturers, and if there are many of them, profits may remain quite modest. On the other hand, if a firm can convince the public through advertising that its product has special properties making it superior to any other, its profits may increase; further, if it can change its product to make it in fact unique, it may achieve a monopoly and set its price accordingly.

administrator

1. In business, a person who directs, coordinates, or controls the activities of subordinates.

2. In law, a person appointed by a court to settle the estate of someone who died without writing a will or without designating an executor.

admission temporaire   See under FREE PORT.

ADR   Abbreviation for AMERICAN DEPOSITARY RECEIPT.

ad valorem   A customs duty or TARIFF that is based on the value of the goods involved. It generally consists of a fixed percentage of, for example, the wholesale price of the item, instead of a fixed amount per unit, ounce, or some other measure. For example, the ad valorem tax on men's woolen trousers is usually set at 25 per cent; thus, if an importer pays $10 for a pair of trousers made in Italy, it must pay a duty of $2.50 per pair, making the total cost $12.50. The opposite of an ad valorem tariff is a *specific tariff*, such as $1 per bottle for champagne, or 10 cents per yard for woolen yard goods. Occasionally both a specific and an ad valorem tariff, a so-called *compound tariff*, are levied on a single item.

The terms *ad valorem* and *specific* also are used for other kinds of tax; among examples of the former are real estate and excise taxes, based on a fixed percentage of the property value or selling price.

advance

1. Any payment made before it falls due, thus representing a loan. For example, authors frequently receive advance payments against future royalties to help them meet expenses while finishing a manuscript.

2. In British terminology, any loan, such as a bank loan.

3. One method whereby a member bank may borrow from its Federal Reserve Bank, that is, by giving its own promissory note, secured by government securities or other satisfactory collateral.

4. In finance, a general rise in market prices.

advance bill An INVOICE submitted before the goods or services itemized therein have actually been delivered or performed. It is usually requested by buyers for tax purposes or some similar reason.

advance refunding An opportunity for holders of bonds due to expire soon to exchange them for new bonds on particularly favorable terms. Used principally by the U.S. Treasury to keep its long-time bondholders from switching to other securities, advance refunding helps lengthen the average maturity of the PUBLIC DEBT without disturbing the general market for capital.

advantage The ability of one nation, region, or supplier to produce a good or service at a lower cost (with less labor, or less land, or less machinery) than others. A producer who makes a single item more cheaply than practically any other is said to have an *absolute advantage*. For example, the Swiss long enjoyed an absolute advantage in the manufacture of fine watches. Despite high wages, they perfected production to such an extent that most other nations found it more advantageous to buy Swiss watches than make their own. With most goods, however, the possible advantage is less clear-cut; the Swiss also made fine cotton handkerchiefs but never had the same advantage as in watch manufacture. The ability to produce a particular good or service more cheaply than some other good or service is called *comparative advantage* (or the principle of *comparative costs*). The so-called *paradox* of comparative advantage was first stated by the 19th-century British economist David RICARDO. In Ricardo's classic example, both England and Portugal could produce wine and tex-

tiles. However, it cost England 120 hours of labor per unit of wine and 100 hours of labor per unit of cloth, whereas Portugal spent only 80 hours of labor per unit of wine and 90 hours per unit of cloth. Ricardo concluded that Portugal should concentrate entirely on wine making, in which it had an advantage of 80 vs. 120 over England, and import cloth from England, since its advantage there was only 90 vs. 100. Without such trading between the two nations, a Portuguese wine producer could obtain only 8/9 unit of Portuguese cloth for 1 unit of wine; with trade, it could obtain 1.2 units of English textiles for 1 unit of wine. Though traditionally associated with international trade, the principle of comparative advantage applies equally to the MAKE OR BUY decisions faced by many business firms, which involve the same kinds of cost comparison.

advertised bidding The practice of publicly obtaining bids for contracts for goods or services, in the United States widely followed in local, state, and Federal government procurement but rarely by private business. Advertised bidding requires highly detailed SPECIFICATIONS, which cannot be restrictive (as for a brand name or patented item) and which must be published. Invitations are sent to all qualified bidders known to the buyer, and also are posted in public places and advertised in newspapers and other media. A specific place, date, and hour are set for opening the bids. The bids are recorded on an *abstract of bids* that is later made available for public inspection. Normally no bidder may withdraw a bid once it is made, nor may the lowest bidder later refuse to honor it. Indeed, the lowest bidder, to whom the contract is invariably awarded provided it is a regular dealer or producer of the item in question, is legally bound to fulfill the precise conditions of the contract. Though advertised bidding is the fairest available procedure, particularly to bidders, it is both expensive and slow. Instead of soliciting bids from a few competing suppliers, one must evaluate the bids of perhaps several hundred. The specifications must be so detailed as to leave no margin for error. Further, apart from price, the lowest bidder may not be the ideal supplier in terms of reliability, quality, or other criteria.

advertising Placing paid public presentations or announcements about products, services, or activities, with the objective of persuading the public to buy particular goods or services or to accept a given point of view or concept. The person or institution paying for such announcements is called the *advertiser* or *sponsor*, and the means of presenting it are collectively known as the *media*. The principal advertising media are newspapers (both national and local, and including CLASSIFIED ADVERTISING), radio and television (network and local), magazines, trade publications (particularly those directed to business, industry, and farmers), outdoor advertising (billboards, signs, posters, etc., in prominent locations on highways, buildings, etc.), and DIRECT-MAIL ADVERTISING. An individual announcement is called an *advertisement*, or *ad*; if presented on radio or television it is also called a *commercial*. Though some advertising is placed by nonprofit organizations, including branches of the government (recruiting for the armed forces, for example), by far the major portion of advertising in the United States is sponsored by private business and industry. Such advertising takes two forms: *product advertising*, aimed at selling a product, and *institutional advertising*, aimed at enhancing the name and reputation of a company (and by extension, its products or services). Either kind of advertising may be local or national or both, depending on the market sought. *Local advertising* is addressed to a neighborhood, town, or other locality, through local newspapers, local radio and television stations or programs, billboards and posters, and direct-mail announcements. It may be sponsored by a local retailer or distributor, or by a large manufacturer on behalf of a local dealer. *National advertising* is addressed to the entire country, through publications circulated nationally and via network radio and television.

Some businesses handle their own advertising entirely through an *advertising* (or *promotion*) *department*. Others use an *advertising agency*, a firm that specializes in creating and placing ads for others, as well as performing a variety of services: planning a coordinated advertising program, or *campaign*; conducting MARKET RESEARCH; recommending packaging, sales promotion, and styling; preparing all kinds of ad, from printed announcements or posters to entire radio or television programs; and selecting the media. (See also MODULAR ADVERTISING.) Agencies usually are paid on a percentage basis, generally 15 per cent of the cost of time and space purchased in the media, but some-

times they work for a fixed fee. (See also ADVERTISING RATES.) In the early 1970s there were 4,800 advertising agencies in the United States, located mostly in Chicago and New York City, and employing about 200,000 persons. An additional 300,000 were employed in the advertising departments of retailers, wholesalers, and manufacturers, as well as in selling advertising time and space for the various media (the job of the *space salesperson*).

Newspaper advertising in the United States began practically with the publication of the first newspaper, but initially it was strictly informational (telling what one could buy where, without even mentioning price). After the Civil War, growing competition led to more aggressive tactics, mostly by manufacturers rather than local merchants. National advertising developed, at first for patent medicines (among the earliest were Sarsaparilla, Castoria, and Lydia Pinkham's Compound), and later for soaps, bicycles, breakfast cereals, cameras and film, razor blades, and chewing gum. Another spurt of growth came after 1914. The radio commercial dates from 1922, and not long afterward soap companies began to sponsor a new "art form," the radio serial, or *soap opera*; television advertising dates from about 1947. Today the average American industry spends only about 1.5 per cent of its sales dollar on advertising, but some industries (notably drugs, and soap and detergents) spend substantially—up to ten times—more. This is particularly true when the products of different manufacturers tend to be essentially identical; large amounts are spent to convince the public that a particular brand is "different" from and "superior" to others, a function of advertising called *product differentiation*. Though some portion of the total is spent on advertising to industrial users, wholesalers, and retailers (chiefly through trade publications), most advertising is directed to the ultimate user, the consumer. Thus it is consumers who pay much (and in some cases, all) of the cost of advertising.

Most consumer advocates, along with some economists, maintain that advertising is basically misleading and wasteful, that it tends to create demand for essentially useless and overpriced goods (particularly in such areas as patent medicines and cosmetics), and that it uses resources that could be more productively employed. Deceptive advertising practices are to some extent restricted by the

U.S. Federal Trade Commission and other agencies, but in practice regulatory agencies have often been slow to take action. (See also CONSUMER PROTECTION LAWS.) In defense of advertising, spokesmen for business and industry hold that it is essential to economic growth and stability, that it plays a major role in stimulating consumption (and hence product development and production), and that it fills the need for information. Certainly advertising today supports the bulk of newspapers and magazines published in the United States, as well as the major broadcasting networks—in fact, the entire mass communications industry. See also CIRCULATION; CLASSIFIED ADVERTISING; PUBLICITY; PUBLIC RELATIONS.

advertising agency See under ADVERTISING.

advertising allowance A deduction permitted by a producer or distributor to a wholesaler or retailer in exchange for advertising a product or service locally. The practice whereby recipients are asked to share the cost of local advertising is called *cooperative advertising*. The Robinson-Patman Act of 1936 prohibits American manufacturers and distributors from discriminating among wholesalers and retailers in offering advertising allowances. Further, unless proof exists that a retailer is actually using the allowance for specific ads, it may be a form of disguised price discrimination, which is also illegal.

advertising rates The rates charged by various media for disseminating advertisements. Newspapers and radio and television stations, which carry considerable local as well as national advertising, usually charge a higher *national rate*, for ads placed by a national or regional advertiser, and a lower *local rate*, for ads placed by local sources, such as retail merchants. Thus national distributors and manufacturers have a real incentive to use advertising agencies to place their ads, since the agencies earn their discount (normally 15 per cent of the media price, paid by the media) only at the national rate, and it costs the advertiser less to use an agency than to employ its own advertising staff. Retailers, on the other hand, who are entitled to the lower local rate, often do not use agencies

since they would have to pay them separately for their services.

affidavit A statement of facts, given voluntarily and sworn and signed before a court officer or other authority.

affirmative action A program made into law by the Equal Economic Opportunity Act of 1972, whereby American employers, labor unions, employment agencies, and labor-management apprenticeship programs must actively seek to eliminate discrimination against and increase employment of women and members of minority groups. Although Title VII of the Civil Rights Act of 1964 had outlawed future discrimination in employment practices, it had done nothing to redress already existing imbalances. The 1972 law, later strengthened by executive orders, required employers to draw up a detailed written plan for equalizing economic opportunity with respect to hiring, promotion, transfers, wages and salaries, training programs, fringe benefits, and other conditions of employment, which included definite numerical goals and timetables for achieving such changes. Affirmative-action programs were administered by three agencies: the Equal Employment Opportunity Commission, for private employers who have no government contracts or grants; the Department of Labor Office of Federal Contract Compliance, for government contractors and holders of grants; and the Civil Service Commission Office of Federal Equal Employment Opportunity, for all Federal employers. See also LABOR LAWS.

affluent society A term coined by J. K. GALBRAITH to describe the post–World War II state of the American economy, which he regarded as rich in private resources but poor in public services. He attributed this disparity to the fact that, because affluence was historically a new condition, people tended to think and behave as though they were still poor. Since publication of Galbraith's *Affluent Society* (1958) the term has lost its original ironic meaning and is now used simply to indicate widespread prosperity.

AFL-CIO Abbreviation for *American Federation of Labor–Congress of Industrial Organizations*.

The most powerful federation of labor unions in the United States, including (in 1975) 80 per cent of the nation's union members. Formed in 1955, after two decades of bitter rivalry, the AFL-CIO is not itself a union engaging in collective bargaining, but rather works to promote cooperation among its 110 or more member unions and to advance the interests of labor politically and legislatively. It receives its income from its affiliate unions through a per capita tax (so much per union member).

The AFL was founded in 1886 by Samuel Gompers (1850–1924) of the International Cigarmakers Union, who aimed at a federation of *craft unions* to oppose the KNIGHTS OF LABOR, the major *industrial union* (see LABOR UNION for explanation of these terms). Gompers's basic principles were *business unionism*, which strove for better wages and working conditions rather than for political or social reform, and *federalism*, which granted each member union autonomy and *exclusive jurisdiction* over its own craft. Later the AFL also supported curbs on immigration, relief from technological unemployment, and the enactment of various labor laws. Under Gompers the AFL soon became the dominant force in the American labor movement, with some 5 million members by 1920. In the 1920s, however, it began to decline. Gompers died, big business prospered, and mass production, which uses more unskilled and semiskilled workers than highly skilled ones, became a growing force. Industrial unions (which embrace all the workers in a given industry) were better suited for mass-production industries, and they were advocated by John L. Lewis (1880–1969), head of the United Mine Workers, and Sidney Hillman (1887–1946) of the Amalgamated Clothing Workers. The AFL, however, continued its traditional policies under Gompers's successor, William Green (1873–1952). As a result, Lewis, Hillman, and others, increasingly dissatisfied, in 1935 formed their own Committee for Industrial Organization to unionize the mass-production industries. Eventually they were expelled from the AFL for running counter to its exclusive jurisdiction policies, and in 1938 their committee became the Congress of Industrial Organizations, with Lewis as president (in 1940 he was succeeded by Philip Murray, 1886–1952). Helped by new LABOR LAWS, especially the National Labor Relations (Wagner)

Act of 1935, the CIO soon succeeded in its aims, and by the beginning of World War II it had organized the steel, rubber, automobile, and electrical industries. By the end of the war the AFL also had begun to organize on an industrywide basis, but the craft unions remained its ruling force. The AFL and the CIO continued to bicker, occasionally wooing members away from one another (thus the International Ladies Garment Workers Union, headed by David Dubinsky, left the CIO and returned to the AFL). Lewis and the Mine Workers eventually left, too, but remained independent. After the CIO's Murray and the AFL's Green both died in 1952, their successors, Walter Reuther and George Meany respectively, set out to mend the rift. The new AFL-CIO of 1955 was headed by Meany, but the CIO had adequate representation. The giant federation aroused some fears of union monopoly and increased corruption, but among its first steps was an internal cleanup. In 1957 three member unions, among them the powerful International Brotherhood of Teamsters, led by David Beck, were expelled for unethical practices.

after date, after sight Terms specifying the due date of a note, bill of exchange, or other credit instrument. *After date* refers to a given period following the date appearing on the instrument; thus, "payable 30 days after date" on a note drawn on February 10 means that payment is due on March 12. *After sight* refers to a given period following presentation of the note for acceptance, and the date for acceptance must similarly be specified.

Agency for International Development Also, *AID*. An agency of the U.S. Department of State set up in 1961 to coordinate economic foreign aid to underdeveloped nations. It replaced the International Cooperation Administration (1955–61) and absorbed the Development Loan Fund, set up in 1957 to grant loans for economic development. Concentrating chiefly on the fields of health, education, and agriculture, AID gave technical assistance by both sending advisers to underdeveloped countries and financing training for their own experts. It also made capital loans on more favorable terms than those offered by private banks (and usually conditional upon matching funds from the government of the borrowing country), made loans and grants to finance imports of needed U.S. commodities, and supported American private investment through loans (in both dollars and local currency), investment surveys, and investment guarantees. More direct assistance was given through child-feeding programs, population- and family-planning programs, disease control and health training, teacher training, introduction of educational radio and television, and similar measures, with considerable emphasis on local participation. AID also administered the *Food for Peace* program, whereby surplus American food and textile fibers were distributed free or sold very cheaply, and the *Alliance for Progress*, a program of economic development for Latin America.

agency shop   See under UNION SHOP.

agent
   1. In law, a person authorized to act under the control and on behalf of another person, called the *principal*, in business transactions with a third party. The agent's actions on behalf of the principal obligate the principal to third parties and give the principal rights against third parties; this is called the *law of agency*. The relation between principal and agent is based on mutual consent and thus is called *consensual*; it may also be based on consideration (pay), and then it is also called *contractual*. A *special agent* is one engaged for a single transaction (such as selling one property); a *general agent* is one engaged for transacting all of the principal's business in a given field (such as a literary agent, who may handle a client's publishing contracts). For other kinds of agent, see under BROKER; MIDDLEMAN; PURCHASING (for purchasing agent); WHOLESALE.
   2. *insurance agent.* A person appointed by an insurance company and, in the United States, licensed by a state insurance commissioner to sell insurance policies for the company. Some firms insist on exclusive representation; others deal with agents who represent more than one firm. In either case they usually are paid on a commission basis. See also BROKER, def. 2.

agent middleman   See under MIDDLEMAN.

aggregate demand   The total market for all goods and services during a specific period of time, including both consumer goods (total consumption) and producer goods (total investment).

aggregative index number   An index constructed from totals rather than from individual categories. For example, a simple aggregative PRICE INDEX compares the total amount spent on a group of selected items (or *market basket*) in any given year to the total spent during the base year. Since this method tends to give more importance to items that show the largest change (for example, a $200 increase in the price of automobiles would greatly outweigh a 20-cent increase in the price of bread, thus distorting the relative importance of change), a weighted aggregative index such as the LASPEYRES INDEX is preferable.

agio   A premium. The term frequently refers to the premium paid for exchanging one currency for another, or for a foreign bill of exchange.

agio theory of interest   See ABSTINENCE THEORY OF INTEREST.

Agrarian Revolution   Also, *Agricultural Revolution.* The transformation of farming from the growing of subsistence crops to a profitable business. Although improvements in agriculture have occurred periodically since earliest times, the term usually refers to the process that took place in England from about 1750 to 1850, which was characterized principally by new uses of land and new techniques and machinery for farming it. By means of ENCLOSURE and other methods, landlords consolidated small holdings into larger ones. Formerly uncultivated land was improved by drainage, fertilizer, and other means. An English lawyer-farmer, Jethro Tull, brought home French methods of deep cultivation (with a horse-drawn hoe) and wrote a book about them (published 1733). Charles, Viscount Townshend, a retired statesman turned farmer, popularized crop rotation (because he insisted that one crop be turnips he was called Turnip Townshend). Selective breeding of livestock was begun by a Leicestershire farmer, Robert Bakewell, who developed the New Leicester breed of sheep.

Increasingly, farmers began to specialize, growing fewer crops and larger quantities, investing more in soil improvement and, as the 19th century progressed, in more complex farm machinery. The Agrarian Revolution paved the way for modern scientific agriculture. In the United States continued improvements were made in farm machinery and chemicals (fertilizer, pesticides, herbicides), particularly during the period 1940–60. As a result, the number of farm workers declined drastically and productivity rose dramatically, with worldwide impact.

In the 1960s came the so-called *Green Revolution*, the development of extremely high-yield hybrid wheat, rice, and corn for use in overpopulated, underfed tropical Asia. Through their use per capita food production increased rapidly. However, the new hybrid strains required improved cultivation (especially more irrigation and fertilizer) than the older types, meaning that a good portion of the farmer's higher return (from greater yield) was needed to finance small pumps, more fertilizer, pesticides, and tools. Since poor subsistence farmers often could not afford these improvements, the rich farmers who could afford them grew richer and, if they were unwilling to raise laborers' wages accordingly, were subject to strikes and other disruptions of production. By the mid-1970s this situation troubled Indian wheat farmers, among others, making some view the Green Revolution as a mixed blessing.

agribusiness The sector of the economy concerned with the production, processing, and distribution of agricultural products, including farm supplies (machinery, fertilizer, pesticides, herbicides) needed for production, various agricultural services (animal husbandry, milling, etc.), and also the economic agencies that serve agricultural producers (credit institutions, marketing associations, etc.).

agricultural carrier A farm truck that is exempted from rate regulation by the U.S. Interstate Commerce Commission. Trucks employed to carry farm produce to a market may then be used to carry industrial goods in the opposite direction as a CONTRACT CARRIER, free of the regulations applying to common carriers.

agricultural cooperative See under COOPERATIVE, def. 3.

Agricultural Revolution See AGRARIAN REVOLUTION.

agriculture Also, *farming*. A general term for the raising of crops, both food and nonfood, and animals on the land. During the past century, the number of farms and of persons employed on farms in North America and Europe has shrunk dramatically, owing to industrialization and the growth of towns and cities, as well as to improved farming methods (see also AGRARIAN REVOLUTION). Just since 1950, the size of farms has grown, owing largely to increased use of heavy machinery. Today there are about 2.7 million farms in the United States, generating a total income of about $35 billion per year (about 3.5 per cent of the total national income). However, only 1.7 million of these are commercial farms (farms whose income comes primarily from agriculture). In fact, about 10 per cent of all American farms produce about 90 per cent of the total farm crops, largely because the various price supports given by the government tend to benefit rich farmers with large acreage (see also AGRICULTURE, AID TO; PARITY PRICE). The most important agricultural products raised, in terms of both number of farms and cash value, are meat animals, grains, and dairy products. See also Fig. 1, page 14; FARM.

agriculture, aid to The various kinds of government subsidy and other help given to farmers, in the United States principally by the Federal government. American farmers have been receiving aid in one form or another since the early 19th century, when the government first began selling them land at low prices and even giving some of it away. Direct payments to farmers reached a peak in 1972 with nearly $4 billion (but dropped to $2.6 billion the following year). In addition, farmers today are aided by price supports (see PARITY PRICE), cheap credit, government purchases of crops, tariffs on imported agricultural products, services such as research and education, and subsidies for irrigation, electrification, crop insurance, and highways. Numerous arguments are advanced in favor of aid to farmers, among them that farm income is lower

Fig. 1. Changes in U.S. farming

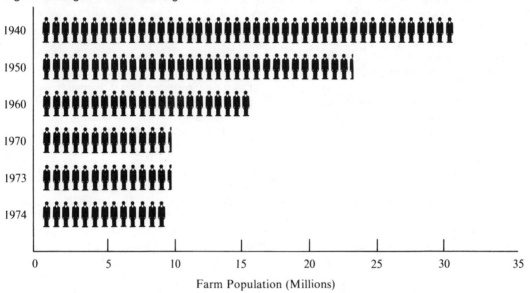

Farm Population (Millions)

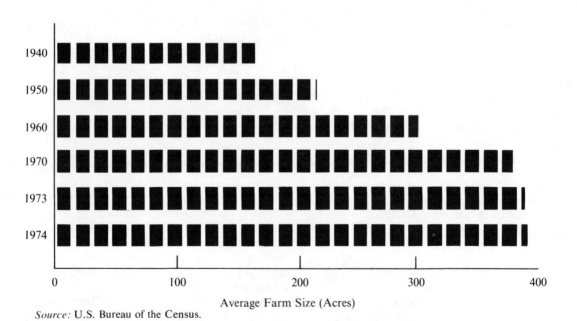

Average Farm Size (Acres)

Source: U.S. Bureau of the Census.

Fig. 2. Some laws aiding U.S. farmers

Law	Date	Provisions
Homestead Act	1862	Farm families given title to 160 acres for settling and cultivating land for 5 years.
Morrill Land-Grant College Act	1862	Donated land to states for endowing agricultural colleges.
Hatch Act	1887	Federal aid to states for agricultural experiment stations.
Newlands Act	1902	Established Bureau of Reclamation, with authority to build irrigation systems in 17 western states and Alaska.
Smith-Lever Act	1914	Federal aid to states for agricultural extension programs.
Federal Farm Loan Act	1916	Established long-term credit facilities for farmers through Federal Farm Loan Banks.
Farm Credit Act	1923	Established system of intermediate credit banks.
Farm Credit Act	1933	Established Farm Credit Administration; facilitated short-term credit.
Agricultural Adjustment Acts	1933 and 1938	Established parity price system and other subsidies, also crop restriction. First Act declared unconstitutional (1936) but modified by new law (1938), which established acreage allotments, marketing quotas, and set up Federal Crop Insurance Corporation.
Frazier-Lemke Act	1935	Established 3-year moratorium on farm mortgage foreclosures.
Rural Electrification Act	1936	Established Rural Electrification Administration to provide loans for electricity and phone service in rural areas.
Bankhead-Jones Farm Tenant Act	1937	Established long-term mortgage loans to help tenant farmers buy small farms.
Sugar Act	1948	Established subsidies for sugar-cane and sugar-beet growers.
Agricultural Act	1949	Price supports for numerous commodities.
National Wool Act	1954	Price supports for wool and mohair producers.
Soil Bank Act	1956	Set up rental payments to farmers for land taken out of production.
Agriculture and Consumer Protection Act	1973	Set target prices and agreed to pay farmers difference between market and target price if former fell; authorized disaster payments; continued subsidies for various commodities.

than that of other businesses, that farmers cannot monopolize markets and are exploited by both suppliers and customers, and that agriculture is more essential to the economy than other industries. The underlying reason, however, is that farm income and farm prices are basically unstable. Unlike prices for manufactured items, farm prices are established by relatively pure competition and tend to respond immediately to changes in supply and demand. Further, demand and supply for farm products are highly volatile: a crop may be destroyed by drought, flood, hail, pests, disease, etc.; demand responds both to the business cycle and to supplies from foreign markets. Also, technological improvements sometimes have increased yields to the point of overproduction (the so-called *farm surplus*). Thus, even with the nation's farm population shrinking drastically since the 1920s, aid to farmers has been continued and expanded.

Cash assistance to farmers today chiefly takes

the form of loans, purchases of crops, and cash payments. Most of these transactions are conducted by the *Commodity Credit Corporation* (established in 1933, and now part of the U.S. Department of Agriculture) and the Agricultural Stabilization and Conservation Service (ASCS), which acts through state, county, and community farmer committees as well as through special local offices. In addition to the PARITY PRICE system, the ASCS also administers *production adjustment programs* (for *crop restriction*) that seek to maintain prices by limiting supply. They take three main forms: *marketing quotas*, whereby only so much of a particular commodity may be sold on the market (see also EVER-NORMAL GRANARY); *acreage allotments*, whereby a farmer may devote only so much acreage to a given crop; and *cropland set-aside* or *diverted acreage provisions*, whereby a certain percentage of a farm's croplands must be set aside for approved conservation uses, either to lie fallow or to be planted in specific crops. Farmers also are able to obtain *nonrecourse loans*, with the commodities they produce serving as collateral. On maturity (at harvest time), if the market price is favorable, the farmer may repossess the crop, sell it, pay off the debt, and pocket the difference; if the market price is low, the farmer forfeits the crop to satisfy the obligation, without having to make any further payment. Products supported in one or another of these ways in the mid-1970s included such *basic commodities* as cotton, peanuts, rice, tobacco, corn, and wheat, and *nonbasic commodities* such as tung nuts, honey, milk and various dairy products, barley, oats, rye, grain sorghums, wool, mohair, sugar cane, and sugar beets. (Fig. 2 shows the principal laws authorizing farm subsidies.) In addition, farmers may obtain crop insurance against drought and other natural risks from the *Federal Crop Insurance Corporation*, created in 1938. Credit is available through other agencies as well. The Farmers Home Administration of the U.S. Department of Agriculture makes loans to farmers who cannot get funds from other sources for operating expenses, emergencies resulting from natural disasters, farm ownership (enabling farmers and ranchers to purchase farms), soil and water conservation projects, and rural housing. The *Farm Credit Administration*, an independent Federal agency created in 1933, which supervises and coordinates the activities of the cooperative farm credit system is, comprised of Federal land banks and land bank associations, intermediate credit banks and production credit associations, and banks for cooperatives, which in turn supply credit to farmers. The *Rural Electrification Administration*, created in 1935, makes loans to finance electric and telephone service in rural areas. In addition, the Department of Agriculture provides marketing and consumer services to farmers, ranging from setting grading standards and disseminating market news to administering marketing agreements and orders, maintaining animal and plant health services, and ensuring fair practices and competition on commodity exchanges, in livestock and meat marketing, and other special areas.

AID Abbreviation for AGENCY FOR INTERNATIONAL DEVELOPMENT.

air express The fastest and costliest method of air shipment. The price includes truck pickup and delivery, and routing via the best available commercial air routes. Costing two to four times as much as AIR FREIGHT, air express generally is used only when time is of the essence.

air freight The cheapest method of air shipment. The shipper delivers goods to the local airport, whence they are carried either by regular scheduled passenger airlines or cargo air carriers. Though normally costing twice as much as truck shipments (twice again that amount if an *air freight forwarder* is used), for some goods the greater speed and the elimination of possible special packaging for ground or water transportation may make air freight economical. Air freight, which has grown enormously since World War II, is used chiefly for high-value items, particularly delicate machinery and parts, and perishable luxury commodities (fresh strawberries, orchids, lobsters).

airline A company that transports passengers and/or freight via aircraft. In the United States a *scheduled airline* is one licensed by the Civil Aeronautics Board (CAB) to fly regularly scheduled flights over specific routes, and whose operations, rates, and fares are closely regulated by the CAB. A *nonscheduled airline* also is licensed by the CAB, but to fly only between certain authorized points according to the demand for such flights (rather than on a fixed schedule).

air rights Rights to space above owned land. For example, railroads often sell or lease the space above large, centrally located terminals to building corporations for office buildings or other facilities.

ALGOL Acronym for Algorithmic Language, a compiler language used in computer PROGRAM-MING, consisting of both algebraic and English components. Created in 1958 by an international committee and intended to become the standard international language for scientific data processing, it has not won so wide an acceptance as FORTRAN.

algorithm A set of computational rules or list of steps (a formula or equation) used to solve mathematical or logical problems. Provided the underlying assumptions are true and the steps are followed correctly, the solution will automatically be correct and, since it involves no judgment, can be performed by a computer. The rule for converting decimals into fractions, or vice versa, is an example of a very simple algorithm.

Alliance for Progress See under AGENCY FOR INTERNATIONAL DEVELOPMENT.

allocated cost In accounting, the assignment of expenditures to various accounts. For example, fire-insurance premium costs might be spread among a firm's departments in proportion to the value of insurable assets located in each department. Similarly, executive salaries might be allocated among different products or plants in proportion to either their sales or their profitability. The term is also used to describe the distribution of the total cost of a lump-sum purchase (for example, a factory and its contents) among the items purchased (land, building, machinery, etc.) See also APPORTIONMENT, def. 1; DISTRIBUTION, def. 3; PRO RATE, def. 1.

allocation of resources See RESOURCE ALLOCATION.

all or any part In the bidding for the underwriting of a new issue of securities, a term used to indicate that the bidder will accept the entire issue or any part allotted to him.

allotment
  1. In government accounting, assignment by an agency of part of an APPROPRIATION to a subdivision of the agency.
  2. In the securities trade, sharing out or apportioning a new issue among underwriters.
  3. *pay allotment.* The assignment of pay to an employee's dependents.

allowance
  1. In commerce and trade, a permitted tolerance in quantity, quality, or some other measurement, based either on custom or on a specific agreement between buyer and seller. Allowances are commonly made for a given percentage of shrinkage, damage, breakage, spoilage, impurities, etc.
  2. In settling a debt, a deduction granted or accepted by the creditor for damages, delays, shortages, or some other imperfection, or for goods accepted as partial payment (see TRADE-IN).
  3. In accounting, an amount set aside for bad debts, depreciation, or some other purpose. See also RESERVES, def. 2.

all-risk insurance See under PROPERTY INSURANCE.

alongside Beside the ship. See F.A.S.

alpha error See under NULL HYPOTHESIS.

alternative cost See OPPORTUNITY COST.

amalgamation See CONSOLIDATION.

American Arbitration Association See under ARBITRATION.

American Depositary Receipt Also, *ADR.* A substitute certificate for stock in a foreign company held in trust by an American bank, which issues receipts for the stock that are traded in American markets much as shares of domestic

Fig. 3. An American Depositary Receipt

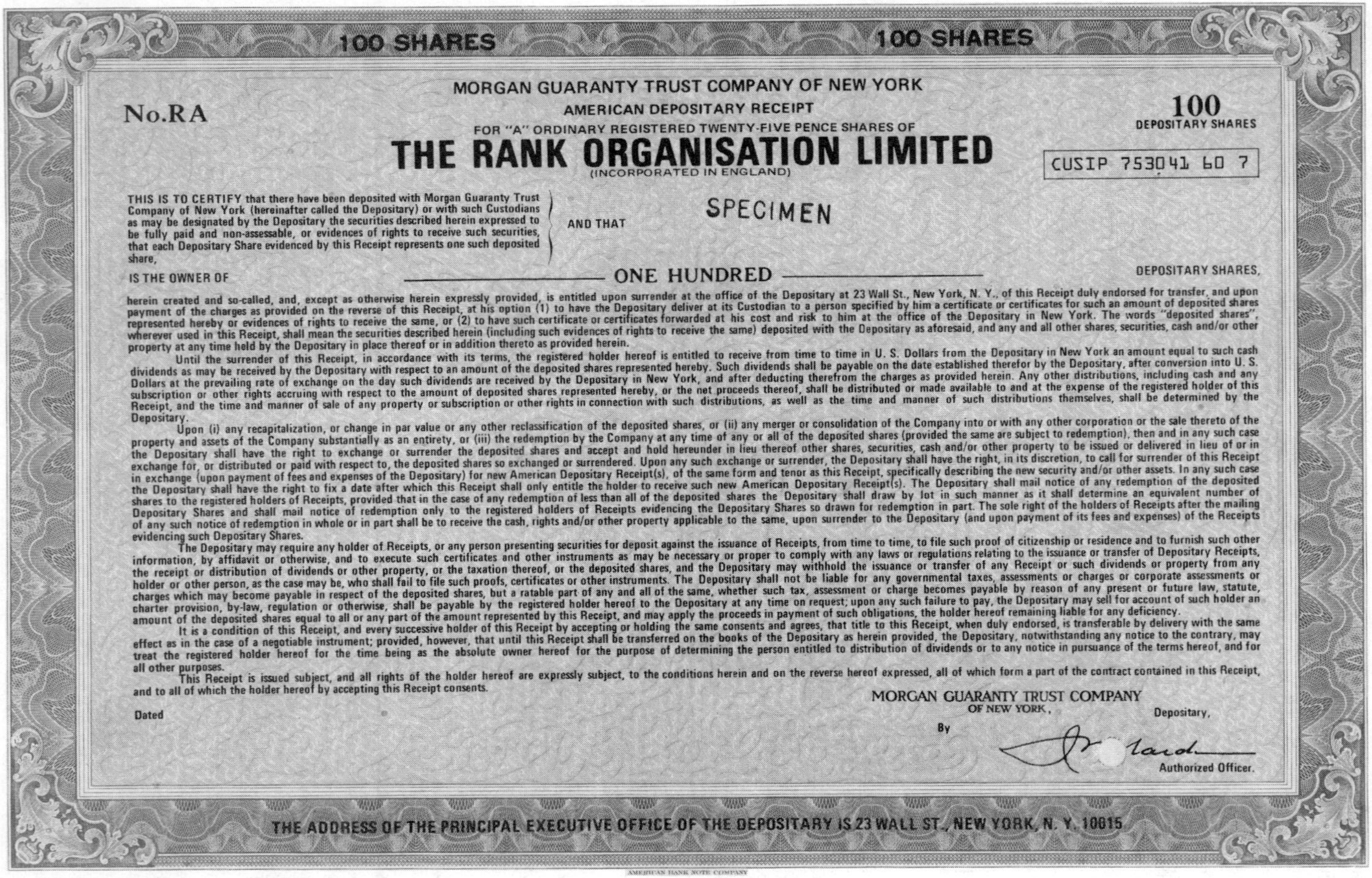

100 SHARES 100 SHARES

MORGAN GUARANTY TRUST COMPANY OF NEW YORK

AMERICAN DEPOSITARY RECEIPT

FOR "A" ORDINARY REGISTERED TWENTY-FIVE PENCE SHARES OF

No.RA

100
DEPOSITARY SHARES

THE RANK ORGANISATION LIMITED
(INCORPORATED IN ENGLAND)

CUSIP 753041 60 7

THIS IS TO CERTIFY that there have been deposited with Morgan Guaranty Trust Company of New York (hereinafter called the Depositary) or with such Custodians as may be designated by the Depositary the securities described herein expressed to be fully paid and non-assessable, or evidences of rights to receive such securities, that each Depositary Share evidenced by this Receipt represents one such deposited share, AND THAT SPECIMEN

IS THE OWNER OF ONE HUNDRED DEPOSITARY SHARES,

herein created and so-called, and, except as otherwise herein expressly provided, is entitled upon surrender at the office of the Depositary at 23 Wall St., New York, N. Y., of this Receipt duly endorsed for transfer, and upon payment of the charges as provided on the reverse of this Receipt, at his option (1) to have the Depositary deliver at its Custodian to a person specified by him a certificate or certificates for such an amount of deposited shares represented hereby or evidences of rights to receive the same, or (2) to have such certificate or certificates forwarded at his cost and risk to him at the office of the Depositary in New York. The words "deposited shares", wherever used in this Receipt, shall mean the securities described herein (including such evidences of rights to receive the same) deposited with the Depositary as aforesaid, and any and all other shares, securities, cash and/or other property at any time held by the Depositary in place thereof or in addition thereto as provided herein.

Until the surrender of this Receipt, in accordance with its terms, the registered holder hereof is entitled to receive from time to time in U. S. Dollars from the Depositary in New York an amount equal to such cash dividends as may be received by the Depositary with respect to an amount of the deposited shares represented hereby. Such dividends shall be payable on the date established therefor by the Depositary, after conversion into U. S. Dollars at the prevailing rate of exchange on the day such dividends are received by the Depositary in New York, and after deducting therefrom the charges as provided herein. Any other distributions, including cash and any subscription or other rights accruing with respect to the amount of deposited shares represented hereby, or the net proceeds thereof, shall be distributed or made available to and at the expense of the registered holder of this Receipt, and the time and manner of sale of any property or subscription or other rights in connection with such distributions, as well as the time and manner of such distributions themselves, shall be determined by the Depositary.

Upon (i) any recapitalization, or change in par value or any other reclassification of the deposited shares, or (ii) any merger or consolidation of the Company into or with any other corporation or the sale thereto of the property and assets of the Company substantially as an entirety, or (iii) the redemption by the Company at any time of any or all of the deposited shares (provided the same are subject to redemption), then and in any such case the Depositary shall have the right to exchange or surrender the deposited shares and accept and hold hereunder in lieu thereof other shares, securities, cash and/or other property to be issued or delivered in lieu of or in exchange for, or distributed or paid with respect to, the deposited shares so exchanged or surrendered. Upon any such exchange or surrender, the Depositary shall have the right, in its discretion, to call for surrender of this Receipt in exchange (upon payment of fees and expenses of the Depositary) for new American Depositary Receipt(s), of the same form and tenor as this Receipt, specifically describing the new security and/or other assets. In any such case the Depositary shall have the right to fix a date after which this Receipt shall only entitle the holder to receive such new American Depositary Receipt(s). The Depositary shall mail notice of any redemption of the deposited shares to the registered holders of Receipts, provided that in the case of any redemption of less than all of the deposited shares the Depositary shall draw by lot in such manner as it shall determine an equivalent number of Depositary Shares and shall mail notice of redemption only to the registered holders of Receipts evidencing the Depositary Shares so drawn for redemption in part. The sole right of the holders of Receipts after the mailing of any such notice of redemption in whole or in part shall be to receive the cash, rights and/or other property applicable to the same, upon surrender to the Depositary (and upon payment of its fees and expenses) of the Receipts evidencing such Depositary Shares.

The Depositary may require any holder of Receipts, or any person presenting securities for deposit against the issuance of Receipts, from time to time, to file such proof of citizenship or residence and to furnish such other information, by affidavit or otherwise, and to execute such certificates and other instruments as may be necessary or proper to comply with any laws or regulations relating to the issuance or transfer of Depositary Receipts, the receipt or distribution of dividends or other property, or the taxation thereof, or the deposited shares, and the Depositary may withhold the issuance or transfer of any Receipt or such dividends or property from any holder or other person, as the case may be, who shall fail to file such proofs, certificates or other instruments. The Depositary shall not be liable for any governmental taxes, assessments or charges or corporate assessments or charges which may become payable in respect of the deposited shares, but a ratable part of any and all of the same, whether such tax, assessment or charge becomes payable by reason of any present or future law, statute, charter provision, by-law, regulation or otherwise, shall be payable by the registered holder hereof to the Depositary at any time on request; upon any such failure to pay, the Depositary may sell for account of such holder an amount of the deposited shares equal to all or any part of the amount represented by this Receipt, and may apply the proceeds in payment of such obligations, the holder hereof remaining liable for any deficiency.

It is a condition of this Receipt, and every successive holder of this Receipt by accepting or holding the same consents and agrees, that title to this Receipt, when duly endorsed, is transferable by delivery with the same effect as in the case of a negotiable instrument; provided, however, that until this Receipt shall be transferred on the books of the Depositary as herein provided, the Depositary, notwithstanding any notice to the contrary, may treat the registered holder hereof for the time being as the absolute owner hereof for the purpose of determining the person entitled to distribution of dividends or to any notice in pursuance of the terms hereof, and for all other purposes.

This Receipt is issued subject, and all rights of the holder hereof are expressly subject, to the conditions herein and on the reverse hereof expressed, all of which form a part of the contract contained in this Receipt, and to all of which the holder hereof by accepting this Receipt consents.

Dated

MORGAN GUARANTY TRUST COMPANY
OF NEW YORK, Depositary,

By

Authorized Officer.

THE ADDRESS OF THE PRINCIPAL EXECUTIVE OFFICE OF THE DEPOSITARY IS 23 WALL ST., NEW YORK, N. Y. 10015

AMERICAN BANK NOTE COMPANY

Source: Courtesy Morgan Guaranty Trust Co.

stock are. ADRs eliminate several problems encountered with foreign investments. First, foreign companies often issue bearer shares (stock whose owner is not registered, so that the possessor, or bearer, is in effect the owner), a practice not customary in the United States and therefore inconvenient. Second, foreign stock often is sold in multiples different from American stocks. For example, Japanese stocks usually have a par value of 50 yen (about 20 cents), and their market value is generally below $1 per share, even for well-known companies. Since higher-priced stocks find better acceptance in American markets, the American bank holding those shares may issue one ADR for every ten Japanese shares. Third, the conversion of dividends from foreign currency to dollars can be accomplished by the bank. Fourth, when foreign companies do not register new issues with the U.S. Securities and Exchange Commission, Americans cannot legally subscribe to rights offers and may find it hard to sell rights. An American bank, however, can handle this problem for ADR owners by selling rights directly in the foreign market (which individual U.S. citizens cannot readily do). See also INTERNATIONAL DEPOSITARY RECEIPT.

American Federation of Labor See under AFL-CIO.

American Stock Exchange The second largest STOCK EXCHANGE in the United States, after the NEW YORK STOCK EXCHANGE. With some 1,500 listed securities, it handles one-third or more of the total volume of stocks traded in the nation yet accounts for only about 10 per cent of the dollar value of trading. Located in New York City, the American Stock Exchange until 1953 was called the *New York Curb Exchange*, because it began as an outdoor, sidewalk ("curbstone") operation, moving indoors only in 1921. In general its operations are very similar to those of the New York Stock Exchange except that it has no odd-lot brokers; instead, the relatively few orders for odd lots are filled by the specialists (they are few because share prices tend to be low enough for most transactions to be in round lots). In the mid-1970s the American Stock Exchange had 650 regular members.

American System See under TARIFF OF ABOMINATIONS.

amortization
1. *of assets*. A method of gradually reducing the book value of a fixed asset by spreading its depreciation over a period of time. This practice is commonly followed for assets whose life is limited but which do not (unlike a machine, which gradually wears out) depreciate in the ordinary way. Examples include patents, copyrights, and leases. On the books they are amortized either by having their value reduced by a set amount for each accounting period or by means of a DEPRECIATION formula.
2. *of debt*. Gradually retiring an obligation by making regular payments of both principal and interest over a period of time. The payments may be made to the creditor, as with a real estate mortgage, or to a sinking fund, as in retiring a bond issue.

Amtorg Acronym for the Soviet Union's STATE TRADING agency.

analog computer See under COMPUTER.

anarchism The theory that all forms of government are based on force and should therefore be abolished, because equality and justice are best served through free agreements among individuals and groups. On the economic level, anarchists would abolish both capitalism and private property; production would be accomplished by voluntary cooperation. While socialists advocate state ownership of the means of production, anarchists maintain that the state itself should be abolished. Historically, anarchism came to be associated on the one hand with various cooperative and utopian theories, such as SYNDICALISM and MUTUALISM, and on the other with violence and revolution. After a small group of anarchists incited the Haymarket riot of workers in Chicago in 1886, American public sentiment led to a law barring anarchists from entering the United States.

annual improvement factor Also, *productivity clause*. A clause in a labor contract that ties wage increases to theoretical long-term increases in productivity. It is based on the theory that workers should receive regular wage increases other than those associated with promotion or a cost-of-living allowance. Typically such increases amount to 3 per cent or so.

annual report A formal financial statement issued once a year by a corporation to all its shareholders, listing assets, liabilities, and earnings, and indicating the company's standing and profits at the end of the business year. In addition to offering a consolidated balance sheet and other financial information, an annual report frequently summarizes the major activities and future plans of each division of the company, announces the annual stockholders' meeting, and includes a statement from the president or other officers on the company's situation during the period covered.

annuity A kind of retirement insurance whereby, after a person has made payments for a given number of years, he or she receives income for a specific period or for life. Since annuities often are purchased from life insurance firms, they are sometimes called *annuity insurance*. There are two basic kinds of annuity. The *straight* or *life annuity* requires the payment of annual premiums until maturity; thereafter the company pays an annual income until death. There is no guarantee of a minimum total payment, and the annuity has no cash value. All payments cease at death. (In the case of a *joint and survivorship annuity*, however, taken out by two persons—usually husband and wife—the annuity pays income as long as either person lives.) The *refund annuity*, in contrast, provides that the company's payments will at least equal the purchase price of the annuity; if the annuitant dies before the total has been paid, the dependents receive the balance, either in installments or in a lump sum (depending on the policy). Refund annuities generally yield less income than life annuities. With a *deferred annuity*, payment

Fig. 4. A consolidated balance sheet for an annual report

XYZ Tobacco Corporation

CONSOLIDATED STATEMENT OF FINANCIAL POSITION
DECEMBER 31, 1999—1998

	1999	1998
ASSETS		
Current assets		
Cash	$ 1,838,000	$ 1,085,000
Short-term bank deposits	120,000	2,896,000
Notes and accounts receivable	26,432,000	34,554,000
Inventories—at cost or market, whichever is lower	80,272,000	141,090,000
Inventories of supplies—at cost	2,216,000	1,967,000
Prepaid taxes and other expenses	3,383,000	2,413,000
Total Current Assets	114,261,000	184,002,000
Investments and advances	15,193,000	12,084,000
Real estate, plant & equipment—at cost, less depreciation	41,175,000	39,464,000
Other assets	2,366,000	1,648,000
Total Assets	$172,995,000	$237,198,000
LIABILITIES		
Current liabilities		
Notes and loans payable	10,220,000	26,023,000
Accounts payable and accrued liabilities	14,972,000	71,512,000
Income taxes payable	4,205,000	8,440,000
Customer advances and deposits	13,860,000	16,818,000
Total Current Liabilities	43,257,000	122,793,000
Long-term debt	3,588,000	4,950,000
Deferred income tax credits	7,159,000	2,994,000
Equity of minority shareholders	3,187,000	3,047,000
Total Liabilities	$ 57,191,000	$133,784,000
SHAREHOLDERS' EQUITY		
Capital	11,545,000	11,618,000
Earnings reinvested	104,259,000	91,796,000
Total Shareholders' Equity	$115,804,000	$103,414,000

begins after a certain number of years (even though premiums may still be required); if the annuitant dies before payment is due to begin, the company pays nothing. This type of annuity is used mainly in company pension plans, since few individuals want to take the considerable risk involved. Still another kind is the *variable annuity*, which takes into account changes in price levels. Rather than invest premium funds in mortgages and bonds, as is done with most conventional life insurance premiums, the company offering a variable annuity invests the funds in common stocks. On maturity the annuitant receives, instead of a fixed dollar income, a given number of units of the total fund. Thus, if stock prices (and other prices) rise, the annuity pays more; if prices decline, it pays less.

annuity bond   See under BOND, def. 1.

antedate   To put a date earlier than the current one on a document such as a life insurance policy, in order to make it take effect sooner. However, changing the date on a negotiable instrument, such as a bill or note, is illegal. See also POSTDATE.

anticipation
  1. See EXPECTATION.
  2. In accounting, recording income or profit before it is actually realized. For example, the total proceeds of an installment sale might be recorded before all the payments have actually been made. See also ACCRUAL BASIS.

antidumping tariff   A tariff enacted to discourage *dumping*, that is, the sale of large quantities of goods at prices well below those charged in their place of origin so as to give the exporter an advantage in the market. The tariff rate usually consists of the difference between the normal selling price and the dumping price. In the United States the Tariff Commission is charged with watching for dumping and with setting a tariff on goods being dumped. Since the precise rate varies, the antidumping tariff is a *flexible tariff*.

antitrust legislation   Any law designed to curtail monopolistic practices on the part of a private business (see TRUST, def. 2) and to ensure competition. In the United States, the growth of big business and

lack of government controls in the latter half of the 19th century led to the creation of numerous monopolies. Small companies merged to create large ones, and big and small colluded to limit the supply of goods and services in order to raise prices. By 1900, half the nation's railroads were controlled by six financial groups, which did not hesitate to manipulate rates to their advantage. John D. Rockefeller's Standard Oil Trust (formally organized under that name in 1882) controlled most of American oil refining, and U.S. Steel controlled most of steel production. Similar powerful trusts developed in the meat-packing, sugar, lead, whiskey, and tobacco industries, among others. By 1890, public sentiment against monopoly was strong enough to ensure passage of the *Sherman Antitrust Act*, which made it illegal to monopolize trade or conspire in restraint of trade but was unclear as to just what constituted a violation. Nevertheless, under the Sherman Act the Supreme Court barred a major railroad merger (Northern Pacific with Great Northern), and in 1911 it ordered both the American Tobacco Company and the Standard Oil Company to break up into smaller, separate organizations. From the latter two cases the Court developed its *rule of reason*, which stated that only those contracts and combinations that are "unreasonable" restraints of trade were to be considered violations of the Sherman Act. The *Clayton Antitrust Act* (1914) tried to define illegal behavior more specifically, prohibiting such important monopolistic practices as price discrimination, the INTERLOCKING DIRECTORATE, and mutual exchanges of stock among competing companies. It also exempted labor and agricultural organizations from regulations applying to other large organizations. The *Federal Trade Commission Act* (1914) set up a government agency to police competition.

  Although the Clayton Act was intended to strengthen the Sherman Act, it was not altogether successful. The U.S. Steel case, for example begun before World War I, was not settled until 1920, with the Court ruling that the mere size of a corporation did not make it a monopoly. Indeed, in practice the effectiveness of all antitrust regulation has depended on the various interpretations and rulings of the courts, and the willingness of the U.S. Department of Justice's Antitrust Division to investigate and prosecute alleged violations of the law. Thus, even though the Clayton Act was supposedly strengthened by two later laws—the Robinson-Patman Act (1936) and the Celler Antimerger Act (1950)—the administrations of Presidents Kennedy, Johnson, Nixon, and Ford (1960–1976) showed little inclination to police big business, and antitrust suits lagged. Moreover, though the Celler Act bolsters the stock-acquisition ban (when such acquisitions hinder competition), the Robinson-Patman Act, which outlaws excessive quantity discounts to large buyers and prohibits "unreasonably" low retail prices, actually limits competition and thus is regarded by some as a perversion of the true purpose of antitrust legislation.

Appalachia The mountain regions of a number of states in the American Southeast—particularly West Virginia, Virginia, Kentucky, Tennessee, North and South Carolina, Georgia, and Alabama—which, owing both to the deterioration of their coal mining industry and to their unsuitability for profitable agriculture, became pockets of extreme poverty in the decades following World War II. The Appalachian Regional Commission, set up by the Appalachian Development Act of 1965, is a Federal agency that helps develop plans and programs for the 13-state area (including, in addition to the above-named states, Maryland, Mississippi, New York, Ohio, and Pennsylvania), ranging from road and low-income housing construction to land reclamation. The term "Appalachia" is occasionally extended to any region suffering from poverty and unemployment owing to depletion or lack of natural resources; thus the northern sections of New Hampshire, Vermont, and Maine are sometimes referred to as New England's Appalachia.

applications programming See under PROGRAMMING.

apportionment
1. In accounting, distributing a cost over several accounting periods in proportion to the benefits received. It is used particularly for long-term costs, such as depreciation or research.
2. In government budgeting, assigning all or part of an APPROPRIATION to a particular period of a fiscal year or to a specific agency or project.
3. See TAX SHARING.

appraisal An evaluation of worth, particularly the worth of real property or businesses, used to determine insurance, taxes, tariffs, sale price, etc. An expert in making appraisals is called an *appraiser* and in some states must be licensed. See also ASSESSMENT, def. 1.

appreciation
1. In accounting and finance, an increase in the value of property. The term is used particularly for an increase in the market value of securities and for one in the estimated replacement cost of fixed assets over their book value; an example of the latter might be land bought for $50,000 five years earlier that today would cost $75,000.
2. In foreign exchange, a rise in the price of one currency in relation to one or more other currencies. See also EXCHANGE DEPRECIATION.

apprentice A person assigned to learn a craft or trade, particularly in the training system that originated in the medieval craft GUILD. In modern times similar training programs have been set up in certain industries, notably in the building, machine-tool, and printing trades, under either employer or union auspices. In the United States the contract terms for such arrangements are usually subject to state regulation, and the general practice is also subject to review by the Department of Labor's Bureau of Apprenticeship and Training, established in 1937. The Labor Department also set up a program to recruit young people (especially from minority groups) for apprenticeship programs operated by labor and management, mainly in the construction trades. For National Apprenticeship Act, see chart under LABOR LAWS (Fig. 44).

appropriation A sum of money granted for a particular purpose. The term is used for government grants, particularly the Federal appropriations voted by the U.S. Congress to various Federal agencies and other bodies for buying goods and services, placing orders, or making other commitments for expenditures. Generally some time elapses between the appropriation of funds and the actual disbursement. (See also under FEDERAL BUDGET.) Federal and other government appropriations are usually for specific uses, but sometimes a *lump-sum appropriation* is made, that is, a sum to be used according to the recipient's discretion. In private business the term is used for permission granted by a board of directors or other officials to invest in new plant and equipment, called a *capital appropriation*. In such cases, not only may there be a time lag between appropriation and expenditure but sometimes the expenditure never takes place, being either postponed or canceled entirely.

approval, sale on A transaction that does not become final until the buyer approves or accepts the goods in question. Title passes only when that approval or acceptance is explicitly indicated, or when the buyer retains the goods beyond the time fixed for their return (or, if no time is fixed, for a reasonable time).

APT An acronym of <u>A</u>utomatically <u>P</u>rogrammed <u>T</u>ools, a computer language used in programs that produce detailed instructions for operating machine tools. APT describes the precise sequence of operations to be performed by numerically controlled machines. See also NUMERICAL CONTROL.

AQL Abbreviation for ACCEPTABLE QUALITY LEVEL.

arbitrage The simultaneous purchase of currency, securities, or goods in one market and their sale in another market at a higher price. The practice of arbitraging itself minimizes price differences in the various world markets, so that profits come mostly from large-volume transactions.

1. *exchange arbitrage*. Buying and selling currency for a profit. For example, if the French franc is quoted at $.29 in New York and at $.285 in London, an arbitrager could make a half-cent profit on each franc bought in London and sold in New York, less any costs incurred in the course of the transaction.

2. *interest arbitrage*. Buying and selling currency in the forward exchange (futures market) to profit from differences between short-term interest rates at home and rates in the foreign-exchange market. Suppose, for example, a foreign-exchange dealer sells francs forward and buys francs on the spot to cover himself. He now has lost interest on the dollars or whatever currency he used to buy the

francs. On the other hand, he may earn interest on the francs bought. If the interest rate is the same for francs and dollars, he breaks even; if one or the other rate is higher, he stands either to gain or to lose.

3. In the securities trade, buying and selling the same security at the same time in different markets to take advantage of a small price difference. If, for example, Stock Q can be bought in New York for $10 per share and sold in London for $10.50, a simultaneous purchase and sale might net the arbitrager 50 cents per share (less expenses). Arbitrage is also used in the simultaneous purchase of RIGHTS to subscribe to a new security and the sale of that security, as well as in the purchase and sale of convertible securities (see CONVERTIBLE, def. 1).

arbitration A means of settling disputes in which a third party, the *arbitrator*, listens to both sides and makes a decision that is binding for both. The arbitrator may be one person or a board of three, five, or more. Such a board may consist entirely of impartial members or it may include representatives from both sides of the dispute. The impartial arbitrator(s) may be selected by the parties to the dispute, or, for labor disputes, by the Federal Mediation and Conciliation Service (an agency set up by the Taft-Hartley Act of 1947), by a state or local agency offering this service, by a public official, or by the privately operated *American Arbitration Association*. Though widely used to settle labor disputes, arbitration is rarely attempted for settling a new labor contract, since generally neither union nor management is willing to leave the final decision to a third party. It is used more to settle grievances, questions of contract compliance, etc., and indeed many labor contracts contain an *arbitration clause* stipulating that it be used in case of disagreement.

There are two kinds of arbitration: *voluntary arbitration* is agreed to and sought by both parties; *compulsory arbitration* is imposed by the government, a court of law, a contract, or some other agency, and forces the disputing parties to submit to an arbitrator for final, binding decision. Compulsory labor arbitration has been invoked when a strike or lockout threatens national security (as in wartime) or the general public welfare (as with critical industries). Many labor experts oppose it on the ground that it discourages collective bargaining and encourages both sides to make extreme demands in the belief that the arbitrator will end by splitting the difference between the two parties. Arbitration also is often used in settling business disputes, particularly in cases involving commercial contracts. Parties to long-term contracts frequently specify that disputes shall be so settled, by either an arbitrator named in the contract or one chosen by both sides.

area sample In statistics, a method of sampling on a geographic basis, for example, all the people living in a given county.

arithmetic mean See MEAN.

array See under FREQUENCY DISTRIBUTION.

arrears In accounting, money due and not paid at the specified time. A person or firm that has not paid a debt when due is said to be *in arrears*. The term is also used in finance for interest or dividends not paid when due.

arrival draft See under BILL OF EXCHANGE.

articles of incorporation See under CORPORATION.

Asian Development Bank A bank set up in 1966 to foster economic growth and cooperation in Asia and the Far East, and to accelerate the economic development of underdeveloped countries there. It has 13 non-Asian members, including the United States, Canada, United Kingdom, West Germany, and Switzerland, as well as 20 Asian members. Capitalized at $1 billion, the bank may make loans to either governments or private entities, and provides technical assistance in preparing, financing, and executing development plans and projects. See also INTER-AMERICAN DEVELOPMENT BANK.

as is A term for secondhand or damaged goods sold at retail without either an express or implied WARRANTY by the seller. The term in effect warns the buyer to inspect the items carefully, since the burden of determining their condition falls on him or her.

ask
1. In business, the price offered by a seller; in effect, the same as a bid (see BID, def. 1).
2. Also, *offer*. In the securities and commodities trade, the lowest price a seller is willing to accept (see also BID, def. 2).

assembler See under PROGRAMMING.

assembly line A manufacturing system of putting parts together into an end-product. The parts and groups of parts (called *subassemblies*) are carried on a series of conveyor belts or other moving lines to machines and/or workers, each of which/whom performs a given operation on each part as it arrives. In highly sophisticated assembly lines, human labor is replaced entirely by automated machinery. One of the earliest assembly lines known was the Brandywine flour mill devised by the American engineer Oliver Evans in 1785. Using water power, it consisted of a series of buckets on an endless conveyor that carried grain to the top floor. There a revolving rake pushed the grain into a chute, which fed it to the grinding millstones. Other buckets on a conveyor then carried the flour to the meal loft, where another rake spread it to cool and dry, and still another device fed it to the hopper of a sifting machine. Though assembly lines of a sort were used in meat-packing in the mid-19th century, their use in large-scale manufacturing dates from Henry Ford's automobile factories in the early 1900s. After trying various devices, including moving workers from car to car, Ford in 1913 tried a moving assembly line on which an automobile chassis was pulled by a rope and windlass. In 1914 he replaced this system with off-the-floor conveyors, improved versions of which are still in use today.

assessment
1. The process of appraising property for tax purposes. Its result, called an *assessed valuation*, becomes the tax base for local property taxes (see also PROPERTY TAX).
2. In insurance, the practice of certain mutual companies or reciprocal exchanges of requiring the insured to pay additional charges to meet losses greater than anticipated. A policy that limits the in-

sured's liability to the amount of premium paid is called *nonassessable*.

asset In accounting, any physical property or right that is owned and has a money value. Accountants view an asset as a source of wealth, usually expressed in terms of its cost, capable of giving its owner future benefits. A *tangible asset* is physical property, such as cash, land, buildings, machinery, claims on property (money owed to a company; see ACCOUNTS RECEIVABLE), investments, goods in process, or prepaid expenses (such as rent, taxes, insurance). An *intangible asset* consists of such nonmaterial benefits as goodwill, franchises, patents, trademarks, or copyrights. Most businesses distinguish between two kinds of tangible asset: *current assets*, which can readily be turned into money (cash on hand, notes and accounts receivable, inventories, marketable securities), and *fixed assets*, which cannot easily be turned into money without disrupting business operations (plant, land, equipment, long-term investments). Assets appear as one of the major categories on a BALANCE SHEET. For net assets, see BOOK VALUE, def. 2. See also CAPITAL ASSET; FROZEN ASSET; HIDDEN ASSET; LIABILITY, def. 1; LIQUID ASSET; NET WORTH.

assigned risk See under RISK, def. 3.

assignment In law, a transfer by a party to a contract of some or all of the rights under the contract to a different party. Rights to money or to performance (of work, etc.) and duties all may be assigned in this way. Accordingly, a lease, sales contract, mortgage, or rents on mortgaged property all may be assigned to someone other than the party named in the contract.

assurance See INSURANCE.

attachment In law, a writ authorizing the seizure of property or rights of the defendant in a legal action as a safeguard for possible satisfaction of a legal judgment. An attachment creates a LIEN on the defendant's property, which can be enforced if the judgment rendered is in the plaintiff's favor. In some states the plaintiff must post a bond to cover any damage or loss the defendant might sustain by

reason of wrongful attachment. See also GARNISHMENT.

at the market Same as MARKET ORDER.

attributes, inspection by See under INSPECTION.

auction A public sale of merchandise, land, or a right to property, in which would-be buyers make successively higher offers, and the person making the highest offer (or bid) becomes the buyer. The person conducting the auction, the *auctioneer*, is legally the seller's agent and so is responsible for getting the highest possible price. The auctioneer may withdraw any or all of the property from the sale if the bids are not high enough. However, once a final bid has been accepted (generally indicated by the fall of the auctioneer's hammer), the sale cannot be canceled. Auctions are commonly used for selling various commodities (tobacco, cattle, used cars), oil exploration leases, land or other real estate, antiques, paintings and other art works, used furniture, and other household goods. The bidding that takes place on stock and commodity exchanges is a form of auction in which brokers represent buyers.

audit An inspection of accounting records and procedures conducted by a trained person, called an *auditor*, to check on their accuracy, completeness, and reliability. An *independent audit* is conducted by an outsider; an *internal audit* is made by a company employee.

Austrian school A name sometimes applied to the three leading Austrian members of the MARGINALIST SCHOOL, MENGER, WIESER, and BÖHM-BAWERK, and for later economists who followed the same general lines of thought, especially F. A. von HAYEK (see under CHICAGO SCHOOL) and L. E. von MISES.

authorized issue The sum of shares of capital stock a corporation may sell under its charter, or the sum of bonds that may be sold under a given mortgage. A corporation wishing to issue more stock must have its charter amended, with the approval of the shareholders.

automatic premium loan See under NONFOR-FEITURE.

automatic stabilizer See BUILT-IN STABILIZER.

automatic wage adjustment See under ANNUAL IMPROVEMENT FACTOR; COST-OF-LIVING ALLOWANCE.

automation The replacement of human labor by more or less automatically run machinery, particularly electronically controlled equipment. Unlike *automatic* production, in which machinery is guided by human operators, *automated* production is at least partly self-regulating, adjusting itself in relation to its own output by means of FEEDBACK (production information relayed back to the machine). From management's point of view, automation in the factory reduces overall costs by cutting labor costs without generally increasing material costs or overhead. Automation in the service industries and in offices of manufacturing industries, involving chiefly the use of electronic data processing to do clerical work, also reduces labor costs and increases efficiency. From the standpoint of labor, automation reduces the total number of jobs available, particularly blue-collar or manual jobs, and increases the need for personnel with the specialized training required for using automated equipment. See also TECHNOLOGICAL UNEMPLOYMENT.

automobile insurance See under LIABILITY INSURANCE; PROPERTY INSURANCE.

autonomous investment Investment that is made independent of current or anticipated economic conditions (such as anticipated increases in national income). The major impetus for autonomous investment is the development of new products and processes. Investment in noneconomic activities, such as philanthropy, is also considered autonomous. See also INDUCED INVESTMENT.

avail In finance, the proceeds of a discontinued loan, that is, the amount the borrower actually receives, the interest having been deducted in advance.

average
1. In statistics, a single number used to represent the central value of a distribution (see DISTRIBUTION, def. 2). Actually, there are several measures of central value, the most important being the MEAN, MEDIAN, and MODE. The term "average" used alone usually refers to the arithmetic mean (see under MEAN). Averages are widely used in accounting, business, finance, and general economic theory.
2. In the securities trade, an average of stock prices that supposedly serves as a barometer of the market. Among the best known is the *Dow-Jones average,* which actually consists of four different averages—for industrial stocks, transportation stocks (formerly only railroads), utility stocks, and a composite average—that are quoted at half-hour intervals throughout every trading day on the New York Stock Exchange. The *Dow-Jones industrial average,* based on 30 industrial stocks, is the most widely quoted one (see DOW THEORY) but has also been much criticized. Most of the 30 stocks included in it are not truly representative issues; they are BLUE CHIP stocks that behave differently from the norm. Further, although the Dow-Jones average is mathematically adjusted to allow for stock splits and dividends (a simple average would be highly misleading, since a stock split automatically reduces the price of shares), it is not entirely accurate no matter how sophisticated the formula used. As a result, sometimes the average goes down while the aggregate value of the stocks it represents rises. Another objection is that, as a result of various adjustments, point changes in the Dow average have virtually no relation to point changes on the exchange (where 1 point = $1); for example, a 1-point change in the average might be the equivalent of a .067-point change (or $.067) on the exchange. This difference becomes even more misleading when the Dow-Jones is compared to other averages that have been devised in attempts at greater accuracy. In 1957 Standard & Poor began publishing a *Composite Index* of 500 stocks, which is computed so that the price of each stock is multiplied by the number of shares outstanding (and thus reflects the greater influence of the large companies). Owing to different computation methods, Standard & Poor's figures are about one-tenth as large as the Dow Jones's; thus, when the Dow-Jones average is about 600, Standard & Poor is about 60. Standard & Poor's index is used by both the Federal Reserve Board and the U.S. Depart-

ment of Commerce, and is said to provide a more reliable long-term view of the market than the Dow-Jones.

In 1966 the New York Stock Exchange began publishing its own *Common Stock Index.* Covering all the common stocks traded on the exchange (some 1,200), it is computed continuously and announced on the exchange ticker tape every half hour. It is *based* on the close of the market on December 31, 1965, as 50.00, and it is *weighted* according to the number of shares listed for each issue (see under INDEX NUMBER for explanation of these terms). Point changes in this index are converted to dollars and cents, thus simplifying its relation to stock prices even more. Also in 1966, the *American Stock Exchange Index* was initiated. Published hourly by the exchange, it is so computed as to give the actual average price of all stocks and warrants listed. In addition, the American Stock Exchange publishes a monthly index showing the average PRICE-EARNINGS RATIO of all stocks traded there.

3. See DOLLAR AVERAGING.

average cost

1. A cost accounting technique in which either purchased material or production costs are averaged to determine the cost of goods sold. It is used in industries where costs of individual lots tend to vary erratically and reported profits become more consistent and meaningful if costs are averaged. For example, if out of 50 units of goods stocked in inventory, 10 units cost $100, 15 units cost $200, and 25 units cost $350, then the average cost per unit would be ($100 + $200 + $350) ÷ 50 = $13.

2. *average-cost pricing.* Also, *full-cost pricing.* A technique of pricing goods for sale whereby the price is based on both average fixed and average variable costs divided by the quantity of goods being sold. Since costs tend to decline as output increases, the price usually also declines. From the seller's viewpoint, therefore, average-cost pricing is useful only when sales volume is fairly predictable; otherwise, if sales are lower than expected, the price will not yield the seller a profit (or perhaps even enough to recoup costs).

average deviation Also, *mean deviation.* The average of all deviations from the mean, or median, regardless of whether the values are positive or negative (higher or lower than the mean). For example, in the following series of observations of workers assembling a part on the assembly line, the MEDIAN and MEAN both are 30. The average deviation is the sum of deviations (8) divided by the total number of values (9), or 8/9 = 0.89. See also STANDARD DEVIATION.

	No. of Parts Assembled	Deviation from Median
Worker 1	28	−2
2	29	−1
3	29	−1
4	30	0
5	30	0
6	30	0
7	31	+1
8	31	+1
9	32	+2
		8

average propensity See under PROPENSITY (TO CONSUME; TO IMPORT; TO SAVE).

averaging down See under DOLLAR AVERAGING.

aviation insurance See under PROPERTY INSURANCE.

backdoor financing A method used by U.S. government agencies to bypass the conventional way of obtaining funds (through congressional appropriations), by instead borrowing money directly from the Treasury. Backdoor financing first came into use in the 1930s, when the Reconstruction Finance Corporation, an agency created to help business revive after the crash, was authorized to borrow in this way. Since then it has been used by a growing number of agencies with increasing frequency.

backdoor selling The practice of attempting to sell a product directly to its ultimate industrial users instead of dealing with the company's authorized purchasing personnel. Most companies discourage backdoor selling, preferring to maintain centralized control of purchasing (and hence of expenses).

backhaul In rail and truck transportation, the practice of carrying a shipment beyond its destination and then returning it, partly over the same route. For example, a shipment bound from Pennsylvania to South Bend, Indiana, might first be carried to Chicago by express and then be backhauled to South Bend.

backlog The total of a business's unfilled orders at any one time. In a manufacturing firm, managers sometimes distinguish between the *total backlog*, meaning all unfilled orders, and the *active backlog*, for which material is on hand but the work has not been completed. From the manufacturer's standpoint, the ideal situation is a backlog of orders large enough to keep all workers and machines constantly employed, but not so large that the firm cannot meet its delivery dates.

back order Also, *open order*. An order accepted by a supplier and marked for future delivery, usually because the item is temporarily out of stock.

back spread See SPREAD, def. 1(d).

backtracking See BUMPING.

bad debt A loan that will not be repaid, in whole or in part, because of the borrower's insolvency or dishonesty. In the United States the National Bank Act defines a bad debt as an unsecured debt on which interest or payment is past due and unpaid for six months (and which is not in process of collection). Some business firms set aside a reserve on their books to offset losses from bad debts.

Bagehot, Walter An English economist (1826–77), banker, and writer remembered for his astute study of finance and banking (*Lombard Street*, 1873) and his criticisms of Smith, Ricardo, and other classical economists (*Postulates of English Economy*, 1876). Beginning his career with a law degree and a job in his father's banking firm, Bagehot later became editor of *The Economist* (1860–77) and helped make it one of the most respected publications in the field. He was one of the first to attribute the business cycle to an alternation of contagious optimism and pessimism that led investment first to expand and then to contract.

bailee See under BAILMENT.

bailment In law, a delivery of personal property by one person (the *bailor*) to another (the *bailee*), who is obligated to hold it in trust for a specific purpose, with the understanding—express or implied—that the property will be returned or duly accounted for when the purpose is accomplished or when the bailor reclaims it. The property must be personal rather than real (that is, not land or buildings), and title to it does not pass to the bailee (who cannot, therefore, sell it to someone else). A bailment exists, for example, when Smith (bailor) parks her car in the garage operated by Green (bailee); when Brown checks his coat in the checkroom of Smith's restaurant; when Jones rents her tractor to Moore. Other, more special bailments are those undertaken by hoteliers and innkeepers, who are to some extent liable for the safety of their guests' belongings, and by warehousemen, who undertake to store goods for consideration (pay). A special kind of bailee is the factor who sells goods on CONSIGNMENT.

bailor   See under BAILMENT.

balanced budget   See BUDGET.

balanced fund   See under MUTUAL FUND.

balanced growth   See under NURKSE, R.; also see GROWTH, ECONOMIC.

balance of indebtedness   A balance sheet that shows, as of a particular date, all the claims for payment held by the residents of one country against foreigners, and all claims held by foreigners against residents. If claims against residents exceed obligations of foreigners, the country is a net international debtor; if the opposite is true, it is a net international creditor. See also BALANCE OF PAYMENTS.

balance of payments   Also, *international balance of payments, balance of international payments*. A double-entry accounting of the money value of all exchanges and transfers of goods, services, capital loans, and gold and international reserves between the individual residents, businesses, and government of one nation and the rest of the world for a given time (usually one year). The exchanges and transfers also include the movement of interest and dividends, gifts, and short- and long-term investment. All entries are either debits (payments) or credits (receipts), whether or not actual payment is made during the period in question; it is the claim for payment that counts. A debit for one nation automatically represents a credit for another; if an American family visits France and

spends $1,000 there, it creates a $1,000 debit for the U.S. balance of payments and a $1,000 credit for the French balance of payments.

A nation's balance of payments is divided into three accounts: current, capital, and gold. The *current account* consists of commodity exports, re-exports, and imports (*visible items* of trade, or merchandise), and services such as tourism, banking, insurance, and transportation, profits earned abroad, and interest (*invisible items* of trade). It also includes *unilateral transfers*, that is, one-way transactions such as grants of foreign aid or individual gifts. The difference between the total export of goods and services and the total imports is called the *balance on current account*. The difference between total goods (merchandise only) imported and exported is the BALANCE OF TRADE.

The *capital account* consists of the inward and outward flow of investment capital. It usually is subdivided into long-term and short-term capital flows, based on when claims fall due (if in a year or more, long-term; otherwise, short-term). Short-term classifications include bank deposits, call loans, short-term government bonds, and currency holdings; long-term categories include bond issues sold abroad and direct investment in foreign plant and equipment.

In the double-entry system, payments must always balance over a given period, that is, debits must equal credits. If the combined capital and current accounts show a deficit (with more goods and services and/or capital investment coming into a nation than going out), the difference is made up by the third account, the *gold account,* which consists of compensatory gold and reserves movements. Thus, if a nation's debits exceed its credits, it must either export gold or spend some of its foreign-currency reserves (usually U.S. dollars) to meet its obligations; if, on the other hand, it has a surplus (credits exceed debits), the statement is brought into balance by an inflow of gold and reserves. Since the creation of SPECIAL DRAWING RIGHTS (sometimes called "paper gold") on the International Monetary Fund, these, too, may be used to offset a deficit.

balance of trade   The difference between a nation's imports and exports of merchandise to and from all other countries over a given period. If exports exceed imports, the balance of trade is said to

Fig. 5. U.S. balances on goods, services, and transfers

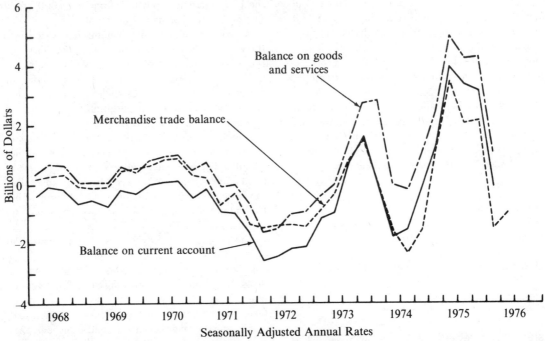

In the first quarter of 1976, the balance on current account was in small deficit, compared with a $3.1 billion surplus in the fourth quarter of 1975. The swing to deficit is mainly accounted for by a $3 billion increase in imports. In the second quarter, the trade deficit narrowed as exports increased more than imports.
Source: U.S. Department of Commerce.

be *favorable* and the nation has a *trade surplus*; if imports exceed exports, it is *unfavorable* and it has a *trade deficit*. Merchandise transactions make up the major part of the current account of a nation's BALANCE OF PAYMENTS. Historically, the United States's balance of trade has varied as it has changed from a new, largely agricultural nation to a highly developed, industrial one. During its first century (until the 1870s), imports exceeded exports, with the deficit made up by loans and investments from Europe. During World War I enormous exports of war materials and food reversed the balance-of-payments position. Foreigners, particularly British firms, were forced not only to liquidate their American investments but also to borrow dollars. After World War II, the U.S. balance of trade continued to run a substantial but steadily declining surplus, but investments by Americans abroad increasingly began to exceed

this surplus. As a result, by 1971 both the balance of payments and the balance of trade were in deficit, and in December of that year, for the first time in modern history, the U.S. dollar was devalued relative to other currencies.

balance sheet   A statement of the financial position of a business firm or other organization at a particular time, indicating its assets, liabilities, and proprietorship (equity of its owners). The typical balance sheet, or *account form* of balance sheet, shows assets on the left side and liabilities and proprietorship on the right (in Europe, however, this order is sometimes reversed). Both sides are always in balance; hence the designation "balance sheet." Another kind of balance sheet is the *report form*, which follows a vertical arrangement of essentially the same information. The assets include all the goods and property owned as well as claims against others yet to be collected. The liabilities include all the debts due—creditors' claims against assets. Proprietorship varies according to the form of organization in question, the most important being the single proprietorship (one owner), partnership (two or more joint owners), and corporation (numerous stockholders). For the first two, proprietorship is listed as the sum of one or more capital accounts; for a corporation it consists of stockholders' equity, normally comprising capital stock, paid-in surplus, and retained earnings.

Balance sheets vary in the amount of detail provided. A long form breaks each element down into its various categories, while an abbreviated balance sheet summarizes the results of each account. A *consolidated balance sheet* combines the assets and liabilities of a parent company with the corresponding items for its subsidiaries, showing the financial condition of the related companies as though they were a single unit. A *parent company balance sheet* would simply consolidate the subsidiaries into a single entry called "investment in subsidiaries."

An organization's balance sheet reveals a great deal about its financial condition, particularly if the figures are analyzed and compared in detail. For example, one figure worth deriving is *net working capital* or *net current assets*, the difference between total current assets and total current liabilities. This amount, in effect, is what the company has left to meet obligations, expand volume, and take advantage of new opportunities. Another way of deter-

Fig. 6. Balance sheet

Typical Manufacturing Company, Inc., and Consolidated Subsidiaries

BALANCE SHEET — DECEMBER 31, 19 ____

ASSETS

Current Assets
Cash		$ 950,000
Marketable Securities, at Cost		1,550,000
(Market Value $1,570,000)		
Accounts Receivable	$2,100,000	
Less: Provision for Bad Debts	100,000	2,000,000
Inventories		1,500,000
Total Current Assets		$6,000,000

Investment in Unconsolidated Subsidiaries		300,000

Property, Plant, and Equipment
Land	$ 150,000	
Buildings	3,800,000	
Machinery	950,000	
Office Equipment	100,000	
	$5,000,000	
Less: Accumulated Depreciation	1,800,000	
Net Property, Plant, and Equipment		3,200,000

Prepayments and Deferred Charges		100,000
Goodwill, Patents, Trademarks		100,000
Total Assets		$9,700,000

LIABILITIES AND STOCKHOLDERS' EQUITY

Current Liabilities
Accounts Payable	$1,000,000	
Notes Payable	850,000	
Accrued Expenses Payable	330,000	
Federal Income Tax Payable	320,000	
Total Current Liabilities		$2,500,000

Long-Term Liabilities
First Mortgage Bonds, 5% Interest, due 1975		2,700,000
Total Liabilities		$5,200,000

STOCKHOLDERS' EQUITY

Capital Stock
Preferred Stock, 5% Cumulative, $100 Par Value Each; Authorized, Issued, and Outstanding 6,000 Shares	$ 600,000	
Common Stock, $5 Par Value Each; Authorized, Issued, and Outstanding 300,000 Shares	1,500,000	
Paid-in Surplus	700,000	
Accumulated Retained Earnings	1,700,000	
Total Stockholders' Equity		4,500,000
Total Liabilities and Stockholders' Equity		$9,700,000

Source: Courtesy Merrill Lynch, Pierce, Fenner & Smith, Inc.

mining this sum is to calculate the *current ratio*, current assets divided by current liabilities. In the balance sheet of Typical Manufacturing in Fig. 6, this ratio is $6,000,000 ÷ $2,500,000 = 2.4 to 1. In other words, for every $1 of current liabilities the company has $2.40 in current assets to back it.

balloon   Also, *balloon payment.* A large final payment made at the end of a term loan or other long-term obligation, following a series of smaller partial payments. For example, a borrower might repay a $100,000 loan in yearly installments of $5,000 for nine years and then pay a balloon of $55,000 in the tenth year.

banana republic   Any of several Central American republics (Costa Rica, Honduras, Panama, etc.) with essentially a one-crop economy—primarily bananas—that became dependent, economically and at times politically, on a large foreign company, the United Fruit Company. Because United Fruit owned not only the banana plantations but the railroads for transporting the crop to the coast, the ships to carry it abroad, and even the wholesaling facilities for marketing it, the company exercised a large measure of control over the countries that depended on this crop.

bank   An establishment that performs one or more of the following functions: accepts custody of money, lends money, extends credit, issues currency, or facilitates the transfer of funds by means of checks, drafts, bills of exchange, or other instruments of credit. Some banks perform nearly all of these functions and hence are sometimes called "department-store banks." Others specialize in one or a few select functions. The principal kinds of bank in the United States are the COMMERCIAL BANK (the kind economists and businessmen usually mean when they speak of banks), SAVINGS BANK, and TRUST COMPANY. In addition, there are numerous credit institutions, such as the CREDIT UNION, MORRIS PLAN BANK, and various kinds of FINANCE COMPANY. The monetary authority of an entire nation is called its CENTRAL BANK, which in the United States is the FEDERAL RESERVE. Finally, in the 20th century several international institutions have arisen that perform some banking func-

tions, principally that of extending loans, among them the ASIAN DEVELOPMENT BANK, BANK FOR INTERNATIONAL SETTLEMENTS, EUROPEAN INVESTMENT BANK, INTER-AMERICAN DEVELOPMENT BANK, INTERNATIONAL BANK FOR RECONSTRUCTION AND DEVELOPMENT, and INTERNATIONAL MONETARY FUND.

Private banking apparently existed as early as 600 B.C. in ancient Greece and was further developed in Roman times. In medieval Europe people often stored their gold in the vaults of goldsmiths, paying a fee for this service and receiving a receipt in return. When a debt had to be paid, it became customary to sign over such receipts to the creditors, thereby avoiding the risk of transporting bullion. The goldsmiths soon realized that the gold tended to remain in their vaults and that they could make a profit by selling the receipts to customers other than the depositors. They thus became bankers, their receipts being the equivalent of modern checks and bills of exchange. Among the famous names in the history of early banking are the Fugger family of Germany, the Medici family of Italy, and the Rothschilds, a family that dominated banking in Germany, Italy, Austria, and France throughout the 18th and 19th centuries. See also INVESTMENT BANKING; MERCHANT BANK. For American banking history, see BANK OF THE UNITED STATES; NATIONAL BANKS.

bank acceptance   See ACCEPTANCE, def. 2

bank call   See under BANK STATEMENT, def. 2.

bank credit   Credit established when a bank adds the proceeds of a loan to the account of a depositor, who may then write checks against it. The term is also used in the broader sense of money created by banks through the creation of demand deposits (see under MONEY).

bank debits   The total of checks and other instruments charged to the accounts of a bank's depositors. A comparison of total bank debits with total deposits during a given period indicates how much money is being used for business transactions and thus represents a measure of business activity for that period. Consequently, figures on bank debits are regularly compiled and published by the

Federal Reserve and are widely used as an economic INDICATOR.

bank deposit See DEPOSIT, def. 1.

bank discount A bank's charge for discounting a promissory note or bill of exchange. It normally is equivalent to simple interest on the face value of the note or bill, from the date of discounting to the due date. See also REDISCOUNTING.

bank draft Also, *banker's draft, bank bill, banker's bill.* An order written by a domestic bank against a foreign correspondent bank to pay a given sum to a particular person. A bank draft thus resembles a personal check except that it is drawn by a bank on a bank, instead of by an individual or firm on a bank. For example, an American wishing to buy a year's subscription to the French newspaper *Le Figaro* would obtain a franc draft payable to *Le Figaro* from a domestic bank and mail it with the subscription order. The draft is an order to the bank's Paris correspondent to pay to *Le Figaro* the stipulated amount upon presentation of the draft. See also BILL OF EXCHANGE.

bankers' acceptance See ACCEPTANCE, def. 2

banker's bank See CENTRAL BANK.

bank examiner A government official who may examine the records and affairs of any bank or similar financial institution in a given district. In the United States examiners are appointed by state banking commissions, the Federal Deposit Insurance Corporation, the Comptroller of the Currency (who appoints all national bank examiners), and the Federal Reserve.

bank failure The inability of a bank to honor the withdrawals of its depositors. Bank failure may be set off by sudden large withdrawals (see BANK RUN). However, it is usually caused by more basic factors, such as competition among too many small banks for a limited amount of business, shifts in the locus of business activity, or an economic recession in which declining incomes and employment impair the ability of debtors to meet their obligations. Until 1934 the United States had one of the highest

rates of bank failure of any advanced country. Nearly 3,000 banks failed between 1864 and 1920, 5,411 more failed by 1929, and these were joined by 8,812 more by the end of 1933 (the period 1929–33 being that of the Great Depression). The reforms of the 1930s did much to give the American banking system greater stability, and since that time bank failures have been rare and depositors' losses virtually nonexistent.

Bank for International Settlements An institution set up in 1930 in Basel, Switzerland, as a kind of central bank for the various European central banks. Its original purpose was to coordinate the receipts and payments arising through German war reparations of World War I. After World War II, however, it became a banker for central banks, accepting deposits and making loans, as well as serving as an agent in international settlements, carrying out transactions for the European Payments Union and (later) the Monetary Fund, European Coal and Steel Community, International Monetary Fund, and similar bodies. Later, it also became active in offsetting the effects of international monetary speculation and as a research center for fiscal and monetary affairs.

bank holiday
1. Any legal holiday or other special occasion when banks remain closed, usually but not always along with most other businesses.
2. Specifically, the period from March 6 through March 9, 1933, when President F. D. Roosevelt ordered the closing of all American banks, to help restore public confidence (by stopping bank runs) and to create some banking controls.

banking laws Legislation that represents the tightening of U.S. government control over banks and savings institutions, primarily for the protection of depositors. The principal laws are listed in Fig. 7, page 34.

banking school A 19th-century English school of thought relating to the role of the central bank in the economy. Its members believed that banks could not increase the circulation of bank notes over and above the needs of trade, since bank notes were convertible into gold and the volume of trade

Fig. 7. Major U.S. banking laws

Law	Date	Provisions
Federal Reserve Act	1913	Set up FEDERAL RESERVE system.
Banking Act (Glass-Steagall Act)	1933	Created Federal Deposit Insurance Corporation; extended open market activities of Federal Reserve; permitted branch banking; separated deposit from investment functions; allowed savings and industrial banks to join Federal Reserve.
Banking Act	1935	Revised structure of Federal Reserve Board of Governors; set up Open Market Committee; empowered Reserve to require higher reserves of member banks; authorized loans to member banks.
Bank Holding Company Act	1956	Made formation of bank holding companies or acquisition of 5% or more of voting shares in a bank by an existing holding company subject to approval of Federal Reserve Board of Governors.
Bank Merger Act	1960	Made bank mergers subject to approval of various central authorities (for national banks, Comptroller of the Currency; state member banks of Federal Reserve, Federal Reserve Board of Governors; other insured banks, Federal Deposit Insurance Corp.).

itself controlled the volume of notes issued. Therefore there was no need for the central bank to control currency, since increased issuance of bank notes could not promote inflation. The banking school was opposed by the CURRENCY SCHOOL, whose views prevailed in a law passed in 1844. In fact, however, both schools erred in their assumption that some ideal formula would automatically provide the economy with precisely the right money supply. Moreover, the banking school ignored the fact that the supply of gold itself might expand (when new mines were discovered) and cause inflation, or, conversely, that population and the general economy would grow faster than the money supply, resulting in declining prices and unemployment.

bank money Money in demand deposits, that is, checking accounts in banks. Since at least 90 per cent of the value of all transactions in advanced countries takes place by means of checks, bank money is by far the most important form of MONEY in use. See also DEMAND DEPOSIT; NEAR MONEY.

bank moratorium See under MORATORIUM.

bank note A kind of paper currency that is, in effect, the PROMISSORY NOTE of a bank. Such notes promise to pay the bearer on demand the amount stated on the face of the note. In the United States NATIONAL BANKS (see def. 2) issued bank notes until 1935, but since then the only kind issued has been the Federal Reserve note.

bank of issue A bank authorized to issue its own bank notes to circulate as currency. In the United States, since 1935 only the twelve Federal Reserve banks have had the authority to issue bank notes.

Bank of the United States Name of two banks that existed from 1791 to 1811 and from 1816 to 1836, respectively, and that functioned as a kind of central bank for the nation. The *First Bank of the United States*, proposed by the first Secretary of the Treasury, Alexander Hamilton, was intended to furnish a stable paper currency and act both as a commercial bank and as a fiscal agent for the government in the sale of bonds and similar transactions. Despite the opposition of Thomas Jefferson and other anti-Federalists (advocates of states' rights over a strong central government), the bank, with a 20-year charter and capital of $10 million, largely succeeded in these functions. It had a central office in Philadelphia and eight branches in major cities, and it accepted deposits, issued bank notes, and extended loans. In that it served both the government and the general public and was operated for profit, it differed from the modern concept of a CENTRAL BANK. Congress defeated renewal of its charter in 1811, largely because the states and the state banks (which had grown in number from 3 in 1791 to 88 in 1811) resented the bank's conservative policies and preferred an "easy money" policy. The financial chaos that ensued, augmented by the War of 1812, engendered sufficient support to charter a *Second Bank of the United States* in 1816. After initial mismanagement it, too, fulfilled its functions adequately, but it also met strong resistance. Some states tried to tax its branches out of existence, but two historic decisions by the Supreme Court under Chief Justice John Marshall—*McCulloch vs. Maryland* (1819) and *Osborn vs. United States Bank* (1824) —declared such taxation unconstitutional. By 1836, however, opposition was so strong that the charter was not renewed. From that time until 1863, when the National Bank Act was passed, American banking was subject to little or no central regulation. As a result, many of the bank notes issued (by more than 1,500 different banks) did not circulate at par, there was a serious shortage of fully backed money, and there was no central monetary authority of any kind. See also NATIONAL BANKS, def. 2.

bank rate   British term for DISCOUNT RATE.

bank reserve   The stock of money a bank must set aside (and not lend) to meet the demands of depositors. Since it is rare for a bank to have all its depositors withdraw all of their funds simultaneously, only a portion of the total deposits are needed as reserves. Some economists, notably Irving FISHER, have objected to such FRACTIONAL RESERVE BANKING, maintaining that greater monetary (and hence economic) stability could be achieved with 100 per cent reserve backing. Nevertheless, no modern banking system heeds such advice.

In the United States all commercial banks are required to retain some percentage of their deposits as reserves. For members of the FEDERAL RESERVE system this percentage is established by the Federal Reserve; for state banks it is set by state law (see also RESERVE REQUIREMENTS). *Legal reserves* consist of currency held in bank vaults (VAULT CASH) or deposits (called *reserve balances*) at one of the twelve Federal Reserve banks. Cash and bank deposits are sometimes also called *primary reserves*; high-grade securities readily converted into cash, such as government bonds, are called *secondary reserves*. A member bank can always obtain reserve balances by sending currency to the Reserve bank and obtain currency by drawing on its reserve balance. Because either can be used to support a much larger volume of deposit liabilities of commercial banks, currency and member-bank reserve balances together are sometimes called *high-powered money*. Reserve balances and vault cash in banks, however, are not considered part of the MONEY SUPPLY held by the public.

bank run   Also, *run on the bank*. A sudden increase in withdrawals of deposits from a bank, usually due to depositors' fear of losing their money. With fractional reserve banking (where only a percentage of total deposits is fully backed), such a run naturally taxes the bank's reserves to the breaking point and may itself bring about the very bank failure the depositors fear. Insurance of deposits (in the United States by the Federal Deposit Insurance Corporation) has helped avert such panics. In fact, no major American bank has been permitted to close its doors to depositors since the 1930s. Instead, when a bank is in financial trouble, the authorities arrange a merger or a transfer of the bank's assets so that depositors can carry on without loss or undue inconvenience.

bankruptcy The legal proceeding whereby the affairs of persons or businesses unable to meet their obligations (see INSOLVENCY) are turned over to a receiver or trustee, in accordance with (in the United States) the Bankruptcy Act. The purpose of this Federal law, first passed in 1898 and amended several times since, is to protect both creditors (from one another and from debtors) and honest debtors (from creditors). Bankruptcy is either *voluntary* or *involuntary*, depending on whether it is the debtor or the creditors who file a petition of bankruptcy in the appropriate Federal district court. For voluntary bankruptcy, any insolvent individual or business—except a municipal, railroad, insurance, or banking corporation, or a building and loan association—may file a petition. In the case of involuntary bankruptcy, the creditors must show that the debtor has committed an *act of bankruptcy*. Such acts include concealing or removing part of one's property to defraud creditors, favoring one creditor (through payment) over others, assigning property, allowing a creditor to obtain a lien on property, admitting insolvency in writing, or letting a receiver take charge of property. The court may then appoint a *referee* to determine the facts of the case, and the debtor is required to make a full disclosure of all assets. If the court decides in favor of the creditors, the referee generally administers the property until a *receiver* or *trustee* has been elected or appointed by the creditors. The receiver takes possession of the bankrupt's property, inventories it, and has it appraised. In the case of a bankrupt business, reorganization may be undertaken in order to satisfy the creditors. When this cannot be done, however, the receiver liquidates the assets (and then becomes a *trustee in bankruptcy*) and distributes the proceeds among the creditors, keeping an accurate accounting of the entire estate.

Banks for Cooperatives In the United States, 12 district banks and a Central Bank for Cooperatives set up through the Farm Credit Act of 1933. They provide a permanent source of credit on a sound business basis to farmer cooperatives, extending both term and seasonal loans. The Central Bank makes direct loans to the district banks and participates in loans that exceed their respective lending limits. See also *Farm Credit Association* under AGRICULTURE, AID TO.

bank statement
1. A periodic statement (usually monthly) that shows all the transactions for a particular bank account during that period, including deposits made, checks drawn, interest earned, etc. The bank sends such a statement to each depositor, along with all checks canceled during the period.
2. A financial statement reporting the condition of a bank. In the United States state-chartered banks must publish such statements at regular intervals, as specified by state law, and national banks must issue them at least three times per year. A request for a bank statement is known as a *bank call*.

bargain
1. A good or service bought for a low price. Hence, *bargain basement*, an area, usually in a department store basement, stocking low-priced goods or selling merchandise at reduced prices.
2. An agreement, particularly a purchase or sales contract. Also, to negotiate such an agreement.
3. See COLLECTIVE BARGAINING.

bargaining power See under COLLECTIVE BARGAINING.

bargaining theory of wages See under WAGE.

bargaining unit See under COLLECTIVE BARGAINING.

barter The direct exchange of goods or services without the use of money.

base pay See under WAGE INCENTIVE.

base period In constructing an INDEX NUMBER, a selected period of time, frequently one year (called a *base year*), against which changes in other years are calculated. The relationship frequently is expressed as base period = 100. For example, suppose the base year chosen is 1967. To calculate the change in average annual income of textile workers, the current year's average annual income—say, $10,000 — is divided by the average annual income for 1967, which was $8,000: $10,000 \div 8,000 = 1.25$. To eliminate the decimal point this figure is multiplied by 100: $100 \times 1.25 = 125$. This would indicate that income in the current year is 25 per cent higher than it was in the base year. See also PRICE INDEX.

base stock method   A method of inventory valuation in which a minimum amount of goods (the so-called *base stock*), carried at all times, is valued at its long-term normal price, while the goods carried in excess of this minimum are valued according to some other method, generally either cost or market, whichever is lower (see COST OR MARKET). This method treats the base stock as an asset like plant and equipment, since it represents a fixed capital investment. It is used particularly in industries where the cost of the finished product is made up largely of some basic raw material, such as hides or crude oil, or if the raw materials being processed are basic and homogeneous (such as cotton or copper), or if processing takes fairly long and a minimum stock of raw material must be kept in process at all times (as with oil refining). The chief drawbacks of the base stock method are its undervaluation of actual inventories and hence its misrepresentation of the amount of working capital, its failure to recognize gains and losses on inventory, and its false assumption that base stock is a fixed asset when in fact it is a constantly changing one intended for eventual sale.

BASIC   In PROGRAMMING, a comparatively simple compiler language for a COMPUTER, invented in the early 1960s, intended for the average layman. It has won wide acceptance, especially in universities, and for initial applications of a computer.

basic commodities   See under AGRICULTURE, AID TO.

basing point system   A system of DELIVERED PRICING in which the price quoted by the seller is the factory price plus the cost of shipping from one or more places called *basing points*, from which the goods may or may not be actually shipped. For example, steel prices used to be uniformly quoted as *Pittsburgh plus*, meaning they included the cost of shipping from Pittsburgh to the buyer's plant. Thus, a steel buyer in Detroit would have to pay the freight charge for steel shipped from Pittsburgh, even though the steel might actually be shipped from a mill in Cleveland or even Detroit itself. Or, a Midwest buyer of sugar might have to pay freight from one or another of the Atlantic seaboard cities that were basing points for the sugar industry, even though shipping costs would be much lower from any number of midwestern refineries. While some industries defend the basing point system, others argue that it violates the antitrust laws, since it means every seller quotes identical prices regardless of destination, and hence all sellers (except those who happen to be located at a single basing point) make different profits on sales to different destinations.

basis point   A unit of measure for the change in interest rates for bonds and notes. One basis point is equal to .01 per cent, so 100 basis points = 1 per cent. Basis points are used because a relatively small change in interest rate—as from 7.50 per cent to 7.75 per cent—can involve a considerable sum of money (on a $10 million bond issue, such an increase in interest amounts to $25,000—from $750,000 to $775,000 per year), and therefore small units are needed to calculate changes in bond yield.

Bastiat, Frédéric   A controversial French economist (1801–50), known as a popular journalist rather than a scholar, who propounded a number of absurd notions in his major work, *Harmonies of Political Economy* (1849), among them that this is the best of all possible worlds, but who is remembered chiefly as a stout defender of free trade. In the most famous of his numerous essays attacking the protective tariff (later collected under the title *Economic Sophisms*), the candlemakers petition the government to remove their major competitor, the sun, so that they—and therefore the nation—may prosper.

batch processing
1. A form of data processing in which information is accumulated over a period of time before being loaded into a computer. For example, data on withdrawals from or additions to inventory might be accumulated daily or weekly, and then processed. The inventory file thus would be up to date only as of the end of the previous day's (or week's) transactions. Formerly the rule for practically all

computer applications, this kind of batch processing became obsolete when computers with large-capacity direct-access memories were developed and the means of input and output improved, so that transactions could be entered as soon as they occurred. However, batch processing still has many other uses. See also TIME SHARING.

2. In manufacturing, a method whereby one stage of processing a single batch or lot of material is completed before another batch is begun. Batch processing, often used in the chemicals, drug, and related industries, is the opposite of a CONTINUOUS PROCESS, where material is constantly fed to a machine, assembly line, etc.

Bayesian decision theory A method of decision-making that applies subjectively determined probabilities (in addition to, or instead of, known data) to the possible outcomes of a particular decision. It differs from classical statistics in that the probability is based in part or entirely on expert opinion rather than solely on actual data (as with the 0.5 probability that a flipped coin will come up heads). It is commonly used (albeit usually unknowingly) by track bookmakers who set odds and take bets on the outcome of a particular race, basing the probability of winners on their own expert judgment and on the actual bets placed. The underlying mathematical principles were developed in the 18th century by Thomas Bayes, an English clergyman, but were not applied to business and economic decision-making until the 1940s. See also DECISION TREE.

bear In the securities trade, a trader who profits from falling prices (by SELLING SHORT) and hence one who believes business is getting worse; by extension, a pessimist. The precise origin of the term is not known. A market characterized by a long-term trend of falling prices is called a *bear market*. The unethical practice of driving stock prices down by repeatedly selling short, so that the trader can profit by covering at lower prices, is called a *bear raid*. Today bear raids are prevented by the stipulation of the U.S. Securities and Exchange Commission that a short sale must be transacted at a price higher than either the previous sale or the last different price. See also BULL.

bearer The person in physical possession of a negotiable instrument payable to the bearer. In such a case, title (legal ownership) is defined by physical possession.

bearer bond See under BOND, def. 1.

Bedaux point system See under WAGE INCENTIVE.

beggar-thy-neighbor policy Also, *beggar-my-neighbor policy.* Any policy designed to enrich one nation at the expense of those it trades with, based on the idea that a surplus of exports over imports is highly desirable. This principle, a basic tenet of MERCANTILISM, survives in the form of trade barriers such as protective tariffs. The policy was attacked by Adam SMITH, among others, who argued that the purpose of economic activity is not the acquisition of more gold but consumption. A modern version of beggar-thy-neighbor occurs when a nation keeps its exchange rate artificially low relative to those of other nations. As a result, its exports will greatly exceed its imports, the low exchange rate making imports expensive on the domestic market but making exports cheap abroad. The exchange rate is kept low by means of a *dirty float*, that is, the central bank of the nation in question keeps selling its own currency and buying foreign currencies. This depresses the price of its own currency (making exports relatively cheap and imports expensive) and makes it pile up large reserves of foreign currencies.

benchmark

1. In statistics, a term for comprehensive data (compiled infrequently) used as a basis for developing and adjusting interim estimates made from sample information. For example, the U.S. Census Bureau's Annual Survey of Manufactures, a review of all manufacturing activity in the economy, is used to adjust the sample reports collected monthly for about 55 major manufacturing industries.

2. A program used as a test to evaluate computer performance. For instance, a program executed in 1 second on a particular computer may serve as a benchmark for a particular series of arithmetical calculations. Other computers can then be com-

pared in terms of how much time they require to finish the same series of calculations.

beneficiary The person who benefits from a trust fund, a contract, a will, or a life-insurance policy. A *donee beneficiary* is not a party to the contract but receives the promised performance as a gift, whereas a *creditor beneficiary*, also not a party to the contract, receives the performance in discharge of an obligation owed to him or her. A life-insurance policy may have a *primary beneficiary*, who receives the benefit if he or she is living when the policyholder dies, and one or more *contingent beneficiaries*, who benefit if the primary beneficiary dies before the policyholder; for example, a woman may name first her husband, and, in the event he predeceases her, her children.

benefit society See SAVINGS AND LOAN ASSOCIATION.

benefits-received principle Also, *benefit theory*. The idea that tax assessments should be based on the extent to which taxpayers benefit from the goods and services paid for by taxes. In effect, it asks people to pay for goods and services provided by government, just as they do for those produced by private business. Taxes such as the HIGHWAY-USER TAX, whose revenues pay for road construction, and the EMPLOYMENT TAX, part of which funds social security payments, illustrate the benefits-received principle. Unfortunately, in most cases the beneficiaries of public services cannot be so readily identified (for example, how should individuals be assessed for the costs of national defense?), so that the principle has limited usefulness in establishing a fair base for taxation. See also ABILITY-TO-PAY PRINCIPLE.

Benelux A customs union of Belgium, the Netherlands, and Luxembourg, conceived during World War II by their governments-in-exile and formed in 1948. Abolishing internal tariffs and reducing mutual import quotas, the three countries adopted a common external tariff as well. According to plans reaffirmed in a treaty of 1960, two years after they had joined the COMMON MARKET, they hoped eventually to combine into a single fiscal and monetary system. Though there was free movement of workers and capital within Benelux, as well as coordination of social security programs and standard postal and transportation rates, its ultimate goal still had not been achieved in the mid-1970s.

Bentham, Jeremy An English social philosopher (1748–1832) remembered as the chief exponent of *utilitarianism*, the theory that society's ultimate goal is the greatest good (happiness) for the greatest number of individuals and that every institution and action should be evaluated on the basis of its *utility*, that is, its contribution to the ultimate goal. Bentham believed that the search for pleasure and the avoidance of pain are intrinsic to human nature and that in essence individuals should be free to follow their self-interest. This latter principle had considerable influence on David Ricardo and other economists of the CLASSICAL SCHOOL, who incorporated the idea of wealth- and pleasure-seeking economic man into much of their thinking. Bentham's major work is *Principles of Morals and Legislation* (1789).

bequest See under WILL.

Berle, Adolph Augustus, Jr. An American lawyer (1895–19   ) who became a specialist in corporation law and finance and wrote a classic text on the subject, *The Modern Corporation and Private Property* (with Gardner C. Means, 1932). A professor intermittently employed in government (he was one of President F. D. Roosevelt's "brain trust"), Berle was among the first to point to the vast concentration of American economic power in the hands of a small number of huge corporations. Further, though these corporations theoretically are owned by a multitude of stockholders, in practice they are managed by relatively few individuals, so that ownership and control are actually quite separate.

Bernoulli distribution See BINOMIAL DISTRIBUTION.

Bernstein, Eduard A German socialist and politician (1850–1932) who was forced into exile (1878–1901) owing to Bismarck's antisocialist policies and who became known for his dissent from the ideas of Karl Marx. In his most important book, *Evolutionary Socialism* (1899), Bernstein, contrary to Marx, held that the downfall of capitalism is not inevitable, that the evolution of society is a much slower process than Marx thought, and that reforms should be won within the system by democratic means rather than by overthrow of the government. Bernstein's concept of socialism, sometimes called *revisionism* (that is, a revision of Marxism), favored government control of monopolies and of working conditions, and government ownership of public utilities and eventually of capital. For another form of revisionism, see FABIAN SOCIALISM.

best-efforts selling See INVESTMENT BANKING.

beta error See under NULL HYPOTHESIS.

betterment Also, *improvement*. In cost accounting, the replacement of an asset or part of an asset with a superior unit or part, resulting in a higher valuation of the asset (and presumably also greater productivity or better quality and/or durability).

Beveridge, William Henry An English economist and educator (1879–1963) who contributed to the establishment of a British government employment service in 1909 and a comprehensive system of social insurance after World War II. During World War I he was employed in the food industry, where he devised a system of wartime rationing. After the war he served as director of the London School of Economics for nearly two decades and then taught at Oxford. His *Social Insurance and Allied Services* (1942) proposed a "cradle to grave" social security system for all Britons, which was subsequently enacted. In *Full Employment in a Free Society* (1944) Lord Beveridge advocated control of private investment, planned public spending, and other measures to insure full employment, but viewed state management as complementing rather than replacing individual economic initiative.

bias In statistics, an error usually due to faulty selection of a SAMPLE. For example, in 1936 a poll based on telephone directory listings showed that Alf Landon would win the U.S. Presidential election by a wide margin; apparently, however, almost every unlisted voter chose Franklin D. Roosevelt. See also ERROR.

bid
1. Also, *quotation*. In business, an OFFER to sell a good or service at a certain price, usually in response to a request from the potential purchaser, which may be publicly announced (see ADVERTISED BIDDING) or addressed to a number of known suppliers (anywhere from 1 to 50 or 100). The request generally includes precise specifications, the quantity required, and the delivery date, which the supplier must take into account in setting the price. Bids usually must be presented within a specified time. Some buyers, notably government agents, require a *sealed bid*, submitted in a sealed envelope. From these the buyer selects the one quoting the lowest price (called *low bid*), a consideration paramount in government purchasing. The idea behind sealed bids is that a seller who does not know what prices others are quoting will be inclined to submit the lowest possible price. With an *open bid*, on the other hand, the seller may agree to lower his quoted price if competitors outbid him. (Actually, the lowest bid often is not the most advantageous; the buyer must also consider the seller's reputation for reliability, quality, and other factors.) When *identical bids* are made, suppliers may have colluded to restrict competition. If all bids submitted are too high, the buyer may either solicit bids from still other suppliers or offer some concessions to induce price-cutting, such as a long-term contract or design changes that make specifications easier to meet.
2. In the securities and commodities trade, the highest price offered for a particular security or commodity at a given time, as opposed to the price *asked*, which is the lowest price any seller will accept at that time. The two are jointly referred to as *bid and asked*. The terms *quotation* and *quote* also are used to mean "bid" in the sense of a price offered, but without the connotation of "highest price offered."

Big Board See NEW YORK STOCK EXCHANGE.

big business
1. A collective term for the large industrial and

commercial enterprises, mostly corporations, that account for the bulk of a developed nation's total private business assets. With but few exceptions, big business is run by professional managers rather than owners, in contrast to the owner-manager setup typical of small business. Big business includes both producers of commodities (automobiles, steel, oil, electric appliances, etc.) and service organizations (banks, insurance companies, etc.). The term is often used to sum up the attitude of large enterprises to various economic policies. From the mid-19th century on, as the United States changed from an agricultural to an industrial economy, businesses tended to grow in size as well as numbers. With abundant cheap labor, improved technology and transportation, a growing market, and a sympathetic government that enacted favorable laws (such as protective tariffs), business was encouraged to expand and use large-scale methods. This trend has continued to the present day, despite the fact that beginning about 1890 the public began to agitate for government controls over big business (see ANTITRUST LEGISLATION).

2. A business firm of a specific size, as defined by local, state, or central government authorities, usually in terms of annual receipts (income) or number of employees, or both. See also SMALL BUSINESS.

bilateralism Exclusive dealings between two countries, as opposed to dealings among a larger group of nations (*multilateralism*). Bilateral trade has numerous drawbacks. First, if the market for a product is confined to only one country, demand is likely to be much less elastic than with a wider market. Second, economic or political instability in the buyer country poses a major threat to the industry in question. Third, very few countries complement one another so perfectly that exclusively bilateral trade is satisfactory. For example, suppose the United States and Canada were to trade with one another solely on a bilateral basis. Both nations are extremely efficient suppliers of wheat. With no American market for Canadian wheat, the Canadians may not be able to buy from the United States products that they themselves do not produce— say, orange juice. If, on the other hand, the Canadians sell their wheat to Germany, which needs it, both they and the Germans can buy American

orange juice, while the Canadians and Americans could buy German cameras and automobiles with the money earned from wheat. Thus all parties involved can benefit from multilateral trade.

bill

1. A list of charges for goods or services. See INVOICE.

2. A piece of paper currency, for example, a dollar bill.

3. Abbreviation for BILL OF EXCHANGE.

4. Abbreviation for TREASURY BILL.

See also BILL OF LADING; BILL OF MATERIAL; BILL OF SALE.

billing

1. In business and trade, the submission of invoices for goods or services. See also DATED BILLING.

2. In ADVERTISING, the total value of all advertising placed by an agency for its clients during a given time, used as a yardstick of the agency's standing.

bill of credit An unsecured promissory note of a government that is intended to circulate as money. The United States Constitution prohibits the states from issuing bills of credit, implying that the Federal government may. The greenbacks issued during the Civil War were in effect bills of credit (see GREENBACK).

bill of exchange Also, *draft, commercial draft.* An unconditional written order by one person upon a second person to pay, on demand or at a specified future time, a sum of money to a third person. The person giving the order is called the *drawer* and is said to *draw* the bill (hence the synonym "draft"). The person on whom the order is drawn is the *drawee.* An order on a bank, particularly a foreign bank, is called a BANK DRAFT; an order on any other drawee is called a *trade draft.* The person to whom payment is to be made is called the *payee.* (In some cases the drawer designates himself as payee.) The drawee is not bound to pay the money unless he *accepts* the order; once he does, he is called the *acceptor.* Accordingly, a bill of exchange or draft is sometimes called an *acceptance.* A bill of exchange sent by a seller of goods to a buyer, which the buyer accepts when he accepts the goods, is called a *trade acceptance*; for bankers' acceptance, see ACCEPTANCE, def. 2.

Among the various kinds of bill of exchange in common use are the *sight draft*, payable on sight or on presentation (a common example is the *personal check*); a *time draft*, payable at a given later time, such as "60 days after sight," or "60 days after date" (meaning the date on the bill); an *arrival draft*, payable when the purchased goods reach their destination; an *inland bill of exchange*, drawn and payable in the same state; and a *foreign bill of exchange*, drawn in one state or country and payable in another. Bills of exchange are negotiable instruments, that is, they can be bought and sold. Foreign time drafts in particular are frequently traded on the FORWARD EXCHANGE.

bill of lading A document issued by a carrier to a shipper, upon acceptance of goods for shipment, that represents both a receipt for the goods and a contract stating the terms of carriage. It normally includes the date of issue, from whom and where the goods were received, to whom and where they are to be delivered, a description of the goods or packages containing them, and the carrier's signature. A *straight bill of lading* states that the goods are to be delivered to one specified person and is not negotiable; an *order bill of lading* states that the goods are consigned to any person named and hence is negotiable. See also WAYBILL.

bill of material In manufacturing, an itemized list of the components for each product, including the name, part number, and usage (amount required) of each component.

bill of sale A receipt signed by a seller, stating that the title of a particular property has been transferred to a specific buyer. It serves as proof that title to the property (if not the property itself) has been transferred, and therefore the buyer may now dispose of that property. In a conditional sale, such as an installment purchase, the seller issues a *conditional bill of sale*, which provides that title passes only after the selling price has been paid in full, and until that time seller retains title.

bills-only policy See under OPEN-MARKET OPERATIONS.

bimetallism A system whereby a country defines its monetary unit in terms of two metals, usually gold and silver, in a specific ratio, called the *mint ratio*. Both metals may be coined in unlimited quantity, and each represents legal tender. Currency can be exchanged for either metal at an agreed upon rate, such as 15 ounces of silver or 1 ounce of gold. Originally instituted to increase the circulating money supply, bimetallism was in use from the late 18th to the 19th century in a number of countries, among them France and the United States. Its chief drawback, which led to its demise, was that the market prices of gold and silver fluctuated independently of one another. Thus, when one metal rose in price it was exported in quantity, leaving the country with the lower-valued metal (or, in effect, on a single-metal standard; see also GRESHAM'S LAW). By 1900 the GOLD STANDARD had replaced bimetallism. Even so, as late as the 1890s, in a time of falling prices, American farmers and laborers tended to blame gold for their problems and demanded that silver supplement it (culminating in William Jennings Bryan's "Cross of Gold" speech at the 1896 Democratic national convention). See also SILVER STANDARD.

binary Based on two values, dual. The binary number system is based on 2 and uses only two digits, 0 and 1, just as the decimal system is based on 10 and uses ten digits, from 0 to 9. Two digits can represent any number, just as ten digits can.

Binary System	Decimal System
0	0
1	1
10	2
11	3
100	4
101	5
110	6
111	7
1000	8
1001	9
10000	16
100000	32

The binary system is basic to the digital COMPUTER, which is activated by electromagnetic impulses that either attract or repel, two conditions usually described as "on" and "off," which can respectively represent the two digits required. Therefore all data loaded into a computer are converted from decimal to *binary digits,* or *bits.* (In the early days of computers this was done beforehand, but today it is usually done by the machine itself.) The memory (storage place of information) in most computers contains a large number of such bits. In addition, several coding systems have been devised to represent letters of the alphabet, decimal numbers, punctuation marks, etc. See also BYTE.

binder
1. In real estate, an agreement to cover a down payment, as evidence of the buyer's good faith.
2. A temporary agreement given to a person who desires insurance, subject to the same conditions as the insurance policy to be issued.

binomial distribution Also, *binomial probability distribution, Bernoulli distribution.* A mathematical estimate of the likelihood of one event occurring instead of another when the outcome must be one of two alternatives and previous experience has no influence on the outcome. For example, it can be used to estimate the number of times a coin will come up heads rather than tails in a given number of tosses, or the percentage of a given number of voters who will vote "yes" rather than "no" on a given amendment. The formula used in this estimate was developed by the Swiss mathematician Jacob Bernoulli (1654–1705). See also CUMULATIVE DISTRIBUTION; NORMAL DISTRIBUTION; POISSON DISTRIBUTION.

bit See under BINARY.

blacklist See under LABOR UNION.

black market
1. In general, any transactions that violate existing laws governing price, supply, or other trading conditions. It is associated particularly with times of scarcity, as in wartime or postwar periods. See also GRAY MARKET.
2. In foreign exchange, a transaction contrary to governmental EXCHANGE CONTROLS. For example, a Russian citizen, forbidden by law to buy U.S. dollars, may wish to build up a private bank account in America; to do so, he or she might sell Russian rubles on the black market to American tourists at a favorable rate in exchange for U.S. currency or traveler's checks.

Blanc, Louis A French socialist and politician (1811–82) who was the first to put a utopian plan into operation with the support of the government. Blanc believed competition to be the source of all economic and social evil, and he visualized a social order in which everyone would produce according to his abilities and receive according to his needs (see also COMMUNISM, def. 1). To this end, he proposed that all goods be produced in *social workshops,* controlled by workingmen and supported financially by the state. In this way the capitalist could be eliminated entirely. The Revolution of 1848 gave Blanc a chance to test his ideas; some social workshops actually were set up, but the plan was sabotaged by opponents of Blanc's views. Involved in a workers' uprising, Blanc was forced into exile in England, where he wrote a 12-volume history of the French Revolution. In 1870 he returned to France and was elected to the National Assembly, where he remained a leader of the left. His ideas had considerable influence on later socialists, especially in Germany.

blank check See under CHECK.

blanket mortgage A MORTGAGE that encompasses more than one parcel of real estate. Once such a mortgage is taken out, the mortgagee is entitled to payment of the mortgage in full and cannot be compelled to release any one parcel upon the payment of a prorated share of the mortgage debt.

blanket order Also, *standing order.* A purchase order for the long-term requirements of a particular item—usually one year's worth—to be shipped "as released." When stocks of such items run low, the buyer asks the supplier for shipment of another part of the outstanding blanket order. Blanket orders on small, regularly used items save paper work, time, and inventory costs, and often result in a price reduction (because the supplier knows a certain quantity will be sold over the year).

blanket policy An insurance policy covering several kinds of property at one location, or one kind of property at several locations. For example, a blanket policy might cover one building and all its contents, or it might cover all of the furniture in three different buildings.

blanket rate See under FREIGHT.

block booking See under TYING RESTRICTIONS.

blocked exchange See under EXCHANGE CONTROLS.

block trader See under THIRD MARKET.

blue chip Describing the common stock of a company known for the quality and wide acceptance of its products or services, and for its ability to make money and pay dividends. Such stocks tend to be relatively high in price and offer a relatively low yield.

blue-collar Describing workers performing predominantly physical labor, ranging from unskilled to semiskilled and highly skilled jobs. The term derives from their work clothes, frequently overalls or similar special outfits. Among those considered blue-collar workers by the U.S. Bureau of the Census are craftsmen and kindred workers (carpenters, construction craftworkers, mechanics, repairers, metalcraft workers, and blue-collar supervisors such as foremen), and operatives of various kinds of machinery, transportation equipment, and motor vehicles. The proportion of blue-collar workers in the labor force has been steadily declining since 1950, as improved technology has decreased the number of workers needed to run machinery. See also GRAY-COLLAR; WHITE-COLLAR.

Blue Cross, Blue Shield See under HEALTH INSURANCE.

blue-sky laws See under ISSUE.

board lot See under ROUND LOT.

board of directors The persons elected by the shareholders of a corporation to set company policy. Normally the directors appoint the company president, vice-presidents, and all operating officers. They also decide if and when stock dividends will be paid. The board of directors and the company officers constitute a company's top management.

Board of Governors See under FEDERAL RESERVE.

board of trade See COMMODITY EXCHANGE.

board room A room in a brokerage office where throughout the trading day customers can see the opening, high, low, and last prices of leading stocks posted on a board (hence the name), also called a *quote board*. The room may also contain a screen on which the TICKER is projected. Since the 1960s various electronic devices, generally involving computers, have replaced older systems of showing price quotations.

bodily injury insurance See under LIABILITY INSURANCE.

body shop See under EMPLOYMENT AGENCY.

bogey In business and industry, a standard of performance, usually a sales or production quota, expected of employees. If the bogey is exceeded, employees are rewarded with bonuses or in some other way.

Böhm-Bawerk, Eugen von An Austrian economist (1851–1914), one of the members of the MARGINALIST SCHOOL, brother-in-law of F. von WIESER. A professor and three-time minister of finance, he is remembered chiefly for his ideas on capital and interest. Böhm-Bawerk regarded capital as a commodity that is created when land, labor, and material are embodied in a product or service and that is destroyed when that product or service is used up. Interest is the price paid for the use of capital, and it exists because consumers prefer present goods to future goods. Further, with modern industry growing more complex, production processes are more "roundabout," to use Böhm-Bawerk's widely quoted term, and hence capitalists must wait longer to get a return on their investment. Interest therefore is a reward for waiting (see also ABSTINENCE THEORY OF INTEREST). Böhm-Bawerk's view of time of production as an important variable and time preference as a vital factor has continued to influence economists to the present day.

boiler insurance See under PROPERTY INSURANCE.

boiler room Also, *boiler shop*. A place devoted to high-pressure selling by telephone of stocks of dubious value. A boiler room is usually lined with desks or cubicles, each with a salesperson and telephone. Sales personnel are given so-called sucker lists, that is, the names and phone numbers of prospective customers.

bona fide In law, a Latin term meaning "in good faith," without FRAUD.

bond

1. An IOU or promissory note from a corporation or government. A bond is evidence of a debt on which the issuer (borrower) usually promises to pay a specified amount of interest for a specified period of time, and usually to repay the principal (in the amount stated on the bond; see FACE VALUE) on the date of expiration, or maturity date (see MATURITY). A bond represents debt; its holder is a creditor and its issuer a borrower. In the event of the issuer's financial collapse, bondholders' claims on assets take precedence over those of stockholders, so bonds are generally considered to carry less risk than stocks. There are many kinds of bond, depending on whether and how they are secured, who issues them, how long they run, how and when principal and interest are paid, the currency of payment, the purpose of their issue, etc.

A *secured bond* is one backed by a mortgage or a pledge of collateral (see also COLLATERAL TRUST BOND; GUARANTEED BOND; MORTGAGE BOND); an unsecured bond is called a DEBENTURE. Bonds may be issued by a central government or one of its agencies (*government bond, Treasury bond*), a local government (*municipal bond*), or a corporation (*corporate bond*). U.S. government bonds are regarded as the highest-grade securities in existence, carrying practically no risk, even though they are secured solely by the credit standing of the government. Municipal bonds, issued by a state, county, city, town, or village (or one of their agencies) generally are *tax-exempt*, that is, the holder of such a bond need pay no Federal (and often no state) income tax on interest earned.

Among the reasons a corporation issues bonds (rather than common or preferred stock) are (1) to avoid diluting the firm's equity (stockholders are owners, bondholders are creditors); (2) to avoid taxes (the interest it pays on bonds is not subject to corporate income tax); (3) management's belief that its earnings will rise, so that bond interest payments will be more economical; (4) management's inability to sell stock, either because of depressed market conditions or because it is not sufficiently well known to investors. American corporate bonds are commonly issued in denominations of $1,000, although there are numerous exceptions (among them the *baby bond* of $100).

A bond usually represents a longer-term obligation than a note or a bill. All bonds run for a year or longer, and most run for 20 to 30 years. A *perpetual bond* or *annuity bond* has no maturity date; interest on it is paid indefinitely, and it is *irredeemable* (cannot be cashed in). Unlike most short-term obligations (and like some preferred stock), a bond may be *callable* or *redeemable*, that is, the issuer may retire it at any time before its maturity date, though usually only by paying a premium (an amount in excess of the face value). Bonds that cannot be redeemed before maturity are termed *noncallable*. An *optional bond* may be redeemed by the issuer on or after a given date prior to maturity. For example, a "5-20" bond was a popular U.S. government bond redeemable after 5 years and payable after 20 years. A *serial bond* is one of a series of bonds issued at the same time but maturing at intervals over a period of time; for example, a total issue of $90 million may be in six series of $15 million each, redeemable at 3-year intervals beginning the fifth year after issue. With an *installment bond,* the principal is repaid in installments over a stated period of time rather than being paid all at once at maturity.

Many bonds pay interest on a regular periodic basis. If one buys a bond between interest payments, the buyer usually pays the seller the interest that has accrued since the last payment in addition to the market price (see also FLAT, def. 1). However, a *noninterest-bearing discount bond* is bought for less than face value (at a *discount*), and interest on it, instead of being paid regularly, accrues to the maturity date, when it is paid together with the principal. An *income bond*, on the other hand, usually receives interest only when it is earned (and thus represents a LIEN on the issuer's income); in some cases unpaid interest is accumulated, as with a discount bond, and is paid on redemption. The various terms of payment for principal and interest are important to the investor in calculating the return on bonds (see also YIELD).

A *coupon bond* is one with interest coupons attached to it; the coupons are *clipped* (detached) by the holder as they become due and are presented for payment of interest. (Thus *coupon rate* has come to mean the stated interest rate on bonds.) A coupon bond usually is a *bearer bond*, that is, because the holder's name is not registered, the bond is payable to the bearer, and therefore negotiable. In contrast, a *registered bond* is recorded on the issuer's books in the holder's name and can be transferred only after endorsement by the registered owner. A *registered coupon bond* is registered for payment of principal but not of interest, which is payable to whoever clips the coupons. An *interchangeable bond* is a bearer bond that may be changed to a registered bond (or, sometimes, vice versa) on the holder's request. A *convertible bond* may be exchanged by the owner for common stock or another security (see also CONVERTIBLE, def. 1).

A *currency bond* is payable in the currency of a particular country rather than in gold or the currency of the holder's country. Some bonds are repayable in several currencies at the option of the holder. A *dollar bond* is one on which both interest and principal are payable in U.S. dollars, no matter where issued (see DOLLAR BOND).

Bonds also can be classified according to the purpose for which they are issued. A *revenue bond* is issued by a government (central or local) to raise funds in anticipation of tax receipts, and is to be redeemed from tax revenues once they have been received. It resembles a *tax bond*, which is actually acceptable as tax payment; such bonds are bought by taxpayers in anticipation of future taxes. An IN-DUSTRIAL REVENUE BOND, on the other hand, is a device for attracting new industry to an area. A *consolidated bond* or *unified bond* is issued to retire and replace two or more previous bond issues, perhaps to take advantage of currently more favorable interest rates or to reorganize the financial structure of the issuing corporation (see also CONSOL); a bond issued for the latter purpose is also called a *reorganization bond* or *adjustment bond*. Sometimes the issuer of a bond extends the maturity date for an additional period, at the same or a different rate of interest; this is known as an *extended bond*. With a *continued bond*, the holder decides whether to present it for redemption at maturity or to continue to hold it, at either the same or a different interest rate. See also SAVINGS BOND.

2. In law, an agreement whereby one party is bound to back another's debt or to indemnify one or more others against loss. For example, a defendant in a court action may be required to post bail (a *bail bond*), and another person may agree to put up the bail, guaranteeing that the defendant will appear in court for disposition of the case. See also FIDELITY BOND; SURETY BOND.

bonded warehouse   See under WAREHOUSE.

bond yield   See YIELD, defs. 1, 2, 3.

bonus   Any compensation to employees over and above the regular wage or salary. See also WAGE INCENTIVE.

bonus stock   Common stock offered as a bonus, either to the underwriter of the issue as additional incentive, or to buyers of bonds or preferred stock in the same company.

bookkeeping   Keeping the financial records (books) of a business or other economic unit, recording all the transactions in which it engages. Bookkeeping is a branch of ACCOUNTING (see def. 1).

book value

1. In accounting, the amount an asset or group of assets is said to be worth in the books of account, which may be quite different from its market value or intrinsic value. *Gross book value* is the amount that appears; to calculate *net book value*, some allowance (for depreciation, etc.) is deducted.

2. In corporate finance, a corporation's value,

computed by subtracting all its debts from its total assets. In effect, book value is the same as *net assets*. In financial reports total book value is often reported on a per-share basis, that is, net assets are divided by the number of bonds or shares outstanding. For example, suppose XYZ Corporation has total assets of $9.6 million and current liabilities of $2.5 million. Further, it has 2,700 $1,000 bonds outstanding. Therefore, the book value of XYZ's assets is $7.1 million ($9.6 million − $2.5 million), and each $1,000 bond is covered by assets equal to $7.1 million ÷ 2,700 = $2,629. To calculate book value per share of stock, one must deduct from total assets not only current liabilities but also long-term liabilities (and, for common stock, the book value of preferred stock) and divide the result by the number of shares outstanding.

boom A particularly rapid expansion in any or all phases of business activity (see under BUSINESS CYCLE). The economy, the stock market, sales, an industry, and a business can all be said to experience a boom (or be "booming"). Also, a business can be said to have a *boom year*.

borrowed reserves See under FEDERAL FUNDS MARKET.

borrowing Obtaining the temporary use of funds, usually for a fee called *interest*. See CREDIT, def. 1; LOAN; LOANABLE FUNDS.

bottleneck A point or stage in a business or manufacturing operation where progress is impeded. For example, in an assembly line, a single machine operating more slowly than the others can prolong one stage of production, and hence reduce overall output.

bottleneck inflation A rise in the general PRICE LEVEL, or in the prices of certain goods, owing either to an unexpected reduction in supply or to a sharp (and usually unexpected) increase in demand. For example, in 1946 the owner of a 1941 automobile could sell it for more than its original price, because almost no civilian cars had been produced during World War II and demand greatly exceeded supply. It was several years before automobile manufacturers were able to eliminate

"bottlenecks" and put enough new cars on the market to satisfy the demand.

bottomry A loan secured by a vessel or its cargo. The borrower may continue to use the vessel, and should it be lost ("go to the bottom," hence the name) the lender loses his money. A *bottomry bond* is a debt secured by a mortgage on a vessel (specifically, the vessel's hull, or bottom). Such bonds are usually issued by shipowners to obtain funds for refurbishing or repairing a vessel; if the vessel is lost the bond is automatically canceled.

Boulwareism A management strategy for negotiating with a labor union, which essentially consists of making a final, "take it or leave it" offer. It is named for Lemuel R. Boulware, a vice-president of the General Electric Company who devised it in the 1950s. After studying union demands, the company announces an offer it describes as fair and the best it can do. If no settlement is made, the company implements its offer for all those workers not represented by the union and states that, unless the union accepts the offer, there will be no retroactive benefits (in case of a wage increase). The company's offer is final, so a strike would be useless. This strategy calls for direct communication between management and workers, circumventing the union, and, though management claims it is trying to be fair, labor not surprisingly resents the one-sidedness of this approach.

bounty A government subsidy or other special payment, used to encourage an industry or product. The most common is the *export bounty*, paid to encourage producers of materials being exported. For most products today export bounties violate the terms of the GENERAL AGREEMENT ON TARIFFS AND TRADE (GATT) or other trade treaties.

bourgeoisie
1. The French word for "middle class," first used in feudal times to distinguish merchants and artisans from the clergy and nobility on the one hand and from common laborers and peasants on the other. During the COMMERCIAL REVOLUTION, the bourgeoisie became the most important economic class in practically all of western Europe; it included merchants, bankers, shipowners, prin-

cipal investors, and industrial entrepreneurs. At first the bourgeoisie was politically both royalist and nationalist, supporting a strong central government that would ensure political stability and favor business interests. Subsequently, in the late 18th century, the bourgeoisie came to support the principles of constitutionality and natural right (as opposed to noble privilege and divine right), and in the 19th century it became a strong political force in its own right.

2. In communist and socialist theory, a name for the capitalist class, which allegedly exploits the proletariat (working class) and hence should be destroyed. See COMMUNISM, def. 1.

bourse The French name for STOCK EXCHANGE, used also for other European exchanges. The German term is *Börse*.

boycott Concerted refusal to cooperate or even deal with a person, organization, or nation to express disapproval and/or effect coercion. The term comes from Captain Boycott, an agent of English landowners who acted so harshly against their Irish tenants that in 1880 they organized against him and refused to sell him supplies or otherwise deal with him. A boycott is principally an economic weapon used by one nation against another, or by a labor union against an employer, involving the refusal to handle, transport, sell, or buy certain goods or materials, and persuading others to do the same. In modern times the boycott became a favorite weapon of labor unions, which resorted to both *primary boycotts* (against employers on whom they were bringing pressure) and *secondary boycotts* (against a third party that in turn would bring pressure on those employers). For example, a union might urge its members and the public to stop buying Company A's products, constituting a primary boycott; then it might urge the employees of Company B to stop processing Company A's products and go on strike, constituting a secondary boycott. Long before the Taft-Hartley Act of 1947 outlawed secondary boycotts, unions had been successfully prosecuted for boycotts under the Sherman Antitrust Act of 1890, which outlawed all contracts, combinations, and conspiracies "in restraint of trade." Courts continued to apply this law to unions even after the Clayton Antitrust Act of 1914

specifically exempted them from this proviso. The most famous Supreme Court decision concerning boycotts was the *Danbury Hatters Case*. In 1902 the United Hatters union called a strike against a hat manufacturer in Danbury, Connecticut, and the national union promoted a nationwide boycott against the company's product. The company sued under the Sherman Act, and the Supreme Court, in 1908 and again on reappeal in 1911, concluded that this secondary boycott was in restraint of trade and that the 248 union members who lived in Connecticut all were liable and could each be sued for damages. Half a century later the United Farm Workers Association, a fledgling union of California agricultural workers led by Cesar Chavez, instituted a nationwide boycott of California wine grapes (1966). Since the union was not officially recognized by either the growers or the government, courts could not rule against this secondary boycott. Soon after, the union began a primary boycott of California table grapes. In 1970 the growers finally agreed to negotiate and signed the first labor contract with the union. In 1975 California passed a state law forbidding secondary boycotts that try to prevent goods from reaching the market but permitted *consumer educational boycotts* against a grower by a union.

brainstorming A technique used to stimulate creative thinking and problem-solving. Introduced in the 1940s in the advertising industry, it has since been used in business, industry, and government. In brainstorming sessions, a group of four to ten persons meets to consider a particular problem. Each participant is encouraged to propose any idea that occurs to him or her, no matter how silly or impractical it may seem, in the hope that at least one good solution will emerge.

branch banking A system whereby a bank may operate more than one office. Though the banking system of many advanced countries, including Canada and the United Kingdom, is characterized by a few large banks with numerous branches, branch banking in the United States is limited to state banks regulated by fairly strict state laws, which specify the location of branches. More than a dozen states forbid branches altogether. Opponents of branch banking believe that it tends to concentrate economic power too greatly. Nevertheless, branch banking has expanded considerably since World War II, and by the mid-1970s about one-third of all American banks operated one or more branches. See also UNIT BANKING.

branching See under PROGRAMMING.

branch store See under DEPARTMENT STORE.

brand A name, term, symbol, or design (or a combination of these) that serves to identify goods or services of one seller or group of sellers and to distinguish them from those of competitors. A *brand name* is a word, letter, or group of words or letters so used; it differs from a TRADEMARK in that the latter is basically a legal term and must meet criteria established by law. Thus, a Ford automobile signifies a brand identifying the Ford Motor Company; its brand name is Ford, whether spoken or printed; "Ford" written in a special script or other distinctive form is a trademark. Both brand names and trademarks are protected by law, their ownership and use having been established by continued usage. In the United States the Lanham Act of 1946 established what types of trademark and brand name can be so protected and provides for their registration. When unregistered, brand names sometimes become common descriptive names, and their owners lose all rights to them. For example, "cellophane," "aspirin," and "kerosene" all were brand names at one time, and such current brand names as Scotch Tape, Lifesaver, and Xerox seem likely to become public property through their widespread use in a generic sense.

The name "brand" comes from the ancient practice of marking property with a hot iron (branding iron), which persists in the livestock industry. Brands were used by medieval craft and merchant guilds to identify and protect their merchandise, so that goods of inferior quality could be traced to their producers and would not reflect on an entire class of goods. The earliest and most aggressive brand promoters in the United States were mid-19th-century manufacturers of patent medicines who were imitated by food manufacturers and soap companies immediately after the Civil War. Some of the brands that originated then are still familiar to consumers, among them Quaker Oats, Vaseline, Borden's Condensed Milk, and Ivory Soap. Today there are some 38,000 brands in American grocery products alone, though the average supermarket stocks only about 6,500.

Brands can be classified according to the number and kind of products they embrace, and according to where in the distribution process a product is branded. A *family brand* or *blanket brand* covers a variety of products (such as Sears, Roebuck's Kenmore brand, used for numerous different appliances and hardware items). An *individual brand* is used for a single product, and in fact a producer may use different brand names for different grades of the same product (such as three names for three grades of motor oil). A *manufacturer's brand* identifies a product branded by the producer and sold as a brand to wholesalers and retailers; such a brand is also called a *national brand* when, as is often the case, it is promoted and distributed on a nationwide basis (which, however, may also be true of other kinds of brand). Examples of well-known American manufacturer's brands include IBM, Kellogg, Coca Cola, and Kleenex. When a wholesaler or retailer brands a product, the brand is called a *dealer brand, distributor's brand, house brand,* or *private brand.* Dealer brands have become quite common in American department stores, supermarkets, service stations, clothing stores, appliance stores, and drugstores, where they frequently—but not always —are offered at slightly lower prices than manufacturer's brands.

Many economists, professional buyers, and consumer advocates point out the disadvantages of buying by brand name. Chief among their objections is that brand names restrict competition (see FAIR TRADE for a glaring example) and that publicizing a brand adds to the product's cost. Nevertheless, many consumers continue to buy by brand, largely because they regard it as an assurance of quality but also for such reasons as snob appeal; moreover, in industrial buying it sometimes is the most practical way for a small firm, which cannot afford elaborate quality-control procedures, to operate.

brassage See under COIN.

breach of contract Failure of one or both parties to a CONTRACT to perform some part of it. In that event the injured party may bring action for damages; in some cases the injured party may also rescind the contract and/or bring a suit in equity to compel the other party to honor the terms.

breach of warranty See under WARRANTY.

break Colloquial term for a drop in prices, particularly volatile securities or commodity prices.

break-even analysis An investigation of how changes in volume of production affect costs and profit, a valuable tool in setting a product's price. A break-even analysis is usually illustrated graphically (see Figs. 8 and 9). On a chart, one curve shows the total cost (fixed plus variable) at various levels of production, while a second shows the total income at various levels of production. The point at which the two curves intersect, called the *break-even point*, indicates the level of production at which the producer neither loses money nor makes a profit.

Fig. 8. Break-even chart and unit cost at standard volume

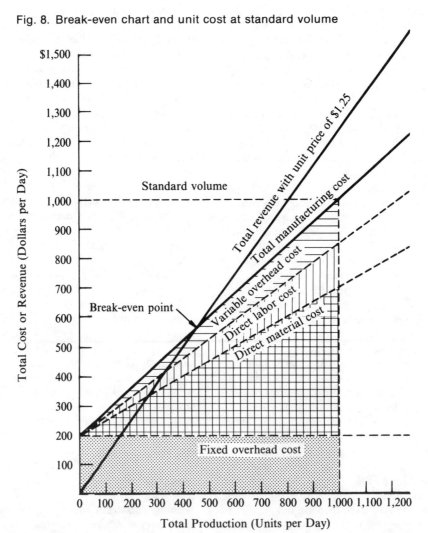

Source: D. S. Ammer, *Manufacturing Management and Control* (New York: Appleton-Century-Crofts, 1968), p. 26. Reprinted by permission of Prentice-Hall, Inc.

Fig. 9. Unit cost at various volumes of output, where variable cost is $.80 and fixed cost is $200

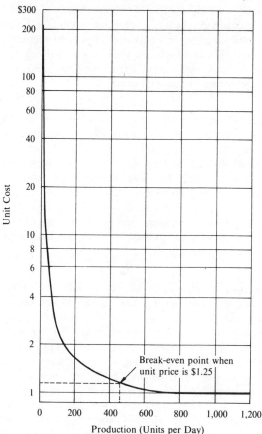

Unit Cost

Break-even point when unit price is $1.25

Production (Units per Day)

Source: D. S. Ammer, *Manufacturing Management and Control* (New York: Appleton-Century-Crofts, 1968), p. 28. Reprinted by permission of Prentice-Hall, Inc.

break point See under ODD LOT, def. 1.

Bretton Woods Conference A meeting held at Bretton Woods, New Hampshire, in July 1944, sponsored by the United Nations and attended by representatives of 44 nations. It established the INTERNATIONAL MONETARY FUND and also the INTERNATIONAL BANK FOR RECONSTRUCTION AND DEVELOPMENT.

broad market See HEAVY MARKET.

broken lot Also, *job lot, odd lot.* In various kinds of trade, an amount smaller than the normal unit of trading, for example, less than 5,000 bushels of wheat.

broker

1. Also, *commission broker.* In the securities trade, an agent who handles customers' orders to buy and sell securities or commodities, in return for a commission or fee (called *brokerage*). A broker may belong to a member firm of a STOCK EXCHANGE or himself be an exchange member. *Stock brokers* specialize in stocks and bonds; *commodity brokers* specialize in commodities. Brokers differ from dealers in that they act as agents rather than as principals (see DEALER, def. 2), but the same individual or firm may, at different times, function as either broker or dealer. See also FLOOR TRADER; REGISTERED REPRESENTATIVE; SPECIALIST; *floor broker,* under STOCK EXCHANGE; TWO-DOLLAR BROKER; *block trader,* under THIRD MARKET.

2. *insurance broker.* In the United States, a person licensed by a state insurance department to sell insurance. He or she need not be appointed as agent of any company (see AGENT, def. 2). Technically a broker does not represent any company (and so cannot make any promises on its behalf); rather, the broker represents the prospective policyholder and tries to obtain the most suitable, economical insurance for him or her.

3. *real estate broker.* A person or company engaged in negotiating the sale, purchase, lease, or exchange of land. Legally the broker is an AGENT (see def. 1) usually working for a commission, which is payable only if the transaction actually takes place. In the United States real estate brokers must have a state license, obtained by passing an examination. A licensed broker may, and frequently does, employ salespersons, who are paid by the broker; they usually may not, unless themselves licensed, collect commissions directly from the broker's customers. Most often brokers are hired by a seller of land, called the *principal,* but occasionally they are hired by the buyer. In some states the broker and principal must have a written contract, called a *listing contract.* See also LISTING.

4. *merchandise broker.* See under MIDDLEMAN.

brokers' loan Money borrowed by brokers from banks to buy or carry securities, finance the underwriting of new issues, or carry their clients' margin accounts. It is sometimes described as a *brokers' call loan* or *call money* since it can be "called" (terminated by the lender or borrower) should the market value of the securities used as collateral decline in value.

Brook Farm   See under FOURIER, F. M. C.

bubble   A high-risk investment, particularly one that leads to inflationary expansion far beyond the original assets or possibilities for profit. In the early 18th century, the rapid expansion of business activity and trade (see COMMERCIAL REVOLUTION) gave rise to orgies of wild speculation, which reached a climax in two "bubbles" that burst in 1720, the *South Sea Bubble* and the *Mississippi Bubble*. The first involved the inflated stock of the South Sea Company in England, whose promoters agreed to take over most of the British national debt in exchange for the exclusive right to trade with South America and the Pacific islands. Since the prospects for profit seemed limitless, the company's stock rose rapidly, soon selling for ten times its original price. Soon, however, investors became disheartened; suspecting that the scheme had been overrated, they unloaded their stock at a frantic rate. The bubble burst, and the investors lost their savings. The Mississippi Bubble involved a similar scheme, in which a Scottish financier, John Law, persuaded the French government to grant his company the exclusive right to colonize and exploit the Louisiana Territory in exchange for taking over the French national debt. As government loans were redeemed through the issuing of paper money, the creditors were encouraged to buy Mississippi stock with the money received. The shares soon soared in price, ultimately reaching 40 times their original value. But as investors came to realize that only a nominal dividend could be paid with the stock thus inflated, they began to sell their shares. In 1720 the bubble burst in a wild panic, and thousands lost their life savings. Though speculative greed was temporarily cooled, bubbles have reappeared and burst periodically in each century. One of the most curious was the *Tulip Bubble*, which occurred in Holland during the mid-17th century. The Dutch had just become large-scale growers and exporters of tulip bulbs (as they still are) and begun to develop new varieties of the flower. Suddenly everyone in Europe became interested in tulips. Prices began to rise, especially of certain new varieties that caught the public fancy. This encouraged speculation in and hoarding of bulbs, in hopes of further price rises. At the peak, some individual tulip bulbs were selling for the equivalent of several thousand dollars. The bubble burst when people realized that almost any bulb could easily be duplicated and thereby lost its scarcity value.

bucket shop   An illegal enterprise in which "brokers" accept but never execute customers' orders to buy and sell securities, pocketing the money instead. So long as a customer's investment declined in price, the bucket shop was safe from exposure; if the price rose and the customer wanted to sell, however, the bucket shop would have to close down, usually opening another office elsewhere. Common in 19th-century America, bucket shops today are virtually extinct.

budget   A plan listing all the expenditures and income expected during some given future period (frequently one year) by an individual, family, or organization (company, government, etc.). An individual or family might expect income from salaries and wages, interest-bearing securities, gifts, sale of securities or other assets, and other sources, and anticipate expenditures for food, housing, entertainment, health care, education, etc. A business budget is usually based on expected output and sales and anticipated expenses. A government budget, on the other hand, is based on anticipated tax revenues and expenditures. The purpose of most budgets is to allocate spending rationally, so that revenues are spent on essential items before luxuries. However, even the most carefully planned budgets can result in excess, in the form of either a *surplus* (when revenues exceed expenditures) or a *deficit* (when expenditures exceed revenues). When revenues and expenditures are equal (over some period of time), the budget is said to be *balanced* (though the term *balanced budget* also is used when revenues exceed expenditures). Whereas a balanced budget is generally desirable for individuals, most modern economists feel it is less important for a government (see under PUBLIC DEBT). See also CAPITAL BUDGET; FEDERAL BUDGET; FULL-EMPLOYMENT BUDGET.

Budget, U.S. Bureau of the See under FEDER-AL BUDGET.

buffer stock plan See under INTERNATIONAL COMMODITY AGREEMENT.

building and loan association See SAVINGS AND LOAN ASSOCIATION.

building code A set of rules and specifications established by local government authorities for the construction of buildings or other permanent structures. Normally a builder requires an authorization, or *building permit*, for a new building or for extensive repairs, and regular inspections by the authority's building inspectors ensure that the work done conforms to the building code.

built-in stabilizer Also, *automatic stabilizer*. An automatic corrective device that offsets the violent price and income swings of the BUSINESS CYCLE. Most such stabilizers are fiscal in nature. The most important are personal and corporate income taxes, which rise and fall with personal and business income and serve both to slow down too rapid expansion (through higher taxes) and to stimulate a sagging economy (through lower taxes); unemployment compensation (and similar forms of welfare payment), which counteract slowdowns by raising payments to the jobless; and farm aid programs, which cushion the sometimes wild fluctuations in farm prices. The American economist Paul SAMUELSON points out that corporate savings (reflected in continuity of dividend payments to shareholders despite short-term changes in corporate income) and family savings (continued propensity to save even if income rises) similarly act as built-in stabilizers.

bulk
   1. A large quantity of merchandise.
   2. A large amount of unpackaged merchandise, such as a carload of fertilizer or a tank car of wine, usually purchased in unpackaged form.
   3. *bulk sale.* The sale of an entire stock of goods, or the entire assets of a business, as in bankruptcy proceedings. In the United States strict laws apply to such a sale to protect the business's creditors.
   4. *bulk-line costs.* The costs of producing most

of the total supply of a particular product. Such costs are calculated in order to set a selling price high enough to attract enough producers to guarantee sufficient supplies of an item, a policy followed by, for example, the U.S. government during World War I.
   5. *bulk buying.* See under STATE TRADING.

bull In the securities trade, a trader who counts on making profits from rising prices (buying low and selling high) and hence believes that business is improving; by extension, an optimist. The precise origin of the term is not known. A market characterized by a long-term trend of rising prices is called a *bull market.* See also BEAR.

bullion Gold or silver of a purity or fineness suitable for coining. Today, since gold and silver are rarely used in coins, bullion is usually cast in bars or ingots of specified weight for convenience of handling. Gold bullion has long been an international medium of exchange and store of value, serving in effect as an international currency. It also is used as a partial reserve by most nations (see GOLD RESERVE), even those whose currency is not on a GOLD STANDARD. Silver is valued principally for its industrial and decorative utility. For the doctrine of *bullionism*, see under MERCANTILISM.

bumping Also, *backtracking.* The displacement of one worker by another with more SENIORITY, common in industries where labor contracts include rigid seniority rules. The term "backtracking" comes from the fact that a senior employee may move to a lower-level job, causing the layoff of a junior employee.

burden
   1. See OVERHEAD.
   2. *of the public debt.* See under PUBLIC DEBT.
   3. *tax burden.* See under TAX.
   4. *burden center.* See under COST CENTER.

business agent The highest official in a local union. Found mostly in the unions of nonfactory workers (building trades, hotel and restaurant workers, barbers, etc.), the business agent, who is usually salaried and either elected or appointed, does the principal work of the local, negotiating contracts, settling grievances, recruiting members, etc.

business barometer See INDICATOR.

Business Conditions Digest A monthly publication of the U. S. Department of Commerce that brings together many of the economic time series found most useful by business analysts and forecasters, including indexes compiled by both government and private agencies. Included are data on national income and product, cyclical indicators, opinion surveys regarding the expectations of businessmen and intentions of consumers, foreign trade and payments, Federal government activities, and price movements.

business cycle Also, Brit. *trade cycle*. A pattern of fluctuation in economic activity, characterized by alternate expansion and contraction. In general, business activity expands, with rising industrial production, employment, prices, wages, interest rates, and profits. It reaches a high point of prosperity and remains there for a time. Then activity begins to contract, with business volume receding, and production, employment, prices, etc., declining for a time until a low point is reached. After a time recovery begins and business activity expands again. Economists distinguish four phases, known by various names: (1) *expansion* (*prosperity, boom*) to an upper *turning point*, or *peak*; (2) *contraction* (*crisis, recession, slump, downturn*) to a lower *turning point*; (3) *depression* (*trough, bust, crash, bottom*); (4) *recovery* (*revival, upturn*).

Although this general pattern prevails, business cycles differ in the duration of each phase, the extent of high and low points, and the overall duration. J. A. Schumpeter classified three types on the basis of overall duration: *Kitchin cycle*, lasting 40 months; *Juglar cycle*, lasting 9 or 10 years; and *Kondratieff cycle* (also called *long-wave cycle*), lasting 54 to 60 years. U.S. National Bureau of Economic Research statistics, on the other hand, claim an average duration of 52 months for the 27 business cycles that occurred in the United States between 1854 and 1971, while the economist Alvin Hansen found an average duration of 8.35 years for the 17 cycles he detected between 1795 and 1937. Obviously, the duration of a cycle depends on how

it is defined. For example, in 1974 there was considerable debate as to whether or not a RECESSION was actually in progress, owing to disagreement as to just what constitutes a recession (as well as the reluctance of policymakers to admit that they had allowed one to occur). By 1975 practically everyone agreed that a recession was indeed in progress, and the debate over when it had begun subsided as economists then disagreed over whether or not the bottom had yet been reached.

The causes of the business cycle have been attributed to a cycle of sunspots (see SUNSPOT-WEATHER THEORY), the presence or absence of innovation (see *innovation theory* under J. A. SCHUMPETER), the expansion or contraction of bank credit (see MONETARY THEORY), overindulgence in investment (the *overinvestment theory*), too much saving and too little consumption (see *underconsumption theory* under J. A. HOBSON), and the so-called *psychological theory* held by W. BAGEHOT and others, which maintains that optimism and pessimism about the future are contagious and therefore actually bring about anticipated events. Practically every theory developed has some element of truth, but no satisfactory comprehensive explanation has yet been found to account for all business cycles. The study of business cycles began in the 19th century with S. de SISMONDI and others. Outstanding among the economists associated with business-cycle study is W. C. MITCHELL. See also FORECASTING.

business failures See under NET BUSINESS FORMATION; also BANKRUPTCY.

business forecasting See FORECASTING; SALES FORECAST.

business-interruption insurance See under PROPERTY INSURANCE.

business organization See CORPORATION; PARTNERSHIP; PROPRIETORSHIP. For internal business structure, see ORGANIZATION, COMPANY.

business panics See PANICS, BUSINESS.

business trust See MASSACHUSETTS TRUST; TRUST, def. 2.

business unionism   See under AFL-CIO.

bust   A particularly rapid contraction in business activity. See under BUSINESS CYCLE.

"Buy American"   A law passed in 1933 prescribing that the U.S. Federal government and its agencies must buy American-made goods for public use unless they are substantially costlier than imported goods. The term is used also for similar provisions of later laws. Though the rule is occasionally modified, usually in response to protests from foreign bidders on U.S. government contracts, by and large preference tends to be given to American producers.

buyer   In a retail business, an executive who undertakes the purchasing and stocking of various items for the store. Buyers are generally associated with department or chain stores rather than small independent stores, where the owner or manager performs this function. For *resident buyer*, see under MIDDLEMAN. See also PURCHASING; VENDOR, def. 3.

buyers' market   A market in which supply is greater than demand, that is, with more goods for sale than customers, giving buyers considerable influence over price and terms of sale. Prices in a buyers' market tend to be low or declining. See also SELLERS' MARKET.

buying   See PURCHASING.

buying office   A centralized purchasing office that serves a number of retail stores. Chain stores are commonly served by a central buying office; independent stores sometimes jointly hire a central buyer to improve their bargaining power. See also DEPARTMENT STORE.

buying on margin   See MARGIN, BUYING ON.

buying policy index   An important LEADING INDICATOR of business conditions. The index measures the percentage of industrial purchasing agents who report buying commitments 60 days ahead or longer. Typically it reaches a peak some months before the general business cycle, when purchasing agents are committing their firms months into the future to assure an adequate supply of materials and parts; at this point 70 per cent of the participants report commitments 60 days ahead or more. The bottom is reached about the same time as the business cycle, with fewer than 50 per cent reporting such commitments. Developed by the National Bureau of Economic Research from data furnished by the National Association of Purchasing Management, the buying policy index is published monthly in *Business Conditions Digest*.

buying power   In the securities trade, the total amount a stock broker will allow a customer to buy on margin without putting up more cash or securities. See MARGIN, BUYING ON.

by-product   Any product resulting from manufacturing or processing a firm's primary product. Some by-products can be sold as is; others require processing to make them marketable. Examples include the cottonseed separated from cotton, used to make oil; molasses left from sugar refining, used to make industrial alcohol; sawmill waste, used to make paper; fish offal, made into oil and fertilizer; mill-feed, bran, and other wastes from milling flour, used mostly for feed; glycerine, from soap; slag (from the top surfaces of molten metals in blast furnaces), used in Portland cement; and dozens of inedible animal parts (hides, hair, fat, bone, glands, etc.) from meat-packing, used in hundreds of products. See also JOINT PRODUCT.

byte   In computers, a unit of storage consisting of the number of binary digits, or bits (see under BINARY), required to represent one character in the code used. Groups of bytes thus are useful for representing large values.

cable transfer In foreign trade, a BANK DRAFT transmitted by cable or telegraph instead of mail. The correspondent bank then notifies the payee of the remittance's arrival.

c.a.f. Abbreviation for *cost and freight*. A price quotation that includes the cost of both merchandise and freight charges for its shipment to a given destination. It does not, like C.I.F., include insurance of the shipment, and the buyer rather than the seller is responsible for any damage or loss occurring during transit.

calculator Any machine that performs arithmetic or other mathematical functions mechanically or electronically. Calculators range from simple, hand-operated adding machines to computers.

calendar variation See SEASONAL VARIATION.

call In the securities trade, an OPTION to buy a given amount of a certain stock at a specified price, called *striking price,* within a specified time. An option to sell is called a PUT. A call is bought by a person who thinks the price of the stock will rise and therefore wants the option to buy it at the current, lower price. It gives the holder the right to buy the stock, and obligates the seller of the contract to deliver the stock at that price and within that time. The price paid to buy the option is called a *premium.* The terms of calls are much the same as those of puts, running 35 days, 65 days, 95 days, 6 months and 10 days (a so-called 6-and-10 call), or 1 year. The shorter the time period, the lower the premium; a 6-and-10 call normally costs about 50 per cent more than a 95-day call, since the opportunity for changes in the stock's market price is pre-

sumably much greater. However, a 1-year call costs nearly the same as a 6-and-10, though writers of such long option contracts are much harder to find. In addition to buying calls directly from those who write them, customers sometimes can purchase a *special offering,* that is, an option originally bought by a dealer who has held it in inventory.

Suppose Mary Jones decides to speculate in a particular stock. She decides to buy a 6-and-10 call on 100 shares of XYZ Corporation at $40 per share (the striking price), which will expire on June 30, and agrees to pay a premium of $600 for the call. According to stock-exchange rules, she must put $600 into her account before she can buy the option, and she must also pay a transfer tax, in this case $5 (if the striking price were under $20 it would be only $3.75; also, there is no transfer tax on puts). Suppose that XYZ stock immediately begins to drop in price, and within a month it is selling at $34. Jones is not happy, since she expected the price to rise, but she is not too alarmed; the most she can lose on this deal is $605 (if XYZ's stock drops to 0, in which case she can simply let the call expire). However, by the end of the second month the stock has rallied and is up to $50 per share. At this moment Jones could make a handsome profit, simply by telling her broker to exercise the call and sell at market. In other words, she would buy her 100 shares at $40 and sell them at $50, making a profit of $1,000 minus dividends and brokerage charges, or approximately $875. Since this is $275 more than Jones's original $600 investment, she will have made a profit of almost 50 per cent in only two months.

Formerly, the only way to purchase calls was on the open market, where brokers negotiated with

56

dealers and writers of options. Beginning in 1972, however, calls in some stocks could be traded on organized exchanges; see OPTIONS EXCHANGE.

callable bond See under BOND, def. 1.

call-back pay Extra pay given to workers who are asked to return to work (called back) outside regular working hours, to make repairs or perform other emergency services.

call-in pay See REPORTING PAY.

call loan See under LOAN, def. 1; also BROKERS' LOAN.

call money See under BROKERS' LOAN.

Cambridge school A name sometimes used for Alfred MARSHALL and his followers.

cameralism Also, *kameralism*. A form of MER-CANTILISM popular in 18th-century Germany and Austria, which extended to government economic policy. The cameralists believed in fostering home industry and economic self-sufficiency, rather than encouraging widespread commerce and development of overseas colonies as earlier mercantilists had done. They also tended to measure a nation's wealth in terms of its tax revenues.

canceled check A CHECK that has been perforated or ink-stamped on its face to indicate that it has been paid by the bank on which it was drawn and so cannot be used again. Banks normally return canceled checks to depositors, who treat them as receipts from payees.

Cantillon, Richard An Irish-born banker and businessman (*c.* 1680–1734) who anticipated some of the ideas of the CLASSICAL SCHOOL. He described the interplay of demand and supply in creating a market price, and he maintained that an item's value is a measure of the amount of land and labor required to produce it. A successful banker, Cantillon realized that less money was required when circulation was speeded up. In his analysis of the circulation of wealth and his stress on agriculture as the only enterprise yielding a true surplus over cost

of production, he may have influenced the PHYSIOCRATS. Cantillon regarded interest as a reward for the lender's risk-taking, its rate being based on the profits entrepreneurs can make from lending and borrowing, and he clearly understood the fact that bankers create credit. Nevertheless, with regard to foreign trade Cantillon upheld the views of MERCANTILISM, believing that a surplus of exports would result in an increased money supply.

capacity
   1. In business and industry, the potential output of a business with existing plant, workers, and equipment. A firm or factory actually producing at this level is said to be working at *full capacity*. *Excess capacity* or *overcapacity*, on the other hand, means the same as *overproduction* (by a firm or entire industry) relative to demand for a product.
   2. In transportation, the ability of a vehicle or vessel to carry freight, measured in terms of volume (cubic feet, etc.) or weight (tonnage, etc.).

capacity utilization rate See OPERATING RATE.

capital
   1. Also, *capital goods, producer goods*. In economic theory, one of the FACTORS OF PRODUCTION, specifically referring to all goods that are used to produce other goods and services, including factories, machinery, and equipment. Such goods are sometimes designated as either *fixed capital*, meaning durable items such as buildings and machinery, or *circulating capital*, consisting of stocks of raw materials and semifinished and finished goods, which are used up fairly rapidly. See also CONSUMER GOOD. For an explanation of the instability of capital-goods industries, see under ACCELERATION PRINCIPLE.
   2. In business, the total assets of a firm. See CAPITAL ASSET; also ASSET.
   3. Also, *contributed capital, invested capital, paid-in capital*. In accounting, the money invested in a firm by the owners (including stockholders) for use in conducting the business.

capital account
   1. See under BALANCE OF PAYMENTS.
   2. In business accounting, the group of records used for transactions involving the equity (in the

assets) of the owner or owners of a business. See ACCOUNT, def. 1.

capital appropriation See under APPROPRIATION.

capital asset In business, any asset needed to create a product (or service), normally acquired with the intention of being kept rather than being resold. Some authorities consider a capital asset identical to a *fixed asset* (see under ASSET), but others distinguish between the two, holding that capital assets include also intangibles (goodwill, patents, etc.) and investments in affiliated companies or other long-term investments.

capital budget A long-range financial plan for acquiring and financing capital assets (see CAPITAL ASSET); also, any annual plan based on such a long-range program. Generally included are expenditures for major repairs, extensions, replacements, and additions to plant and equipment. The term *capital budgeting* is used for the analysis and evaluation of various capital investments, a process that must take into account such factors as general business conditions (and their influence on current and future prices), funds available for capital expenditures, sources of financing, and choices among investments. In most large corporations, each project is considered and evaluated separately in terms of estimated cost, return on investment, urgency of need, etc. For two methods commonly used to determine return on investment, see DISCOUNTED CASH FLOW and PAYBACK PERIOD.

capital coefficient See CAPITAL-OUTPUT RATIO.

capital consumption allowance In national income accounting, the equivalent of what is called DEPRECIATION in private business accounting. A capital consumption allowance is an accounting charge reflecting estimates of wear and tear, obsolescence, destruction, and accidental loss of physical capital. In the NATIONAL INCOME AND PRODUCT ACCOUNTS, it comprises depreciation charges by business and nonprofit institutions, depreciation of owner-occupied dwellings, and accidental damage to fixed business capital; it does not include allowances for depletion of natural resources. Gross national product (GNP) minus capital consumption allowances constitutes NET NATIONAL PRODUCT.

capital cost See COST OF POSSESSION; OPPORTUNITY COST.

capital expenditure Also, *capital investment, capital outlay*. The purchase price of a CAPITAL ASSET (plant, equipment, vehicles, etc.). Individual firms budget their capital expenditures, usually on an annual basis. Changes in aggregate spending on plant and equipment (that is, the sum of capital expenditures in the nation during a given period) are a major factor in determining the course of the business cycle. See also CAPITAL BUDGET.

capital flight See FLIGHT OF CAPITAL.

capital formation Net investment in capital assets (plant, equipment, vehicles, etc.), that is, the total value of GROSS PRIVATE DOMESTIC INVESTMENT minus depreciation and other physical deterioration of existing stock. Capital formation, which is the basis of future production, is essential to economic growth. Fluctuations in such investment are major contributors to the ups and downs of the business cycle.

capital gains Personal income earned through the sale of such capital assets as securities and real estate. If the asset has been owned for six months or longer and is sold at a profit, the profit is considered a *long-term capital gain* and is taxed at a lower rate by the U.S. Federal government than other income. However, *short-term capital gains*, earned on assets held for less than six months, do not receive a similar favorable rate; thus investors and speculators often must consider the tax advantages (or disadvantages) in deciding whether to buy or sell. *Capital losses*, incurred when an asset is sold for less than its cost, can be deducted from capital gains. Thus, if a taxpayer has made $3,500 on the sale of some stocks and lost $2,000 on the sale of others, only $1,500 of the capital gain is taxable. Also, if losses exceed gains, at least part of them usually can be applied to reduce tax liability, and the balance carried over for a period of years to reduce taxes on possible future capital gains. Some economists believe these rules to be loopholes benefiting the rich, who use them to escape paying their fair share of taxes. Others believe that the entire income-tax structure discourages the risk-taking essential to economic growth and that capital gains therefore should be taxed less than other income, or even not at all.

capital good See CAPITAL, def. 1; also CONSUMER GOOD.

capital-intensive Describing an industry, economic sector, or economy that requires a large proportion of capital input relative to labor or land. For example, the oil industry requires extremely expensive refining equipment, representing heavy capital investment, but relatively little manpower or land area. See also LABOR-INTENSIVE.

capital investment See CAPITAL EXPENDITURE.

capitalism Also, *free enterprise, free enterprise system*. An economic system characterized by private ownership of the means of production and all other kinds of property, and considerable individual freedom in the pursuing of economic activities for the sake of personal profit. Thus, private property, individual freedom, and the profit motive are basic to capitalism. Implicit in capitalism is the use of CAPITAL, or wealth, to earn income for its owner, the *capitalist*. In all capitalist systems, the government plays some economic role, restricting enterprise when it threatens public well-being and engaging in those enterprises that are necessary but not lucrative enough to attract private investment (national defense, police, postal service, etc.).

capitalization
1. The sum of the various securities issued by a corporation. It may include bonds, debentures, preferred and common stock, and surplus. Bonds and debentures are usually carried on the books of the company in terms of their FACE VALUE. Preferred and common stocks may be carried in terms of PAR VALUE or some arbitrary stated value determined by the firm's directors (which may or may not be based on the amount received by the firm for the securities at the time of issue). The capitalization also includes all paid-in and earned surplus that has accrued for the stockholders.

2. The conversion of something into capital, that is, to treat expected earnings (of a bond, machinery, etc.) as though they were part of the firm's capital. Also, the addition to capital of money spent for a long-term benefit, rather than charging it to operating expense. For example, some oil companies "expense" the cost of drilling new wells, while others "capitalize" such expenditures. See also CAPITALIZED VALUE.

capitalized value The value of business assets in terms of their expected future earnings, as calculated according to the DISCOUNTED CASH FLOW method.

capital market The market for buying and selling long-term loanable funds, in the form of bonds, mortgages, and the like. Unlike the MONEY MARKET, where short-term funds are traded, the capital market tends to center on well-organized institutions, such as the stock exchange. However, there is no clear-cut distinction between the two markets, other than that capital market loans generally are used by businesses, financial institutions, and governments to buy capital goods, whereas money-market loans generally fill a temporary need for working capital. The same institutions usually are involved in both markets.

capital movements In economic theory, the movement of money capital from one country to another. In practice, it involves both the long-term and short-term loans made to or received from foreign private citizens, and the long- and short-term government loans and credits extended, either directly or through intermediate channels. The sum of these transactions make up the capital account of a nation's BALANCE OF PAYMENTS. Long-term loans are differentiated from short-term loans (accounting convention sets the dividing line arbitrarily at one year) because their economic effect can differ. A rapid rise in short-term foreign investments, or FLIGHT OF CAPITAL, can help create a balance-of-payments deficit, whereas long-term foreign investments can stimulate domestic economic growth. Short-term capital movements primarily reflect international differences in short-term interest rates and speculators' collective assessment of relative exchange rates. Capital tends to leave nations with low short-term interest or weak currencies in danger of devaluation. In contrast, long-term capital movements are much less speculative, reflecting government or private investment in another country. For example, the Ford Motor Company created a long-term capital movement when it bought a minority interest in its British subsidiary for $400 million, which was converted into British pounds sterling and used to buy the shares. In contrast, American corporations create short-term capital movements when they use U.S. dollars to buy Deutschmarks in the New York, London, or Frankfurt markets because they fear that the dollar will decline in value relative to the Deutschmark. After World War II, the need for more investment capital than either private persons or individual governments could generate led to the creation of the World Bank (INTERNATIONAL BANK FOR RECONSTRUCTION AND DEVELOPMENT) as well as other agencies, such as the INTERNATIONAL MONETARY FUND. See also INTERNATIONAL INVESTMENT.

capital-output ratio Also, *capital coefficient.* The ratio of net investment to change in output, that is, the proportion of capital invested in plant and equipment, minus depreciation, to the total value of a firm's (or industry's or country's) output. The amount of capital required to produce one additional unit of output, which varies widely from industry to industry, depends on both technology and relative prices of factors of production (capital, labor, land). For example, if interest rates are high and wages relatively low, comparatively little investment will be needed to obtain an increase in output. In general, industries that convert basic raw materials into markedly different end-products—such as wood into paper, or crude oil into plastics—require considerable capital investment in order to increase output, and hence have a high capital-output ratio. In contrast, industries that manufacture consumer goods, such as tobacco, leather, clothing, and furniture, require relatively little investment to increase output, and hence have a low capital-output ratio.

capital productivity See under PRODUCTIVITY.

capital stock See under STOCK, def. 1.

captive item A good that is both manufactured and used by the same firm, generally in different divisions of the company. Similarly, a *captive shop* is a factory producing items used in other divisions of the same company.

card punch See under PUNCHED-CARD DATA PROCESSING.

Carey, Henry Charles An American economist (1793–1879) who developed a theory of rent different from that of the English economist David RICARDO. Whereas Ricardo maintained that the best land always was cultivated first and the poorest last, Carey said that in America the process had been reversed. As the population grew and technological progress was made, men cultivated better and better land, and therefore rents fell owing to higher productivity. Carey also believed that increasing prosperity benefits all levels of society and, unlike MALTHUS, he held that as mankind grew in numbers, so would its mastery of nature and its ability to provide food. Though at first a supporter of Adam Smith's views on free trade, Carey later became a protectionist, opposing international trade as wasteful, decadent, and harmful to the internal development of a nation's resources. Since Carey criticized the pessimistic outlook of the CLASSICAL SCHOOL, his views are sometimes called *optimist.*

cargo Any FREIGHT, that is, merchandise transported by a carrier. Usually (but not always) the term is confined to freight carried by ships or other vessels.

carryback A device for reducing a business's income tax by using past capital or operating losses to offset present or future taxable profits. Under certain circumstances this procedure is perfectly legal.

carry forward In accounting, to transfer a balance from one page, account ledger, or accounting period to the next one (or any subsequent one).

carrying cost See COST OF POSSESSION.

cartel An association of producers of the same or similar goods that seeks to obtain MONOPOLY advantages for its members. In the United States cartels are in violation of antitrust laws except insofar as they cover patented items or are concerned solely with the export trade of their members; many other developed countries, including those of the Common Market, now impose similar limitations. (Before World War II, however, cartels were common and perfectly legal in most of Western Europe.) Today, therefore, the term is used chiefly for international associations seeking to control a world market. Control is effected by such practices as prescribing the conditions of sale, setting prices, restricting output, allocating customers and sales territories among the members, or awarding a fixed share of the market to each member. The most powerful cartels are those that control various vital raw materials. For example, in the 1970s the major crude-oil-producing nations functioned as a cartel through the Organization of Petroleum Exporting Countries (OPEC). Their power was felt the world over when, in late 1973, they cut off sales to some nations entirely and quadrupled prices to the rest. Nations producing other relatively scarce raw materials have tried at various times to group together to restrict output and raise prices; generally their success is directly related to the availability of substitutes for their product and the cohesiveness of the group. Cartels also have affected manufactured products such as chemicals, plastics, dyes, electric appliances, light bulbs, steel, and explosives, as well as numerous services. The large airlines of all countries belong to the International Air Transport Association, which sets air fares on all major international routes. See also INTERNATIONAL COMMODITY AGREEMENT.

cash

1. Same as CURRENCY, def. 1; see also LEGAL TENDER.

2. Money in the form of coins, as opposed to paper money.

3. In accounting, a category made up of currency, negotiable money orders, checks, and demand deposits. Listed under current assets, cash is money that is almost instantly available for any ordinary use. See also CASH BASIS; CASH FLOW.

4. To convert a negotiable instrument into money, as, to cash a check or a coupon.

cash and carry A retail business that provides no credit or delivery services, requiring customers to pay cash and pick up their purchases (or pay extra for delivery). By extension, any business that offers lower prices and fewer services.

cash basis In accounting, a system of recording income and expenses when the cash is actually received or paid out, without regard to when it was earned or incurred. See also ACCRUAL BASIS.

cash discount See under DISCOUNT, def. 1.

cash flow In accounting, a company's net profits (sales minus operating expenses) plus allowances for depreciation, representing the funds available as working capital and for expansion. The term "flow" reflects the fact that a company's cash position is in a constant state of flux as a result of continuing activity. *Gross cash flow* is made up of total profits plus depreciation; *net cash flow* is composed of retained earnings (profits remaining after taxes and dividends have been paid) plus depreciation. A company's cash position is affected not only by its cash flow but also by changes in debt, accounts receivable and payable, inventory, prepaid expenses, and interest payments. See Fig. 10, page 62; see also DISCOUNTED CASH FLOW; SOURCE AND APPLICATION OF FUNDS STATEMENT.

cashier's check See under CHECK.

cash market See SPOT MARKET.

cash on delivery See COD.

cash sale

1. In business law, a transaction in which title to goods passes when the buyer pays the seller, as opposed to a CONDITIONAL SALE, in which the seller retains title.

2. In retail selling, a transaction paid for with cash on the spot, as opposed to a credit, COD, or charge account sale. A personal check is usually, though not always, considered a cash payment.

3. In industrial and wholesale selling, a transaction for which payment is made within a specified

Fig. 10. Flow of funds into and out of a business (viewed as a continuous process)

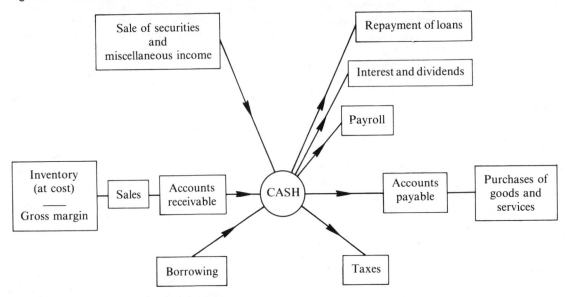

time, such as 30 days. See also under TERMS OF SALE.

cash surrender value See under LIFE INSURANCE.

Cassel, Gustav A noted Swedish economist (1866–1945) remembered principally for his theory of interest and his formulation of the PURCHASING POWER PARITY THEORY. Cassel observed that a lower interest rate might make individuals either save less (by living on capital, or buying an annuity) or save more (so as to receive the same return with the lower interest rate as they received at the higher rate). Suppose, for example, a person has capital of $100,000 and, investing at a 6 per cent interest rate, receives $6,000 per year. If the rate drops to 5.5 or even 5 per cent, the person may be willing to cut back and live on $5,500 or $5,000. But it would be impossible to live on a 3 per cent income from capital, to make ends meet at $3,000. If this person expects to live another 15 years, he could maintain the former standard of living ($6,000) by gradually using up some of the capital. Thus life expectancy enters into the calculation: with a long life expectancy the purchased annuity becomes smaller; with a low interest rate and short life expectancy, it

becomes more tempting to consume savings. Thus it is likely, said Cassel (in *The Theory of Social Economy,* 1918), that at an interest rate below 3 per cent most people will decide to consume their savings. Cassel's theory, however, tends to ignore the real rate of interest (that is, interest in relation to price levels) and the fact that interest is only one of a number of considerations affecting saving.

casual Describing an employee or a job that is irregular in some way, in that it is occasional, temporary, or part-time. Casual workers usually do not accrue seniority, and often they do not share in benefits such as pension plans.

casualty insurance A term still used in the name of many American insurance firms though it no longer describes a specific kind of insurance. In the 19th century, American insurance companies were divided into underwriters of life insurance, fire insurance, and casualty insurance. Fire insurance firms, besides insurance against fire and other perils, often issued marine insurance. Casualty companies wrote many kinds of insurance, such as against glass breakage, theft, forgery, and liability. Most states had laws to the effect that a fire company could not issue liability insurance, or a casualty company fire insurance. In time these distinctions became blurred as companies merged or expanded into other fields, and in the early 1950s many states changed their laws so that non-life insurance companies could write just about any insurance other than life insurance. (Life insurance remained separate, largely because it tends to be much longer-term than the others, which seldom run for terms longer than five years.) The new laws were called *multiple-line laws*, and the practice of issuing many kinds of insurance is called *multiple-line insurance.*

caveat emptor   A Latin term meaning "let the buyer beware," used to signify that the seller offers no WARRANTY and the buyer purchases at his own risk.

caveat venditor   A Latin term meaning "let the seller beware," used to signify that the seller must tell the whole truth or else risk prosecution.

ceiling price   The maximum price that may be charged under a system of PRICE CONTROL.

Celler Antimerger Act   See under ANTITRUST LEGISLATION.

census   A count of a given portion of the population or some other characteristic in a given area (housing, industry, etc.) and the statistical information derived from it. The U.S. Bureau of the Census, since 1972 part of the Department of Commerce's Social and Economic Statistics Administration, conducts nationwide censuses of population and housing every ten years, and censuses of agriculture, business, governments, manufacturers, mineral industries, and transportation every five years. In addition, it compiles statistics on construction activity, retail and wholesale sales, foreign trade, and numerous other activities of economic and business interest. One of the best summaries of national statistics is found in its annual publication, *Statistical Abstract of the United States.*

central bank   A nation's principal monetary authority, whose chief function is the regulation of the money supply and credit so as to promote econom-

ic growth without inflation. The central bank acts both as the government's bank and as a *banker's bank*, accepting deposits by and extending loans to commercial banks. It also sets the DISCOUNT RATE, on which most other interest rates are—directly or indirectly—based, and it conducts transfers of money and gold with foreign central banks. Most advanced countries have a single central bank with official government standing, such as the United Kingdom's Bank of England, West Germany's Deutsche Bundesbank, France's Banque de France, and Canada's Bank of Canada. The United States, with its traditional emphasis on decentralization and states' rights, has the FEDERAL RESERVE, a system composed of a board of governors and twelve regional Reserve banks. See also GOSBANK.

centralized planning   See under PLANNED ECONOMY.

central limit theorem   In statistics, the concept that if all possible random samples of size n are drawn from a universe, the arithmetic mean of the sampling distribution will be equal to the mean of the universe, and the means of the samples drawn even from skewed universes will tend to approach a NORMAL DISTRIBUTION as the size of the sample is increased. Also, the general idea that the values of most distributions tend to cluster around their own mean. For example, a half-inch drill is more likely to produce a .500-inch hole than one measuring .501 inch, and, moreover, is more likely to produce a .501-inch hole than a .502-inch hole, so long as the process is operating normally.

central processing unit   See under COMPUTER.

central reserve city bank   See under NATIONAL BANKS, def. 2.

certificate of beneficial interest   See under MASSACHUSETTS TRUST.

certificate of deposit   Also, *CD*. A certificate for a TIME DEPOSIT in a commercial bank, earning a specified rate of interest over a given time. Increasingly popular in the United States since the early 1960s, certificates of deposit are negotiable credit instruments that are traded in the MONEY MARKET along with other short-term paper, such as Treasury bills.

certificate of incorporation   Another name for corporation charter; see under CORPORATION.

certificate of origin   In the United States, a statement required of all importers as to the country of origin of imported goods. As a rule, a label or other means of giving this information must be affixed to the goods.

certificate of public convenience and necessity   A form of permission frequently required of transport, communications, and utilities firms wishing to enter into business. In effect they must prove to a state commission or other authority that their service is needed and will benefit the public. Having obtained the certificate, a utility can then apply for use of the right of eminent domain to construct its plant or run its lines over private property. The system of certificates can also be used to prevent competition in those service industries where it is generally believed that a monopoly will provide better service.

certificate of title   See under TITLE.

certification
   1. A written assurance by an officer or other authority of the truth of a statement or event, that is, that certain conditions exist, requirements have been met, etc.
   2. The award of a license or franchise to engage in a particular activity.
   3. In labor, the declaration by a government agency that a particular union may bargain for a given group of workers.

certified check   See under CHECK.

certified public accountant   Also, *CPA*. In the United States, an accountant with a special state license indicating that he or she meets certain requirements for the public practice of accounting. Though the requirements vary from state to state, all demand passing a rigorous examination prepared by the American Institute of Certified Public Accountants. No unlicensed person may use the title of certified public accountant. However, some states do permit the public practice of accounting without this license (see PUBLIC ACCOUNTANT).

chain discount   In business, one or more discounts on a price that has already been subject to a DISCOUNT (see def. 1). For example, a furniture dealer may be allowed a standard trade discount of 20 per cent on all merchandise. In addition, a given manufacturer may offer a second discount of 10 per cent on all wrought-iron garden furniture, and a third discount of 5 per cent on all such furniture paid for before April 1. Thus, for a set of furniture with a list price of $150, the dealer pays $120, from which he may deduct another $12 (.10 × $120) if it is wrought-iron furniture and $5.40 more (.05 × $108) if he can pay for it by April 1. Thus, the dealer has paid only $102.60 for $150 worth of furniture. The chain discount of 20, 10, and 5 per cent, however, is less advantageous than a straight 35 per cent discount, equivalent to a price to the dealer of only $97.50.

chain of command   See SPAN OF CONTROL.

chain store   One of a group of essentially identical, centrally owned retail stores, which have, to varying degrees, centralized control over their operations. Though both department stores and the retail outlets of mail-order houses have been organized as chains, this form of organization is far more common among variety stores (e.g., the F. W. Woolworth chain, founded in 1879), grocery stores, and service enterprises such as hotels. The advantages of chain-store operations include large-scale buying direct from the manufacturer (some stores even operate their own warehouses) and the use of private brands; standardization of systems and procedures, making for lower administrative costs; and eliminating customer services (chiefly credit and delivery, though some chains have reinstated the former). The chief disadvantage is that, because of its centralized control, the chain may be slow to respond to changes in local conditions.

   The American chain store first appeared after the Civil War. It became very popular after World War I and grew rapidly during the 1920s, especially in the grocery business. By 1929 the A & P (Great Atlantic & Pacific Tea Company, founded about 1859) had 15,418 stores, Kroger had 5,575, and

Safeway, 2,340. In 1929 more than 7,000 chains existed in the United States, controlling more than one-fifth of all retail sales (and an even higher portion in some fields). As a result, a number of states passed anti-chain legislation, and the Robinson-Patman Act of 1936 specifically eliminated some of the purchasing privileges claimed by chain stores, such as their demand for special discounts. Nevertheless, chains continued to proliferate, although less rapidly. In the late 1970s they accounted for about 30 per cent of all retail sales (and about 80 per cent of variety-store sales).

Two special kinds of chain store have evolved to compete with ordinary chains. The *cooperative chain* is formed by independent retailers to set up a cooperative wholesaling organization (not a CONSUMER COOPERATIVE); the *volunary chain* is similar but is formed by the wholesalers themselves, some of whom unite independent retailers by specifying common operating procedures, storefront design, store name, and promotional efforts. See also FRANCHISE, def. 2.

chairman of the board In a corporation, the highest-ranking executive, usually elected by the board of directors. The chairman normally outranks the president, but in some cases they are one and the same person, while in others the chairman leaves the company's operations largely to the president.

Chamberlin, Edward Hastings An American economist (1899–19) who was one of the first to see that most markets operate under IMPERFECT COMPETITION (which he called *monopolistic competition*). Unlike earlier theorists, Chamberlin held that markets in which either pure monopoly or perfect competition operates are rare; in most instances elements of both are present, with one or a few buyers or sellers materially influencing price. Chamberlin also pointed out the role of advertising and product differentiation in promoting monopoly in the case of allegedly "unique" products, as well as the restriction of output to maintain artificially high prices.

chamber of commerce An association of business and professional men and women and of trade and professional organizations, formed to promote the interests of the business community. In the United States some 4,000 such organizations—local, regional, and state—belong to the Chamber of Commerce of the United States of America (organized in 1912), which in turn belongs to the International Chamber of Commerce. In 1976 the U.S. Chamber of Commerce announced plans to merge with the National Association of Manufacturers (NAM), a group organized in 1895 to promote trade and commerce.

chancery See under EQUITY, def. 5.

charge account Also, *open-account credit.* A system of allowing retail purchases on credit widely used by department stores, hotels, airlines and other transportation companies, oil companies, and others, as well as by banks that offer central charge plans. There are several kinds of charge account. With a *regular charge account*, the customer simply charges purchases and is billed once a month. This bill is payable in full within 10 days after the billing date, without extra charge. Most department stores allow 30 days for payment; thereafter any unpaid balance may go into a revolving account (see below). With a *depositor's account*, the customer deposits a given amount of cash with a store and charges purchases against the account. Sometimes interest may be paid on whatever balance remains, usually at a rather low rate. With a *divided charge account*, large items may be purchased and paid for over a specified period, usually 3 months, with (normally) no extra charge. With a *revolving* or *budget charge account* the store establishes a specified credit level, for example, $500. The customer then may buy goods up to a cost of $500 and pay for them over a 6- to 12-month period (the time period depends on the retailer). Usually there is a service charge for such an account, about 1 to 1.5 per cent per month on any unpaid balance. With a *central charge plan*, purchases can be charged at designated stores in an area and the customer is billed for the total spent each month. He may pay either in full or on an "extended terms" basis, for which a service charge is leveled.

charging what the traffic will bear A form of pricing based on what a seller thinks customers are willing to pay. When this involves charging different prices for the same goods, it constitutes a form of PRICE DISCRIMINATION.

charter A document issued by a legislature or other government authority granting certain rights and privileges to a bank or corporation, and also imposing certain restrictions on it. In the United States banks may be chartered either by the Federal government or by a state government. (See also NATIONAL BANKS, def. 1; STATE BANKS.) A charter for creating a corporation, often called *articles of incorporation*, may be granted by the Federal government whenever appropriate, to carry out the powers expressly granted to it by the U. S. Constitution. In addition, Congress may authorize the creation of corporations in U. S. territories and the District of Columbia. Individual states may create any kind of corporation for any purpose; most have a general corporation code that, if its requirements are met, automatically confers corporate status on any group desiring it. See also CORPORATION.

charter rate A fee charged for leasing a ship (most often a tanker) for one or more voyages, or for leasing some or all of its cargo space. Charter rates fluctuate widely and are used as a barometer of the health of the shipping industry and, by extension, of the shipbuilding industry.

Chartist

1. An English working-class reform movement (1838–48) that presented its demands in a People's Charter (hence the name) that called for universal male suffrage, vote by ballot, equal electoral districts, annual meetings of Parliament, abolition of property qualifications for membership in the House of Commons, and salaries for Members of Parliament. The movement, also called *Chartism*, grew out of dissatisfaction with low wages, high prices, and a new poor law (1834). It was considered radical at the time largely because some of the Chartists advocated violence, and several mass meetings and general strikes took place. After a decade of activism the movement disintegrated, but its aims were taken over by other groups, especially the trade-union and cooperative movements, and all of its demands, except for the annual meeting of Parliament, eventually were enacted.

2. *chartist*. In investment, an analyst who forecasts securities prices from charts of past prices and price movements.

chattel mortgage A MORTGAGE on personal property, legally called *chattels*, rather than on real property (land, buildings, etc.). It is most commonly used in buying high-priced consumer goods on credit, such as automobiles and large appliances. Like a real mortgage, a chattel mortgage can be viewed either as a transfer of title from borrower to lender or as a LIEN on the goods, and it terminates when the debt (plus accumulated interest) has been paid in full.

cheap money Same as *easy money*; see under MONETARY POLICY.

check Also, *bank check*, Brit. *cheque*. A written order drawn on a bank to pay on demand a specified sum to the bearer or to a designated person or firm. A check, unlike an ordinary BILL OF EXCHANGE drawn on a bank, is always payable on demand. Further, it is drawn against funds presumably already on deposit and hence needs no acceptance to make it valid. Once signed, it can be invalidated only by means of a STOP PAYMENT order. In an advanced economy checks are freely used in lieu of currency, and indeed it is by means of checking accounts—which economists prefer to call DEMAND DEPOSITS—that banks are able to create money (see also MONEY; MONEY SUPPLY). Except in small day-to-day transactions, currency rarely changes hands, and "cashing a check" often means simply exchanging it for another check for credit to some other account.

Numerous special kinds of check are in general use. Of these, the most important are the *blank check*, a check left blank in any of the particulars (amount, payee, date) except the drawer's signature, which must appear; *cashier's check*, drawn by a bank on itself (not against a particular depositor's account) and signed by a bank officer (such as the cashier, hence the name), used as a convenience to customers who wish to write checks but do not have a checking account at that bank; *certified check*, bearing the guarantee of a bank officer that the drawer has funds with the bank to cover the amount of the check and in effect making the bank assume liability for it (such checks therefore are regarded as reliable as actual currency); *counter check*, in effect a kind of withdrawal slip banks keep on hand (at a counter) for depositors who wish to

Fig. 11. Personal check

This check is drawn on a joint checking account held by Dean S. Ammer and Christine Ammer. Christine Ammer is the drawer, Harvard Trust Company is the drawee, and Ulysses S. Grant is the payee. The face value of the check is $10.00, and the transit number is 53-60/113.

withdraw money from their own accounts; *memorandum check*, a postdated check drawn by a borrower and payable to his creditor with the understanding that it will be redeemed only if the loan has not been paid when due (in this instance, "check" is a misnomer since it is not payable on demand; "promissory note" would be more accurate); *personal check*, a check drawn by an individual rather than a firm; *registered check*, a check written by a bank teller and drawing on special funds set aside by the bank to accommodate persons who have no accounts (checking or otherwise) with the bank but want to write checks and hence must pay a fee for the privilege (it is very similar to a MONEY ORDER). See also CANCELED CHECK; CHECKING ACCOUNT; DRAWER; DRAWEE; ENDORSEMENT, def. 1; TRAVELER'S CHECK; VOUCHER CHECK.

checkbook money See DEMAND DEPOSIT.

checking account A bank account from which withdrawals can be made simply by writing a CHECK. In the United States checking accounts usually are with commercial banks and do not earn interest. Most though not all banks require that a minimum balance be maintained on all checking accounts. Others may offer a *special checking account*, for which no minimum balance is required, a small fee is charged for each check drawn (and sometimes for each deposit made), and there may be a monthly or other periodic service charge for handling the account. See also DEMAND DEPOSIT.

checkoff The automatic deduction of union dues from a paycheck, so that it is the employer who remits the worker's dues to the union. In part an assurance that the union will get its dues and in part a bookkeeping convenience, the practice has been much resented by some employers and was outlawed by the Taft-Hartley Act of 1947 except where it is specifically authorized in writing by the individual employee. Numerous states have similar laws regulating the checkoff so that it is not automatic.

Chicago Board Options Exchange See under OPTIONS EXCHANGE.

Chicago school A group of economists associated with the University of Chicago who, although they did not necessarily agree on how to achieve their goals, believed that competition in a free-market economy would provide the best all-round allocation of resources. They tended to support many of the tenets of Alfred MARSHALL, retaining his microeconomic approach, and to repudiate most of the theories of J. M. KEYNES and his followers, opposing government interference in economic affairs. Its leading member is Milton FRIEDMAN. Others are George J. Stigler and Henry C. Simons, who both believed that large firms should be broken up into small ones to enhance competition; Frank H. Knight, who held that all true profit must be linked with uncertainty or risk-taking; and Austrian-born Friedrich A. von Hayek, who, in the tradition of the Austrian marginalists (especially BÖHM-BAWERK and von MISES; see also MONETARY THEORY), believed that government interference leads to socialism (antithetical to freedom and democracy), and in 1974 shared the Nobel Memorial Prize in Economic Science with Gunnar MYRDAL (with whom he otherwise had little in common).

child labor The employment of children under a particular legal age. Child labor was a mainstay of the early Industrial Revolution, particularly in the British coal mines, where youngsters were hired to work in places too small for adults, and it continues to be widely used in underdeveloped as well as developed countries, especially in agriculture. The U.S. Congress began to intercede in the hiring of children as early as 1918 (against strong opposition from employers, who usually pay children much less than adults), and twenty years later it passed the Fair Labor Standards Act, prohibiting the employment of persons under 16 (and in certain hazardous jobs, under 18). However, exceptions are permitted in agriculture, entertainment, and family-run businesses. Today nearly every state has statutes dealing with the employment of children under a certain age (which varies from 14 to 18, depending on the state). Theoretically children may not work on farms during the time they legally should be in school, but in practice this provision is widely violated, particularly by migrant workers, who are seldom in one place long enough to enroll their children in school and who often lack funds to buy clothes and school supplies.

Christian socialism
1. In England and later in the United States, a movement that tried to counter capitalism with a combination of Christian and socialist ideals. Beginning in England after the demise of the CHARTIST movement (1848), Christian socialism was based largely on the writings of two clergymen, Charles Kingsley (1819–75) and Frederick Denison Maurice (1805–72). It did not advocate overthrow of the government or even state ownership of the means of production (see SOCIALISM) but championed free cooperation among producers and social reform. The Christian Socialists published journals and tracts, promoted a few short-lived self-governing workingmen's associations, founded a workmen's college (1854), and supported factory legislation and the cooperative movement. Their traditions were carried on by followers of FABIAN SOCIALISM, GUILD SOCIALISM, and various Roman Catholic groups. In the United States a Society of Christian Socialists was formed in 1889, though there had been earlier proponents, among them the clergyman Washington Gladden (1836–1918) and the economist Richard Theodore Ely (1864–1943). There the the movement addressed itself even more to specific industrial and social problems than to political socialism.
2. Name of several European political parties. Those prominent after World War II, as in Belgium, tended to be more conservative than socialist. In those predating World War I, however, as in Austria, Roman Catholics and moderate socialists sometimes worked together to promote social legislation.

chronic unemployment Long-term unemployment, that is, lasting six months or longer. It is caused by a variety of factors, among them structural changes in the economy (STRUCTURAL UNEMPLOYMENT), technologic changes (TECHNOLOGICAL UNEMPLOYMENT), or a slowdown in the economy as a whole (CYCLICAL UNEMPLOYMENT). The U. S. Department of Labor compiles a statistical series of persons unemployed for 27 weeks or longer. The National Bureau of Economic Research considers unemployment lasting 15 weeks or longer long-term and deems it an important LAGGING INDICATOR of business conditions. Chronic unemployment is sometimes called *hard-core unemployment*, though the latter term often is associated with workers who are not employable regardless of the state of business, usually owing to lack of either skill or motivation.

churning The practice of unduly stimulating security trading by customers to increase a broker's commissions. If blatant, churning is illegal.

c.i.f. Abbreviation for *cost, insurance, and freight.* A price quotation that includes cost of merchandise, shipping insurance, and freight charges to a specific destination. The seller is responsible for shipment to the buyer and is liable for any loss or damage during shipment. Once the shipment reaches its specified destination, however, the buyer is responsible for unloading it and, if necessary, payment of customs duties and delivery to a plant or some other place. See also C.A.F.

CIO See AFL-CIO.

circular flow In economic theory, the continual flow of income—in the form of payments and receipts for goods and services—in an economy. This concept is actually an abstract, oversimplified model of the economic transactions constantly taking place. Households buy goods and services. The payments for these become the income of the firms producing the goods and services. To produce them in the first place, the firms must pay the factors of production: rent (land), wages (labor), interest (capital), and profit (entrepreneur). These payments in turn are the source of household income, spent on the consumption of goods and services. When all income is spent on consumption, the circular flow is complete. The flow of demand is said to be unending and unchanging, and the economy is static, experiencing no expansion, contraction, or growth. From the microeconomic viewpoint, circular flow describes the market for goods and the market for factors of production, with both households and businesses operating as buyers in one market and sellers in the other. From the macroeconomic viewpoint, circular flow describes national income, which will remain the same so long as withdrawals (in the form of saving, taxes, and spending for imports) are exactly equal to input (investment spending, government spending, selling goods abroad). In both cases, the static equilibrium is theoretical rather than actual.

circulating capital See CAPITAL, def. 1.

circulation In publishing, the number of copies of a single issue of a periodical (newspaper, magazine, journal, etc.) that are sold or distributed. This figure is particularly important to advertisers, who want to know the size of the audience they can reach through a particular publication. Moreover, a given circulation figure furnishes a clue about the total *readership* (the number of persons who actually read all or part of the periodical). Thus, a circulation figure of 30,000 may mean a total readership of 90,000 or more, since the issue may be passed among family members, friends, colleagues, etc. *Average circulation* is the average number of copies distributed over several successive issues, usually over a six-month period. *Paid circulation* refers to the number of copies actually bought, on both an individual and a subscription basis. This figure can be verified by an independent agency, such as the publishing industry's own *Audit Bureau of Circulation* (established for that very purpose); once verified and averaged for some months, it is called *net paid circulation*. Some periodicals are distributed free to persons considered potential customers for the products and services advertised in them; such distribution, called *controlled circulation*, is used principally for trade, technical, and other specialized magazines, either alone or in conjunction with paid circulation. For example, magazines dealing with infant and child care often are distributed to the offices of obstetricians and pediatricians for their waiting rooms.

Civil Aeronautics Board Also, *CAB.* An independent U.S. government commission, established in 1938, with broad authority to promote and regulate the civil air-transport industry within the United States and between the United States and other countries. It authorizes carriers to engage in interstate and foreign commerce, reviews and regulates rate schedules of commercial carriers, grants subsidies to maintain service in places where the volume of traffic is not large enough to meet costs, acts on proposed mergers and other agreements among carriers, and prescribes a uniform system of accounting and reporting for carriers.

Civilian Conservation Corps Also, *CCC.* A Federal agency established in 1937, during the Great Depression, to provide vocational training and employment for young men in useful public works projects connected with conservation and development of natural resources (reforestation, flood control, etc.). It attracted 300,000 recruits during its first year, and continued to function until 1942, when Congress ended its appropriations.

civil law Originally, the body of law that dates from the ancient Roman civil law. Today, the term usually refers to the body of written law that deals with rights of and disputes between private individuals, as opposed to *criminal law*, which deals with offenses against the public interest or the state. In civil suits both defendant and plaintiff are private individuals or organizations; in criminal suits the plaintiff is always the public or government, usually in the person of a district attorney.

Clark Name of two American economists, father and son. The father, John Bates Clark (1847–1938), was the leading American exponent of the MARGINALIST SCHOOL and the first major American economic theorist. A teacher for most of his long life (his most famous pupil, Thorstein VEBLEN, became one of his sternest critics), Clark appears to have discovered marginalism by himself, without having read the works of Jevons or Marshall. His principal contribution was the MARGINAL PRODUCTIVITY THEORY, which was based on his application of the law of diminishing returns to all factors of production (land, labor, capital). According to Clark, the distribution of the income of society (wages, profits, interest, the last including also rents) depends on the marginal productivity—the extra unit contributed to value, up to the point of diminishing returns—of each factor of production. So long as there was competition, Clark believed, economic harmony could and would exist. In its absence, government has to intervene to curb monopolies and restore competition. Clark's analysis, however, was based on a static economy in which such elements as population, supply of capital, technology, and consumer tastes remain fixed.

John Maurice Clark (1884–1963), who succeeded his father as professor of economics at Columbia University in 1926, is best known for his formulation in 1917 of the ACCELERATION PRINCIPLE. Also, Clark was one of the first to recognize that independent economic action cannot offset the fluctuations of the business cycle, and he proposed that coordinated action—by business, labor, government, banking, and insurance—might produce economic stability and full employment. In this respect the younger Clark's views are considered a bridge between the neoclassical ideas of his father and the newer Keynesian economics (see under J. M. KEYNES).

classical school A group of 18th- and 19th-century British economists whose ideas dominated economic thought from about 1775 to 1850 and therefore came to be called "classical." Its founder was Adam SMITH, and it included David RICARDO, Thomas MALTHUS, and James Stuart MILL, as well as Jeremy BENTHAM and Nassau SENIOR. Underlying their ideas was the belief that, without government interference—that is, with *laissez-faire* policies—individual initiative and perfect competition would result in the best possible economic development, assuring full employment and adequate profits (see also SAY'S LAW OF MARKETS). Individuals, said Smith and his followers, are naturally guided by self-interest, but each man's selfishness is curbed by the selfish interests of other individuals (which may conflict with his). Therefore, it is to everyone's best interest to work for the greatest good for the greatest number. Economic behavior—that is, production, consumption, and the distribution of wealth—is governed by natural laws, which the economist can merely deduce and with which one should not interfere. Competition alone determines prices, wages, profits, and rents. (See IRON LAW OF WAGES; WAGES-FUND THEORY.) To the mercantilists' emphasis on trade (which, however, the classical school believed should be free and unrestricted) and to the physiocrats' emphasis on agriculture, the classical economists added industry, which they felt was equally productive, and for which they developed first a LABOR THEORY OF VALUE and later a COST OF PRODUCTION THEORY OF VALUE. Though the classical economists were among the first to analyze the economy as a whole (macroeconomics) and the laws they believed to be operative in it, their analysis was essentially static. They took into account neither the increasingly inequitable distribution of wealth nor the realities of technological change. They did not grasp that economic laws are not immutable but subject to change by individuals and institutions. Nor did they understand the role of demand in a free enterprise system, any more than they understood the roles played by money and interest. Nevertheless their influence remained strong. Long after most of their specific theories had been rejected, their abstract deductive approach, their assumption of pure competition, their belief in laissez faire, and their faith that economic forces tend toward an equilibrium all reappeared in the "neoclassic" theories of Alfred MARSHALL and others. See also Richard CANTILLON; David HUME; MANCHESTER SCHOOL.

classified advertising Also, *want ads*. A form of advertising in special sections of newspapers and magazines, consisting of relatively brief announcements appearing under such headings as "Help Wanted," "Work Wanted," "For Sale," "For Rent," "Lost and Found," "Personal (Announcements)," "Legal Notices," etc. The rates for classified ads are usually based on space—number of words, inches, or lines of print.

classified stock A stock issue that is divided into two or more classes, carrying different rights and privileges. For example, a firm might issue both Class A and Class B common stock, with one carrying voting rights and the other not. The purpose of classifying stock is to give control of the corporation to the minority group owning the stock with greater voting privileges.

class interval See under FREQUENCY DISTRIBUTION.

Class I A classification assigned to American railroads and motor carriers of goods and passengers on the basis of their annual gross operating revenues. Set by the U.S. Interstate Commerce Commission, this system extends to three different classes (I, II, III) and is used for both rate-making and general statistical purposes. Class I carriers have the biggest revenues, usually representing by far the major proportion of total revenues (80 per cent for freight-carrying trucks, 95 per cent for line-haul railroads). The precise amount of revenue differentiating the classes has, of course, changed over the years. In the mid-1950s Class I trucks were those grossing $200,000 per year or more, and

Class I railroads were those with $1 million per year or more; by 1969 these figures had risen to $1 million and $3 million, respectively.

class price See under PRICE DISCRIMINATION, def. 1.

class rate See under FREIGHT.

class struggle See under COMMUNISM, def. 1.

Clayton Antitrust Act See under ANTITRUST LEGISLATION; also under LABOR LAWS.

clearance An approval given to persons, carriers, etc., indicating the settlement of an account. Thus, a ship must receive a *clearance paper* in order to leave a harbor, indicating that applicable duties and other charges have been paid, and all legal requirements have been fulfilled. For similar settlement of financial transactions, see CLEARING HOUSE.

clearance sale A retail sale of merchandise at reduced prices, to clear out seasonal stock, overstock, or slow-moving items.

clearing house An association of commercial banks, brokerage houses, central banks, or other institutions established to settle simultaneously the claims of its members on one another. For example, representatives of the banks of the city of Springvale might meet daily to exchange checks drawn on one another, each bank reducing the claims to a net balance that it must pay or be paid. Ordinarily the balance is not paid in cash but simply entered on the books of the local Federal Reserve bank (or, if Springvale is too small, it is settled via a draft on a correspondent bank). Many bank clearing houses exchange not only checks but drafts on businesses and other negotiable instruments.

For international payment transactions, payment for nearly half a century was made by hand delivery of checks to a central New York location. By the late 1960s this system no longer proved adequate for handling the greatly increased number of transactions growing out of expanded world trade, investment, and tourism. In 1970 a *Clearing House Interbank Payment System* (CHIPS) began to handle these transactions by computer. Members, including commercial banks, foreign bank branches and agencies, and bank subsidiaries from coast to coast, are tied in by computer terminals through which payment orders are transmitted and received. More than 25,000 items per day are cleared through CHIPS, which expedites interbank international dollar payments on behalf of foreign banks and their clients, domestic banks or companies and their overseas branches, foreign corporations, and even foreign central banks. See also CLEARING UNION. For an example of brokerage clearing, see STOCK CLEARING CORPORATION.

clearing union A kind of international CLEARING HOUSE, composed of the central banks of member countries, whereby international payments are settled by means of each nation's trading surplus or deficit. The chief advantages of a clearing union are that it permits nations to concentrate on efficient production—without worrying about exporting to one nation (or group of nations) while importing from another—and that it reduces the need for FOREIGN EXCHANGE RESERVES. J. M. Keynes proposed the establishment of a worldwide clearing union after World War II (see under INTERNATIONAL MONETARY FUND for his plan), but his proposal was turned down. In 1950 16 European nations formed a clearing union (the European Payments Union), which survived in the European Monetary Agreement of 1958. Since its creation of SPECIAL DRAWING RIGHTS in 1969, the International Monetary Fund has in effect performed some of the functions of a clearing union.

Cleveland panic See under PANICS, BUSINESS.

closed account See CLOSING ENTRY.

closed corporation Also, *close corporation, private corporation.* A CORPORATION in which most or all of the stock is owned by a few persons, and little or none is available for sale to the public. Frequently the owners will agree not to sell their stock without offering it to the other stockholders. The most common examples of a closed corporation are small, family-owned businesses, but occasionally a very large enterprise is so organized. The Ford Motor Company formerly was a closed

corporation, owned and run by Henry Ford and his family. See also OPEN CORPORATION.

closed-end investment trust See under INVESTMENT COMPANY.

closed mortgage See under MORTGAGE.

closed shop A firm or part of a firm that agrees to hire only union members. A means of providing security for the union, the closed shop traditionally existed chiefly in industries where a high level of skill or short-term employment was involved. Thus, even though the closed shop was outlawed by the Taft-Hartley Act of 1947 and was further declared illegal under numerous state laws, it still exists in effect for musicians, longshoremen, and crafts workers in the building trades, among others. See also OPEN SHOP; UNION SHOP.

closed stock Merchandise sold only in sets, such as silverware or china, with no guarantee that replacements for lost, broken, or damaged pieces will be available. *Open stock*, in contrast, can be purchased piece by piece, and, at least for a time, replacements will be available.

closed union A labor union that restricts its membership through high initiation fees, long apprenticeship requirements, or similar means. By so doing, it may seek to create a scarcity of skilled workers to keep wages high, but often religious and/or racial prejudice and nepotism also are operative. For example, in the 1960s many of the American building-trade craft unions had rules that effectively prevented blacks and other minorities from joining. In contrast, an *open union* tends to set low fees and accepts as a member anyone working or trained in its field.

closing In real estate transactions, the delivery of the deed by the seller to the buyer upon payment of the full purchase price. Normally a closing date is specified in the contract of sale. Documents exchanged at closing may include the deed, abstract of title, mortgage, mortgage note, survey of the property, leases, insurance policies, assignments (of service contracts, etc.), and receipts for taxes, special assessments, and utilities.

closing entry Also, *closed account.* In accounting, an entry in an ACCOUNT (see def. 1) or set of accounts that transfers the net balance (either plus or minus) to some other statement, such as an income statement.

closing price The price at which a listed security last changed hands at the end of a trading day. Stock prices listed in the financial pages of leading newspapers normally are the closing prices.

Cobb-Douglas production function A well-known PRODUCTION FUNCTION relating input to output in such a way that returns to scale are constant—that is, an increase in all input factors will result in a proportionate increase in output. First published in 1928 by two American economists trying to explain the relative constancy of capital input and labor input in the national income, the formula reads thus:

$$O = k_0 \, F_1^{\,k_1} \, F_2^{\,k_2} \, F_3^{\,k_3} \ldots F_n^{\,k_n}$$

where O = output; $F_1 \, F_2 \ldots F_n$ are factors of production; $k_0 \, k_1 \, k_2 \ldots k_n$ are positive constants; and $k_1 + k_2 \ldots + k_n = 1$.

This production function is widely used in theory of production and theory of distribution (see DISTRIBUTION, def. 2). If each factor is paid a return equal to the value of its marginal product, each factor will always receive a constant proportion of the value of total output.

COBOL An acronym of Common Business-Oriented Language, a compiler language used in computer PROGRAMMING, particularly for business problems. Developed by the U.S. Department of Defense in 1959, it resembles a stylized form of business English.

cobweb theorem A theory that tries to account for the cyclical character in the supply and price of certain commodities, so called because the pattern traced by the price movements on a graph resembles a cobweb. For example, take the growing of cranberries and, for simplicity, say that they have a market only from November through Christmas. Cranberries in Year 1 are selling for 40 cents a pound. All the growers assume this price will hold for Year 2 and plan production accordingly, planting the quantity (C_2) they are willing to offer at 40

cents. However, when the crop is harvested, it sells for only 35 cents a pound. Accordingly, growers now plan their next crop, C_3, on the basis of a 35-cent price. When C_3 reaches the market, however, it fetches a price of 42 cents. And so the cycle continues. The output of Year 1 determines a price that influences output of Year 2, which in turn determines a price guiding output for Year 3, and so on. The cobweb theorem clearly shows that not all markets automatically produce equilibrium prices. Actually, in most markets, changes in demand, supply, and price occur more gradually than in this example. But where supply is relatively elastic, price and output can move sharply up and down.

COD Abbreviation for *cash on delivery*, which in business refers to the practice of paying for an item at the time of delivery. In industrial purchases, COD is required principally of buyers whose credit is either poor or not yet established.

code For *machine code*, see under PROGRAMMING; for *Hollerith code*, see under PUNCHED-CARD DATA PROCESSING.

codetermination The policy of giving labor unions representation on a company's board of directors to an extent equal to that of the stockholders. Begun on a small scale after World War I in Germany, where it is called *Mitbestimmung*, codetermination became the rule after World War II in the German coal and steel industries and was made mandatory in 1951. A similar policy became common in France. Supporters of codetermination hold that a company's workers should have a voice in policy-making; its opponents contend that it is a form of socialism.

coin A piece of metal of prescribed size, shape, and weight, usually stamped with a number denoting its face value as well as other special markings, that is used as MONEY. Today just about all coins are TOKEN MONEY and are issued only by governments. As recently as the mid-19th century, however, *full-bodied* gold and silver coins, actually containing their face value in metal, were in common use, and any gold- or silversmith could make one. In U.S. currency the cent (penny) and five-cent (nickel) coins are sometimes called *minor coins* because they traditionally contained no precious metal. Also, coins under the denomination of one dollar were called *subsidiary coins* because they never contained as much metal as their face value, whereas the silver dollar at one time did. The production of coins, or *coinage*, is carried on by the government (see MINT). The charge for coinage is called *brassage* if it just covers the cost of making coins; if it is higher, yielding a profit over cost, it is called *seigniorage*.

coincident indicator Also, *roughly coincident indicator*. An INDICATOR that experiences the peaks and troughs of the business cycle at approximately the same time as general economic activity. Coincident indicators therefore provide an analytic basis for determining just when the overall economy reaches these peaks and troughs. According to the U. S. Bureau of Economic Analysis, which regularly publishes statistics on indicators, there are 26 coincident indicators. Of these, 8 are considered particularly important by the National Bureau of Economic Research and therefore comprise its short list of coincident indicators (see Fig. 12). See also LAGGING INDICATOR; LEADING INDICATOR.

coinsurance In property insurance policies, a requirement that the insured, in order to buy insurance at a given rate, agrees to carry at least a specified proportion of insurance to the value of the property—such as 80 per cent—at the time of loss. To the extent that the insured fails to carry this much insurance, he will not collect in full for partial losses. For example, suppose Green and White both own buildings worth $100,000 and the fire-insurance rate on each building is 10 cents per $100 of insurance. Green carries $80,000 of insurance

Fig. 12. "Short list" of coincident indicators

- Employees on nonagricultural payrolls
- Unemployment rate, total
- Gross national product in current dollars
- Gross national product in 1972 dollars
- Index of industrial production
- Manufacturing and trade sales
- Personal income
- Sales of retail stores

on her building and pays a premium of $80; White, knowing that fires rarely destroy an entire building, decides to buy only $20,000 worth for a $20 premium. Suppose, now, that fire causes $20,000 of damage to each building. Without a coinsurance clause, both owners would collect $20,000, even though Green had paid four times the premium of White. With a coinsurance clause specifying 80 per cent of value, however, White would recover only $5,000 of the loss, according to the formula:

$$\frac{\text{insurance carried}}{\text{insurance required}} \times \frac{\text{amount}}{\text{of loss}} = \frac{\text{limit of}}{\text{recovery}}$$

Colbert, Jean-Baptiste A French statesman (1619–83) who served Louis XIV as minister of finance (1661–83) and was France's leading exponent of MERCANTILISM. Colbert believed that a country's strength depends entirely on tax revenues, which in turn depend on an abundant money supply. Like most mercantilists, he supported expanded exports, reduced imports, retention of bullion within the country, colonization, and a powerful navy and merchant fleet. Unlike some mercantilists, however, Colbert believed that with these policies one nation could prosper only at the expense of another, so that commerce represented a form of warfare. On the other hand, he believed in free internal trade and made considerable efforts to overcome the feudal traditions whereby each lord treated his domain almost as a nation. Most of Colbert's ideas, among them establishing uniform weights and measures, eliminating internal tolls and tariffs, and doing away with heavy local taxes, were not put into effect during his lifetime. A strong believer in the centralized regulation of business and commerce, Colbert instituted government controls over production methods and the quality of goods produced, and offered monopoly privileges and subsidies to certain new industries.

collateral A tangible security, with monetary value and usually readily convertible into cash, that is deposited with a creditor to guarantee repayment of a loan. Either the property itself or a document of title to it is held by the creditor until the loan is repaid.

collateral loan A loan secured by some kind of property, which is either held by the lender until repayment is made or is merely pledged. The collateral often is in the form of stocks, bonds, or some other security.

collateral trust bond A BOND (see def. 1) secured by collateral deposited with a trustee. The collateral often consists of the stocks or bonds of companies controlled by the issuer but also may consist of other securities.

collator See under PUNCHED-CARD DATA PROCESSING.

collection The presentation of an invoice or other request for payment. The *collection period* is the average time that elapses between the presentation and payment of a business firm's total accounts receivable, and is computed by dividing the average value of accounts receivable by average daily sales. Some enterprises, particularly physicians, attorneys, and other professional services, occasionally hire a *collection agency*, which specializes in obtaining payment from delinquent accounts.

collective bargaining The negotiations between an employer and the labor union that represents the employees concerning the terms and conditions of employment (wages, work hours, hiring and layoff practices, vacations, rest periods, pensions, sick leave, etc.). The terms agreed upon, which must be mutually acceptable, are incorporated into a written LABOR CONTRACT, which is binding on both employer and employees. Until the passage of the National Industrial Recovery Act of 1933, American workers did not have the express right to organize for collective bargaining, and though such negotiations could and did take place, employers could refuse to participate in them and/or to honor the agreements made. The National Labor Relations Act provided further safeguards for collective bargaining (see under UNFAIR LABOR PRACTICES; also LABOR LAWS).

The underlying rationale of collective bargaining is that (1) the individual worker alone is not strong enough to stand up for his or her rights, and hence can be effective only through collective action, and (2) employers and workers each want to work for their own interests through means that are often—although not always—in direct conflict. Man-

agement seeks to keep its costs, including labor costs, to a minimum; labor seeks to improve its welfare through changes that usually (but not always) require larger expenditures by management. The ability of one side to gain concessions from the other is called *bargaining power*, which itself can become an issue. For example, the presence or absence in a contract of a no-strike clause (allowing no strike while the contract is in force) obviously affects the two parties' relative bargaining power. Bargaining power to some extent depends on the size of the *bargaining unit*, that is, the employees covered in a particular labor contract or represented in negotiations with an employer. A bargaining unit may consist of two or three mechanics working in an entrepreneur's garage or of the work force of an entire industry. It may cover all or part of one plant, or one or several firms, or one or many kinds of worker. Every labor contract clearly identifies the bargaining unit it covers, as, for example, "All the nonsupervisory employees in Plant X of ABC Products Corporation." Obviously, the larger the unit, the greater its bargaining power.

The bulk of collective bargaining involves *negotiation*, that is, the direct discussion of proposals and counterproposals by the two sides, with or without representation by attorneys. It has been estimated that 95 per cent of all agreements are made in this way. If agreement cannot be reached, the next resort is MEDIATION, with a third party trying to bring the two sides together. If mediation fails, more drastic pressure may be brought, by the union in the form of a STRIKE and/or BOYCOTT, or by management through a LOCKOUT; or alternatively, both sides may agree to submit to ARBITRATION (decision by a third party).

collective farm A cooperative association of farmers who are chartered to work state-owned land but who own the means of production (other than land or some heavy machinery). It differs from a *state farm*, which is owned and run by the government and is operated by hired workers whose wages are geared to productivity. In the Soviet Union collective farms were first established in 1929; at first, the average collective farm comprised about 75 families and 3,800 acres, of which one-third were planted. Collectivization continued over the next few years, and by 1936 virtually all the country's cultivated land was so organized. Today collective farms account for about 90 per cent of Russian agricultural production; state farms account for the remainder. Each farm's management is carried on by a committee, usually chaired by a Communist party member, in accordance with central government plans for agriculture. Heavy equipment for plowing and harvesting is provided by a Machine Tractor Station, which is remunerated in crops. Crop and livestock production is subject to quotas, as is the amount of work performed by each farmer. No person may leave the farm or community without permission.

Larger and more diversified than the collective farm is the Chinese *commune*. First set up in the People's Republic of China in 1958, the communes originally were combinations of numerous smaller collective farms or agricultural cooperatives, averaging 200 to 300 households each. The first commune, named Sputnik, combined 27 cooperatives and included 10,000 families, or 44,000 persons. In a massive campaign lasting about six months, 99 per cent of China's rural population of 550 million was organized into 26,500 communes of about 4,750 households each. A commune welds together all the industrial, educational, cultural, administrative, and military activities for its entire area. All property except for houses, clothing, bicycles, and personal possessions belongs to the entire community. Schools, factories, and shops similarly are considered communal. Families eat in communal mess halls, and children are cared for in nurseries, releasing their parents for work. Workers are paid a wage that depends on skill, hours of work, quality of work, and enthusiasm, with a system of bonuses and fines. Food, clothing, rent, education, medical care, and similar personal services are free. Communes handle their own supplies, marketing, and credit, control their own accounting, and bear profits and losses as a single entity. During the 1960s the commune system was extended to China's urban population of 100 million. Smaller communes were formed in the cities to operate workshops and factories, staffed largely by housewives released from domestic tasks through the communal mess halls and nurseries.

Israel is the principal non-Communist country in which agricultural collectives have played a major role. There, two types have existed side by side since the early 1920s, the moshav and the kibbutz. The *moshav* is a kind of cooperative, with land divided equally among families (except for a portion set aside for common cultivation, to which all must contribute), cooperative marketing of produce, and arrangements for mutual aid, for provision of services, and usually for credit facilities and purchases of equipment and consumer goods. At first subordinate to the more popular *kibbutz*, the moshav gained prominence during the 1950s, attracting many of the new immigrants from Europe and, even more, from Asia, and by about 1970 the number of moshavim had trebled. In the *kibbutz,* on the other hand, all means of production are owned collectively, all work is collectively arranged, and there often are arrangements for communal housing, meals, and child care. In recent decades, however, as the kibbutz increasingly began to include industrial production along with farm work, usually requiring high levels of technical competence, the original emphasis on shared manual labor and rotation of tasks became less feasible. For larger enterprises, several kibbutzim may join in putting up capital, and occasionally even private capital is used. See also COOPERATIVE, def. 2.

collective ownership See COLLECTIVISM, def. 1; also PUBLIC OWNERSHIP.

collectivism

1. Collective ownership, that is, joint ownership of an economic enterprise, as in a producer cooperative (see COOPERATIVE, def. 2), or ownership by the government (see PUBLIC OWNERSHIP).

2. Centralized economic planning, ranging from outright state ownership and control (as under FASCISM, COMMUNISM, or SOCIALISM) to various degrees of economic planning in which private property may be retained but where private individuals and organizations are not free to act as they wish. See also PLANNED ECONOMY.

3. A concept championed by various 19th-century opponents of Marxism. Rejecting Marxist emphasis on a strong central government, which they believed would simply replace other forms of tyranny over the working class, collectivists instead ad-

vocated some form of voluntary cooperative association. Among them are some of the proponents of ANARCHISM, SYNDICALISM, and MUTUALISM.

collect on delivery Same as *cash on delivery*; see COD.

collision insurance A form of PROPERTY INSURANCE for owners of motor vehicles that compensates them for damage caused by collision with another object or vehicle. Comprehensive automobile insurance usually covers damage from causes other than collision. Collision insurance tends to be quite costly.

colonialism The policy of acquiring colonies to gain power and wealth. Colonialism is intimately linked with *nationalism*, the idea that one's own nation should be bigger, richer, and stronger than any other, and, by extension, with the concept of economic self-sufficiency, the idea that one's own nation should not depend on any other. From an economic standpoint, colonialism, which became the national policy of all the powerful West European countries with the discovery of the New World in the 15th century, gave rise to MERCANTILISM. Since the sole reason for colonies was a nation's self-aggrandizement, at first they were regarded chiefly as sources of precious metals and other valuable raw materials. With the expansion of manufacturing in the home countries, colonies also provided markets for manufactures and investment opportunities. To serve these purposes, the strict rules and regulations advocated by the mercantilists were enacted, prohibiting certain industries in the colonies, invoking protective tariffs, and regulating commerce. The colonial system began to break down as early as 1776, when the American colonies broke away from Britain, but in some parts of the world, notably Africa, it persisted until the mid-20th century. The economic efficiency of colonialism has long been questioned, since it has most of the same disadvantages as ABSENTEE OWNERSHIP.

comaker A person who, together with one or more others, signs a negotiable instrument and hence is liable for its payment.

combination In business, the joining of two or more companies in order to pool resources, cut costs, and/or limit competition. According to U. S. law, a combination whose chief purpose is to limit or eliminate competitors may be declared illegal (see ANTITRUST LEGISLATION). For the principal kinds of business combination, see CARTEL; CONSOLIDATION; HOLDING COMPANY; MERGER; POOL, def. 2; SYNDICATE, def. 1; TRUST, def. 2.

combination rate A transportation rate computed by adding two different rates, such as domestic and foreign air rates, or freight rates for goods carried in two districts with different rates.

commerce Also, *trade.* Buying and selling goods and services, particularly on a large scale, between firms, communities, states, or nations. In the United States commerce between different states is regulated through the *Interstate Commerce Commission.* The *U.S. Department of Commerce,* created as the Department of Commerce and Labor in 1903 and separately constituted in 1913, is the principal government agency charged with fostering, serving, and promoting the nation's economic development and technological advancement.

commercial bank A bank whose principal functions are to accept demand deposits and to make short-term loans, chiefly to business firms. In addition, American commercial banks may make many other kinds of loan (on real estate, to consumers, for buying and carrying securities, to governments, some long-term loans), and they also may issue time and savings deposits, operate trust departments, act as agents in buying and selling securities, underwrite and sell new security issues for state and local governments, sell insurance, etc. Though commercial banks do not issue currency, they do issue money in the form of checking deposits, and as such they are the only financial institution with the power of creating and destroying money (see also under MONEY). In Great Britain commercial banks were formerly called *joint-stock banks,* and in Western Europe they are known as *credit banks* (for example, *Kreditbank, Kreditanstalt, Crédit Suisse,* etc.) as opposed to investment banks (see INVESTMENT BANKING). In the United States all national banks, though not all state banks, are commercial banks, and practically all are insured by the FEDERAL DEPOSIT INSURANCE CORPORATION. See also DEMAND DEPOSIT; DEPOSIT, def. 1.

commercial credit company See FINANCE COMPANY, def. 3.

commercial draft See BILL OF EXCHANGE.

commercial loan theory of banking See REALBILLS DOCTRINE.

commercial paper Short-term promissory notes of highly reputable business firms. Though unsecured, these notes are backed by excellent credit ratings and therefore are eminently negotiable. (To indicate their high standing, they often are called *prime commercial paper*.) Normally a firm sells commercial paper to a dealer, who in turn sells the notes, most often to commercial banks, after deducting interest at the current rate plus a small commission. (Finance companies, however, sell notes directly to investors.) Most commercial paper represents liabilities of $50,000 to $1 million or more, payable in less than 90 days. Commercial paper is traded in the MONEY MARKET. Interest rates, which are published monthly in the *Federal Reserve Bulletin*, tend to be lower than those on ordinary bank loans.

Commercial Revolution The steady economic expansion of Europe from the late Middle Ages (15th century) until 1700, marked by the increasing importance and growth of towns and cities, the advent of a money economy (replacing BARTER) and private banking, and the development of trading organizations such as the Hanseatic League (see under GUILD). Its greatest stimulus came from the voyages of overseas discovery and exploration of the 15th and 16th centuries, which promoted worldwide trade and also brought treasures of gold and silver from the New World. Companies were organized, shipping expanded greatly, and modern credit facilities appeared to finance the new trade, including state banks, exchanges, and the futures market. The medieval craft guild system began to decline as technical advances changed industry; it was replaced in part by COTTAGE INDUSTRY. At the same time the old-style family business began to give way to larger forms of organization—first the partnership, later the regulated company (an association of merchants), and, in the 17th century, the joint-stock company, early model of the modern corporation. The Commercial Revolution gave rise to the concepts of MERCANTILISM, embodied in a system of government intervention to promote economic prosperity and enhance the power of the national state. In establishing competitive enterprise as the foundation of production and trade, the Commercial Revolution paved the way for the INDUSTRIAL REVOLUTION, creating both a class of capitalists to invest in industry and colonial empires to provide sources of raw materials and markets for manufactured goods.

commission A fee paid to an agent or broker for negotiating a sale, based on a percentage of the selling price. Though it may be calculated in precisely the same way, a commission differs from a FUNCTIONAL DISCOUNT, which is a fee paid to middlemen who take title to the property being sold. For *commission house*, see under MIDDLEMAN; for *commission merchant*, see CONSIGNMENT; see also BROKER; MERCHANT WHOLESALER.

commodity
1. Any physical good or product, whether agricultural, mineral, or manufactured.
2. A basic product, usually but not always agricultural or mineral, traded on a COMMODITY EXCHANGE. Products commonly traded in this way include wheat, corn, other grains, cotton, sugar, coffee, rubber, lead, zinc, and copper.

commodity agreement See INTERNATIONAL COMMODITY AGREEMENT.

Commodity Credit Corporation See under AGRICULTURE, AID TO.

commodity exchange Also, *board of trade, produce exchange*. An organized market where traders buy and sell contracts for immediate or future delivery of certain commodities. The contracts specify the amounts, quality, and delivery terms for the commodities, which themselves never actu-

Fig. 13. Principal U.S. commodity exchanges

Commodity Exchange	Commodities Handled (Regulated under Commodities Exchange Act)	Commodities Handled (Not Regulated under Act)
Chicago Board of Trade	Corn; oats; soybean meal; soybean oil; soybeans; wheat	Gold; iced broilers; plywood; stud lumber; silver
Chicago Mercantile Exchange	Eggs (frozen and shell); frozen pork bellies; grain sorghums; live beef cattle, feeder cattle, hogs; potatoes	Lumber; turkeys
International Monetary Market of Mercantile Exchange		Copper; foreign currencies; gold; silver coins
Commodity Exchange, Inc. (NY)		Copper; gold; mercury; rubber; silver
Kansas City Board of Trade	Corn; grain sorghums; soybeans; wheat	
Mid America Commodity Exchange (former Chicago Open Board of Trade)	Corn; oats; soybeans; wheat	Gold; silver; U.S. silver coins
Minneapolis Grain Exchange	Durum wheat; wheat	
New York Cocoa Exchange		Cocoa; rubber
New York Coffee and Sugar Exchange		Coffee; sugar
New York Cotton Exchange	Cotton	
Citrus Associates of Cotton Exchange	Frozen concentrated orange juice	
Wool Associates of " "	Wool	
LPG " " " " "		Liquid propane gas
Petroleum " " " "		Petroleum
New York Mercantile Exchange	Imported frozen boneless beef; potatoes	Fuel oil; foreign currencies; gold; heating oil; platinum; plywood; palladium; silver coins
Pacific Commodities Exchange	Coconut oil; eggs (shell); live cattle; palm oil	Silver

ally appear on the exchange. Contracts for immediate delivery are traded in the SPOT MARKET; contracts for future delivery are traded in the FUTURES MARKET. By far the majority of transactions are in futures. The biggest U.S. commodity exchange is the Chicago Board of Trade, where numerous commodities are traded, and Canada's largest is the Winnipeg Grain Exchange. Some exchanges specialize in particular commodities, such as cotton or coffee, whereas others handle a variety. Only commodities whose quality can readily and accurately be determined are suitable for trading on ex-

changes. Further, buyers often inspect samples to assure themselves of their quality. The commodities traded, in addition to those listed in Fig 13, include rice, barley, rye, flaxseed, mill feeds, butter, other fats and oils (lard, tallow, peanut oil, etc.), and peanuts. Although anyone can purchase spots or futures through a broker, most commodity trading is done by professional speculators. In the United States commodity exchanges are regulated by the *Commodity Futures Trading Commission* (which replaced the Commodities Exchange Commission) of the Department of Agriculture.

commodity futures See FUTURES MARKET.

commodity money A medium of exchange consisting of a given commodity or group of commodities, as opposed to some kind of paper money or currency. Numerous commodities have been used in this way (and in less developed areas of the world still are): human beings (slaves, wives), cattle, gold, silver, diamonds, wampum beads or shells, furs, olive oil, tobacco, etc. In general, commodities used as money are those in relatively short supply and in great demand. Ideally they should also be readily identifiable and divisible into small units; clearly some of the commodities mentioned above lack some of these characteristics (a wife, for example, is identifiable but, unlike olive oil, not divisible). Some drawbacks of commodity money were overcome by the use of full-bodied coins of silver and gold, which had relatively stable values and were readily measurable (by weighing). However, most societies in which many economic transactions take place prefer paper money to commodity money.

commodity price index
   1. General term for any PRICE INDEX for commodities, including consumer, wholesale, and prices-received-and-paid-by-farmers indexes.
   2. A PRICE INDEX for raw materials (raw wool, cotton, etc.) that are usually but not always traded on commodity exchanges (for example, scrap iron is not). Two such indexes are the Dow-Jones spot and futures commodities indexes. The spot index measures prices paid for immediate delivery of such basic commodities as cotton and copper. The futures index measures current prices for delivery as much as one year in advance. Both indexes are much more volatile—that is, they move up and down more rapidly—than the U.S. Bureau of Labor Statistics WHOLESALE PRICE INDEX, which includes many manufactured items whose prices are administered (see ADMINISTERED PRICE).
   3. The 22 Basic Commodities Index, a supplement to the U.S. Bureau of Labor's WHOLESALE PRICE INDEX, which attempts to measure price change at an even earlier stage of exchange for selected sensitive commodities, such as cotton and copper.

commodity rate See under FREIGHT.

commodity theory of money A theory that attempts to explain the fluctuating value of money in terms of changing demand for and supply of the commodity by which money is backed, chiefly gold and silver. For example, with a GOLD STANDARD, the value of a monetary unit would depend on the price of gold, partly determined by the demand for it as a commodity (used in manufactures, arts, etc.). If this were true, the purchasing power of money would decline—that is, prices would rise—whenever the gold content of the monetary unit was reduced. In fact, however, this does not necessarily happen—it did not in 1934, with the U.S. dollar—and today the commodity theory of money has largely been discarded.

common carrier An individual or firm providing public transportation for any passengers or goods at a uniform rate. It usually operates under a franchise given by an official regulatory body. A common carrier may decide to carry only certain classes of passenger or freight, but if so, it must accept any passengers or freight within those categories, and it must maintain regular service. To discontinue service or change its rates, it usually must obtain special permission. The principal common carriers are railroads, trucks, buses, barges, and pipelines. See also CONTRACT CARRIER.

common law A body of law that has grown out of previous court decisions, customs, and usage, rather than resulting from specific legislation (statutory law). Originally developed in England following the Norman Conquest (1066), it was brought to North America by English colonists, along with numerous English statutes, and is still largely valid in most states of the United States. A notable exception is Louisiana, which adhered to French law in the form of the Napoleonic Code.

common-law trust See MASSACHUSETTS TRUST.

Common Market
   1. Popular name for the *European Economic Community* (*EEC*), originally a customs union of six European countries (France, West Germany, Italy, Belgium, Netherlands, Luxembourg) formed in 1958, which has since become a more inclusive

economic union, in terms of both membership and functions. Conceived by the French economist Jean Monnet, who favored political unification of Europe but realized the need for a sound economic basis, the Common Market aimed to establish the free movement of goods, services, capital, and labor among its members, as well as common commercial transport and agricultural policies and a common tariff and trade policy toward nonmembers. It also established the *European Investment Bank* to provide money for helping the less developed areas of its members; a *European Social Fund* to help find employment for laid-off workers, especially those affected by the formation of the EEC; and an *Overseas Development Fund* aimed at helping the former colonies of its members that had become independent (by the early 1960s these included all the former French and Belgian possessions in North and Central Africa). By 1968 a common external tariff had been set and most import duties and quotas among members had been eliminated. Also, workers could move freely among the member countries without special work permits. However, by 1975 common agricultural and transportation policies had not yet been determined, and numerous discrepancies in excise and other taxes remained.

The Common Market's greatest achievement by far was the increased prosperity of the members, particularly during the early years. With the creation of a much larger market for producers, who were for the first time not hampered by trade barriers, factory production in the Common Market countries increased by 50 per cent in the first five years alone. Moreover, at the same time that other industrial nations, including Canada and the United States, were suffering from growing unemployment, the Common Market countries experienced a labor shortage. The Market also raised some new problems. By levying preferential tariffs on former colonies of its members, it created problems for underdeveloped countries that lacked this trade advantage. In addition, political pressures within the Common Market forced it to set preferential tariffs and quotas to protect some of its relatively inefficient industries—especially agriculture. As a result, European consumers had to pay high food prices, and major agricultural exporters (the United States, Canada, New Zealand, etc.) were prevented from exploiting the full potential of the European market by a complicated system of trade barriers and price supports.

2. A name for other groups of nations banded together for a form of cooperation similar to the European Common Market (see def. 1). Among them are the Andean Pact (Peru, Chile, Bolivia, Ecuador, Colombia), Latin American Free Trade Association (Brazil, Argentina, and the Andean Pact nations), Central American Common Market (Guatemala, El Salvador, Nicaragua, Costa Rica), Caribbean Free Trade Association, East African Common Market, and the EUROPEAN FREE TRADE ASSOCIATION.

Commons, John Roger An American economist (1862–1945), member of the school of INSTITUTIONAL ECONOMICS, remembered for his emphasis on social reform. Commons strongly supported trade unions and labor laws, and helped formulate such reform legislation as workmen's compensation and unemployment insurance in Wisconsin under Gov. Robert M. LaFollette. Defining institutions as "collective action in control of individual action," Commons believed that a society must develop institutions in order to curb individual power.

common stock A SECURITY that represents an ownership interest in a corporation (see also STOCK, def. 1). If a company has not issued PREFERRED STOCK, its common stock is synonymous with *capital stock*. If it has also issued preferred stock, the latter usually has prior claim on dividends and, in case of liquidation, on the company's assets. Common stockholders thus assume more risk, but they also exercise more control over a company because they usually have VOTING RIGHTS. Also, they may realize a greater return on their investment in terms of both dividends and capital appreciation. By far the majority of stocks traded today, both on and off organized exchanges, are common stocks, which have much greater potential yield for investors than any other kind of security.

common trust fund A trust fund to provide for the combination of several individual trust funds, such as a number of small pension funds. This practice both reduces administrative costs and permits greater diversification of investment.

commune See under COLLECTIVE FARM.

communism

1. The political, economic, and social doctrine of Karl MARX, also called *Marxism*, *Marxist communism*, and, at the time Marx formulated it, "socialism." Its principal features are the economic interpretation of history, dialectical materialism, the class struggle, the surplus labor and value theory (or doctrine of surplus value), and the theory of socialist evolution. According to Marx, all important events in human history were determined by their economic environment, that is, the methods of producing and exchanging goods and services of their time. Every successive economic system, based on a particular pattern of production and exchange, has some weaknesses and internal strains, and the inevitable clashes growing out of a system result in its destruction and replacement by another system. This process is continual until an ideal system—communism—is finally attained. All history has seen struggles between classes—masters vs. slaves, patricians vs. plebeians, masters vs. journeymen, lords vs. serfs. The current (19th-century) struggle is between capitalists (employers) and proletariat (workers), that is, between the owners of the means of production and the wage earners. True value is created not by capital but by the labor that produces a product (see LABOR THEORY OF VALUE). The worker, who should receive full value for his labor, instead receives only a portion, in the form of a wage, while the remainder, the surplus value, goes to the capitalist as profit, interest, or rent. Marx believed workers should cease to allow such exploitation, rise up against the capitalist, and set up a dictatorship of their own (dictatorship of the proletariat). During this "socialist" stage of evolution the state will own and operate all the means of production, distribution, and exchange, and each person will be paid according to work performed. In time, however, the state will no longer be necessary and hence disappear. Society will then be classless, and everyone will work according to his ability and receive according to his needs (an idea originated by Louis BLANC). It is this ideal condition that Marx called "communism."

2. Also, *Communism*. Various versions of Marx's doctrines (see def. 1 above) adopted in those countries whose political and economic systems are dominated by a Communist party, including the Union of Soviet Socialist Republics, German Democratic Republic, the nations of eastern Europe, Federal Socialist Republic of Yugoslavia, Republic of Cuba, People's Republic of China, Democratic Republic of Vietnam, and Democratic People's Republic of Korea. In all these countries the respective Communist party took power by military force, on which it has continued to rely, and all are characterized by elements of dictatorship and a strong central government with strict control over economic affairs. Actually, none of the Communist countries claims to have achieved the ultimate ideal described by Marx. Most hold that they are in some earlier stage of socialism. The most highly industrialized of them, Russia, calls itself an "industrial democracy." Its state planning commission, *Gosplan*, decides what goods should be produced and in what manner. All land and capital goods are government-owned, private property being limited to homes, furniture, personal effects, and individual savings from wages. The government sets both wages and consumer prices.

3. Marx's doctrine as it appears in branches of the Communist Party where it is one of several political parties, as in France, Italy, and the United States. See also SOCIALISM. For other communist theorists, see F. ENGELS; V. I. LENIN.

Communist Manifesto, The   A declaration of political, social, and economic ideas that became the basis of Marxist communism. Written by Friedrich Engels and Karl Marx and published in Paris in 1848, the manifesto states some of the main communist precepts: dialectical materialism, inevitable class struggle, and a predicted worldwide communist revolution ending in the abolition of private property and the creation of a classless society. See also COMMUNISM, def. 1; F. ENGELS; K. MARX; SOCIALISM.

community property   Property that is accumulated by the efforts of either husband or wife while living together. In the United States certain states recognize this system of ownership. In addition to his or her interest in the community property, either spouse may own separate property, which usually consists of property owned prior to marriage or acquired after marriage by gift, devise, descent, or in exchange for property owned separately.

company General term for any business enterprise. The most common forms of business organization are the CORPORATION, the PARTNERSHIP, and the PROPRIETORSHIP. See also ESTABLISHMENT; FIRM, def. 1; HOLDING COMPANY; JOINT-STOCK COMPANY, def. 2; SUBSIDIARY.

company store A retail store operated by a firm for its employees. In places where it is the only readily accessible retail outlet, the company store can be (and has been) used to cheat employees by charging exorbitant prices, allowing credit purchases that are automatically deducted from wages, etc. At one time some companies even paid wages in scrip that was redeemable only in the company store, a practice now illegal in the United States. Today company stores are found largely in remote areas (such as Alaska's North Slope) and, if anything, tend to sell merchandise at lower prices than an independent merchant in a comparable location could afford to charge. In the mid-1970s some large American companies operated retail shops on their premises in urban and suburban areas, where, in effect, these heavily subsidized enterprises, offering low prices, were a form of fringe benefit for employees.

company town A community established by a company for its employees, usually in a remote, unpopulated area. Traditionally the company or a subsidiary owns all the real estate and other property, which it rents to employees. Commonly built by mining companies, steel mills, and other industrial concerns in 19th- and early 20th-century America, the company town is rare today except in areas like the Alaskan oil fields, where workers must be housed in a naturally inhospitable environment.

company union A union set up by management for its employees. Meetings and elections take place in the plant during working hours, and the employer pays all union "expenses." Company unions generally petition management for changes but rarely, if ever, make demands. Essentially a device to satisfy workers' desire to unionize without losing control over their activities, American company unions were made illegal by the National Labor Relations Act of 1935, which forbids employer interference with unions. Even before this law was passed, some company unions circumvented their original purpose by affiliating with national unions.

comparative advantage See under ADVANTAGE.

comparative costs, principle of Same as comparative advantage; see under ADVANTAGE.

comparative statics A method of economic analysis that compares different states of EQUILIBRIUM. For example, in the market for a given good, such as automobiles, the initial equilibrium price is determined by supply and demand, in turn influenced by consumer taste, income levels, prices of other products, technology, cost of production, etc. The economist constructs a MODEL based on the condition of all these influences at one moment in time (a *static* model). A single factor then is changed. For example, suppose this change is a decline in consumer income. This will cause demand for new automobiles to fall and prices to decline. The output of cars also will decline until a new equilibrium is reached. By comparing the new equilibrium with the old, one can presumably predict the effect of a decline in income on the future price and output of automobiles. One cannot, however, determine how the market will behave between the two equilibrium points, nor how long it will take to move from one to the other. See also DYNAMICS.

comparison shopping Investigating different sellers for the best merchandise or services on the most favorable terms. Though it is primarily a technique used by actual buyers, large retailers sometimes employ comparison shoppers to check on their competitors, and manufacturers and distributors sometimes use them to check on retailers who carry their products.

compensating balance The balance a borrower must keep on deposit in a bank, representing a given percentage of the loan (typically about 20 per cent). In effect, the compensating balance is an extra cost to the borrower, since it is money that cannot be used for some other purpose. For example, suppose a businessman borrows $100,000 at an interest rate of 8 per cent and must maintain a compensating balance of $20,000. He then really gets the use of only $80,000, and his $8,000 interest payment represents an effective rate of 10 per cent. The minimum balance required by many commercial banks for maintaining a checking account is a form of compensating balance for consumers.

compensatory fiscal policy See under FISCAL POLICY.

compensatory tariff A kind of protective TARIFF (see def. l) used to offset either a tariff on raw materials or an excise tax on domestic goods. It is levied on imported manufactured goods to offset a domestic manufacturer's costs (which include a tariff on raw materials used in the product) or on imported commodities on whose domestic equivalent an excise tax is levied. For example, the United States is a major exporter of cotton, which is sold at world market prices. During periods of depressed prices, the price of domestic cotton might be deliberately kept higher than world prices in order to help growers of cotton. However, this makes the costs of U.S. textile producers higher than those of their foreign competitors. The solution is a compensatory tariff on imported cotton goods, which prevents the foreign producer from exploiting the advantage gained by buying cotton at the lower world market price.

competition A state of rivalry among sellers, each of whom tries to gain a larger share of the market and greater profits. In the business sense of the term, sellers are vying for customers, and in so doing they both adapt to existing market conditions (by switching to more profitable items, for instance, or through more efficient operation) and attempt to change market conditions (by creating additional demand through product differentiation, combining with other sellers in cartels, etc.). Competition may exist not only among sellers of the same product or service, but among different industries—so-called *interindustry competition*—with buyers being urged to substitute butter for margarine, synthetic for natural fibers, natural gas for oil, etc.

In economic theory competition refers to market conditions in terms of how much control sellers can exercise over price. It ranges from complete control (in monopoly) to no control whatever (pure

competition). More common than either extreme is a market where sellers have some degree of control over prices (imperfect competition). In all cases the seller's objective is the same: to maximize profit. The difference lies in the structure of the market—the number of competing firms, how easily firms can enter or leave the business, the individual character of their products. Most economists regard *price competition* as the only true form of competition, as distinguished from a competition based almost entirely on brand preference (for example, the competition between Ford and Chevrolet, Anacin and Bayer Aspirin, etc.). See also CUT-THROAT COMPETITION; FREEDOM OF ENTRY; IMPERFECT COMPETITION; MONOPOLISTIC COMPETITION; MONOPOLY; NONPRICE COMPETITION; OLIGOPOLY; PERFECT COMPETITION; PURE COMPETITION; UNFAIR COMPETITION.

competitive exchange depreciation See EXCHANGE DEPRECIATION.

compiler See under PROGRAMMING.

complementation agreement An agreement between a company and two or more countries whereby tariffs on specified goods are reduced or abolished. For example, in 1962 an American firm, International Business Machines (IBM), signed an agreement whereby Argentina, Brazil, Chile, and Uruguay abolished tariffs on punched-card data-processing equipment, its components, and the paper for the cards when produced in any of the four countries. Because this agreement gave IBM a large enough market to justify local production, it built plants in Argentina and Brazil, and arranged for a license for Chile to produce the paper for the cards. Exports in these products increased rapidly for the countries concerned, and IBM, by reducing its costs through the elimination of tariffs, also profited.

complements and substitutes Also, *complementary and substitute goods*. Goods so related that a change in the price of one good affects consumption of the other. For example, if the price of gasoline falls, demand for gasoline will probably rise, as will demand for motor oil. Motor oil and gasoline are complements. In contrast, if the price for coffee rises, some coffee drinkers may switch to tea. Coffee and tea are substitutes. See also CROSS-ELASTICITY, def. 1.

composite demand The total demand for a given good or service from all sources, even though it involves a variety of uses. For example, low-carbon steel sheets are used in a wide range of manufactured products, including automobiles, refrigerators, office furniture, etc. Similarly, *composite supply* refers to the total supply of a variety of goods and services that satisfy a particular demand. For example, the demand for construction materials may be satisfied by brick, cement, concrete block, lumber, aluminum siding, etc.

composition of creditors An arrangement whereby a debtor who cannot pay all his creditors in full pays each of them the same fixed percentage of the amount owed, in exchange for their freeing him from the balance of the indebtedness. For example, if Bowman has only $30,000 but owes Adams $15,000, Hancock $18,000, and Clarke $12,000, the three creditors might agree to release Bowman from the debt, provided he pays each of them two-thirds of what is owed ($10,000, $12,000, and $8,000 respectively). If this procedure will prevent Smith from going bankrupt, in which case the three might have to share his total assets with still other creditors, it is to their advantage to conclude such an agreement.

compound entry Also, *combined entry.* In accounting, an entry in a journal involving three or more elements, as opposed to a simple entry involving just one credit and one debit. A compound entry might consist of two debits and one credit, or two credits and two debits, or some other combination. For example, suppose a company sells 100,000 shares of $1 par value stock for $3 per share. Cash is debited $300,000; common stock is credited for the stock valued at par, or $100,000, and capital surplus is credited for $200,000.

compound interest An interest charge computed by applying the percentage rate of interest not only to the principal of the loan, but also to successive increments of simple interest—that is, to the principal plus the simple interest on it after the periodic due dates. For example a principal of $100 invested at 10 per cent interest, compounded annually, would yield $10/100 \times \$100 = \$10$ in the first year, $10/100 \times (\$100 + \$10) = \$11$ in the second year, $10/100 \times (\$100 + \$20) = \$12$ in the third year, and so on, provided that the $10 earned in the first year remained invested (was not paid out as a dividend). If the interest is compounded more frequently than once a year, it is calculated proportionately, for example, 5/6 per cent monthly at an annual rate of 10 per cent. Compound interest is based on the idea that the interest itself becomes principal and therefore also earns interest in subsequent periods. Since compound interest is the most common form of interest charge in practically all loan transactions, numerous formulas have been devised for calculating it, and compound-interest tables are widely available.

compound tariff See under AD VALOREM.

comprehensive insurance See under PROPERTY INSURANCE.

comptroller See CONTROLLER.

compulsory arbitration See under ARBITRATION, def. 1.

computer An automatic, high-speed calculating machine that performs a variety of mathematical operations by reducing them to arithmetical operations by means of electronic devices. The difference between the computer and other calculators lies in its ability to be programmed to perform limitless sequences of operations. Its importance is largely due to its capacity to store enormous amounts of readily retrievable data, to perform very rapid arithmetical operations, and to accomplish all of this with extreme accuracy.

Modern computers are used to solve problems by organizing them into separate steps, using the results obtained in one step to execute the next (a feature called FEEDBACK), and storing intermediate results until they are needed for a subsequent step or for the final solution. They operate by means of a *program,* a set of instructions that represent the steps of a given task (such as computing a payroll, printing out the appropriate checks, and updating all accounting records affected by these operations; see also PROGRAMMING). In addition to accepting and storing information, moving it from place to place inside the memory (see below), and performing arithmetic, the computer can compare information and perform different program steps depending on the results of the comparison, a process called *logic*.

The earliest computers, developed in the 1920s, were *analog computers,* electromechanical (rather than wholly electronic) devices that measured physical quantities (the amount a shaft turns, varying electrical voltages, etc.), which represented mathematical quantities. (The slide rule is an example of a simple mechanical analog computer, on which varying physical lengths represent different logarithms.) In the 1940s *digital computers* were developed; instead of measuring, they use discrete numbers. Most present-day computers are digital, but some combine analog and digital features.

A digital computer consists of four kinds of equipment (called *hardware*): (1) *input-output devices,* whereby data are put into the computer (paper-tape readers, card readers, magnetic-tape readers, optical scanners, magnetic-ink readers, console typewriters, analog-digital converters, etc.) and produce the desired results (printers, magnetic-tape writers, paper-tape punches, card punches, voice-response units, console typewriters, cathode-ray display, etc.); (2) *arithmetic and logic units,* which perform the required operations on the data; (3) *storage* or *memory,* which holds information until it is needed (in a magnetic core, magnetic tapes, magnetic disks, magnetic cards, etc.; see also STORAGE, def. 1); (4) a CONTROL UNIT, whereby the computer controls its own operations. The arithmetic-logic and control units frequently are combined in what is known as the computer's *central processing unit* or *main frame.*

General-purpose computers can be used for making economic forecasts, helping decide how to allocate government revenues, guiding production managers in planning the most profitable output mix from week to week, aiding cattle raisers in preparing the lowest-cost feed for their animals, determining the most advantageous locations for plants and warehouses, guiding account executives in finding the most effective advertising methods for their clients, and similar purposes. They can serve as general business information systems, particularly in accounting, inventory control, production scheduling, and sales analysis. *Special-purpose* or *dedicated computers,* designed to carry out only a single task or group of tasks, can be used for any of the applications above when the quantity of data and repetition of limited operations are sufficiently large to warrant the expense of building a specially adapted machine. They also are widely used to control physical operations, as in NUMERICAL CONTROL of machine tools and process control, as well as in aerospace and other scientific research.

concentration ratio   A measure of the extent of concentration of business volume in any given industry among a small number of firms. It generally is measured in terms of the percentage of total assets, production, employment, sales, or profits that is accounted for by the top three to eight firms. The higher the percentage, the more concentrated the industry. For example, about 95 per cent of the automobiles made in the United States are produced by Chrysler, Ford, and General Motors. Another way of measuring concentration is to see how many firms account for a given percentage (60, 70, or 80 per cent) of an industry's sales, profits, etc.; in this case, the smaller the number, the greater the concentration. One drawback of the concentration ratio is that it tends to ignore the size distribution of the producers in a given industry. Thus, it does not differentiate between Industry A, where three firms account for 60 per cent of volume and three others for the remaining 40 per cent, and Industry B, where three firms account for 60 per cent and 40 others for the remainder; in reality, however, Industry A is less competitive than Industry B.

concession

1. Permission to conduct a business enterprise in a particular place. Also, the business so conducted. Thus, a city may grant a concession for the operation of a guided tour within its limits, or a sports club may grant a concession for refreshment sales in its stadium. The person or firm operating a concession is called the *concessionaire.*

2. A price reduction or rebate from an established price or rate, such as a tariff concession on a particular import.

conciliation Helping to settle a dispute by keeping open the lines of communication between the two parties. In current usage it is generally the same as MEDIATION.

concurrent processing Also, *multiprocessing.* The simultaneous operation of two or more programs on one computer.

condemnation The acquisition of privately owned land for some public use through the power of EMINENT DOMAIN. In the United States such power is exercised by the Federal or local governments, by school boards or other public bodies, and by quasi-public corporations such as railroads and public utilities. However, the purpose must be a public one, and the owner must be paid just compensation. Normally the exerciser of eminent domain institutes a court proceeding, and the compensation to the owner, based on the fair market value of the land at the time, may be determined by a jury. By condemnation the condemnor acquires either an easement or title to the land (technically, a *fee simple title,* meaning complete ownership). However, Federal law permits the United States government to acquire by condemnation the right merely to occupy land for a given period of years if that is preferred to outright ownership.

conditional sale A common method of credit sales of durable goods when the purchase price is paid in installments. In a conditional sale, the buyer gets possession of the goods even though they are not paid for in full, but the title to the goods is retained by the seller. The seller thus remains the legal owner and may repossess the merchandise if the buyer fails to pay as agreed. See also INSTALLMENT BUYING; SALE, def. 1.

conditional value In statistics, the influence of the occurrence of one event on the occurrence of another but related event. For example, the probability of a college student's election to Phi Beta Kappa is related to (or conditional upon) his or her grade-point average. The probability of event A occurring conditional (or given) that B has occurred is expressed as $p(A|B)$.

condominium In real estate, an arrangement for buying a dwelling unit whereby the buyer receives a deed conveying absolute ownership of the unit itself plus an undivided interest or share in certain common elements (such as the land, the roof, basement, halls, stairs, heating and air-conditioning plant, etc.). The purchaser of a condominium may be an individual, a married couple, or two or more unrelated persons. The buyer can take out a mortgage to finance the purchase, covering both the dwelling and the share of the common elements. However, such a mortgage may make it harder to dispose of the condominium than, for example, a cooperative apartment. See Fig. 14; see also COOPERATIVE, def. 5.

confirmation An informal or verbal offer put into final written form, which may be required to make a contract valid.

confiscation The appropriation of property by the government or a public agency, with or without

Fig. 14. Differences between cooperative and condominium

Condominium	Cooperative
Individual takes title to unit.	Individual owns stock in the cooperative and right of occupancy to a specific unit.
Individual owners vote on proportionate basis.	Each individual has one vote, regardless of unit's size.
Individuals are taxed separately on their units.	Cooperative as a whole is taxed, and individuals pay their share through monthly rent or maintenance charges.
Individuals are liable only for mortgage and taxes on their own unit.	Each individual is dependent on solvency of the whole cooperative.

compensation to the owner. For example, the owner of land condemned for a public use would normally be paid, whereas the possessor of confiscated illegal narcotics or firearms not only would fail to be compensated but would probably be penalized.

conflict of interest In business, finance, and government, any situation where a decision made by an individual in an official capacity is likely to bring personal benefit. For example, a conflict of interest exists when a purchasing agent selects a supplier in whose company he has a financial interest, or when an investment counselor advises customers to buy stock in a company in which she herself has invested heavily and hopes to stimulate demand and drive up the price. Brokers often find themselves in potential conflict of interest when forced to decide whether or not to counsel their customers to buy or sell securities for which they also act as underwriters.

conglomerate Also, *multi-industry firm, multimarket firm.* A business concern consisting of a corporation with large, diversified holdings, acquired through a series of mergers. It differs from other business combinations in that there need be no relationship among the businesses acquired. For example, in the 1970s an American corporation, Textron, owned, among others, firms manufacturing helicopters, electronic instruments, hydraulic equipment, solar energy products, sterling silver and stainless steel flatware, stationery, garden equipment, hearing aids, snowmobiles, pens, watchbands, and zippers.

Congress of Industrial Organizations See under AFL-CIO.

conservation The care and preservation of natural resources—water, minerals, soil, forests, fish and wildlife, energy—in order to prolong their usefulness. With a steadily growing human population using the earth's resources in increasing quantities, and with the proliferation of industrial processes that deplete or ruin resources (strip mining, industrial-waste pollution, etc.), economists and scientists alike have become increasingly concerned lest the resources become exhausted. Frequently such conservation interests conflict with the interest, at least in the short run, of the business community. The manufacture of automobiles that give off less fumes is more expensive; subterranean mining is more costly than stripping ore from surface lodes.

In the United States numerous government agencies administer conservation measures. The Department of the Interior, created in 1849, is charged with reclamation of arid lands (see also RECLAMATION, def. 2.), management of hydroelectric power facilities and mines, and the conservation and development of mineral, water, fish, and wildlife resources. Soil and water conservation programs are carried out by the Soil Conservation Service of the Department of Agriculture. An independent Federal agency, the Environmental Protection Agency, created in 1970, deals with pollutants. In 1974, after restriction of Arab petroleum exports focused attention on energy sources, the Federal Energy Administration was formed to administer American energy resources, developing programs to increase domestic production of energy from coal, petroleum, natural gas, nuclear fuels, etc., and reducing energy waste. See also PUBLIC DOMAIN, def. 1.

conservatism In economics as in politics, views and policies that tend to resist change and uphold the status quo. Since the status quo obviously varies from era to era, so does a more specific definition of economic conservatism, and ultimately the term has very limited usefulness. What was conservative in the 18th century—retaining governmental restrictions on trade (see MERCANTILISM)—might today be called "liberal," since present-day conservatism is identified with the absence of government interference. See also CHICAGO SCHOOL; ECONOMIC LIBERALISM.

consideration In law, the price demanded and received in exchange for a promise. It may consist of payment in money, goods, or services, or the performance or nonperformance of a given act. Without consideration a CONTRACT is not considered enforceable.

consignment A form of selling in which the owner of property, called *consignor*, turns it over for sale by another party, called *consignee, com-*

mission merchant, or *factor.* The consignee does not take title to the property but merely acts as selling agent and is paid a fee, usually a percentage of the selling price, called a *commission* or *factorage.* Title passes only when the property is sold to a final buyer. A consignment differs from a CONDITIONAL SALE in that the consignee is not obliged to keep the goods, nor does he assume risk of loss; if the final purchaser fails to pay for the goods, the consignee does not have to compensate the owner for the loss. However, he is supposed to exercise due care that the purchaser is a reasonably good credit risk.

consol Abbreviation for *Consolidated Annuity,* a kind of long-term security issued by the British government beginning in 1751, when they were issued in place of nine separate loans (hence "consolidated"). Consols pay a fixed interest rate but have no maturity date. However, they are callable, that is, they may be redeemed at the government's option, and as cheaper ways of financing became available many consols have been redeemed. A similar obligation issued by the French government is the *rente.* The term "consol" is sometimes loosely used to mean any British government bond, or any consolidated bond (see under BOND, def. 1).

consolidated balance sheet See under BALANCE SHEET.

consolidated bond See under BOND, def. 1.

consolidation Also, *amalgamation.* The union of two or more formerly independent business firms into a third, new firm under single ownership. Unlike a MERGER, in which the acquiring company retains its identity, a consolidation involves the liquidation or dissolution of the old companies, which cease to exist when it takes effect.

conspicuous consumption See under Thorstein VEBLEN.

constant cost See FIXED COST.

constant-cost industry An industry that does not benefit from economies of SCALE, its unit cost remaining the same regardless of increased or decreased output, as, for example, a barbershop or dentist's office.

constant-dollar value Also, *real-dollar value.* A value expressed in dollars adjusted for purchasing power. Constant-dollar values represent an effort to remove the effects of price changes from statistical series reported in dollar terms. The result is a series as it would presumably exist if prices were the same throughout as they were in the base year—in other words, as if the dollar had constant purchasing power. Any changes in such a series would reflect only changes in the real (physical) volume of output. The simplest way to obtain a constant-dollar value is to divide the dollar value of a given year by the price-index number for that year. See also GNP DEFLATOR; INDEX NUMBER; PRICE INDEX.

construction contract awards An important INDICATOR of future investment spending. No construction proceeds without a contract, and construction is an important component of investment spending, which in turn helps determine overall gross national product. Statistics on U.S. construction contract awards are reported monthly and published in the Department of Commerce's *Survey of Current Business.* The awards are reported in terms of their dollar value for just about every kind of structure—residential, nonresidential, and nonbuilding (utility and public works)—except farm buildings.

consular invoice An INVOICE for a shipment of imported goods that has been reviewed and signed by the receiving country's consul in the country of origin. Consular invoices are generally required for all imports and are used to calculate customs duties and other charges.

consumer In economics, an individual who buys goods and services for personal use rather than for manufacture, processing, or resale. See also CONSUMER GOODS.

consumer cooperative A retail business (and sometimes also a wholesale business) that is owned and may be operated by some or all of its customers in order to reduce the costs of marketing. The members of a cooperative ordinarily save through a *patronage dividend,* a portion of the net earnings that is distributed periodically to each member in proportion to the value of his or her purchases from the cooperative during the period since the last dividend. In the United States the most important fields in which consumer cooperatives operate are lending (see CREDIT UNION), electric power, rural telephone service, health plans, farm supplies (producer goods, petroleum products), and foods. A less formal version of the consumer cooperative is the *food cooperative,* in which a small number of consumers—perhaps only fifteen or twenty in all—combine their weekly and monthly grocery orders so as to buy direct from wholesalers. In these the saving is in direct cost rather than through a patronage dividend. Still another form is the cooperative apartment (see COOPERATIVE, def. 5).

The consumer cooperative originated in England in the 1820s, when workers joined together to buy goods in quantity, and the savings made through volume discounts were passed on to their members. In 1844 the first formal consumer cooperative, the Rochdale Society of Equitable Pioneers, was established. Through it goods were sold to members at the same prices charged by retail merchants, but the profits were distributed to members at year's end in proportion to their purchases. Membership was unrestricted, but each member had only one vote, regardless of the amount he or she invested. These principles, which came to be called the *Rochdale Plan,* still are followed by many present-day cooperatives. The cooperative movement spread rapidly, and by the early 1900s local cooperatives were joining together in national organizations. By 1940 cooperatives had spread throughout Europe, especially the Scandinavian countries, where they are among the largest retail enterprises. In the United States the movement never achieved the same eminence but continues to keep a share of the market, particularly in rural areas.

consumer credit   Credit extended to consumers for purchasing goods and services through charge accounts, credit cards, service credit, installment purchases, and personal loans. Such credit is largely short- or intermediate-term, usually to be repaid within six months to three years. (Long-term loans, such as home mortgages, are not considered consumer credit.) A number of financial institutions specialize in consumer loans, notably the personal finance company (see FINANCE COMPANY, def. 2), MORRIS PLAN BANK, and CREDIT UNION. Total consumer credit is an important element in the American economy. About two-thirds of all automobiles and about half of consumer durable goods (television sets, washing machines, etc.) are bought on one or another installment plan (see also INSTALLMENT BUYING). In the mid-1970s consumer credit accounted for about 20 per cent of all personal disposable income in the United States. Control over consumer credit, largely in the form of setting minimum down payments on installment purchases, is one way the Federal Reserve implements its monetary policy. See Fig. 15.

consumer expenditure   See PERSONAL CONSUMPTION EXPENDITURES.

consumer finance company   See FINANCE COMPANY, def. 2.

consumer good   A product used directly to satisfy human needs or desires, such as food or clothing, as opposed to a capital good, used to produce some other product or service. (See CAPITAL, def. 1.) The differentiation depends more on how a product is used than on the product itself. A washing machine or electric range used by an individual or family for their own washing or cooking is a consumer good; the identical machine used by a commercial laundry or restaurant is a capital good. Consumer goods, like capital goods, can be categorized as *nondurable* or *soft goods,* expected to last less than three years (food, clothing, tobacco, gasoline), and *durable goods,* expected to last longer than three years (books, automobiles, appliances, furniture). Some authorities also use a third category, *semidurable goods,* which last from six months to three years (clothing, shoes, etc.). Because of their nature, nondurable goods are generally purchased when needed, that is, demand tends to be relatively inelastic and expenditures grow roughly parallel to population growth. In the United States personal consumption expenditures for food and beverages comprise about half of nondurable spending, with clothing and shoes accounting for another 20 per cent. In contrast, purchases of durable goods often

Fig. 15. Consumer installment credit (millions of dollars; monthly data seasonally adjusted)

Period	Installment Credit Extended			Installment Credit Liquidated			Net Change in Amount Outstanding		
	Total[1]	Auto-mobile	Bank credit cards	Total[1]	Auto-mobile	Bank credit cards	Total[1]	Auto-mobile	Bank credit cards
1969	109,146	32,553	4,398	99,786	29,974	3,066	9,360	2,579	1,332
1970	112,175	29,965	6,768	107,385	30,432	5,615	4,790	−468	1,153
1971	123,086	34,778	8,377	113,788	31,303	7,679	9,299	3,476	699
1972	140,072	40,266	10,390	124,513	34,705	9,472	15,559	5,561	918
1973	160,228	46,105	13,863	140,552	40,137	12,433	19,676	5,968	1,430
1974	160,008	43,209	17,098	151,056	42,883	15,655	8,952	327	1,443
1975	163,483	48,103	20,428	156,640	45,472	19,208	6,843	2,631	1,220
1975: June	13,187	3,865	1,678	12,738	3,727	1,555	448	138	123
July	14,089	4,104	1,684	12,803	3,719	1,591	1,286	386	94
Aug	14,048	4,143	1,743	13,211	3,884	1,634	838	259	110
Sept	14,194	4,330	1,806	13,201	3,869	1,670	993	461	135
Oct	14,609	4,354	1,781	13,429	3,860	1,696	1,181	494	85
Nov	14,579	4,441	1,842	13,255	3,835	1,762	1,324	606	80
Dec	15,228	4,642	1,839	13,738	3,883	1,832	1,490	759	6
1976: Jan	15,132	4,505	1,921	14,029	3,966	1,815	1,103	539	106
Feb	15,045	4,523	2,012	13,923	3,909	1,881	1,123	614	132
Mar	15,521	4,689	2,118	14,048	4,026	1,926	1,473	663	192
Apr	15,003	4,583	1,985	13,576	3,851	1,846	1,427	732	139
May	15,041	4,471	2,103	13,566	3,819	1,911	1,474	652	193
June	15,592	4,600	2,088	14,261	4,074	1,990	1,330	526	98

[1]Includes some items not shown separately.
Source: Board of Governors of the Federal Reserve System.

can be postponed, at least for a time, so that total demand varies with the state of the economy. During a business slump, people tend to put off redecorating their homes or buying a new car. In the United States, automobiles and auto parts, and furniture and other household goods account for 80 to 90 per cent of durable spending. Since durable-goods demand reflects the condition of the economy, it is used as a LEADING INDICATOR of business conditions (both the value of manufacturers' NEW ORDERS and the change in manufacturers' UN-FILLED ORDERS are taken into account).

consumer price index Formerly *cost-of-living index.* A PRICE INDEX constructed monthly by the U.S. Bureau of Labor Statistics from the retail prices of about 400 goods and services sold in a large number of cities across the country. Like other price indexes, the consumer price index weights products by their importance (in terms of the dollar value of purchases, reflecting their importance in the individual consumer's budget) and compares prices to those of a selected base year, expressing current prices as a percentage of prices in the base year. A major drawback of the consumer price index is the difficulty in assessing changes in quality of the goods purchased, which obviously affects their price. For example, how can one compare present prices of an appliance such as an oven with those of ten or fifteen years ago when the product itself has been greatly improved, an improvement reflected at least partly in the current higher price. Another problem is assessing the effect of changes in taste on demand. However, the consumer price index is useful for determining not only price changes in individual products but changes in REAL INCOME (the purchasing power of the dollar) and the COST OF LIVING.

Fig. 16. Major U.S. consumer protection laws

Law	Date	Provisions
Pure Food and Drug Act	1906	Outlawed adulteration and misbranding of food and drugs sold in interstate commerce.
Meat Inspection Act	1907	Provided for veterinarian inspection of slaughtering, packing, and canning facilities whose meat is shipped across state lines.
Sea Food Act	1934	Permitted inspection of sea food processors (at their request); rarely invoked.
Food, Drug, and Cosmetic Act	1938	Strengthened Pure Food and Drug Act; defined adulteration; empowered FDA to set minimum standards of identity and fill for all foods; extended law to cover cosmetics; instituted factory inspection. Subsequent amendments have strengthened this law, especially with respect to drugs, pesticides, and food additives.
Wheeler-Lea Act	1938	Strengthened FTC to act against deceptive advertising and selling practices for food, drugs, corrective or curative devices, and cosmetics (in particular).
Wool Products Labeling Act	1940	Required labels detailing percentage of new wool, reused or reprocessed wool, and other fibers used in any product containing wool.
Fur Products Labeling Act	1951	Required sellers to use official Fur Products Name Guide in labeling all furs, to state part of animal used, and whether furs are new or used.
Flammable Fabrics Act	1953	Outlawed sale of highly flammable fabrics.
Poultry Products Inspection Act	1957	Required inspection of poultry sold in interstate commerce.
Automobile Information Disclosure Act	1958	Required manufacturers to tag new passenger cars and station wagons with suggested retail price and prices for optional equipment.
Textile Fiber Products Identification Act	1958	Required sellers of yarns, fabrics, and manufactured articles made of natural or synthetic fibers to label products showing percentage of each fiber used.
Hazardous Substances Labeling Act	1960	Required warnings printed on labels of dangerous household articles (cleaning agents, polishes, etc.).
Fair Packaging and Labeling Act	1966	Regulated packaging and labeling of consumer goods to prevent deception and facilitate value comparisons; required labels to identify commodity, producer, and net quantity of content.
National Traffic and Motor Vehicle Safety Act	1966	Required safety and emission standards for all automobiles sold.
Truth in Lending Act (Consumer Credit Protection Act)	1969	Required all finance companies, retailers, credit unions, and other grantors of consumer credit to reveal cost of credit, both in dollar amount of finance charges and as annual percentage rate computed on unpaid balance of loan, as well as to disclose other credit terms. Amended (1970) to regulate issuance, holder's liability, and fraudulent use of credit cards.
Cigarette Labeling and Advertising Act	1970	Required statement on cigarette packages about health hazards of smoking; outlawed cigarette advertising on television.

Fig. 16. Major U.S. consumer protection laws (*continued*)

Law	Date	Provisions
Fair Credit Reporting Act	1970	First Federal regulation of consumer reporting industry (credit bureaus, investigative reporting agencies, detective and collecting agencies, lenders' exchanges, etc.); upheld consumer's right to privacy; gave consumer right to notice of reporting activities and access to information in such reports.
Equal Credit Opportunity Act	1974	Forbade discrimination in granting credit on basis of sex or marital status.
Fair Credit Billing Act	1974	Amended Truth in Lending Act (above) so it also protected against inaccurate and unfair credit billing and credit card practices.
Hobby Protection Act	1975	Protected collectors of stamps and political articles (campaign buttons, posters, etc.) against fakes by requiring that they be marked as imitations.
Magnuson-Moss Warranty-Federal Trade Commission Improvement Act	1975	Required certain disclosure standards for consumer product warranties; extended FTC authority to include matters "affecting" commerce.

consumer protection laws In the United States, any of numerous Federal, state, and local laws specifically designed to protect consumers against unfair or deceptive trade practices. Many of these Federal laws are partly or wholly administered by the FEDERAL TRADE COMMISSION. See Fig. 16.

consumer sovereignty Also, *consumer preference.* The influence of consumers on resource allocation, that is, on the kinds and amounts of goods produced. Theoretically, in a free-market economy purchases should guide producers to supply those goods for which there is a demand. In practice, however, consumers no more control production than they control prices, their power being greatly limited by monopolies and oligopolies, by their ignorance of products and production methods, by the deceptive practices of sellers, and by overall economic conditions (inflation, interest rates, etc.).

consumer's surplus See under Alfred MARSHALL.

consumption The purchase and use of goods and services to satisfy needs and desires. The purchaser/user, either an individual or an institution, is called the *consumer.* Goods and services used by individuals and families are called *consumer goods.*

In modern industrialized nations practically all disposable personal income—90 to 94 per cent for most Americans—is used for consumption. The remainder is used for saving, which actually means merely a postponement for future consumption. PERSONAL CONSUMPTION EXPENDITURES make up about two-thirds of GROSS NATIONAL PRODUCT (its single largest component). For the effect of income on consumption, and for *consumption function, consumption schedule,* see under PROPENSITY TO CONSUME.

consumption tax See under ABILITY-TO-PAY PRINCIPLE.

containerization Also, *containerized freight.* The use of giant standard-size containers to transport goods, which can then be transferred intact from trucks to railroad flatcars, ships, and airplanes almost entirely by mechanized equipment. Considered a revolutionary development in the transportation industry, containerization, which became common in the 1970s, eliminates much of the need for workers to load and unload freight. See also FISHYBACK; LAND BRIDGE; PIGGYBACK.

contingent liability See under LIABILITY, def. 2.

continued bond See under BOND, def. 1.

continuous process A method of manufacturing whereby material undergoes an uninterrupted series of operations or processes, with new material constantly being fed in as completed products are removed. Examples range from a blast furnace, which may operate night and day for months on end, to an automobile assembly line, where car after car is put together by round-the-clock work shifts. In all such cases a single homogeneous or standardized product is produced in large quantities (see also MASS PRODUCTION). Many firms using a continuous process also use a *process system of cost accounting,* in which costs are determined for each department or process, added together to determine total cost, and divided by total output to obtain unit cost. Because like units of product are involved, it is assumed that the same amount of material, labor, and overhead is chargeable to each unit processed. See also BATCH PROCESSING, def. 2.

contra account An ACCOUNT (def. 1) that partially or entirely offsets another account, so that its balance may be subtracted from the other. For example, the balance of an accumulated depreciation account might be subtracted from the plant and equipment account balance, or an account receivable from Firm XYZ might be deducted from the account payable to Firm XYZ (when XYZ is both a supplier and a customer).

contraband General name for goods illegally transported over national borders to evade payment of duties, or simply to import or export merchandise ordinarily not permitted.

contract An agreement that creates an obligation, that is, a binding, legally enforceable agreement between two or more competent parties. It generally consists of an exchange of promises—an *offer* and an *acceptance*—resulting in an obligation to perform (or not perform) some particular act. In order to be valid, a contract must have the genuine assent of the parties to it, that is, it must involve both offer and acceptance. It also must be supported by CONSIDERATION (payment), be for a lawful object, and be in proper legal form. Some of the contracts commonly used in business transactions are available in printed form, so that only the date, price, name of commodity or service, name of par-

ties, and similar particulars need be filled in. Examples of such *standard contracts* include leases, contracts for installment purchases of automobiles and major appliances, and life insurance policies. A party to a contract may be an individual, partnership, corporation, or government. A person may act for himself or on someone else's behalf. Actually there is considerable latitude concerning contracts: not only may they be either *oral* (called *parol contracts*) or written—if both parties agree, a contract can be made in sign language—they need not even be *express* (include all the terms of the transaction) but can be *implied* (inferred from the acts of the parties; for example, an order for material that is accepted implies that the buyer will pay for the material). See also OPEN-END CONTRACT; SALE, def. 1.

A contract can terminate in any of several ways. If all its terms and conditions have been fulfilled, it is an *executed* contract and hence exists in name only. If it cannot be completed immediately but depends on some future event (for example, if if calls for building a house after land has been purchased), it is called *executory.* If a contract involves an illegal act it is *void,* since it cannot be enforced. A *voidable* contract is one that can be declared invalid by one of the parties, as, for example, in cases where one party was deceived or coerced into making the agreement in the first place. See also BREACH OF CONTRACT; RESCISSION.

contract carrier A person or firm that transports goods or passengers under contract, either for a particular trip or over a given time period. Unlike a COMMON CARRIER, a contract carrier need not maintain regular service, and it may negotiate a rate for each contract. Many truck companies and some bus lines operate on a contract basis.

contraction See RECESSION; also BUSINESS CYCLE; DEPRESSION.

contractor An individual or firm signing a contract to perform services or do work for another party for pay, but operating with less direct supervision than either an employee or an agent. In the construction and garment industries, contractors sometimes work with materials belonging to their customers; in other cases they supply the material themselves and include its cost in the price charged the client. An *independent contractor* works with virtually no supervision or control. A *prime contractor* takes responsibility for the completion of an entire project with the understanding that portions of the work will be *subcontracted* (or *farmed out*) to others (called *subcontractors*). In building a house, for example, a *general contractor* may work with the architect in planning the construction details of the overall structure and then subcontract the electrical wiring, plumbing, flooring, masonry, painting, and roofing to specialists in each of those areas.

contract rent   The actual rent paid for land, as agreed to by landlord and tenant, as distinguished from the economic concept of RENT (see defs. 1, 2).

contributed capital   See CAPITAL, def. 3.

contributory pension   See under PENSION.

controller   Also, *comptroller*. The chief accountant of a firm or other organization, responsible for instituting and operating a system of accounts and external financial reports, preparing and filing tax returns, countersigning checks, and preparing and implementing the budget. In some companies the controller also supervises the company treasurer, purchasing agent, and office manager. In the U.S. Federal government the *Comptroller General* heads the General Accounting Office, an agency that assists Congress in matters concerning the receipt, disbursement, and application of public funds and audits the accounts of all Federal agencies and departments. The office of the *Comptroller of the Currency* is charged with supervising the operations of the country's NATIONAL BANKS.

control unit   In a COMPUTER, the part of the central processing unit that takes instructions from the memory, interprets them, and initiates appropriate action.

convenience goods   Retail merchandise for which customers rarely engage in COMPARISON SHOPPING but which they tend to buy routinely, with minimum effort. Examples include cigarettes, newspapers and magazines, and some foods, drugs,

and cosmetics. *Convenience foods,* on the other hand, are processed food products whose appeal is based on timesaving and convenience features, since they require little or no additional preparation. See also IMPULSE BUYING; SHOPPING GOODS.

conversion   The exchange of a preferred stock or a bond for common stock, at a specified price, called the *conversion price,* at the owner's option. Also, the exchange of one currency for another. See also CONVERTIBLE.

convertible
   1. Designating a bond, debenture, or stock that can be exchanged by its owner for common stock or another security, usually but not always of the same company. The terms of the exchange usually are very specific as to price and time. The most common convertible securities are debentures and preferred stock.
   2. Paper money that can be turned in for gold or silver coin or bullion, meaning that a reserve is maintained in gold or silver for all or part of its face value. In practice this reserve is usually a FRACTIONAL RESERVE, meaning that the nation with convertible currency assumes that its promise will never be put to the test. In 1971, when the United States stopped the convertibility of its currency into gold (by foreigners), the outstanding claims against gold were at least $50 billion while no more than about $10 billion was theoretically available.

conveyance   In real estate law, the document whereby a title or some interest in land is transferred from one person to another.

cooling-off period   See under STRIKE.

cooperative
   1. In general, an organization of persons who pool their resources to buy or sell more efficiently and profitably than they could individually.
   2. See CONSUMER COOPERATIVE.
   3. *producer cooperative.* An organization of producers who cooperate in buying supplies and equipment and marketing their output (*marketing cooperative*). From the producer's standpoint, the most effective cooperative takes on monopoly characteristics, restricting output so as to keep prices

high. The most successful kind of producer cooperative in the United States has been the *agricultural cooperative*, in which growers not only pool their capital to purchase machinery and supplies but also provide themselves with storage facilities, processing, transportation, and other services, eliminating the costs of wholesalers (see also under WHOLESALE). At least one reason for the success of farm cooperatives is the *Capper-Volstead Act* of 1922, which gave them broad exemption from antitrust legislation. According to this law, farmers may use cooperatives to sort, grade, and pack their crops, to process such foods as butter, cheese, and canned goods, to market their output, and to fix prices and terms of sale. Though these privileges are not to be exercised to monopolize or restrain trade, in fact they may give farm cooperatives (and those involved in processing farm products) marked advantages over other industries. Further, while these advantages matter little in the case of the major staple products, whose producers tend to be widely scattered, they in effect grant a license to the monopolies possible when producers are geographically concentrated (as, for example, with certain fruits, vegetables, and nuts).

   4. *cooperative bank.* See under SAVINGS AND LOAN ASSOCIATION.

   5. *cooperative apartment.* An arrangement by which a tenant can own an apartment. Cooperatives are organized on either a trust or a corporate basis, the latter type being more common. Usually a corporation is formed, which acquires ownership of the land and the building (if existing). The corporation obtains a mortgage for buying the land and/or putting up a building. Since no mortgagee puts up the full value, the balance of the funds needed is raised by selling stock to the prospective tenants. With the purchase of a given number of shares, the tenant also gets a *proprietary lease*, which grants the right of possession of the apartment for a specified term but requires payment of rent to the corporation. The rent payments, often called *maintenance* rather than rent, consist of the prorated share of the amounts needed to cover mortgage debt, taxes, and operating expenses. The annual cash needs for the building are established by the corporation's board of directors, and the sum is divided among the tenants in proportion to the number of shares allocated to each apartment (the large ones having larger shareholdings and assessments). As a rule, tenants may not assign or sublet without approval of the corporation. See also CONDOMINIUM and Fig. 14, which compares cooperatives and condominiums.

copy   In printing, publishing, and advertising, any material that represents text, as opposed to illustrations. A *copy editor* employed by a publisher puts such material into final form, ready to be set in type. A *copywriter*, employed by an advertising agency, writes the texts of advertisements.

copyright   A grant of the exclusive right to possess, make, publish, and sell copies of a literary, musical, or artistic work, or to authorize others to do so, for a specified period of time. Copyrights may be obtained for lists of addresses, books, maps, musical compositions, motion pictures, and similar works, provided they are original expressions of an idea and are not seditious, libelous, immoral, or blasphemous. Independent of statute, the creator of a literary or artistic work has an absolute property right in his or her production so long as it remains unpublished. Infringement of copyright—copying or reproducing a copyrighted work substantially—is illegal, and the owner may collect damages (and sometimes also profits) for such infringement. Abbreviated ©. See also PATENT.

core memory   See MAGNETIC CORE.

corner   Virtually complete control of the supply of a given stock, so that buyers who may have sold it short and must now buy it back to cover themselves are forced to pay ruinously high prices. (See also SELLING SHORT.) Market corners created by an individual or small group were common in the United States during the latter half of the 19th century, when unscrupulous and powerful financiers—among them Jay Gould, Cornelius Vanderbilt, and Jay Fiske—used this technique to drive competitors out of business.

corn-hog cycle   A readily observable cycle illustrating the process of pure competition. High hog prices lead to increased demand for feed corn, pushing up corn prices. This in turn increases the cost of raising hogs, so farmers sell some of their stock rather than letting it mature or using it for breeding. This extra supply depresses hog prices. In time, it also reduces demand for corn, since there are fewer hogs to feed. Corn prices then drop, both because of declining demand and because farmers have increased corn production in response to the previous high corn prices. Corn is now cheap. Farmers expand their hog production again, cheap corn having made hog-raising profitable. They also withhold stock from the market in order to breed still more hogs, so hog prices go up again, the demand for corn also rises, and the entire cycle repeats itself. But the cycle works perfectly only when the market is completely free from other influences and corn is the only source of hog feed.

Corn Laws A series of laws in force in England from about 1400 to 1846 intended to protect the domestic grain industry. ("Corn" in Britain can mean any grain but usually means wheat.) In order to keep domestic prices high, heavy duties were levied on imported grains. In effect these laws benefited landowners and kept the prices of flour and bread artificially high, working a hardship on the poor. The effect was devastating in Ireland, which could not raise enough of its own grain and could not afford imported grains at high prices, and so became wholly dependent on its potatoes. When the potato crop failed several times during the 1840s owing to blight, more than 1 million persons starved to death and some 2 million more emigrated. Although agitation against the Corn Laws had existed for some years (see MANCHESTER SCHOOL), the Irish situation, along with a poor wheat harvest in England in 1845, finally gave Prime Minister Robert Peel the backing needed to repeal the Corn Law then in effect (1846), over the protests of the rich, the Conservative Party, and opposition leader Benjamin Disraeli.

corporate bond See under BOND, def. 1.

corporation A form of business organization consisting of an association of owners, called *stockholders*, who are regarded as a single entity (person) in the eyes of the law. Accordingly, apart from the actual individual stockholders, a corporation may own property, earn profits, incur debts, and sue or be sued. The chief advantages of the corporation are *limited liability*, that is, each owner (stockholder) is liable for the debts of the business only to the extent of his or her investment (if, for example, one buys 100 shares of stock at $10 per share and the corporation goes bankrupt, the most one can lose is $1,000); *simple transfer of ownership* (anyone can buy or sell stock at any time, provided it is available and/or a buyer can be found); and *continuity*, or *permanence* (the corporation continues to exist even if all the stockholders die). Also, a corporation can raise much larger amounts of capital than the two other principal forms of business organization, the proprietorship and partnership, because it can issue either stock or bonds (or both; see BOND, def. 1; STOCK, def. 1). On the other hand, in the United States corporations must pay Federal income tax on their profits and individual stockholders also must pay tax on whatever share of those profits they receive as dividends; such DOUBLE TAXATION can be avoided only by paying no dividends, since undistributed corporate profits are not subject to personal income tax. Finally, corporations are subject to a variety of government controls, and in the United States they lack legal status outside the state in which they are chartered.

Unlike the proprietorship and partnership, an American corporation is created by statute law, which varies from state to state. All states, however, require reports on corporations' activities and levy fees on their operations. In some states *incorporation* (forming a corporation) is easy, and in others difficult. A corporation normally is first planned by a group of *promoters*, who usually agree to buy some of its stock and apply for a charter from the state. The application includes the corporation's name; its purpose (which should—but in practice does not—limit its activities); the amount, type, and value of stock it will issue; location of main office; intended life of the corporation; and names of officers and directors. When the application is approved and all appropriate fees are paid, the corporation formally comes into existence, as verified by a *certificate of incorporation* (or *articles of incorporation*, or a *corporate charter*; see also CHARTER). Its name usually will include the word "Corporation" (Corp.), or "Incorporated" (Inc.), or, particularly in Great Britain, "Limited" (Ltd.).

Though a corporation may have as few as two

stockholders (and many do), the major corporations (in terms of production) in an advanced economy tend to have thousands. Control is legally in the hands of the stockholders, who exercise it through their voting rights, but in practice most small stockholders—and often very large ones also—take little interest in their company provided it is making money. As a result, unlike either partnership or proprietorship, large corporations tend to be run by professional managers rather than by their owners. To the extent that both managers and owners want to make the greatest possible profit, their interests coincide; when managers seek to draw huge salaries or use all profits for expansion rather than pay out dividends, their interests may clash.

As a form of business the corporation is believed to date from the time of ancient Rome, when individuals would pool their capital for various business ventures. It became more common in medieval Europe, and by the 16th century many such organizations existed, especially in shipping and foreign trade (enterprises requiring considerable capital). The most successful corporation of this era was the *Dutch East India Company*, chartered by the Netherlands government in 1602. With its monopoly on Dutch trade in Asia, it helped make the Netherlands one of Europe's wealthiest nations for two centuries. Any Dutch citizen could invest in the company simply by buying shares; almost 6.5 million guilders were thus invested. Actual control was held by the directors, who decided, among other things, if and how much of a dividend would be paid to shareholders. Unlike many early corporations, the Dutch East India Company always used a large share of its profits for expansion, building more ships and adding to warehouses and other assets. During the Industrial Revolution, as labor-saving machinery began to make large-scale production profitable, manufacturing began to require large capital investment and many manufacturing corporations came into being. In the United States corporations were formed mostly after the Civil War. By 1919 they employed 86 per cent of all American wage earners and accounted for 87.7 per cent of the total value of products.

The simplest way for a corporation to grow is by producing more goods to sell to the public. The Ford Motor Company had fewer than a dozen employees when it was founded in 1903; by 1925 the public was buying so many Ford automobiles that it employed 165,000 workers. Another way to grow is through the acquisition of other companies. The General Motors Corporation was originally a group of separate companies until General Motors absorbed them all, either buying up their stock directly or exchanging it for General Motors stock. Some corporations today own virtually no physical assets, their principal possession being the stock of other companies (see HOLDING COMPANY). See also CLOSED CORPORATION; CONGLOMERATE; HORIZONTAL INTEGRATION; MERGER; NONSTOCK CORPORATION; OPEN CORPORATION; PUBLIC CORPORATION; VERTICAL INTEGRATION.

corporation income tax Also, *corporate income tax.* A tax imposed on the annual net earnings of a corporation. In the United States such taxes are levied by the Federal government and by most states on all incorporated businesses, the rate depending on the size of earnings. In addition, the government may impose an *excess profits tax,* an additional tax on earnings in excess of earnings during a given "normal" year; this tax generally is levied only during emergencies, such as wartime. Corporate income actually is taxed twice, since dividends are subject to personal income tax (see DOUBLE TAXATION). Corporation income taxes are the second-largest source of Federal revenue (after personal income taxes).

corpus The Latin word for "body," used sometimes for the principal or capital of a TRUST or other fund or estate, as distinguished from the income or proceeds from it. See also PRINCIPAL, def. 1.

correlation analysis See under REGRESSION ANALYSIS.

correspondent bank A bank that holds deposits of and acts as agent for another bank in various transactions, such as clearing checks, buying and selling securities or foreign exchange, or participating in large loans. For domestic transactions the system of correspondent banks is peculiar to the United States, since most other banking systems consist of a few large banks with numerous branches (see BRANCH BANKING). The use of foreign correspondent banks, on the other hand, is worldwide and virtually essential for effecting international payments with some efficiency. (See also BANK DRAFT.)

The center of domestic correspondent banking is New York, with almost every large bank in the United States maintaining correspondent relations with at least one New York bank. There are many secondary centers as well, and the overall network of correspondent banks is quite complex, with numerous banks holding deposits in more than one center, and correspondent banks themselves having correspondents in other cities. For banks not belonging to the Federal Reserve System, such interbank deposits often serve as legal reserves.

cost

1. In economic theory, the value of the factors of production in a given enterprise. See FACTOR COST; also OPPORTUNITY COST.

2. In accounting, an expenditure of money, goods, or services for the purpose of acquiring goods or services. Also, the object of any such expenditure (materials cost, labor cost); further, to estimate or determine the expenditure required ("to cost a lawnmower"). Accountants classify business expenditures in various ways—by function (for selling, manufacturing, finance, etc.); by the firm's departments, divisions, or units; by product line; by location of operations; etc. They also distinguish between *nonvariable cost* or FIXED COST (also called associated OVERHEAD or INDIRECT COST— note that these terms all are used inconsistently), which is incurred no matter how much or how little a firm is producing (or even if it is not producing at all), and VARIABLE COST (or DIRECT COST), which varies directly in proportion to production volume. (It should further be noted that while all direct costs are variable, not all variable costs are direct.)

In manufacturing enterprises the term "cost" is frequently reserved for expenditures directly related to the end-product, no matter when they are incurred, while the term "expense" is used for general operating costs, independent of end-product, that are incurred during a particular accounting period. (See also EXPENSE, def. 2.) Allocating a firm's total costs to determine just what can be attributed to a specific product is the job of COST ACCOUNTING.

cost, insurance, and freight See C.I.F.

cost accounting A branch of accounting concerned with the collection, determination, and control of costs, particularly the costs of producing a particular product or service. Numerous methods and systems have been devised to carry out these functions, but basically they all involve recording costs (either projected or actually incurred), allocating costs to the appropriate accounts, and analyzing and comparing costs with those of other products, processes, firms, time periods, etc. For an example, see *process system of cost accounting* under CONTINUOUS PROCESS. See also COST CENTER.

cost and freight See C.A.F.

cost-benefit analysis Also, *benefit-cost analysis*. A systematic technique for judging among alternative ways of trying to achieve the same or related objectives, frequently requiring use of a computer to handle the large quantity of data and equations involved. In effect it consists of quantifying and comparing the expected cost and benefit of each alternative and choosing the option whose cost-benefit ratio is smallest. Originally applied to water-resource development in the United States, cost-benefit analysis is now widely applied to virtually every kind of government spending.

cost center In cost accounting, any department, process, machine, or other element of a firm for which cost records are maintained and to which fixed costs are allocated along with direct labor and material costs. Some cost accountants distinguish between two kinds of cost center: a *productive* or *direct cost center,* consisting of certain equipment, with the product made on that equipment then being charged with the equipment's expenses; and a *nonproductive* or *indirect cost center* to group

Fig. 17. Cost centers for small machine shop

- Lathe and screw machine department
- Grinder department
- Assembly department
- Warehouse and shipping department

items of expense connected with a particular activity that is not, of itself, actually productive. The principal purpose of cost centers is to assign final responsibility for costs incurred to the top manager of each center. In manufacturing enterprises a cost center is often called a *burden center.*

cost curve A graphic representation of a company's costs in relation to the quantity of output. Several kinds of cost can be so represented, singly or in combination. For example, *fixed cost* remains the same even if output is zero. *Variable cost,* on the other hand, rises with output. Fixed cost plus variable cost represents *total cost,* which also rises with output. *Average* or *unit cost* is derived by dividing total cost by the number of units of output. Whereas the total cost curve tends to slope upward, average cost tends to be U-shaped, beginning high because fixed cost then is spread over but a small number of units of output, gradually declining with quantity, and then rising again as average variable costs begin to outweigh the drop in average fixed cost. See also MARGINAL COST.

cost depletion See under DEPLETION ALLOWANCE.

cost of acquisition See ACQUISITION, def. 2.

cost of living The money cost of maintaining a particular STANDARD OF LIVING, in terms of purchased goods and services. It is nearly always described in comparative terms, such as a rise or decline in cost of living from one year to the next. The CONSUMER PRICE INDEX, sometimes thought to measure such changes, was called the *cost-of-living index* until 1945. However, it measures changes not in standard of living but in the cost of fixed quantities of the same goods and services. Standard of living, in contrast, is determined subjectively by the consumer, who in practice shifts purchases in response to changing prices, either to avoid giving up a customary living standard or to reach a higher level. A true cost-of-living index would have to take such adjustments into account, a virtually impossible task.

cost-of-living allowance An increase in wages to all employees during a period of rapidly rising

Fig. 18. Cost curves

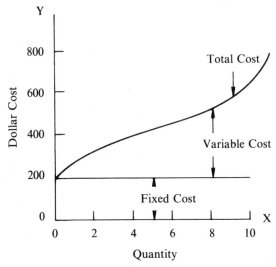

Fixed + Variable Cost = Total Cost

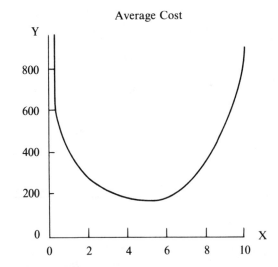

Average Cost

prices so as to keep wages in line with the current cost of living. Based on a consumer price index, such allowances were negotiated by a number of American labor unions following World War II. Some economists argue that this practice contributes to inflation. See also COST-PUSH INFLATION.

cost of possession Also, *carrying cost.* In business, the cost of owning plant, equipment, inventory-ries, and other assets, calculated in terms of alternative uses of the funds so tied up. Since in most cases businesses own only the plant and equipment they absolutely require, reductions in the cost of possession can be made only through changing inventory management. Many American companies estimate that it costs as much as 20 to 25 per cent per year to carry inventories, that is, it costs $200,000 to $250,000 to maintain each $1 million worth of inventory. The chief costs of carrying inventory are storage, obsolescence, and capital cost. *Storage cost* involves rent for storage facilities, salaries of personnel and related storage expenses, taxes, etc. *Obsolescence* includes shrinkage, spoilage, and loss of stored materials. *Cost of capital* refers simply to the alternate, more profitable uses to which money tied up in inventories could be put. See also OPPORTUNITY COST.

cost of production   In a manufacturing business, total cost of materials, labor, and overhead charged to producing a particular item. It is the single most important factor in determining that item's ultimate price.

cost-of-production theory of value   The idea, held by David Ricardo and other classical economists, that the relative value of different commodities depends on the cost of production, which to Ricardo meant wages and profits. Since neither land nor capital was considered a separate factor of production, Ricardo's theory is a version of Adam Smith's LABOR THEORY OF VALUE. Its drawbacks are that it ignores rents (the cost of land), reduces all capital to previously expended labor plus interest, and does not take into account the demand for a product and its utility.

cost of sales   In accounting, all costs associated with sales made during any particular period. Therefore, subtracting cost of sales from sales gives the net profit for the period before income taxes. The two basic components of cost of sales are the cost of goods sold and applicable overhead expenses. See also under INCOME STATEMENT.

cost or market   A method of inventory valuation in which stock is valued at either the price for which it was bought (cost) or the price at which it could currently be replaced (market), depending on which figure is lower. This method, long favored by a majority of accountants, is based on the idea that, if the current replacement cost is lower than the original purchase cost, the sales price will have to be lowered, a factor that inventory valuation should take into account. The chief drawback of the method is that, while taking future losses into account, it fails to account for future profits. It also does not show the true results of business operations during a given period, demands that both cost and market price be determined for every item, and is inherently inconsistent, swinging back and forth between two types of cost.

cost-plus contract   A purchase contract whereby the seller is paid whatever it costs him to supply a given item, plus some extra fee as profit. In a *cost-plus-fixed-fee contract*, the extra fee is set in advance; in a *straight cost-plus contract*, the fee is usually a fixed percentage of total costs. Since such a contract gives the seller little or no incentive to keep costs down, it normally is used only for an item so novel that neither buyer nor seller has any idea what the costs will be. When a cost-plus contract must be used, detailed audits of cost are usually made by the buyer.

cost-plus pricing   A very common method of setting prices. Management first determines the cost of goods to the company, adds a percentage of this cost to cover expenses and profits, and arrives at a selling price. Though practically all pricing methods must take the seller's costs into account, a simple cost-plus method may fail to take into account changes in costs owing to changes in sales volume. See also AVERAGE COST, def. 2.

cost-push inflation   Also, *price-wage spiral, wage-price spiral, wage push*. A situation in which consumer and industrial prices keep rising (see INFLATION) owing to a continuing demand for higher wages. Powerful labor interests negotiate increasingly high wage settlements to enable the workers they represent to meet rising consumer prices. Industries then raise prices to meet their higher labor costs (and usually also a little more, to increase profits), in turn leading workers to demand still higher wages. In extreme cases the government may intervene and impose *wage controls*, either by urging unions and management to hold wage increases within a particular "guideline" or, if the situation is considered an emergency, by setting mandatory limits. See also DEMAND-PULL INFLATION.

cottage industry   Also, *domestic system, home industry, putting-out system.* A system whereby a manufacturer hires laborers to work in their homes. The manufacturer supplies materials and sometimes tools or machines, and markets the finished product. The name "cottage industry" arose in the British Isles, where the system originated and where workers generally lived in simple thatched cottages in rural or semirural areas. The system made for greater division of labor than the *handicraft system* it replaced, but it required less capital investment than the more efficient FACTORY SYSTEM, which eventually superseded it. During Japan's rapid industrialization following World War II, cottage industry was widely used, and even after large factories were built industry continued to rely on thousands of small suppliers that really were just expanded cottage industries.

Council for Mutual Economic Assistance Also, *COMECON.* An international agency for economic cooperation set up in 1949 by the Union of Soviet Socialist Republics and its satellites in eastern Europe. Conceived by Soviet Foreign Minister Vyacheslav M. Molotov, it was for a time called the *Molotov Plan.* COMECON was modeled originally on the European Recovery Program. Later it devoted itself primarily to coordinating long-range production planning among its members, promoting the exchange of goods among them, undertaking bulk purchases from other nations, and handling some foreign-aid programs for underdeveloped nations. It is widely regarded as the Communist equivalent of the European Common Market.

counter check   See under CHECK.

countercyclical fiscal policy   See under FISCAL POLICY.

counterfeit   Describing a false coin or currency made in imitation of a lawful one. Also, to make such an imitation. The word originally meant to press a soft mold against something, and therefore refers to items that are engraved, as coins and paper money are.

counteroffer   An OFFER (see def. 1) made by an offeree to an offeror, accepting some terms, changing other terms, etc. See also ACCEPTANCE, def. 4; PURCHASE ORDER.

countervailing power   A term used by J. K. Galbraith for powerful interest groups that offset some of the bargaining power of monopolies and near-monopolies. Among the ones cited in his *American Capitalism* (1952) are labor unions, which raise corporate labor costs, and large retail chains (such as Sears, Roebuck, or A & P), which as big buyers are able to influence the prices charged by their suppliers. Similar but less direct influence may be exerted by consumer interest groups, such as conservationists, who through political channels have affected the technology—and therefore the costs—of numerous industrial enterprises.

countervailing tariff   See under TARIFF, def. 1.

country bank   See under NATIONAL BANKS, def. 2.

coupon bond   See under BOND, def. 1.

Cournot, Antoine Augustin   A French mathematician and economist (1801–77) who was among the earliest to apply mathematics to economic theory. He developed a system of equations to describe GENERAL EQUILIBRIUM, defined the downward-sloping demand curve, and identified the equilibrium price as the intersection of quantity demanded with quantity supplied. Cournot also was one of the first to realize that pure competition is rare, and that when a firm's output continues to grow while its costs decline it begins to enjoy a degree of monopoly. Then, as progress is made and large firms can increase their output and cut costs, they undercut the smaller firms, and monopoly becomes more widespread. Cournot's work on these issues, published in 1838, was overlooked for nearly a century but was given credit when E. H.

CHAMBERLIN published his views on monopolistic competition in 1935.

covenant A legal agreement; a CONTRACT. Also, a clause or provision of a contract.

covenants of title See under WARRANTY DEED.

cover See under SELLING SHORT.

craft guild See under GUILD.

craft union See under LABOR UNION.

crash See under BUSINESS CYCLE; also DEPRESSION.

crawling peg See under EXCHANGE RATE.

credit
   1. In general, the ability to obtain goods, services, or money now in exchange for promise of payment in the future. The degree of this ability is often described either as *good credit* (or as a good CREDIT RATING, *standing*, or *risk*), or as *bad credit*, depending on the estimated likelihood that payment will be made in full when expected. Credit either may be *secured*, that is, granted on the basis of COLLATERAL pledged or deposited to back the borrower's promise of repayment, or it may be *unsecured*, guaranteed simply by the borrower's reputation.
   Credit is essential in any advanced economy owing to the time lag between the production of goods and their ultimate consumption. For this reason, numerous written forms, called *instruments of credit*, have been developed to cover the variety of ways in which credit can be extended, that is, how funds can be transferred from one person to another. Among those most commonly used in business, commerce, and banking are the ACCEPTANCE, BILL OF EXCHANGE, LETTER OF CREDIT, and PROMISSORY NOTE. Often these instruments are negotiable (see NEGOTIABLE INSTRUMENTS), are regarded much the same as currency, and are traded in the MONEY MARKET. See also BANK CREDIT; COMMERCIAL PAPER; CONSUMER CREDIT; PAPER.
   2. In accounting, an entry on the right, or liability, side of an account, indicating the reduction or elimination of an asset or expense, or the creation of or addition to a liability or item of net worth or revenue. See also DEBIT.

credit, letter of See LETTER OF CREDIT.

credit card A card or other document indicating that the holder is entitled to credit for goods or services. Credit cards are issued by banks, hotels, travel agencies, oil companies, and other organizations, which generally first investigate an applicant's CREDIT RATING. Some organizations require payment of an initial fee, while others do not. See also CHARGE ACCOUNT.

credit control See MONETARY POLICY.

credit money
   1. Same as FIAT MONEY.
   2. Money created by banks on the basis of deposits. Since bank loans may be in excess of deposits, provided RESERVE REQUIREMENTS are maintained, banks actually create money by granting credit.

creditor
   1. In general, anyone to whom a debt is owed.
   2. *creditor nation.* A country whose investments abroad exceed the value of foreign investments within its borders, so that it owes less than it is owed. Until the outbreak of World War I Great Britain was by far the world's largest creditor nation, accounting for nearly half of all long-term foreign investments outstanding. By the end of World War II it had been replaced by the United States, which by the mid-1970s was facing competition from West Germany and Japan.

credit rating An evaluation of the financial trustworthiness of a company or individual, particularly with regard to meeting obligations. Credit ratings for business firms are normally supplied by a *mercantile agency*, which specializes in this work. The most famous such agency in the United States, Dun & Bradstreet, whose name has become synonymous with credit rating, was founded as the Mercantile Agency by Lewis Tappan in 1841. Two kinds of firm specialize in investigating consumers' credit ratings. The *credit bureau* reports to its clients—department stores, banks and other lending institutions, credit-card companies, etc.—on an individual's past record in meeting obligations (based on existing records). The *consumer-investigation agency* actually compiles and disseminates all kinds of personal information about applicants for insurance, home mortgages and leases, and employment. Because such investigations and reporting have caused considerable harm to numerous individuals, in 1971 the Fair Credit Reporting Act was passed to control these activities and prevent excesses (see Fig. 16 under CONSUMER PROTECTION LAWS for its provisions).

credit theory See under MONETARY THEORY.

credit union A form of CONSUMER COOPERATIVE that makes short-term personal loans to its members, usually at much lower interest rates than are available elsewhere. Its funds come from the deposits of members, which are regarded as purchases of shares, usually in small denominations ($5 shares are common). All earnings are paid out to the members as dividends. Credit unions are most often formed by the members or employees of a particular organization. In the United States the National Credit Union Administration, an independent government agency set up in 1970, regulates all Federally chartered credit unions (numbering about 13,000 in the mid-1970s).

creeping inflation A slow, steady increase in the general price level, about 2.5 per cent per year. Some economists, such as Alvin H. Hansen, believe that creeping inflation is an inevitable by-product of economic growth and is a stimulant to both employment and income. Others, such as Arthur Burns of the CHICAGO SCHOOL, maintain that the economy can grow when prices are stable (or even declining) and point out that, compounded over the years, creeping inflation can raise prices by 100 per cent in 25 years. Further, they warn that creeping inflation can easily get out of hand and turn into RUNAWAY INFLATION.

creeping socialism See under WELFARE STATE.

Critical Path Method See PERT.

crop insurance See under AGRICULTURE, AID TO.

crop-lien system See SHARECROPPING.

crop restriction See under AGRICULTURE, AID TO.

cross-elasticity
1. *of demand.* The effect of a change in the price of Product A on the demand for Product B. This effect is generally expressed as the percentage change in the amount of B bought, divided by the percentage change in the price of A. Thus, suppose the price of butter rises from $.80 to $1.20 per pound, or by 50 per cent; some consumers undoubtedly will buy more margarine instead of butter, perhaps twice as much (100 per cent increase). The cross elasticity of demand can then be expressed as $1.00 \div .50 = 2$, and is positive. Positive cross-elasticity indicates that butter and margarine are substitute goods (see also COMPLEMENTS AND SUBSTITUTES). On the other hand, suppose the price of baseball bats doubles. How will that affect demand for baseballs? It is safe to assume that the demand for baseballs will decline, and the cross-elasticity of demand between these two items will be negative, indicating that balls and bats are complementary goods. It should be noted, however, that cross-elasticity is a valid measure of complements and substitutes only if the items in question represent a minor part of total spending (otherwise the INCOME EFFECT of the price change must be taken into account), and if no other factors (such as changes in taste or fashion, in prices of other goods, in disposable personal income, etc.) are operative.
2. *of supply.* The effect of a change in the price of one good or service on the supply of another. The principle works exactly the same as for cross-elasticity of demand (see def. 1. above). For example, the wage paid to auto mechanics by service stations in a given area will undoubtedly affect the supply of mechanics available for work in a local machine shop, since mechanics can be expected to seek work in the business offering the highest wage.

cross-licensing See under LICENSE, def. 2.

cross order In the securities trade, an order to a broker to buy and sell the same security. If the order is placed by a single customer, it constitutes a WASH SALE and is illegal. If the order actually consists of two or more orders from different customers, the broker must execute them through the stock exchange rather than privately (provided the stock is listed and the broker is a member of the exchange). See also under STOCK EXCHANGE.

cross-rate An EXCHANGE RATE between two currencies calculated in terms of a third currency. For example, if on a given day the Swiss franc is quoted at $.3324 in New York and the German Deutschmark at $.2923, their cross-rate is 1 franc = 1.137 Deutschmark.

cultural lag The failure of political, social, and economic views and policies to keep pace with environmental or technological changes. Examples include the present-day problem of pollution in industrialized countries and the population explosion and food shortages in underdeveloped countries.

cum dividend Literally, "with dividend," meaning that the price of a stock offered for sale includes the next dividend, which has been declared but not yet paid. The buyer of the stock thus will be paid the dividend. See also EX-DIVIDEND.

cumulative distribution In statistics, a measure of the tendency of items in a FREQUENCY DISTRIBUTION to have a value equal to or greater than certain values, or a measure of how many will tend to have a value less than certain values. In effect, this is calculated by restructuring the data in the basic frequency distribution. For example, Fig. 19 shows the probable demand for a specialized machine during one day, with the cumulative probability plotted on the accompanying graph. The table shows that there is a 5 per cent probability that demand will range between 5 and 10 hours and a 10 per cent cumulative probability that demand will be between

Fig. 19. Probable demand for a specialized machine during one day

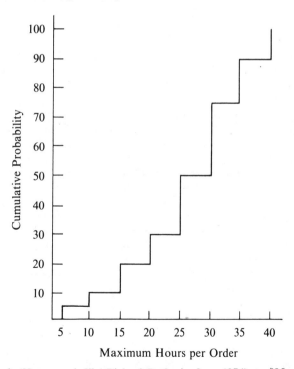

(1) Demand Hours (Machine Time)	(2) Number of Occurrences	(3) Probability	(4) Cumulative Probability
0-5	50	0.05	0.05
5-10	50	.05	.10
10-15	100	.10	.20
15-20	100	.10	.30
25-30	200	.20	.50
30-35	250	.25	.75
35-40	150	.15	.90
40-45	100	.10	1.00
	1,000	1.00	

Average 27.0 hours demand per day

Source: D. S. Ammer, *Materials Management,* 3d ed. (Homewood, Ill.: Richard D. Irwin, Inc., 1974), p. 585. Reprinted by permission.

0 and 10 hours. Similarly, there is a 10 per cent probability of daily demand for 10 to 15 hours and a cumulative probability of 20 per cent for demand ranging from 0 to 20 hours.

cumulative dividend See under DIVIDEND, def. 1; also under PREFERRED STOCK.

cumulative preferred stock See under PRE-FERRED STOCK.

cumulative voting A system of voting for the directors of a corporation that enables a shareholder to multiply the number of his or her shares by the number of directorates being voted on and cast the total for one director or a selected group of directors. For example, suppose there are ten nominees to the board. A holder of 100 shares normally casts 100 votes for each nominee, making a total of 1,000 votes. With cumulative voting, however, he or she may cast all 1,000 votes for a single nominee, or 500 votes for each of two nominees, or 250 for each of four, or any other desired combination. Cumulative voting is required under the corporate laws of some states and allowed in most others.

curb exchange See under AMERICAN STOCK EXCHANGE.

currency
  1. Also, *cash*. The portion of a nation's MONEY SUPPLY actually in circulation, comprising coins, bank notes, and government notes. A synonym for LEGAL TENDER, currency is popularly called *hard cash* to distinguish it from credit. In the United States commercial banks obtain currency in the form of VAULT CASH from Federal Reserve banks, drawing on their reserve on deposit with the Federal Reserve. Currency may or may not be convertible into precious metals. See CONVERTIBLE, def. 2; MONEY.
  2. In popular usage, paper money as opposed to metal coins.

currency, conversion of See CONVERTIBLE, def. 2.

currency school A 19th-century English school of thought concerning the role of the central bank in the economy. Its adherents believed that only currency (bank notes and coin) was actual money, and that the central bank should regulate the money supply to keep it in a fixed proportion to the amount of gold backing it. Any necessary adjustments to economic need would come about automatically through changes in the balance of trade. The currency school was opposed by the BANKING SCHOOL. Its stand was embodied in Prime Minister Robert Peel's Bank Charter Act of 1844, a law that, had it been obeyed to the letter, would have stunted the growth of the British economy through too inelastic a money supply. Fortunately for Britain the law was circumvented, and greater elasticity was effected through the use of deposit money (the law did not regard demand deposits as money), various suspensions to permit more FIDUCIARY MONEY, and credit expansion and contraction.

currency swap Also, *swap agreement*. An exchange of currency between two nations, at the official EXCHANGE RATE, made because they wish to acquire a ready source of foreign exchange in case of need. The agreement is usually on a standby basis, being executed only when one country needs the other's currency to prevent relative values from getting out of line during a crisis. For example, following widespread rioting in France in 1968, that country concluded swap agreements with the United States and West Germany, obtaining dollars and Deutschmarks to offset the flow of French francs being converted into other currencies. Similar swap agreements exist between the United States and the rest of the GROUP OF TEN.

current account See under BALANCE OF PAYMENTS.

current asset See under ASSET.

current liability See under LIABILITY, def. 1.

current ratio In analyzing a BALANCE SHEET, the proportion of current assets to current liabilities. Most analysts hold that for a manufacturing company the minimum current ratio should be 2 to 1, that is, current assets should be at least twice as great as current liabilities. However, companies with small inventories and easily collected accounts receivable can safely operate with a lower current ratio than companies that have a large proportion of current assets tied up in inventories and sell their output largely on credit. See also QUICK RATIO.

current yield See YIELD, def. 2.

customer classification See FUNCTIONAL DISCOUNT; PRICE DISCRIMINATION.

customer's man See REGISTERED REPRESENTATIVE.

customs See TARIFF, def. 1.

customs broker An individual or, more often, a firm that brings imported goods through customs and prepares export shipments to go through customs at their port of entry. This work is frequently undertaken by a FORWARDING AGENT specializing in imports and exports (also called *foreign freight forwarder*).

Customs Service The agency of the U.S. Department of the Treasury charged with collecting customs duties (see TARIFF, def. 1), preventing fraud and smuggling, and processing and regulating the passage of persons, carriers, cargo, and mail in and out of the United States. It suppresses illegal traffic (in narcotics, arms, etc.) and enforces regulations of various kinds imposed on articles in international trade.

customs union An agreement between two or more countries to abolish tariffs and other trade restrictions among the members of the union, and to establish uniform tariffs against nations outside the union. (The latter provision distinguishes it from a FREE TRADE AREA.) Because of its common tariff policy, a customs union calls for some integration of fiscal and monetary policy of the member nations. The advantages of a customs union lie in its creating a larger market for its members, making possible economies of scale, additional trade, and more efficient specialization. One disadvantage, apart from the fact that no member may protect any of its domestic industries against other members, is that it gives preference to imports from member countries, who may be less efficient producers than

outsiders. For a 19th-century customs union, see ZOLLVEREIN; for a more recent one, see COMMON MARKET.

cutthroat competition The use of price-cutting by a large seller for the purpose of eliminating smaller competitors and ultimately controlling a product's price. In the 19th century cutthroat competition was widely and ruthlessly practiced in a number of American industries, which ultimately established monopolies in the form of trusts over such products as tobacco, sugar, oil, iron, and steel. By the turn of the century cutthroat competition was made illegal by ANTITRUST LEGISLATION. See also UNFAIR COMPETITION.

cybernetics A term invented in 1947 by an American mathematician, Norbert Wiener, for a new field of control and communications theory, that is, the theory behind self-regulating logical processes. The principal nonhuman embodiment of such processes is the computer, which through FEEDBACK (def. 1) is to some extent self-controlling. Wiener was particularly interested in the similarities between such machines and the human nervous system and their relationship to mathematical logic.

cyclical fluctuations Regular changes in the BUSINESS CYCLE, characterized by fluctuations in employment, money income, and output, especially of capital goods. Such fluctuations also affect credit, which expands during an upturn and contracts during a downturn, as well as a country's balance of payments and balance of trade, both of which tend to become more favorable during a recession (since demand for imports lags, owing to decreased income, and manufacturers work harder to increase exports).

cyclical industry An industry whose sales and profits reflect to a great extent the ups and downs of the business cycle. Practically all the capital goods industries (steel, machine tools, etc.) are cyclical, because a moderate decline in demand for a consumer product may virtually eliminate demand for the capital goods needed to make that product (see ACCELERATION PRINCIPLE for further explanation).

cyclical stock The stock of a company whose fortunes are closely tied to the business cycle, usually one engaged in a CYCLICAL INDUSTRY.

cyclical unemployment Unemployment caused by a downturn in the business cycle, specifically by lack of demand for labor. Generally the lowest-paid, least skilled workers are the first to be laid off, but in a prolonged period of business contraction layoffs gradually affect all groups. Hardest hit are workers in capital goods industries, whose volume of output fluctuates most widely with business-cycle fluctuations. See also UNEMPLOYMENT.

damages In law, compensation for loss or injury.

Danbury Hatters case See under BOYCOTT.

data
1. In statistics, the quantitative raw material of any study, as, for example, the head count in a census. *Primary data* are those originally collected in the process of investigation; *secondary data* are those collected by others, sometimes for a quite different purpose.
2. In computer technology, information consisting of numbers, letters of the alphabet, punctuation marks, or symbols that are to be processed in a computer program.

data base A term loosely used to mean sample size (see SAMPLE, def. 1). More specifically, it is used for a file (or series of files) of data so structured that its contents can be used in a computer to provide input to several systems, with the object of holding each basic item of data only once on file.

data processing The gathering, interpreting, and transmitting of data for reference and/or to furnish the basis for decisions, and the relaying of instructions to effect the actions whereby decisions are carried out. The term is used chiefly in connection with mechanical and electronic equipment—automatic or electronic data processing (ADP or EDP)—developed to facilitate these activities, particularly the high-speed computer, but also PUNCHED-CARD DATA PROCESSING and other equipment.

data transmission The rapid transfer of information between distant points, either into or from a computer, or between computers. Various methods are used for this purpose. Telephone and telegraph lines can be employed to transfer electrical impulses generated by a business machine at one point to another machine miles away, the impulses first being converted into tones suitable for such transmission and then reconverted into electrical impulses at the other end. Both existing long-distance lines and special private lines have been so utilized, as has microwave radio transmission. See also TIME SHARING.

dated billing Also, *dating.* The practice of giving credit beyond a stated period by forward dating of an invoice. For example, a buyer technically obliged to pay for a purchase within 30 days may be given a postdated invoice, one bearing a date perhaps a month later than the actual date of purchase; in effect, the buyer now has 60 days in which to make payment. Dated billing is often used to encourage orders for seasonal goods (such as sleds or air conditioners) well in advance of need.

day order An order to buy or sell a security that, if not executed, expires at the end of the trading day on which it was entered. A day order also is a LIMIT ORDER (that is, one specifying price) for most stocks, but not necessarily in the case of bonds.

days of grace See GRACE.

deadheading Describing a freight or passenger vehicle returning empty to a terminal or to its point of origin. Also, carrying passengers or freight free of charge.

dead weight The weight of a carrier without any load. See also TONNAGE.

dealer
1. In business and commerce, an individual or firm buying and selling goods to make a profit. A dealer is distinguished from a BROKER or AGENT in that he takes title to the goods bought. Some authorities also maintain that a dealer is one who sells to the ultimate consumer rather than to another middleman, but others do not make this distinction. See also MERCHANT WHOLESALER.
2. In the securities trade, a trader who buys and sells for his or her own account rather than as an agent for customers. Unlike a broker, who is paid a commission, a dealer profits by selling for a higher price that he paid. However, he also may collect the standard brokerage commission in addition to the profit earned by the price difference.

dear money Same as tight money; see under MONETARY POLICY.

death tax Also, *death duty, estate tax, inheritance tax*. A tax levied on the property of a person who has died. Strictly speaking, an estate tax is levied against the property (estate) itself, whereas an inheritance tax is levied against those to whom the property is bequeathed, but the terms often are used interchangeably. Death taxes generally are in proportion to the value of the property. Also, a system of exemptions prevents a surviving spouse with dependent children, for example, from being taxed

as heavily as an already wealthy person who inherits an estate. In the United States death taxes are levied by both the Federal and state governments.

debasement A reduction in intrinsic value, especially referring to reducing the amount of precious metal contained in a coin.

debenture A BOND (see def. 1) backed by the general credit of the issuer but not secured by a mortgage or lien on any specific property. It normally has a stated maturity date and rate of interest. Debentures are the most common kind of bond issued by large, well-established corporations (with good credit ratings). They frequently are in convertible form, that is, exchangeable for common stock (see CONVERTIBLE, def. 1). The written agreement whereby debentures are issued, setting forth the maturity date, interest rate, and other terms, is called an INDENTURE (see def. 1.).

debit In accounting, an entry on the left, or asset, side of an account, indicating the creation or addition to an asset or an expense, or the reduction or elimination of a liability. See also CREDIT, def. 2.

debt Money, goods, or services owed by one person or organization to another. See CONSUMER CREDIT; DEBT MONETIZATION; FLOATING DEBT; LIABILITY, def. 1; NET NATIONAL DEBT; PRIVATE DEBT; PUBLIC DEBT. For consumer installment debt, see under INSTALLMENT BUYING.

debt limit In public finance, the maximum indebtedness permitted to a government by law. In the United States, the Federal debt was first limited by the Liberty Loan Act of 1917, since amended many times. The debt limit of most state governments is stated in their constitutions, and the states themselves impose debt limits on local governments within their boundaries.

debt management See under PUBLIC DEBT.

debt monetization Literally, turning a debt into money, describing a method of increasing the amount of currency in circulation by increasing the PUBLIC DEBT. The chief means of debt monetization in the United States is the issue of new government securities, which are purchased by the Federal Reserve (through member banks). They are paid for with Federal Reserve notes or with a check drawn on the Federal Reserve, which then becomes part of the primary reserves of the banking system. If notes are used, they enter into general circulation, thus increasing the money supply. Debt monetization also increases the money supply by expanding credit. The notes, representing newly created reserves, become the basis for the creation of new demand deposits by commercial banks. This represents a much larger increase in the money supply than the notes alone could effect since, for example, with a 20 per cent reserve requirement, banks can grant credit for five times the amount of the new notes; a $20 million increase in reserves thus would add $100 million to the money supply.

debtor nation   A nation whose collective foreign debt exceeds the foreign debts owed to it. Some countries become debtor nations because their BAL-ANCE OF TRADE is consistently unfavorable, that is, their imports exceed their exports. However, a nation can be a debtor, as the United States was until the end of World War II, even with a favorable trade balance when there is a persistent flow of investment capital into it from abroad. See also CRED-ITOR, def. 2.

debugging   The process of detecting and correcting errors in a computer program.

decentralization   See under ORGANIZATION, COMPANY.

decile   In statistics, a name for the nine values in a FREQUENCY DISTRIBUTION that divide the items into ten equal groups; that is, dividing the first tenth from the second tenth, the second tenth from the third tenth, etc. See also PERCENTILE; QUARTILE.

decision rule   Any rule set up to help make decisions in the face of uncertainty. It may be a complex mathematical formula involving various conditional probabilities or a simple rule such as "Use mortar only when the outdoor temperature is at least 40° F. by 8:00 A.M."

decision tree   A graphic representation of *conditional probabilities*, that is, various possible alter-

natives each of which in turn affects still other alternatives. For example, suppose a contract with a steelworkers' union is about to expire, giving rise to the probability that steel prices will increase after a new contract is negotiated, either through peaceful settlement or a strike. Assume that prices will increase not at all or by 2 per cent or by 4 per cent. However, they take on different values with different strike outcomes. If there is no strike, assume a 50 per cent probability of no price increase, 30 per cent probability of a 2 per cent increase, and 20 per cent probability of a 4 per cent increase. These probabilities can be expressed by the following formulas:

$$P(0)|NS = .50 \text{ (probability of zero price increase after no strike)}$$
$$P(.02)|NS = .30$$
$$P(.04)|NS = .20$$

If there is a strike, however, wages will rise more and so prices are more likely to increase. With a strike, therefore, assume a 20 per cent probability of no price increase, 50 per cent probability of a 2 per cent increase, and 30 per cent probability of a 4 per cent increase. According to the best estimates of experts, there is a 70 per cent probability of peaceful settlement and 30 per cent probability of a strike, expressed as:

$$P(NS) = .70$$
$$P(S) = .30$$

Fig. 20 shows a decision tree that represents the eight different probabilities under consideration.

declining balance method   Also, *diminishing balance method.* In accounting, a method of calculating depreciation of a fixed asset in which the annual depreciation charge is equal to a fixed percentage of the diminishing balance of the asset (that is, the balance remaining after previous depreciation has been deducted) or by applying a declining rate to the asset's original cost. For example, suppose a $1,000 machine is considered to depreciate at a fixed rate of 10 per cent. Annual depreciation would be $100 the first year, $90 ($1,000 − $100 × .10) the second year, $81 ($1,000 − $190 × .10) the third year, and so on. With this method, higher depreciation costs are charged to the early years of the asset's life than to its later years. Another version is the *double declining balance method,* whereby the annual depreciation

Fig. 20. Decision tree for steel

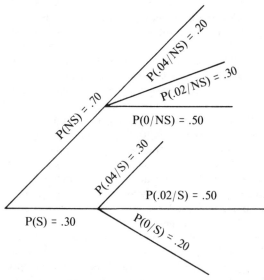

Source: D. S. Ammer, *Materials Management,* 3d ed. (Homewood, Ill.: Richard D. Irwin, 1974), p. 218. Reprinted by permission.

charge is exactly twice the percentage determined by the STRAIGHT-LINE METHOD applied to the undepreciated balance at the start of each year. For example, a $10,000 machine with a service life of five years has, according to the straight-line method, a depreciation rate of 20 per cent ($10,000/5 = $2,000 ÷ $10,000 = 20%). This rate is now doubled, to 40 per cent, and annual depreciation the first year is .40 × $10,000 = $4,000; the second year, .40 × ($10,000 − $4,000) = $2,400; the third year, .40 × ($10,000 − $4,000 − $2,400) = $1,440; and so on. With this method the asset's book value never reaches zero (as it does with the SUM-OF-DIGITS METHOD). Therefore, when the asset is scrapped, sold, or exchanged, the remaining book value at that time determines whether the final transaction involves a gain or a loss.

declining marginal efficiency of capital   See under PRODUCTIVITY.

dedicated computer   See under COMPUTER.

deductible coverage   An insurance clause providing that the insured will assume any losses below a given amount. For example, an automobile collision insurance policy with a $50 deductible clause will require the insured to pay the first $50 worth of damage caused in any collision; if damages amount to $300, the company will pay the remaining $250. In contrast, *full coverage* would cover all of the loss, no matter how small.

deduction

   1. In general, any cost or expense set off against revenue.

   2. *payroll deduction.* Funds withheld from wages prior to their being paid, for purposes such as employee savings plan contributions, insurance premiums of various kinds, repayment of employer loans, payment for goods purchased from the company, donations to charities, etc. See also WITHHOLDING TAX.

   3. *tax deduction.* Any sum that is charged as business expense or capital loss and hence reduces taxable income. In preparing an income-tax return, such sums are subtracted before the tax is calculated. The regulations and laws governing Federal and state income-tax deductions are quite complex and often subject to varying interpretations.

deed   A written agreement whereby an owner or *grantor* conveys title to, or an interest in, land to another person, called a *grantee* or *transferee.* There need be no consideration (payment) to make a deed valid, since land may be either sold or given away. However, the deed usually must be signed and sealed by the grantor, and, in order to be recorded by a public officer (known as a *recorder, registrar, commissioner of deeds,* or some similar title), it usually must be signed by witnesses and acknowledged by the grantor before a notary public or other official. Title does not pass until the deed is actually delivered, and generally it must also be accepted by the grantee. See also ABSTRACT OF TITLE; *deed of trust,* under MORTGAGE; QUITCLAIM DEED; WARRANTY DEED.

deed of trust   See under MORTGAGE.

deep organization   See under SPAN OF CONTROL.

defalcation   In law, a broad term for EMBEZZLEMENT and other misappropriation of funds or property.

default Failure to perform a duty, whether arising under a contract or otherwise. Also, failure to meet an OBLIGATION (def. 1) when it is due.

defensive investment Any investment, domestic or foreign, undertaken principally to insure against loss rather than to make a profit. Most often such investments are made in response to the actions of competitors. For example, in the 1970s the United States government was encouraging the domestic development of processes to produce petroleum from shale and coal. While such a synthetic fuel probably could never be produced as cheaply as natural petroleum in the Near East, it represented a defensive investment to help ensure a source of supply.

deferred annuity See under ANNUITY.

deferred charge Also, *deferred expense*. See PREPAID EXPENSE.

deferred demand Demand that must be postponed owing to a shortage of the desired good or service.

deferred income Also, *deferred credit, deferred revenue*. Income that has been received but not yet earned (and hence is sometimes called "unearned" income). Examples include an advance to an author against royalties, rent paid in advance, and payment for a magazine subscription. On the BALANCE SHEET deferred income is listed under liabilities, offsetting the increase in cash assets resulting from such payments.

deficit In accounting, the precise excess of liabilities over assets, or of expenditures over receipts. See also LOSS, def. 1.

deficit financing A deliberate policy of heavy government spending that is not expected to be offset by increased revenues but is financed by increasing the public debt (through issuing new government securities, etc.). It represents a compensatory FISCAL POLICY, that is, an attempt to offset declines in private investment during a business slump. (See also PUMP PRIMING.) Though deficits in the United States national budget were not unknown prior to the 1930s, they have since become the rule, to the dismay of those economists who believe that expenditures and revenues should balance (if not every year, then at least over the span of each business cycle). Others, however, maintain that so long as GROSS NATIONAL PRODUCT increases at a healthy rate, budget deficits are unimportant.

deflation A decrease in the general PRICE LEVEL, owing to a decrease in total spending relative to the supply of goods on the market. The immediate effect of deflation is to increase purchasing power: if prices fall, the same amount of money will buy more. However, it tends to benefit only persons on fixed incomes and creditors, whereas businesses suffer sharp declines in income and workers lose their jobs. Deflation may occur during a contraction phase of the BUSINESS CYCLE, representing part of a general decline in overall economic activity. There has been no genuine deflation—drop in the general price level—in the United States since the 1930s, although policies aimed toward DISINFLATION have caused declines of particular prices. For example, a policy of disinflation may eventually lead to lower food prices, but it does not significantly lower the overall cost of living; many manufactured products have ADMINISTERED PRICES, which are not sensitive to such programs and may actually be increased during this period by corporations trying to maintain profits despite lower sales. See also REFLATION.

deflationary gap An excess of saving over the investment spending needed to maintain full employment. Thus, for example, though consumers may be willing to save 20 per cent of national output, businesses may be willing to invest only 15 per cent. As a result of lagging demand, prices tend to decline and, since lower prices mean lower income, the result may be a *deflationary spiral*, greatly augmented by the multiplier effect (see MULTIPLIER PRINCIPLE, def. 1). For example, a $30 billion gap in investment spending may cause national income to fall by as much as $90 billion, a decline that reflects not only lower prices but lower physical output as well. In reality, however, lower prices often will stimulate consumers to buy more and save less, so that saving and investment will tend to be brought back in line with one another, closing the deflationary gap. See also INFLATIONARY GAP.

deflator See GNP DEFLATOR.

degressive tax A PROGRESSIVE TAX whose rate rises decreasingly. Most personal income taxes are degressive, the maximum tax rate in the United States being about 50 per cent, whether annual income totals $300,000, $500,000, or $1 million.

delinquent tax A tax not paid when due. Usually penalties are invoked, which for a property tax may involve a TAX LIEN.

delisting Removing a stock that was formerly listed on an organized exchange. In order to be listed, the issuing company needs to fulfill the qualifications set by the exchange (see under STOCK EXCHANGE for more details). Moreover, it must continue to meet these requirements; otherwise it can be suspended or removed entirely.

delivered pricing Also, *freight-allowed pricing.* A system of pricing whereby the price of goods includes the cost of moving them to the buyer's place of business or the receiving station nearest it. A delivered price may be computed simply by adding the cost of freight to an ordinary price; in that case it differs from an F.O.B. price only in that the seller retains title to the goods during transit and is the one to file claims with the carrier in case of damage. However, a seller may also quote a *uniform delivered price*, that is, the same delivered price to any destination. In that case the price will include a charge to cover the seller's average freight expenditures, and hence it necessarily discriminates against nearby buyers in favor of distant ones. If the cost of transportation is too high to allow a uniform delivered price throughout the country, the seller may use *zone pricing*, dividing the country into zones and charging a uniform delivered price within each zone. This price discriminates in the same way as the overall uniform delivered price, depending on a buyer's location within a zone. Also, a seller may quote a delivered price that covers the freight charge from a competitor's mill closer to the buyer than the seller's mill and pay for the extra freight cost himself (*freight absorption*); this practice,

called *freight equalization*, is also discriminatory, since the seller's return on identical goods will differ, depending on the location of the buyer. For still another form of delivered pricing, see BASING POINT SYSTEM.

delivery
1. In a business transaction, the transport and arrival of purchased goods at a designated destination. The terms of delivery are an important feature of a purchase contract, particularly in industrial buying, where failure to deliver material when promised can be very costly to the buyer. Many companies employ EXPEDITERS to deal with shortages caused by delivery failure.
2. In law, the final surrender of goods or other property to which title is being transferred. In real estate transactions title normally does not pass until the deed to the property is delivered into the buyer's hands. In a sale of goods, if the contract requires the seller to deliver the goods or pay for transportation to some designated place, title does not pass until the goods have been delivered or have arrived at their destination.

Delphi forecast Also, *jury-of-executive opinion.* A method of forecasting first used extensively in military technological planning and later applied in business and economic planning. A panel of experts is chosen, each of whom is given all the information pertinent to the forecast and asked to make an individual forecast. Each then has the opportunity to read the other's forecasts and modify his or her own if desired. The result allegedly is a superior (more accurate) projection.

demand In economic theory, the willingness of buyers to purchase a given amount of goods or services for a given price at a given time. The only kind of demand of interest to economists is *effective demand*, that is, not only the desire to purchase but the ability to pay. The relationship of amounts of goods that will be bought at various prices can be charted in the form of a *demand schedule* (see Fig. 21) or be portrayed graphically (see DEMAND CURVE). As a rule, the lower the price, the greater the demand for a product or service, at least up to a point; this rule is known as the *law of demand.* However, demand for some goods will not increase

Fig. 21. Demand schedule for automobiles

Price per Car	×	Quantity Demanded per Week	=	Gross Revenue per Week
$9,500		1,000		$ 9,500,000
8,000		1,250		10,000,000
6,000		2,000		12,000,000
4,500		3,000		13,500,000
2,750		4,500		12,375,000
2,000		5,500		11,000,000

Fig. 22. Demand curve for automobiles

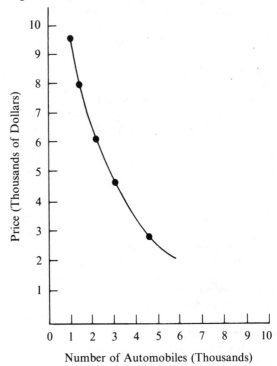

Number of Automobiles (Thousands)

much no matter how low the price. Even if bread cost only a penny per loaf, most families would buy only a little more bread than they do when the price is 50 cents. Similarly, a reduction in the price of a drug such as insulin would probably have no effect on demand (which is the reason producers do not cut its price). The degree to which demand responds to price changes is called its ELASTICITY (see def. 1). See also AGGREGATE DEMAND; COMPOSITE DEMAND; DEFERRED DEMAND; DERIVED DEMAND; FORECASTING; INFERIOR GOOD; JOINT DEMAND; SUPPLY.

demand curve A graphic representation of the quantities demanded of some commodity at various prices. For example, to show the demand for a new model of automobile at various price levels, prices are indicated on the Y-axis (vertical axis) and quantities demanded on the X-axis (horizontal axis). The demand curve drawn by connecting the points on the graph usually slopes downward and to the right, showing a definite relationship between price and quantity bought: the lower the price, the higher the demand. (See Fig. 22.) The curve also shows the relative ELASTICITY (def. 1) of demand; the curve for automobiles is fairly flat compared to a demand curve for bread, for example, which would be much steeper, because when prices rise people are more inclined to postpone auto purchases than to stop buying bread. See also SUPPLY CURVE.

demand deposit A bank DEPOSIT (def. 1) from which withdrawals can be made at any time simply by writing checks, but which in the United States generally earns no interest. Since checks are used just about as readily as currency, they are considered part of a nation's MONEY SUPPLY, and demand deposits are sometimes called *checkbook money*. Further, demand deposits are the basis on which banks create money: a bank extending a loan can simply create a demand deposit by crediting the amount of the loan to the borrower's account, against which the borrower then can write checks. (See also MONEY.) The ratio of a bank's debits to its demand deposits (that is, checks written against accounts, versus deposits) represents its *deposit turnover*. The deposit turnover of all commercial banks indicates how fast money is being used in the economy (see VELOCITY OF MONEY). Economists regard deposit turnover as a COINCIDENT INDICATOR, that is, its ups and downs coincide with those of the business cycle. See Fig. 23.

demand note See under PROMISSORY NOTE.

demand-pull inflation A situation in which consumer and industrial prices keep rising (inflation),

Fig. 23. Bank debits and deposit turnover (seasonally adjusted annual rates)

Period	Debits to Demand Deposit Accounts[1] (billions of dollars)					Turnover of Demand Deposits				
	Total 233 SMSA's[2]	Leading SMSA's		Total 232 SMSA's (excl. N.Y.)	226 other SMSA's	Total 233 SMSA's	Leading SMSA's		Total 232 SMSA's (excl. N.Y.)	226, other SMSA's
		N.Y.	6 others[3]				N.Y.	6 others[3]		
1975—June	22,503.5	10,612.2	4,756.7	11,891.3	7,134.6	124.4	328.6	114.2	80.0	66.7
July	22,827.9	10,709.5	4,841.1	12,118.3	7,277.2	126.2	331.0	115.7	81.6	68.2
Aug	23,269.4	10,628.8	5,125.1	12,640.5	7,515.4	130.4	335.0	124.4	86.2	71.2
Sept	23,181.9	10,585.0	5,153.0	12,596.9	7,443.8	128.8	330.7	123.8	85.1	70.0
Oct	24,137.1	11,801.5	4,921.3	12,335.6	7,414.3	134.0	364.0	118.7	83.5	69.8
Nov	24,067.7	11,529.9	4,937.3	12,537.8	7,600.5	134.0	360.8	119.5	84.9	71.5
Dec	23,565.1	10,970.9	4,932.5	12,594.2	7,661.8	131.0	351.8	118.4	84.7	71.6
1976—Jan	23,845.0	11,517.7	4,789.0	12,327.3	7,538.3	132.4	366.0	115.4	82.9	70.3
Feb	ʳ25,528.4	12,212.0	ʳ5,324.6	ʳ13,316.4	7,991.8	140.9	375.4	ʳ128.1	89.6	74.6
Mar	ʳ26,474.4	12,629.6	ʳ5,560.9	ʳ13,844.8	8,283.9	144.6	377.5	131.4	92.5	77.2
Apr	ʳ25,792.8	12,482.8	ʳ5,302.4	ʳ13,310.0	ʳ8,007.7	140.3	374.9	ʳ124.6	ʳ88.4	ʳ74.2
May	ʳ25,490.9	12,179.0	ʳ5,327.1	ʳ13,311.9	ʳ7,984.7	139.3	380.2	126.9	88.2	73.3
June	26,636.6	12,844.3	5,566.9	13,792.4	8,225.5	145.1	400.8	132.0	91.0	75.2

[1]Excludes interbank and U.S. government demand deposit accounts.
[2]SMSA means "standard metropolitan statistical area." Total SMSA's include some cities and counties not designated as SMSA's.
[3]Boston, Philadelphia, Chicago, Detroit, San Francisco–Oakland, and Los Angeles–Long Beach.
ʳRevised.
Source: Federal Reserve Bulletin, August 1976.

triggered by a continuing high demand for bank loans. These loans, when granted, add to bank deposits and hence to the total money supply. When the deposit money so created is spent, the resulting demand pulls up prices still more. Demand-pull inflation can also be triggered by a sharp rise in exports; the extra demand that pushes up prices then is external, but the result is the same. The American economy periodically is subject to at least mild demand-pull inflation when poor crops abroad cause demand for American farm products to rise, which in turn pushes up domestic food prices. See also COST-PUSH INFLATION.

demonetization The removal of one kind of currency from circulation, accomplished by eliminating its status as LEGAL TENDER. For the demonetization of silver, see under SILVER STANDARD.

demonstration effect The stimulation of consumer demand through advertising, displays of greater varieties of goods, and similar means. Such actions may increase consumer purchases even when consumer income has remained stable (see PROPENSITY TO CONSUME), both on an individual or family level and on an international level. For ex-

ample, through massive international distribution (and advertising), the Coca-Cola Company manages to sell its products in many countries where per capita income is well below the subsistence level and cash might more rationally be spent on necessities.

demurrage An extra charge made when carriers (barges, freight cars, trucks, special shipping containers) are held over the usual time allowed for loading or unloading (normally two days).

denationalization Turning over public property to private ownership. For example, following World War II, the British government divested itself of the trucking industry, which it had taken over while the Labour Party was in power (1945–50), and also of some 90 steel mills. Following the return of a Labour government in 1964, the British steel industry was *renationalized* (restored to state ownership). Denationalization often involves a considerable loss for the government, as seller, and can have considerable influence on the future course of an industry, depending on whether it is sold to many buyers, a few, or one. Prior to World War II a single American company,

ALCOA, was responsible for all of the nation's aluminum output; soon after the Federal government sold the aluminum facilities it had built during the war, ALCOA was producing only half the national output, the market now being shared with two other large firms (Kaiser and Reynolds).

denominational value See FACE VALUE.

department store A large retail store that handles a wide variety of goods—clothing, housewares, home furnishings, furniture, etc.—and is organized into separate departments for purposes of promotion, service, and control. Usually the different departments, each with its own buyer, are divisions owned by the central management, but occasionally a store will have one or more *leased departments* for items requiring special merchandising skills, such as shoes or optical goods. Though the sales volume in some of a big store's departments justifies buying directly from manufacturers, smaller departments often have to buy from middlemen and therefore must charge more for their merchandise. As a result, some department stores have joined *buying groups,* combining their purchasing operations in order to obtain greater bargaining power. Also, some previously independent stores have been absorbed by *ownership groups,* originally put together by financiers but later often making use of the advantages a centralized management can offer. Though in essence operating much the same as a CHAIN STORE, the ownership group stores usually retain their own name, image, and customer orientation in the cities in which they operate. Thus, few customers of the 1970s knew (or cared) that Filene's of Boston, Shillito's of Cincinnati, Bloomingdale's of New York, Abraham & Straus of Brooklyn, Bullock's of Los Angeles, and Burdine's of Miami all belonged to Federated Department Stores.

The department store was invented in France in the mid-19th century (Paris's Bon Marché, still active, was one of the earliest) and grew rapidly in America after the Civil War. American department stores were pioneers in marketing, especially in aggressive advertising. R. H. Macy's of New York, which claimed its prices were the city's lowest, offered not only delivery service but a restaurant for shoppers, and its departments grew from 12 in 1869

to 91 in 1914 (when its annual sales were $17.3 million). Traditionally department stores were located in downtown shopping districts. After World War II, however, many stores opened *branch stores* in suburban shopping centers to serve the middle- and high-income groups living outside the cities. Often the shopping center itself was built around the branch store. See also RETAIL.

dependent In tax law, a person whose chief support is provided by another person and for whom the latter may claim an *exemption* in computing his or her personal INCOME TAX.

dependent variable See under REGRESSION ANALYSIS.

depletion allowance In accounting, an allowance made for depletion, that is, the shrinkage or exhaustion of a product, nearly always a natural resource (mineral deposit, stand of timber, etc.). The cost of such depletion must periodically be assigned to the accounts in question to keep reported profits from being excessive. In some cases, U.S. Federal tax laws permitted the deduction of a flat *percentage depletion* allowance in determining taxable income from petroleum, natural gas, and other mineral deposits. This allowance is essentially arbitrary and apparently reflects a desire on the part of a majority of Congress to augment the after-tax profits of certain industries. See also SUBSIDY.

deposit

1. In banking, a credit to an individual's or firm's account. The cash deposited in a bank is not a tangible property held there for safekeeping. Rather, it is there for the bank to use, in exactly the same way as a bank loan is money the borrower may use. In exchange for a deposit the depositor gets a receipt and a credit on his or her bank statement. The conditions under which a depositor can withdraw money depend on the type of account. The two main kinds of bank deposit are the DEMAND DEPOSIT, which may be withdrawn at any time ("on demand") and the TIME DEPOSIT, which stipulates when withdrawals may be made. Bank deposits represent the principal kind of MONEY in circulation. See also MONEY SUPPLY.

2. In business, a down payment on merchandise,

to reserve it for the buyer until payment is complete.

depositary An individual or institution with whom property is deposited for safekeeping, and who therefore is put into a position of trust. See also DEPOSITORY.

deposit insurance See FEDERAL DEPOSIT INSURANCE CORPORATION; FEDERAL SAVINGS AND LOAN INSURANCE CORPORATION.

deposit multiplier See under FRACTIONAL RESERVE BANKING.

depository A place of safekeeping for goods or other property, such as a safe-deposit box or warehouse. See also DEPOSITARY.

depreciation
1. In general, any decline in the value of a physical asset. Depreciation results from normal usage and from age; it is not a function of changes in style (see OBSOLESCENCE) or of being used up little by little (see SHRINKAGE). Accountants record depreciation by allocating part of the cost of an asset that will be used up over time to each accounting period during its life. The consideration of depreciation as a cost is necessary to ensure that the prices a company charges for its products or services will cover that cost as well as the more direct costs of production. Since depreciation represents a deduction from taxable income, its method of calculation can materially affect a company's finances. (Many nonprofit institutions, which neither have to price their output nor pay income tax, do not bother to calculate depreciation at all.) Depreciation can be measured accurately only at the end of an asset's SERVICE LIFE, so that any prior calculations necessarily involve estimates, both of the total amount of depreciation and of the length of service life. Consequently, numerous accounting methods are used, some allocating total cost equally over an asset's life (see STRAIGHT-LINE METHOD), and others weighting the early years (see ACCELERATED DEPRECIATION) or considering usage (see PRODUCTION METHOD) or replacement cost (see REPLACEMENT METHOD). See also DEPRECIATION RESERVE.
2. See EXCHANGE DEPRECIATION.

depreciation reserve A series of credits on the asset side of the balance sheet that show the reduced value of a fixed asset. The term "reserve" does not refer to a fund set aside but merely indicates a valuation reserve. In the United States the ratio of a company's total depreciation reserves for a given kind of asset to the original cost of its total capital assets still in use—called the *depreciation reserve ratio*—is a measure of whether or not its depreciation policy is in keeping with the tax rules laid down by the U.S. Treasury.

depression A prolonged period in which business activity is at a very low point (see BUSINESS CYCLE). Production is greatly reduced and there is little or no new capital investment, income is sharply lowered, there is massive unemployment, many businesses fail, and banks are slow to create credit. The depression following the panic of 1873 (see PANICS, BUSINESS) lasted five and one-half years, and the Great Depression of the 1930s lasted nearly four. Both these depressions began with a *crash*, a sudden sharp drop in stock-market prices, followed by the failures of many banks, brokerage houses, and other businesses. See also RECESSION.

derived demand The demand for a good or service that arises from the demand for some other good or service. For example, consumer demand for shoes gives rise to demand for leather, plastic materials, shoelaces, rubber, and other components, as well as for machines making lasts and stitching leather, for shoe factory workers, factory buildings, land, etc. All demand for FACTORS OF PRODUCTION—so-called *factor demand*—is derived demand, stemming from ultimate consumer demand for finished products.

determination coefficient See under REGRESSION ANALYSIS.

devaluation A decrease in the value of a nation's currency relative to gold and/or other currencies, or, conversely, a rise in the price of gold and/or other currencies relative to a particular currency. In 1973, for example, the U.S. dollar was officially devalued through an increase in the price of gold from $38 per ounce to $42.22 per ounce. In practice, the actual devaluation varied from country to country, depending on payments balances with each. Thus, the devaluation relative to the Swiss and German currencies was greater (as determined by floating rates; see EXCHANGE RATE for explanation) than the change in the official price of gold, whereas the dollar actually gained value relative to the British pound sterling and Italian lira.

Devaluation is most often used to correct a serious BALANCE OF PAYMENTS deficit, that is, when import values far exceed export values and there is an increasing shortage of foreign exchange to pay for the imports. Devaluation corrects such a deficit by lowering the price of exports in terms of foreign currencies and raising the price of imports at home. See also DOLLAR SHORTAGE; EXCHANGE DEPRECIATION.

developing nation See UNDERDEVELOPED NATION.

Development Loan Fund See under AGENCY FOR INTERNATIONAL DEVELOPMENT.

devise A gift of real estate by will.

dialectical materialism The view that only economic matters are of ultimate importance (materialism) and that all change takes place through the conflict and reconciliation of opposites (dialectic). It is a basic theory of Marxist thought (see COMMUNISM, def. 1).

diffusion index An INDEX NUMBER showing the percentage of the members of a series that has increased during a given period. For example, stock market speculators often use a diffusion index showing the percentage of stocks traded whose prices have risen during a given trading day. If the index number is 50, exactly half of all stocks traded have gone up; if it is higher, the majority of stock prices has risen; if it is lower, the majority of stock prices have either remained stable or declined.

digital computer See under COMPUTER.

diminishing balance method See DECLINING BALANCE METHOD.

diminishing marginal productivity See under DIMINISHING RETURNS, LAW OF; also, MARGINAL PRODUCTIVITY THEORY.

diminishing marginal utility Also, *diminishing utility*. See under MARGINAL UTILITY.

diminishing returns, law of Also, *law of variable proportions*. The economic principle that, as successive units of a factor of production (land, labor, or capital) are added in a particular enterprise, the additional output they generate decreases (diminishes). For example, suppose 100 man-hours of labor produce 20 bushels of beans on a one-acre plot of land. Adding 10 man-hours will produce an additional 2 bushels of beans. Will each additional 10 man-hours continue to yield still another 2 bushels? No. At some point, 10 additional man-hours will increase yield by only $1\frac{1}{2}$ bushels, or even only by 1, and eventually the yield will not increase at all. The 18th-century French economist TURGOT was one of the first to state this principle clearly. When capital or labor (rather than land) is the constant factor, the principle is sometimes called the law of *diminishing marginal productivity*.

diminishing substitution, law of See SUBSTITUTION, LAW OF.

direct access In computers, a technique that permits retrieval of data stored on magnetic cores, disks, or drums without "reading" the entire file in sequence. See also RANDOM ACCESS.

direct cost A business cost that is directly related to producing a product or service. Direct cost consists chiefly of the materials and supplies used to make a product and the wages and salaries of personnel working in its production. Such direct cost is usually readily identifiable, as opposed to *indirect cost*, which is allocated among the various products or services produced, often quite arbitrarily. Direct cost is important to a firm because it usually represents the minimum figure at which it is advantageous to sell in a very weak market. Selling prices frequently are the sum of direct cost plus a markup, the markup being designed to yield the ex-

pected profit provided anticipated sales are great enough to absorb all overhead. See also LABOR COST; MATERIALS COST. For *direct costing*, see under ABSORPTION COSTING.

direct investment　See under INTERNATIONAL INVESTMENT.

direct labor　See under LABOR COST.

direct-mail advertising　A form of advertising through letters, cards, and other literature sent by mail to potential customers. It is used either to solicit mail-order purchases or to direct customers to particular products or retail stores. Direct-mail advertising, which is the third-largest kind of advertising in the United States, relies heavily on *mailing lists* containing the names and addresses of prospective customers (from hundreds to literally millions). Normally advertisers buy or rent such lists from companies that specialize in collecting and preparing them. Direct-mail advertising, which recipients often refer to as *junk mail*, is regulated to some extent by the U.S. Postal Service. Mailing of obscene material or potentially harmful samples is generally illegal, nor can recipients be compelled to pay for merchandise they did not actually order (such as books sent "on approval"). See also ADVERTISING. For direct-mail selling, see MAIL ORDER.

directors　See BOARD OF DIRECTORS.

direct placement　Selling an entire issue of securities directly to investors, without using the intermediary of UNDERWRITING. Bonds in particular often are sold in this way to a few large institutional investors, thereby eliminating underwriting costs. An issue of stock sold to fewer than 25 buyers normally is not classified as a public offering and hence need not be registered with the U.S. Securities and Exchange Commission.

direct tax　See under TAX.

dirty float　A floating EXCHANGE RATE that is manipulated by the central government. See also under BEGGAR-THY-NEIGHBOR POLICY.

disability insurance　See under SOCIAL SECURITY.

disadvantaged　A euphemism for "poor"; see POVERTY.

disagio　In exchanging one currency for another, a charge paid for exchanging a depreciated currency. The term is supposed to mean the opposite of AGIO.

disbursement　In accounting, a payment in cash or by check. It is an actual payment, as opposed to an EXPENDITURE, which simply means incurring a liability (not necessarily paying it). See also CASH BASIS.

discount
1. In business, an amount deducted in advance from a payment that is due, as a reward for paying cash (*cash discount*), buying in quantity (*quantity discount, volume discount*), making early payment (*trade discount*), or granting some other advantage to the seller. See also CHAIN DISCOUNT; HIDDEN DISCOUNT; TERMS OF SALE, def. 2.
2. In banking and finance, interest on a loan charged in advance and deducted from the amount lent. For example, a bank lending $1,000 to a business firm for a one-year period may in advance deduct $75; the borrower then receives only $925, representing a discount of $7\frac{1}{2}$ per cent. In the same way a bank may purchase an obligation, such as a BILL OF EXCHANGE, and deduct a discount from its face value, which serves as interest until the bill falls due. See also DISCOUNTED CASH FLOW; DISCOUNT RATE; REDISCOUNTING.
3. In investment, the difference between the FACE VALUE and market value of a security when the face value is higher.

discount bond, noninterest-bearing　See under BOND, def. 1.

discounted cash flow　Also, *present value method*. A method of measuring return on a capital investment, such as a machine, in terms of a compound interest rate discounted over the life of the asset. Based on the idea that the value of money

Fig. 24. Present value for future payment of $1 discounted at various rates*

Year	15%	18%	20%	22%
1	$.929	$.915	$.909	$.901
2	.799	.764	.751	.731
4	.592	.533	.513	.482
6	.439	.372	.350	.317
8	.325	.260	.239	.209
10	.241	.181	.164	.138

*Calculations assume continuous return from the investment throughout the year.

depends on when it is received, discounted cash flow takes into account the fact that, given a current interest rate of 4 per cent, for example, today's $.96 will grow to $1.00 within the next year. Hence the *present discounted value* of $1 payable a year from today would be only 96 cents (100 ÷ 1.04). To obtain figures for longer periods, a compound interest table is used. Suppose, for example, that the ABC Company is trying to decide whether or not to buy a $10,000 machine to replace one worker earning $5,000 per year. The machine, which has a ten-year life, yields a net cash flow of $3,000 (see under PAYBACK PERIOD for how to compute this figure); ABC executives believe the firm must earn at least 20 per cent after tax on any new equipment. The $3,000 return must therefore be discounted to present value at 20 per cent. It is assumed that the return is spaced out evenly over the year. The payment of $1 spread out over the year (at $.004 for each of 250 working days, for instance) has a present discounted value of $.909 at 20 per cent. Therefore, ABC multiplies this figure by $3,000 (.909 × $3,000 = $2,727) to obtain discounted present value for the first year. Using this approach for the ten years of the machine's expected life, it is calculated that the machine yields a present discounted value of $13,377, or about one-third more than its purchase price, which ABC considers an adequate return on investment.

discount house

1. A retail business enterprise that sells largely consumer durables (appliances, cameras, furniture, etc.) at low prices and offers a minimum of customer service. Discount houses range from small stores with open showrooms and catalogs describing other available merchandise to huge stores that in most respects resemble, a conventional DEPARTMENT STORE but offer fewer services (no credit, no free delivery, little or no servicing or repairs of merchandise, etc.). Discount houses became very popular in the United States after World War II. At that time most appliances were sold by small dealers who took big markups, often 35 to 40 per cent of the retail price. Discount-house operators found they could do very well with a markup of only 30 per cent. By the 1960s the discount houses, originally located in dingy warehouses in low-rent neighborhoods, were moving uptown and expanding. They began to sell soft goods as well—clothing, linens, bedding, etc.—and stopped relying solely on nationally advertised brands. Some were organized into chains (see CHAIN STORE). Discount houses buy both from wholesalers and directly from manufacturers, and, like supermarkets, rely on big sales volume and rapid turnover for their profits. See also MASS MERCHANDISER.

2. See FINANCE COMPANY, def. 3.

discount rate Also, *rediscount rate*. The interest rate charged by Federal Reserve banks on loans to their member banks (see FEDERAL RESERVE BANK CREDIT). Discount rates are set every 14 days by the regional Federal Reserve banks, subject to approval by the Board of Governors. A high discount rate discourages commercial banks from lending in excess of their required reserves, since it makes borrowing from the Federal Reserve (called "going to the discount window") too costly; the general effect on the economy is to slow down business expansion, which relies heavily on bank loans. A low discount rate has the opposite effect, encouraging member banks to borrow in order to finance lending, which stimulates business activity. The discount rate therefore is an important instrument of MONETARY POLICY (although it is not as critical as the Federal funds rate; see FEDERAL FUNDS MARKET). It also is considered a financial barometer of the general condition of the credit market and the direction of current Federal Reserve policy.

In general banks borrow from the Federal Reserve only when they are hard pressed, both because the discount rate is often higher than other sources of funds (such as the Federal funds rate) and because the Federal Reserve refuses loans unless it considers them absolutely essential. Credit to commercial banks is usually extended on a short-term basis (up to 15 days), and member banks tend to borrow in one of two ways. First, they may *rediscount* short-term commercial, industrial, agricultural, or other business PAPER, with recourse on the borrowing bank; such loans are called *discounts*. Second, they may give their own promissory notes secured by paper eligible for discounting, by government securities, or by other satisfactory collateral; such loans are called *advances*. In practice the method of using government bonds as collateral is the more common. See also REDISCOUNTING.

discretionary account A brokerage account in which the customer gives the broker or some other person discretion as to the purchase and sale of securities or commodities on his or her behalf, including selection, timing, amount, and price. Such discretion may be complete or limited in various ways, and it is usually granted by means of a power of attorney. Many brokers do not like to accept so much responsibility for an account, preferring to act on specific instructions, and some won't accept them at all. Others favor it because it provides an opportunity for higher commissions (through more frequent trading) and also, perhaps, because they feel their investment decisions are inclined to be sounder than those of their customers.

discretionary income Also, *supernumerary income*. Any portion of DISPOSABLE INCOME not committed to essential purchases (food, etc.), taxes, and payments due on previous purchases, and therefore available for spending or saving at the owner's discretion.

discrimination
1. In employment, different treatment of workers based on race, sex, age, religion, ethnic or national background, or union membership (or nonmembership), concerning hiring, wages, promotions, training programs, or any other terms and conditions of employment. In many cases such discrimination is illegal. In the United States it is prohibited by such Federal laws as the Age Discrimination in

Employment Act, Equal Pay Act, and Civil Rights Act of 1964 (see also Fig. 44 under LABOR LAWS), as well as by laws passed in various states. However, although employers cannot discriminate against union members without violating the National Labor Relations (Wagner) Act of 1935, unions may insist on a PREFERENTIAL SHOP, in which union members are hired before and laid off after nonunion members. See also AFFIRMATIVE ACTION; CLOSED UNION; LABOR FORCE; UNFAIR LABOR PRACTICES.
2. See PRICE DISCRIMINATION.
3. For discrimination in international trade, see CUSTOMS UNION; EXCHANGE CONTROLS; EXPORT QUOTA; FREE TRADE AREA; IMPORT QUOTA; TARIFF.

diseconomy of scale See under SCALE, ECONOMY OF.

disequilibrium, international payments A persistent deficit or surplus in a nation's current account (see under BALANCE OF PAYMENTS) not matched either by long-term capital inflows or outflows or by regular unilateral transfer payments. In the case of a persistent deficit, the nation's foreign exchange reserves may be depleted or even exhausted. In the case of a persistent surplus, the necessarily related deficit in the current account of one or more other nations will eventually cause similar difficulties. See also DOLLAR GLUT; DOLLAR SHORTAGE.

disguised unemployment See UNDEREMPLOYMENT.

dishoarding See under HOARDING.

disinflation A deliberate attempt by a government or central bank to arrest an inflationary trend in the general PRICE LEVEL by means of tax increases, cuts in government spending, high interest rates, and similar policies. However, disinflationary policies directed at the general price level may lead to declines of particular prices, though they are rarely so vigorous as to lead to genuine DEFLATION, that is, a severe decline in the general price level. See also INFLATION; REFLATION.

disintermediation A tendency for money to be drawn out of savings institutions (banks, savings and loan associations, life insurance companies, etc.) when the short-term interest rate (on Treasury bills, commercial paper, etc.) exceeds the savings dividend. For example, when Treasury bills pay $7\frac{1}{2}$ per cent interest, people are likely to withdraw funds from savings accounts earning $5\frac{1}{2}$ or 6 per cent interest to buy Treasury bills. Disintermediation generally occurs when the money supply for business firms is so low that they are willing to pay higher interest rates, and tends to continue either until the money supply becomes more plentiful or until there is less demand for loans. Disintermediation has a particularly serious effect on the construction industry, which depends heavily for mortgage loans on the very institutions from which funds are being withdrawn. It also represents a serious problem for savings institutions, whose major assets—mortgages—cannot readily be converted into cash in periods of tight credit without serious losses. As a result, the institutions quickly use up available cash to accommodate withdrawals and must borrow heavily from government agencies such as the Federal Home Loan Bank.

disinvestment Also, *negative investment*. A decrease in capital goods, either because worn out equipment is not replaced or because inventories are reduced, affecting the total supply of capital goods. An individual firm may disinvest simply by getting along with the equipment it already owns. In this case, the DEPRECIATION allowance for the existing equipment is not offset by new purchases, so that the company's net investment after depreciation declines. Another way a firm can disinvest is by selling some of its equipment.

disk memory See MAGNETIC DISK.

dismal science Thomas Carlisle's sardonic term for political economy (or economics), coined after he read Thomas Malthus's pessimistic essay on population. In 1850 Carlisle referred to RICARDO and MALTHUS as the "Respectable Professors of the Dismal Science."

dispersion In statistics, the total spread of the values in a FREQUENCY DISTRIBUTION. The STAN-DARD DEVIATION is the most common measure of dispersion, but the most direct way of expressing dispersion is by means of the *range*, that is, the difference between the greatest and smallest values in a distribution. For example, if wages in a firm range from $70 to $150 per week, the range is $80. See also DECILE; PERCENTILE; QUARTILE.

disposable income Also, *disposable personal income*. An individual's income after payment of personal taxes (income, property, estate, gift, etc.) and any other payment to local, state, or central government (such as traffic fines, state college tuition, etc.). It is disposable income that is spent on consumer goods and services and used for net personal saving (the latter representing any portion of income *not* spent for consumption). Since income is regarded as the chief determining factor of consumption expenditures—one can only spend as much as one has—disposable personal income is an important measure of consumption expenditures, and statistics on it are regularly published by the U.S. Department of Commerce in its *Survey of Current Business*.

dispossess To deprive a person of the use of real estate by legal means. For example, a tenant who defaults on rent payments may be dispossessed by the landlord, who usually must obtain an order from a court, sheriff, or other authority.

dissaving An excess of spending over income, popularly described as "living beyond one's means." Spending more than one earns is possible by using past savings or through loans. On the level of the overall economy, dissaving can be measured only partially by overall consumer credit, since consumers may be borrowing at lower interest rates in order to use their cash for a lucrative investment. Dissaving also occurs when a business allows its buildings and equipment to wear out gradually without spending equivalent sums on replacement or expansion. For example, a railroad dissaves if it lets its roadbed deteriorate and does not spend equivalent amounts on other improvements. See also PROPENSITY TO SAVE.

dissolution The termination of a partnership, corporation, or other business organization. A corporation may voluntarily surrender its charter, take part in a merger or consolidation, forfeit its charter (through state action), or be dissolved by its stockholders. Insolvency or bankruptcy alone does not effect such a dissolution, though either may become grounds for voluntary or involuntary dissolution. A partnership is dissolved when its term expires or its aim (as stated in the original agreement) is accomplished, when either partner or all partners wish to withdraw from it, or when a partner is expelled, dies, etc. In contrast to a corporation, the dissolution of a partnership involves a change in the relation of the partners but does not actually end the partnership; a partnership is terminated officially only when its affairs are completely wound up.

distribution

1. Also, *physical distribution*. In business, the process of conveying goods and services from the producer to the market. Unlike MARKETING, distribution involves the physical movement of goods (transportation, traffic) but does not include advertising and selling. Some writers, however, use "marketing" and "distribution" interchangeably, while others interpret distribution as the entire movement of goods from producer to ultimate consumer, including their preparation, selling, shipping, and storing, but describe the selling and promotion function as "merchandising." The different stages goods go through—from producer to wholesaler to retailer—are sometimes called *channels of distribution*.

2. In economics, the division of a society's or nation's total income, in the form of profit, rent, interest, and wages. The division of income among the factors of production (land, labor, capital) is called *functional distribution*; the division of income among individuals is called *personal distribution*.

3. In accounting, the term "distribution" is used in two ways: (a) the assignment of revenues or expenditures to various accounts, also called *allocation* (*double distribution* means redistributing or prorating some cost from one account to one or more other accounts), and (b) any payment of part of a company's assets to owners, stockholders, or creditors, including any form of dividend payment.

4. In statistics, the spread of events over a series of measurements. See FREQUENCY DISTRIBUTION.

distribution expense In accounting, any expense associated with selling and distributing a product or service, including warehousing, advertising, sales commissions, and delivery charges.

distributor An individual or firm selling manufactured products, either to retail outlets (dealers) or directly to consumers. A distributor thus is virtually identical to a wholesaler (see WHOLESALE). An *industrial distributor* sells directly to the industrial user of a product.

disutility Also, *negative utility*. The dissatisfaction, in the form of pain, discomfort, or fatigue, rendered by acquiring a good or through performing work. See also MARGINAL UTILITY.

diversification

1. In business and industry, expanding the scope of output. A job printer, for example, might begin by printing labels and tags for garment manufacturers and gradually expand to produce handbills, business stationery, booklets, and pamphlets, etc., for other customers, thereby diversifying both in terms of product and customer. The printing firm may even go on to acquire a paper mill or other business and conceivably end up as a CONGLOMERATE. See also SPECIALIZATION, def. 1.

2. In investment, the degree to which funds are invested in the securities of numerous enterprises engaged in different activities. In this way, if one company or industry faces problems that depress the value of its securities, the investor is protected by holdings in other areas. Most professional investors believe that 20 to 30 well-chosen stocks usually will provide adequate diversification.

diversion A change in ROUTING while a shipment is under way. Some railroads permit shipping of a carload of goods in a given direction without a specific destination—for example, Florida oranges moving north—allowing the shipper to specify the destination when market conditions are known. The railroad then reroutes the car for a small fee. This practice allows a producer to ship goods yet remain flexible as to their final market.

divestiture Getting rid of a SUBSIDIARY, either through sale or through a SPINOFF to stockholders of the parent company. It may come about through an antitrust decision against the parent company (ordering it to divest itself of some of its holdings), or because a company finds the subsidiary has ceased to be profitable, or because the parent company needs cash or some such reason.

dividend

1. The part of a corporation's profits that is distributed among the stockholders in proportion to their share of ownership. The rate of return on stock investments is measured in terms of the dividend (see *dividend yield*, under YIELD, def. 1). Whether or not a dividend will be paid, and its amount, is decided by the board of directors. The amount of the dividend for preferred stock is ordinarily fixed over a period of time, whereas the amount for common stock varies more with the current success of the company and the amount of cash it has on hand. A *regular dividend* is one that is declared and paid over regular intervals (monthly, quarterly, annually). If business is poor or the directors decide to withhold earnings in order to invest in new plant and equipment or for some other reason, either or both the common-stock and preferred-stock dividends may be omitted (called a *passed dividend*). Some companies, however, pay a dividend out of past earnings if currently they are not making a profit. Preferred stocks may earn a *cumulative dividend*, that is, if the dividend is not paid at the normal time it is accumulated and paid at some future date (see also PREFERRED STOCK). Dividends usually are paid in cash. However, they may also be paid in stock, usually (but not always) in the stock already owned by the stockholder. On rare occasions companies pay dividends in something other than cash or stock; a large distillery once declared a dividend payable in barrels of whiskey. Many companies offer a *dividend reinvestment* plan, whereby a cash dividend is automatically reinvested in stock, purchased on the open market by a bank that administers the plan for the company. See also CUM DIVIDEND; EX-DIVIDEND; EXTRA DIVIDEND; STOCK DIVIDEND; YEAR-END DIVIDEND.

2. A payment made to the holders of equity in a cooperative, such as a mutual life insurance company (insurance dividend), savings and loan association, or consumer cooperative. In the case of a savings institution it represents a kind of interest; in the case of insurance companies and cooperatives it is regarded more as a refund due to previous overpayment (of an insurance premium or retail price).

division of labor The principle of dividing a job into all of its component operations and having each operation (or a small number of operations) performed separately by one worker. Each worker thus becomes a specialist in one or a few operations, presumably achieving maximum efficiency in his or her specialty and eliminating the time needed to shift from one kind of work to another. While it is usually the fastest, most efficient, and most productive way of tackling a complicated job, division of labor may carry the inherent disadvantages of monotony, fatigue, and consequent job dissatisfaction. Nevertheless it is essential to many forms of MASS PRODUCTION (except where machines have replaced human labor altogether) and is also applied to some services. For example, a dentist, although quite able to clean a patient's teeth, usually delegates the task to a lower-paid dental technician.

dole A RELIEF payment by government or a charitable agency to the needy. Also, a pejorative term for unemployment compensation and other forms of WELFARE, which strictly speaking differ from a dole in that they are based on insurance.

dollar averaging Also, *dollar cost averaging*. A system of buying securities at regular intervals with a fixed amount of money (for example, $100 per month) over a long period of time. As a result, the investor buys more securities with the same amount of money when prices are low and fewer when they are high, and eventually, owing to the law of averages, makes a profit. The choice of securities is up to the investor. If a stock drops in price, it is advantageous to keep on buying that stock (provided that one believes it is essentially sound) as it continues to decline; this process, called *averaging down*, can yield good profits, since the more low-cost shares one acquires, the more one owns and can sell when the price goes up again. The chief difficulty is that the average buyer wants to sell when prices drop for fear of losing too much, and dollar averaging can work only if one continues to buy the same amount in both good times and bad. See also FORMULA INVESTING; MONTHLY INVESTMENT PLAN.

dollar bond A bond on which both principal and interest are payable in U.S. dollars. Foreign governments and corporations sometimes issue such bonds to attract investors who distrust other currencies. American corporations sometimes do the reverse: borrow with bonds denominated in foreign currency, usually to take advantage of more favorable credit conditions in another country or because they intend to use the funds there.

dollar exchange Bills of exchange in international trade that are payable in U.S. dollars. Also, use of the dollar as a reserve currency or a valuation for an EXCHANGE RATE.

dollar gap See DOLLAR SHORTAGE.

dollar glut A situation in which gold and currency reserves leave the United States at such a rate that the nation suffers a BALANCE OF PAYMENTS deficit. This situation occurred in the late 1950s and prevailed through the 1960s into the mid-1970s, beginning at first with large-scale FOREIGN AID programs following World War II, continuing with heavy military spending abroad, and climaxing with greatly increased direct investments abroad (see under INTERNATIONAL INVESTMENT). As a result, the dollar was overvalued in relation to other currencies—that is, there was an oversupply of dollars and a shortage of foreign currencies—and consequently had to be devalued (as it was in 1971 and 1973). See also DOLLAR SHORTAGE.

dollar shortage Also, *dollar gap*. The situation in which the demand for U.S. dollars greatly exceeds their supply. After World War II, the demand abroad for dollars to finance American imports was much greater than the total in dollars that private American sources wished to supply (through tourism, imports, direct investment, etc.). Had the market been allowed to operate freely, the dollar would have appreciated considerably, perhaps doubling in value with respect to foreign cur-

rencies (for example, $1, then equivalent to 5 British shillings, might have been revalued at 10 British shillings); this would have corrected the dollar's *undervaluation*. However, in practice the dollar shortage was handled by means of exchange and import controls on the part of nations with currencies suffering from *overvaluation*, as well as being diminished by the vast American FOREIGN AID programs of the postwar period. The dollar shortage thus ended in the 1950s, and by 1971 had turned into a DOLLAR GLUT.

domain Immediate or absolute ownership of land. See also EMINENT DOMAIN.

domestic
1. In business, any transaction within a state (of the United States) or a nation, as opposed to one involving two or more states or countries.
2. *domestic corporation.* A corporation that received its charter within the state in question; if chartered in another state it is termed a *foreign corporation.*
3. *domestic export.* An item that originates in the country from which it is exported, to distinguish it from goods that are being re-exported.
4. *domestic system.* See COTTAGE INDUSTRY.

domicile Also, *permanent residence.* A place where a person lives or has a permanent home to which he or she will, if absent, eventually return. Also, in the United States, the state in which a company is formed and is chartered or otherwise licensed.

door-to-door selling Also, *house-to-house selling.* A method of retail distribution in which individual salespersons call on customers in their homes, either by prior appointment or by ringing the doorbell. Originating in the 18th century with the Yankee peddler, door-to-door selling today accounts for only about 1 per cent of U.S. retail sales. It is confined largely to products thought to require demonstration (e.g., sewing machines, vacuum cleaners), to a well-advertised line of related products (cosmetics, brushes, plastic housewares), or to some products that consumers generally will not consider in stores but may be willing to buy when approached in this way (encyclopedias, magazine subscriptions, Bibles). Though door-to-door selling eliminates the cost of operating retail stores, it requires travel, personal contact, and the training and administration of a large sales staff. Also, the commission earned by sellers usually ranges from 25 to 50 per cent of the list price. Although it is admittedly old-fashioned and expensive, door-to-door selling has been extremely successful for certain products in the United States; the Fuller Brush man and the Avon lady, reinforced by heavy advertising, are practically part of the national landscape.

double entry A system of BOOKKEEPING in which every transaction is recorded twice, representing a debit in one account and an equivalent credit in another. The total debits therefore always equal the total credits, and the net balance of accounts always is zero. The general rules of the system are (1) increases in assets are debited to asset accounts and decreases in assets are credited; (2) increases in liabilities and proprietorship accounts are credited to those accounts and decreases are debited. For example, suppose Mary Smith invests $100,000 in her new drugstore, the MS Pharmacy.

Fig. 25. Double-entry system

CASH		
(debits)	(CASH)	(credits)
$100,000		
		$1,500
		$8,000
$ 75,000		
$175,000		$9,500
$175,000 – $9,500 = $165,500		

MS. CAPITAL		
(debits)	MS. CAPITAL	(credits)
		$100,000

MS. PREPAID RENT

$ 1,500		

MS. AUTOMOBILE

$ 8,000		

FURNISHINGS SUPPLY CORP.

		$ 2,000

MS. STORE FURNISHINGS

$ 2,000		

INVENTORY SUPPLY CO.

		$ 10,000

MS. STORE INVENTORY

$10,000		

ABC REAL ESTATE

		$ 75,000
$21,500		$187,000
$187,000 – $21,500 = $165,500		

She pays $1,500 cash in advance rent on the premises and $8,000 cash for a small delivery van, and buys $2,000 in store furnishings and $10,000 worth of stock on credit. At the same time, she receives $75,000 from the sale of her father's real estate agency's building and equipment. The $100,000 investment increases her equity in the MS Pharmacy by that amount while decreasing her cash balance by $100,000. The store's capital account is credited with $100,000 and its cash account debited by $100,000; the prepaid rent account is debited by $1,500 and cash credited by $1,500 (because the right to occupy the store during the period of prepaid rent is considered an asset); for the van, the automobile account is debited by $8,000 and the cash account credited $8,000; for store furnishings, the furnishings account is debited by $2,000 (because the furnishings were bought on credit, representing a liability) and the account of the furnishings supplier is credited; the same is done for the stock bought on credit, inventory being debited and the supplier(s) credited; finally, $75,000 from the building's sale means cash is debited by that amount and XYZ Real Estate Agency, which owed her the money, is credited.

With double-entry bookkeeping, the system is periodically checked by taking a *trial balance,* that is, adding all the credits and all the debits and making sure they cancel one another exactly. If they do not, an error has been made.

double indemnity Also, *accidental death benefit.* A clause in life-insurance policies whereby twice the face value of the policy will be paid in case of accidental death. Usually this provision commands a slightly higher premium.

double option See STRADDLE, def. 1.

double taxation Taxing the same income twice. The U.S. corporation income tax involves some double taxation, since a corporation pays income tax on its earnings and stockholders pay personal income tax on whatever part of those earnings are paid to them as dividends.

Dow-Jones average See under AVERAGE, def. 2.

down payment A partial payment of the total purchase price rendered by a buyer to a seller at the time of purchase, with the understanding that the rest will be paid later, according to the terms of their agreement. A down payment may signify that title to the property changes hands at the time (as is usually the case for a down payment on a house) or that title remains with the seller until the total purchase price is paid (as in installment buying). In some cases the down payment is forfeited if the transaction is not completed; in others it is not.

down tick Also, *minus tick.* In the securities trade, a term for a stock price lower than that of the preceding transaction. It is designated by a minus sign immediately preceding the price displayed for that stock at the STOCK EXCHANGE trading post. A *zero-minus tick* means a price the same as that of the transaction immediately preceding it but lower than the preceding different price. See also UP TICK.

down time A period when machinery or other equipment is idle, owing to breakdowns, adjustments, etc. See also FIXED COST.

Dow theory A theory of stock-market analysis based on the performance of the Dow-Jones industrial and transportation stock-price averages (see under AVERAGE, def. 2). According to the theory, the market is moving upward if one of these averages rises above a previous important high point, accompanied or followed by a similar advance in the other average. When both the averages decline below previous important low points, however, the market basically is moving down. Whatever its intrinsic merits, enough people may believe in the Dow theory—or are thought to believe in it—for it to have some influence on market sentiment.

draft See BANK DRAFT; BILL OF EXCHANGE.

drawback The repayment of an import duty, in part or in full, made when imported goods are re-exported rather than retained for domestic consumption. A device to encourage exports, the drawback sometimes is used for imported raw materials or semifinished goods that are incorporated into a finished product and then re-exported.

drawee, drawer The person on whom an instrument, such as a check or bill of exchange, is drawn, and the person who draws it. For example, the writer of a personal check is the *drawer*, the bank holding his or her account is the *drawee*, and the person to whom the check is made out is the *payee*.

drive-in A business enterprise whose customers drive their cars to the establishment and conduct their business without leaving the automobile. The most common are drive-in restaurants, serving food to customers seated in their own cars; drive-in theaters, showing motion pictures on a large outdoor screen to viewers seated in their cars; and drive-in banks, with special teller's windows to serve customers in their cars.

drop shipment A shipment sent directly from a manufacturer to a retailer or industrial customer, even though it was ordered through a wholesaler who takes title to the goods and collects the usual wholesale discount. Drop shipments thus do not eliminate the cost of the middleman, though they may offer a saving in shipping costs.

drum memory See MAGNETIC DRUM.

drummer Also, *bore*. A name for the 19th-century American traveling salesman employed by wholesalers or manufacturers. They were so called because of their persistence in selling merchandise to rural storekeepers and other merchants.

dry goods Older name for cloth sold by the yard rather than being made up into a garment or other item. Before the widespread availability of ready-made clothing, the dry goods store was an important form of retail establishment.

dual pricing See PRICE DISCRIMINATION.

due bill See IOU.

dummy A person who serves in another's place, either briefly or for an extended period. For example, a newly organized corporation required to name its directors may list several *dummy directors* until such time as the stockholders can elect the actual directors. Similarly, stock may be issued to a *dummy stockholder*, who holds the shares for another person who does not wish to be named as owner. Likewise, title to real estate may be held by a *dummy owner* because the real owner wants to conceal his or her identity. The term "dummy" also can be used for a firm that acts on behalf of another company whose name remains secret.

dumping See ANTIDUMPING TARIFF.

dunnage Packing material of various kinds—straw, glass fiber, etc.—used to keep goods from being damaged while in a ship's hold, freight car, etc.

duopoly, duopsony Exclusive control over a particular product or service by two sellers (*duopolists*) or two buyers (*duopsonists*). Since each seller or buyer has only one competitor—the other—the competitor's reactions must usually be taken into account in determining both price and output. As a result, duopolists generally cooperate rather than compete with another, in effect creating a MONOPOLY.

durable goods See under CONSUMER GOOD.

duty See TARIFF, def. 1.

dynamics The analysis of economic change over time and the processes of adjustment to change. Necessarily such study involves analyzing changes that have occurred in the past. Increasingly sophisticated mathematical methods enable analysis of many variables over time, which are of special importance in economic forecasting and planning. See also COMPARATIVE STATICS.

earmarking Setting aside specific tax revenues for specific services or projects. For example, in the United States many states use their gasoline tax revenues exclusively for road maintenance and construction. Similarly, the Federal government uses employer contributions to social security exclusively to finance social security benefits.

earned income Income derived from actual work or services performed, as opposed to income from investments, rent, etc. See also RETURN, def. 1; UNEARNED INCOME.

earnings

1. Same as EARNED INCOME.

2. The operating profits of a business. See under PROFIT, def. 1. For *earnings statement*, see INCOME STATEMENT. See also PRICE-EARNINGS RATIO.

3. See RETAINED EARNINGS.

easement In real estate, the right acquired by the owner of one tract of land to use the land of another for a special purpose. For example, in the case of adjoining property, owner A may grant owner B an easement over his land at a particular place giving B access to the highway. This particular easement is a *right of way*, a term also used for the property over which a railroad or a utility may run its tracks, pipes, or lines.

easy money See under MONETARY POLICY.

econometrics A branch of economics that seeks to verify economic theory and measure economic relationships by statistical and mathematical methods, chiefly for the purposes of forecasting future events and choosing desirable policies. Though the term was introduced only in 1926 (by the Norwegian economist Ragnar FRISCH), the statis-tical-mathematical approach dates back at least to the 17th century, when economics itself was called "political arithmetic." As a separate discipline, however, econometrics was developed mainly after World War I and expanded even more after World War II with the invention of high-speed computers and other sophisticated equipment facilitating the gathering and analysis of data. Present-day econometrics focuses on measuring the impact of economic variables—prices, costs, wages, consumer spending, interest rates, etc.—on one another. These interrelationships are expressed in the form of one or more equations (see MODEL), the variables being included in the equations if deemed appropriate by the economist. The appropriateness of the equations is then tested (usually with the help of a computer) by employing data for the different variables. Since most economic relations are STOCHASTIC, the methodology of econometrics is taken from mathematical statistics, using such tools as REGRESSION ANALYSIS.

economic

1. Pertaining to the economy, or to the field of economics (as in "Council of Economic Advisers").

2. Also, *economical*. Economically advantageous, because of reduced costs, increased profits, or some other benefit (as in "economic order quantity").

Economic Advisers, Council of An executive agency of the United States government, established by the Employment Act of 1946 to analyze the national economy, advise the President on economic developments, appraise Federal economic programs and policies, make recommendations, and help in preparing the President's economic reports to Congress. It consists of three

129

members appointed by the President with the advice and consent of the Senate. Two other advisory bodies were formed later. The *Council on International Economic Policy*, created in 1971, is charged with coordinating policy on international economic issues. The *Council on Economic Policy*, created in 1973, helps ensure better coordination in forming and executing economic policy and performs various special tasks in this regard when needed.

Economic and Social Council   Also, *ECOSOC*. An agency of the United Nations responsible for the organization's economic and social programs. Its studies, reports, and recommendations concern national and international problems in the areas of economics, culture, education, health, and related matters. Consisting of 27 members elected by the U.N. General Assembly for staggered three-year terms (9 elected each year), it usually holds two sessions a year.

economic determinism   The view that social and political changes are ultimately the result of economic forces. For example, Karl Marx believed that all important events in man's history result from his contemporary economic environment (see COMMUNISM, def. 1). Thomas Malthus's view that the human population will eventually and inevitably outstrip the earth's food supply is similarly deterministic.

economic growth   See GROWTH, ECONOMIC.

economic imperialism   See COLONIALISM.

economic indicator   See INDICATOR.

economic liberalism   A name sometimes used for the doctrines of the CLASSICAL SCHOOL, especially laissez faire and extreme individualism. (A 20th-century version of these ideas is also called *neoliberalism*.) To some degree the term has become a misnomer, for policies that were considered liberal in the 18th and 19th centuries—that is, doing away with the trade restrictions of mercantilism—are now regarded as "conservative," and the social welfare policies (administered by a central government) advocated by some Keynesian econo-

mists are considered "liberal." See also CONSERVATISM; SOCIAL DARWINISM.

economic life   See SERVICE LIFE.

economic man   A view of human beings as being motivated by purely economic considerations, always searching for the biggest profit. This notion, hypothesized by the CLASSICAL SCHOOL, is obviously limited, failing to take into account such real and noneconomic human goals as security and individual freedom.

economic model   See MODEL.

economic order quantity   Also, *EOQ, optimum lot size*. The amount of a particular material or good that should be purchased or manufactured at one time so as to incur the least expense—in both ordering cost and carrying cost—while still meeting the needs for that material or good. Among the factors that affect this calculation are storage cost, obsolescence (through shrinkage or spoilage), the amount of cash tied up in inventories (which then cannot be used for some other purpose), the reduction of unit cost through mass production (or, for purchased materials, a quantity discount), and the administrative cost of ordering, handling, and shipping numerous lots. A mathematical formula can be used to determine the economic order quantity. For items that have no quantity discount (so that the unit price is the same regardless of the amount ordered), the formula is:

$$EOQ = \sqrt{\frac{2 \times U \times OC}{UC \times CC}}$$

with *EOQ* standing for economic order quantity, *U* for annual usage of the item in number of units, *OC* for the ordering cost in dollars per order, *UC* for the unit cost of the material in dollars per unit, and *CC* for the carrying cost in per cent per year. For example, suppose that the annual usage of a certain casting is 1,200 units and it costs $10 to handle an order of castings. The price is $1 per casting and the carrying cost of castings in 24 per cent per year. Then,

$$EOQ = \sqrt{\frac{2 \times 1,200 \times 10}{1.00 \times .24}} = 316 \text{ units}$$

For items where a discount is given for buying larger quantities, the buyer must use a table showing total procurement cost (price plus order cost plus carrying cost) for a series of order quantities and annual requirements. Fig. 26 shows the total annual cost for various values of annual use and various order quantities for a casting whose price is reduced from $1.00 to $.95 when 500 to 999 units are ordered, and to $.925 when 1,000 or more units are ordered.

Unfortunately, in cases where the need for an item fluctuates unpredictably, no formula or table will work. Even when the variables in the formula (ordering cost and carrying cost) are known, the

Fig. 26. Total annual cost for various values of annual use and various order quantities

Value of Annual Use	Order Quantity in Months' Supply						
	1	2	3	4	5	6	7
$ 100	221	162	143	134	129	126	124
102	223	164	145	136	131	128	126
104	225	166	147	138	133	130	128
106	227	168	149	140	135	132	131
108	229	170	151	142	137	134	133
⋮	⋮	⋮	⋮	⋮	⋮	⋮	⋮
1,050	1,181	1,131	1,122	1,122	1,127	1,133	1,141
1,060	1,191	1,141	1,132	1,132	1,137	1,144	1,151
1,070	1,201	1,151	1,142	1,143	1,148	1,154	1,162
1,080	1,211	1,162	1,152	1,153	1,158	1,165	1,173
1,090	1,221	1,172	1,163	1,164	1,169	1,175	1,183
1,100	1,231	1,182	1,173	1,174	1,179	1,186	1,194
1,110	1,241	1,192	1,183	1,184	1,190	1,197	1,205
1,120	1,251	1,202	1,194	1,195	1,200	1,207	1,216
1,130	1,261	1,213	1,204	1,205	1,211	1,218	1,226
1,140	1,271	1,223	1,214	1,216	1,221	1,228	1,237
1,150	1,282	1,233	1,225	1,226	1,232	1,239	1,248
1,160	1,292	1,243	1,235	1,236	1,242	1,250	1,258
1,170	1,302	1,253	1,245	1,247	1,253	1,260	1,269
1,180	1,312	1,264	1,255	1,257	1,263	1,271	1,280
1,190	1,322	1,274	1,266	1,268	1,274	1,281	1,290
1,200	1,332	1,284	1,276	1,278	1,284	1,292	1,301
1,210	1,342	1,294	1,286	1,288	1,295	1,303	1,312
1,220	1,352	1,304	1,297	1,299	1,305	1,313	1,323
1,230	1,362	1,315	1.307	1,309	1.316	1,324	1,333
1,240	1,372	1,325	1,317	1,320	1,326	1,334	1,344
⋮	⋮	⋮	⋮	⋮	⋮	⋮	⋮
19,750	20,068	20,205	20,383	20,570	20,762	20,955	21,150
19,800	20,118	20,256	20,434	20,622	20,814	21,008	21,203
19,850	20,169	20,307	20,486	20,674	20,867	21,061	21,257
19,900	20,219	20,358	20,537	20,726	20,919	21,114	21,310
19,950	20,270	20,409	20,589	20,778	20,972	21,167	21,364
20,000	20,320	20,460	20,640	20,830	21,024	21,220	21,417

This table shows the cost for various values of annual use and various order quantities when carrying cost is 24 per cent, ordering cost $10. Total annual cost = value of annual use + order cost + carrying cost.

Source: D. S. Ammer, Materials Management, 3d ed. (Homewood, Ill.: Richard D. Irwin, Inc., 1974), p. 336. Reprinted by permission.

calculation is not foolproof. Often, owing to certain fixed costs (such as salaries of employees involved in placing an order), one could arrive at two different EOQ results, one for short-term inventory management and another for long-term management. Further, the calculation of carrying cost and order cost is in itself costly and time-consuming; for small orders it may not be worth the effort. Nevertheless, EOQ formulas can be very useful, especially in cases where the need for an item is fairly steady and predictable, the cost of the item is relatively low, and it can be delivered in relatively short time.

economic organization   The way in which an economy is organized, that is, who owns or controls the means of production and distribution of goods and services. The most important modern types of economic organization are CAPITALISM, COMMUNISM, and SOCIALISM. See also ANARCHISM; COLLECTIVISM; SYNDICALISM.

economic planning   See PLANNED ECONOMY.

economic rent
   1. The theory of rent advanced by David RICARDO.
   2. A term sometimes used for QUASI-RENT.

economics   The study of the production, distribution, exchange, and consumption of goods and services. Owing to the complexity of modern society, economics has been subdivided into numerous specialized areas, such as macroeconomics, microeconomics, consumer economics, labor economics, international economics, banking and finance, econometrics, public finance, and others. Although the methods and tools of economists have become more and more sophisticated, economics retains the essential drawbacks of any social science, dealing as it does with vagaries of human nature. No matter how elaborate the tools and how extensive the data, economic predictions and theories cannot be totally reliable or accurate.

economic sanctions   See SANCTION, ECONOMIC.

economy of scale   See SCALE, ECONOMY OF.

EDP   Abbreviation for electronic data processing; see COMPUTER; DATA PROCESSING.

EDR   Abbreviation for European Depositary Receipt; see under INTERNATIONAL DEPOSITARY RECEIPT.

EEC   Abbreviation for European Economic Community; see COMMON MARKET, def. 1.

effective demand   See under DEMAND.

effective interest rate   See Fig. 40, accompanying INSTALLMENT BUYING.

efficiency   Maximum output with minimum input of labor and/or capital. Efficiency is a goal not only for manufacturing enterprises, where it has given rise to the entire field of industrial engineering (with its so-called efficiency experts), but also for service industries and other enterprises, where simpler, more accurate accounting methods, machines ranging from electric typewriters to computers, and changes in operations and procedures can reduce costs and increase profits.

EFTA   Abbreviation for EUROPEAN FREE TRADE ASSOCIATION.

elasticity
   1. *of demand.* Changes in demand for a good or service resulting from changes in its price. It usually is expressed as a percentage change in the rate of buying divided by the percentage change in price:

$$\text{elasticity} = \frac{\% \text{ increase in quantity bought}}{\% \text{ decrease in price}}$$

The response of buyers to price changes naturally varies from item to item, depending on the urgency of need. A patient in need of emergency surgery usually will buy this service regardless of price; here demand is said to be *inelastic*. A person interested in cosmetic surgery, on the other hand, is more likely to shop around for a less expensive surgeon; here demand is more *elastic*. A price reduction in appendectomies would have little or no effect on the number of operations performed; a price cut in face lifts might increase demand, even if only slightly. In general, necessities are characterized by inelasticity of demand and luxuries by elasticity. However, the *degree* of elasticity of demand for a particular good can vary considerably, depending on price variations. Thus, though the demand for ballpark tickets might rise considerably as prices drop, at 1 cent a ticket the demand might well become inelastic, with no more tickets being purchased than if they were being given away. Similarly, if the price of milk rose, people would continue to buy just about as much milk as they needed so long as it did not go up much more than other food prices. But if milk rose to $1 per cup while other food prices remained unchanged, they would certainly think twice before buying milk, and the demand for milk would become more elastic. The degree of elasticity is measured like this: if a 1 per cent price cut increases demand by *less* than 1 per cent, demand is said to be inelastic; if a 1 per cent price cut increases demand by *more* than 1 per cent, demand is considered elastic; if a 1 per cent price cut increases demand by *exactly* 1 per cent, demand is said to have *unitary elasticity*. At any given point in time, a change in total revenue (the total spent on one item) will indicate whether demand is elastic, inelastic, or unitary.

Though demand elasticity was recognized for many years, the first economist to analyze it fully was Alfred Marshall. See also CROSS-ELASTICITY; PROPENSITY TO IMPORT.

2. *of supply*. Changes in the supply of a good or service relative to its market price. Just as consumers are willing to buy more when prices are low, producers are willing to produce more when prices are high. If supply varies considerably with price, it is termed elastic; if it remains constant, it is inelastic.

electronic data processing See COMPUTER; DATA PROCESSING.

eleemosynary Pertaining to charity or alms. The term is used for a corporation organized solely for charitable or benevolent purposes, such as some hospitals.

embargo
1. In international trade, a government prohibition restricting either commerce or transportation. For example, the Embargo Act of 1807 prohibited American ships from sailing to foreign ports and restricted foreign trade through certain bonding conditions. This law was designed to retaliate against British and French blockades and other hostile acts at sea during the Napoleonic Wars, but in practice it hurt American shipping more than it punished the Europeans. More recently, the Neutrality Act of 1937 forbade the export of arms and munitions to belligerent countries, an embargo lifted in November 1939.

2. In transportation and shipping, the refusal of a company to accept or move freight on account of some emergency, such as a strike.

embezzlement Fraudulent use or appropriation of funds or other property being held in trust or otherwise in one's lawful possession.

Emerson efficiency plan See under WAGE INCENTIVE.

emigration The movement of people out of a country. From an economic standpoint it represents a movement of one factor of production: labor. Emigration, like IMMIGRATION, is usually undertaken primarily for economic reasons; emigrants move elsewhere to improve their standard of living. Underemployment and/or low income are major factors, in turn caused by a relative scarcity of capital and land. Whether or not emigration results in a more than temporary increase in the per capita supply of capital and land is questionable, especially since population often tends to increase rapidly in just those areas where capital is most scarce.

eminent domain The right of government to take private property for public purposes. Usually some legal or constitutional provision requires that the owner be paid fair compensation for such property.

Empire preference system See under TARIFF, def. 1.

employers' association An organization established by employers in a particular area or industry for mutual cooperation in collective bargaining or other matters of common interest. In the United States employers' associations were formed as early as 1809 for making wage agreements, contributing to a fund to help fight labor organizations, agreeing not to employ union members, and, during a strike, farming out work to shops not affected by the strike. Such groups became more numerous in the 1830s, stimulated by the many strikes then occurring. They began to use the YELLOW-DOG CONTRACT and to break up strikes with the aid of militia. Though their hostility to unions continued, at least one association, the Pittsburgh iron manufacturers, negotiated a wage with a union—the iron puddlers' union in 1867—representing one of the first MULTIEMPLOYER AGREEMENTS. More often, however, employers' associations militantly fought unions, using blacklists, lockouts, and every other conceivable device. Nevertheless, collective bargaining expanded, and during the 1890s it was common for unions to deal with employers' associations. Among the strongest of them in the early 1900s were the National Metal Trades Association and the National Association of Manufacturers; the latter led the war on labor unions for the next three decades, at first militantly and later also in the form of WELFARE CAPITALISM. Only in 1937, when the U.S. Supreme Court upheld the National Labor Relations (Wagner) Act, which outlawed UNFAIR LABOR PRACTICES, did the employers' associations begin to lose power. See also LABOR UNION.

employment Engagement in some occupation, usually but not always for pay, such as a profession, trade, business, or other form of work. The number of persons actually employed, compared to the total willing to work if they could find jobs (that is, the total LABOR FORCE), is an important indication of an economy's well-being. The U.S. Department of Commerce, which compiles statistics on employment, defines *employed persons* as: (1) all civilians who, during a particular week, did any work at all as paid employees or in their own business or profession, or on their own farm, or who worked fifteen hours or more as unpaid workers on a family farm or in a family business; and (2) all those who were not working but who had jobs or businesses from which they were temporarily absent (owing to illness, vacation, a strike, etc.). Not included are persons whose activity consisted of housework in their own home, repair or maintenance of their own home, or volunteer work. See also ACCESSION RATE; FULL EMPLOYMENT; UNEMPLOYMENT.

employment agency An individual or firm in the business of finding jobs for persons seeking employment and employees to fill vacant positions. Most private employment agencies charge either the employee or the employer a fee that represents a fixed percentage of the job's weekly, monthly, or annual wage. In the United States, many states operate employment agencies, usually in conjunction with their unemployment compensation programs, that charge no fee, and some labor unions also provide such a service for their members (see also HIRING HALL). Some private employment agencies specialize in certain fields (medical, clerical, legal, etc.). Others specialize in certain levels of employment, such as top-level executive positions. The latter kind of agency, popularly called *body shop*, often goes to considerable effort to recruit executives who might be persuaded to change jobs if the offer were right. (Executive recruiters are sometimes called *headhunters*.)

Employment Service A division of the U.S. Department of Labor that helps the individual states establish and maintain a system of local public employment offices (numbering more than 2,400 in 1975), as well as providing special services for veterans, rural workers, and young people.

Employment Standards Administration The division of the U.S. Department of Labor responsible for administering and directing programs concerning minimum wage and overtime standards, equal pay for equal work, age discrimination, promotion of women workers' welfare, standards to improve employment conditions other than safety, nondiscrimination and affirmative action in government contracts and subcontracts, and workers' compensation for Federal and certain private employers and employees. It includes both the Office of Federal Contract Compliance and the Women's Bureau, as well as a Wage and Hour Division.

employment tax Also, *payroll tax*. A tax levied on a business firm's payroll, paid by the employer and based on the total of wages and salaries paid by the firm. In the United States the Federal government levies an employment tax on all employers to finance social security; employees also must contribute part of their wages to this insurance plan.

Thus, if the premium rate is 10 per cent (of all wages and salaries), half (5 per cent) is paid by the employer and half by the individual employee. These employment taxes are imposed under the Federal Insurance Contribution Act (or FICA) and hence are sometimes called *FICA taxes*. The employee's share is deducted from his or her paycheck, just as income tax is (see WITHHOLDING TAX), and periodically remitted to the government. A record of each employee's FICA taxes appears on his or her annual W-2 FORM.

enclosure Also, *inclosure*. In British history, the practice of enclosing (with fences, ditches, or other barriers) woods and pastures formerly considered *common lands*, or *commons*, open for use by anyone. In England this practice began during the 12th century and was greatly expanded after the 14th century, as the wool trade became more important and profitable. Landlords now coveted more and more large fenced-in areas for sheep pastures, and they would evict their tenants to obtain them. As a result, a large class of dispossessed paupers —without land or occupation—came into being, and a series of POOR LAWS was enacted to check vagrancy and begging. The practice of enclosure reached a peak during the late 17th century in England and about 100 years later in Scotland, where large portions of the Highlands were very nearly depopulated. Although enclosure encouraged more efficient farming of tillable soil and served to reclaim lands not suitable for cultivation but adequate for grazing, it dispossessed hundreds of thousands of rural workers, who, as it happened, were to provide a built-in labor supply for the factories of the Industrial Revolution. By the middle of the 19th century, there were no more lands left to enclose, and laws were passed against the practice. See also AGRARIAN REVOLUTION.

encomienda In Spanish and Latin American history, a royal land grant that gave rise to a system of tributory labor, also called *encomienda*. It was used in Spain over the conquered Moors, and later in Latin America over the native Indians. The Indians were required to pay tribute from their lands, which had been "granted" to deserving Spaniards, that is, supporters of the conquistadors, and often they had to render services as well. In return the grantee of the land was to provide protection and instruction in Christianity. In the West Indies the encomienda system effectively wiped out the Indian population, leading the Spanish crown to suppress it. It gradually died out after about 1542, to be replaced by *repartimiento*, a system whereby the Indians were required to give goods and services to the conquistadors, to their staff and soldiers, and to officials and missions. In effect this was a system of forced labor. For a later version, see PEONAGE.

encumbrance Any claim, interest, or right in property, such as a LIEN, MORTGAGE, dower right (widow's interest in husband's property), or EASEMENT. Such encumbrances generally do not prevent a property from being bought or sold, but they lessen its value. In real estate transactions a buyer often will insist that the seller have clear title to the property, free of encumbrances, and a deed normally must state what encumbrances, if any, do exist.

endogenous variable In econometrics, any variable in a MODEL or system whose value is determined by the relations in the model. For example, a model of a market is likely to include three STRUCTURAL (or causal) equations—one describing the demand for the commodity in question, one describing its supply, and a third stating that the amounts demanded and supplied must be equal to one another. These three equations will then simultaneously determine the value of three endogenous variables: the commodity's price, the quantity supplied, and the quantity demanded. A factor that is external to the model, such as rainfall, is called an *exogenous variable*. A variable may be exogenous to one model but endogenous to another. For example, rainfall is exogenous to an economist's model of the corn market but endogenous to a meteorologist's model of climate. See also REDUCED FORM; STRUCTURAL EQUATION.

endorsement
  1. Also, *indorsement*. A signature placed on the back of a negotiable instrument such as a check, which transfers the amount of that instrument to someone other than the payee, such as the bearer, a bank, etc. The endorser thereby automatically implies that he or she has title to the instrument and may legally transfer it to another party. An endorsement may be either unrestricted or qualified

(or restrictive) in some way. For example, John Doe may simply sign his name on the back of a check made out to him by XYZ Company; this endorsement specifies no payee and therefore is a *general endorsement* to the bearer, a form commonly used on bank checks being passed on to other persons. On the other hand, Jane Doe may write on the back of a check made out to her "For deposit only, Jane Doe," a *restrictive endorsement*, which means the check may not be transferred further until it has been deposited in her personal bank account, or she may sign it, "Pay to the order of John Doe," a *special endorsement* in which the new payee is clearly indicated.

2. See ACCOMMODATION ENDORSEMENT.

3. In insurance, a form attached to a policy that includes any alterations to the original terms of the policy. See also RIDER.

endowment insurance   See under LIFE INSURANCE.

energy   See under CONSERVATION.

Engels, Friedrich   A German socialist (1820–95) remembered chiefly for his collaboration with Karl MARX. A successful businessman working in his family's textile business in Manchester, England, Engels wrote about the English working class as early as 1844, the year he met Marx in Paris. For the next five years he was active on the Continent, helping to orgainze various revolutionary movements, and also found time to collaborate with Marx on the COMMUNIST MANIFESTO. Returning to England, Engels continued to work with Marx, whom his income helped to support. After Marx's death, Engels completed the second and third volumes of his friend's book *Das Kapital* (*Capital*). Engels is thought to be the originator of the theory of DIALECTICAL MATERIALISM and, with Marx, is still considered the founder of COMMUNISM (see def. 1).

Engel's law   A rule discovered by and named for the German statistician Ernst Engel (1821–96), which states that a family spends steadily smaller shares of its income on food as income rises, and that the percentage of family income spent on food is therefore a valid measure of standard of living.

One obvious inference from this observation is that, as income rises, an increasing proportion is spent on luxuries, that is, unnecessary, readily postponable purchases (see DISCRETIONARY INCOME). See also PROPENSITY TO CONSUME.

enterprise   A business undertaking. See also ENTREPRENEUR. For *free enterprise*, see CAPITALISM.

entrepreneur   A French term for a person who undertakes and develops a new enterprise at some risk (of failure or loss). Although the words *innovator, proprietor,* and *capitalist* are used in the same sense, there are subtle differences that make the term "entrepreneur" preferable. The idea for the undertaking may not be the entrepreneur's own invention, he or she is not simply an "owner" of the business, and the capital raised for it may or may not be his own. In the modern corporation, owned by hundreds or thousands of shareholders who usually have nothing to do with running the business, the distinction between the entrepreneur, who founded the business, and the manager, who is paid to run it, is particularly clear-cut. Hence such economists as Joseph A. Schumpeter differentiate between *profit*, the entrepreneur's reward for innovation and risk-taking, and the wages of managers, which they regard as no different from those of clerks, factory workers, and other employees. The term "entrepreneur" dates back to at least the early 18th century, when it was used by Richard Cantillon, François Quesnay, and others.

Environmental Protection Agency   See under CONSERVATION.

EOM   Abbreviation for *end of month*. A term used chiefly in specifying the TERMS OF SALE in purchase orders, invoices, and similar documents. It refers to the last day of the month *following* that of the date on the document. Thus, *net EOM* means payment in full must be made by the last day of the month following the month of the invoice date; for an invoice dated September 3, it would mean October 31.

EOQ   Abbreviation for ECONOMIC ORDER QUANTITY.

Equal Employment Opportunity Act See Fig. 44, accompanying LABOR LAWS.

Equal Employment Opportunity Commission An independent Federal agency established by the Civil Rights Act of 1964 to help end discrimination in employment practices and promote voluntary AFFIRMATIVE ACTION. It deals with charges of discrimination against public and private employers who do not hold government contracts (those that do are under the jurisdiction of the Office of Federal Contract Compliance) and, if necessary, brings legal action against them.

equal pay The principle that a particular kind of work should command a given rate of pay, no matter who performs it. In the United States the Equal Pay Act of 1963, an amendment to the Fair Labor Standards Act, prohibited discrimination on the basis of sex in wage payments for equal work on jobs requiring equal skill, effort, and responsibility, and performed under similar working conditions. At first, executive, administrative, and professional employees were exempt from this provision, but an amendment passed in 1972 extended it to them as well.

equation of exchange Also, *quantity equation of exchange, transaction equation.* A mathematical expression of the QUANTITY THEORY OF MONEY devised by Irving FISHER, which states $MV = PT$ where M is the quantity of money (currency in circulation plus demand deposits), V is the velocity of its circulation (or rate of turnover), P the general price level (or a price index), and T the total number of transactions (or the value of real output). The equation thus states that total spending is always equal to total receipts. While true by definition, the equation can be used to predict changes in the value of output only if the speed with which people spend money balances (V) tends to remain constant. If real output is also relatively stable, which depends primarily on the full-employment capacity of the economy, the equation states that changes in the money supply will cause a proportional change in output.

equilibrium In economics, a condition of perfect balance, in which opposing forces are of equal weight, countering any tendency to change in any direction. Thus *market equilibrium* (or *momentary equilibrium*) means a market at the point where the supply of and demand for a particular item at the prevailing price (*equilibrium price*) are precisely equal. (If supply were greater than demand, the price would drop; if demand were greater, the price would rise. In either case demand and supply would *tend* to move toward equilibrium but would not necessarily attain it.) While markets are almost never in precise equilibrium, most free markets appear to be operating near their equilibrium levels or moving toward them. The concept of equilibrium is applied also to workers and wages, international trade (see BALANCE OF PAYMENTS; BALANCE OF TRADE; DISEQUILIBRIUM, INTERNATIONAL PAYMENTS), interest rates and prices, and numerous other economic phenomena. Economists use the concept of equilibrium not only to define a final position but to describe the direction in which variables are moving. See also EQUILIBRIUM OF FIRM; GENERAL EQUILIBRIUM THEORY; PARTIAL EQUILIBRIUM THEORY.

equilibrium of firm Also, *best-profit equilibrium.* The point at which marginal cost is equal to marginal revenue. For example, suppose a hat manufacturer increases output by 1,000 hats per month at a unit cost of 90 cents more per hat. The firm realizes a profit of $1 per hat, so it now stands to gain an extra $100 ($.10 × 1,000) per month. So long as the extra cost of making more hats does not exceed the extra revenue, it is advantageous for the firm to expand output. As soon as it needs to hire more workers (at higher cost) or cannot sell more hats without reducing prices, it no longer pays to make additional hats.

Exactly the same concept can be applied to an industry in terms of the number of firms engaged in the same work. *Equilibrium of industry* is reached when profits are not so high that anyone else is encouraged to enter the industry, but not so low that anyone currently in it wishes to leave.

equipment Also, *capital equipment.* Goods that are used to produce other goods or services but are not themselves used up in the process. The term is used chiefly for such capital assets as machinery, tools, furnaces, appliances, and vehicles of various kinds. Along with plant (buildings), equipment represents a major investment for most manufacturing enterprises.

equipment trust certificate Also, *equipment trust bond.* A type of obligation where security for the loan depends almost entirely on the value of the collateral rather than the credit rating of the borrower. It is used primarily to finance the purchase of railroad rolling stock and airliners. The trustee, usually a bank, is the legal owner of the equipment and is free to foreclose on the loan and sell the equipment if the borrower—who has use of the equipment—does not meet prescribed payments of interest and principal. Since there is a ready market for used rolling stock and aircraft, the lender need not worry too much about the borrower's credit rating, especially if the amount of the loan represents only a fraction of the lowest price for which the equipment could be sold.

equitable tax See PROGRESSIVE TAX; also TAX EQUITY.

equity
1. The excess of a firm's assets over its liabilities; see NET WORTH.
2. Also, *equity capital, stockholders' equity.* The portion of a corporation's assets—all or part—that is owned by the holders of common and preferred stock.
3. In a margin account, the excess of value of securities over the debit balance. See MARGIN, BUYING ON.
4. In real estate, the interest or value an owner has in real estate over and above any mortgage on it. For *equity (right) of redemption,* see under MORTGAGE.
5. In law, a body of rules and precedents based on fair and just dealing, as opposed to statutory law (written laws). The law of equity developed in England after the Norman Conquest (1066) and was administered in a separate court, the *court of chancery.* Equity deals principally with conflicting claims and rights of individuals, and its remedies are considerably more flexible than those of either common or statutory law. Courts of equity, for example, might grant injunctions, require a specific

performance, rewrite contracts and other instruments, and divide disputed property. In the United States some states still maintain separate courts of equity, but in others equity is administered in ordinary courts of law.

error In statistics, the difference between an observed value and its true value. Also, the mistaken acceptance or rejection of a hypothesis. See also under NULL HYPOTHESIS; SAMPLING ERROR; STANDARD ERROR.

escalation In purchase contracts, a provision for unforeseen changes in basic costs—labor or materials or both—that may make it necessary to increase the final price. Construction contracts often permit escalation if wages paid to the various building-trade workers rise as a result of union negotiations. Similarly, contracts issued by auto manufacturers for batteries may permit escalation if prices of lead and antimony, the key raw materials for batteries, change. Escalation clauses are part of most long-term contracts. However, it usually pays to set some limit to price escalation, lest the item in question become prohibitively costly and the substitution of another item or design change would make more sense; a 10 to 15 per cent increase over the original price is the top limit commonly used.

escape clause
1. See under MAINTENANCE-OF-MEMBERSHIP CLAUSE.
2. An amendment to the Reciprocal Trade Agreements Act of 1934 (see chart under TARIFF OF ABOMINATIONS) whereby a tariff concession on any imported item may be withdrawn, wholly or partly, when the volume of imports of that item has increased so as to cause or threaten "serious injury" to domestic producers of the same or similar items. In individual cases the U.S. Tariff Commission decides whether or not the escape clause should be invoked, and then recommends to the President (who is empowered by the same 1934 law to negotiate tariff reductions) to withdraw or modify the concession or impose an import quota on the item. If the President disagrees, he must report to Congress on the entire matter; if he agrees, the escape clause is used.

escheat The reversion of property to the state when its deceased owner has left no will and no legal heirs are found.

escrow The deposit with a third party of a real estate DEED or some other item of value until the performance of some specified condition. For example, in a real estate transaction, both deed and purchase money may be delivered to a third party, called the *escrow holder* or *escrowee*, with written instructions to record the deed and order an examination of title. If the title shows clear, the escrowee turns the purchase money over to the seller. If the title proves defective, the buyer is entitled to the return of the purchase money upon reconveying title to the seller. One benefit of escrow is that if objections to the title can be removed by use of the purchase money (for example, a lien for unpaid taxes), the escrowee may use part of the money for that purpose. Another benefit for the buyer is the protection it offers against the seller's changing his mind and conveying the property to someone else. On the other hand, escrow assures the seller of receiving the purchase price once the title is clear, and enables him to use the buyer's money to pay off any liens against title.

establishment A term used by the U.S. Bureau of the Census for any business office, store, or plant at a specific location that has one or more employees. It differs from a *firm*, which may include several offices, plants, etc., under one ownership or corporation. Statistics concerning establishments are used chiefly for market analysis.

estate
1. In common usage, the total property left at death.
2. In law, an interest in land, also called *estates in land*, describing the degree, quantity, nature, duration, and extent of such an interest. Complete ownership of land is called an *estate in fee simple*, of unlimited duration. An owner in fee simple may do as he or she chooses with the land, and upon death title passes either to the heirs or to whoever is designated in the will. An *estate for life* is an interest for the duration of the owner's life only; on death all rights to the land cease. Both an estate in

fee simple and an estate for life are *freeholds*, as opposed to a *leasehold*, an interest based on a LEASE for a definite number of years (no matter what number).

estate tax See DEATH TAX.

Euratom Abbreviation for EUROPEAN ATOMIC ENERGY COMMUNITY.

Eurodollar A U.S. dollar held outside the United States, usually as a deposit in a commercial bank. Funds from such deposits are lent either to other banks or to corporate or governmental borrowers throughout the world. Eurodollars were created after World War II, when the United States bought more goods and services with dollars than other nations bought from it with foreign currency, creating a substantial BALANCE OF PAYMENTS deficit. Part of the deficit was made up by American sales of gold, but most of the surplus dollars simply remained in circulation in bank deposits owned by foreigners. These deposits, which until 1971 were freely convertible into gold (by foreign central banks), became FOREIGN EXCHANGE RESERVES for the foreign country in which they were held; since they were convertible into gold they were treated as though they were gold. Thus foreign banks could indirectly use Eurodollars as a basis for deposit expansion, and the Eurodollar became a substitute for increased gold production, permitting economic expansion. It remained in circulation only so long as European interest rates were somewhat higher than those in the United States; if the American rate was higher, the Eurodollar owner (usually a bank) would "repatriate" the Eurodollar by investing it in securities in America, and the Eurodollar would thus become an ordinary U.S. dollar. However, European countries tended to keep their interest rates slightly higher in order to prevent excessive domestic inflation. Thus the Eurodollar benefited both lenders, who earned more interest on them, and borrowers, who could use them to circumvent American EXCHANGE CONTROLS and raise money overseas. Further, Eurodollar funds increased when American businesses bought European firms or set up branches and built new plants in Europe with U.S. dollars that remained in circulation abroad (as Eurodollars). Earnings from these properties enabled the American owners to pay off their loans and repatriate the dollars if they wished. In practice, however, they have continued to use them, along with even more Eurodollars, to acquire other European assets. Other key currencies used in this way are called *Eurocurrency*, but none has found so large a market as the Eurodollar. The center for Eurodollar transactions is London.

European Atomic Energy Community Also, *Euratom*. An agency formed at the same time and by the same countries as the COMMON MARKET (def. 1) for the purpose of pooling atomic energy resources and eliminating tariffs on nuclear materials. Under its auspices several experimental and commercial nuclear reactors and a number of nuclear laboratories were built in member nations.

European Coal and Steel Community Also, *ECSC*. A customs union established by Germany, France, Italy, Belgium, Luxembourg, and the Netherlands in 1952 to eliminate all import duties and quota restrictions on coal, iron, and steel among the members. By 1958 the union had adopted a common external tariff; later it coordinated its activities with the COMMON MARKET (def. 1). Though originally conceived by the French economist Jean Monnet, the ECSC came into being largely through the efforts of French Foreign Minister Robert Schuman and was therefore known as the *Schuman Plan*.

European Depositary Receipt See under INTERNATIONAL DEPOSITARY RECEIPT.

European Economic Community See COMMON MARKET, def. 1.

European Free Trade Association Also, *EFTA*. A free trade area established in 1959 by Great Britain, Norway, Sweden, Denmark, Austria, Portugal, and Switzerland (called the *Outer Seven* because they were outside the COMMON MARKET) and later joined by Finland (1961) and Iceland (1970). The members agreed to abolish tariffs among themselves but left each member in full control of its own foreign trade and tariff policies toward outsiders (thus differing from a CUSTOMS UNION). Because each member can set its own tariffs for trade outside the bloc, rules were made to prevent nonmembers' products from being sold in a high-tariff member after being sold first to a low-tariff member; to qualify for entry into the free-trade area, at least half the value of the import must be accounted for by domestic manufacture. In addition, there is a list of commodities that are treated as though they originated in EFTA countries even though they may actually come from outside the bloc. Established to give its members some of the benefits of economic integration achieved by the Common Market countries, EFTA lost Great Britain and Denmark to the Common Market in 1973. The remaining EFTA countries then negotiated an agreement with the enlarged Common Market to liberalize trade between the two groups.

European Investment Bank See under COMMON MARKET, def. 1.

European Monetary Agreement Also, *EMA*. A clearing house for international payments set up in 1958 to replace the EUROPEAN PAYMENTS UNION after postwar recovery, when currency convertibility in Europe had been restored. It continued the banking function of the Payments Union, but now all settlements were made in gold or in convertible currencies, and automatic credit was no longer granted. It also established a European Fund, capitalized at $600 million, to extend two-year loans to countries with temporary balance of payments deficits.

European Payments Union Also, *EPU*. An agency set up in 1950 among the 16 members of the Organization for European Economic Cooperation (the implementing agency of the EUROPEAN RECOVERY PROGRAM) as a temporary system to provide Europe with currency convertibility during the postwar period. The EPU served as a clearing house for the debits and credits among member countries, and it also extended credit to any member with a balance of payments deficit with fellow members. Each member had a quota based on its trade with member countries during 1949, and it could receive automatic credit for up to 20 per cent of its quota in case of a deficit (beyond this deficits were payable in gold or U.S. dollars). The agent for the union was the BANK FOR INTERNATIONAL SETTLEMENTS at Basel, Switzerland. In 1958 the EPU was terminated and succeeded by the EUROPEAN MONETARY AGREEMENT.

European Recovery Program Also, *ERP*, *Marshall Plan*. A program proposed in 1947 by U.S. Secretary of State George C. Marshall to help the recovery of western Europe following World War II. In July 1947 the plan was approved by 16 nations that formed the Organization for European Economic Cooperation (OEEC), and the following spring it was launched with a U.S. appropriation of $5 billion. Each country receiving aid was required to match any sum from its own treasury and to submit a four-year development program (1948–51). General distribution of the funds, which included loans as well as gifts, was handled by the *Economic Cooperation Administration* (ECA). The funds were put to many uses, including the building of highways, bridges, railroads, power installations, housing, factories, and farm improvements. The chief recipients were Great Britain (which no longer needed aid after two years), France, Germany, and Italy. By 1951, industrial production had risen well beyond prewar levels and the expansion of Communism had been halted. However, western Europe still had a severe dollar shortage, which continued to require alleviation through U.S. aid programs. Total ERP aid, exclusive of military aid, is believed to have amounted to $30 billion. The Soviet Union in 1949 set up a similar program (see COUNCIL FOR MUTUAL ECONOMIC ASSISTANCE).

event In statistics, an occurrence whose frequency is being measured, such as the purchase of a particular brand by a consumer, or the production of a defective part by a machine. Events can be *independent*, *related*, or *mutually exclusive*. The result of tossing a coin—heads or tails—is an event that is totally independent of any previous or subsequent tosses of the coin. The cancellation of a ballgame and a snowstorm are related events, whereas a snowstorm and a temperature of 75° F. (simultaneously) are mutually exclusive events.

ever-normal granary A concept developed in U.S. government programs to support farm prices, according to which the surplus from a good harvest is stored (hence "granary," a storage place for grain) until the time of a poor harvest, when it is sold on the market. The government made loans to farmers against the value of the stored grain, so that they in effect received income from it before it was actually sold and could avoid glutting the market (and thus lowering prices) when they had a bumper crop. See also AGRICULTURE, AID TO.

eviction In general usage, ousting of a tenant by a landlord. Technically, however, eviction is a violation of some part of a lease by the landlord (not the tenant), while *ejectment* is a landlord's action to regain possession of leased premises because of the tenant's default on rent payments or some other reason. See also under LEASE.

exception rate See under FREIGHT.

excess-profits tax See under CORPORATION INCOME TAX.

excess reserves Any stock of cash and deposits a commercial bank holds over and above what it is required to hold (see RESERVE REQUIREMENTS). The amount of this surplus indicates, at least in part, a bank's potential for granting additional loans or for investing in government securities. The Federal Reserve itself can increase (or decrease) the reserves of member banks by buying (or selling) government bonds, notes, or bills on the open market, either from commercial banks or from the public. If securities are bought from a commercial bank, the bank's reserve balance in its district Federal Reserve Bank is increased by the amount of the purchase. If securities are bought from the public, the seller of the security is paid with a check drawn by a Federal Reserve Bank on itself, which the seller deposits in a commercial bank. This bank sends the check to the Federal Reserve for collection and in return receives an increase in its reserve balance. Because excess reserves are not the only source of a bank's expansion of lending or purchase of securities (it also can borrow from the Federal Reserve), financial analysts prefer to assess the banks' lending potential in terms of *free reserves*, that is, total excess reserves *minus* total borrowing from Federal Reserve banks. A bank also may lend its excess reserves on an overnight basis; see FEDERAL FUNDS MARKET.

exchange, foreign See FOREIGN EXCHANGE.

exchange controls Any of numerous government policies designed to maintain the international value of a nation's own currency and improve its BALANCE OF PAYMENTS position by regulating the purchase and sale of foreign currency. Their major drawback is that they limit trade. The principal methods used include *exchange licenses*, which permit only certain foreign-exchange transactions and prohibit all others (called *blocked exchange*); rationing of exchange, whereby holders of bills of exchange must give them to the government in exchange for domestic currency at a fixed rate, and only the government may issue bills of exchange to importers; *bilateral trade agreements*, whereby payments for transactions are made through balances held in the respective countries' central banks (to avoid imbalance, such agreements frequently involve trade quotas as well); STATE TRADING, in which some or all foreign trade is conducted through government agencies; *multiple exchange rates*, where different rates of exchange are set for different foreign currencies or for different types of international transaction (to encourage exports and/or discourage imports, rates are pegged high; to discourage exports they are set low); and *stabilization funds*, accounts controlled by the central bank, which buys and sells its own currency for gold and other currencies purely to offset fluctuations in the exchange rate (the United States version is the Treasury's Exchange Stabilization Fund, established in 1934). The last-named practice, also called *pegging*, became so widespread that in mid-1974 it received the official sanction of the INTERNATIONAL MONETARY FUND, which, however, called on all nations to follow its guidelines so as to prevent pegging from favoring only certain nations to the detriment of others and of world trade in general.

exchange depreciation A fall in the price of a foreign currency in relation to one or more other currencies, but particularly a RESERVE CURRENCY. Sometimes exchange depreciation is deliberately used by a government anxious to improve its balance of payments position, even at the expense of its neighbors. This device, called *competitive exchange depreciation*, consists of the purposeful un-

dervaluation of its currency, which results in raising foreign demand for its own currency, the acquisition of foreign exchange (which is used to pay for its currency), and the consequent depletion of other nations' reserves. See also DEVALUATION.

exchange rate Also, *rate of exchange*. The price at which one currency can be bought with another currency or with gold. For example, on any given day an American may, for the price of $1.00 (U.S.), buy 25 Portuguese escudos, 93 Canadian cents, 18 Austrian Schillings, 2.42 Swiss francs, or whatever currency he wants from his local bank, at the exchange rate for that currency on that day. Were there no government or other interference of any kind, the precise rate would be determined by supply and demand in the FOREIGN EXCHANGE MARKET. Supply and demand in turn would depend on the BALANCE OF PAYMENTS position of each country and the demand for a currency in terms of both obligations incurred and speculators' expectations about its future exchange rate. Such a rate is called a freely *fluctuating* or *floating exchange rate*. If this were to obtain, no government would need FOREIGN EXCHANGE RESERVES, since the rate would continue to adjust until supply and demand attained equilibrium.

From the end of World War I until 1971, the major trading nations preferred a *fixed rate of exchange*, with each country setting a *par value* for its currency (known as the *official exchange rate*). In practice this rate varied only slightly. Before World War II the par value of each major currency normally was fixed in relation to gold; in the postwar period it was set (by the INTERNATIONAL MONETARY FUND) in relation to the U.S. dollar, which itself was tied to gold (the U.S. Treasury was by law committed to buying gold at a fixed price of $35 per ounce). But in 1971 the United States, with a serious balance of payments deficit, suspended the convertibility of the U.S. dollar, so that it could no longer be freely exchanged for gold at a fixed price. In the absence of a single stable currency unit, exchange rates now floated, determined largely by supply and demand but also influenced by various government exchange controls. This situation was called a *dirty float*. The next few years brought continued monetary crises, aggravated by widespread inflation and, late in 1973, by a quadrupling of oil prices. As a result, gold, officially valued at $42.22 per ounce, fetched four times that price on the open market. The members of the International Monetary Fund (IMF), who had hoped to devise some kind of stable system of currency valuation to replace fixed par values, agreed in mid-1974 to continue with a kind of *managed floating rate*, that is, a floating rate influenced by individual governments trading in their own currencies (*pegging*) in order to stabilize its market value (but not imposing other, more restrictive EXCHANGE CONTROLS). This agreement was formalized in 1976 at a conference in Kingston, Jamaica. At the same time the IMF formally abolished any fixed price for gold.

A floating exchange rate theoretically has the same basic advantage as free trade: efficient allocation of resources through a freely operating market mechanism. Its chief disadvantages are that changes in the exchange rate directly affect domestic price and income levels, as well as creating inconvenience for commerce, especially when they are highly volatile, and that speculation is likely to promote rapid changes (see FORWARD EXCHANGE). A fixed exchange rate, on the other hand, may provide stability, but it is too rigid; it does not respond fast enough to changing conditions, particularly differences in rates of inflation in different countries. For example, a fixed relationship between the German Deutschmark and the British pound sterling cannot possibly be maintained indefinitely if export prices of one country are increasing at a rate of 3 per cent per year while in the other they are rising at a rate of 5 to 6 per cent per year. The managed floating rate is closer to a *flexible* exchange rate, which combines features of both extremes.

Another kind of flexible rate-setting that has been proposed is variously known as *crawling peg*, *gliding bands*, or *moving (sliding) parity*. Such rate-setting involves a gradual adjustment of exchange rates—no more than 1 to 2 per cent per year—to bring them in line, slowly but surely, with changes in growth, productivity, costs, and income in the respective countries. Ideally, this compromise between a fixed and floating rate would provide sufficient stability to encourage trade but permit adjustment to take into account variations in the rates of inflation and productivity of the individual na-

tions. In the mid-1970s the Common Market members and several other nations of western Europe were using this method in a so-called *joint float* (see SNAKE IN THE TUNNEL), and some authorities believed the U.S. dollar should be linked with it as well. See also DEVALUATION; OVERVALUED; REVALUATION.

Exchequer

1. The British counterpart of the U.S. Department of the Treasury. Originating in the reign of Henry I, the Exchequer imposes and regulates taxes and the collection of revenues, controls public spending, and generally oversees the nation's monetary and financial affairs. The Chancellor of the Exchequer is the chief financial minister and Second Lord of the Treasury (the Prime Minister is, by tradition, the First Lord of the Treasury).

2. Also, *Consolidated Fund*. The account of the British government with the British central bank, the Bank of England.

excise tax A kind of SALES TAX on certain commodities, in the United States levied by the Federal government and by some states. It is imposed on the manufacture or distribution of consumer goods, usually luxury items, and often is paid by means of *tax* or *revenue stamps*, which must be bought and affixed to the merchandise before its sale. An excise tax may be either a unit tax, based on a fixed price per unit of product (such as 10 cents per gallon of gasoline), or an ad valorem tax, based on a fixed percentage of the selling price. In the United States, Federal excise taxes are levied on tobacco products, alcoholic beverages, gasoline, playing cards, slot machines, travel, cosmetics, and other items. Excise taxes, like sales taxes, are usually regressive, placing a heavier tax burden on the poor than on the rich. They often are used to increase the cost (and thereby discourage consumption) of goods subject to social disapproval, such as liquor and cigarettes.

exclusive agency listing See under LISTING.

exclusive contract An agreement to purchase all of one's needs of a particular item or material during a given period from a certain supplier. See also TYING RESTRICTIONS.

exclusive representation See under LABOR UNION.

exclusive right to sell See under LISTING.

ex-dividend "Without dividend," that is, an indication that the purchaser of a given stock will not receive the dividend that has already been declared, which instead will be paid to the seller. Every corporate dividend is payable on a fixed date to all shareholders on the company books as of a previous date of record. For example, a dividend may be declared as payable to holders of record on the company books on a given Friday. However, a certain number of business days are allowed for delivery of stock in a regular stock-exchange transaction (five days on the New York Stock Exchange). Thus the exchange would declare the stock "ex-dividend" as of the opening of the market the given number of days earlier (in New York, the previous Monday). Then anyone who bought the stock on or after Monday would not be entitled to that particular dividend. This provision is taken into account in various kinds of customer's orders to brokers, the price of a stock usually being reduced by the amount of the dividend in question.

executive In business, a loosely used term for a manager, one who makes decisions and sees that they are carried out. See also under MANAGEMENT.

exemption In Federal income tax accounting, a deduction from gross income allowed to an individual for his or her own support and the support of children or other dependents.

exogenous variable See under ENDOGENOUS VARIABLE.

expansion A period when economic activity is moving from a low point to a new peak; see under BUSINESS CYCLE.

expectation Also, *anticipation*. A belief or state of mind concerning a future event. Expectations concerning price changes, profit, the behavior of

buyers and sellers, or other aspects of the market frequently influence future conditions. In recognition of their importance, surveys of businessmen's and consumers' expectations have become an important element in economic forecasting.

expediting In business and industry, the job of seeing that materials are at the right place when needed. In the case of purchased materials, the expediter tries to ensure delivery of the material to the buyer, and also sees that it reaches the right department as soon as possible. Expediters who do their work largely at the supplier's facility are called *field expediters*. Within a company, especially a processing or manufacturing enterprise, expediters are used to track down specific orders, sometimes conducting a physical department-wide search. In larger companies much of this work has been eliminated by computers, which can print out summaries of key-punched cards that show every operation completed on an order.

expenditure In accounting and finance, the act of acquiring an asset or settling a loss by paying cash, transferring property, or borrowing. Also, the amount of money or property so committed. See also DISBURSEMENT; EXPENSE, def. 1.

expense
1. In general, any kind of business cost incurred in operating an enterprise, maintaining property, etc.
2. In accounting, any kind of general operating cost related to a particular accounting period rather than to a particular product or service. Also, to charge a past or current EXPENDITURE to the accounting period to which it applies. For example, a firm's electric-power bill during a particular period is charged against operating expenses. In some cases companies have a choice as to whether or not to expense some cost that has been incurred. For example, if a company purchases a drill press, the cost must be capitalized (added to an asset account rather than expensed). But if it rebuilds a drill press, thereby achieving the same economic objective, it can (and probably will) charge the cost to current operating expenses, thereby reducing stated profits for the period and, consequently, income-tax liability. See also COST, def. 2; PREPAID EXPENSE.

expense account A statement of special expenses incurred while conducting business outside the office, for such items as business-related travel and entertainment. Normally such expenses must be authorized before reimbursement.

exponential smoothing A statistical technique for adjusting data so that they reflect recent rather than past experience and thus prove more useful for forecasting. In inventory control, for example, suppose a demand of 80 units of a material is forecast for a week in which the actual usage is 90 units. To compute average needs, the old average is adjusted to current demand, using the formula:

$$\text{new average} = \text{old average} + A \, (\text{current demand} - \text{old average})$$

where A stands for a fractional constant, arbitrarily set at 0.1. Accordingly, the new average is $80 + 0.1$ $(90 - 80) = 81$. Then, if demand during the following week drops to 75 units, the new average will be $81 + 0.1 \, (75 - 81) = 80.4$ units.

export Any good or service sold to a foreign country. While exports are essential for providing foreign exchange, some economists believe it is dangerous to rely on exports for growth, especially for an underdeveloped nation, because that makes for a tendency to ignore needed internal economic and social improvements. Argentina, for example, from the late 19th century until the 1930s, had a highly profitable beef export trade, selling huge quantities to Great Britain. The proceeds, however, were not used either to improve the Argentine cattle industry or to develop other Argentine industries. Consequently, when the British began to turn elsewhere for beef in the 1930s, Argentina's industry declined, and by the 1970s it was in a state of constant crisis. See also BALANCE OF PAYMENTS; BALANCE OF TRADE; EXPORT QUOTA; INTERNATIONAL INVESTMENT; INVISIBLE ITEMS; TERMS OF TRADE.

Export-Import Bank of the United States Also, *Eximbank*. An independent U.S. government agency formed in 1934 to promote the country's foreign trade by extending loans to foreigners that must be spent in the United States and be repaid in U.S. dollars. The first public agency ever to finance large-scale economic development projects, the bank stimulated U.S. exports by financing the purchase of American capital equipment, materials, and services. The bank has a capital stock of $1 billion and may borrow up to $6 billion more from the U.S. Treasury. At any one time it may have outstanding loans, guarantees, and insurance of up to $20 billion, and it may not compete with private capital. In addition to promoting trade, the bank has collected interest on its loans that represents a substantial contribution to the U.S. Treasury.

export license A permit to export specific goods to a particular country. It may be used to administer an EXPORT QUOTA by setting specific limits on the quantity that may be exported over a certain period of time, to limit shipments to neutral countries during wartime, or to limit the export of military or other critical materials, art objects, etc.

export multiplier See MULTIPLIER, def. 2.

export quota

1. A limit on the amount of a particular item that may be exported during a given period of time, usually set in order to protect a domestic industry. For example, the United States set a quota on the export of logs in order to keep prices low for American lumber mills.

2. *"voluntary" export quota*. A device used either to prevent imports from gaining too large a share of the domestic market or to ensure an adequate supply of raw material for a domestic industry. As an example of the former, the United States has in the past asked the Japanese to impose "voluntary" quotas on their exports of both textiles and steel. Japanese manufacturers agreed to adhere to these specifically negotiated quotas because they rightly feared that they otherwise would be replaced with mandatory quotas. Similarly, the United States has periodically limited (on both a voluntary and a mandatory basis) exports of scrap iron and steel in order to ensure the availability of an adequate supply at low prices for domestic industry.

express warranty See under WARRANTY.

expropriation The right of a government to take over private property, usually but not always with compensation for the owner. See also EMINENT DOMAIN.

ex-rights "Without rights," meaning that a stock whose present owner has RIGHTS to buy a new issue of that stock at a discount is being sold without those rights. The term *cum rights* ("with rights") is used when a stock sale includes the rights to a new issue.

extended bond See under BOND, def. 1.

extended coverage See under PROPERTY IN-SURANCE.

extended term insurance See under NONFOR-FEITURE.

extensive cultivation A method of farming large areas of land with relatively few workers and little capital equipment and fertilizer, which is possible only where land is cheap and plentiful. Traditionally practiced in Canada and the United States,

extensive farming has gradually given way to more intensive cultivation as land became costlier and as more expensive, complex farm equipment was developed. See also INTENSIVE CULTIVATION.

external debt The total sum collectively owed by a country—both privately and publicly—to foreigners.

extractive industry Any industry that removes irreplaceable natural resources, such as petroleum, iron ore, and other minerals.

extra dividend A dividend in the form of stock or cash that the board of directors votes to distribute to shareholders in addition to the regular dividend the company has been paying.

extra product See MARGINAL PHYSICAL PRODUCT.

extra utility See MARGINAL UTILITY.

Fabian socialism A branch of SOCIALISM that believes socialist doctrines can be put into effect gradually and peacefully, by democratic means, rather than by revolution. Thus Fabianism is a form of "revisionism" (see also Eduard BERNSTEIN). The name comes from the Fabian Society, founded in 1889 in England, which in turn took its name from the Roman general Fabius Cunctator, who fought Hannibal by avoiding confrontations and using delaying tactics. Among the most notable Fabians were Sidney Webb, Beatrice Potter Webb, and George Bernard Shaw. The British Labour Party, founded in 1900, based itself largely on Fabian views. The Fabian Society continues to exist as an independent research agency.

face value The value of a security, insurance policy, or coin, expressed as a specific sum of money, which is printed, stamped, or otherwise marked on its face. The face value of coins is also called their *denominational value*; gold or silver coins may have a face value that is actually less than their market value (the price they could fetch at a given time). The face value of a bond is usually the amount the issuer promises to pay at maturity; it is sometimes called PAR VALUE, a term nearly always used for the face value of stocks.

factor
1. A financial organization that takes responsibility for collecting accounts receivable and for the

customers' credit, a process called *factoring*. A factor buys the accounts receivable of manufacturers—that is, money owed them by wholesalers and/or retailers—in the same way as a sales finance company buys the accounts receivable of retailers (money owed them by consumers, chiefly through installment buying; see FINANCE COMPANY, def. 3). In buying their accounts receivable, factors provide their clients with working capital, a service for which they charge a fee, usually a percentage of the total (6 to 18 per cent, depending on the risk that the factor may not be able to collect). Factors are commonly used in highly competitive industries such as textiles, where the term also is used as a synonym of *selling agent* (see under MIDDLEMAN for further explanation).

2. In business law, a seller of goods on CONSIGNMENT, sometimes also called a *commission merchant*.

factor cost The costs of the FACTORS OF PRODUCTION used in making a commodity, that is, the wages and fringe benefits paid to labor, rent paid on property, profits paid to the entrepreneur, and materials costs. Factor cost does not include indirect costs, such as depreciation on the machinery used, or excise or sales taxes. Calculating factor cost can be useful in assessing how various industries within an economy absorb the available factors of production.

factors of production The resources required to produce a commodity. They are usually divided into three categories—LAND, LABOR, and CAPITAL (def. 1)—which, however, are admittedly arbitrary, since often a given resource may belong to more than one category. Broadly defined, land consists of natural resources in fixed supply, which cannot be used up; its earnings are called *rent*. Labor consists of both physical and mental efforts and skills expended, influenced by biological and social conditions as well as economic need; its earnings are called *wages*. Capital consists of goods that themselves have been produced and are used for further production of goods and services; its earnings are called *interest* or *return on investment*. This largely traditional analysis of the factors of production was first formulated by the 18th-century French economist J.B. Say (see under SAY'S LAW OF MARKETS). Some economists consider entrepreneurial or managerial ability a fourth factor of production; its earnings are called *profits* and represent a surplus that is earned over and above a normal rate of interest on the capital employed in a business. See also ENTREPRENEUR.

factory system A system of manufacturing in which production takes place in a building where workers are supplied with materials, tools, and machinery, and the workers, who are paid wages, are directed by either the owner or a salaried manager. The factory system began to supplant COTTAGE INDUSTRY in the late 17th century and had replaced it almost entirely by the mid-19th century in Great Britain and somewhat later in the United States and other countries. See also INDUSTRIAL REVOLUTION.

failure

1. In quality control, the inability of an item to perform its required function.

2. For business failure, see BANKRUPTCY; also NET BUSINESS FORMATION.

fair A public exposition or market, usually held at regular intervals, for the purpose of exhibiting, exchanging, and/or selling goods. The practice of holding fairs dates from ancient times and became an important feature of economic life in medieval Europe. Today fairs are used less for actual trading than for exhibiting merchandise, both to producers within a field or industry and to the public. The *agricultural fair* became a rural diversion in the United States during the 19th and early 20th centuries, as the emphasis of state and county fairs gradually shifted from commerce to amusement. *Industrial fairs*, also called *trade fairs* or *trade conventions*, have been popular since the latter half of the 19th century and often are international in scope. They have become particularly important in the Communist countries, where they are in part a substitute for the advertising and sales promotion undertaken in capitalist economies.

fair rate of return See under PUBLIC UTILITY; RATE BASE.

fair trade Also, *resale price maintenance*. An agreement between a manufacturer and a distributor, or a distributor and a dealer, stipulating that the latter will not resell an item below a specified minimum price. In the United States such agreements seemed in theory to violate Federal ANTI-TRUST LEGISLATION; in practice many states passed statutes called *fair trade laws*, permitting such agreements for products bearing a brand name or trademark. Moreover, two Federal laws, the *Miller-Tydings Act* of 1937 and the *McGuire Act* of 1952, upheld resale price maintenance. Dealers and distributors sometimes circumvented fair trade restrictions by giving buyers substantial discounts on other items not so restricted. Nevertheless, by the 1970s it was clear that consumers were paying several billion dollars per year more than necessary because of fair trade. In December 1975, Congress repealed the 1937 and 1952 Federal laws, thereby effectively doing away with state laws permitting fair trade. See also MINIMUM MARKUP LAW.

falling-rate-of-profit theory   Another name for declining marginal efficiency of capital; see under PRODUCTIVITY.

family income insurance   See under LIFE INSURANCE.

Fannie Mae   Nickname for FEDERAL NATIONAL MORTGAGE ASSOCIATION.

farm   A term used by the U.S. Bureau of the Census for a tract of land used for raising animals or crops intended for sale. A tract of fewer than 10 acres is a farm if estimated annual sales of agricultural products amount to at least $250; a tract of 10 or more acres is a farm if estimated annual sales amount to at least $50. In addition to farms raising livestock, poultry, or conventional crops, the Census Bureau includes such enterprises as nurseries, greenhouses, hothouses, sod farms, mushroom houses, and cranberry bogs, but does not include fish or oyster farms, fish hatcheries, kennels, or game preserves. See also AGRICULTURE.

farm aid   See AGRICULTURE, AID TO.

Farm Credit Administration   See under AGRICULTURE, AID TO.

Farmers Home Administration   See under AGRICULTURE, AID TO.

farming   See AGRICULTURE.

farm out
1. To subcontract; see under CONTRACTOR.
2. To delegate all or part of a job, often on a freelance basis.

farm surplus   See under AGRICULTURE, AID TO.

f.a.s.   Abbreviation for *free alongside ship*. Describing a price quotation, usually for an export shipment, and meaning that the seller is responsible for getting the shipment to a designated port (for example, *f.a.s. Boston, Mass.*). The seller assumes all transportation and other costs up to that point. Upon arrival the buyer takes title to the goods and is responsible for having them loaded from the dock to the vessel and for further shipping costs, including loss or damage.

fascism   A political and economic system in which the state is all-powerful and all activities are to be directed toward its advancement. Politically, fascism generally is characterized by a dictator, a single political party, and the abrogation of civil rights. Economically, the government has unlimited regulatory power, even though capital may be privately owned; thus an individual might own a shoe factory, but the government would determine how it was to be run and could, moreover, take it away from the owner at any time. The name "fascism" comes from a political party formed by Benito Mussolini in Italy in 1919, the *Fascio di Combattimento* ("fighting band").

favorable balance of trade   See under BALANCE OF TRADE.

FDIC   Abbreviation for FEDERAL DEPOSIT INSURANCE CORPORATION.

featherbedding   Requiring an employer to pay union wages for work that either is not performed at all or is only partially performed. Union requirements for using a given number of workers, even if not needed, for a particular job—for example, four stagehands to change scenery—may be a form of featherbedding. Blatant featherbedding is forbidden by the Taft-Hartley Act of 1947, but unions find ways to sidestep this provision of the law. See also MAKE-WORK.

Fed Colloquial abbreviation for the FEDERAL RESERVE.

Federal Advisory Council See under FEDERAL RESERVE.

Federal Aviation Administration Also, *FAA*. A division of the U.S. Department of Transportation that regulates air commerce to foster safety, promotes civil aviation and a national system of airports, and develops and operates a common system of air traffic control and air navigation for both military and civilian aircraft. Founded as the Federal Aviation Agency in 1958, it also registers aircraft ownership, publishes current information on airways and airport service, and issues technical aeronautical publications.

Federal budget The budget of the U.S. Federal government, a detailed statement of expected Federal expenditures and revenues for the coming fiscal year, running from July 1 to June 30. In preparing this budget, the executive branch of government decides its expenditures and tax policies, which are then considered by the legislature and voted into law. This complicated process is set in motion the previous spring or summer, when the various government agencies seeking funds prepare preliminary outlines of their programs, showing projected costs. These proposals are reviewed by the executive branch, which then sets forth guidelines indicating either what funds may be available or what general principles of allocation will be followed. The agencies then present detailed budget requests in the fall. For the next few months the President, working with the *Office of Management and Budget* (formerly U.S. *Bureau of the Budget*), reviews and alters agency requests (which normally exceed the total to be spent) and prepares a budget. This budget is sent to Congress early in January for review, usually first by the committees for each program (foreign relations, health care, etc.) and then by both houses of Congress. A committee

must vote *authorization* of a particular program before funds can be released for it. Then the appropriations committees and both houses of Congress must vote *appropriations* of money. This process usually takes Congress from January to the beginning of the fiscal year (July 1).

Appropriations empower the President to spend the money, but often there is a considerable time lag between an appropriation and actual disbursement of funds. For this and other reasons several sets of budgetary figures are actually in use. The most comprehensive is the *unified budget*, which takes into account both *Federal funds* (money collected by the Federal government and used for its general purposes) and *trust funds* (revenues earmarked for specific uses, notably social security payments, unemployment compensation, some grants-in-aid to states, etc.). An important item for economic analysis is the *national income and product accounts budget*, which attempts to take into consideration the economic impact, both in terms of time and magnitude, of an expenditure or income. It includes Federal trust fund transactions but excludes loans and similar transactions, since the latter involve the exchange of financial assets or physical assets that are not newly produced and hence do not contribute to current income. Another budget is the nation's *economic budget*, which allocates transactions to each of four sector accounts (government, business, consumers, international), so that each of them balances in terms of receipts and expenditures. It is primarily an analytical tool, used to compute indicators and similar data. See also FULL-EMPLOYMENT BUDGET.

Federal Communications Commission Also, *FCC*. An independent regulatory agency, created in 1934, which supervises interstate and foreign communications, including radio and television broadcasting; telephone, telegraph, and cable television operation; two-way radio and radio operators; and satellite communications. It issues construction permits and licenses for broadcasting, and it oversees compliance with laws on fair competition. In 1970 two other Federal agencies were created for the field of communications. The *Office of Telecommunications Policy*, part of the Executive Office of the President, is responsible for overall supervision of national communications matters, particularly in helping to establish policies and propose legislation for the executive branch. The *Office of Telecommunications* of the Department of Commerce was established largely to conduct research in the field of telecommunications and provide technical support and advice.

Federal Contract Compliance, Office of An agency of the U.S. Department of Labor that is responsible for establishing policies and goals and for providing leadership and coordination to eliminate discrimination in employment by government contractors and subcontractors and in federally assisted construction programs. It works with the Equal Employment Opportunity Commission and the Department of Justice in matters relating to Title VII of the Civil Rights Act of 1964 (see Fig. 44 under LABOR LAWS). See also AFFIRMATIVE ACTION.

Federal Crop Insurance Corporation See under AGRICULTURE, AID TO.

Federal debt See NET NATIONAL DEBT; PUBLIC DEBT.

Federal Deposit Insurance Corporation Also, *FDIC*. An agency originally established by the Federal Reserve Act of 1933 to insure up to $20,000 the individual deposits in all Federal Reserve member banks and in any state bank that qualifies for such insurance. The FDIC also may make loans to or buy assets from insured banks to help effect mergers, and it can help a closed bank to reopen (or prevent a bank from closing) when it considers the bank's operation important to the local community. In addition, the FDIC has various powers over insured nonmember banks concerning the opening of branches, mergers with other banks, issuing of securities, etc. The corporation's income comes chiefly from assessments on deposits held by insured banks and from interest on the government securities it must buy with its surplus funds.

Federal Energy Administration See under CONSERVATION.

Federal funds market A market in day-to-day lending or borrowing of EXCESS RESERVES among commercial banks. For example, suppose that Bank A closes a business day with an excess of $1 million over its required reserve (see RESERVE REQUIREMENTS) and is willing to lend $1 million to Bank B, which has closed that day with a reserve deficiency of $1 million. Buyer (Bank B) and seller (Bank A) are brought together by a broker who specializes in this market. The rate of interest charged for the overnight loan, called the *Federal funds rate*, depends on conditions of supply and demand. The Federal funds rate is nearly always lower than the DISCOUNT RATE, which in effect acts as a ceiling for it (were the discount rate lower, member banks would prefer to "go to the discount window," that is, borrow from the Federal Reserve). Borrowers in the Federal funds market tend to be large commercial banks in important financial centers, principally New York and Chicago, which frequently find themselves short of reserves owing to sudden large outflows of deposits. Lenders tend to be smaller banks whose depositors are more likely to be small business firms and individuals, rather than the giant corporations and foreign concerns served by big-city banks.

Federal Highway Administration A division of the U.S. Department of Transportation in charge of the nation's highway system. It administers Federal aid for new highway construction (in which the Federal government contributes 90 per cent of the cost and the states the balance), develops safety standards and programs, and exercises jurisdiction over the safety performance of commercial motor carriers engaged in interstate or foreign commerce.

Federal Home Loan Bank system A system of 12 regional banks established by the Federal Home Loan Bank Act of 1932 to provide a credit reserve for savings and home-financing institutions. Each bank is owned by its members, mostly savings and loan associations, mutual savings banks, and insurance companies, that is, the chief investors in home mortgages. Every Federal SAVINGS AND LOAN ASSOCIATION is required to belong to its regional Federal Home Loan Bank. The bank lends to these institutions when they are short of funds, and in turn raises money by issuing notes and bonds.

Federal Housing Administration Also, *FHA*. A government agency created by the National Housing Act of 1934 and today part of the U.S. Department of Housing and Urban Development. Its chief function is to insure loans and mortgages issued by private lending institutions for the purchase of single-family dwellings, private residences, rental housing, cooperative housing, condominiums, and mobile homes.

Federal intermediate credit bank Any of 12 banks set up by the Agricultural Credit Act of 1923 (superseded by the Farm Credit Act of 1971) to make loans to and discount agricultural paper for production credit associations, state and national banks, agricultural credit corporations, livestock loan companies, and similar institutions lending money to farmers and cattleraisers. The intermediate banks do not lend directly to individual farmers nor do they conduct a general banking business. The capital stock of the banks is owned by farmers through their local production credit associations, and the banks obtain funds for lending primarily from sales of short-term debentures (unsecured bonds) to the public. See also *Farm Credit Administration*, under AGRICULTURE, AID TO.

Federal land banks A system of banks, administered by the U.S. Farm Credit Administration, that grant long-term mortgage loans to farmers and ranchers for buying land, refinancing debts, or other general agricultural purposes. There are 12 Federal land banks, one in each Farm Credit district, and some 600 local land bank associations, whose stock is owned by their member-borrowers. A farmer who wishes a loan purchases stock in the land bank association equal to 5 per cent of the loan, and the association purchases a like amount of stock in the land bank. When the loan is repaid, the stock in the bank and association is retired. The money for the loans is obtained chiefly from the sale of consolidated Federal farm loan bonds to the public. See also *Farm Credit Administration*, under AGRICULTURE, AID TO.

Federal Maritime Commission See under MERCHANT MARINE.

Federal National Mortgage Association Also, *Fannie Mae*. A government-sponsored private corporation that buys mortgages from banks and other lending institutions and sells them to investors in order to create a fund for mortgage lending. First created in 1938 as a Federal agency, it became private in 1968. See also GOVERNMENT NATIONAL MORTGAGE ASSOCIATION.

Federal Open Market Committee See FEDERAL RESERVE; OPEN-MARKET OPERATIONS.

Federal Power Commission Also, *FPC*. The principal Federal regulatory agency for the electric power and natural gas industries. It issues licenses and permits for non-Federal hydroelectric power projects; regulates interstate power and gas rates; issues certificates for interstate gas sales and for the construction and operation of interstate pipelines; and enforces regulations dealing with environmental pollution by power installations and pipelines. In the 1970s the FPC was particularly concerned with long-range planning for power supplies and facilities.

Federal Railroad Administration A division of the U.S. Department of Transportation concerned with consolidating Federal support of rail transport, providing a unified national policy, administering and enforcing rail safety laws and rules, administering financial aid for certain lines, research and development of improved intercity ground transport, and operating the Alaska Railroad.

Federal Reserve The central monetary authority of the United States, established by the Federal Reserve Act of 1913. Unlike most other advanced countries, the United States has no single CENTRAL BANK. Instead, it operates under a system of 12 Federal Reserve banks owned by the member banks in their respective districts. All national banks must belong to the Federal Reserve; state banks may join if they wish and are eligible for membership (see NONMEMBER BANK). In the mid-1970s about 40 per cent of all American commercial banks were members, accounting for more than three-fourths of all demand deposits. The 12 district banks are controlled by the Federal Reserve *Board of Governors*, consisting of a chairman and 6 other members who are appointed by the President of the United States to a 14-year term. Each of the Federal Reserve banks has 9 directors, 6 chosen by the member banks and 3, including the chairman, by the Board of Governors. The chief function of each Federal Reserve Bank is to hold the reserves of its members and extend credit to them by discounting notes, bills of exchange, and other obligations (see also DISCOUNT RATE; REDISCOUNTING). It also issues currency; *Federal Reserve notes,* backed by gold, U.S. government securities, and commercial paper, constitute the bulk of money in circulation. In addition, it acts as a clearinghouse for its members, facilitating the collection and clearing of checks, and as a fiscal agent for the Federal government, holding government funds on deposit and acting as a selling agent for government bonds.

Acting through the Federal Reserve banks, the Board of Governors implements the general monetary, credit, and operating policies it formulates for the system as a whole. Its chief function by far is its influence on credit, exerted through regulating RESERVE REQUIREMENTS for its members, the discount rate (interest charged to its members), and OPEN-MARKET OPERATIONS. For the last, there is a *Federal Open Market Committee,* made up of the 7 members of the Board of Governors plus 5 elected representatives from the Federal Reserve banks. The Board of Governors also relies on the advice of the *Federal Advisory Council,* made up of one member from each Federal Reserve District who is chosen annually by the board of directors of the Reserve bank of that district. See also BANK RESERVES; DEBT MONETIZATION; FEDERAL RESERVE BANK CREDIT; MONETARY POLICY.

Federal Reserve bank credit The monetary base for the American economy's financial structure, consisting largely of U.S. government securities but also including loans to commercial banks and floats (checks in process). When credit is expanded (that is, when the Federal Reserve's holdings of government bonds increase), the banking system has more primary reserves (see BANK RESERVES); when credit shrinks, reserves contract. Each addition to the Federal Reserve bond portfolio is paid for with a check drawn by the Federal Reserve on itself, which becomes primary reserves when deposited in a commercial bank by the seller of the bond. Therefore the effect of a $1 loan to a member bank is exactly the same as a $1 purchase of a Treasury bill on the open market. For how banks borrow from the Federal Reserve, see under DISCOUNT RATE. See also Fig. 27.

Federal savings and loan association See SAVINGS AND LOAN ASSOCIATION.

Federal Savings and Loan Insurance Corporation An agency established by the National Housing Act of 1934 to insure the safety of savings in thrift and home-financing institutions. It insures each investor's account in an insured institution for up to $20,000. Institutions so covered include all Federal SAVINGS AND LOAN ASSOCIATIONS (required by law to be so insured) and those state-chartered savings and loan associations that qualify. The corporation's income comes chiefly from premiums paid by insured institutions and interest earned on investments.

Federal Trade Commission Also, *FTC*. The principal Federal regulatory agency for maintaining free and fair competition in American business and industry and for preventing any practices likely to hinder competition or create a monopoly. Formed as an independent agency in 1915, it administers both ANTITRUST LEGISLATION and various CONSUMER-PROTECTION LAWS.

fee A payment for a service, particularly a professional service, such as rendered by a physician, lawyer, accountant, etc. See also *brokerage*, under BROKER, def. 1; RETAINER.

feedback
   1. The ability of a COMPUTER to use the outcome of one step of a problem to proceed to the logical next step.
   2. In marketing, a return flow of ideas and opinions from buyers and consumers to sellers and producers. Obtaining relevant feedback is a major objective of market research.

fee simple See under ESTATE, def. 2.

feudalism The prevailing social and political system in Europe during the Middle Ages. It involved an intricate series of relationships among *lords* of varying rank (from lowly noble to king) who, in return for land grants (called *fiefs*) made to lesser lords (*vassals*), were entitled to their military services. The arrangement was essentially reciprocal and based on barter: the lord gave land, the right to govern it, and some measure of protection; in re-

Fig. 27. Total Federal Reserve bank credit

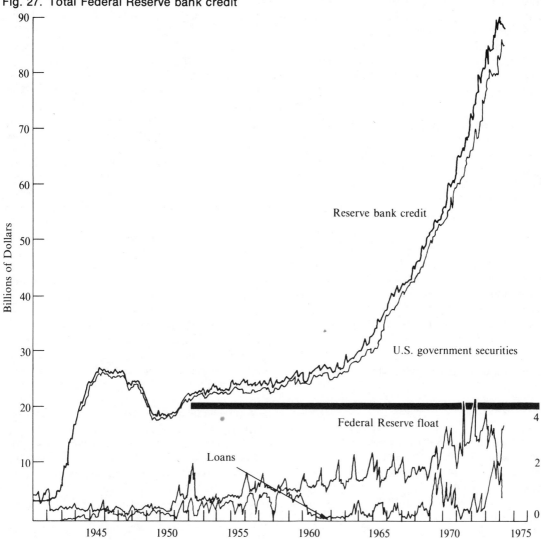

Source: Board of Governors of the Federal Reserve System.

turn the vassal rendered military services and also provided hospitality and some financial support. See also MANORIAL SYSTEM.

FHA Abbreviation for FEDERAL HOUSING ADMINISTRATION.

fiat money Paper money whose value derives from the fact that the issuing government has so decreed and people generally accept it as such. (The Latin word *fiat* means "let there be.") Fiat money need not be backed by (or be convertible into) gold or silver; its value depends largely on people's confidence in it. All present-day currency is essentially fiat money; even coins normally have considerably less intrinsic value than their declared monetary value. See also FIDUCIARY MONEY; GREENBACK.

FICA See under EMPLOYMENT TAX.

fidelity bond A kind of insurance against an employer's loss of money, goods, or other property through the dishonesty or treachery (lack of fidelity) of an employee. It thus differs from a SURETY BOND, which protects against failure to fulfill an obligation, but in practice the two are frequently combined.

fiduciary Literally, involving trust. A term applied to a person on whom a trust has developed, that is, a trustee (see under TRUST, def. 1). It is also used to describe a transaction based on faith or confidence, such as a loan unsecured by collateral. See also FIDUCIARY MONEY.

fiduciary money Money only partly backed by gold or silver, so that only part of a total issue is convertible into gold or silver. Its value therefore is partly dependent on faith (fiduciary means "involving trust"). Since 1933, when the U.S. government declared that no American could exchange dollars into gold, U.S. currency has been fiduciary money. See also FIAT MONEY.

field warehousing loan See under LOAN, def. 1.

FIFO Abbreviation for FIRST-IN, FIRST-OUT.

file In computer terminology, a collection of data records (see RECORD). Most computer applications in business consist of processing such files, which may contain personnel records, accounts-payable records, salary records, inventory records, etc. See also STORAGE, def. 1.

final utility theory of value Also, *utility theory of value*. See under MARGINALIST SCHOOL.

finance, international See BALANCE OF PAYMENTS; CAPITAL MOVEMENTS; EXCHANGE CONTROLS; EXCHANGE RATE; FOREIGN AID; FOREIGN EXCHANGE; INTERNATIONAL INVESTMENT; INTERNATIONAL MONETARY FUND; SPECIAL DRAWING RIGHTS.

finance, public See PUBLIC FINANCE.

finance bill A long-term BILL OF EXCHANGE drawn by a bank on another bank in a foreign country, usually against security held.

finance company

1. General name for a firm that specializes in making loans to business or individuals or both.

2. *personal finance company*. Also, *consumer finance company, personal loan company, small loan company*. A firm that specializes in making small short-term loans to consumers for the purchase of consumer goods or some other purpose. Such loans usually range from $300 to $3,000 and are made for periods from six months to three years, with an interest rate of $1\frac{1}{2}$ per cent to 3 per cent *per month* on the unpaid balance. The loans may be unsecured or secured by a CHATTEL MORTGAGE on an automobile or other personal property. In the United States the operations of personal finance companies are closely controlled by state laws.

3. *sales finance company*. Also, *commercial credit company, discount house*. A firm that specializes in buying, at a discount, the ACCOUNTS RECEIVABLE of other firms, especially installment contracts from retailers. Since funds for these purchases are normally obtained through bank loans, sales finance companies must charge considerably more interest than banks in order to cover expenses and make a profit. Retailers benefit, however, by passing on the risks and capital involved in carrying unpaid installment balances. Sales finance companies also may extend credit to retailers such as automobile dealers, paying in cash for the dealer's purchases from the manufacturer and being repaid, as the automobiles are sold, by the dealer. See also FACTOR, DEF. 1.

financial intermediary An institution or organization that brings together borrowers and lenders, making available loanable funds to those willing to pay for their use. A great many credit institutions, ranging from commercial banks, mutual savings banks, and trust companies to credit unions and various kinds of finance company, fall into this category.

financial statement See BALANCE SHEET; also STATEMENT.

finder's fee In real estate, a fee or commission paid to a broker for obtaining a mortgage loan for a client or for referring a mortgage loan to another broker. Also, a commission paid to a broker for locating a property.

fink Slang for a person hired to replace an employee on strike.

fire insurance See under PROPERTY INSURANCE.

firing See under LAYOFF.

firm
1. A business enterprise. Some confine the term to any noncorporate business (see CORPORATION), but most use it in a more general sense. See also ESTABLISHMENT; PARTNERSHIP; PROPRIETORSHIP.
2. Describing prices or demand that are relatively stable, with little fluctuation.
3. Describing an offer, bid, price, delivery promise, or other term or condition that is binding when accepted. In some states a written offer stating that it will be irrevocable for a given time may not be revoked during that period. The Uniform Commercial Code adopts this concept for contracts to sell goods but sets a maximum of three months on their duration.

firm, theory of the See under MICROECONOMICS.

firm market See under SOFT MARKET.

first-in, first-out Also, *FIFO.* A system of inventory accounting in which the items that are bought earliest are regarded as being used first during an accounting period. In some businesses, inventory is actually handled in this way; in grocery stores, stock is turned over physically on a first-in, first-out basis to minimize spoilage. In manufacturing enterprises, the concept is less logical, particularly for nonperishable goods; steel sheets or zinc slabs will be just as useful two years after purchase as they are on the day of arrival. From an accounting standpoint, however, it is assumed that the goods bought first are used first, and hence the goods remaining in stock are the most recently bought and are valued at the most recent market prices. As a result, the first-in, first-out method tends to show lower costs

and higher profits in times of rising prices (because it records material cost at the earlier, lower price level), and consequently indicates higher taxable income. Many companies therefore prefer *last-in, first-out* accounting, because general inflation tends to cause both stated profits and tax payments to be consistently lower with this method.

first mortgage bond See under MORTGAGE BOND.

fiscal policy The overall program for directing government spending and taxation so as to achieve the desired economic goals. Today these goals (at least in capitalist countries) consist principally of modifying the ups and downs of the business cycle and achieving full employment with relatively stable price levels (without excessive inflation). During a business decline, the government can stimulate overall output by increasing its spending and/or by cutting taxes. The former increases government purchases from the private sector, thereby adding to income; the latter leaves more spendable income for consumers, businesses, or both, depending on whose tax rates are changed. Conversely, in times of overexpansion, the government can work to lower overall output (and to counter inflation) by cutting back spending and/or by raising taxes. Less government spending puts less income into the private sector; higher taxes mean less spendable income, leading to reduced demand and eventually lower prices. Not all United States fiscal policy is *discretionary*, that is, not every change in policy requires a separate decision by Congress and the President. Much change is built into the fiscal system, so that it can respond to changing economic conditions. For example, when income declines, income tax payments also decline, and there is a rise in unemployment benefits being paid out. (For other such automatic changes, see under BUILT-IN STABILIZER.)

Fiscal policy that is primarily directed toward offsetting fluctuations in income and employment is called *countercyclical* or *compensatory fiscal policy.* Though American fiscal policy has always been directed at one or another economic goal (ever since tariffs first were enacted to protect INFANT INDUSTRY), until the 1930s the goal of economic stability was largely secondary to that of a "balanced budget," so that government revenues (chiefly taxes) would be sufficient to cover government expenditures. Even though an excess of outgo over income—the PUBLIC DEBT—was regarded as "a national blessing" by such authorities as Alexander Hamilton, for more than a century people were inclined to regard DEFICIT FINANCING with suspicion and dismay. Today, however, it is generally accepted that economic growth and prosperity are more important than the precise size of the public debt, and that fiscal policy can and should be used, as J. M. KEYNES maintained, to bring about full employment. Also, the U.S. government today is more inclined to execute policy through changes in tax rates than through crash programs of spending on public works or through severe austerity programs to curtail spending. See also PUBLIC SPENDING.

fiscal year
1. Any 12-month period ending with a date other than December 31.
2. Any ACCOUNTING PERIOD, usually consisting of 12 successive months, 52 successive weeks, or 13 successive 4-week periods. If 1- or 4-week intervals are used, adjustment may be made for leap year. A few companies use a 48-week year in order to have 12 months of 4 weeks each, and they make periodic adjustments to make their financial statements consistent with the calendar.

Fisher, Irving An American mathematician and economist (1867–1947) who is remembered for his contributions to econometrics, statistics, and index numbers (see IDEAL INDEX), and for developing the EQUATION OF EXCHANGE, a modern version of the QUANTITY THEORY OF MONEY. Because he believed that the amount of money in circulation determines price levels, and vice versa, Fisher came to think that overall prices could be stabilized by controlling the amount of currency in circulation, to be effected by adjusting the price of gold. If prices rose by 2 per cent, for example, lowering the dollar's purchasing power by 2 per cent, the weight of the gold dollar should rise accordingly (by 2 per cent). After the crash of 1929, however, in which Fisher lost a considerable personal fortune, he formulated the *debt-deflation theory*, holding that excessive debts were responsible for a depression. Excessive debts lead to business bankruptcies and the consequent dump-

ing of goods on the market, lowering prices still more and causing more bankruptcies and more dumping. Realizing that changing the price of gold would not sufficiently alter average price levels, Fisher proposed that all commercial banks be required to hold a reserve of 100 per cent against their demand deposits. This reserve would consist of currency, reserve accounts with the Federal Reserve banks, and government bonds. In this way banks would not be able to create money on the basis of fractional reserves, since all credit would be 100 per cent backed, and the monetary authority would have full control over the money supply. Like the quantity theory of money itself, however, Fisher's *100 per cent plan* ignored the fact that borrowing and spending depend on numerous factors besides the supply of money.

fishyback A freight shipment that combines the use of truck and ship. Goods are loaded into truck trailers and are driven from the shipper's plant to the dock. There the trailers are loaded into ships or barges for shipment between cities or countries. At the dock nearest their destination, they are reloaded onto trucks that drive them to the customer's plant. Fishyback shipments reduce handling expense and special export packaging, and hence make for both lower rates and faster service. See also PIGGYBACK.

five-and-ten See under RETAIL.

Five-Year Plan A plan for economic development. Specifically, the series of such plans established under the regime of Josef Stalin (1879–1953) whereby the Soviet Union was converted from a nation of backward peasants to an industrialized world power. The first Five-Year Plan, introduced in 1928–29, set up machinery for the collectivization of agriculture (see COLLECTIVE FARM) and the industrialization of manufacturing. Although as late as 1929 less than 5 per cent of arable land was under state control, by the spring of 1930 more than half had been collectivized, and by 1936 the process was virtually complete. For industrialization, a State Planning Commission was established to allocate production, set goals for output, and otherwise control manufacturing. Both consumption and production of consumer goods were strictly rationed, so that the nation's resources could be fully directed toward the capital goods it so badly needed. The Soviet government continued the system of Five-Year Plans even after Stalin's death, and there is no doubt that they accelerated Russia's long overdue Industrial Revolution. Five-year plans have been used in several other countries, notably India.

fixed asset   See under ASSET.

fixed capital

1. See CAPITAL, def. 1.

2. In finance, the money invested in the fixed assets of a business.

fixed charge   In accounting, principally in railroad accounting, rental and interest charges that must be paid regardless of business volume.

fixed cost   Also, *constant cost, fixed expense, standby cost.* An operating expense of a business that does not vary, at least over the short term, with the volume of output, as for example rent on buildings, interest on bonds, depreciation of plant and equipment (sometimes only in part), property taxes, and salaries of top management. Of course a fixed cost can fluctuate, but such fluctuation is usually for reasons independent of production volume. Owing to the similarity between fixed cost and INDIRECT COST, some authorities equate the two, but they are not precisely the same. See also OVERHEAD; VARIABLE COST.

fixed investment trust   Also, *nondiscretionary trust.* An investment company that may invest its assets only in a given list of securities, set forth when the trust is organized. Further, the proportion of total assets to be invested in specific securities is also usually predetermined.

fixed liability   See under LIABILITY, def. 1.

fixed overhead   See under OVERHEAD.

fixed-price contract   Any purchase order in which the price of the purchased item is quoted as a specific figure, as opposed to a contract including an ESCALATION clause to protect the seller if costs rise, or a *price redetermination clause*, to allow for review and renegotiation of the selling price after

the seller acquires experience with the item being sold. See also INCENTIVE CONTRACT.

fixture   An article that has been installed in or attached to a building or land in a more or less permanent way, so that legally it is considered part of the real estate. Prior to such installation, however, the article is regarded as PERSONAL PROPERTY. For example, a faucet displayed in a plumbing supply store is legally personal property; the same faucet installed in a house is a fixture.

flat

1. In the securities trade, describing the sale of a bond in which the new owner receives 100 per cent of the next interest payment. Normally bonds are sold "full," meaning that the former owner receives from the new owner that portion of the next interest payment that accrued up to the date of the sale. For example, if a bond that pays interest on January 1 and July 1 is sold on January 31, the new owner pays the seller not only the agreed on purchase price but also 30 days' worth of interest at the coupon rate (about $5 for a $1,000 bond with a 6 per cent coupon rate). Usually bonds sell flat only when the issuer of the bond has failed to make one or more of the interest payments, or where interest is payable only if earned (that is, the interest is not certain and becomes similar to a dividend on stock that is payable at the option of the company's directors).

2. *flat lease.* See under LEASE.

flat organization   See under SPAN OF CONTROL.

flat rate

1. An overall price for an entire job or group of jobs. For example, a painter may offer a flat rate covering both time and materials, rather than working for an hourly fee plus the cost of the paint.

2. A uniform rate charged for every unit of a service, regardless of actual use. A telephone company or water utility may charge a flat rate payable by each customer at regular intervals, regardless of how many units of the service (number of phone calls or gallons of water) are actually used during that period.

flea market   A market, held either outdoors or indoors, where numerous merchants at separate stalls sell old or used household goods, antiques, and curios. Prices are usually subject to bargaining. Some flea markets are held only on certain days of the week or during certain seasons; others are open daily and the year round. The flea market of Paris, France, is one of the oldest and best known.

flexible hours The concept that work need not always be done within a traditionally accepted time period, such as the business hours of 9:00 A.M. to 5:00 P.M. For example, a company might consider a work week of four ten-hour days, or allow some employees to work from 7:30 A.M. to 3:30 P.M., or various other arrangements. Flexible hours have been proposed to ease traffic and commuting problems, to enable parents to work while their children are at school, to use computers and other expensive equipment more efficiently, and similar reasons.

flexible tariff A tariff whose rate can be varied to offset changes in the rate of exchange, cost of production, or some other variable. For an example, see ANTIDUMPING TARIFF.

flight of capital The international transfer of short-term funds—investments or loans maturing within a year or less—as well as long-term funds to escape domestic taxation, inflation, political instability, devaluation, or some other unfavorable circumstance. Such flights of capital can cause serious BALANCE OF PAYMENTS problems, since they can rapidly deplete domestic reserves. Before World War II, numerous countries experienced severe flights of capital, which they tried to counter by imposing exchange restrictions and other government controls. In 1971, after a long period in which interest rates in the United States lower than those available abroad caused a heavy outflow of short-term funds, there was a run on the dollar in the foreign-exchange market as speculators became convinced that the dollar would have to be devalued. This actually helped create a balance of payments deficit so large that the anticipated devaluation had to be carried out. See also CAPITAL MOVEMENTS.

float The total of checks outstanding at any one time, owing to the time lag between the writing of a check and its collection at the bank on which it is drawn. In effect, the float represents a short-term loan over the period it takes a check to clear. In the United States such large sums of money are involved that the Federal Reserve compiles and publishes statistics on the float, which appear at least once a week in the financial pages of large newspapers. For *dirty float*, see under EXCHANGE RATE; also BEGGAR-THY-NEIGHBOR POLICY.

floater A kind of inland marine insurance that follows movable property, covering it wherever it may go. Floaters are generally all-risk, that is, they offer protection against all hazards except for a few specifically excluded. They generally are worldwide, paying for losses anywhere, and they usually are scheduled, that is, each item listed in the policy has an up-to-date appraised value. Floaters are available for specific kinds of valuable personal property (works of art, jewelry, furs, securities, etc.), as well as for general personal property, giving overall protection for virtually all the items the policyholder owns. They also are available for business property, such as contractor's equipment, livestock, theatrical equipment, neon signs, scientific instruments, samples, patterns, vending machines, stocks of goods in transit, etc.

floating an issue See under ISSUE.

floating debt Also, *unfunded debt*. Any short-term obligations (current liabilities) of a business or government, as opposed to long-term obligations such as bonds (see FUNDED DEBT). In the case of a government it consists largely of bills and other short-term notes. Among businesses it consists chiefly of bank loans or commercial paper.

floating exchange rate See under EXCHANGE RATE.

floating interest rate See under MORTGAGE.

floor trader Also, *registered trader*. A member of a STOCK EXCHANGE who trades for his or her own account rather than for customers. Floor traders pay no commissions, since they do their own trading, and they tend to take advantage of small price fluctuations to make a quick profit. Most exchanges have strict regulations for floor traders so that they have no special advantage over the general public (which deals through brokers). On the New York Stock Exchange floor traders account for but a small fraction of the shares traded (about 1 per cent).

flow chart

1. A graph or other chart that illustrates the movement of money, credit, goods, or some other economic element through various stages. A flow chart might, for example, show the various stages of manufacturing, beginning with raw material and ending with finished product, or the international movement of dollars.

2. In computer terminology, a diagram showing the processing of a problem in a computer by means of boxes and interconnecting lines. Preparing such a diagram often is the first step in PROGRAMMING, since it provides a clear graphic analysis of the steps involved in the desired computation. An example is shown in Fig. 28.

Fig. 28. Flow chart for converting present serum storage data

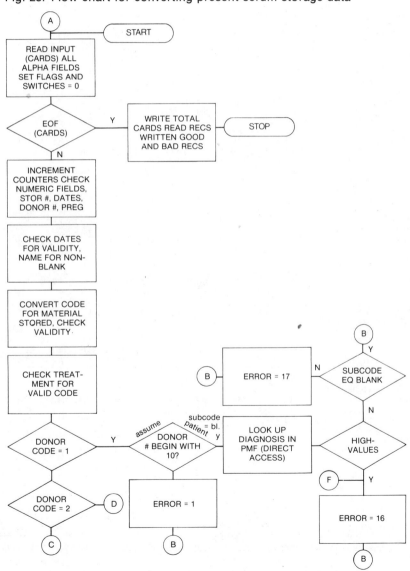

Fig. 29. Summary of funds raised in U.S. credit markets (seasonally adjusted annual rates; in billions of dollars)

Transaction Category, or Sector	1966	1967	1968	1969	1970	1971	1972	1973	1974	1975	1975 H1	1975 H2
				Credit market funds raised by nonfinancial sectors								
1 **Total funds raised by nonfinancial sectors**	**67.9**	**82.4**	**96.0**	**91.8**	**98.2**	**147.4**	**169.4**	**187.4**	**180.1**	**204.6**	**186.7**	**222.2**
2 *Excluding equities*	**66.9**	**80.0**	**96.0**	**87.9**	**92.4**	**135.9**	**158.9**	**180.1**	**176.2**	**194.6**	**176.2**	**212.8**
3 U.S. government	3.6	13.0	13.4	−3.7	12.8	25.5	17.3	9.7	12.0	85.2	84.1	86.3
4 Public debt securities	2.3	8.9	10.4	−1.3	12.9	26.0	13.9	7.7	12.0	85.8	85.4	86.4
5 Agency issues and mortgages	1.3	4.1	3.1	−2.4	−.1	−.5	3.4	2.0	*	−.6	−1.2	−.1
6 **All other nonfinancial sectors**	**64.3**	**69.4**	**82.6**	**95.5**	**85.4**	**121.9**	**152.1**	**177.7**	**168.1**	**119.4**	**102.6**	**135.9**
7 Corporate equities	1.0	2.4	*	3.9	5.8	11.5	10.5	7.2	3.8	9.9	10.5	9.4
8 *Debt instruments*	63.3	67.0	82.6	91.6	79.7	110.4	141.6	170.4	164.2	109.4	92.1	126.5
9 *Private domestic nonfinancial sectors*	**62.7**	**6.45**	**79.7**	**91.8**	**82.7**	**117.3**	**147.8**	**170.1**	**152.7**	**106.3**	**93.0**	**119.4**
10 Corporate equities	1.3	2.4	−.2	3.4	5.7	11.4	10.9	7.4	4.1	9.9	10.3	9.5
11 *Debt instruments*	61.5	63.0	79.9	88.4	77.0	105.8	136.9	162.7	148.6	96.4	82.7	109.9
12 Debt capital instruments	38.2	44.5	49.5	49.6	56.7	83.2	93.8	96.1	92.9	97.8	101.7	93.8
13 State and local obligations	5.6	7.8	9.5	9.9	11.2	17.6	14.4	13.7	17.4	15.4	17.1	13.8
14 Corporate bonds	10.2	14.7	12.9	12.0	19.8	18.8	12.2	9.2	19.7	27.2	35.3	19.1
15 *Home mortgages*	11.7	11.5	15.1	15.7	12.8	26.1	39.6	43.3	31.7	36.1	31.2	41.0
16 *Multifamily residential mortgages*	3.1	3.6	3.4	4.7	5.8	8.8	10.3	8.4	7.8	2.4	2.9	1.9
17 *Commercial mortgages*	5.7	4.7	6.4	5.3	5.3	10.0	14.8	17.0	11.5	11.0	9.4	12.6
18 *Farm mortgages*	1.8	2.3	2.2	1.9	1.8	2.0	2.6	4.4	4.9	5.6	5.8	5.4
19 Other debt instruments	23.3	18.5	30.4	38.8	20.3	22.6	43.0	66.6	55.6	−1.3	−19.1	16.1
20 Consumer credit	6.4	4.5	10.0	10.4	6.0	11.2	19.2	22.9	9.6	5.3	−1.5	12.0
21 Bank loans n.e.c.	10.9	9.8	13.6	15.5	6.7	7.8	18.9	35.8	27.3	−11.3	−20.2	−2.5
22 Open market paper	1.1	1.7	1.8	3.0	3.0	−1.2	−.5	−.4	6.6	−2.0	−1.5	−2.5
23 Other	5.0	2.6	5.0	9.9	4.6	4.8	5.5	8.3	12.1	6.7	4.2	9.2
24 By borrowing sector	62.7	65.4	79.7	91.8	82.7	117.3	147.8	170.1	152.7	106.3	93.0	119.4
25 State and local governments	6.3	7.9	9.8	10.7	11.3	17.8	14.2	12.3	16.6	13.2	14.8	11.6
26 Households	22.7	19.3	30.0	31.7	23.4	39.8	63.1	72.8	44.0	45.2	36.2	54.1
27 Farm	3.1	3.6	2.8	3.2	3.2	4.1	4.9	8.6	7.8	9.2	8.2	10.2
28 Nonfarm noncorporate	5.4	5.0	5.6	7.4	5.3	8.7	10.4	9.3	7.2	2.9	.2	5.4
29 Corporate	25.3	29.6	31.6	38.9	39.5	46.8	55.3	67.2	77.1	35.8	33.6	38.1
30 *Foreign*	**1.5**	**4.0**	**2.8**	**3.7**	**2.7**	**4.6**	**4.3**	**7.5**	**15.4**	**13.0**	**9.6**	**16.4**
31 Corporate equities	−.3	.1	.2	.5	−.1	*	−.4	−.2	−.3	*	.1	−.1
32 *Debt instruments*	1.8	4.0	2.7	3.2	2.7	4.6	4.7	7.7	15.7	13.0	9.5	16.6
33 Bonds	.7	1.2	1.1	1.0	.9	.9	1.0	1.0	2.2	6.3	5.9	6.7
34 Bank loans n.e.c.	−.2	−.3	−.5	−.2	−.3	1.6	2.9	2.8	4.7	4.0	1.4	6.6
35 Open market paper	−.1	.5	−.2	.3	.8	.3	−1.0	2.2	7.1	−.1	−1.2	1.0
36 U.S. government loans	1.3	2.6	2.2	2.1	1.3	1.8	1.8	1.7	1.7	2.8	3.4	2.3
37 Memo: U.S. govt. cash balance	−.4	1.2	−1.1	.4	2.8	3.2	−.3	−1.7	−4.6	2.9	2.7	3.1
Totals net of changes in U.S. govt. cash balances:												
38 Total funds raised	68.3	81.3	97.1	91.4	95.4	144.2	169.7	189.0	184.7	201.7	184.0	219.1
39 By U.S. government	4.0	11.8	14.6	−4.1	10.0	22.3	17.6	11.4	16.6	82.3	81.4	83.2
				Credit market funds raised by financial sectors								
1 **Total funds raised by financial sectors**	**11.7**	**2.0**	**18.3**	**33.7**	**12.6**	**16.5**	**28.9**	**52.0**	**38.0**	**12.1**	**4.9**	**19.3**
2 Sponsored credit agencies	4.8	−.6	3.5	8.8	8.2	3.8	6.2	19.6	22.1	11.0	9.1	13.0
3 U.S. government securities	5.1	−.6	3.2	9.1	8.2	3.8	6.2	19.6	21.4	10.2	8.0	12.3
4 Loans from U.S. government	−.2	−.1	.2	−.3	.....	.....	.....	.....	.7	.9	1.1	.6
5 Private financial sectors	6.9	2.6	14.9	24.9	4.3	12.7	22.8	32.4	15.9	1.1	−4.2	6.3
6 Corporate equities	3.7	3.0	6.4	6.1	4.6	3.3	2.4	.8	1.7	1.8	2.1	1.5
7 *Debt instruments*	3.2	−.4	8.5	18.8	−.3	9.3	20.3	31.6	14.2	−.7	6.3	4.8
8 Corporate bonds	.9	1.3	1.1	1.5	3.1	5.1	7.0	2.3	1.4	3.1	3.0	3.3
9 Mortgages	−.9	1.0	.4	.2	.7	2.1	1.7	−1.2	−1.3	2.3	2.0	2.6
10 Bank loans n.e.c.	−1.0	−2.0	2.5	2.3	−.5	3.0	6.8	13.5	7.5	−5.3	−7.9	−2.7
11 Open market paper and RP's	3.3	1.9	3.6	10.7	−5.0	1.8	4.9	9.8	−.1	3.1	4.6	1.5
12 Loans from FHLB's	.9	−2.5	.9	4.0	1.3	−2.7	*	7.2	6.7	−4.0	−8.1	.2

Only part of summary is shown.   *Insignificant amount   *Source: Federal Reserve Bulletin*, August 1976.

flow-of-funds analysis

1. Also, *money-flow analysis.* A type of accounting that focuses on the circular flow of money throughout the economy, where every expenditure is someone else's receipt and every asset is someone else's liability. Such an analysis gives an overview of the financial relationships among the various economic sectors, showing how the saving of one sector finances the investment of another. It also presents a summary of total borrowing, spending, and lending. Flow-of-funds analyses are published monthly in the *Federal Reserve Bulletin*; part of one is shown in Fig. 29.

2. A type of financial statement that focuses on the funds flowing into and out of an individual firm. See SOURCE AND APPLICATION OF FUNDS STATEMENT.

f.o.b. Abbreviation for *free on board*, a price quotation indicating that the seller is responsible for all costs of a shipment of goods, including responsibility for damage or loss, up to a certain named point. For example, *f.o.b. buyer's plant* means the seller is responsible for the cost of the goods and their transportation and arrival in good condition at the buyer's plant. The buyer takes title to the goods only when they are delivered to its loading dock. Most low-value materials purchased locally are bought on these terms. Similarly, *f.o.b. shipping point* means the seller is responsible for the shipment until it is loaded onto a carrier at a particular shipping point; at that point the buyer takes title to the goods, pays transportation charges direct to the carrier, and is responsible for negotiation of freight damage claims (if any) with the carrier. Many companies prefer to buy key materials on these terms because it gives their traffic department better control over inbound shipments and often makes for a considerable reduction of freight costs.

Food and Agriculture Organization Also, *FAO.* An autonomous special agency of the United Nations engaged in raising the level of nutrition and standard of living of people the world over, through improving the production and distribution of food and other agricultural products and through bettering the living conditions of rural populations. The FAO recommends and promotes national and international action toward these ends, furnishes technical aid when requested by a member govern-

ment, and furthers the exchange of information relating to nutrition, agriculture, forestry, and fisheries, as well as production, distribution, and consumption. The FAO has international headquarters in Rome, Italy, and regional offices on every continent.

Food and Drug Administration Also, *FDA.* A division of the U.S. Department of Health, Education, and Welfare concerned with protecting the nation's health against impure and unsafe foods, drugs, and cosmetics, and other potential hazards by means of regulation, inspection, licensing, development of standards, and extensive product research. It was first established by the Agriculture Appropriation Act of 1931, though similar activities had been carried on under different names from the time the Food and Drug Act of 1906 took effect. See also CONSUMER-PROTECTION LAWS.

food cooperative See under CONSUMER COOPERATIVE.

Food Stamp Program A United States government program of public assistance to low-income American families, which provides food coupons for needy persons. Participants in the program, which is administered by the Food and Nutrition Service of the Department of Agriculture, pay a certain sum of money they might normally spend on food for food coupons with higher monetary value. For example, a family might pay $143 in cash for coupons that will buy $230 worth of food.

forced loan

1. A LOAN (def. 1) that cannot be collected when it matures and hence is extended, by necessity rather than choice.

2. In banking, the loan a bank must make when a depositor overdraws his or her account. By covering the overdraft, the bank extends a loan, which may be converted into a more formal (voluntary) loan if the depositor cannot immediately cover the overdraft.

3. In public finance, a loan to the government that the public is required to extend, through some form of tax, by accepting payment in the form of interest-bearing notes, or some other means. Some economists believe that RESERVE REQUIREMENTS represent a forced loan, since banks must keep definite cash deposits with the central bank that earn no interest.

forced sale An involuntary sale, through a foreclosure or similar circumstances, usually bringing the owner a lower price than he might otherwise have received. The term is sometimes used for a voluntary sale at reduced prices to get rid of overstock, raise cash quickly, or for some other reason.

forced saving The prevention of spending by individuals, which compels them to save more than they ordinarily would. It may occur through a shortage of consumer goods (as in wartime), or as the by-product of a fiscal policy to curb inflation through levying higher taxes, thus limiting consumption. The withholding of earnings from shareholders by a corporation, whose officers may wish to reinvest them rather than pay out dividends, is another form of forced saving, since it prevents shareholders from spending these earnings.

Forced saving also occurs when businesses and governments try to invest more than is available through voluntary saving. For example, if voluntary saving amounts to $1 million, a business can invest $1.5 million in new plant, equipment, and inventory only by drawing additional factors of production (used in making consumer goods), which it accomplishes by simply paying more for them. For example, a farmer may be encouraged to work on a construction project instead of growing corn if the construction company pays sufficiently high wages. This shift in turn causes the supply of consumer goods (corn) to decrease relative to demand. Consequently corn prices rise, and this inflation is a form of forced saving: consumers involuntarily consume less simply because their money buys less, and their saving, due to reduced physical consumption, permits resources to be diverted to capital goods industries. An equivalent form of forced saving occurs in wartime, when the government simply commandeers the factors of production needed to make munitions, leaving a reduced civilian supply that automatically becomes more costly and hence creates a forced saving.

forecasting Predicting future business conditions and the state of the economy on the basis of various statistics describing past and current condi-

tions, particularly those selected as INDICATORS. Forecasting may be concerned with anticipating the ups and downs of the overall BUSINESS CYCLE for the purpose of guiding business and economic planning so as to smooth the peaks and valleys. It also may focus on particular economic phenomena, such as the future price of soda ash or the demand for sheet steel. For business planning, *short-term forecasts,* predicting conditions 3 to 18 months ahead, are used to plan purchasing, inventories, production, and sales. Essentially the business forecaster is concerned with future prices of purchased materials and parts, and future demand for the goods produced. For forecasting demand, a *long-term forecast,* predicting conditions 5 to 15 years ahead, is essential for planning capital investment (increasing production by building new factories, developing new products, acquiring subsidiaries, etc.).

In economic planning, both short- and long-term forecasts are used, chiefly to determine what government policies will best promote growth and price stability. In addition, economists often use *medium-term forecasts,* predicting conditions two to three years ahead. Economists also use the forecasts of the business firms themselves as a basis for forecasting, on the assumption that expectations concerning business conditions will actually influence those conditions. Since about 1950, increasingly sophisticated mathematical techniques have been used in forecasting. In economics the use of the mathematical MODEL has become popular, giving rise to the new discipline of ECONOMETRICS. The gathering and manipulation of data have been enormously facilitated through widespread use of increasingly larger, faster, and more complex computers. Yet despite all these rapid advances, forecasting still involves considerable guesswork and error, and so is far from approaching any true certainty. See also SALES FORECAST.

foreclosure A proceeding undertaken when a mortgage is in default and all efforts to salvage the property for the mortgagor by sale, refinancing, and other means have failed. Through foreclosure the mortgagee can acquire ownership of the property. In the United States methods of foreclosure vary from state to state. In a few states foreclosure is simply by decree, the mortgagee declaring that the mortgagor has lost the right to redeem the property; this procedure, called *strict foreclosure,* is rarely used today. In other states the mortgagee files a foreclosure suit and a court orders the mortgaged property sold at a public auction conducted by an officer of the court. Up to the time of the sale the mortgagor or certain others (a spouse, a second mortgagor, etc.) may pay off the mortgage and ward off foreclosure. Otherwise the highest bidder at the sale usually receives either a certificate of sale stating he will be entitled to a deed if no redemption is made (see under MORTGAGE for explanation) or a deed to the property conveying ownership, free and clear of the rights of the mortgagor. (In some states there is *statutory redemption,* that is, by state law the mortgagor may, within a given period after the sale, still redeem the property upon payment.) In many states the mortgagee himself may hold a sale, usually a public auction, without any court proceedings. Unless specifically stated in the mortgage, the mortgagee may not purchase the property at his own sale (nor, if the mortgage is in the form of a deed of trust, may the trustee), a rule designed to encourage mortgagors to use impartial third parties to run such sales and thereby prevent future disagreement and lawsuits.

foreign aid A policy of giving financial and technical aid to other countries. Such a policy may be undertaken for various reasons: emergency relief in time of war, famine, flood, or other disaster; military aid for defense against a common enemy; enlightened self-interest, that is, building up a poor country in order to improve one's own commerce or to help world trade in general. Aid may take a variety of forms: direct gifts of money (*grants,* or *grants-in-aid*) and equipment; short- or long-term loans, with or without specific conditions of use and/or terms of repayment (see LOAN, def. 2); technical assistance and training programs; aid for particular projects or for broad development programs; sales of surplus food and other goods at advantageous prices. Since World War II American foreign aid, which has averaged roughly 0.2 to 0.5 per cent of gross national product, has gone through three phases. Immediately after the war the emphasis was on relief to wartorn countries. During the 1950s, during the Korean conflict in Asia and the so-called cold war in Europe, emphasis shifted to

building up nations, both economically and militarily, to contain the spread of Communism. By the mid-1970s, with the end of American participation in Vietnam, the emphasis had shifted again, to helping underdeveloped countries. Since 1961 most American aid programs have been coordinated under the AGENCY FOR INTERNATIONAL DEVELOPMENT, but there also has been increasing participation in cooperative ventures with other countries, through the INTERNATIONAL BANK FOR RECONSTRUCTION AND DEVELOPMENT, INTER-AMERICAN DEVELOPMENT BANK, ASIAN DEVELOPMENT BANK, and similar bodies. See also UNDERDEVELOPED NATION.

foreign bill of exchange See under BILL OF EXCHANGE.

foreign corporation In American terminology, a corporation created in a different state or nation. For example, in California corporations chartered either in Ohio or in Germany would be considered foreign.

foreign exchange The mechanism whereby international transactions are settled, that is, the exchange of one country's currency for another's. (Foreign currency itself is also called "foreign exchange.") Such transactions are effected through various instruments, among them bank drafts, bills of exchange, letters of credit, and acceptances. The demand for foreign exchange arises from debts incurred through trade, foreign investment, tourism and other travel abroad, various government needs, and speculation concerning changes in the EXCHANGE RATE. The supply of foreign exchange arises from payments for exported goods and services, gifts and contributions from abroad, the sale of loans and other obligations to foreigners, and the like. Both demand and supply of foreign exchange reflect a nation's balance of trade, the relation of its imports to its exports. These forces, influenced also by government-imposed EXCHANGE CONTROLS, interact in the FOREIGN EXCHANGE MARKET.

foreign exchange market A market where foreign exchange transactions take place, that is, where different currencies are bought and sold. In practice this market is not located in any one place, most transactions being conducted by telephone, wire service, or cable. The modern market is dominated by banks, financial institutions, and exchange brokers who buy and sell foreign currencies and make a profit on the difference between the EXCHANGE RATES and interest rates among the various world financial centers. In addition to the settlement of obligations incurred through investment, purchases, and other trading, the foreign exchange market involves speculation in exchange futures (see FORWARD EXCHANGE). New York and London are the major centers for these transactions. See also ARBITRAGE, def. 1.

foreign exchange reserves The stock of foreign currencies (including bank deposits), gold, and Special Drawing Rights held by a nation to pay its debts to foreigners. See also LIQUIDITY, def. 2.

foreign investment See INTERNATIONAL INVESTMENT.

foreign lending See FOREIGN AID; INTERNATIONAL INVESTMENT.

foreign trade See INTERNATIONAL TRADE.

foreign trade multiplier See MULTIPLIER PRINCIPLE, def. 2.

foreign trade zone See FREE PORT.

foreman In manufacturing, construction, and similar industries, a person in direct charge of production workers, generally considered a member of MIDDLE MANAGEMENT. In the 1930s and early 1940s in the United States, foremen, wanting the advantages of union membership but aware of the disadvantages of belonging to the same unions as the workers they supervised, formed unions of their own. This action was strongly opposed by top management, on the theory that it encouraged foremen to view themselves as employees rather than as management. Foremen, on the other hand, wanted bargaining power, particularly in dealing with employers who sometimes paid them less than some production workers. Under the Taft-Hartley Act of 1947, foremen were allowed to join unions but could be disciplined by their com-

pany if they actually did. The law, together with management's subsequent reappraisal of the foreman's role, greatly undermined the strength of the Foremen's Association, and as a result American foremen have remained largely unorganized.

formula investing A system of investment that attempts to keep a given balance between the stocks and bonds in an investor's portfolio, the ratio of one to the other being altered in accordance with changes in market prices. Basically, the formulas operate on the assumption that one should buy bonds and sell common stocks in a rising market, and sell bonds and buy common stocks in a declining market. There are at least three kinds of formula. One holds that a fixed amount of dollars must always be kept in stocks (or bonds); a second holds that a fixed percentage of the value of total investment should be in stocks, which causes the investor to buy stocks as prices fall and sell them when they rise; a third varies the percentage of the portfolio in common stocks as the market rises and falls. See also DOLLAR AVERAGING.

FORTRAN Acronym for <u>For</u>mula <u>Tran</u>slator, a compiler language used in computer PROGRAMMING, consisting of combinations of algebraic and English statements that can be translated into algebraic notation. It is used chiefly for scientific and mathematical applications.

forward buying Buying at a current price for future delivery, based on the anticipation that prices will rise. The term is used particularly for purchases of commodities whose price is largely determined in a free market (with relatively PURE COMPETITION), such as cotton, wool, copper, lead, sugar, zinc, crude rubber, tin, wheat, and soybeans.

forward exchange A kind of futures market in foreign exchange, used to take advantage of or protect oneself against future changes in the EXCHANGE RATE. For purposes of pure speculation, a buyer may buy the French franc 90 days ahead, for example, hoping that during this period of time the dollar value of the franc will increase by more than the interest that could have been earned on the money during this period. The foreign-exchange dealer who sells these francs, on the other hand, will probably cover the purchase by buying francs at the spot (current market) rate. Forward buying is also used for hedging against the risk that an obligation due in the future will have less than the current value. Thus, a Japanese auto manufacturer selling cars to a British dealer may draw a 90-day bill of exchange for £20,000 on the importing dealer's bank, thus deferring the payment for 90 days. Suppose today the pound sterling is worth $1.60 and in 90 days its value has dropped to $1.55. The exporter stands to lose $.05 × £20,000, or $1,000 on the deal. To protect against such a loss, the exporter might sell £20,000 forward, that is, enter a contract with an exchange dealer whereby the latter agrees to buy, 90 days from now, £20,000 at a price agreed on today. The exporter is then relieved of any risk of loss owing to change in the exchange rate. Similarly, an importer who must pay for goods in a foreign currency at some future time can protect against loss by buying the currency forward at a rate agreed on in advance. Foreign-exchange dealers, like stockbrokers, work on a commission basis and further protect themselves against loss on forward sales by making either forward or spot purchases. Interest may also figure in the transaction (see ARBITRAGE, def. 2).

forwarding agent   See FREIGHT FORWARDER.

foundation   A nonprofit organization set up for charitable or other benevolent purposes, such as supporting scientific research, artistic endeavor, educational institutions, etc. Generally tax-exempt, a foundation usually is organized through a large gift or bequest administered by a board of trustees. Since World War II, a number of foundations have grown so wealthy and powerful that their investment policies have had considerable influence on the securities market, as for example the Ford and Rockefeller foundations, both based in New York, the Gulbenkian Foundation in Lisbon, and the Nuffield Foundation in London.

Fourier, François Charles   A French critic of capitalism (1772–1837) who sought to cure economic and social ills through the establishment of cooperative communities called *phalanstères* ("phalanxes"). Each community of 300 families was to support itself, chiefly through agriculture

and handicrafts, and share in the profits. Of the utopian communities following Fourier's model, the most famous were the North American Phalanx (1843–56) at Red Bank, New Jersey, and Brook Farm (1841–46), near Boston, Massachusetts, with which such intellectual leaders as Ralph Waldo Emerson, Henry David Thoreau, Theodore Parker, Bronson Alcott, Margaret Fuller, and William Ellery Channing were associated. Though some 40 phalanxes were organized in America before the Civil War, largely through the work of Fourier's principal American disciples, Albert Brisbane, George Ripley, and Horace Greeley, none survived after 1860. Traces of Fourier's ideas are to be found in the cooperative movement. Also, they have resurfaced in some of the informal communes set up by young people since the late 1960s, where the emphasis is on sharing possessions, little or no specialization of labor, and a return to rural life and values.

fractional reserve banking   A system of banking in which only a portion (fraction) of deposits are backed by primary BANK RESERVES, used today in all the capitalist countries of the world. In the United States the reserve ratio—the proportion of reserves relative to total deposits—is determined by the Federal Reserve for its member banks and by state law for nonmember banks (see RESERVE REQUIREMENTS). In Great Britain commercial banks are ruled by custom alone in maintaining cash reserves of 8 to 10 per cent of deposits, and an additional 18 to 20 per cent in *secondary reserves* (assets readily convertible into cash, principally short-term government notes). Fractional reserve banking developed early in the history of banking, as bankers realized how remote was the possibility that all depositors would withdraw all their funds at the same time. Regulated by government, fractional reserve banking today is a basic means whereby the monetary authority can control the supply of money (see under MONETARY POLICY for more detailed explanation).

The outstanding feature of fractional reserve banking is the multiplier effect of small changes. Suppose, for example, that for every dollar deposited a bank is required to keep a reserve of $.15. The bank now may lend the remaining $.85 to borrowers or, if it prefers, may invest it in some interest-bearing security. Now suppose a dealer sells $1 million of securities, and the $1 million is deposited in the bank. The bank is obliged to keep only $150,000 in the form of reserves and may lend up to $850,000. In making the loan, no currency actually changes hands. Rather, the bank accepts promissory notes from the borrowers and in exchange credits their accounts. On its balance sheet, loans (assets) and deposits (liabilities) both rise by $850,000. This is the first step, or Stage 1, of what is variously called the *pyramid of credit, multiple expansion of deposits* (or *credit*), or *deposit multiplier*. At the end of Stage 1, deposits have risen by $1,850,000—the original dealer's $1 million plus the borrowers' $850,000 credit. Of the second deposit ($850,000), 85 per cent ($722,500) now may be lent to other borrowers (Stage 2). Again the borrowers' accounts are credited with this amount, of which 15 per cent must be retained as reserves; the remainder may be lent. By means of this process, continued to its theoretical limits, the initial $1 million can, under a 15 per cent reserve requirement, give rise to an expansion of $5.67 million of commercial bank credit and support a total of $6.67

million of new deposits. The deposit-expansion factor for a given amount of excess reserves is the reciprocal of the required reserve ratio: $1/.15 = 6.67$.

In practice, of course, borrowers do not necessarily deposit their checks in the lending bank. However, where they deposit their checks does not affect the outcome: the deposits and reserves are created within the banking system. Further, an individual bank is less concerned with the stage of expansion in which it is participating than with the deposit that it receives, which represents new money, whatever the source. If it maintains a policy of making loans and investments equal to whatever reserves it has in excess of legal requirements, it will be carrying on the expansion process. However, the stages of expansion occur neither simultaneously nor in chronological sequence. Some banks do not use all of their excess reserves, or do so only after a considerable time lag, and others may expand assets on the basis of expected reserve growth (borrowing in order to do so). The process is, in fact, continuous, and may never reach the "final stage" described in Fig. 30.

The opposite process, *deposit contraction*, works

Fig. 30. Stages of fractional reserve banking

	Assets				Liabilities
	Reserves			*Loans and Investments*	*Demand Deposits*
	Total	(Required)	(Excess)		
Initial reserves provided	1,000	150	850	0	1,000
Expansion—Stage 1	1,000	278	722	850	1,850
Stage 2	1,000	386	614	1,572	2,572
Stage 3	1,000	478	522	2,186	3,186
Stage 4	1,000	556	444	2,708	3,708
Stage 5	1,000	623	377	3,125	4,152
Stage 6	1,000	680	320	3,529	4,529
Stage 7	1,000	728	272	3,849	4,849
Stage 8	1,000	769	231	4,121	5,121
Stage 9	1,000	803	197	4,352	5,352
Stage 10	1,000	833	167	4,549	5,549
⋮	⋮	⋮	⋮	⋮	⋮
Stage 20	1,000	961	39	5,448	6,448
⋮	⋮	⋮	⋮	⋮	⋮
Final stage	1,000	1,000	0	5,667	6,667

Through stage after stage of expansion, "money" can grow to a total of 6⅔ times the new reserves supplied to the commercial banking system, as the new deposits created by loans at each stage are added to those created at all earlier stages and those supplied by the initial reserve-creating action.

Source: D. M. Nichols, *Modern Money Mechanics*, rev. ed. (Federal Reserve Bank of Chicago, 1971).

in precisely the same way. Thus, for instance, suppose the Federal Reserve sells a $1 million Treasury bill and is paid with a check drawn on commercial Bank A. When the check clears, Bank A's reserve account at its Federal Reserve Bank is reduced by $1 million. As a result, all commercial banks taken together have $1 million less in deposits and reserves than they had before. The amount of reserves freed by the decline in deposits is $150,000. Unless the banks had excess reserves, they now are left with a reserve deficiency of $850,000. To make up this amount, they will probably sell securities. The buyers of the securities pay for them with checks drawn on their deposit accounts, resulting in a $850,000 decline in securities and deposits, Stage 1 of the contraction process. Now deposits have been reduced by a total of $1.85 million, but there is a reserve deficiency of $722,500, which then is made up by selling more securities or by reducing loans, continuing the contraction process. The contraction multiple is the same as that of deposit expansion, that is, with a reserve requirement of 15 per cent, $1/.15 = 6.67$.

fractional share   Any portion of a single share of stock. Many companies have dividend reinvestment plans, where the cash dividend is automatically reinvested in shares of stock purchased on the open market. This procedure inevitably creates fractional shares.

frame   In statistical sampling (see SAMPLE, def. 1), an analytical layout of the universe from which sample units are to be drawn. For example, in a statistical study of workers, the frame might consist of the files on them kept by the personnel department, or a system of accounts or records kept by the Internal Revenue Service.

franchise
1. A right, usually an exclusive right, granted by a government to an individual or firm, to perform some service or activity of a public nature. For example, the operation of municipal transportation facilities (bus lines, subways) or of public utilities is normally awarded under a franchise. A franchise is similar to a contract in that its terms can be enforced in a court of law. Its duration may vary, from a limited period to perpetual. Franchises usually are administered through a regulatory com-

mission (see PUBLIC SERVICE COMMISSION). See also LICENSE, def. 1.
2. Also, *dealer franchise*. A continuing relationship between a manufacturer or specialist in a service and a retailer, in which the former supplies the latter with manufacturing and/or marketing techniques, a brand image, and other expertise, for a price. This type of operation, common for many years in such American industries as petroleum and auto marketing, has become increasingly prevalent in the hotel, restaurant, and fast-food industries. Such franchises are similar to a voluntary chain (see under CHAIN STORE) except that the latter usually works with established retailers, whereas franchisers prefer to draw newcomers into the business, training them and otherwise helping them get started. Sometimes the franchiser determines the new retailer's site, supervises construction of the store, and handles the initial promotion and opening.

fraud   In law, the intentional misrepresentation of a material fact in order to induce another person to act on it, and consequently to part with some property of value or to surrender some legal right. Fraud is a TORT. The *statute of frauds,* originally enacted by the English Parliament in 1677 and since imitated by a number of states in the United States, stipulates that certain kinds of informal contract must be in writing to be enforceable; among them are contracts for the sale of real estate and for the sale of goods of a certain value. The Uniform Commercial Code instructs courts to construe the statute of frauds liberally, so as to conform to its underlying purposes.

free alongside ship   See F.A.S.

free coinage   Coinage of unlimited quantities of a given metal (or metals). Under this system any person may bring metal—usually gold or silver—to the mint to be made into coins, usually upon payment of a minting charge. (If the minting is performed free of charge the system is called *gratuitous coinage.*) Free coinage into silver dollars was at one time available to the silver miners of the American West.

freedom of entry   The relative ease of going into a business. It usually is calculated in terms of the new seller's costs and revenues compared with those of established sellers. The degree of freedom of entry is an important measure of how competitive a market will be. If entry into an industry is virtually unrestricted, there will be a fairly large number of sellers with little or no influence over the product's price. If barriers—in the form of higher costs or some other restriction—to entering the industry are high, established sellers will have considerable control over price (see IMPERFECT COMPETITION). Barriers to entry may involve technological considerations, economic conditions, or both. Thus, a market in which products are clearly differentiated by brand names—for example, the cigarette industry—may require so great an initial investment in advertising to lure consumers away from established brands that a new producer's costs will be significantly higher than those of established producers. In some industries, such as automobiles and steel, the initial capital investment needed is so high that it constitutes a barrier. Still other barriers to free entry are limited access to raw materials, distance from customers (and concomitant higher transportation costs), legal restrictions such as franchises and patents, and technology. In the United States, among the industries easiest to enter are retailing and textile manufacturing.

free enterprise   See CAPITALISM.

free good   See GOODS.

free lance   A person who works on an independent basis, taking on assignments from one or more employers. The term is used particularly for writers and artists who sell their work to various publishers rather than being employed by one, for musicians who take on temporary engagements rather than working with one particular band or orchestra, as well as for various kinds of business and industrial consultant. The term originally meant a mercenary, a knight or soldier who offered his military services to any ruler for pay, and whose lance was thus free to be hired.

free list   A list of goods that may be freely imported into a country, without payment of customs duties.

free-market commodity   A commodity whose price is largely determined by the impersonal forces of supply and demand, rather than being an ADMINISTERED PRICE. In most modern industrial nations only a few agricultural commodities fall into this category. See PURE COMPETITION.

free on board   See F.O.B.

free port   Also, *admission temporaire, foreign trade zone, free trade zone, free zone.* An area, usually (but not always) adjacent to a port, into which goods may be imported directly without customs inspection or payment of a TARIFF (def. 1). The goods may be stored, processed, and/or repackaged in this area, and then either imported in the normal way (going through customs) or re-exported (without tariff payment). See also FREE TRADE AREA.

free reserves   See under EXCESS RESERVES.

free silver   In American history, the movement for free coinage of silver. See under SILVER STANDARD.

free trade   The removal of all trade barriers in international trade. Supporters of free trade, from Adam Smith and others of the CLASSICAL SCHOOL to present-day economists, argue that only completely unrestricted commerce will give free rein to the principle of comparative ADVANTAGE, resulting in the most efficient production and optimum general economic welfare. Opponents of free trade believe restrictions necessary for protecting health and welfare, national security, encouraging or protecting domestic industries, stimulating home employment during times of economic slowdowns, improving the nation's balance of payments, and assisting the development of poorer countries. See also CORN LAWS; CUSTOMS UNION; FREE TRADE AREA; GENERAL AGREEMENT ON TARIFFS AND TRADE; TARIFF, def. 1; TRADE BARRIER.

free trade area   An agreement between two or more countries to abolish tariffs and other mutual trade barriers. It differs from a CUSTOMS UNION in that each country may retain its own tariffs against other countries, rather than agreeing on a common uniform tariff between the free trade area members and the rest of the world. The European Free Trade Association is a free trade area, whereas the Common Market is a customs union.

freeze A form of PRICE CONTROL and wage control, usually invoked by a central government as a temporary measure to check inflation until some longer-term measures can be formulated or take effect. In essence it holds all prices and/or wages at existing levels, forbidding any increase for a stated period of time. For example, in the United States in August 1971 all prices and wages were frozen for a 90-day period.

freight In general usage, any goods transported by a vehicle or vessel, and/or any charges made for such transport. Strictly speaking, the former should be called *cargo* and the latter *freight,* but in practice the two terms are used interchangeably, and transport charges often are called *freight rates.* The principal carriers of freight in the United States in terms of tonnage carried are the railroads, followed by pipelines, motor vehicles (trucks), barges, and airlines. In revenues, however, trucks account for more than half the combined freight rates paid to all carriers. *Rail freight* for most commodities is the cheapest mode of overland shipment, particularly for commodities in bulk shipped in full carloads (such as wheat, coal, steel ingots). However, companies relying on rail freight need to be located near a railroad siding or have some special arrangement to minimize handling of goods between railroad cars and their final destination (see also PIGGYBACK). *Truck freight* eliminates this problem, since most factories are equipped with a dock to receive truck shipments. For finished manufactured products on short hauls, trucks often are cheaper and faster than rail. *Air shipments,* the most expensive mode of transport, are slowly capturing an increasing share of freight, but still account for only 2 or 3 per cent of total revenues. They are fast and often eliminate the expensive packaging required in trucks or railcars. (See also AIR EXPRESS; AIR FREIGHT.) *Barges* and *pipelines* tend to be very cheap indeed but have several serious limitations. Barges are slow and require either a terminal located at a deep-water port or inland waterway, or some means of economically handling goods between barge and delivery point (see also FISHYBACK). Pipelines are limited to liquids, and in the United States are used primarily for oil and natural gas. They also are the least flexible means of transportation in terms of routes: once laid, they simply cannot be rerouted.

Though some American companies operate their own ships and aircraft, and many have their own trucks, a considerable volume of transportation is purchased, mostly from common carriers. (See COMMON CARRIER; also CONTRACT CARRIER.) Railroads and trucks are classified by the U.S. Interstate Commerce Commission according to the value of the freight they carry (see under CLASS I), which affects how they may set their rates, and they in turn base their rates on the kind and quantity of goods being shipped. Pipelines are regulated by the Federal Power Commission. There are three main kinds of *rail freight rate* (and comparable kinds for other carriers), called class, commodity, and exception; each is quoted for a whole *carload* (*CL,* 60,000–100,000 pounds) and *less-than-carload* (*LCL,* under 60,000 pounds). The trucking equivalents are whole *truckload,* or *TL,* 24,000 pounds or more, and *less-than-truckload,* or *LTL,* under 24,000 pounds. (However, truckload rates for certain light and bulky articles may be much lower, since some expanded plastic items, for example, weigh less than 3 pounds per cubic foot and the average 40-foot truck trailer holds 2,600 cubic feet.) Rates for LCL and LTL vary, but they can be twice as high as those for full loads. These differentials have given rise to numerouse WHOLESALE enterprises that buy and ship in economical large quantities and sell in the smaller amounts their customers need. (See also FREIGHT FORWARDER; POOL CAR.)

A railroad *class rate* is based on a freight classification system that includes some 10,000 different items or groups of items, spelled out in the *Uniform Freight Classification* (the trucking equivalent is the *National Motor Freight Classification*). Each class is assigned rates based on the cost and value of the service, size of shipment, and distance shipped. Most goods handled under class rates are general manufactured items shipped in quantities too small to justify negotiation by shippers. Only about 2 to 4 per cent of the volume of rail-shipped freight falls into this category, which represents the highest rail rates. A *commodity rate* is a rate specifically set for a given commodity, usually shipped between specific points or over particular routes. There are special commodity rates for most items in bulk that are shipped regularly in large volume (wheat, coal, lumber, etc.). Some commodity rates are *blanket rates* (also called *group rates*), with the same rate applying over a large geographical territory regardless of the distances between shipping points within that territory. About 90 per cent of rail freight commands a commodity rate. An *exception rate* is a special lower rate set in consideration of competition, either that faced by the railroad from other carriers or that faced by a producer in more distant markets.

Owing to the many different rates, choosing the most economical means of transportation for a product becomes a highly specialized job (see also TRAFFIC). Moreover, transportation can account for a sizable percentage of cost—55 per cent in the case of sand and gravel (traveling by rail), 20 per cent for iron ore (but less than 2 per cent for cigarettes or butter). In practice, however, large shippers are able to exert some influence on the rates they pay, so for them, at least, it is more a question of successful negotiation than of having to choose among a wide range of rates.

freight absorption   The practice of a seller's paying part or all of the freight charges for goods sold. When this practice results in charging different prices to different buyers of the same goods (because distant buyers ordinarily would have to pay more freight than nearby ones), it may constitute a violation of antitrust laws. (See also DELIVERED PRICING.) Occasionally a carrier pays for some of the freight charges by not passing on the charges for switching, terminals, etc. to the shipper.

freight-allowed pricing   See DELIVERED PRICING.

freight equalization   See under DELIVERED PRICING.

freight forwarder   Also, *forwarding agent*. A middleman in the business of wholesaling transportation. A freight forwarder accumulates small shipments from numerous shippers and combines them into larger quantities (full truckloads or carloads) to obtain lower freight rates, making a profit on some of the difference in rates for small and large shipments. Such firms are particularly useful for export shipments, where they help take care of much of the complicated paperwork involved. See also FREIGHT.

frequency distribution   In statistics, the organization of data to show how often certain values or ranges of values occur. For example, a frequency distribution might show the number of families with annual incomes between $5,000 and $6,000, $6,000 and $7,000, $7,000 and $8,000, and so on, or the weekly wages of production workers, the populations of towns and cities, etc. An important feature of a frequency distribution is the *class interval*, that is, the size of grouping selected. For example, the class interval in the family income distribution cited above is $1,000 (6,000 − 5,000 = 1,000). (If class intervals were not used, one would have to cite every single individual income between $5,000 and the highest value; such specific figures are termed an *array*.) Ideally class intervals are equal (as above, not $5,000−6,000, $6,000−7,500, $7,500−8,000) and neither so narrow nor so wide that too few or too many values fall into each class, concealing the pattern of distribution. A frequency distribution may be presented graphically by means of a *histogram* or bar chart (see Fig. 31), by a polygon, or by a curve (see Fig. 59). See also BINOMIAL DISTRIBUTION; CUMULATIVE DISTRIBUTION; NORMAL DISTRIBUTION; POISSON DISTRIBUTION.

frictional unemployment   Unemployment owing to job changes that result from a changing demand for labor, in turn caused by changes in consumer demand, new legislation, plant relocations, or similar factors. The term "frictional" comes from the theories of the MARGINALIST SCHOOL of economics, which held that "frictions" interfere with the free, smooth interaction of demand and supply in a perfect market. Frictional unemployment differs from

Fig. 31. Histogram of nonproduction workers' wages

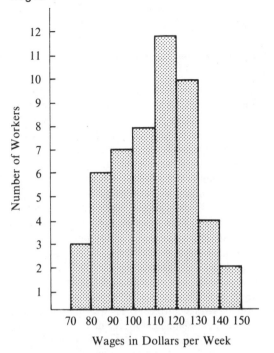

Wages in Dollars per Week

pansion, the rigid rate of money increase would automatically check inflation, since in effect the economy would run out of money. The period of adjustment would be mild, and the economy then would gradually expand again as the money supply continued to grow at its fixed rate. Another idea he subscribed to is the PERMANENT-INCOME HYPOTHESIS.

Friedman opposed the full-employment goal of J. M. KEYNES and his followers; he believed it would automatically cause inflation, since with such a policy the money supply would have to grow unduly fast. In general Friedman stood for a high degree of individual freedom and minimum government interference with the market mechanism. He proposed abolishing such institutions as the postal system and the public schools (instead of the latter, the state would give students coupons to attend private schools of their choice). He also advanced the idea of a *negative income tax*, whereby all unemployable persons would simply be given a check, enabling abolition of the elaborate bureaucratic apparatus of welfare (including the social security system). Friedman was awarded the Nobel Memorial Prize in Economic Science in 1976.

STRUCTURAL UNEMPLOYMENT in that it is generally short in duration, lasting only as long as it takes to find a new job. However, delays may be caused by lack of information about jobs, lack of mobility (transportation problems, time needed to relocate), or the need for retraining. Frictional unemployment is unrelated to the business cycle and other large-scale economic factors, and presumably will continue to exist even when jobs outnumber workers.

Friedman, Milton An American economist (1912–), noted member of the CHICAGO SCHOOL. In essence a follower of Alfred MARSHALL, Friedman adhered to the QUANTITY THEORY OF MONEY, holding that the size of the money supply regulates prices and employment. He therefore advocated a fixed annual increase of 3 to 4 per cent in the U.S. money supply, to be made regardless of economic conditions, on the theory that this would be just enough to equal the long-term trend of American economic growth. During periods of business ex-

fringe benefit Any of a number of payments—in the form of cash, goods, or services—made to employees in addition to basic wages and salaries. They range from time off with pay (for coffee breaks, lunch hours, vacations) and provisions against various contingencies (accident, illness, disability) to profit-sharing plans and deferred wages (pay after retirement), as well as a variety of miscellaneous services. In the United States some fringe benefits are required by law, notably old-age, survivors, disability, and health insurance, unemployment compensation, workmen's compensation, and, in some industries, certain taxes. On the whole, however, these compulsory benefits amount to but a fraction of the cost of fringe benefits to American employers, which represents a substantial (and growing) part of total labor costs, in some cases as much as 30 per cent of the total payroll.

Frisch, Ragnar A Norwegian statistician and economist (1895–19), originator of the term ECONOMETRICS. In 1969 he was awarded the first

Nobel Memorial Prize in Economic Science (along with the Dutch economist Jan Tinbergen). He is regarded as the father of the modern planned economies of Scandinavia.

front-end load plan Also, *contractual plan.* A form of MUTUAL FUND that allows an investor to accumulate shares in the fund by regularly paying a given sum of money over a period of time, such as $50 per month for ten years. However, the contract usually provides that about half of the payments in the first year are deducted for the "load"—that is, sales commissions and other expenses, consisting of a percentage of the *total* contract. Therefore, unless the investor remains in the plan for some years, he or she loses out because of the high commission paid at the beginning (whence the name "front-end"). See also UNIT INVESTMENT TRUST.

front-end processor An auxiliary device that handles the input and output of data to a main computer's central processing unit. Generally used as part of a TIME SHARING system, the front-end computer may either be local or operate as a remote terminal station.

frozen asset An ASSET not readily convertible into cash within a reasonable time or without a considerable loss. Examples include inventories of obsolete goods, land that for some reason is not readily salable (perhaps because of some defect in title), or some property that cannot legally be sold.

full cost In accounting, the direct cost of a product (purchased direct material plus direct labor) plus allocated overhead. A company's "full cost" is equal to the actual total unit cost of a product only if sales volume is equal to expectations. For example, suppose a product has direct material cost of $1 per unit and direct labor cost of $.50, making its total direct cost $1.50. If the company has general overhead expenses of $1 million per year and expects to sell 1 million units of that product, it must recoup $1 of overhead from each sale if it is to recover its full cost, which is then equal to $2.50 ($1.50 direct cost plus $1 overhead). If sales fall short of 1 million units, overhead is said to be *underabsorbed* and profits are less than expected; if

sales exceed 1 million units, overhead is *overabsorbed* and profits will exceed expectations.

full-cost pricing See AVERAGE COST, def. 2.

full coverage See under DEDUCTIBLE COVERAGE.

full employment The availability of work at prevailing wage rates for all persons who desire it. Full employment does not mean 100 per cent employment. There always is some unemployment, owing to job changes, seasonal factors, etc. Most economists define full employment as meaning that a given percentage—conventionally 96 per cent —of the work force is employed, or that unemployment is no higher than 4 per cent. Most economists (but not all) consider full employment a highly desirable goal for any economy, since it often is equated with maximum utilization of economic resources: land, labor, capital. In real life, full-employment programs focus primarily on providing jobs for all who want them. However, difficulties arise when aggregate demand is not large enough (in which case there is unemployment) or when it is too large (producing inflation). An additional problem is that workers' skills are not necessarily compatible with either demand or technology. Thus, it is possible simultaneously to experience excessive unemployment of persons whose abilities do not fit employers' needs and shortages (with accompanying inflation) of personnel whose skills are in high demand. Governments try to help through training programs and other means to assist workers adjust to employer needs. To maintain aggregate full employment, the government may enact monetary and fiscal policies to encourage business expansion. However, these policies also stimulate price inflation. Indeed, the United States has begun to suffer from severe inflation whenever unemployment has fallen much below 4 per cent, and even this goal has been achieved only occasionally since 1950. See also under J. M. KEYNES.

full-employment budget A theoretical FEDERAL BUDGET that projects what receipts, outlays, and surplus or deficit would occur under given U.S. tax laws and spending programs if the economy were operating at full capacity (traditionally defined as employment of 96 per cent of the civilian labor force). A concept developed after World War II, the full-employment budget discounts the effect of the BUILT-IN STABILIZERS that operate automatically when the economy is not at full employment, and thus helps disclose the effect of discretionary (purposeful) fiscal policy.

full-employment output See POTENTIAL GROSS NATIONAL PRODUCT; also FULL EMPLOYMENT.

full-line forcing See TYING RESTRICTIONS.

full-service Describing a bank, wholesaler, or other enterprise that provides all of the services traditionally associated with that line of business. A full-service bank provides saving, checking, lending, and other facilities; a full-service advertising agency provides market research, creation of ads and campaigns, placing of ads with media, and various other services. For *full-service wholesaler*, see under WHOLESALE.

functional discount A discount granted according to the buyer's position—or function—in the chain of distribution from manufacturing to retailing. The greater the distance between the ultimate consumer and buyer, the larger the discount; thus wholesalers and other middlemen get bigger discounts than retailers. Sellers have long followed the practice of classifying customers in this way, dividing them into noncompeting groups (manufacturing, wholesaling, retailing). Were the buyers competing with one another, such discounts would represent price discrimination and would be illegal. Therefore the U.S. Federal Trade Commission has strict rules as to how customers may be classified. The classifications may not be arbitrary and must conform closely to the nature of the operations undertaken by the customers. Further, all buyers at the same level—for example, independent retailers, chain stores, and mail-order houses, all of which are on the retail level—must be considered to be in the same class.

funded debt The debt of a business or government in the form of outstanding bonds and other long-term notes. The debt is "funded" to differentiate it from short-term borrowing (called FLOATING DEBT) that presumably covers temporary needs for cash. See also FUNDING, def. 2.

funding
1. In general usage, providing money to finance a particular project. Thus one speaks of a grant "funding" a research study, and such a study is said to be "funded."
2. The conversion of short-term obligations (accounts payable) into long-term obligations, such as a bond. Funding is frequently undertaken when businesses wish to take advantage of the more favorable terms of long-term debt (specifically lower interest rates) and also to postpone the date when loans must be repaid. It is used also by governments in their efforts to manage the PUBLIC DEBT.
3. The establishment of a reserve of cash or other assets (often in a separate account or a trust) to enable payment of a future liability, such as taxes, pensions, etc.

futures market A market in which contracts for the future delivery of commodities are bought and sold. (For a similar market in foreign exchange, see FORWARD EXCHANGE.) The contracts themselves are called *futures*. Futures trading often takes place on an organized COMMODITY EXCHANGE, such as the Chicago Board of Trade, and futures prices are commonly listed in the financial pages of leading newspapers. A futures contract is an agreement to deliver or to receive some commodity at a specified price at some specified future time. If, in April, a trader believes the price of cotton will fall by September, he may sell futures contracts for September delivery; if, on the other hand, he believes the price will rise, he may buy futures contracts. The chief function of speculation in futures is to protect processors, manufacturers, and other users of basic commodities against unfavorable price fluctuations. Such protection is afforded by hedging, that is, taking an opposite position in futures from the position taken in the SPOT MARKET (for immediate delivery; see further explanation under HEDGING). The U.S. Commodity Futures Trading Commission sets a limit, called the *trading limit*, on the quantity of futures that may be bought or sold by one individual or in one trading day. See also RINGING OUT.

In recent years, the futures market has been extended to U.S. Treasury bills and to government-guaranteed mortgages, or Ginnie Maes (see GOVERNMENT NATIONAL MORTGAGE ASSOCIATION), in effect allowing traders to speculate on changes in future interest rates.

Fig. 32. Futures trading (partial listing)

CHICAGO BOARD OF TRADE

Season's High	Low		Week's High	Low	Close Last	Prev.	Open Int.
WHEAT (5,000 bu)							
5.13	2.98	Sep	4.50	4.02	4.47½	4.16¾	31,585
	3.07½	Dec	4.67	4.14	4.63	4.33½	99,010
4.79½	3.16½	Mar	4.79½	4.25½	4.76¾	4.45½	40,715
4.81	3.20	May	4.81	4.29	4.77½	4.49	20,910
4.64½	3.82	Jul	4.64½	4.09½	4.56½	4.29½	5,525
Sales: Sep 55,185; Dec 197,080; Mar 39,120; May 8,125; Jul 5,535							
CORN (5,000 bu)							
3.88½	2.46	Sep	3.30¾	3.11½	3.21	3.20½	51,005
3.55	2.32½	Dec	3.30¼	3.10	3.22¼	3.18¾	208,385
3.59½	2.39	Mar	3.37½	3.18	3.29¼	3.27¼	116,460
3.41	2.44½	May	3.41	3.22	3.32½	3.31¾	59,190
3.42	2.48	Jul	3.42	3.24	3.33½	3.33	7,275
Sales: Sep 80,170; Dec 314,305; Mar 87,420; May 22,155; Jul 5,545							
OATS (5,000 bu)							
1.80	1.22¼	Sep	1.80	1.70½	1.74¼	1.72½	2,900
1.88	1.24½	Dec	1.77¼	1.67	1.72½	1.71	7,275
1.76½	1.36½	Mar	1.76½	1.67	1.73¼	1.70½	2,970
1.76	1.39	May	1.76	1.67	1.73½	1.71½	980
Sales: Sep 3,240; Dec 9,080; Mar 2,670; May 890							
SOYBEANS (5,000 bu)							
9.61	4.82	Aug	6.49	6.05	— —	6.25	560
9.15	4.74	Sep	6.45	6.07	6.16	6.29¼	24,395
8.69	4.76	Nov	6.52½	6.12	6.22¾	6.34	113,345
8.60	4.81	Jan	6.63½	6.21	6.31	6.43½	59,800
6.59	4.91	Mar	6.72	6.30½	6.41¼	6.55	60,845
6.80	4.98	May	6.80	6.38	6.48½	6.62½	40,245
6.85	5.04	Jul	6.85	6.43	6.52	6.68	13,160
6.81	5.04	Aug	6.81	6.42	6.51	6.67	4,630
Sales: Aug 7,990; Sep 38,780; Nov 284,645; Jan 51,390; Mar 19,960; May 15,585; Aug 95							
SOYBEAN OIL (60,000 lbs)							
44.30	19.75	Aug	28.80	26.92	— —	28.70	311
43.70	19.15	Sep	27.82	25.10	26.18	27.82	5,234
32.75	18.40	Oct	27.00	24.20	25.20	27.00	4,569
30.90	17.75	Dec	26.20	23.30	24.38	26.15	6,984
28.50	17.55	Jan	25.75	23.30	24.03	25.70	3,026
27.35	17.45	Mar	25.45	23.10	23.90	25.45	2,993
27.10	17.25	May	25.30	23.05	23.70	25.20	2,498
26.65	16.90	Jul	25.00	23.00	23.62	25.00	2,264
26.00	16.90	Aug	24.50	23.00	23.50	24.75	512
Sales: Aug 2,303; Sep 7,522; Oct 3,773; Dec 11,890; Jan 1,635; Mar 1,069; May 468; Jul 288; Aug 26							
SOYBEAN MEAL (100 tons)							
212.00	115.00	Aug	145.00	140.00	— —	148.00	39
211.00	118.00	Sep	159.00	142.00	151.70	149.80	3,111
170.00	121.10	Oct	161.50	145.00	153.50	153.00	4,246
167.00	123.00	Dec	167.00	150.50	157.90	158.50	7,045
170.00	125.50	Jan	170.00	154.50	160.00	161.20	1,992
175.00	128.30	Mar	175.00	157.00	163.50	164.50	1,772
173.50	132.00	May	173.50	163.00	166.50	166.00	501
178.50	136.00	Jul	178.50	169.00	170.00	171.30	273
180.50	144.00	Aug	180.50	167.00	171.50	172.50	62
Sales: Aug 745; Sep 3,954; Oct 2,831; Dec 11,252; Jan 1,980; Mar 760; May 54; Jul 60; Aug 73							

Season's High	Low		Week's High	Low	Close Last	Prev.	Open Int.
GOLD BULLION (100 troy oz)							
209.00	159.00	Sep	163.90	161.30	162.20	162.90	2,205
215.00	162.80	Dec	167.90	165.30	166.00	166.90	3,165
200.50	167.20	Mar	172.50	169.90	170.50	171.40	1,983
227.00	172.00	Jun	176.90	174.50a	175.10	175.80	1,573
195.00	177.00	Sep	181.60b	179.60	179.90	178.80	480
197.00b	181.50a	Dec	180.60b	184.50a	185.00	185.00	48
Sales: Sep 3,731; Dec 2,407; Mar 324; Jun 69; Sep 21; Dec 14							
N.Y. MERCANTILE EXCHANGE							
MAINE POTATOES (500 CWT)							
8.94	4.15	Nov.	8.94	7.17	8.70	7.65	5,926
11.50	5.00	Mar	11.50	8.75	11.50	9.14	4,141
12.56	5.40	Apr	12.56	9.97	12.56	10.06	1,526
14.28	5.92	May	14.28	11.88	14.28	11.78	9,953
Sales: 24,398.							
PLATINUM (50 troy oz)							
253.00	144.30	Oct	178.00	168.60	177.50	169.50	2,351
244.50	149.00	Jan	183.00	173.10	182.60	173.70	1,574
211.00	151.70	Apr	187.50	178.40	187.20	178.20	1,730
193.70	156.30	Jul	192.00	182.30	192.00b	182.50	313
196.00	162.40	Oct	195.00	187.00	193.70	178.80	149
198.50	189.50	Jan	198.50	192.10	199.70b	191.00	5
Sales: 2,376.							
SILVER COINS (10-$1,000 bags)							
4300	2965	Oct	3525	3365	3410a	3475	1,066
4040	3020	Jan	3526	3450	3490b	3560	1,452
3890	3085	Apr	3575	3540	3575b	3645	857
3960	3125	Jul	3760	3640	3663b	3730	641
4010	3395	Oct	3820	3701	3748	3815	658
4164	3935	Jan	3950	3935	3850a	3900	88
Sales: 287.							
a-Asked. b-Bid. n-Nominal. s-Split.							
N.Y. COFFEE AND SUGAR EXCHANGE							
SUGAR NO. 11 (112,000 lbs)							
56.05	10.40	Sep	20.70	17.05	17.15	20.88	2,300
535.55	11.00	Oct	20.35	16.95	16.95	20.33	7.961
18.90	14.10	Jan	17.70	17.70	17.29n	19.75	3
45.45	11.00	Mar	19.40	15.89	15.89	19.35	11,969
28.65	11.10	May	19.10	15.64	15.64	19.00	3,271
25.10	11.05	Jul	18.95	15.40	15.40	18.75	2,974
19.08	11.05	Sep	18.60	15.25	15.35n	18.45	1,228
18.95	11.00	Oct	18.45	15.10		18.30	1,776
Sales: 23,318.							
COFFEE 'C' (37,500 lbs)							
87.75	49.10	Sep	87.75	83.35	83.86b	86.20	467
86.50	49.70	Nov	86.50	85.00	85.50	85.40	41
87.00	49.75	Dec	87.10	84.25	84.60s	84.65	1,076
86.10	49.80	Mar	86.10	83.80	84.10	84.35	821
86.90	51.80	May	86.90	84.10	84.35b	85.10	338
86.90	83.50	Jul	86.90	85.25	85.00n	85.70	72
Sales: 1,509.							
B+Bid. n-Nominal. s-Split.							

Source: Barron's Weekly, September 25, 1976.

Galbraith, John Kenneth A Canadian-born American economist (1908–) who became known for his biting criticism of neoclassical economics (Alfred MARSHALL and his followers) and his attempt to construct new theories to explain modern economic realities, particularly the large corporation, economic planning, and a market in which producers exercise considerable control. In *American Capitalism* (1952) Galbraith said that the market is far from competitive; instead, the large corporations are extremely powerful, and to counteract their influence and restrain them, the COUNTERVAILING POWER of government and labor unions has developed. In *The Affluent Society* (1958) he attacked the concept of economic growth for its own sake, which has produced a supposedly rich society in which the rich become richer and the poor poorer. In such an economy, advertising "creates" new "needs," inflation is rampant, much of the nation's budget goes to military spending, and there is no market machinery to allocate national resources to needed public spending. In *The New Industrial State* (1967) Galbraith claimed that the large corporations have created a new social class, the *technostructure*, which is more interested in perpetuating itself than in profit-making.

galloping inflation See RUNAWAY INFLATION.

gambling In economics, making predictions on the basis of one or more unknown variables. See GAMES THEORY; PROBABILITY THEORY.

games theory A branch of mathematics first introduced in 1928 by the Hungarian-American mathematician John von Neumann (1903–57) and subsequently elaborated, by him and others, to be applied to economic problems. Essentially, games theory uses mathematical processes that take into account variables beyond the mathematician's control, a situation prevailing in games of strategy, in wartime, and in the real-life economy. For example, indefinitely declining retail prices eventually must result in lower profits for the retailer (if wholesale prices do not also drop). Charging higher prices than a competitor's also results in lower profits if customers are lost to the competitor. Yet if Retailer A lowers prices in order to win back customers, Retailer B may follow suit, and if they continue in this fashion, both A and B must lose. It is to A's advantage, then, to figure out just what price will make customers keep on buying from him without stimulating a price-cutting reaction from B. Games theory can help determine the most advantageous strategy. The classic text on the subject, *Theory of Games and Economic Behavior* (1944), was written by Von Neumann in collaboration with Oskar Morgenstern.

gang punching See under PUNCHED-CARD DATA PROCESSING.

Gantt chart A graphic means of comparing a production schedule with actual performance, or an employee's performance with a predetermined standard. Named for its inventor, H. L. Gantt, an American engineer, the chart includes a schedule for all the elements of a job, or, in the case of a job order shop, for each job. Slack time, if required (to guard against bottlenecks or to allow for readjusting machines to accommodate new work), is also included, and movable arrows indicate the actual progress being made. Fig. 33 shows a Gantt chart for a job shop with just three machines (lathe, milling machine, and drill press). The chart shows progress against the backlog of orders as of week 7; the arrows show actual progress on the machines, while the line after week 7 shows scheduled

Fig. 33. Gantt chart

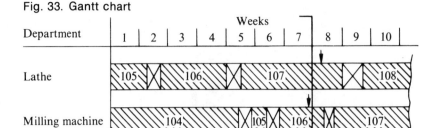

Source: D. S. Ammer, *Manufacturing Management and Control* (New York: Appleton-Century-Crofts, 1968), p. 129. Reprinted by permission of Prentice-Hall, Inc.

progress. The areas marked X are scheduled slack time for setting up machines, and the white areas represent periods for which no work was scheduled. Probably because of its essential simplicity, which enables managers to tell at a glance which operations are behind schedule, the Gantt chart is one of the most widely used instruments of PRODUCTION CONTROL. See also PERT.

Gantt premium plan See under WAGE INCENTIVE.

garnishment In law, a procedure whereby the property, wages, money, or credits of a debtor are taken away and paid to his or her creditors. The term is most often used for the taking of wages, which then are paid direct to the employee's creditor. In the United States, state laws concerning garnishment differ widely, some prohibiting it entirely. See also ATTACHMENT.

GATT Abbreviation for GENERAL AGREEMENT ON TARIFFS AND TRADE.

General Accounting Office, U.S. See under CONTROLLER.

General Agreement on Tariffs and Trade Also, *GATT*. An international body devoted to eliminating import quotas, lowering tariffs, and otherwise promoting free, nondiscriminatory international trade. Begun as an agreement among 23 nations at the *Geneva Trade Conference* of 1947, it has sponsored negotiations and agreements among many more nations (76 members by 1971) and effected literally thousands of tariff concessions. One round of negotiations, known as the *Kennedy Round* (for U.S. President John F. Kennedy) and lasting from 1964 to 1967, ended in a one-third across-the-board reduction of all tariffs by 49 countries (accounting for about 80 per cent of world trade; China and the Soviet Union were the only big trading nations that did not participate). Members of GATT also agree to honor the *most-favored-nation clause*, whereby trade concessions are passed on to other trading countries (see under TARIFF, def. 1). However, members of CUSTOMS UNIONS, which have no tariffs among themselves, are exempt. Also, various special concessions have been made to aid underdeveloped countries, notably to lower tariffs and quotas for their products in particular, and, from 1971 on, the United States, Common Market, and European Free Trade Association agreed to give preferences in certain manufactured goods to the underdeveloped nations for at least a ten-year period.

Although GATT was made possible by growing sentiment in favor of freer trade after World War II, by the 1970s it faced a new wave of protectionism on the part of both the Common Market and the United States. Both tended to make preferential trade agreements with other nations, and the

United States also resumed protecting home industry (by such means as basing tariffs on imports on the selling price of similar domestic products).

general equilibrium theory The theory that in many instances the interrelationships among the many variables in an economy as a whole, particularly concerning prices and outputs, must be analyzed so as to yield valid principles and policies. Developed in the 19th century by Léon WALRAS, general equilibrium theory attempts to show mathematically the effect of a single change—as in the price of milk—on the entire economy. Where PARTIAL EQUILIBRIUM THEORY might conclude that consumers will simply buy less milk when the price rises, general equilibrium analysis would also consider related changes in both production and consumption of various milk-based products (butter, cheese, ice cream, etc.), the use of substitutes (margarine, nonfat dry milk, etc.), shifts in capital investment and labor and machinery, and so on. However, a modern economy is so complex that it is difficult to specify all the interrelationships among the many variables. INPUT-OUTPUT ANALYSIS, developed half a century later, can be used to quantify the theoretical relationships of general equilibrium theory, as can the large MACROECONOMIC models developed by the Brookings Institution and other research organizations.

general journal See under JOURNAL.

general mortgage bond See under MORTGAGE BOND.

General Services Administration Also, *GSA*. An independent U.S. government agency that serves as the Federal government's housekeeper, managing both property and records. The GSA is in charge of constructing and operating buildings, procuring and distributing supplies, using and disposing of property, managing transport, traffic, and communications, stockpiling STRATEGIC MATERIALS, and administering automatic data processing.

general store See under RETAIL.

general strike A STRIKE called by all or most of the workers in all or most industries simultane-

ously. It may involve a city (as did the San Francisco general strike of 1934) or an entire country. Its purpose usually is not so much one of gaining specific concessions as it is to put political pressure on a government or to demonstrate the unity of the labor movement. General strikes have occurred periodically in France and Italy since World War II.

Geneva Trade Conference See under GENERAL AGREEMENT ON TARIFFS AND TRADE.

gentlemen's agreement In business and industry, an informal agreement secured by the word of the parties involved rather than by a written contract. Since there is no written evidence of its existence, such an agreement nearly always involves illegal or unethical practices, such as dividing markets, fixing prices, discriminating against particular buyers or sellers, etc.

George, Henry An American social reformer and public figure (1839–97) remembered chiefly for his proposal to have a *single tax*, on land, replace all other taxes. A firsthand observer of land speculation (in San Francisco in 1868, after the first transcontinental railroad was completed), George protested against the evils of profiteering and political corruption in *Progress and Poverty* (1879), which was published partly at his own expense and became a runaway bestseller. George maintained that a nation's produce was equal to the sum of rent, interest, and wages. Or, transposing the equation, produce minus rent is equal to interest plus wages. Since economic progress brings rises in rent (because the supply of land is fixed), most of a nation's gains in production will be absorbed by increasing rents instead of being reflected in higher wages and interest. The only solution, George said, is to tax all rent accruing from land ownership; improvements on the land (buildings, etc.), however, should remain untaxed. With such a tax, there would be no land speculation and no monopolies on land holdings. Moreover, tax revenues would be large enough to allow for the abolition of all other taxes. Further, land is the only factor of production where supply cannot be reduced if it is taxed. Hence, a single tax on land is ideal because in the absence of taxes all other factors would expand, bringing general prosperity. Although George was no doctrinaire socialist, his ideas influenced the Fabian socialists and other social critics, among them Leo Tolstoy and Thorstein Veblen. George ran for Mayor of New York City in 1886 as the labor candidate but lost. In 1897 he ran again as a third-party candidate but died suddenly just before the election.

German historical school   A group of 19th-century thinkers who, reacting against the abstract, deductive approach of the CLASSICAL SCHOOL, maintained that economic theory must be based on the documented history and actual observation of real economic institutions. Since economic affairs are constantly changing and evolving, economic laws cannot be static principles if they are to be valid. Further, they felt that the classical economists had overemphasized human materialistic concerns and had neglected the influence of ideals, both individual and group (nationalistic). Opposing the doctrine of LAISSEZ FAIRE, the historical school believed that the state had to interfere in economic affairs. The most important members of the school, which was influential from the 1840s until the beginning of World War I, were Friedrich LIST, Wilhelm ROSCHER, Gustave SCHMOLLER, Werner SOMBART, and Max WEBER. Some historians distinguish between an "older" and "younger" historical school, the former seen as wanting to supplement classical theory, and the latter as wishing to replace it entirely with historical studies.

Giffen goods   Also, *Giffen paradox*. See under INFERIOR GOOD.

gift tax   A tax on gifts of property, levied by the U.S. Federal government and by many state governments, primarily to prevent evasion of inheritance and estate taxes. The Federal gift tax is levied against the donor, and, like the DEATH TAX, its rate is proportionate to the value of the gift.

Gilbreth, Frank B.   An American engineer, building contractor, and management consultant (1868–1924) who was a pioneer in motion study, as well as in other areas of business and industrial management. Gilbreth devised methods of detecting wasteful, unproductive movements, breaking each job down into its minutest components. First applying his ideas in his own contracting firm, from 1912 on he devoted himself entirely to management engineering, concentrating especially on developing efficient physical working methods. Gilbreth was the first to use a motion-picture camera to record and analyze work motions. After his death his work was carried on by his widow and long-time collaborator, *Lillian E. M. Gilbreth* (1878–1972), a trained psychologist and teacher who lectured on and taught management extensively until her death. See also TIME AND MOTION STUDY.

gilt-edged security   Any security of exceptionally high quality, very likely to pay interest or dividends. The term is used more for bonds than for stocks. See also BLUE CHIP.

Ginnie Mae   Nickname for GOVERNMENT NATIONAL MORTGAGE ASSOCIATION.

glut   An oversupply on the market, which is then said to be "glutted." One of the first to use the term was Thomas MALTHUS, who feared the consequences of what he called a "general glut," a flood of goods on the market, leading to a widespread depression. Unlike his contemporary, David RICARDO, Malthus believed that human demand was not insatiable and that effective demand can be reduced by the process of saving. Though he never worked out his ideas in detail, Malthus appears to have discovered the phenomenon of the business cycle. See also DOLLAR GLUT.

GNP   Commonly used abbreviation for GROSS NATIONAL PRODUCT.

GNP deflator   A revision in the calculation of GNP, or GROSS NATIONAL PRODUCT, based on the appropriate indexes for each of its components, in order to take into account current inflation. The GNP deflator thus is an index obtained from other indexes. For example, the consumer expenditure component of GNP is adjusted for price change—that is, deflated—by dividing each category of consumer spending by the appropriate CONSUMER PRICE INDEX. Business expenditures for capital equipment, raw materials, and semifinished goods similarly are deflated by the relevant index of wholesale prices. In addition, other indexes—of construction costs, prices paid by farmers, import prices, etc.—are used to deflate the other components of GNP. The resulting aggregate index is a mixture of the effects of all these different indexes.

go-go fund See under MUTUAL FUND.

going public See under ISSUE.

gold bloc The major trading countries of the world that continued to adhere to the GOLD STANDARD in the 1930s, after Great Britain and most other nations using the pound sterling had abandoned it (see STERLING AREA). As a result, France, Belgium, and other gold-bloc countries had currencies that were overvalued in relation to the devalued pound sterling (and U.S. dollar) and, unwilling to devalue, were forced to impose import controls and other measures restricting trade.

gold certificate In the United States, a form of paper money fully backed by gold bullion and issued by the Treasury. Gold certificates were in free circulation from 1865 to 1933, when the United States went off the gold standard, so that certificates, no longer convertible into gold, were withdrawn from circulation. Thereafter they were issued only to Federal Reserve banks, which were required to back at least 25 per cent of all deposits and notes in circulation with this GOLD RESERVE. However, the Federal Reserve did not really control gold certificates, since it had to buy all the gold certificates issued to it by the Treasury. The Treasury in turn used the gold certificates to reimburse itself for gold purchases. See also GOLD STERILIZATION.

gold-exchange standard A form of the GOLD STANDARD in which a central bank's reserves are held in the form of both gold and RESERVE CURRENCY convertible into gold. Adopted by various countries after World War I, countries on the gold-exchange standard do not convert their currency into gold on demand (as those on the gold standard must) but instead buy or sell the currency of some gold-standard nation at a fixed price.

gold flow Also, *gold movements*. The movement of gold into and out of a country, which directly affects its GOLD RESERVE and therefore its money supply. According to the classical economists, who believed in the QUANTITY THEORY OF MONEY (that the amount of money in circulation directly affects price levels), the gold flow in the long run automatically rectifies imbalances in international payments. Although this concept would appear to work in theory, governments have always intervened to offset or prevent this effect. The government receiving the gold "sterilizes" it to prevent inflation (see GOLD STERILIZATION), and the government losing gold either borrows or devalues its currency and thereby prevents the deflation that would otherwise occur.

gold point See under GOLD STANDARD.

gold reserve The stock of gold held by a country to cover its own currency issues, make international payments, and provide a reserve for future expansion of its money supply. In the United States the Gold Standard Act of 1900 created a reserve fund of about $150 million in gold and set up various regulations for maintaining a gold reserve. The Gold Reserve Act of 1934 nationalized gold—that is, from then on all gold produced domestically or imported automatically had to be bought by the U.S. Treasury—and specified that Federal Reserve banks had to cover at least 25 per cent of their notes and deposits with gold certificates. (In 1974 a new law was passed that once more allowed Americans to buy and sell gold freely.) Today most Western nations' reserves tend to be in RESERVE CURRENCY as well as in gold, and, at times when these reserves are too low to pay their debts, they may resort to using SPECIAL DRAWING RIGHTS or some other means of payment.

gold standard A system whereby a country defines its monetary unit in terms of a given gold content, which is the same as establishing an official price per ounce of gold. Since gold is a commodity traded in world markets, it becomes the job of that country's central bank to buy and sell gold in such a way as to maintain its official price. The exchange rates of gold-standard currencies are quite stable, depending on the ratio of their values in gold (or the ratio of the gold prices in each currency), which is known as their *mint par of exchange* (or *mint rate,* or *mint parity*); the market rate tends to fluctuate closely around this figure. For example, in 1930 the Bank of England sold gold at £4.2477 per ounce, and the U.S. Treasury bought and sold gold at $20.67 per ounce. The exchange rate therefore was set at £1 = $4.87 (20.67 ÷ 4.2477). If the demand for dollars exceeded the demand for pounds, the dollar value of pound sterling began to fall. If it fell enough, it would pay British citizens buying American goods to pay for them with gold (bought from the Bank of England at its fixed rate) and ship it to America at their expense, instead of paying in the more expensive dollars. Conversely, if the sterling value of dollars fell, it would pay Americans to ship gold to their British creditors. The exchange rate could vary enough to cover the shipping rate for gold. Now suppose the shipping rate was $.05 per ounce. If the exchange rate fluctuated by more than $.05—up *or* down—it paid to ship actual gold. The rate at which it pays to ship actual gold is called the *gold point.* A sizable outflow of gold would cause a BALANCE OF PAYMENTS deficit. The country's money supply would shrink and prices would fall; therefore imports would tend to decline and exports of its now cheaper domestic goods would increase. Eventually the payments deficit would be corrected. (This *gold-flow* or *price-specie mechanism* was first pointed out by David HUME in the mid-18th century.)

The main advantage of a gold standard is that it promotes stable rates of exchange, produced automatically by the operation of the world market, without artificial restrictions on international payments. Its chief disadvantage is that, if it is to function smoothly, all the countries using it must have relatively similar price structures and income levels. If prices and income decline in one country, the others must follow suit to maintain equilibrium. Further, the nation that is losing gold must be politically willing and able to suffer the rising unemployment that is an inevitable by-product of deflation, and workers there must be willing to accept wage cuts so that costs will be reduced.

The gold standard prevailed among the world's major trading nations from about 1870 until 1914. After World War I it was restored in most countries, but the depression of the 1930s led to its gen-eral abandonment (by Great Britain in 1931, by the United States in 1934). For a modified version of the gold standard, see GOLD-EXCHANGE STANDARD. See also EXCHANGE RATE.

gold sterilization A monetary policy that prevents the accumulation of a country's GOLD RESERVES from expanding the amount of money in circulation within the country. In the United States the Treasury can sterilize gold either by failing to issue GOLD CERTIFICATES to the Federal Reserve (which then cannot back the extra commercial bank reserves that gold might generate) or by selling securities to commercial banks (or their customers), thus reducing the commercial banks' reserves. The first method prevents credit expansion on the central bank level; the second counteracts credit expansion on the commercial bank level. Even though the United States is no longer on the gold standard, the term continues to be used with the understanding that not gold but other reserves (RESERVE CURRENCY) are being sterilized.

goods Material or physical objects, either natural or manmade, used to satisfy human needs or desires. They are sometimes distinguished from services (actions performed to satisfy needs or desires). A *free good* is a commodity so abundantly furnished by nature that it does not command a price—for example (usually), fresh air or water. An *economic good,* on the other hand, is in short supply relative to demand for it, so that people will pay for it. A *final good* is one that is purchased by its ultimate consumer, whereas an *intermediate good* is one purchased for further processing or resale. For *capital good,* see under CAPITAL, def. 1. See also CONSUMER GOOD.

goodwill An intangible business ASSET arising from a firm's high reputation, good relations with customers and/or suppliers, favorable location, etc. For example, if a corporation pays $1 million for acquiring a profitable firm with tangible net assets of just $800,000, it probably is paying $200,000 for that firm's goodwill, and its accountants might treat this as an asset that may or may not be amortized over a period of years. Usually, however, accountants prefer not to list goodwill as an asset unless some specific sum is actually paid for it.

goon Slang for a person hired to break up meetings, damage property, and otherwise threaten or terrorize individuals or groups. Goons were used by some employers against the early labor unions.

Gosbank The state bank of the Union of Soviet Socialist Republics, keystone of the Soviet banking system. It acts as the government's fiscal agent, grants commercial credit to all kinds of enterprise, carries the accounts of all businesses in the country, prepares the credit and cash plans for the Ministry of Finance's overall financial plan, issues currency, and holds all specie and foreign exchange owned by the government. Since 1966 all Soviet savings banks also have been part of Gosbank. Unlike the CENTRAL BANK of capitalist nations, Gosbank is not the chief determinant of monetary policy, which is under still more direct government control. Rather, it serves as an instrument of control whereby all transactions can be verified (since they all must be conducted through Gosbank), banking thus being a government monopoly.

Similar in scope and operations to Gosbank is the *People's Bank of China,* the central bank of the People's Republic of China. It, too, is responsible for issuing currency, furnishing credit to state enterprises, supervising expenditures of state enterprises, and developing the credit and cash plans. Like Gosbank, it represents a financial control mechanism for carrying out overall economic plans.

Gosplan The state planning agency of the Union of Soviet Socialist Republics, responsible for the country's overall economic planning. See also PLANNED ECONOMY.

Gossen, Hermann Heinrich A German thinker (1810–58) who, in a book published in 1854, anticipated the principal ideas of W. S. JEVONS and other economists of the MARGINALIST SCHOOL. Gossen's book was a failure and he died soon after its publication, but it was rediscovered by Jevons and others, who gave Gossen full credit for his ideas. Gossen formulated both the law of diminishing MARGINAL UTILITY and the idea that consumers allocate their spending to equalize maxium satisfaction, that is, so that the last unit of money spent for any one item gives equal satisfaction with the last unit spent for any other item. Like Jevons and later marginalists, Gossen used a highly statistical, mathematical approach.

government, economic role of The scope and influence of government, both local and central, on the economy, which in the United States and most other industrialized capitalist nations has been gradually increasing since the late 19th century. (In socialist countries government exercises primary control over—if not outright ownership of—all the factors of production.) Among government's principal functions are the provision of security (police protection and defense), necessary for the continuity of all economic enterprise, and the creation of a stable monetary system. In addition, government uses public expenditures and taxes to influence the level of employment and business activity (see FISCAL POLICY), and a central banking authority to control the availability of money and credit (see MONETARY POLICY). To some extent it also regulates the factors of production, principally capital and labor, so as to create and maintain competition and curb monopoly (see ANTITRUST LEGISLATION; LABOR LAWS), in some cases directly controlling or owning monopolistic industries (see PUBLIC OWNERSHIP). Government also can—and does—assist particular business interests by reducing or restricting supply (through tariffs, import quotas, etc.) and/or providing aid through subsidies (price supports, depletion allowances, tax benefits, etc.; see also AGRICULTURE, AID TO). In addition, government exerts increasing influence on the redistribution of income, through transfer payments (pensions, welfare, etc.), taxation, and by providing employment in public works. See PUBLIC SPENDING; also PUBLIC SECTOR.

government bill General name for a very short-term obligation, such as a TREASURY BILL.

government bond See under BOND, def. 1.

Government National Mortgage Association Also, *Ginnie Mae.* A U.S. government-owned corporation formed in 1968 when the FEDERAL NATIONAL MORTGAGE ASSOCIATION ("Fannie Mae") became private, in order to invest in mortgages not suitable for Fannie Mae. Administered by the U.S. Department of Housing and

Urban Development, Ginnie Mae buys mortgages such as those for government-subsidized housing, which carry greater risk than a private firm can afford. To obtain funds for this purpose, it issues securities backed by Federal Housing Authority and Veterans Administration mortgages and guaranteed for timely payment of principal and interest, making them attractive to investors.

government ownership See PUBLIC OWNERSHIP.

government sector See PUBLIC SECTOR.

government spending See PUBLIC SPENDING.

grace Also, *days of grace*. Any extra time granted by a creditor beyond the date when payment of an obligation is due.

Grange Any of the individual local lodges of the *Patrons of Husbandry*, an American farmers' organization formed in 1867 which, during the next decade, became a channel for voicing farmers' grievances, particularly against the railroads. As a result of Grange agitation, most of the midwestern states passed laws to regulate rail rates and to prevent railroads from unfairly discriminating among their customers, through setting schedules of maximum rates, forbidding higher charges for short hauls than for long ones, prohibiting the consolidation of parallel rail lines, and eliminating the practice of furnishing public officials with free passes. Some individual Granges functioned as farm cooperatives, not only for marketing but in some cases even manufacturing farm machinery. By the 1890s the Grangers had joined forces with other farm groups in the Populist Party, which advocated unlimited coinage of silver and a number of reforms, among them government ownership of railroads, an eight-hour work day, and a graduated income tax.

grant-in-aid
1. A grant of funds from a central government to a state or local government, or from a state government to a local unit, usually earmarked for a specific purpose. In the United States Federal grants-in-aid have been awarded to states to help build roads, supply lunches to schoolchildren, for old-age pensions, and similar purposes. A *matching grant* is a conditional payment that requires the recipient to put up some part of the funds needed (sometimes but not always one-half). For road renovation, for example, the state may agree to pay 90 per cent of resurfacing costs if the locality will put up the rest.
2. In foreign affairs, an outright gift of money from one nation to another. A grant is preferable to a loan when the probability of repayment is slight or when questions of repayment might cause embarrassment or ill will. Its chief disadvantages are that it may carry an implication of charity and that it may be used less efficiently than a loan (which has a price tag). See also FOREIGN AID.

graphic See VISUAL DISPLAY.

graveyard shift See under SHIFT, def. 1.

gray-collar Describing workers whose jobs lie midway between BLUE-COLLAR and WHITE-COLLAR employment, or jobs containing elements of each. For example, a construction contractor who employs both building-trade specialists (carpenters, electricians, etc.) and on-the-job supervisors, and hence does no manual labor and little direct blue-collar supervision, might be considered a gray-collar worker. The term also may be applied to such service workers as police officers and letter carriers, whose work involves physical activity.

gray market A term for transactions that are unethical but not illegal. For example, in a time of scarcity, a supplier might offer goods for immediate delivery at triple the normal price. See also BLACK MARKET.

grazing lands Lands used by ranchers to feed their livestock. In medieval England most villages had common lands for use by anyone for this purpose, but from the late 14th century on the ENCLOSURE movement began to fence off all lands as private property, until no commons remained. In the United States, with its vast unsettled areas, ranchers freely used public lands. During the 19th century much of the public domain was sold or given to settlers, and gradually the better range lands became private property. Nevertheless ranchers continued to graze the public lands without permission, regulation, or payment of any kind. In some cases they even tried to fence such lands, claiming that by using them over the years they had acquired proprietary rights. Not until 1900 was a law passed to prevent grazing in national forests, and the Taylor Grazing Act of 1934 finally forbade free grazing on the remaining 142 million acres of public range lands, and instituted a system of permits, regulations, and fees. Today the grazing lands, principally located in the Far West, are administered by the U.S. Bureau of Land Management, which is also responsible for leasing mineral rights on public lands.

Great Depression   The slump in the BUSINESS CYCLE that began in 1929 (sometimes dated from October 29, the so-called Black Friday, the day of the biggest stock market crash) and continued until 1933. During that period the United States' gross national product fell from $104 billion to $56 billion, and unemployment rose from 1.5 million to nearly 13 million (which meant that 25 per cent of the labor force was jobless). Some 9 million savings accounts were wiped out owing to bank failures, and 85,000 businesses failed. Although the precipitating cause of the Great Depression was the feverish stock speculation in the year preceding the crash, the boom of the 1920s held the seeds of its own destruction. During a period of seemingly unparalleled prosperity, the nation's agricultural producers were having increasing problems. Even though farm prices dropped, domestic demand did not increase, and Europe, not yet recovered from World War I, could not afford to import enough American grain. Manufacturing boomed, especially in the rapidly growing new auto industry (which spurred road construction and related industries), but employment did not rise along with it. Indeed, though manufacturing output rose by nearly 50 per cent between 1920 and 1929, employment in manufacturing remained unchanged. In mining, output increased by more than 40 per cent yet employment actually declined by 12 per cent, as it did in the transportation and utility industries. During the Great Depression, private capital investment—in construction, in producers' durable equipment, and in inventories—came to a virtual standstill, and consumers' expenditures declined by nearly one-half. With the private sector unable or unwilling to turn the tide, it became necessary for the Federal government to step in. In the months following President F. D. Roosevelt's inauguration in March 1933, his administration's emergency measures—the beginning of the NEW DEAL—addressed themselves to the most urgent of the nation's economic problems. See also DEPRESSION.

greenback   A name of U.S. Treasury notes authorized in February 1862 (during the Civil War), so called because green ink was used to print the backs of the notes. Plagued by a shortage of money backed by gold or silver to finance the war, the Treasury issued a total of $450 million in notes backed solely by the credit of the United States, which were noninterest-bearing and simply were declared to be legal tender. The question of redeeming these greenbacks remained a burning political issue for the next two decades, and they gave their name to a political party, the Greenback Labor Party, which showed considerable strength in the Congressional elections of 1878. In that year Congress decided that the $346,681,000 outstanding in greenbacks should remain a permanent part of the currency, and by the end of that year greenbacks for the first time attained a face value in gold (they had declined as low as 39 cents in July 1864). Today the term "greenback" occasionally is used for ordinary American paper currency, which is printed in green ink on one side.

Green Revolution   See under AGRARIAN REVOLUTION.

Gresham's law   The principle formulated by Sir Thomas Gresham (1519–79), adviser to Queen Elizabeth I, that "bad" money drives out "good" money, which is the the chief argument against a bimetallic money standard (see also BIMETALLISM). When two metals are used to valuate currency, the ratio of value is always fixed. Thus, in the early days of the United States, the dollar was equal to either 15 units of silver or 1 unit of gold. But gold and silver also are commodities whose price in the world market depends, to some extent at least, on supply and demand. If the market price of gold goes up (owing to relative scarcity) and the price of silver remains the same, it stands to reason that

Americans will want to export gold dollars at their new high price. As a result, the country will soon lose its gold dollars and be, in effect, on a silver standard. Thus silver, which is "bad" (that is, less valuable) money, will have driven out gold ("good" money). More recently, American dimes, quarters, and half-dollars containing several metals have driven older coins made of pure metals out of circulation, even though it is illegal to melt down coins for their silver content.

grievance   A complaint, usually by an employee but sometimes by an employer, concerning some work-related decision or action. Labor contracts nearly always specify what will constitute such complaints and how they are to be handled. A typical *grievance procedure* involves a series of steps whereby a complaint is considered by union and management at successively higher levels of the organization. (The union is particularly closely involved if the grievance is thought to constitute a violation of the contract.) An aggrieved employee thus might first complain, usually in writing, to his or her direct supervisor. If the outcome is not mutually satisfactory, the employee then takes the problem to the next higher level designated in the contract. Eventually, if no satisfactory decision is reached, the problem may be submitted to ARBITRATION. Though many grievances undoubtedly stem from matters simply perceived as injustices or from hurt feelings, some do involve provisions of the labor contract, and it is these that tend to reach the arbitration level. The most common such issues concern discipline, seniority (in both promotion and demotion), job classification and work assignment, management's rights, and overtime.

gross cash flow   See under CASH FLOW.

gross income   See INCOME, def. 2.

gross national product   Also, *GNP*. The total monetary value of a nation's output of goods and services during a given period, usually a year. It can be described either as expenditures (consumption expenditures, net foreign and domestic investment,

Fig. 34. Summary of U.S. gross national product (in billions of dollars)

Item	1929	1935	1945	1955	1965	1970	1972	1974 (prel.)
Gross national product	**103.1**	**72.2**	**211.9**	**398.0**	**684.9**	**977.1**	**1,158.0**	**1,397.3**
By type of expenditure:								
Personal consumption expenditures	77.2	55.7	119.7	254.4	432.8	617.6	729.0	876.7
Gross private domestic investment	16.2	6.4	10.6	67.4	108.1	136.3	179.3	209.4
Net exports of goods and services	1.1	.1	−.6	2.0	6.9	3.6	−6.0	2.0
Govt. purchases of goods and services	8.5	10.0	82.3	74.2	137.0	219.5	255.7	309.2
By major type of product:								
Goods output	56.1	39.9	128.9	216.4	347.2	471.2	543.8	670.3
Services	35.6	28.3	76.5	132.6	262.9	410.3	488.1	590.1
Structures	11.4	4.0	6.5	49.0	74.8	95.6	126.1	136.8
By sector:								
Business	95.1	64.1	172.3	352.9	594.4	827.0	977.9	1,177.8
Households and institutions	2.9	1.9	4.1	9.1	18.5	30.8	37.2	47.0
Rest of the world	.8	.4	.4	1.8	4.2	4.6	6.5	11.7
General government	4.3	5.9	35.2	34.2	67.8	114.7	136.4	160.8

Source: U.S. Department of Commerce.

Fig. 35. U.S. gross national product

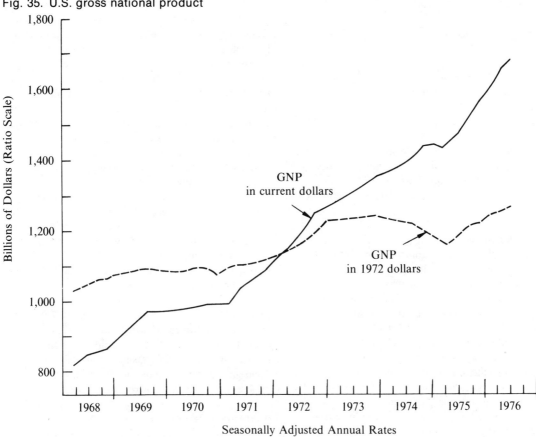

Seasonally Adjusted Annual Rates

In the second quarter of 1976 GNP rose $37.9 billion, or at an annual rate of 9.6 per cent. Real output (GNP adjusted for price changes) rose at a rate of 4.3 per cent compared with 9.2 per cent, and the inflation rate rose from 3.2 per cent to 5.1 per cent (annual rate).
Source: U.S. Department of Commerce.

and government purchases of goods and services) or as total earnings of factors of production (wages, rents, interest, profits). GNP is a *gross* measure because no deductions are made for capital consumption allowances, that is, depreciation of the capital goods used in production. Used principally to compare national output from one year to the next, or from decade to decade, GNP is considered the most comprehensive single barometer of a nation's overall economic well-being. It also is used to compare the contribution to the economy of various sectors (consumer, business, government) or various industries (auto, health services, construction, etc.). See also GNP DEFLATOR; NATIONAL INCOME; NET NATIONAL PRODUCT.

gross private domestic investment The total value of private spending for capital assets (durable equipment, machinery, new buildings, etc.) plus INVENTORY CHANGE. The spending for capital assets, also called *gross private fixed investment,* differs from CAPITAL FORMATION in that depreciation is not taken into account (hence "gross"). Gross private domestic investment is a major component of GROSS NATIONAL PRODUCT, accounting for roughly 15 per cent of the U.S. GNP. It is reflected there in two ways: first, through increasing GNP by the value of the asset in the period during which it is purchased; second, through the effect of fixed investment made during previous periods, appearing in the goods produced with the aid of that capital.

gross profit   See under PROFIT, def. 1.

gross spread   See SPREAD, def. 1(b).

gross weight   The entire weight of a package, including both wrapping and/or packing materials and the contents. See also NET WEIGHT; TARE.

ground rent   See under LEASE.

group banking   A system whereby a corporate holding company controls two or more separate incorporated banks, usually through ownership of a controlling interest (sometimes 100 per cent) in their stock.

group insurance   An INSURANCE plan subscribed to by an employer, labor union, or professional organization for various kinds of insurance, most often LIFE INSURANCE and/or HEALTH INSURANCE. The premiums either are paid solely by the employer or are shared by employer and employees; often employees' premiums are collected by means of a payroll deduction. Normally all employees who contribute to group insurance pay the same rate, regardless of health status, age, or occupational risks, with the differences in actual cost averaged out. As a result of low selling and administrative costs, group insurance tends to be one of the least expensive kinds for policyholders.

Group of Ten   Also, *Paris Club*. The ten nations responsible for the largest share of international trade in the 1960s and subsequent years: the United States, United Kingdom, West Germany, France, Belgium, Netherlands, Italy, Sweden, Canada, and Japan. So called since 1962, when they signed a General Agreement to Borrow in order to make $6.2 billion in credit available to the INTERNATIONAL MONETARY FUND (IMF), they continued to meet regularly to map cooperation in international finance by such means as currency swaps. Switzerland, although not a member of the IMF, occasionally participated in its activities.

group rate   See under FREIGHT.

growth, economic   An increase in the productivity of a nation or area. In general economists agree that such an increase is reflected in an improved standard of living. The basic measure of such growth is GROSS NATIONAL PRODUCT (GNP) after adjustment for price inflation, but since population increases may offset such growth GNP should be regarded on a per capita basis. The calculation is only as good as the statistics that provide information about GNP, which in turn depend on the definitions and methods used in national income accounting. Further, these tend to vary among different countries, making comparisons misleading. Certain factors are not taken into account at all, such as the number of work hours per week, which has decreased sharply since about 1900, improving the quality of life but not in a directly measurable way. Nevertheless, growth theory can be useful for assessing the state of a nation's economy at a given time, and for attempts to speed up the progress of an UNDERDEVELOPED NATION. See also MATURE ECONOMY; *balanced growth* under R. NURKSE; SECULAR STAGNATION; STAGNATION.

growth stock   The stock of a company with good prospects for future growth, whose earnings are expected to increase fairly rapidly. Such stocks frequently pay out only a small share of earnings as dividends because funds can be reinvested in the business at high rates of return.

guarantee   To offer a GUARANTY.

guaranteed annual wage   A plan whereby a company guarantees employment to some or all of its employees for most or all of a full year, at full-time pay (or less). Used mostly in industries where output varies cyclically or seasonally, guaranteed annual wage plans differ significantly in detail, both as to which workers will be covered and to what extent. Some plans are initiated by management; others are responses to union demands. Used as early as the 1920s in the United States, guaranteed annual wage plans have to some extent been replaced by *supplemental unemployment benefits* (SUB), a system in which the employer contributes a set amount per man-hour into a fund from which laid-off employess can collect benefits to supplement state UNEMPLOYMENT COMPENSATION.

guaranteed security   A bond (or stock) whose interest or principal (or dividend) is backed by some company other than the issuing one. Usually the company making the guarantee is leasing property from the issuer and guarantees its securities as part of the lease agreement. Guaranteed bonds in particular were common in the railroad industry, where large companies often leased track from smaller ones, or several roads using one terminal would guarantee its bonds.

guaranty The undertaking of responsibility by one person for another's debt or obligation to perform some act or duty, or generally to assure that a thing will be done as promised. The original debtor is still liable for payment or performance, but in case of default the maker of the guaranty, called *guarantor*, can be called on. (See also under SURETY BOND.) In common business usage, a guaranty often is an assurance of quality, that is, an assurance that goods being offered for sale are effective, or contain certain ingredients, or will last for a given period, etc. In case of quality failure, the guarantor then can be held liable. However, a guaranty is less binding than a WARRANTY.

guideline, industry-labor In the United States and Europe, a suggestion from government officials concerning a wage settlement, which industry and labor unions are asked to follow but which does not have the force of law. The suggestion generally is supposed to keep wages low enough not to contribute to inflation. See also COST-PUSH INFLATION.

guild An economic and social organization of persons working in the same business or plying the same trade, a vital feature of economic life in medieval western Europe. The earliest *merchant guilds* were organized in the 11th century. Originally formed for protection against highway dangers as the merchants traveled from manor to manor, the merchant guilds became more and more powerful during the COMMERCIAL REVOLUTION, as trade became worldwide. In some cases they grew from local associations of merchants to huge intercity leagues devoted to promoting as well as protecting their trade. The best known of these was the Hanseatic League of northern Europe, which actually established and controlled its own trading cities.

Alongside the merchant guilds developed associations of artisans, or *craft guilds*, whose chief function was to establish local control over a profession or trade by setting standards of workmanship and price and by limiting the number of workers in a given field. Each craft guild had three classes of member: *apprentice, journeyman,* and *master.* An apprentice usually was a boy bound to a master craftsman for a period of some years during which the master taught him the trade and provided him with a bare living. A journeyman had finished his apprenticeship but had not reached the status of master, since the guild limited the number of masters. The master, who achieved this rank by virtue of training, examinations, and fees, owned the shop and was in full charge. Each guild had an effective monopoly over its specialty—how it was produced, its standard of quality, and method of sale. In the more industrialized towns the guilds assumed political power as well. As central governments became more powerful, however, the guilds became weaker, increasingly subject to royal or other central national authority. The system was too rigid to allow guilds to adapt to changing conditions. In England, therefore, the guilds' power had withered by the 17th century. In France they persisted until the French Revolution, and in Germany and the Italian city-states they lingered into the 19th century. Outside Europe, in China, Japan, India, and elsewhere, organizations comparable to guilds flourished also, in some cases persisting into the 20th century. Today the term "guild" can be used for any association organized for mutual benefit and is found in the names of some labor unions.

guild socialism A moderate form of SOCIALISM that advocated social ownership of the means of production but management of industrial activity by the workers themselves, who were to be organized into guilds modeled after the medieval craft guilds (see GUILD). Local guilds would federate to form national guilds for the various industries, which in turn would be represented in a national guild congress with ultimate responsibility over industry but no effect on the existing government structure. Popular mainly in England just before and after World War I, guild socialism was formulated by G. D. H. Cole and other British intellectuals. In 1915 the National Guilds League was formed, along with a number of working guilds, but by 1925 the movement had waned and the league collapsed; its influence survives only in the British trade unions.

handicraft system The practice of pursuing a craft or trade in a small shop, largely by hand or with only simple machinery. This kind of business was common in Europe in the late Middle Ages, as the growth of villages and towns gradually led craftsmen to move out of their homes into shops, and was promoted with the development of the craft GUILD. It was later replaced by COTTAGE INDUSTRY.

hand-to-mouth Describing the practice of operating with a bare minimum of inventory. Thus a company anticipating price declines in the near future might limit itself to hand-to-mouth purchases of raw materials, buying just enough to carry on production.

Hansen, Alvin H. See under SECULAR STAGNATION.

hard-core unemployed See under CHRONIC UNEMPLOYMENT.

hard goods
1. Same as durable goods; see under CONSUMER GOODS.
2. Also, *hardware*. Consumer durable goods made principally from metal, such as most electrical appliances, cutlery, and tools.

hard loan See under SOFT LOAN.

hard money Cash or currency, as opposed to credit.

hardware
1. The electrical, electronic, and mechanical devices that make up a COMPUTER. See also PROGRAMMING.

2. Synonym for HARD GOODS, def. 2.

harmony of interests The belief that individuals pursuing their own selfish economic interests will ultimately promote the good of society as a whole. This idea was popular with Adam Smith and others of the CLASSICAL SCHOOL.

Hawthorne studies A well-known experiment on the relation of worker morale to productivity conducted by several Harvard Business School professors between 1927 and 1932 at the Hawthorne plant of Western Electric, near Chicago. Testing a group of six women who assembled relay units, the researchers successively varied their working hours, work week, pay rate, lighting, and other working conditions. Finally all the changes were shelved and the original working conditions restored. Nevertheless, the workers' productivity continued to rise, increasing to 25 per cent above the original level. It was concluded, therefore, that factors such as informal group relationships and the special attention focused on the group by the study had more influence on productivity than physical or other objective conditions.

Hawtrey, Sir Ralph George See under MONETARY THEORY.

Hayek, Friedrich A. von See under CHICAGO SCHOOL; also under MONETARY THEORY.

hazard Also, *peril*. In insurance, a cause of probable loss. See Fig. 69 under PROPERTY INSURANCE for a list of hazards covered by various kinds of homeowner's insurance.

headhunter See under EMPLOYMENT AGENCY.

head tax See POLL TAX.

health insurance Also, *accident and sickness insurance, medical insurance*. In general, any INSURANCE program covering medical expenses and/or income lost owing to illness or accidental injury. Such insurance may cover some or all of the expense of hospitalization; surgery; physicians' fees; drugs and medicines; laboratory tests, X-rays, and other diagnostic procedures; radiation therapy; maternity and nursing care; eyeglasses, crutches, prostheses, etc.; so-called *major medical* expenses, that is, the expenses incurred in a serious or long-term illness; and compensation for earnings lost through illness or injury (*loss of income* or *disability insurance*). In the mid-1970s the United States was the only major industrial nation without a comprehensive program of tax-supported health insurance (whereby the government assumes the major burden of health-care expenses). Though some government programs did exist, chiefly for the aged (through Medicare and SOCIAL SECURITY) and for those suffering job-related illness or injury (WORKMEN'S COMPENSATION), the choice left to the major part of the population was between private health insurance or none.

Private health insurance policies in the United States take one of two forms: *cancellable* (at the insurer's option, usually when the insured person grows old or has had the warning signs of serious illness, such as a heart attack), and *noncancellable* (renewable at the client's option), which usually cost more than cancellable policies. In addition, nonprofit plans for *prepaid medical care* have been instituted by medical societies, groups of physicians, consumer cooperatives, fraternal groups, and others. The two largest nonprofit plans, *Blue Cross* (for hospitalization) and *Blue Shield* (for medical, surgical, and maternity expenses), were originally sponsored by the American Hospital Association. Although designed primarily for group enrollment, they accept individuals and families as well. In each case, a chapter is organized by a local hospital, and cost arrangements are determined with member hospitals in the area and with participating physicians who offer a wide range of services to plan members. Premium costs, benefits, and enrollment regulations vary with each plan (there are at least a hundred different ones). Though relatively inexpensive compared to commercial health insurance, the coverage given by nonprofit plans may cover only a fraction of medical expenses incurred. With the cost of health care rising faster than practically any other major service, owing both to inflation and to the development of increasingly sophisticated and costly methods of treatment, the cost of private health insurance was becoming prohibitive. Hence by the mid-1970s it was widely believed that the United States would have public health insurance and health care within the next decade.

heavy market Also, *active market, broad market*. In the securities and commodities trade, a market in which there is a very active trading, with many shares changing hands. The term does not describe the direction of prices, which may be moving up or down or remaining stable. However, owing to the large volume of trade, individual price fluctuations in a heavy market tend to be small. See also THIN MARKET.

hedge fund A MUTUAL FUND that may borrow money and/or sell short (see SELLING SHORT) in an attempt to make quick profits for its stockholders, no matter what the direction of the general market.

hedging In the commodities trade, a method of buying and selling in the FUTURES MARKET that minimizes the risk that unfavorable price changes might wipe out one's profit. It is associated particularly with commodity speculators (and dealers), and with manufacturers and processors who require large quantities of basic commodities (flour millers, suger refiners, leather tanners, etc.). Hedging is best illustrated by an example. Suppose that George Smith, a flour miller, receives an order in June for 10,000 barrels of flour, to be delivered over the next three months at a given price. If the price of wheat should rise during these three months, Smith's costs may rise above the contract price, and he stands to lose money. If he could buy all the wheat he would need for the next three months in the SPOT MARKET, there would be no problem, but he lacks sufficient storage space and also does not want to tie up that much cash (the spot market requires cash payments). To avoid the risk of loss, Smith decides to hedge. He buys wheat for cash as he needs it, at $3 per bushel, and buys an equal amount of wheat futures for $3.25 per bushel for delivery later. If wheat prices rise, he will lose money on the flour (because his materials cost will rise) but he will profit on the futures contract; for example, if wheat rises to $3.40 per bushel, he can sell the contract at a profit high enough to compensate for his loss on the flour. Should the price of wheat fall to $2.75 per bushel, Smith makes an extra profit on the flour (owing to lower costs) but loses on the futures contract. Either way he is protected, for Smith's risk of loss has been assumed by the speculator in wheat futures. Hedging succeeds largely because the spot and future prices of commodities tend to rise and fall by approximately equal amounts.

For a similar technique in securities trading, see under SELLING SHORT and STRADDLE, def. 1. For hedging in foreign exchange, see under FORWARD EXCHANGE.

hedonism The doctrine that each individual should seek his or her own greatest happiness, or pleasure. Originating in ancient Greece, hedonism was adapted by Jeremy BENTHAM in his social philosophy of utilitarianism, which described not individuals but society as seeking the greatest good for the greatest number. Both the classical economists and the marginalists adopted it in their view of self-seeking economic man, which was scathingly repudiated by Thorstein VEBLEN.

heuristic rules In solving a problem, rules that permit the results of tests on each step to be used in formulating the next step. For example, if Machine 4 produces only 95 units instead of the expected 100, this actual output is used as the basis of the next computation.

hidden asset Also, *hidden reserve, secret reserve.* An ASSET whose value on the company books is deliberately understated, to avoid taxes or for some other reason. An asset also may be "hidden" on a balance sheet simply because it represents intangibles or has previously been charged to expense. For example, some large oil companies charge off as operating costs the money spent in drilling new wells, even though these wells represent a very real asset that will generate profits for years to come.

hidden discount A way of giving price reductions that is used largely in industrial purchasing, where the prices of some items are fixed by the industry as a whole. In such cases, the buyer obtains a discount by buying, from the same supplier, other items whose price is open to negotiation and deducts some agreed-on percentage from their purchase price. See also under FAIR TRADE.

hidden inflation A price increase disguised by offering smaller quantity or poorer quality for the same price. For example, food processors might change the quantity in a package of food without changing the package size, charging the same price for an 8-ounce box of cereal that they had been charging for a 9.5-ounce box.

hidden tax An indirect tax paid by the buyer without his or her knowledge. For example, most purchasers of imported cameras do not know what percentage of the camera's price reflects import duties (and some may not even realize that they are paying such duties).

high flyer A stock whose price climbs very rapidly compared to other stocks.

high-level language See under PROGRAMMING.

high-powered money See under BANK RESERVES.

highway-user tax A tax levied in several ways on the principal users of highways, with the revenues generally being reserved for highway maintenance and construction expenditures. The principal highway-user taxes are those on gasoline sales (usually a fixed amount per gallon sold) and license fees for motor vehicles. In the United States highway-user taxes are imposed by both the state and Federal governments.

hiring hall A kind of employment service run by a labor union. Employers needing workers to load and unload cargo, for example, may call on the longshoremen's union, which keeps a rotating list of members' names and sends workers out as needed. Hiring halls are found mostly in industries and trades where practically all of the workers are union members, such as the printing and building trades. Although the Taft-Hartley Act of 1947 requires hiring halls to handle nonunion members as well, the unions generally get around this rule in labor contracts by insisting on seniority clauses, which give preference to older workers who tend to be union members.

hiring rate See ACCESSION RATE.

histogram See under FREQUENCY DISTRIBUTION.

historical school See GERMAN HISTORICAL SCHOOL.

hoarding In general usage, the accumulation of currency, goods, or some other commodity in excess of normal needs, usually motivated by a fear of future scarcity and/or high prices. In economic theory, however, any money that is saved but not invested is considered to be hoarded. Because such funds are removed from the normal stream of circulation, total income is reduced and the VELOCITY OF MONEY slowed down. The opposite of hoarding—putting hoarded funds back into circulation—is called *dishoarding*.

Hobson, John Atkinson An English social reformer, economist, and journalist (1858–1940), an early proponent of WELFARE ECONOMICS. At the outset of his career Hobson formulated the idea, originally proposed to him by a businessman friend, A. F. Mummery, that thrift can be detrimental to economic growth and prosperity. Hobson believed that income was distributed so unequally that the rich received too much in profits, rent, and interest to do anything with it but save. The poor, on the other hand, received too little to increase consumption. Consequently the economy could not grow, and unemployment was inevitable. Thus *oversaving* and *underconsumption*, said Hobson, were ultimately responsible for the ups and downs of the business cycle. Underconsumption also led to imperialism. Colonies were needed as an outlet for both surplus goods that could not be sold and surplus profits that could not be invested at home. The remedy Hobson proposed was nothing less than a redistribution of income, accomplished through government regulation and operation of industry and through taxation. It included such measures as stringent labor laws, government ownership of certain industries, and taxation of high incomes, particularly those derived from rents and from excessive interest and profits. Considered a flaming radical by his contemporaries, Hobson was forced out of his post at the University of London and thereafter excluded from other academic positions. J. M. KEYNES was among the first to give Hobson the recognition he deserved.

holder In law, a person in possession of a negotiable instrument payable either to his own order, as payee or endorsee, or to the bearer. If the holder buys the instrument or accepts it as payment of a debt, he becomes a *holder for value*.

holding company A business firm with the primary or sole purpose of dominating other corporations through the ownership or control of their stock. A dominant form of organization during the period of great business consolidation in the United States in the early 20th century, holding companies were formed then by some of the industrial giants that are still influential—American Tobacco, Standard Oil, and U.S. Steel, among others—and they remain a leading form of corporate organization. The holding company has several advantages. It may represent a simpler, cheaper way of acquiring another company than a merger or purchase of assets; it retains the subsidiary's good name and goodwill without necessarily acquiring its liabilities; it may perform marketing, financial, and other overall management functions for all the subsidiaries more advantageously, and, because different states and countries have different laws governing corporations, it can, by acquiring strategically located subsidiaries, take advantage of laws in its favor. However, holding companies may be subject to higher taxes and are governed by a variety of special laws. In fact, when they represent a monopoly in an industry, they may be declared illegal and forced to divest themselves of some, if not all, of their holdings.

A holding company potentially can wield enormous power, because one firm can control a number of other companies with combined capital much greater than its own: it need control only half or less than half of the shares outstanding. Thus, a

$50,000 firm can conceivably control a $150,000 company, which, if it too is a holding company, may in turn control an $800,000 company, whose sole function may be the control of a $7 million company. This sort of *pyramid of control* can be dangerous if misused, as it was—especially by American public utility holding companies—prior to the stock market crash of 1929. See also CONGLOMERATE.

holding the line Maintaining a given economic position, such as opposing further wage or price increases. The term is often used with regard to controlling inflation.

Hollerith Code See under PUNCHED-CARD DATA PROCESSING.

homeowner's insurance A general term for a package of home-insurance policies covering damage caused by fire, wind, hail, blasting, dust, industrial smoke, frozen plumbing, vandalism, tenants, damage to the contents, etc. They also may provide protection against liability for personal injuries. Such policies normally cannot be assigned (for example, to the buyer when the house is sold).

homesteading The legal acquisition of land in the western United States by living and working on it. The Homestead Act of 1862 provided that a prospective landowner could stake out up to 160 acres of public land designated for homesteading. Up to 1974 one could still do so, if one farmed at least 20 acres of the land and lived on the tract at least seven months a year for three years. In May 1974, however, Alaska, the last state to offer homesteading land, withdrew its remaining 15 million acres of such lands, and the practice of homesteading was officially ended. Although some feel that the Homestead Act and subsequent legislation making land available at little or no cost aided the rapid settlement of the American West, in practice less than 50 million acres were granted under the Homestead Act between 1862 and 1890, and only about one-third of these claims were finally proved. Often the homesteading land was distinctly second-rate; better land was reserved for sale. Further, by means of special clauses—laws that could be used to advantage—and collusion, mining and lumber companies were able to obtain huge tracts of land originally intended for small homesteading tracts. About 1900, conservation interests finally began to win support for the view that public lands should be reserved for public uses and administered by government agencies, and increasing amounts of land came permanently into the public domain.

homework Work supplied to employees to be done in their own homes, usually on a PIECEWORK basis. Formerly common in the American garment industry, it is still used in other countries, such as Japan, for various kinds of assembly work. See also COTTAGE INDUSTRY.

horizontal equity See under ABILITY-TO-PAY PRINCIPLE.

horizontal integration Also, *horizontal expansion*. The expansion of a business through the acquisition of additional divisions or other firms engaged in essentially the same stage of production of the same product. Buying out competitors is the most common means of horizontal integration. See also VERTICAL INTEGRATION.

hospitalization insurance See under HEALTH INSURANCE.

"hot cargo" agreement A form of secondary BOYCOTT whereby an employer agrees not to handle, use, sell, or transport the products of another employer to whose labor policies a union objects. Widely sought by the American teamsters union, "hot cargo" agreements were limited by the Taft-Hartley Act of 1947 and outlawed completely by the Landrum-Griffin Act of 1959.

house brand See under BRAND.

household According to the U.S. Bureau of the Census, all the occupants of a group of rooms or single room that constitutes a housing unit when occupied as separate living quarters. Data concerning households are used chiefly in market analysis, as, for example, in forecasting demand for consumer durables (furniture, refrigerators, etc.).

household system The system of producing goods needed by a household within the household itself. Thus the American pioneer family, isolated from village or town, often produced its own soap, candles, cloth, and other goods, with little or no reliance on outside sources of supply.

house organ Also, *company magazine.* A periodical issued by a business enterprise either for its own employees or for its customers, distributors, stockholders, or other outsiders with whom it has regular dealings. For example, large pharmaceutical manufacturers often publish house organs addressed to physicians featuring articles about their own products as well as other medical subjects.

house-to-house selling See DOOR-TO-DOOR SELLING.

housing investment See CONSTRUCTION CONTRACT AWARDS.

housing loan insurance See MORTGAGE LOAN INSURANCE.

Hume, David A Scottish philosopher and political economist (1711–76) remembered for developing the *price-specie flow mechanism* (as it is now called), an idea that became basic to the theory of international trade held by the CLASSICAL SCHOOL. Hume accepted the QUANTITY THEORY OF MONEY (that the amount of money in circulation directly determines the general price level). However, whereas the mercantilists believed that a surplus of exports is required for a nation's money supply to grow, Hume maintained that even if imports exceed exports, the system is self-regulating and will reach equilibrium without government interference. Thus, if Country A loses gold through increased imports, the gold it pays to Country B, the exporter, will increase B's money supply and, in time, its general price levels. At the same time, the contracted money supply in A will cause its price levels to drop. As a result, B will begin to buy more from A (at A's lower prices) and A will import less from B (at B's high prices). Thus the changes in relative price levels caused by the flow of gold will remedy a trade imbalance before it becomes too extreme. Today, when money supply is essentially independent of precious metals and central banks exert a major influence on internal price levels and exchange rates, the mechanism is no longer automatic (and some doubt that it ever was).

hyperinflation See RUNAWAY INFLATION.

hypothecation The pledging of property as collateral for a loan. The lender is not given title to the property but is given the right to sell it in case of default. Hypothecation is widely used in buying securities on margin. The buyer signs a hypothecation agreement for the securities with the broker who handles the margin transaction. The broker is then free to use the securities as collateral for a bank loan or even for other customers making short sales. See also MARGIN, BUYING ON; SELLING SHORT.

ideal index An index devised by Irving FISHER to compensate for opposing tendencies toward bias in two different indexes. In effect the ideal index can combine any two indexes whose biases tend to offset one another. The ideal index is constructed by taking the geometric average of the two indexes, that is, the square root of their product (which always results in a slightly lower value than a simple arithmetic average). For example, two formulas are commonly used for obtaining a price index. One, the LASPEYRES INDEX, uses a ratio of hypothetical current expenditures to actual base-period spending expenditures (a base-weighted index). The other, the *Paasche index*, relates actual current spending to hypothetical base-period spending (a current-weighted index). The former tends to produce a higher measure of price change than the latter. To offset these tendencies, the ideal index can be computed:

$$I.I. = \sqrt{\frac{\Sigma Q_1 P_2}{\Sigma Q_1 P_1} \times \frac{\Sigma Q_2 P_2}{\Sigma Q_2 P_1}}$$

(Fischer)   (Laspeyres)(Paasche)

where $I.I.$ = ideal index; Σ = sigma, the standard symbol for "sum of"; Q = quantity; P = prices of individual items; and the subscripts 1 and 2 represent the base year and current year respectively. Owing to the difficulty of applying the ideal index to large samples, a similar but more manageable version was devised by the British economist Francis Y. Edgeworth.

It generally is easy to state how much a single price has increased from one period to another, but it usually is not possible to state in an unambiguous way how much a group of prices has increased if they have not all changed at the same rate. Thus, if hamburger cost $1 per pound last year and $1.05 per pound this year, the rate of that price increase is

194

5 per cent. Suppose, however, that during the same period the price of steak has increased 20 per cent and rents have risen by 12 per cent. Clearly one cannot simply average the three items to see how prices have changed since they are not of equal importance. One could weight the items according to importance, but how is importance to be measured? If a family bought more steak last year, when it was cheaper, does one weight the price of steak by the amount bought then or by the amount bought today? The former method will produce a higher measure of price increases (just as the Laspeyres index does) than the latter, but obviously neither is preferable. Fisher's ideal index—and Edgeworth's version of it—tried to get around this problem, yet despite the name it is still subject to the same limitations as other indexes. In fact, most economists today agree that no really "ideal" index can be constructed. See also INDEX NUMBER; PRICE INDEX.

idle In cost accounting, equipment or labor that is not being used productively and hence represents a loss to the firm. *Idle capacity*, referring to equipment not being employed either because workers cannot use it or because a plant for some reason must close, represents a cost chiefly in terms of fixed maintenance charges for the equipment, incurred whether it is used or not. *Idle time*, referring to workers standing by rather than actually working, representing labor costs, may be due to machine breakdowns, materials shortages, poor scheduling, administrative errors, or external factors (seasonal, cyclical, or industrial fluctuations).

IDR Abbreviation for INTERNATIONAL DEPOSITARY RECEIPT.

ILO Abbreviation for INTERNATIONAL LABOR ORGANIZATION.

image In advertising and public relations, the general view or overall reputation of a person, product, firm, or organization, as it is presented to (or perceived by) the public.

immigration The movement of people into a country for permanent settlement. From an economic standpoint, it constitutes a movement of one factor of production—labor—nearly always in the direction of greater prosperity, that is, immigrants are motivated at least partly by a desire to improve their economic lot. Historically, the largest movements of people took place during the 19th century, when certain areas of the world were rich in resources but sparse in population, the opportunities for economic growth were well publicized, and there was considerable freedom of movement across national boundaries. The chief recipients of immigrants were the United States, followed by Canada, Argentina, Brazil, Australia, and New Zealand. Between 1820 and 1950 an estimated total of 32 million immigrants settled permanently in the United States. Although the United States began to impose selective immigration controls as early as 1882 (when the Chinese began to be excluded), largely in response to pressure from those economic interests that feared a large influx of cheap labor, widespread restrictions were not imposed until the end of World War I. With the institution in 1922 of a stringent quota system, which put an absolute limit on total annual immigration and apportioned it among the various nationalities, immigration to the United States from any place other than northern and western Europe was severely curtailed. In the mid-1970s U.S. immigration policy was still basically restrictive, but quotas were less heavily skewed in favor of northwestern Europe. Countries that still welcomed immigrants after 1950 included Israel, Australia, and New Zealand, although all three exercised selectivity (Israel admitted practically all Jews, and Australia welcomed Europeans but set limits on the number of Asian immigrants).

imperfect competition Describing a market in which sellers can exert influence (but not full control) over selling prices for reasons such as increased demand caused by product differentiation, through advertising, brand names, patents, etc. (this type of market also is described as MONOPOLISTIC

COMPETITION); control over supply owing to a limited number of sellers and relative difficulty of entry by new sellers into the market (because of collusion, high initial investment requirements, etc.; see also FREEDOM OF ENTRY); limited knowledge on the part of buyers about prices and profits. The selling price under imperfect competition is known as an ADMINISTERED PRICE. In the so-called free-market economies of present-day capitalist nations, where price supposedly results from the interaction of supply and demand, imperfect competition tends to prevail for most goods and services. See also OLIGOPOLY; PURE COMPETITION.

imperialism The policy of extending a nation's rule over foreign territories and peoples. See COLONIALISM; also MERCANTILISM.

implied warranty See under WARRANTY.

import Any good or service purchased from a foreign country. See BALANCE OF TRADE; IMPORT QUOTA; INTERNATIONAL INVESTMENT; INTERNATIONAL TRADE; INVISIBLE ITEMS; TARIFF, def. l; TERMS OF TRADE.

import duty See TARIFF, def. 1.

import license A permit to import a given amount of a specific item. The purpose of such licenses usually is to enforce an IMPORT QUOTA. Since the quota limits the total quantity of an item permitted into a country, its domestic selling price may be artificially high, allowing importers to make an enormous profit. The value of an import license, therefore, may become very high, so in order to eliminate exorbitant profits on the licenses themselves a system of auctioning them off to the highest bidders is often used.

import quota A limit on the quantity of a particular item that may be imported during a given period of time. The limit may be in physical terms (such as total tonnage) or in terms of value (total dollar value); it also may be based on country of origin (so much from country A, so much from B, etc.), or it may be a simple total. Unlike such absolute quotas, a *tariff quota* admits unlimited amounts of an item but above a certain quantity imposes higher customs duties. The GENERAL AGREEMENT ON TAR-

IFFS AND TRADE has attempted to limit the use of import quotas. See also EXPORT QUOTA; IMPORT LICENSE.

import substitution The substitution of a costlier domestic product for a cheaper import for the purpose of improving one's BALANCE OF TRADE or for some other reason. For example, for many years the British continued to use domestic coal as boiler fuel in their electric power stations even though Arab crude oil was normally cheaper; this practice was intended both to guarantee an assured domestic supply and to reduce the deficit in Britain's balance of trade.

impulse buying The purchase of nonessential consumer goods without prior planning. The decision to buy usually is made at the point of purchase, as, for example, an ice-cream cone or popcorn purchased from a street vendor, a candy bar or magazine picked up in a supermarket, or an inexpensive pair of socks in a clothing store. In department stores goods likely to be bought on impulse often are placed on the first floor near the main doors; in grocery stores and drugstores, they are near the cash register or checkout counter.

imputed income Income in some form other than money, most often in the form of goods or services. In computing the national income and product accounts, the U.S. Department of Commerce assigns a value, based on estimated market value, to such imputed income so that it can be counted as part of total national income. Four major imputations are made: for wages and salaries paid in kind (food, clothing, lodging); rental value of owner-occupied houses; food and fuel produced and consumed on farms; and interest payments by financial intermediaries that do not otherwise explicitly enter the accounts (such as noninterest-bearing demand deposits).

inactive stock A stock issue in which there is a relatively low volume of trade, perhaps a few hundred shares per week or less, traded on an organized exchange or in the over-the-counter market. On the New York Stock Exchange some high-priced inactive stocks are traded in 10-share units instead of the customary 100-share round lots, transactions for these being concluded at a trading post called the *inactive post* or *Post 30*.

in-and-out trader Also, *in-and-outer*. A speculator who trades for quick small profits, buying and selling the same security within a short time. He or she is usually more interested in profiting from day-to-day price fluctuations than from dividends or long-term growth.

incentive See WAGE INCENTIVE.

incentive contract A purchase contract in which the seller is allowed to share in savings resulting from successful cost-cutting. Such a contract usually specifies a target cost, target profit, ceiling price, and percentage of savings in cost that will go to the seller as extra profit (or conversely, what percentage the seller will lose if its costs rise). For example, buyer and seller may set a target price of $100,000, of which $7,500 should be profit. They agree that even if costs rise, the selling price will not exceed $115,000. If costs can be minimized and the price can be kept below $100,000, the savings will be split, the seller receiving 25 per cent and the buyer 75 per cent. If costs are greater than anticipated and the buyer must charge $110,000, the buyer will pay for 75 per cent of the excess, or $7,500, but the seller's profit will be reduced by $2,500 because it must foot one-fourth of the excess cost. Incentive contracts are used chiefly for items with which the supplier has had little or no production experience.

In another kind of incentive contract, called a *special incentive contract*, the seller is encouraged to exceed the specifications. For example, with a contract for an engine that uses one gallon of fuel for every 25 hours of running time, the seller may be offered a bonus for producing an engine able to run even longer on the same amount of fuel.

incidence See under TAX.

income
1. In economic theory, the payment received by—or earnings of—a factor of production (land, labor, or capital), or the total of these payments. The concept of NATIONAL INCOME was given prominence by J. M. KEYNES and his followers, whose

theory is in effect based on INCOME ANALYSIS. See also the succeeding entries beginning with INCOME; also DISPOSABLE INCOME; PERSONAL INCOME; PSYCHIC INCOME; REAL INCOME.

2. Also, *gross income.* In accounting, a general term for money earned or accrued during a particular accounting period from any source (sales, rentals, investments, gifts, etc.), which increases previously existing net assets. Any excess of such money over costs is called NET INCOME. See also DEFERRED INCOME; EARNED INCOME; EARNINGS; PROFIT, def. 1; REVENUE, def. 2; UNEARNED INCOME.

income, disposable personal See DISPOSABLE INCOME; PERSONAL INCOME.

income analysis Also, *income determination.*

Analysis of the level of total spending, which is determined by the interplay of the monetary forces of saving and investment. Usually calculated on a national level (NATIONAL INCOME), income analysis is one of the major concerns of macroeconomics and a basic element of Keynesian economics (see also under J. M. KEYNES).

income bond See under BOND, def. 1.

income determination See INCOME ANALYSIS.

income distribution

1. The apportionment of total national income among all the individuals and families in a country. The amount of one's income depends on a variety of factors, including education, ability, social status, sex, and age. Income distribution is general-

Fig. 36. U.S. money income—per cent distribution of families, by income level, by race of head of household

| Race of Head and Year | Per Cent Distribution by Income Level | | | | | | | | | | | Median | |
	Under $1,000	$1,000–$1,999	$2,000–$2,999	$3,000–$3,999	$4,000–$4,999	$5,000–$5,999	$6,000–$6,999	$7,000–$9,999	$10,000–$14,999	$15,000–$24,999	$25,000 and over	Income	Index (1950 =100)
All families													
1950	11.5	13.2	17.8	20.7	13.6	9.0	5.2	5.8		3.3		3.319	100
1955	7.7	9.9	11.0	14.6	15.4	12.7	9.5	12.9	4.8	1.4		4.421	133
1960	5.0	8.0	8.7	9.8	10.5	12.9	10.8	20.0	10.6	3.7		5.620	169
1965	2.9	6.0	7.2	7.7	7.9	9.3	9.5	24.2	17.7	7.6		6.957	210
1970	1.6	3.0	4.3	5.1	5.3	5.8	6.0	19.9	26.8	22.3		9.867	297
1971	1.5	2.6	4.2	4.8	5.4	5.7	5.5	18.5	26.9	19.5	5.3	10.285	310
1972	1.3	2.2	3.7	4.5	4.9	5.0	5.2	16.8	26.1	23.0	7.3	11.116	335
1973	1.1	1.8	3.1	4.1	4.5	4.6	4.8	14.9	25.5	26.2	9.3	12.051	363
1974	1.3	1.3	2.7	3.6	4.1	4.4	4.4	13.8	24.3	28.3	11.5	12.836	387
White													
1950	10.0	12.2	17.3	21.3	14.4	9.6	5.5	6.1		3.5		3.445	100
1955	6.6	8.7	10.4	14.3	16.0	13.4	9.9	13.9	5.3	1.5		4.605	134
1960	4.1	6.9	8.1	9.4	10.5	13.3	11.2	21.3	11.2	4.1		5.835	169
1965	2.5	5.2	6.3	6.9	7.6	9.3	9.8	25.5	18.8	8.3		7.251	210
1970	1.4	2.4	3.7	4.6	4.9	5.5	5.8	20.1	27.9	23.7		10.236	297
1971	1.3	2.1	3.5	4.3	5.0	5.4	5.4	18.6	28.0	20.6	5.8	10.672	310
1972	1.1	1.7	3.1	4.1	4.5	4.7	5.0	16.7	27.0	24.2	8.0	11.549	335
1973	1.0	1.3	2.6	3.5	4.1	4.3	4.5	14.6	26.3	27.6	10.0	12.595	366
1974	1.1	1.0	2.2	3.1	3.7	4.2	4.2	13.5	25.1	29.7	12.4	13.356	388
Negro and other													
1950	28.1	25.3	23.5	13.5	4.3	1.9	1.5	1.7		0.3		1.869	100
1955	19.0	20.7	17.6	17.2	11.1	5.8	4.8	3.1	0.6	(z)		2.549	136
1960	13.4	18.3	14.8	14.0	10.4	8.7	6.7	8.7	4.3	0.6		3.233	173
1965	7.1	13.6	14.6	14.8	10.8	9.5	6.8	13.7	7.6	1.4		3.994	214
1970	3.4	7.7	9.0	8.8	8.2	9.0	7.4	18.2	17.3	10.9		6.516	349
1971	2.9	6.6	9.9	8.7	8.9	8.1	7.1	17.8	17.9	10.5	1.7	6.714	359
1972	2.7	6.3	8.7	9.0	8.5	7.5	6.5	17.1	18.1	13.2	2.4	7.106	380
1973	2.5	5.3	7.6	8.4	8.3	7.2	6.8	16.9	19.1	14.4	3.5	7.596	406
1974	2.2	4.4	7.0	8.2	7.8	6.3	6.7	16.2	19.0	17.9	4.5	8.265	442

z = less than 0.05 per cent.   *Source:* U.S. Department of Commerce.

ly assessed by means of a FREQUENCY DISTRIBUTION, that is, by sorting income into classes (under $1,000 per year, $1,000–1,999, $2,000–2,999, etc.) and counting the number of individuals and families within each class. A look at such distributions indicates that a much larger proportion of the population has low incomes than high ones. Although over time the general pattern of income distribution has tended to shift upward, the fact remains that there are far fewer wealthy individuals than poor ones (bearing out *Pareto's law*; see under V. PARETO). Also obvious is the fact that the distribution pattern of incomes is far from uniform, that is, the lowest 10 per cent receive far less than 10 per cent of national income, and the highest 10 per cent far more than 10 per cent of the total. This inequality of distribution has been diminished somewhat by government policies such as a PROGRESSIVE TAX on income and various welfare programs.

2. The apportionment of income among different areas, both within a nation and throughout the world, usually measured in terms of *per capita income* (total income divided by total population).

income effect The effect on the overall demand for a product of a price change that increases or decreases consumer purchasing power. For example, if the price of gasoline is cut by 50 per cent, an individual who loves driving will not only be able to buy more gas but, assuming that the amount of driving he does won't actually double, be able to buy more of other goods and services as well.

income elasticity of demand for imports See PROPENSITY TO IMPORT.

income equation See under J. M. KEYNES; for *income velocity of money equation*, see under VELOCITY OF MONEY.

income statement Also, *earnings report, operating statement, profit-and-loss statement.* A summary of the revenues and expenses of a business firm or other organization for a particular period of time, generally one year. Serving as a record of the organization's operating activities, the income statement matches the amounts received from selling goods or services, or other items of income, against the cost of goods sold and other outlays made in the operation of the company. The result is *net income*—a *net profit* if it is positive and a *net loss* if negative (sales minus costs equal net profit or loss). The most important source of revenue usually makes up the first item on the income statement: in a manufacturing firm it is *net sales*; in a utility or transportation service it is *operating revenues*. In either, it represents the primary source of money received by the company from its customers for goods sold or services rendered, after taking into consideration returned goods and allowances for price reductions. A secondary source of income, called "other income" or "miscellaneous income," is derived from dividends and interest received by the firm from its investments in securities, which are carried as assets in the balance sheet. In a manufacturing company, *cost of sales* represents all the costs incurred in the factory (including depreciation, which may or may not be stated separately) in the course of converting purchased materials into the finished products sold during the accounting period. These costs include raw materials and semifinished goods, direct labor, and such factory overhead items as supervision, rent, electricity, supplies, maintenance, and repairs. *Depreciation* is the decline in useful value of an asset due to wear and tear. *Selling and administrative expenses* often are grouped separately from cost of sales because they may be incurred independently of the cost of goods sold. They include salesmen's salaries and commissions, advertising and promotion, travel, entertainment, executives' salaries, office payroll, office expenses, etc. The interest paid to bondholders sometimes is referred to as a *fixed charge* because it must be paid year in and year out, regardless of whether the company is making a profit, whereas stock dividends generally are directly related to profits. The last important expense is *taxes*, especially (in the United States) Federal income tax.

Subtracting the total costs and expenses from the total income results in *net income*, the sum available for dividend payments on preferred and common stocks and for use in the business. The examination and comparison of the components of a firm's income statement can be very revealing. One useful figure is the *operating margin of profit ratio*, calculated by dividing sales into operating profit. In the Typical Manufacturing income statement in Fig. 37, this ratio is $700,000 ÷ $6,500,000 = 10.8%; that is, for each $1 of sales, there remains $.108 as gross profit. Similarly, one can calculate *operating cost ratio,* either by subtracting the operating margin of profit ratio from 100 or by dividing total operating costs by net sales; in our example, this is $5,800,000 ÷ $6,500,000 = 89.2%. Another useful figure is the *net profit ratio,* also called *profits per dollar of sales,* calculated by dividing net profit by net sales; in our example, $355,000 ÷ 6,500,000 = 5.5%. These figures are even more meaningful when compared from one year to the next for an individual company, or among a number of companies for a given year, serving as a useful means for inves-

tors to evaluate the basic financial soundness of different firms.

income tax Also, *personal income tax.* A tax levied on the annual incomes of households and unincorporated businesses after certain deductions and exemptions have been taken into account. (For income tax on businesses, see also CORPORATION INCOME TAX.) In the United States the Federal government and most state governments levy an income tax. These taxes are PROGRESSIVE, that is, the larger the *taxable* income (gross income minus exemptions and allowable deductions), the higher the tax rate. The higher rates apply not to the total income but to *increments* of income; thus no tax at all is paid on a basic income that is exempt, a small percentage is paid on the next few thousand dollars,

Fig. 37. Income statements
Typical Manufacturing Company, Inc., and Consolidated Subsidiaries

(1)   INCOME STATEMENT — YEAR 19 ____

Net Sales		$6,500,000
Cost of Sales and Operating Expenses		
Cost of Goods Sold	$4,400,000	
Depreciation	900,000	
Selling and Administrative Expenses	500,000	5,800,000
Operating Profit		$ 700,000
Other Income		
Dividends and Interest		110,000
Total Income		$ 810,000
Less: Interest on Bonds		135,000
Profit before Provision for Federal		
Income Tax		$675,000
Provision for Federal Income Tax		320,000
Net Profit for the Year		$355,000

(2)   **CONDENSED INCOME STATEMENT**

Plus Factors		
Net Sales	$6,500,000	
Other Income	110,000	
Total		$6,610,000
Minus Factors		
Cost of Sales and Operating Expenses	$5,800,000	
Interest on Bonds	135,000	
Provision for Federal Income Tax	320,000	6,255,000
Net Income		$ 355,000

Source: Courtesy Merrill Lynch, Pierce, Fenner, & Smith, Inc.

a larger percentage on the next few thousand, and so on. The principal *deductions* allowed from gross income to determine taxable income are business costs and expenses incurred in earning income, gifts to charity, interest payments, certain medical expenses, most other tax payments, and a per capita *exemption* for the taxpayer and each of his or her dependents (for many years $600 each, but increased in the 1970s owing to inflation).

Unlike some other taxes, the *burden* of income tax tends to fall squarely on the individual taxpayer; it rarely can be shifted elsewhere. However, U.S. tax law, which has become immensely complicated, offers a number of *loopholes* whereby the rich in particular can escape what would otherwise be a very high rate (80 per cent or more). First, interest on state and municipal bonds is not taxed at all. Second, and even more important, CAPITAL GAINS are taxed at a much lower rate than other income, as are high-risk investments, such as drilling for oil. By investing in fairly risky enterprises, therefore, the wealthy are able to keep much more of their income than the tax-rate tables would indicate. Finally, a person whose income comes primarily from owning or operating a corporation may be able to leave a large share of the profits in it; this income, in effect being reinvested, also is not taxable to the individual.

Instituting a Federal income tax, which today is the source of about half of the U.S. government's total revenues, was tried several times in the 19th century. At one point (1895) it was declared unconstitutional by the Supreme Court, but it was finally declared legal by the Sixteenth Amendment to the Constitution (adopted 1913). In addition, by 1975 all but six states had some kind of personal income tax. The Federal agency responsible for income taxes is the INTERNAL REVENUE SERVICE. See also SURTAX; WITHHOLDING TAX.

income velocity circulation of money   See VELOCITY OF MONEY.

inconvertibility   See CONVERTIBLE.

incorporation   The act of forming a CORPORATION.

increasing returns, law of   A principle that counteracts the law of diminishing returns. A firm

that, for any of several reasons, can effect an increase in production greater than its increase in costs will enjoy increasing returns—that is, higher profits. The most common way of achieving increasing returns is mass production (see SCALE, ECONOMY OF). Other ways include improved technology and use of higher-skilled labor.

indemnity   In insurance, compensation for a loss, in most cases equal to the face value of the insurance policy. See also DOUBLE INDEMNITY.

indent   A purchase order to an exporter or middleman to import certain goods within a specified time. In the case of an *open indent*, the exporter may obtain the goods from any source whatever; with a *closed indent* they must come from a particular manufacturer or producer. The name "indent" comes from the old practice of tearing ("indenting") the duplicate and other copies of such purchase orders for purposes of indentification, a practice made obsolete by carbon paper.

indenture
1. Also, *deed of trust, trust indenture*. An agreement that governs the conditions under which bonds are issued and that empowers one or more trustees to act on behalf of all the bondholders. The indenture states the total amount of the bonds secured by it (and hence the amount that may be issued and sold). The trustee, who must (according to the Trust Indenture Act of 1939) be independent, is normally a bank or trust company. Only after the indenture is deposited may the bonds actually be sold.
2. A system of bound labor whereby an individual is committed to work for a particular employer for a certain period of time. The name comes from the form of the contract, which originally was written on a sheet of paper and then torn in half (the jagged tear being called an "indent"). One form of indenture dates from medieval times, when an APPRENTICE was bound to work in exchange for learning a trade (see also under GUILD). Although most children who were apprenticed at least had the consent of their parents, in some instances poor children were apprenticed through public authority; in 1619, for example, the London Common Council sent to Virginia 100 children as "Bound apprentices." During the American colonial period it was

common for immigrants to bind themselves as servants (*indentured servants*) for a number of years, usually two to seven, in exchange for passage to America. Involuntary indenture consisted chiefly of three kinds: convicts serving their sentences through bound labor; victims of piracy or kidnapping forced to work; and servitude for debt (see also PEONAGE; POOR LAWS). Indenture furnished a considerable proportion of colonial labor.

index   See INDEX NUMBER; also under INDEXING.

indexation   See under RUNAWAY INFLATION.

index fund   A portfolio of stocks so weighted by their relative values that the fund performs virtually the same as the overall market over a period of time. Setting up the portfolio is called *indexing.* Such a fund is based on some general weighted market average, most often Standard & Poor's Composite Index of 500 stocks (see under AVERAGE, def. 2). The index fund adjusts its investment in each stock to reflect the market value of all shares outstanding in that company relative to the cumulative market value of all the other stocks in the index. For example, if General Motors represents 5 per cent of the total value of the Standard & Poor Index on a given day, the index fund should have 5 per cent of its total holdings in General Motors. The principal advantage of this system of investment is that it greatly lowers administrative costs; it requires no costly research of the market, and the decisions of what to buy and sell may be left to a properly programmed computer. Critics point out, however, that while an index fund will perform no worse than the overall market, neither will it perform significantly better. Further, some believe that if indexing becomes too popular the process itself will alter the values of the stocks in the index, driving up their prices in relation to those of stocks outside the index. For a similar means of tying monetary policy to the general price level, see *indexation* under RUNAWAY INFLATION.

indexing
1. In computers, the technique of adding a number called an *index* (or *offset* or *displacement*) to a "base address" to determine the location of a specific piece of information stored on a magnetic disk or magnetic core.

2. Another name for *indexation*; see under RUNAWAY INFLATION.
3. Creating an INDEX FUND.

index number   A measure of relative value compared with a base quantity for the same series. In a TIME SERIES in index form, the base-period value is often set at 100, and data for other periods are expressed as percentages of the value in the base period. Index numbers are used primarily to compare the changes in various economic phenomena over time (year to year, month to month, or even hour to hour in the case of stock indexes). The U.S. Federal government publishes numerous indexes concerning the overall economy, among them the CONSUMER PRICE INDEX and WHOLESALE PRICE INDEX. In addition, indexes are published by industries, private foundations, state and local governments, university bureaus of business research, the United Nations Statistical Office, and others.

There are four principal kinds of index: *price* (see PRICE INDEX); *quantity* (such as the Federal Reserve Board Index of Industrial Production); *value* (such as the Total Retail Sales Index); and *special-purpose*, most often involving some combination of the other three (such as the Forbes Index, combining production, money turnover, employment, department store sales, etc.). A *composite index* is one made up of other indexes (see under INDICATOR for an example.)

All indexes have three features in common. First, every index number has a *base period*, which is assigned a given value (usually 100, but 10 in the case of Standard & Poor's Composite Stock Price Index, 50 in the New York Stock Exchange's Composite Index, etc.). Second, all indexes measure a representative *selection* of items—a given list of products, employment in certain industries, etc. This selection is but a sample from which more general information is inferred, and obviously the inference can be only as good as the sample and the procedures used in obtaining it. Third, every index is computed according to some statistical formula, so that the index numbers for different time periods are comparable. The two principal kinds of formula used are *simple* (*unweighted*) and *weighted*. A simple form of price index is the ratio of one price to another for a specific commodity. For example, consider a gallon of milk, with a base-year price of $1. If milk goes up to $1.10 in Year 2 (the following year), to $1.15 in Year 3, $1.40 in Year 4, it is simple to calculate the index number, using the formula

$$I = \frac{P_n \times 100}{P_1}$$

where I = index number, P_n = price in any chosen year, and P_1 = base-year price of $1. (This formula is known as a *simple average of relatives*.) The index numbers would be 110 for Year 2, 115 for Year 3, and 140 for Year 4; one also might say that the price of milk had risen 10 per cent from the base period to Year 2, 15 per cent to Year 3, and 40 per cent to Year 4. A simple average works well for one commodity but falls down as soon as several commodities (milk, meat, cranberries) or, for a quantity index, different units of measure (liters, kilograms, meters) enter the picture. For the former, it distorts matters because the different foods mentioned have unequal importance in the total budget, a fact that becomes even more obvious if the items are not food but automobiles, milk, and funerals. In that case, a conversion to a common measure would be required. The same drawback holds true for a *simple aggregative average*, in which the prices of all the commodities under consideration are added and divided by the price they commanded in the base year. A single item that rises by a considerable sum will make the overall average rise too much, thereby distorting the picture. These drawbacks can be avoided in part by working with a WEIGHTED AVERAGE; of these, one of the most common used is the LASPEYRES INDEX. (See also IDEAL INDEX.)

Indexes have been used since the 18th century. An Italian, G. R. Carli, reputedly published the first such index in 1764, in a report on price changes in Europe from 1500 to 1750. The U.S. government has been publishing indexes since about 1900. A highly convenient way to measure changes in data made up of many unlike quantities (such as the production of lumber, automobiles, oil, shoes, and fish), indexes are useful for describing changes over time in employment, production, retail sales, and numerous other economic activities. For some specific indexes, see CONSUMER PRICE INDEX; INDUSTRIAL PRODUCTION INDEX; PURCHASED MATERIALS INDEX; VENDOR PERFORMANCE INDEX. For stock price indexes, see under AVERAGE, def. 2.

indicator Also, *cyclical indicator*. A set of data that serves as a tool for analyzing current economic conditions and future prospects. Included are data concerning employment, capital investment, inventories, prices, costs and profits, the money supply, bank loans, income, industrial production, and trade. The indicator approach was developed in the late 1930s by the American economists W. C. MITCHELL and Arthur F. Burns, among others. The 78 indicators currently recognized by the U.S. Bureau of Economic Analysis are classified according to their timing in relation to the ups and downs of the BUSINESS CYCLE, that is, whether they anticipate (lead), coincide with, or lag behind general business conditions. (See COINCIDENT INDICATOR; LAGGING INDICATOR; LEADING INDICATOR.) The government also publishes *composite indexes* that combine selected indicators from each classification into weighted, representative indexes. The indicators chosen measure related aspects of business change and are sensitive to business cycles. The procedure used allows for the fact that some indicators, such as new orders, move in wide swings, whereas others, such as the average workweek, are subject to narrow (though still significant) fluctuations.

indifference curve A graphic representation of the various amounts of two items that will yield equal satisfaction. A *consumer indifference curve* can be used to show, for example, what combination of apples and oranges would equally satisfy a particular consumer. In Fig. 38, quantities of apples are plotted on the Y-axis (vertical axis) and oranges on the X-axis; the line connecting these points forms the indifference curve. Though the term is generally used only in connection with consumer commodities, the same concept applies to factors of production, that is, to show what combination of two factors of production will yield the same amount of product; this representation is generally called the *isoquant* or *iso-product curve*. It can show, in theory at least, the varying quantities of labor and land that will yield, for example, the same quantity of tomatoes. Like the consumer indifference curve, the isoquant slopes downward to the right, indicating that as less of one factor is needed, more of the other is required to yield the same output. In both cases the slope of the curve represents the marginal rate of substitution between the two

Fig. 38. Indifference curve

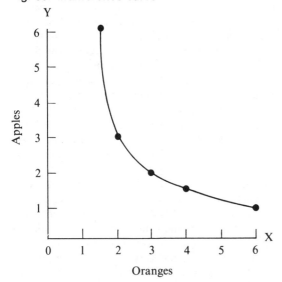

factors (or goods), the amount of one factor (good) that is needed to replace one unit of the other, although in one case it is substitution in consumption and in the other, in production. Because the rate of marginal substitution is usually diminishing, the curve tends to be convex to the point of origin (zero on the graph). If, however, the two goods (or factors) are perfect substitutes for one another, the curve will be a straight line, since the marginal rate of substitution then will be constant. See also ISOCOST CURVE.

indirect cost   Also, *indirect expense*; *manufacturing cost*. A business cost incurred by a firm producing goods or services that usually cannot be directly associated with any particular good or service but rather results from general productive activity. In effect, indirect cost is any cost of production other than direct labor and direct materials cost. Examples include the wages of supervisory personnel, maintenance of buildings and machinery, property taxes, and power costs. Since indirect cost tends to vary little with volume of output, some authorities identify it with fixed cost. See also DIRECT COST; FIXED COST; OVERHEAD.

indirect labor   See under LABOR COST.

indirect material   See under MATERIALS COST.

indirect production   See ROUNDABOUT PRODUCTION.

indirect tax   See under TAX.

indivisibility   See under SCALE, ECONOMY OF.

induced investment   Investment made in response to actual or anticipated increases in demand, either for a specific good or service or throughout the entire economy (owing to increased national income, larger population, etc.). Induced investment usually consists of purchases of capital equipment to increase productive capacity. According to some economists, specific increases in income or output will generate specific increases in investment. Most economists, however, feel that although a relationship undoubtedly exists it is not numerically fixed. See also ACCELERATION PRINCIPLE; AUTONOMOUS INVESTMENT.

industrial average   See under AVERAGE, def. 2.

industrial bank   See MORRIS PLAN BANK.

industrial democracy   The concept of giving workers a voice in how they do their jobs, so that to some extent they help manage a firm or industry. Practiced widely in Sweden since the 1930s, the concept also has been used in some West German companies where workers are represented on top management councils.

industrialization   The development of industry, considered by most economists essential for economic growth and prosperity. Though a largely agricultural economy can in theory be as prosperous as an industrial one, in modern times it usually finds itself at a distinct disadvantage (see under UNDERDEVELOPED NATION). In the 1970s New Zealand was one of the few very prosperous nations that was still largely agricultural, and it was gradually becoming industrialized. See also INDUSTRIAL REVOLUTION.

industrial migration   The relocation of industries, prompted by the location of markets, supply of labor or resources, transportation considerations, tax benefits, and other reasons making a new location seem more profitable than the old. For example, most of New England's textile industry moved to the South because of its lower wage levels and lower taxes. Similarly, while the American steel industry at first was centered near Pittsburgh because of a ready access to both raw materials and labor, most newer steel mills have been located closer to major markets (as in Detroit or California) or to deep-water ports giving ready access to imported iron ore.

industrial production index An index of U.S. industrial output in the mining, manufacturing, and utilities industries that is an important COINCIDENT INDICATOR of general business conditions. Officially entitled the *Federal Reserve Index of Industrial Production,* it is made up each month from a representative group of products, of which nearly 90 per cent are manufactured goods. Output is measured against a base year. The index is published in both the Federal Reserve's *Business Indexes* and the *Survey of Current Business,* as well as in the financial sections of many newspapers.

industrial relations A broad term for all relations between management and individual employees or employee groups (labor unions, etc.), concerning promotions, layoffs, transfers, wage scales, wage increases, fringe benefits, affirmative action, and similar conditions and terms of employment. It thus embraces both PERSONNEL ADMINISTRATION and LABOR RELATIONS.

industrial revenue bond A tax-exempt bond issued by a local government to attract industrial enterprises. The bond is for a plant nominally owned by the municipal government but actually secured by the long-term lease of a firm that negotiates with the local government. The firm therefore has the advantage of lower-cost borrowing on a tax-free bond, and the municipality gets a new industry. Utilities also use industrial revenue bonds for pollution control projects.

Industrial Revolution A period of rapid industrial growth, characterized by mechanization in industry and agriculture, new uses of energy in industry, the FACTORY SYSTEM, division of labor both within factories and throughout particular industries, large-scale production, development of trans-

portation and communications systems to effect large-scale distribution, and attendant economic growth and development. The term is most often used for the developments that took place in Great Britain from about 1750 to 1850, beginning with the substitution of coke for charcoal in iron smelting, continuing with the invention of new textile manufacturing machines (spinning jenny, power loom) and the steam engine, and climaxing in the development of a railway system. Some historians describe the period from about 1850 to 1950 as a Second Industrial Revolution, characterized by further technological innovation, the growth of mass production and automation, and the increasing reliance of industry on a complicated financial structure (investment banks, separation of ownership from management, holding companies and conglomerates). Whereas the first Industrial Revolution centered chiefly in England, spreading a little later to the United States, the United States led the so-called Second Revolution.

industrial union See under LABOR UNION.

Industrial Workers of the World Also, *IWW, Wobblies.* A union federation formed in 1905 by American Western miners to compete with the AFL, which they felt ignored unskilled labor and was too conservative generally (see AFL-CIO). Organized with the help of the Socialists, the IWW sought to stir up worker discontent and help win strikes. However, its violent tactics and blatant opposition to capitalism and to American involvement in World War I made it unpopular not only with business but also with less militant labor interests, and aroused public distrust of organized labor in general.

industry
1. A collective term for many of the productive activities of an entire nation or other large group, embracing manufacturing, processing, and mining, but usually excluding distribution and agriculture.
2. A specific branch of mining, manufacturing, or processing, in which a number of firms produce the same kind of commodity or service, or are engaged in the same kind of operation, for example, chemicals industry, steel industry, auto industry, construction industry, trucking industry, etc.

inelasticity See ELASTICITY.

infant industry A new or relatively new manufacturing enterprise. The argument that such new businesses need help against foreign competitors in the form of protective tariffs was a basic tenet of MERCANTILISM and a popular idea in 19th-century America (see also under TARIFF OF ABOMINATIONS).

inferior good Also, *Giffen good, Giffen's paradox.* A commodity for which demand declines as income rises and increases when real income falls, that is, a commodity whose DEMAND CURVE rises. For example, a poor family may substitute dried beans or eggs for meat. When income rises, the family will eat less beans and more meat; when the price of beans rises, it will be forced to eat still more beans and still less meat (because its real income will decline with this price increase). Thus, in the case of an inferior good, INCOME EFFECT outweighs both the effect of a change in price and the substitution effect (assuming there is no cheaper protein substitute for beans). Among the first to point out this phenomenon was the British economist Sir Robert Giffen (1837–1910).

inflation An increase in the general PRICE LEVEL, owing to increased total spending relative to the supply of goods on the market. Inflation is generally also associated with rising wages and rising costs of production, a large money supply (in relation to output), and a decrease in purchasing power (since prices usually rise faster than income does). Most economists agree that some rise in the general price level is inevitable with economic growth, and many feel that a price-increase rate of up to 2.5 per cent per year is normal (assuming that output and wages also increase by at least that much). Anything in excess of that figure, however, is considered inflation. Inflation may occur during the expansion phase of the BUSINESS CYCLE as part of a general increase in overall business activity, or it may result from overenthusiastic government action in the form of REFLATION. It frequently follows a war; for example, in Germany after World War I the general price level increased a trillionfold between 1920 and 1923 (see also RUNAWAY INFLATION). Other causes are high demand for bank loans (see DEMAND-PULL INFLATION); heavy government spending; continuing demand for wage increases (see COST-PUSH INFLATION); increasing demand for goods in short or fixed supply; a growing tendency to spend savings for fear that, with further declines in purchasing power, they otherwise will shrink in value. In the United States, inflation has occurred during every war and its aftermath, beginning with the American Revolution, but until the end of World War II a general price decline always set in sometime during the postwar period. Between World War II and the Korean conflict, however, prices continued to rise at varying rates, a pattern that continued into the late 1970s. See also BOTTLENECK INFLATION; HIDDEN INFLATION; SUPPRESSED INFLATION; STAGFLATION.

inflationary gap An excess of investment spending over the real saving that becomes available at full employment. For example, if consumers are willing to save (that is, not spend on goods and services) only 15 per cent of national output, while businesses would like to invest 20 per cent of that output, there is a gap of 5 per cent between investment and saving. Prices will tend to rise because the demand for investment funds raises business costs. The higher prices in turn will become someone else's higher costs, and the result is what is known as an *inflationary spiral*, in which all prices and costs rise by an amount equal to the inflationary gap times a given multiplier (see MULTIPLIER PRINCIPLE, def. 1). Thus, in an economy with full employment, a $30 billion inflationary gap may cause prices to rise by an amount equal to $90 billion per year. In reality, however, higher prices will tend to make consumers put off some of their purchases and save more, so that saving and investment gradually will tend to be brought back in line with one another, closing the inflationary gap. See also DEFLATIONARY GAP.

infrastructure Also, *social overhead capital.* Basic facilities and services upon which an economy's industry and commerce depend. Among them are transportation systems, sanitation, communications networks, and public utilities. Also included are less tangible requirements, such as the level of health and education of the population, the availability of administrative skills, and technological sophistication. A nation's infrastructure generally is created and operated or controlled by the government.

inheritance tax See under DEATH TAX.

injunction In law, a writ obtained from a judge which forbids specified acts by certain persons for a given length of time. This legal device was much used against labor unions by employers, who, in the name of protecting property, called for and received injunctions that forbade strikes and boycotts. The Norris-LaGuardia Act of 1932 virtually eliminated such interference by the courts in labor disputes, and today an employer cannot obtain a Federal court injunction against a peacefully conducted primary strike, although injunctions still may be issued against sympathy strikes and similar tactics, particularly by state courts. The Taft-Hartley Act of 1947, moreover, ruled that a strike in an essential industry can be halted by a temporary court injunction.

in kind, payment Strictly speaking, an exchange of equivalent goods, such as buying merchandise in exchange for other, comparable items. In general usage, however, the term refers to payment in any form other than money, chiefly goods or services. For example, a tenant farmer may pay some or all of his rent in the form of a share of his crop.

inland bill of exchange See under BILL OF EXCHANGE.

inland marine insurance See under PROPERTY INSURANCE.

innovation The practical application of a new product, service, or method following its original invention and representing an improvement important to economic growth. For the *innovation theory*, see under J. A. SCHUMPETER.

in-process inventory See WORK-IN-PROCESS INVENTORY.

input Information fed into a COMPUTER.

input-output analysis An analysis, usually in table form, that shows statistically how a nation's industries interact with one another. Its ultimate purpose is to answer such questions as, "How will a 10 per cent rise in steel prices affect the oil industry?" Devised principally by Wassily W. Leontieff (1906–), a Russian-American economist who won the 1973 Nobel Memorial Prize in Economic Science for his contribution, detailed input-output tables are very complex. They show, for each of several hundred industries, the amount of each industry's output that goes to every other industry in the form of either raw materials or finished products, as well as the amount that goes to its ultimate market in the economy. They also show, for each industry, its consumption of the products of other industries, as well as its contribution to the production process (in the form of value added). They thus permit tracing the industrial repercussions of changes in exports, government procurement, demand for investment goods, and other variables.

Modern input-output tables, used in several countries besides the United States, are in effect an elaboration of the *tableau économique* of F. QUESNAY. The entire approach, however, has certain serious drawbacks, apart from the fact that, owing to its complexity, a table for a given year is usually not published until five or six years later. It is based on the assumption that constant quantities of input are needed to produce a given output; with increased efficiency or improved technology this simply is not true. A woodcutter sawing down trees may become more efficient at his job, or wage cuts may permit hiring two woodcutters for the former price of one, or a chain saw may reduce the woodcutter's work time even more, or—the variables are considerable. Moreover, input-output analysis assumes constant consumer demand for products, given prices, and similar constants that in reality are quite variable and affect production. Hence input-output analysis would be truly useful only in a totally planned economy, where consumer demand changes are irrelevant to production, prices are controlled, and input materials have long since been allocated by a central planning committee.

inside price Also, *dealer price, wholesale price.* In finance, the price quoted by dealers to one another in the OVER-THE-COUNTER MARKET, as opposed to the *outside prices* they charge other customers. (For the difference between the two, see SPREAD, def. 1.)

insolvency In general usage, inability to pay one's debts as they fall due. According to U.S. Federal law (the Bankruptcy Act), a person is insolvent if the sum of his or her property, at a fair valuation, is not sufficient to pay his or her debts. See also BANKRUPTCY.

inspection In quality control, the process of measuring, examining, testing, gauging, or otherwise comparing one or more units of a product with product specifications. The unit of product may be a single item, a pair, a set, a specimen, a length, an area, a volume, or some other quantity, or it may be an operation, service, or performance. No matter what the method of inspection, however, none is foolproof. Even when every single item is carefully inspected, roughly 15 per cent of the defective items will be passed as acceptable. There are two main kinds of inspection. One, called *inspection by variables*, measures the cogent characteristics precisely, as, for example, a particular dimension on a machined part. The other, *inspection by attributes*, simply sorts the items into two groups, one acceptable and the other not. With the first method, the variations from the standard are sorted according to the degree of deviation (for example, by .001 centimeter, .002 centimeter, .003 centimeter, etc.). The second method encompasses only two groups, one usable and the other not. Although inspection by attributes is both cheaper and faster, it cannot reveal the cause of defects. However, if the dimensions of a given part are found to be gradually getting larger and larger, the inspector may be able to deduce at what stage of production the defect is occurring and thus help prevent further recurrence.

installment bond See under BOND, def. 1.

installment buying Also, *buying on time.* Purchasing consumer goods, usually relatively expensive ones, and paying for them over a period of time, in periodic partial payments called *installments.* This practice allows buyers to use goods before they are paid for, an obvious advantage, and

enables sellers to charge more for the goods, since the buyer must pay interest on the unpaid balance of the purchase price. Also, even though the seller may retain title to the goods, the buyer is responsible for them and must bear the loss if they are damaged or destroyed while in his or her possession. Should the buyer default on payments, the seller has the right of *repossession,* that is, he may take back the goods. The charges for installment sales, commonly called *interest* or *carrying charge,* usually cover not only pure interest (what the seller presumably could earn by investing the total purchase price were it paid in full at once) but also insurance against estimated risks (losses from bad debts, extra collection expenses for would-be evaders) and administrative expenses (credit investigation, legal help with contracts, bookkeeping, billing, collection). Until 1968, when the Truth in Lending Act was passed, less sophisticated American consumers could be deceived into thinking that installment purchases cost only little more than cash sales, with sellers quoting charges, for example, of $1\frac{1}{2}$ per cent (failing to mention that this meant $1\frac{1}{2}$ per cent per month, or 18 per cent per year). Since then, sellers have been required to disclose not only the total dollar amount of finance charges but the annual percentage rate as well. (See also under CONSUMER PROTECTION LAWS.)

Installment buying involves a contract between buyer and seller, which ordinarily takes either of two forms: a CHATTEL MORTGAGE, in which the seller transfers title to the buyer but then takes the mortgage as security; or a *conditional sales contract,* whereby the buyer gets possession of the

Fig. 39. Typical installment purchase of automobile

Price of automobile		$3,075
Trade-in value of old car	$ 375	
Cash down payment	+ 700	
Total down payment	$1,075	− 1,075
Balance to be financed		$2,000
Car insurance		+ 149
Total to be financed		$2,149
24 payments of $111 each		2,664
Dollar cost of credit		$ 515

Fig. 40. Dollar cost of credit charges on $1,000 loan at different credit rates, repaid in different number of installments

Credit Rate	Dollar Cost of Charges When Number of Monthly Installments Is					
	12	18	24	30	36	42
"Add-on" rate (added to beginning amount of debt):						
$ 4 per $100 per year	$ 40	$ 60	$ 80	$100	$120	$140
$ 6 " " " "	60	90	120	150	180	210
$ 8 " " " "	80	120	160	200	240	280
$10 " " " "	100	150	200	250	300	350
$12 " " " "	120	180	240	300	360	420
Per cent of unpaid balance:						
$\frac{3}{4}$ of 1 per cent per month	49	73	96	120	145	169
1 per cent per month	66	98	130	162	196	230
$1\frac{1}{2}$ " " " "	100	149	198	249	301	355
2 " " " "	135	201	269	340	412	488
$2\frac{1}{2}$ " " " "	170	254	342	433	528	627

goods but the seller retains title until the last payment has been made (see also CONDITIONAL SALE). Typically, the customer makes a cash down payment and agrees to pay the remainder in monthly installments, over a period ranging from a few months to several years. With a special contract, called an *add-on contract*, the customer may make additional purchases, add them to the original contract, and extend the payments.

Originating in the mid-19th century and at first largely confined to low-income consumers, installment buying in the United States has expanded greatly and is now common on all income levels. Though it remains a fairly expensive form of credit, about one-sixth of all personal income in the 1970s was going to installment payments. The single item most often bought "on time" is the automobile, with about half of all American car purchases being made in this way. Installment credit, which in the mid-1970s exceeded $145 billion, is basically financed by commercial banks, which lend funds on deposit in checking accounts or obtained through certificates of deposit. The banks lend both directly to consumers and to finance companies, which in turn lend (at higher interest) to consumers. See also CONSUMER CREDIT; FINANCE COMPANY, def. 2. For installment buying of real estate, see LAND CONTRACT.

institutional advertising See under ADVERTISING.

institutional economics A school of economic thought that emphasizes the influence on human behavior of institutions, which are broadly defined as well-established organized patterns of group behavior. This view would regard as institutions such practices as slavery or laissez faire. For the most part, however, the institutionalists concentrated on economic institutions that they believed required reform, principally credit, monopoly, labor-management relations, and the distribution of wealth and income. Though the institutionalists believed one must study the economy as a whole, they tended to use an empirical approach (like the German historical school). They also emphasized that customs, feelings, and habits were at least as influential as rational forces. Unlike the MARGINALIST SCHOOL, they believed that society and its institutions were constantly changing, and hence they stressed the importance of a dynamic view. Equilibrium, they said, is not a normal condition, whereas the business cycle itself *is* normal, but government interference is needed to offset its more harmful effects. Moreover, they denied the existence of a basic underlying harmony of human interests; rather, they thought that conflict between different economic groups was inevitable. The institutionalists favored liberal reforms and believed government should play a greater role in economic affairs. Principally an American school, institutional economics was founded by T. VEBLEN, whose principal followers were W. C. MITCHELL and J. R. COMMONS.

institutional investor A buyer of securities acting on behalf of an institution, such as a pension fund, trust fund, mutual fund, or insurance company. Though such an "institution" may consist of a relatively small trust fund—for example, $50,000 or so—institutional investors more often are associated with considerable investment capital, and today they account for about three-fourths of the trading on the New York Stock Exchange. Indeed, a THIRD MARKET has developed as a result of their dealings, which often involve blocks of stock too large for the ordinary stock exchange SPECIALIST to handle. Since institutional investors frequently decide to buy and sell the same securities at the same time, their growth has also contributed to the existence of a more volatile THIN MARKET.

instruction See under PROGRAMMING.

insurable interest See under INSURANCE.

insurance Also, *assurance.* A contract whereby one party promises to pay a sum of money to another if the latter suffers a particular loss. Insurance protects against hazards to life or property (of death, theft, fire, etc.) by charging losses against a fund created by the payments of many individuals. In effect, the risk and financial burden of such losses are distributed among thousands of persons instead of falling on one or a few. The person or firm who undertakes the risk is called the *insurer* or *underwriter*; the person or firm who receives the promise is the *insured* or *policyholder;* the contract in which the promise to pay is made is the insurance *policy*; and each policyholder payment is called a PREMIUM. For a policy to be enforceable, the policyholder must have an *insurable interest* in whatever is being insured. With property, a person has an insurable interest when he or she has any interest or right in a property whose destruction or damage might cause him or her a direct loss, and when this

interest exists at the time the loss occurs (not necessarily when the insurance contract is originally made). The insured thus need not have title to the property but may simply be in possession of it or hold a lien against it. With life, everyone has an insurable interest in one's own life and therefore can insure it and name anybody else as *beneficiary*. Further, a person may have an insurable interest in the life of another person if he or she can expect to suffer financial loss from that person's death. A creditor, for example, may have an insurable interest in the life of a debtor, and a business PARTNERSHIP has an insurable interest in the life of each partner (as does any business in the life of any key executive). Unlike property insurance, however, life insurance requires that the insurable interest exists at the time the policy is taken out (rather than when the loss occurs).

The modern insurance business originated in 17th-century England, which, as a major maritime nation, became an early center of *marine insurance*. At first signed by private individuals (called *underwriters* because they signed their names at the bottom of a policy), insurance policies for shipping became a burgeoning business, and in the late 1680s Edward Lloyd established a coffeehouse in London where underwriters and shippers could get together. The organization that still bears his name, Lloyd's of London, is not a conventional company but an association of individual underwriters operating through a system of syndicates. Each underwriter represents a group of investors who pool their funds to put up insurance. Though this form of organization (sometimes called a *Lloyd's association*) does exist in the United States, it is rare compared to stock and mutual companies. The first American MUTUAL INSURANCE COMPANY (in which the policyholders are the owners) was chartered in 1752 by, among others, Benjamin Franklin. The oldest American STOCK INSURANCE COMPANY (set up like a corporation) still in existence was founded in 1792. Other forms of American insurance organization are the *reciprocal exchange*, an association in which each member insures all the others; *government insurance*, in which a government (state or Federal) serves as the insurer (for workmen's compensation, life insurance, or other kinds); and *self insurance*, in which a large business sets up an insuring fund to which, for example, each of its many retail outlets contributes a "premium" and from which losses are paid.

The principal hazards for which one may buy insurance today can be broadly classified as loss of income and/or loss of property. Income may be lost through death, retirement, unemployment, or some kind of disability resulting from accident or illness. Property may be damaged or lost through dishonesty (burglary, robbery, theft), fire, explosion, storms (lightning, wind, hail, rain), civil disturbances (riots), traffic accidents, etc. Consequently the principal kinds of insurance are LIFE INSURANCE, UNEMPLOYMENT COMPENSATION, HEALTH INSURANCE, WORKMEN'S COMPENSATION, and PROPERTY INSURANCE. For insurance against the claims of a third person suffering loss or injury, see LIABILITY INSURANCE. For surety and fidelity insurance, see FIDELITY BOND; SURETY BOND. See also ANNUITY; GROUP INSURANCE; NO-FAULT INSURANCE; TITLE INSURANCE.

intangible asset   See under ASSET.

intangible cost   Also, *intangible expense.* A cost incurred in order to acquire an intangible asset, such as goodwill or a patent.

integration   See HORIZONTAL INTEGRATION; VERTICAL INTEGRATION.

intensive cultivation   Methods whereby a farmer seeks to obtain the greatest possible yield from a given acreage, using large amounts of fertilizer, irrigation, and special seed, as well as a great deal of labor and equipment. Traditionally used where land is relatively scarcer and costlier than labor or equipment, intensive farming has long been practiced in such small and technologically advanced countries as Denmark and the Netherlands, and more recently Japan. It also is practiced—though with less success—in overpopulated but underdeveloped nations with fertile soil, such as Indonesia. See also EXTENSIVE CULTIVATION.

Inter-American Development Bank   A credit agency established in 1959 by the United States and 20 Latin American nations (later joined by Canada and several others) to promote the economic development of its members by making loans, either to governments or to private entities, usually for specific projects. It also provides technical help for development projects and administers the Social Progress Trust Fund, which concentrates on loans for land settlement and improved land use, low-income housing, water and sanitation facilities, and training technical personnel. See also ASIAN DEVELOPMENT BANK.

interchangeable bond   See under BOND, def. 1.

interchangeable part   A part of a machine so designed that it can be used as the corresponding part in any other machine of the same kind. The use of interchangeable parts is intrinsic to MASS PRODUCTION.

intercorporate dividend credit   In U.S. tax law, a provision that exempts 85 per cent of the dividend income distributed by a taxpaying corporation from corporation income tax for the corporation receiving the dividend. It is intended to eliminate DOUBLE TAXATION.

interest

1. In banking and finance, the charge, usually quoted as an annual percentage, for borrowing money. See COMPOUND INTEREST; INTEREST RATE; SIMPLE INTEREST; USURY.

2. In economic theory, the return earned by capital, one of the FACTORS OF PRODUCTION. See also INTEREST RATE; PRODUCTIVITY OF CAPITAL. For various economic theories of interest, see ABSTINENCE THEORY OF INTEREST; LIQUIDITY PREFERENCE; LOANABLE FUNDS; TIME PREFERENCE THEORY OF INTEREST; *natural interest rate,* under K. WICKSELL.

3. A share in the ownership of property, as, for example, a 10 per cent interest in a business.

4. A right to the benefits of ownership short of having title to the property. For example, a will may grant a *life interest* in a parcel of land, which becomes someone else's property when the legatee dies. The first legatee benefits from the property, that is, he or she may keep whatever income the land earns, without holding title to the land. That title then passes to someone else.

interest rate The price paid for borrowing money (see INTEREST, def. l). It is based on such factors as the borrower's having immediate use of the money while the lender must postpone its use, the lender's risking nonrepayment and the possibility that economic changes will have reduced the purchasing power of the funds by the time they are repaid, the administrative costs of processing a loan, etc. Since these factors vary under different circumstances, there is no single interest rate but many different ones, depending on the kind of loan, its period, the credit standing of the borrower, collateral for the loan, the nature of the lender (private individual, bank, etc.), and so on. In addition, the interest rate depends on the market for a particular loan, that is, the demand for that kind of loan by borrowers and the supply of funds available for such lending. See also DISCOUNT RATE; MARKET RATE OF INTEREST; PRIME RATE; REDISCOUNTING.

interindustry competition See under COMPETITION.

interlocking directorate A method of limiting competition by securing a directorship on the board of a rival company and then influencing that board's decisions in one's own favor. A common monopolistic practice in the late 19th-century United States, the interlocking directorate was outlawed by the Clayton Antitrust Act of 1914, which said that a person cannot serve as a director of two companies if both have assets of $1 million or more, are engaged in interstate commerce, and are natural competitors. However, since a major stockholder still can serve as director of a competing firm, the intent of this provision can readily be circumvented.

intermediate goods See under GOODS.

Internal Revenue Service Also, *IRS*. The principal Federal agency administering and enforcing all U.S. tax laws except those relating to alcohol, tobacco, firearms, and explosives. Chief among the taxes it administers are the personal income tax and the social insurance and retirement taxes; also important are corporation income, excise, death, and gift taxes. Disputes between the IRS and taxpayers are heard by the U.S. TAX COURT.

international balance of payments See BALANCE OF PAYMENTS.

International Bank for Reconstruction and Development Also, *World Bank*. An institution affiliated with the United Nations and organized at the Bretton Woods Conference in 1944, whose chief purposes are to assist in the reconstruction and development of its members by facilitating capital investment, making loans out of its own funds where private capital cannot be obtained, and promoting foreign investment by guaranteeing and participating in private loans and private investment. It extends loans to member governments or to their agencies, or to private enterprises guaranteed by member governments. Each member nation contributes to the bank's stock according to its ability. The bank also raises funds by selling bonds in the world market, as well as from the sale of part of its loans, and from earnings and repayment of loans. It operates chiefly through two affiliates, the INTERNATIONAL DEVELOPMENT ASSOCIATION (IDA) and INTERNATIONAL FINANCE CORPORATION (IFC).

International Commerce, Bureau of An agency of the U.S. government charged with the promotion of American foreign commerce and assisting American business with its operations abroad. It provides commercial, economic, and marketing information for exporters, participates in international trade conferences, and negotiates with other nations, both directly and through such organizations as the GENERAL AGREEMENT ON TARIFFS AND TRADE (GATT).

international commodity agreement An agreement among the producers of a particular commodity, such as wheat or sugar, to set the prices and quantities at which the commodity will be traded. Aimed at stabilizing the prices of primary commodities, which normally are extremely volatile, such agreements usually involve setting export quotas in a commodity (such as the Coffee Agreement of 1962, renewed in 1968) and, where importing countries also are involved, import quotas as well. Another device used in such agreements is the accumulation of surpluses in times of good or excessive supply to offset times of relative scarcity (as in the Tin Agreement of 1956, renewed in 1971), along the lines of the EVER-NORMAL GRANARY concept; this practice is also called a *buffer stock plan.* Designed mainly to protect producer interests and therefore essentially collusive, if not outright monopolistic, commodity agreements serve to protect the less efficient producers and maintain high prices, which naturally does not help consumers. In practice, however, the difficulties of accurately predicting demand, supply, and other vital factors have made such agreements less than fully effective. The International Wheat Agreement of 1949, for example, floundered when wheat prices shot up wildly during the Korean War. Nevertheless, some economists believe that price-support agreements could be used to help poorer countries—especially those dependent on one or a few commodities for the bulk of their income—to improve their TERMS OF TRADE position. See also CARTEL; UNDERDEVELOPED NATION.

International Confederation of Free Trade Unions A world body founded in 1949 to counteract Communist influence over the labor movement. With headquarters in Brussels, Belgium, it has about 135 member unions in more than 100 nations. The confederation is largely an educational body, aimed particularly at underdeveloped nations. It has set up programs for training labor leaders and also administers a fund to help victims of mine disasters, strikes, earthquakes, and so on.

international corporation See MULTINATIONAL COMPANY.

International Depositary Receipt Also, *IDR.* A substitute stock certificate that makes it easier for a citizen of one country to own stock in a firm located in another country. For example, a Mexican who wished to invest in a German firm might find it easier to purchase IDRs for stock in that firm than to buy the stock directly. An IDR is essentially the same as an AMERICAN DEPOSITARY RECEIPT, except that the owner of the receipt is not an American. In fact, when an IDR for a non-American firm is sold to an American citizen, it becomes an American Depositary Receipt. Another version is the *European Depositary Receipt,* or *EDR,* created for the convenience of European investors.

International Development Association Also, *IDA.* An affiliate of the International Bank for Reconstruction and Development (World Bank) that lends money at no interest other than a service charge of 1 per cent or less and over long terms (up to 50 years) to underdeveloped countries unable to obtain investment capital through conventional channels at normal rates. Established in 1960, the IDA is open to all members of the World Bank. It draws its funds chiefly from 18 of its more than 120 members, who are known as Part I countries and are highly developed. Though projects seeking IDA funds are expected to meet the same criteria as World Bank loans, IDA loans cover a wider range, including the development of transportation, agriculture, electric power, industry, water supply, and education.

International Finance Corporation Also, *IFC.* An affiliate of the International Bank for Reconstruction and Development (World Bank) that lends money to private industry in underdeveloped member countries. Established in 1956, the IFC aims to provide equity and loan capital for productive private enterprise in association with private investors and management, to encourage the development of local capital markets, and to stimulate the international flow of private capital. It therefore invests in a wide variety of industries, always in association with private business that has no government guarantee, but it may not provide more than half of the total financing required (in practice it usually supplies only 25 per cent). The IFC makes available financing for both foreign exchange and local currency expenditures. The borrower can use IFC funds for fixed assets or for working capital, and it may spend them in any country. The IFC may borrow funds from the World Bank to re-lend to investors who lack the government guarantee the Bank requires. Financed by subscriptions from member nations, IFC loans have been bought by private financial institutions (by 1968, one-third of the total IFC investment had been so purchased), releasing the funds for reinvestment.

international investment Also, *foreign investment*. Ownership by a private individual, business, institution, or government of assets—in the form of securities; titles to land, buildings, or equipment; bank deposits; etc.—in a foreign country. In effect, such investment represents the export of money capital from one country to another, and in fact it is so represented in that country's BALANCE OF PAYMENTS. International investment may be undertaken either to obtain higher profits (through higher dividends or interest, greater political stability, lower taxes, or expected changes in the exchange rate) or for political, diplomatic, military, or long-term economic reasons. Investment purely for higher profits is usually private, whereas that for political and other purposes is nearly always made by governments (see also FOREIGN AID). Both private and government investment may consist of either *portfolio investment*—that is, securities traded in the conventional securities market of the foreign country in question—or *direct investment*, that is, the purchase of a controlling interest in a foreign business or subsidiary, which usually involves managerial control over the business and generally also technological input.

Foreign investment holds both advantages and disadvantages for the investor country. If too much capital is invested abroad relative to trade surplus or loans that bring in money, a balance of payments deficit may result. On the other hand, foreign investment not only may lower the prices of imports, but the higher yield on capital invested abroad will eventually return to the domestic economy as dividends are remitted from abroad. Advantages and disadvantages exist for the foreign country as well. Foreign capital can be a good means of stimulating rapid growth, particularly in countries where savings are insufficient compared to potential investment opportunities (as in Australia). On the other hand, most people do not always welcome the idea that their destiny is controlled by foreign capitalists, even when they benefit economically. In addition, direct investment can lead to ruthless exploitation (as in the past in Africa and Latin America), as well as create economic and political rivalries among the investors that sometimes erupt in warfare. Supporters of foreign investment for underdeveloped nations say that private investment does not have these pitfalls. Nevertheless, since World War II many individual underdeveloped nations have complained that foreign capital is akin to colonialism and imperialism, and some have responded by nationalizing some or all of the foreign enterprises within their borders.

In the United States an independent Federal agency, the Overseas Private Investment Corporation, was created in 1969 to encourage private American citizens to invest in some 90 underdeveloped nations. One of its functions is to insure investors against the risks of political expropriation and other losses by guaranteeing loans made to eligible private foreign enterprises. See also CAPITAL MOVEMENTS.

International Labor Organization Also, *ILO*. A specialized agency associated with the United Nations, created by the Treaty of Versailles in 1919 as part of the League of Nations. The United States became a member in 1934. Today the ILO has more than 120 member nations, each of which appoints four delegates (two from government, one from labor, and one from employers). Its major purposes are to improve labor conditions, raise living standards, and promote economic and social stability. It develops standards concerning employment, freedom of association, work hours, migration for employment, protection of female and child labor, prevention of industrial accidents, workmen's compensation, social security, and similar matters, which serve as guides for its members.

international liquidity See LIQUIDITY, def. 2.

International Monetary Fund Also, *IMF*. An institution affiliated with the United Nations and set up at the Bretton Woods Conference in 1944 to promote international monetary cooperation, facilitate the expanded and balanced growth of international trade, promote exchange stability, help establish a multilateral system of payments for current transactions among members, and make available to members the fund's resources. Thus the overall aim of the IMF is to minimize imbalances in the international BALANCE OF PAYMENTS of any of its members and to tide them over temporary deficits. A member with a balance of payments deficit can borrow foreign currency from the IMF in exchange for its own currency; it must then repurchase that currency within three to five years with gold or some acceptable currency. In 1962 ten member countries and Switzerland signed a General Agreement to Borrow, making available an additional sum of $6.2 billion in credit should it be required. (See also GROUP OF TEN.)

In 1969 the IMF established a kind of international paper money in the form of SPECIAL DRAWING RIGHTS (SDRs), providing for annual increases in international credit. In the next few years SDRs became an important medium of exchange in international trade. In 1974 the IMF decided to expand both its long-term and its short-term lending. The former, represented by an extended "fund facility," was designed particularly to aid underdeveloped nations. The latter, a so-called oil facility, was an attempt to tide over nations whose balance of payments had been thrown badly into deficit by the fourfold increase in Arab oil prices begun in 1973. At the same time the IMF decided to support a managed floating EXCHANGE RATE. In 1976 it was agreed to set up a new gold trust fund to make more internationally usable money available to the poorer nations.

international reserves See FOREIGN EXCHANGE RESERVES; GOLD RESERVE; RESERVE CURRENCY; RESERVES, def. 1.

international trade Also, *foreign trade, world trade*. The buying and selling of goods and services among different nations, which plays a major role in their respective economies. Aside from the basic fact that many nations cannot feed their populations without importing food—whether the population is vast and fast-growing as in India or small and relatively stable as in Switzerland—international trade is intimately related to general economic well-being. One of the chief determinants of the size of a country's trade is its real income. Countries with low income levels lack the purchasing power to import much. Not surprisingly, therefore, the countries with the highest incomes account for the lion's share (more than half) of all international trade, which in the 1970s meant just 11 countries: the GROUP OF TEN plus Switzerland. All highly industrialized, they exported chiefly manufactured goods and imported foodstuffs and raw materials. Even before World War II manufactures

accounted for about 40 per cent of all trade, and that proportion has been growing steadily. Though the United Nations has classified internationally traded commodities into hundreds of different items, in fact relatively few items make up the bulk of those traded. Among manufactures, machinery, iron and steel products, transportation equipment, chemicals, plastics, and textiles account for a huge proportion of the total. Among raw materials, petroleum, wool, cotton, wood pulp, timber, coal, copper, rubber, jute, tin, lead, and zinc are outstanding; among foods and related commodities, wheat, meat, fruit, sugar, vegetable oils, coffee, cocoa, tea, alcoholic beverages, and tobacco are the most important. For more information about international trade and finance, see ADVANTAGE; BALANCE OF PAYMENTS; BALANCE OF TRADE; COMMON MARKET; EXCHANGE CONTROLS; EXCHANGE RATE; FOREIGN AID; FOREIGN EXCHANGE; GOLD STANDARD; INTERNATIONAL INVESTMENT; TARIFF, def. 1; TERMS OF TRADE.

international union See under LABOR UNION.

Interstate Commerce Commission Also, *ICC*. An independent Federal regulatory agency, established by the Interstate Commerce Act of 1887 to regulate carriers engaged in U.S. interstate commerce. Under its jurisdiction are railroads, trucking companies, bus lines, freight forwarders, water carriers, oil pipelines, transportation brokers, and express agencies. The ICC regulates rates and charges, lays down accounting rules, grants operating rights to truckers, buses, freight forwarders, water carriers, and transportation brokers, and processes applications to construct or abandon rail lines.

interview In market research, a face-to-face meeting or telephone conversation in which a person is asked to give opinions and views relating to a product, service, company, etc. In a *quantitative interview* the questioner asks a series of fixed questions so designed that the answers lend themselves to statistical analysis. In a *qualitative* or *depth interview* the respondent is encouraged to talk freely about the issue rather than answering set questions, and the answers are open to more subjective interpretation.

in the red Also, *red ink, red-ink entry.* Losing money, or otherwise indicating a loss. The term comes from the accounting practice of making negative or reverse entries on the books in red (or red ink) to show that these amounts must be deducted from the other figures, written in black ink (hence, "in the black").

inventory

1. The materials owned and held by a business firm, including raw materials, intermediate products and parts, work-in-process, and finished goods, intended either for internal consumption or for sale. In this sense inventory differs from the fixed assets of a business, such as its office furniture, machinery, buildings, or land, which are referred to as "plant and equipment."

2. A detailed list of all the items owned by an individual or firm, showing the value of each. Such inventories often are required for purposes of property insurance.

inventory change Also, *inventory investment.* The total value of the increase or decrease in the physical stock of goods (see INVENTORY, def. 1) held by private businesses, stated in current prices. An inventory increase represents production not matched by current consumption, and hence is regarded as an investment, while a decrease reflects consumption in excess of current production, and hence is regarded as a "negative investment." An important LEADING INDICATOR of future business conditions, which it anticipates by some months, inventory change has always played a role in the business cycle. (See also under INVENTORY CONTROL.) Inventory changes are a component of GROSS NATIONAL PRODUCT, and in times of recession a reduction in inventories will show up as a decline in GNP. Data on inventory change in the United States are published monthly by the Department of Commerce in the *Survey of Current Business.* See also GROSS PRIVATE DOMESTIC INVESTMENT.

inventory control Also, *inventory management, material requirements planning.* The management of inventories so that there is always enough stock on hand for production yet no investment of capital that could more profitably be used otherwise. Inventory control involves determining how much

stock must be kept on hand, the rate at which stock will be consumed, the most ECONOMIC ORDER QUANTITY for purchasing or manufacturing, and the lead time required to obtain the needed materials. The most difficult phase of this process is forecasting demand for stock. Too little inventory leads to stockouts, which delay production and thus raise costs, as well as delaying deliveries to customers, who may then turn to other suppliers. Too much inventory ties up capital, increases storage cost, and may result in waste if materials deteriorate or spoil during storage.

The management of inventory affects not only an individual business but the entire economy. When growing demand is anticipated, businesses tend to accumulate inventories, which helps raise the level of economic activity. When demand tapers off and the accumulated inventory stocks prove to be excessive, businesses try to offset this by buying less than normally. As a result, economic activity slackens dramatically, sometimes to the point of recession or even depression. When an equilibrium is reached, demand again begins to rise in excess of production, business finds itself short of inventory and steps up its purchasing, and the entire cycle repeats itself.

Because inventory control is so costly and vital to an individual business, since World War II numerous sophisticated mathematical techniques, often involving computers, have been used in this field. See also ABC CONTROL; JOB-LOT CONTROL; ORDER POINT CONTROL; PERIODIC ORDERING; PERPETUAL INVENTORY SYSTEM; TWO-BIN CONTROL.

inventory-sales ratio The proportion of stock on hand to sales during a given period. Since a high ratio (large amounts of unsold stock) indicates that production is exceeding sales, it is desirable to keep the inventory-sales ratio as low as possible. Calculated for an industry rather than for an individual firm, the inventory-sales ratio over a period of time is a useful economic INDICATOR, a rising ratio indicating that production is outpacing demand and a falling one that production is lagging.

inventory valuation

1. In accounting, determining the cost of inventories. Normally manufacturing inventories are divided into three categories: raw materials to be used in the end-product; semifinished goods in process of manufacture (or work-in-process); and finished goods ready for shipment to customers. Like other assets on the balance sheet, inventories usually are valued at original COST OR MARKET price, whichever is lower. With this method, the inventory value will be equal to cost or less than cost if, as a result of deterioration, obsolescence, price declines, or other factors, less than cost would be realized were the inventories to be sold.

Inventory valuation is influenced by the way in which stocks are charged out of inventory as they are used. Suppose, for example, that an inventory consists of 50 tons of steel purchased at $300 per ton and another 50 tons purchased at $250 per ton. The total cost of the inventory is $27,500 (50 × $300 + 50 × $250). Suppose, now, that 10 tons are withdrawn from inventory. If the company uses FIRST-IN, FIRST-OUT accounting, the value of this withdrawal would be $3,000, leaving 90 tons in inventory carried at $24,500. But if the company uses LAST-IN, FIRST-OUT accounting, the more recent purchase would be assumed to have been withdrawn. Its value is $2,500, leaving an inventory of $25,000. (It should be noted that this difference relates only to accounting practice. The warehouse workman in either case could probably use the steel that was physically most accessible.) For other frequently used accounting methods, see AVERAGE COST, def. 1; BASE-STOCK METHOD; RETAIL INVENTORY METHOD.

2. In national income accounting, the total value of business inventories. Economists try to distinguish between total profits that businesses earn from their operations and those that merely reflect inventory profit, that is, the speculative profit made when rising prices cause the value of inventories to rise between the time of their acquisition and the time of their incorporation into an end-product and sale. The latter may appear as an *inventory valuation adjustment* on each firm's income statement. Whereas operating profits are a measure of economic health, an inventory valuation adjustment resulting from higher prices is simply a measure of inflation.

inverted economic series An economic INDICATOR in the form of a TIME SERIES whose behavior is opposite (and hence inverted on a graph) to that of

the business cycle, that is, the indicator declines when general business activity rises, and vice versa. Examples include the layoff rate in manufacturing, unemployment insurance claims, liabilities of business failures, and delinquency rate on installment loans. For purposes of comparison with other indicators, such indicators often are inverted, either by turning the graphic representation upside down (as in Fig. 41) or by adding plus or minus signs to tables showing percentage changes (plus for a negative change, minus for a positive one). Inverted in this way, the indicator will be seen to rise when general business improves and decline when it deteriorates.

invested capital
1. See CAPITAL, def. 3.
2. The equity of all security-holders in a business, that is, both stockholders and holders of long-term liabilities (such as bonds). This can also be described as net worth plus long-term debt, and is sometimes called *capital structure*.

investment
1. In general usage, the purchase of some form of property that will be held for a relatively long period, during which it is expected to increase in value. The property may consist of shares in a corporation, real estate, plant and equipment to produce goods, a work of art, etc. The period of time varies from a few months to many years, but conventionally considered it is longer than that used for purposes of SPECULATION (usually associated with the expectation of a quick return). The increase in value is called a *return on capital*.
2. In economic theory, the purchase of capital goods by individuals, businesses, and institutions (see GROSS PRIVATE DOMESTIC INVESTMENT; INVESTMENT SPENDING), which is an important determinant of national income. See also INDUCED INVESTMENT; MULTIPLIER PRINCIPLE, def. 1; PROPENSITY TO INVEST.

investment, foreign See INTERNATIONAL INVESTMENT.

investment banking The marketing of new securities, usually through a firm known as an *investment bank*, or *banker*. Normally such banks buy

Fig. 41. Inverted economic series

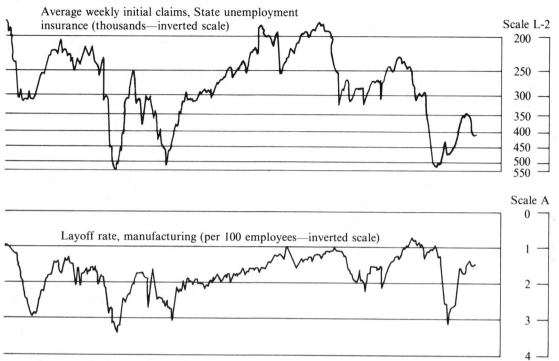

Average weekly initial claims, State unemployment insurance (thousands—inverted scale)

Scale L-2

Layoff rate, manufacturing (per 100 employees—inverted scale)

Scale A

1953 54 55 56 57 58 59 60 61 62 63 64 65 66 67 68 69 70 71 72 73 74 75 76 1977

The graphs showing weekly initial claims for unemployment (upper) and the layoff rate in manufacturing (lower) are inverted, because these statistics, which lead (anticipate) the business cycle by some months, run exactly counter to it. In other words, *increases* in unemployment claims and layoffs anticipate a *decline* in business activity.
    Source: Business Conditions Digest, July 1976.

entire stock or bond issues from the issuing corporation and either distribute them to dealers or sell them to investors, taking a profit on the selling price. The issuing corporation thus is assured of a definite price for the security, and the investment bank is rewarded for undertaking the risk of resale. In purchasing an entire issue, called *underwriting,* several investment banks may combine their resources into a syndicate in order to put up enough capital. Occasionally an investment bank only sells a new security, without underwriting it (taking possession of it), in which case it acts as an agent rather than a middleman; this practice is called *best-efforts selling* or *agency marketing.* Investment banking is not banking in the sense of creating deposits, and by law (the Banking Act of 1933) it may not, in the United States, be engaged in by a commercial bank.

investment company Also, *investment trust.* A company or trust formed for the purpose of pooling the members' resources to invest in other companies. The chief advantage of such arrangements is that they offer more diversified holdings, in terms of both different companies and different industries, than most individuals could hope to acquire, thus reducing risk. Presumably they also benefit from professional management, but in practice their performance has not been significantly better than investments selected at random without professional analysis. There are two main kinds of investment company, the *closed-end investment trust* and the *open-end investment trust* (see MUTUAL FUND). Capitalization of closed-end trusts remains the same, that is, the trust is restricted to the original capital of the original members, unless special action is taken to change it (a rare occurrence). Shares in closed-end trusts, some of which are listed on the New York Stock Exchange, are readily traded in the open market, just as other stocks are.

investment counselor An individual or firm whose principal business consists of guiding the investments of its clients, generally making for them all decisions to buy and sell securities and/or commodities and seeing that these decisions are executed. Typically, a client of an investment counselor would simply indicate the total amount he or she wants to invest, and perhaps also the return expected from this total. Investment counselors charge sizable fees for their services, which may make them uneconomic for individuals with less than about $100,000 to invest. Investment counseling is also available in some large banks that offer *investment advisory accounts.* Customers deposit funds for investment into the account, and the bank manages the investments for a small annual fee (1 per cent or less). However, a substantial minimum deposit is normally required. In addition, there are numerous kinds of *investment advisory service,* ranging from ones that merely provide statistical information to help investors make their own decisions, to others giving advice about specific firms and current market conditions, to still others that formulate specific plans for individual investors. All these services tend to be concerned more with short-term than long-term conditions. The quality of the advice varies widely, and though in the United States these services technically are under the jurisdiction of the Securities and Exchange Commission they are not very strictly regulated.

investment multiplier See MULTIPLIER PRINCIPLE, def. 1.

investment plan See CAPITAL BUDGET.

investment spending Expenditures for products and services not consumed during the accounting period in question. In addition to GROSS PRIVATE DOMESTIC INVESTMENT, it includes government spending for capital assets (buildings, vehicles, equipment, etc.), and in the broadest sense it includes all consumer spending for durable goods. Investment spending is important because, unlike purchases for food, it is postponable and hence

fluctuates with the business cycle. See also CAPITAL EXPENDITURE.

investment tax credit See under TAX CREDIT.

investment trust See INVESTMENT COMPANY.

invisible hand A term used by Adam SMITH in stating his belief that the pursuit of individual self-interest will benefit society as a whole. He wrote: "Every individual . . . intends only his own gain, and he is in this, as in many other cases, led by an invisible hand to promote an end which was no part of his intention . . . . By pursuing his own interest he frequently promotes that of the society more effectually than when he really intends to promote it." See also CLASSICAL SCHOOL; HARMONY OF INTERESTS.

invisible item In international trade, any paid for item other than tangible merchandise. Invisible items are largely services, such as insurance, freight charges, banking services, tourist expenditures, and dividends or interest on foreign investment. Unlike tangible commodities (*visible items*) such items do not pass through customs, and formerly they were not recorded in trade statistics. However, both visible and invisible items must be considered in drawing up a nation's BALANCE OF PAYMENTS.

invoice An itemized statement of goods or services bought or sold, usually including (or implying) a request for payment. The same invoice is called a *sales invoice* by the seller and a *purchase invoice* by the buyer.

IOU Also, *due bill.* A simple acknowledgment of indebtedness whose name is a phonetic rendition of the phrase "I owe you." It includes a date, the stated sum of money owed, and the borrower's signature. However, unlike many instruments of credit, an IOU is not negotiable, does not imply interest payments, and does not necessarily indicate when the debt must be repaid.

iron law of wages Also, *brazen law of wages, subsistence theory of wages.* The theory propounded by various writers in the late 18th and early 19th centuries that in the long run workers receive the bare minimum wage they require to survive. When wages rise, workers tend to have larger families, eventually increasing the labor force. As competition for jobs grows, wages drop. Then poverty among workers' families causes the working population to decline, and wages rise again. The iron law of wages is most fully stated in David Ricardo's *Principles of Political Economy and Taxation* (1817). Before long, however, it became evident that this "law" did not operate in actual practice, and by the mid-19th century it had been largely replaced by the WAGES-FUND THEORY.

irregular With reference to consumer goods, a term indicating a slight flaw in an article that may affect its appearance but usually not its durability, but that generally leads the seller to reduce its price. For example, an "irregular" coat may have a lining that does not quite match the outer fabric, or a glass dish may have one or more bubbles in the glass. See also SECOND.

isocost curve Also, *iso-outlay curve.* A graphic representation of the various possible combinations of two resources that can be purchased with the same amount of money, assuming that their cost remains in a fixed proportion. It can be used, for example, to show how much natural gas and how much petroleum can be bought for $4 million, assuming that the cost of one unit of petroleum is exactly twice that of one unit of natural gas. Despite its name, the isocost curve is actually a line. When a family of isocost curves is combined on the same graph with a set of isoquants (see under INDIFFERENCE CURVE), the points of tangency can be connected to form a *scale locus*, which indicates the cheapest combination of factors for each given quantity of output. See Fig. 42.

iso-product curve See under INDIFFERENCE CURVE.

isoquant See under INDIFFERENCE CURVE.

issue Any securities or obligations of a company that are put into the hands of the public. Also, the act of distributing such securities, also called *floating an issue.* If the company is issuing any kind of STOCK for the first time—that is, if it is selling equi-

Fig. 42. Isocost curve

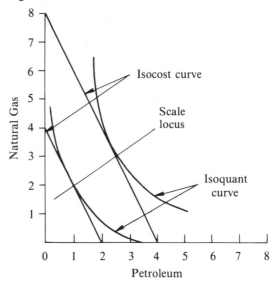

ty in itself—it is popularly said to be *going public.* If the security has never been sold before, it is called a *new issue* (or *primary offering* or *primary distribution*); if, on the other hand, it is selling a large block of securities formerly held by itself or by one or more large stockholders, the issue is called a *secondary offering* or *secondary distribution.* If the secondary offering is made according to a definite plan registered with the U.S. Securities and Exchange Commission (SEC) in which the price, commission, and other terms are specified, it is called a *special offering.*

Companies float issues in order to raise money for working capital, for new plant and equipment, to retire outstanding securities, or yet other purposes. They nearly always sell an issue to one or more investment bankers, who for a commission assume the risk of selling it to the public. However, in order to do so, they must first comply with both Federal and state regulations. First, a firm must file a lengthy *registration statement* with the SEC giving full information about its financial condition, its performance (profits and losses) for several years past, its outstanding securities, its directors and officers, and numerous other details concerning its operations. It also must prepare a printed *prospectus* (called a *red herring*) making available the most important of these facts to any potential buyers of the new issue. Other than this prospectus, the company must for a given period refrain from advertising the issue beyond a brief announcement stating its name, price, and size, and the names of the underwriters and dealers from whom it can be bought (a so-called *tombstone ad*). Further, it must comply with applicable state laws concerning the registration and sale of new securities (called *blue-sky laws*).

Because complying with Federal and state regulations can be quite expensive, the SEC instituted a shorter registration form for small issues (under $300,000 total value), under a rule called *Regulation A*, which permits the company to issue a shorter *offering circular* instead of a 20- to 30-page prospectus. Still smaller issues (valued at less than $50,000) do not even require the offering circular. Further, if a new issue is to be offered to only a few buyers (25 or fewer), it is called a *private placement* (as opposed to a public offering) and does not have to be registered with the SEC. See also INVESTMENT BANKING; RIGHTS; UNDERWRITING.

jawboning Public criticism by the President of the United States or members of the administration of price or wage increases that they consider unjustifiably large or contributory to inflation. The term came into use in the 1960s during President L. B. Johnson's administration. See also MORAL SUASION.

Jevons, William Stanley An English economist and philosopher (1835–82), a founder of the MARGINALIST SCHOOL, who began his *Theory of Political Economy* (1871) with the statement that "value depends entirely upon utility." According to Jevons, it is not labor that determines the value of a product (see LABOR THEORY OF VALUE); rather, the value of labor itself is determined by the value of the product it is expended on. Moreover, labor is essentially painful, a *disutility*, offset only by the pleasure of the laborer's earnings. When the pain exceeds the pleasure, the laborer will stop working. One of Jevons's chief contributions was his mathematical, statistical approach to economic questions. He made wide use of graphs and tables; in his studies of variations in price and the value of currency he improved the use of the INDEX NUMBER; and he was among the first to apply calculus to illustrate

the law of diminishing marginal utility, drawing a graph quite similar to that of the modern DEMAND CURVE. When Jevons discovered that much of his work had already been done independently by H. H. GOSSEN, he gave the other man full credit. For Jevons's view of business cycles, see SUNSPOT-WEATHER THEORY. See also under C. MENGER.

jobber An older name for wholesaler; see under WHOLESALE.

Job Corps A U.S. Department of Labor division that administers a nationwide training program offering comprehensive training for young people from low-income families. Operating largely through residential training centers, it aims to provide education, vocational skills, and useful work experience in rural, urban, or inner-city centers. Enrollees may spend a maximum of two years in the Job Corps, but the average period is six months to a year. Recruiting is done primarily through state employment services, which also help enrollees find jobs after they complete their training. The Job Corps was created by the Comprehensive Employment and Training Act of 1973.

job cost system See JOB ORDER SYSTEM.

job enlargement Broadening the scope of a particular job so that the worker performing it can see some relation between it and the end-product.

job evaluation A complete analysis of all the positions in a company, with a view to establishing their comparative value to the firm. Each job is ranked according to such factors as physical and/or mental effort required, responsibility, skill, and working conditions. A complete ranking presumably enables management to adjust wages to make them consistent with the relative worth of each job and make sure that jobs of the same type receive the same pay, an important consideration for employee satisfaction and morale.

job lot See BROKEN LOT.

job-lot control A system of INVENTORY CONTROL that essentially involves buying the materials needed for each order (or "job"). The purest example of such a system is found in the construction industry, where, when a firm wins a construction contract, it simply orders the materials it needs for the job to be delivered to the construction site. There are no inventories to draw on, since storage and additional transport of construction materials would add too much to costs. Manufacturers that work with a JOB ORDER SYSTEM—principally makers of custom-made items —operate similarly, ordering nearly all materials and parts only as they are needed. While seemingly foolproof, job-lot control has several major drawbacks: some of the material ordered may be defective or be damaged on the job, so that more will be needed than the original bill of material indicates; unforeseen shortages of a key material or part can hold up the entire job; and buyers cannot take advantage of volume discounts or a period of low prices, since needs cannot be anticipated. For these reasons job-lot control is avoided whenever material can be purchased in advance of demand without risk. For example, job order shops may try to use as many standard materials and parts as possible in their custom-made products, so that they can lower costs by drawing on existing inventory.

job order system Also, *job-cost system, job-lot system, order-cost system.* A system of cost accounting in which costs are collected separately for each job, order, or job lot accepted by the plant. (A *job* may be a single product manufactured to the specifications of a particular customer; a *job lot* is a given amount of identical items, such as 25 executive desks, made together for a single order.) Job order systems thus are used chiefly by firms that do custom work or manufacture to order, and usually are organized to treat each order as a separate entity. Examples include construction contractors, job printers, custom tailors, shipbuilders, machine shops and foundries, and in nonmanufacturing industries, motion-picture makers (each film is different) and magazine publishers (each issue is different).

job rotation A technique of training employees by moving them from one job to another in a systematic way. For example, a purchasing agent who supervises six buyers, each of whom specializes in a particular group of production items, might rotate them on a two-month basis, so that after one year each buyer presumably will know how to purchase any of the commodities needed.

joint account See under ACCOUNT, def. 2.

joint and survivorship annuity See under ANNUITY.

joint cost The cost of materials, facilities, or services to produce two or more products or services, called a *joint product.* In such cases it generally is difficult to assign costs to one product or the other. For example, a railroad must maintain its roadbed for both passenger and freight services, and this joint cost must be allocated in some way (usually arbitrarily). Similarly, almost all silver and most nickel are found jointly with copper deposits, making it impossible to distinguish clearly the cost of mining the copper from that of mining the other metals. In most cases the allocation is made on the basis of the value of the end-product; this means, for example, that the cost of mining copper may rise when the market price of silver (a by-product of copper) declines.

joint demand   The simultaneous demand for two or more goods or services that generally are used together. For example, numerous commodities are nearly always sold in pairs, notably earrings, shoes, and gloves; one is of little use without the other. Similarly, there is a joint demand for automobiles, gasoline, and tires; tennis rackets and tennis balls; bricks and mortar; etc.

joint float   See SNAKE IN THE TUNNEL. Also under EXCHANGE RATE.

joint product   Two or more products that inevitably result from processing a single raw material and that are of equal importance, so that none can be designated as the major or primary product. For example, refining crude petroleum produces gasoline, fuel oil, and lubricants, as well as paraffin wax, coal tar, and asphalt; all these are joint products. See also JOINT COST.

joint rate   A transportation rate between two points on the routes of different carriers that is quoted as a single rate.

joint return   An income tax RETURN (def. 3) filed by a husband and wife together, reporting the total income of both. Such a return may be filed even if only one spouse earned the entire family income, and often makes for a lower tax liability than a *separate return* (filed by each spouse alone and reporting only his or her share of income and expenses).

joint-stock bank   British name for COMMERCIAL BANK.

joint-stock company   A form of business organization that has some features of a partnership and others of a corporation. As with a CORPORATION, the original investor in a joint-stock company receives shares of stock and may sell them whenever he or she wishes. Also, shareholders elect the company's directors, who are in charge of management. However, as in a PARTNERSHIP, membership in a joint-stock company does not confer LIMITED LIABILITY; rather, each shareholder is legally liable for all the debts incurred by the company.

joint tenancy   In law, a kind of co-ownership of property. In a valid joint tenancy, the tenants must have one and the same interest and title, beginning at the same time, and they share possession equally, that is, they have equal shares in the property. While the joint tenants are alive, they are co-owners of the property; when one dies, his or her title passes automatically to the surviving joint tenant(s). In this respect joint tenancy differs from *tenancy in common*, in which a deceased co-owner's title passes to his or her heirs. Some states, however, have passed laws to abolish the joint tenant's right of survivorship, eliminating this difference. In some states there is a form of joint tenancy called *tenancy by entirety*, in which husband and wife are the co-owners. Unlike a joint tenancy, such a tenancy need not be explicitly stated. When either spouse dies, the other automatically acquires the deceased's share of the title. If the couple are divorced, the tenancy is automatically converted into a tenancy in common.

joint venture   A business relationship similar to a PARTNERSHIP but formed for the purpose of carrying out a single project rather than as an ongoing business. For example, an agreement to buy, develop, and resell a particular parcel of real estate might be a joint venture for the promoters involved.

journal   In accounting, a book in which original entries concerning transactions are recorded and later transferred to the appropriate accounts in a ledger. A company may use a *general journal* in which any or all transactions are entered, or it may have several specialized journals for different kinds of transaction, such as a *cash-receipts journal* to record all money collected, a *purchase journal* showing all items bought, a *sales journal* recording all sales, etc.

journeyman   See under GUILD.

Juglar cycle   See under BUSINESS CYCLE.

junior financing   See under MORTGAGE.

junk   Also, *junk value*. See SCRAP.

jurisdictional strike   See under STRIKE.

jury-of-executive opinion   See under DELPHI FORECAST.

kameralism See CAMERALISM.

Kennedy Round See under GENERAL AGREEMENT ON TARIFFS AND TRADE.

keyed advertising A method of identifying the source of an advertisement that prompted a customer's order or inquiry. For example, in a classified advertisement different box or department numbers in the return address might serve as keys to identify each publication that draws customer response.

key industry An industry that, by virtue of its size or the importance of its product or service, is vital to a nation's economic activity and whose condition is therefore considered a barometer of the entire economy. Key industries in the United States are steel, electric power, and automobiles, among others.

Keynes, John Maynard An English economist and government adviser (1883–1946) who founded an important school of thought known as *Keynesian economics,* and whose *General Theory of Employment, Interest, and Money* (1936) is considered by many to be the single most important book on economics of the 20th century. Unlike Alfred Marshall and other marginalist economists under whom he studied at Cambridge University, Keynes adopted a macroeconomic approach, preferring to deal with large aggregations of data, such as national income and employment. In keeping with his time, which was characterized by declining economic activity, severe depression (including the Great Depression), and widespread unemployment, Keynes addressed himself chiefly to problems of income and employment. Over the short term, Keynes said, the level of national income determines the level of employment. Both in turn depend on consumption and investment spending, for every penny spent—either for consumer goods or for investment—becomes someone's income. Consumption in turn is determined by the size of individual income and tends to represent a stable proportion of income at various income levels (a proportion that decreases as income increases; thus, the percentage of income spent on milk is much smaller with a $900 weekly salary than with a $90 weekly salary). On any income level, people tend to spend a certain fixed proportion on consumer goods; Keynes called this figure the PROPENSITY TO CONSUME. Investment, on the other hand, is determined by the interest rate and by what Keynes called "the marginal efficiency of capital," that is, the expected rate of return on new investments. The interest rate in turn depends on LIQUIDITY PREFERENCE and on the quantity of money; marginal efficiency of capital in turn depends on the expectations of future profits and the supply price of capital assets. (Note that three of the important influences on income and employment are largely psychological in nature: the propensity to consume, the desire for liquid assets, and the expectation of profits from investment.)

The business cycle depends basically on saving and investment, which according to Keynes and his followers are always equal. If savings increase relative to investment, money that was being used productively in the economy is idle. As a result, overall output declines; this automatically reduces income and brings savings back in line with investment. Conversely, if investment tends to race ahead of saving, overall national income rises and creates increased saving. If the economy is operating well below full employment, the rise in national income triggered by an increase in investment will be largely "real"; if the economy is already at or near full employment (of either labor or capital), then the rise in national income comes entirely from rising prices. In either case, saving will be brought back in line with investment.

Keynes described his theory with the following equations, in which Y = national income, C = consumption, I = investment, and S = saving:

$$Y = C + I$$
$$S = Y - C$$

Therefore, $S = I$

Saving and investment always are equal; it is income that varies. The equation $Y = C + I$ is sometimes called the *income equation* or *income and expenditure equation*.

Note that Keynes, unlike the classical economists or the marginalists, does not assume full employment. The classical economists believed that variations in the rate of interest and in other factor prices (such as wages) would automatically cause the savings-investment part of national income to come into balance at a level of output that brought full employment. When savings were not equal to the investment needed for full employment, rising interest rates would encourage abstinence from consumption and bring savings up to the desired level. When savings exceeded the level of investment, interest rates would decline, businesses would be encouraged to invest because of the low interest rates, and saving would also be discouraged. Again the economy would come into equilibrium at a savings-investment level equal to full employment.

As Keynes knew full well, however, in the real world this never happened. Interest rates always declined sharply during recessions, but so did investment spending. In the 1930s in particular, it became obvious to Keynes and his followers that an economy could suffer from permanent SECULAR STAGNATION in which a tendency to save pushed down interest rates without any response from investment, which continued to decline. As a result, lower income allowed lower saving, bringing it into balance with income but with the economy at equilibrium at less than full employment and with no built-in tendency to swing back to full employment. In fact, the declining national income tended to produce even greater declines in investment, which in turn reduced national income still more. Finally, at the bottom of the Great Depression, the United States (along with Germany) appeared to reach

Fig. 43. Aggregate volume of employment

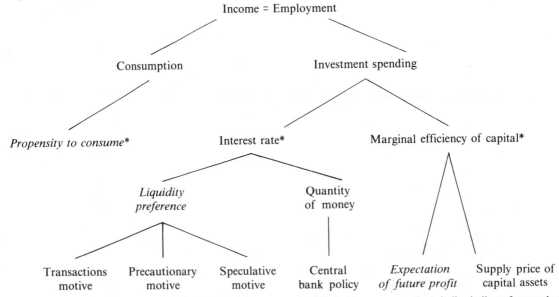

Asterisks indicate independent variables (whose values cannot be inferred from one another); italics indicate factors that are largely psychological.

equilibrium at a stage when investment was not even equal to capital consumption and a huge part of the labor force—one-fourth in the United States —was unemployed.

How then could investment, on which economic health so desperately depended, be expanded? Keynes said that if private investment lagged, the government must step in to take up the slack. He not only repudiated the laissez-faire policy advocated by both the classical and marginalist schools, but he strongly supported international financial cooperation, and he devoted his last years to helping create the financial organization of the United Nations.

The Keynesian idea that propensity to consume is related to income encouraged a "soak the rich" tax philosophy in the United States and much of western Europe. High and progressive income and death taxes not only help redistribute income but also promote economic stability, since the surplus funds of the wealthy are taxed away by the government and, when spent, become a substitute for private investment spending, helping to bring the economy toward full employment. While Keynes's main ideas have been accepted by every Western government, they continue to be controversial. In some cases, it is not the theory that is rejected but its implications of government economic control and equalization of income. Its practical applications also have been challenged. Both critics and followers of Keynes agree that, while governments have successfully applied Keynesian principles to prevent widespread unemployment, they have yet to learn how to control the inflation that appears to be an inevitable by-product. Economists such as Milton FRIEDMAN say, in effect, that human beings and their elected governments are not wise enough to manage their economic affairs along Keynesian lines, and hence would be much better off if government interference were limited to increasing the money supply at a fixed rate of 3 or 4 per cent per year. This last point is anti-Keynesian in the extreme, for Keynes and his followers believed that the interest rate, dictated by central bank policies, had little influence on either saving or investment (actually, Keynes believed it did influence investment, but his later followers found that it seldom actually influenced real-life business decisions), and hence monetary changes had little relationship to fluctuations in economic activity.

keypunch See under PUNCHED-CARD DATA PROCESSING.

kibbutz See under COLLECTIVE FARM.

kickback A portion of a fee, salary, sales commission, or other payment that is given to a third party for having assisted—or refrained from preventing—the payment in the first place. For example, salespersons may be required to return part of their commission to the district sales manager in return for being assigned a lucrative territory, workers may pay part of their wage to a union official in order to keep their seniority ranking, etc. Most kickbacks are clearly unethical if not outright illegal.

Kingsley, Charles See under CHRISTIAN SOCIALISM.

Kitchin cycle See under BUSINESS CYCLE.

kiting
1. Writing a check for an amount greater than the balance on deposit to take advantage of the time lag between credit and collection. Such a check itself is called a *kite*.
2. Fraudulently increasing the face value of a check by altering the figures.

Knights of Labor The first large industrial LABOR UNION in the United States. Officially called the Noble Order of the Knights of Labor, it was founded in Philadelphia in 1869 and slowly grew in strength. By 1886 it had some 700,000 members, including unskilled and semiskilled workers as well as craft unions, and both native Americans and new immigrants. However, like other large labor groups of the 19th century, it tended to concentrate on political and social reform more than on specific labor grievances. Conflict among the highly diverse membership grew, some of the craft unions withdrew, and by the late 1880s the federation was weakened beyond the point of recovery.

Kondratieff cycle See under BUSINESS CYCLE.

kurtosis See under SKEWNESS.

labor In economics, one of the FACTORS OF PRODUCTION, consisting of human effort expended to acquire income. As a factor, labor usually refers only to hired workers, not to capitalists or entrepreneurs. The people who seek to expend labor are known collectively as the LABOR FORCE, and they, together with those who seek to employ them, constitute the LABOR MARKET. The term "labor" also is used to mean physical work as opposed to mental work (see MANUAL LABOR), and to describe the organized efforts of workers to further their common interests (see LABOR MOVEMENT). The *U.S. Department of Labor,* first created as a Bureau of Labor in 1884 and separately constituted in 1913, is charged with promoting the welfare of the nation's wage earners, improving their working conditions, and advancing their opportunities for profitable employment. See also EMPLOYMENT, the entries below through LABOR UNION, and WAGE.

labor contract Also, *collective bargaining agreement, union contract.* A formal contract between a union and one or more employers concerning wages, working conditions, job security, and numerous other issues of mutual interest. Most labor contracts are negotiated in a give-and-take process called COLLECTIVE BARGAINING and are in effect for a limited period, most often one year. They not only spell out all the conditions of employment, which apply to both members and nonmembers of the union in a given area (see *exclusive representation,* under LABOR UNION), but they generally also include judicial procedures for settling grievances and disputes arising out of the contract, through ARBITRATION if necessary, and sometimes contain a *no-strike clause* banning strikes and lockouts during the life of the contract.

labor cost In a business, the total salaries and wages paid to workers. (Executive and clerical salaries are usually considered separately, as administrative OVERHEAD.) Cost accountants distinguish between *direct labor,* which includes all work performed directly on the firm's end-product, and *indirect labor,* which may be involved with production activities in general but is not concerned with the actual production (product inspection, materials handling, maintenance, and supervision of workers all are considered indirect labor). Sometimes the distinction is not entirely clear. For example, an operator of a machine that simultaneously produces and packages a product technically performs both direct and indirect labor, though most accountants would charge his or her wage to direct labor alone. Further, roughly one-third of total direct labor cost, which reflects workers' fringe benefits (social security taxes, vacation pay, etc.), may be charged as overhead, since the accountant regards as direct labor cost only the cash wages paid to workers (or deducted from paychecks for taxes, etc.). See also WAGE.

labor economics A branch of economics concerned with productivity, wage determination, job security, unemployment, labor markets, occupational structure, and similar questions concerning labor as a factor of production. See also LABOR STATISTICS, BUREAU OF.

labor exchange bank An institution that functions as a market where products can be exchanged for notes that represent hours of labor. In 1832 Robert OWEN founded a National Equitable Labour Exchange in Britain to function in this way, but it foundered after two years.

labor force According to the U.S. Bureau of the Census, all persons over 16 years of age who either are employed or are seeking employment. In the mid-1970s about 93 million Americans were in this category, including members of the armed services, employees in business and industry, self-employed persons, unpaid family workers in stores and on farms, and the unemployed. Of these, more than 33 million were women. About 60 per cent of employed women worked in white-collar jobs (as opposed to 40 per cent of the men), and their median income was $117 per week as opposed to $188 per week earned by men (or about 60 per cent that of men). With implementation of equal pay and other laws (see under LABOR LAWS), it was expected that women's wages would more closely approach those paid to men, though part of the differential was accounted for by interrupted careers (leading to loss of seniority) and the practice of offering training only for lower-level jobs.

labor-intensive Describing an industry, economic sector, or economy that requires a large proportion of labor input relative to capital investment. Many agricultural enterprises are labor-intensive simply because many crops require work that cannot be performed by machinery, among them grapes, coffee, tea, cork, and silk. All handicraft industries are labor-intensive, along with most service industries. See also CAPITAL-INTENSIVE.

labor laws A general term for legislation that partly or wholly relates to matters of employment and the activities of employers and workers in relation to one another. Such laws, together with their interpretation in the courts, have had considerable influence on the course of the labor movement in the United States. Labor unions in the early 19th century had scarcely been formed before they were brought into court on the ground that, in the absence of specific statutes, the English common law applied, and they represented a conspiracy against the public and hence were illegal. By the early 1900s a number of states had enacted laws protecting workers by limiting work hours, setting minimum wages, establishing compensation for on-the-job accidents, etc. Some of these laws were declared unconstitutional by the courts or were simply ignored (as was the Clayton Antitrust Act; see under BOYCOTT). The most important of the Federal laws that relate partly or wholly to labor are listed in Fig. 44. See also RIGHT-TO-WORK LAW.

Fig. 44. Major Federal laws affecting U.S. labor

Law	Date	Provisions*
Clayton Antitrust Act	1914	Exempted labor unions from antitrust laws; declared peaceful picketing was legal.
LaFollette Seamen's Act	1915	Established working conditions on ships of American registry.
Adamson Act	1916	Established 8-hour work day on interstate carriers.
Esch-Cummins (Transportation) Act	1920	Set up machinery for peaceful settlement of labor disputes to avoid disruption of rail service by strikes.
Railway Labor Act	1926	Upheld right of rail workers to organize and bargain collectively. Amended (1934) by provisions for settling disputes.
Davis-Bacon Act	1931	Required paying prevailing local wage to workers on public buildings or public works, in full, at least weekly.
Norris-LaGuardia Act (Anti-Injunction Act)	1932	Made yellow-dog contracts unenforceable and severely limited issue of court injunctions against unions.
National Industrial Recovery Act (NIRA)	1933	Section 7a guaranteed labor's right to organize and bargain collectively through representatives of their own choosing.
Federal Unemployment Tax Act	1935	Established unemployment insurance tax payable by employers to the Federal government.
National Labor Relations Act (Wagner Act)	1935	Supported right of collective bargaining and banned management's anti-union activities as UNFAIR LABOR PRACTICES; required employers to bargain in good faith with a union selected by majority vote; set up National Labor Relations Board (NLRB).

*Only those provisions pertaining to labor are described here.

Fig. 44. Major Federal laws affecting U.S. labor (*continued*)

Law	Date	Provisions*
Social Security Act	1935	Set up Federal old-age insurance system and basis for Federal-state system of unemployment compensation.
Byrnes Act (Antistrike-breaking Act)	1936	Together with 1938 amendment, forbade interstate transport of persons hired to hamper picketing, collective bargaining, or self-organization of employees; common carriers exempted.
Walsh-Healy Public Contracts Act	1936	Established that Federal contractors must pay prevailing minimum wage for the industry and conform to 8-hour day, 40-hour week in calculating overtime.
National Apprenticeship Act	1937	Established labor standards to safeguard apprentices; set up agency to support apprenticeship programs.
Fair Labor Standards Act (Wage-Hour Law)	1938	Established minimum wage and maximum work hours; banned goods produced by child labor from interstate commerce.
Full Employment Act	1946	Set goal of maximum employment and production, with government taking responsibility.
Taft-Hartley Act (Labor-Management Relations Act)	1947	Revised National Labor Relations Act to curb power of unions, attaching list of "unfair union practices"; outlawed closed shop, secondary boycotts, mass picketing; encouraged state right-to-work laws (aimed against union shops); established *cooling-off period* before strike could be called; outlawed automatic checkoff (deduction of union fees from paycheck); required unions to publish their finances, and allowed employers to sue union for broken contract or damage inflicted during strike.
Welfare and Pension Plans Disclosure Act	1958	Required employers and unions to keep records and submit reports on their welfare and pension plans (aimed at preventing misuse of such funds).
Landrum-Griffin Act (Labor-Management Reporting and Disclosure Act)	1959	Required unions to give detailed reports of finances (to protect their members against corrupt union officials); provided safeguards against officials' conflicts of interest and regulated internal government of unions; strengthened Taft-Hartley Act provisions against hot-cargo clause and limited picketing.
Manpower Development and Training Act	1962	Established broad program for retraining unemployed and underemployed workers.
Work Hours Act	1962	Established uniform standard of 8-hour day, 40-hour week, and time-and-a-half pay for overtime in excess of the standard for any work performed under Federal contracts or subcontracts.
Equal Pay Act	1963	Prohibited discrimination in pay on basis of sex.
Civil Rights Act (Title VII)	1964	Outlawed discrimination against any worker because of race, color, religion, sex, or national origin, with regard to pay, terms, conditions, or privileges of employment, on the part of employers, employment agencies, and labor unions.
Economic Opportunity Act	1964	Set up Office of Economic Opportunity to help open opportunities for job training and employment.

*Only those provisions pertaining to labor are described here.

Fig. 44. Major Federal laws affecting U.S. labor (*continued*)

Law	Date	Provisions*
Age Discrimination in Employment Act	1967	Outlawed discrimination against persons aged 40–65 in hiring, job retention, wages, and other work conditions in industries affecting interstate commerce.
Federal Coal Mine Health and Safety Act	1969	Established mandatory health and safety standards for coal mines, and disability payments for black lung disease.
Occupational Health and Safety Act	1970	Set job safety and health standards for all employees, and a system of inspection and complaint procedures.
Emergency Employment Act	1971	Authorized public-service employment program when national unemployment rate exceeds 4.5% and special aid to areas with high unemployment.
Equal Employment Opportunity Act	1972	Expanded Title VII of 1964 Civil Rights Act; called for *affirmative action* with definite goals and timetables to redress past discrimination in employment against women and minorities.
Comprehensive Employment and Training Act	1973	Provided Federal funds to local and state governments to identify manpower needs in their areas and provide training and other services to meet those needs.

*Only those provisions pertaining to labor are described here.

labor market The contacts between buyers and sellers of a given kind of labor. For the majority of jobs such contacts occur in a relatively small geographic area, limited by the distance people are willing to travel to work. For certain occupations, however, the labor market is nationwide, or even worldwide, with both employers and would-be employees willing to search far afield for the positions of a high-level specialist or professional. In most cases, however, the labor market area consists of a medium-sized or large urban center and the territory surrounding it, in effect a metropolitan area. About 150 such areas in the United States are considered major labor market areas by the U.S. Department of Labor's Bureau of Employment Security, which publishes monthly statistics on the subject. See also LABOR MOBILITY.

labor mobility The relative flexibility with which workers change jobs. Labor mobility in the economy as a whole is measured by the *net turnover rate*, that is, the number of persons (relative to the total labor force) who left their jobs and were replaced. The degree of labor mobility in any given LABOR MARKET has a direct bearing on the elasticity of the labor supply. There are three kinds of labor mobility, each influenced by different factors. *Vertical labor mobility* refers to changing to a better or worse job, through the acquisition of new skills or work experience, or, in the case of a downward shift, because of the inability to find work at the existing level of skill. Since it usually involves a change of social status and income, vertical mobility is at least partly a function of social flexibility. *Horizontal labor mobility* refers to changing jobs on the same level, usually contingent on some change in working conditions—wages, hours, fringe benefits, etc.—with a new employer. It can be limited by such factors as fear of losing seniority or promotion potential through a change, reluctance to move, preferential hiring practices, etc. *Occupational mobility* refers to changing to an entirely new occupation, either from desire or from necessity (such as technological change). Owing to the financial and other difficulties of changing fields in which considerable skill or knowledge is involved, occupational mobility is most common among unskilled workers.

labor movement A general term embracing all efforts of workers to improve their lot, individually as well as collectively, and through political as well as economic means. The first major collective effort of this kind was the CRAFT GUILD, but the labor movement as a larger force developed chiefly after the INDUSTRIAL REVOLUTION had made individual workers virtually powerless, and employers were able to impose on them starvation wages, long hours, and wretched working conditions. In the 19th century the labor movement tended to take one of two directions. The first was an attempt to bargain with employers over rates of pay, hours, apprenticeship requirements, and other conditions, an approach that culminated in the modern LABOR UNION and its collective bargaining procedures. The second direction was that of collective ownership of the means of production, which manifested itself in various kinds of COOPERATIVE on the one hand and in political attempts to change the entire economic structure on the other; the latter ranged from political parties representing labor (such as the British Labour Party) to various forms of SOCIALISM and COMMUNISIM. See also under L. BLANC; CHRISTIAN SOCIALISM; FABIAN SOCIALISM; C. FOURIER; GUILD SOCIALISM; MUTUALISM; R. OWEN; SYNDICALISM; UTOPIAN SOCIALISM.

labor relations Also, *labor-management relations*. The relations and transactions between employers and groups of employees, especially labor unions, concerning such matters of mutual interest as wages, working conditions, job security, etc. After initial refusals to deal with any unions or their members, management has gradually been forced to accept them as a powerful economic force (more in some industries than in others). Nevertheless, the course of labor relations probably will never be entirely smooth, since the aims of organized labor and of management often represent diametrical opposites. See also COLLECTIVE BARGAINING; LABOR UNION.

Labor Statistics, Bureau of Also, *BLS*. The United States government's principal fact-finding agency in the field of LABOR ECONOMICS, particularly with respect to the collection and analysis of data on manpower and labor requirements, the labor force, employment and unemployment, hours of work, wages and other compensation, prices, living conditions, labor-management relations, productivity, technological developments, occupation-

al safety and health, structure and growth of the economy, urban conditions and related socioeconomic issues, and international aspects of some of the subjects. Practically all the data it collects are supplied voluntarily by workers, businesses, and government agencies. Its chief publications include the *Monthly Labor Review, Consumer Price Index, Wholesale Prices and Price Indexes,* and *Employment and Earnings.*

labor theory of value The idea that the value of a commodity depends on the amount of labor required to produce it, either directly or indirectly. Thus the value of a head of lettuce, for example, depends on the farmer's work in growing it, as well as in improving the soil, the labor used to build the machinery for cultivating that soil, etc. This theory was developed by the CLASSICAL SCHOOL, notably by Adam Smith, and David Ricardo expanded it to include profits (see COST OF PRODUCTION THEORY OF VALUE). It also was taken over by Karl Marx, who used it to denounce capitalists for selling goods at prices higher than the cost of labor and thereby exploiting the working class (see SURPLUS LABOR AND VALUE THEORY). The labor theory of value and its derivatives embody several serious fallacies. They fail to take into account (1) the effect of demand, which may make lettuce sell for 25 cents a head one week and 35 cents the next; (2) the time taken by the productive process; (3) interest on invested capital; (4) the fact that varying amounts of capital are required for producing different commodities (costly machinery is needed to produce cloth, relatively few tools to produce tomatoes or lettuce); and (5) that identical commodities can be made with varying amounts of labor and capital (for example, infertile land needs a great deal more labor per unit of product than fertile land).

labor turnover See TURNOVER, def. 2; also under LABOR MOBILITY.

labor union An organization of workers formed for the purpose of collective bargaining with employers concerning wages, working hours, job security, fringe benefits, seniority, and similar matters of common interest. A labor union is sometimes referred to as *organized labor*, but more often this term is used for labor unions collectively. It also may be called a *trade union*, a term also used for a union that limits its membership to workers doing the same kind of work. The latter is more accurately called a *craft union*, which nearly always is limited to workers in one or a few closely allied skilled trades. In contrast, an *industrial union* will admit any workers from a single industry, ranging from unskilled to highly skilled—for example, the United Auto Workers admits any automobile company employee. In addition there are *professional unions*, such as those for teachers and for some civil service employees. In Europe there also are huge *general unions*, whose members come from many branches of industry and often are semiskilled or unskilled; the broad scope of these unions enables workers in such countries as France periodically to call a GENERAL STRIKE that virtually paralyzes the nation.

In the 1970s more than one-fifth of the American labor force—more than one-fourth of nonagricultural workers—belonged to labor unions. Of these, about 10 per cent worked in government and the rest were just about equally divided between manufacturing and nonmanufacturing industries. In certain key industries, notably transportation, steel and auto manufacturing, coal mining, and the garment industry, practically all eligible workers were union members. Moreover, many nonunion members were covered by union contracts, for according to the rule of *exclusive representation* established by the National Labor Relations (Wagner) Act of 1935, a union contract must apply equally to all persons, both members and nonmembers, in the area covered by it.

Present-day American unions are organized on two or three levels. The most important to the individual workers is the *local union*, which a worker joins in his or her plant or town and to which both dues and initiation fee are paid. It is normally the local union that negotiates the contract determining wages and working conditions. The local union is but a chapter (or lodge) of the *national union*, to which it pays a percentage of each member's dues. (If the national union also includes some Canadian local unions, it is called an *international union*.) The national union lays down broad overall policies for the members, and it sometimes becomes involved in local collective bargaining. It also administers the union's benefit and strike funds, aids or supervises strikes, and carries on lobbying and other political activities on behalf of its members. Although many national unions are autonomous (including two of the nation's largest, the International Brotherhood of Teamsters and the United Auto Workers), more than 100 of them belong to a *federation of national unions*, the AFL-CIO (see below; see also separate entry).

The earliest American unions, craft unions made up of highly skilled workers (printers, tailors, carpenters, shoemakers), were formed in the late 18th century. Periodically these local unions would combine in city or national federations, usually for purposes of political reform, but until after the Civil War the larger associations tended to be short-lived. The war, with its rising living costs and labor shortages, gave a strong impetus to organized labor, and many more workers joined unions. The first important industrial union was the KNIGHTS OF LABOR, founded in 1869, which for a time achieved considerable strength, but by the late 1880s it had begun to decline. Meanwhile the craft unions had started a new organization, which in 1886 became the American Federation of Labor (AFL), soon the dominant labor organization in the United States. By the 1930s, however, individual crafts had become far less important than the rapidly growing mass-production industries, and a rival industrial union, the Congress of Industrial Organizations

Fig. 45. Largest U.S. labor unions, 1972

Union	No. of Members
Teamsters*	1,855,000
Steelworkers	1,400,000
Automobile workers*	1,394,000
Electrical workers	957,000
Carpenters	829,000
Machinists	758,000
Retail clerks	633,000
Laborers	600,000
Food workers and meat cutters	529,000
State and county workers	529,000
Service employees	484,000

*Independent, that is, not members of AFL-CIO (as all of the other unions are).

(CIO), was founded by dissatisfied AFL members who now concentrated on unionizing mass-production workers. The next two decades saw a phenomenal growth in union membership, largely stimulated by the passage of favorable LABOR LAWS. Union membership grew from 6.9 per cent of the labor force in 1934 to 14 per cent in 1939, 22.9 per cent in 1949, and 26.8 per cent in 1953. In 1955 the two big federations overcame their differences and merged, and by the 1970s, the AFL-CIO embraced 113 separate unions, accounting for 80 per cent of American union membership (see also AFL-CIO). Among individual unions the trend toward consolidation also continued, mill and smelting workers merging with steelworkers, packinghouse and food workers with meatcutters and butchers, bakers with confectioners, bookbinders with lithographers, etc.

Unions did not develop and grow without bitter opposition from management, which used both fair and foul means of fighting back. (See EMPLOYERS' ASSOCIATION.) Supported by government and the general public, employers fired union members and put their names on a blacklist circulated among other employers (who then would not hire them). They employed labor spies to inform on union plans and strikebreakers to undermine strikes, and they obtained court orders to stop strikes (see INJUNCTION). Violence and bloodshed characterized many strikes before World War I, and some well into the 1930s. (See also COMPANY UNION; LOCKOUT; STRIKE; YELLOW-DOG CONTRACT.) Government also played a prominent role in opposing unions until the mid-1930s, when the passage of key labor laws upheld union status once and for all. The unions themselves were not entirely innocent victims. Certainly much of the violence was committed by them. Further, as early as 1900 corruption had become entrenched in the labor movement. Employee collusion and extortion from employers (for "strike insurance") were common, particularly in the construction industry. Local union officials sometimes acquired immense personal power, and some appropriated union funds for their private use (among them Peter J. McGuire of the Carpenters Union, the founder of Labor Day, who was convicted of fraud in 1901). In the 1950s such practices were uncovered in a number of unions, and public pressure led to passage of the Landrum-Griffin Act of 1959, mandating public disclosure of union finances. By the 1970s the growth of union membership had slowed considerably, largely because technological changes had reduced the number of blue-collar jobs. By then, many labor unions tended to have an elaborate bureaucracy not unlike that of big business, with leaders who were professional administrators, far removed from the 19th-century concept of the working class.

lagging indicator An INDICATOR that experiences the peaks and troughs of the business cycle some months after changes in general economic activity have occurred. Some economists believe that lagging indicators serve merely to complete the entire history of a particular cycle, but others feel they can themselves exert an important influence on other, coincident or leading indicators. For example, a belated decline in interest rates, plant and equipment spending, and unit labor cost could conceivably bring about a new decline in already rising leading indicators, such as profits and materials inventories. According to the U.S. Bureau of Economic Analysis there are 12 major lagging indicators; of these, 6 are considered particularly significant by the National Bureau of Economic Research and therefore constitute its *short list* of lagging indicators (see Fig. 46).

laissez faire A French term meaning "allow (them) to do" that connotes nonintervention by government in economic affairs. It may have been first used in this sense by Vincent de Gournay (1712–59), a quality inspector in France during the mercantilist period, when even internal trade was strictly regulated by the government (see under

Fig. 46. "Short list" of lagging indicators

• Unemployment rate, 15 weeks and over
• Business expenditures for new plant and equipment
• Manufacturing and trade inventories, book value
• Labor cost per unit of output, manufacturing
• Bank rates on short-term business loans, 35 cities
• Commercial and industrial loans outstanding, weekly reporting large commercial banks

PHYSIOCRATS). Disgusted with his job and the system in general, de Gournay supposedly said, "Laissez faire, laissez passer," presumably meaning, "Let them be free to manufacture, let them be free to trade." (Others, however, attribute the term to a French manufacturer of the time of COLBERT.) The doctrine of laissez faire in both foreign trade and domestic industry was basic to the physiocrats and to the CLASSICAL SCHOOL, dominating economic thought from the early 18th to the late 19th century. From about 1900 on, demands for government regulation gradually grew more influential than protests against interference. Nevertheless, a modified 20th-century doctrine of laissez faire developed alongside welfare economics and Keynesian economics, with their heavy stress on government's active role in economics. Its supporters believe that government should not regulate either prices or trade, but should control the money supply, undertake some social welfare activities, and restrict monopolies to ensure competition (see also CHICAGO SCHOOL). See also FREE TRADE.

land In economic theory, one of the FACTORS OF PRODUCTION, consisting not only of bare earth but of all natural resources (minerals, forests, wildlife, water, etc.). Since land is fixed in supply, it commands a price for its scarcity, which is called RENT (def. 1). See also CONSERVATION.

land bank
  1. In colonial America, a bank backed by assets in land that issued a form of currency called "bills of credit." In Massachusetts such a bank was organized in 1740 to issue 150,000 pounds in bills of credit based on mortgages at 3 per cent interest. However, its operations were declared illegal by an act of Parliament in 1741, and a later act (1751) prohibited the New England colonies from organizing new land banks and from using bills of credit as legal tender.
  2. See FEDERAL LAND BANKS.

land bridge Shipping goods in truck trailers or other sealed containers by a combination of overland and sea routes, using freighters, railroad flatcars, and trucks. The trailers are simply transferred from vehicle to vehicle without being opened or unpacked until they reach their final destination.

land contract Also, *contract for deed, installment contract.* A contract for the sale of land that provides for a down payment, with the rest of the purchase price payable in monthly installments. The buyer receives the DEED to the property when all installments have been paid or when the unpaid balance reaches a specified sum; in the latter case the buyer then gives the seller a purchase-money mortgage for the balance (see under MORTGAGE). A land contract thus resembles both a mortgage and an installment purchase of consumer goods (see INSTALLMENT BUYING).

landlord The granter of a LEASE, or lessor.

land reform Government-enforced changes in land ownership. In most countries, land reform means breaking up large estates worked by landless peasants into smaller plots that can be owned and worked individually. In such cases it is hoped that the political and social goals of every peasant working his own plot may offset the economies of SCALE that theoretically accrue to the larger plot. However logical it may seem on paper, in reality land reform is generally a painful process giving rise to bitter resentment in those who are dispossessed. See also COLLECTIVE FARM; ENCLOSURE; GRAZING LANDS; HOMESTEAD.

Landrum-Griffin Act See under LABOR LAWS.

land tax See PROPERTY TAX; also under H. GEORGE.

language, programming See under PROGRAMMING.

lapping Falsifying accounting records to conceal a shortage caused by theft or loss, usually by means of postponing cash receipts or some other asset from one accounting period to the next. A cashier, for example, might steal cash received from one customer and at a later date make good and credit that customer's account by stealing cash from another customer, continuing this process indefinitely. Such practices may have become more difficult to execute as more and more accounting procedures are executed by automated equipment.

lapse provision The clauses in an insurance policy relating to what will happen if the insured stops paying premiums. See also NONFORFEITURE.

Laspeyres index An index devised by French statistician Etienne Laspeyres in 1864 that is frequently used in constructing price indexes, notably the CONSUMER PRICE INDEX and WHOLESALE PRICE INDEX. The Laspeyres index is a weighted aggregative index, that is, it weights the items according to importance (see WEIGHTED AVERAGE) and considers the sum (aggregate) of expenditures for a given period. Importance is measured by the quantity purchased in the base year; thus it remains constant so long as the same base year is used. (This is sometimes called a *base-weighted index*.) The index number is computed by dividing the sum of current purchases of goods at base-year prices by actual base-year quantity at base-year price. Thus,

$$I = \frac{\Sigma Q_1 P_2}{\Sigma Q_1 P_1} \times 100$$

where I = index number; Σ = sigma, the standard symbol for "sum of "; Q_1 = quantity bought in the base year; P_2 = prices of individual items paid in the current year; and P_1 = prices paid in the base year; also, to avoid decimals index numbers normally are multiplied by 100. See also IDEAL INDEX; INDEX NUMBER; PRICE INDEX.

last-in, first-out Also, *LIFO*. A system of inventory accounting in which the items that are received last are regarded as being used first during an accounting period. As a result, cost of production is charged the most recent purchase cost. The reasoning behind this method is that a going concern must always keep some stock on hand; therefore goods used up must be replaced, making their value equal to the replacement cost. In industries that depend on raw materials whose prices fluctuate considerably, the type of inventory accounting method used can substantially influence reported profits. For example, suppose a firm making zinc die castings has 1 million pounds of zinc in stock, half of which was bought at 15 cents per pound and half six months later, at 10 cents per pound. The current market price for zinc is 11 cents. The company now gets an order for which 100,000 pounds of zinc will be required, and the price in the purchase contract is set accordingly. What will be the company's direct materials cost? On a last-in, first-out basis, materials cost can be based on the 10-cent price paid for the second 500,000 pounds, or $10,000, which is $1,000 cheaper than material bought at the current market price (11 cents, or $11,000), and the accounts may designate that $1,000 as a "profit." Were the company using the older FIRST-IN, FIRST-OUT accounting method, it would have to charge $15,000 to direct material, or $4,000 over the current market price. With last-in, first-out accounting, therefore, changing prices of raw materials have a smaller effect on stated profits. One drawback of last-in, first-out accounting is that it tends to undervalue inventory when prices are rising.

lawful money Same as LEGAL TENDER.

law of agency See under AGENT, def. 1.

laws For important U.S. legislation concerning business or economic affairs, see under the following entries: AGRICULTURE, AID TO; ANTITRUST LEGISLATION; BANKING LAWS; CONSUMER PROTECTION LAWS; FAIR TRADE; LABOR LAWS; TARIFF; UNIFORM COMMERCIAL CODE.

layaway plan A form of retail selling in which merchandise is held by the retailer while the customer makes periodic partial payments on it. It is similar to INSTALLMENT BUYING except that the customer does not have the use of the goods until they are paid for in full, and the seller usually does not receive more than the standard list price (which may, however, be higher than for cash purchases). Also, the seller does have the use of the partial payments without relinquishing the merchandise.

layoff The temporary or permanent removal of a worker from the payroll, usually owing to production cutbacks or to technological change (such as replacement of human labor with machinery). A layoff for disciplinary reasons—inadequate performance, infraction of company rules, etc.—is called a *discharge* or *firing*. Since layoffs are always involuntary from the worker's standpoint, in unionized organizations the labor contract generally governs both order of layoff and method of recall. Some labor contracts include provisions for supplemental unemployment benefits (paid in addition to state unemployment compensation). Occasionally they provide for *severance pay*, a lump-sum payment at the time of a permanent layoff, although this practice has been more common for nonunion salaried white-collar employees than for unionized production workers. See also SEPARATION RATE.

LCL See under FREIGHT.

leader See LOSS LEADER.

leading indicator An INDICATOR that anticipates the ups and downs of the business cycle, reaching peaks and troughs anywhere from 1 to 12 months ahead of general economic activity. Leading indicators therefore provide significant clues to future changes in business activity and are an important tool of economic FORECASTING. According to the U.S. Bureau of Economic Analysis, which regularly publishes statistics on leading indicators, there are 40 such indicators. Of these, 12 are considered particularly significant by the National Bureau of Economic Research and comprise its *short list* of leading indicators (see Fig. 47). It should be noted that these 12 are not all the same 12 leading indicators that make up the bureau's *Composite Index* of leading indicators, which is periodically revised. This difference—and the fact of revision—show that leading indicators are not totally reliable as a forecasting tool. Considerable time may elapse before the data from which the indicators are derived can be compiled, or a turning point may not be obvious until well after the fact. Hence economic forecasting can never consist simply of counting rising or falling indicators. See also COINCIDENT INDICATOR; LAGGING INDICATOR.

lead-lag relationship The more or less stable relationship in the timing and nature of changes between one set of economic indicators and another. For example, approximately six months after an increase in the number of construction contracts awarded, there is a corresponding increase in construction material sales. Similarly, an increase in the price of grain will be followed within a few months by higher-priced chicken and eggs, and,

Fig. 47. "Short list" of leading indicators

- Average workweek of production workers, manufacturing
- Average weekly initial claims for state unemployment insurance
- Index of net business formation (1967 = 100)
- Value of new orders in durable goods industries
- Value of contracts and orders for plant and equipment
- Index of new building permits for private housing units (1967 = 100)
- Index of stock prices for 500 common stocks (1941–43 = 10)
- Change in book value of manufacturing and trade inventories
- Index of industrial materials prices (1967 = 100)
- Corporate profits after taxes
- Index of ratio of price to unit labor cost, manufacturing (1967 = 100)
- Change in consumer installment debt

somewhat later, by price rises in pork and beef. If these relationships are fairly stable, relatively accurate forecasts of construction material sales and meat prices can be made. The CORN-HOG CYCLE is the classic example of such a relationship. See also LEADING INDICATOR.

lead time The interval between the time a need for material is determined and the time of its actual delivery. For example, if an office manager requisitions a typewriter on March 10, the buyer issues a purchase order on March 13, and the typewriter is delivered on March 26, the total lead time for the typewriter is 16 days; of these, 3 days represent administrative lead time and 13 days represent supplier lead time. Lead time for items that must be manufactured to order by out-of-town suppliers may be a matter of months or even, for very complex equipment, several years. Lead time also varies from supplier to supplier, and it may shorten as the business cycle dips into recession and lengthen dramatically during a boom. Fluctuating lead time is one of the biggest problems of industrial buyers, particularly for items that are critical for production. For this reason most firms must depend on a SAFETY STOCK as a safeguard against late deliveries.

leakage

1. In general, any diminution in the full effect of a policy.

2. In particular, a diminishing of the full effect of the MULTIPLIER PRINCIPLE (def. 1). For example, when bank reserves change, the multiplier principle makes for a much larger change in the granting of credit. If banks need a $.15 reserve for every $1 of credit they grant, deposits theoretically could expand $6\frac{2}{3}$ times (the reciprocal of the required reserve percentage, or $1/.15 = 6\frac{2}{3}$). But the real-life relationship between changes in reserves and changes in money is rarely so precise. Reserves are not always fully utilized as a basis for lending. Some reserves are required against bank liabilities other than demand deposits, such as time deposits. There frequently is a time lag in the flow of funds between one bank and another, between the conversion of deposits into currency and vice versa, and in shifts from demand deposits to other bank liabilities. All these drains from the full utilization of reserves as a basis for lending are called "leakage."

learning curve A graphic representation of a worker's increasing efficiency as he or she performs a given job again and again. Although a correlation between efficiency and experience had long been observed, the first attempts to measure it were made during World War II, when studies showed that labor hours per unit of product in the air-frame industry declined by about 20 per cent whenever output was doubled, a change representing an 80 per cent learning curve. Thus, if the first unit of a product takes 100 hours of labor, the second unit will take only 80 per cent of that time, or 80 hours, the fourth unit will take 64 hours, the eighth unit 51.2 hours, and so on. As a result, labor costs will decline as a manufacturer gains experience with a new product, and overall costs should decline accordingly. To calculate the precise percentages and appropriate cost reductions for specific cases, formulas involving logarithms are used, or the results are plotted on a chart using log-log paper.

lease A contract granting possession and use of property in return for rent or some other compensation. The most common kind of lease involves real estate. Legally a real estate lease is not only a con-tract but a CONVEYANCE by the *landlord* (or *lessor*), who is usually but not always the owner, to the *tenant* (or *lessee*) to occupy the land (premises) for the term specified in the lease. The lessee's interest in the land for that period is called a *leasehold*. In theory, a lease may run for any period of time, from 1 day to 99 years or longer; in the United States some states have statutes limiting the duration of leases. Generally a lease running for 10 years or longer is considered a *long-term lease*, and anything less a *short-term lease*, but these terms often are used quite loosely. A written lease (necessary for a period of more than 1 year in most states in order to be legally enforceable) normally includes a description of the leased premises, the term of the lease (beginning and end), and the amount of rent and how it is to be paid. Unless stated otherwise, rent is payable at the end of each rental period; however, most landlords want it payable in advance, at the start of each period. A *flat*, *straight*, or *fixed lease* calls for a fixed rent for the entire term, whereas some leases call for periodic increases. Leases of retail premises often are *percentage leases*, that is, in addition to a minimum fixed rent they call for payment of a fixed percentage of the tenant's gross sales. This amount may be as low as 2 per cent for large department stores and as high as 75 per cent for a parking lot. A *net lease* requires the tenant to pay all operating costs, including real estate taxes and insurance, which with other leases are normally paid by the landlord. Such leases are commonly confined to large commercial and industrial properties leased for long periods as well as to investors in offshore properties (for extracting oil and gas) who use purchase and LEASEBACK agreements. A *ground lease* covers the use of vacant land on which the tenant usually agrees to erect a building or other structure. Built at the tenant's expense, the building legally still is the property of the landlord (though it remains in the tenant's possession for the term of the lease); usually some provision is made for reimbursing the tenant. The rent for a ground lease, or *ground rent*, is often calculated on the basis of the land's value, and the tenant usually pays taxes and other charges, as with a net lease.

Unless a lease states otherwise, a tenant may *assign* it, or *sublet* the premises. In ASSIGNMENT, the entire unexpired remainder of the term of the lease is transferred; in subletting, only part of the remaining term or only part of the premises is transferred. The difference is important, since an assignee is liable to the original landlord for rent, whereas a sublessee is liable only to the lessee under the original lease. Also, unless stated otherwise, a tenant may mortgage the leased property, taking out a *leasehold mortgage*. Such mortgages sometimes raise legal problems; for example, if a tenant defaults on rent payments, the landlord may declare the lease forfeited, thereby extinguishing the mortgage.

A lease ends when its term runs out (it is then said to *expire*). Also, landlord and tenant may agree to end the lease by means of *surrender*, the tenant simply giving the premises up to the landlord; surrender releases the tenant from liability for rent. Some leases contain a clause allowing the landlord to cancel it if the property is sold (after giving due notice to the tenant). However, often the landlord simply sells, with the buyer accepting the property subject to existing leases, and the tenant then pays rent to the new landlord. Most leases stipulate that they may be *forfeited* and the tenant *dispossessed* for nonpayment of rent or violation of other terms; in such cases the tenant usually is not liable for rent following ejectment. However, the tenant's departure before the lease expires is considered *abandonment* and the tenant remains liable for the rent. In the event that the tenant leaves because the premises have become uninhabitable owing to the landlord's delinquency in maintenance and repairs, the tenant is not liable for rent; this is sometimes called *constructive eviction*. See also EVICTION; TENANCY.

leaseback Also, *sale and leaseback*. A way of acquiring capital that would otherwise be tied up in fixed assets. For example, a manufacturing firm might sell a building to an insurance company and then sign a long-term lease for its use. The building becomes the equivalent of collateral on a loan for the insurance company, and the lease includes a rent high enough to cover depreciation of the property over its life as well as a return on the insurance company's investment. Sale and leaseback is particularly beneficial when a company cannot raise money more cheaply through a direct bank loan or does not wish to impair its credit standing by having

such a loan appear on its balance sheet, or when the profit from selling the asset is larger than the amount of the rent it must pay.

leased department See under DEPARTMENT STORE.

leasehold See under ESTATE, def. 2; also under LEASE.

least squares method See under REGRESSION ANALYSIS.

ledger In accounting, the final book of entry for recording a business's financial transactions. Normally entries in a ledger are transferred from a book of original entry (see JOURNAL) or from vouchers. A ledger has a separate page or group of pages for each account (see ACCOUNT, def. 1; also DOUBLE ENTRY). A firm may have several ledgers, such as a *general ledger* in which it posts the chief accounts that make up the balance sheet and income statement, and one or more *subsidiary ledgers* devoted to specific accounts that are later transferred to the general ledger.

legal list A list of investments selected by various states in which certain institutions and fiduciaries, such as banks and insurance companies, may invest. Legal lists tend to include only high-quality securities meeting certain specifications. See also PRUDENT-MAN RULE.

legal reserve See BANK RESERVES; RESERVE REQUIREMENTS.

legal reserve life insurance A LIFE INSURANCE company that, to comply with state laws, maintains a minimum reserve of assets for each policy it issues.

legal tender Any authorized coin or paper money that may lawfully be offered—"tender" means "offer"—in payment of a debt or other obligation and that creditors must accept as payment. Until the Civil War, legal tender in the United States consisted of gold and silver coins and paper money backed by gold and silver. (Unlike most countries, in the United States money had to be declared legal tender for it to be so.) To finance the war, however, Congress in 1862 passed the first Legal Tender Act, which provided for an issue of $150 million in paper notes that had no specie backing and were not convertible into gold or silver, but that could be used to buy Treasury bonds. These notes were sometimes called "legal tenders," but more often "greenbacks" (see GREENBACK). In 1870 the U.S. Supreme Court declared the issuing of legal tenders unconstitutional, but the following year it reversed its decision and held they were a properly constitutional means of borrowing money. A law passed in 1893 made all currency and coin, including Federal Reserve notes and other notes, full legal tender. However, there are limits on the use of coins as legal tender. For example, a debt of $.31 may be paid in pennies, but a creditor need not accept repayment of a debt of $31.00 in pennies.

leisure class See under T. VEBLEN.

lending, foreign See INTERNATIONAL INVESTMENT; also FOREIGN AID.

Lenin, Vladimir Ilyich The assumed name of Vladimir Ilyich Ulyanov, a Russian socialist (1870–1924) and first chairman of the Council of People's Commissars, the ruling body of what became the Union of Soviet Socialist Republics. Involved in revolutionary activities from an early age, for which he was exiled for a time to Siberia, Lenin became a faithful disciple of the doctrine of Karl Marx (see COMMUNISM, def. 1). In his book *Imperialism,* Lenin explained that imperialism had delayed the collapse of capitalism that Marx had predicted, because the acquisition of colonies had temporarily postponed the breakdown of the capitalist system. Lenin lived for some years abroad, mostly in Switzerland. In 1903 at a conference in London he organized the Bolsheviks, who became the extremist faction of the Russian socialists. In November (October according to the old-style Russian calendar) 1917, the Bolsheviks overthrew the provisional government under Kerensky that had been set up after the abduction of the Tsar and seized control. Soon after they broke with the other wings of the socialists and established a new government. Calling themselves *communists,* they asserted they had set up a proletarian dictatorship, and Lenin himself, returning from exile, was made chairman of the Council of People's Commissars, which controlled the entire hierarchy of soviets (councils) down to the local level. Under Lenin the government abolished private ownership of land and announced it would distribute land among the peasants. The banks were nationalized, a supreme council was set up to administer the disrupted economy, and workers' councils were established to control the factories. In 1919 Lenin set up the *Third International* (or *Comintern*) to further the cause of world revolution, and enacted extensive nationalization of industry and food requisitioning from farms for factory workers. This policy proved an economic disaster, leading to a sharp decline in output, and was modified in 1921 through the *New Economic Policy (NEP),* which permitted some private enterprise and return to a market economy. Lenin, who combined a mastery of Marxist theories with extremely shrewd political instinct, is still revered in the Soviet Union as its founding father.

Leontieff, Wassily W. See under INPUT-OUTPUT ANALYSIS.

less developed nation See UNDERDEVELOPED NATION.

lessee See under LEASE.

lessor See under LEASE.

letter of credit A letter or instrument authorizing that credit up to a particular amount be extended to the person named therein, and guaranteeing the reimbursement of the funds so advanced. Most letters of credit are issued by a bank and are addressed to one or more correspondent banks. They are widely used in foreign trade, where they eliminate the need for transferring funds to banks in different countries. There are numerous kinds of letter of credit, differing chiefly in how they are used and in the liability assumed by the issuing bank. A *commercial letter of credit* is one purchased by a prospective buyer of goods and forwarded to a correspondent bank in the place where the purchase is to be made; the seller is notified and presents a draft for payment, along with any required documents verifying the shipment, to the correspondent bank. Such a letter of credit may cover a single transaction or a whole series; in the latter case it is sometimes called a *revolving letter of credit*. A *traveler's letter of credit* is one purchased by a person planning to travel abroad to obtain funds in different currencies; it is presented at any of several foreign correspondent banks listed. A *confirmed* letter of credit guarantees payment of all drafts drawn against it; an *unconfirmed* letter of credit is one for which credit has been established but the correspondent bank itself does not guarantee payment of drafts against it. An *irrevocable* letter of credit cannot be canceled until a specified date unless the person to whom it is issued agrees; a *revocable* letter of credit may be canceled at any time by the issuing bank.

letter of lien In foreign trade, a document signed by a buyer stating that the seller retains a lien, or possession of the goods, until they have been paid for.

letter stock A stock that is not registered with the U.S Securities and Exchange Commission and that therefore cannot be resold by its owner on the open market. Such stocks are sold directly by the issuer to the investor; the issuer thus saves a registration fee and the investor benefits from a slightly lower price. The investor can sell letter stock only privately to another investor and cannot use a broker or other intermediary unless the stock has been registered.

leverage The effect on the earnings per share of a company's common stock when large sums must be paid out for bond interest or dividends on preferred stock (or both) before the common stock may share in the earnings. When earnings are good, common stock benefits; when they decline, it suffers. For example, suppose Company A has one million shares of common stock outstanding and no other securities. Earnings now drop from $1 million to $800,000, or from $1 to $.80 per share, a 20 per cent decline. Company B also has one million shares of common stock but in addition must pay $500,000 in bond interest. If earnings are $1 million, $500,000 is available for common stock dividends, meaning $.50 per share. But if earnings

drop to $800,000, only $300,000 is available for common stock dividends, which drop to $.30 per share, representing a 40 per cent decline. With Company A there is no leverage, but with Company B there is quite a bit. Actually, a company having only common stock may still feel the effect of leverage if it faces relatively large fixed charges for leasing important plant assets. Thus the stocks of most supermarket chains are quite highly leveraged even if there is no debt because the actual premises are almost always leased rather than owned outright.

liability

1. A debt owed by a business or individual. In accounting the term, usually in the plural (*liabilities*), refers to the credit side of a balance sheet, where the sum of liabilities and NET WORTH exactly offset assets on the debit side of the balance sheet. (See ASSET.) Accountants generally distinguish between *current* (or *floating* or *short-term*) *liabilities*, to be paid within one year or less (such as salaries, taxes due, accounts payable, short-term notes, accrued interest, etc.), and *long-term* or *fixed liabilities*, running one year or longer (mortgages, bonds, long-term notes). See also FUNDED DEBT.

An *accrued liability* is an expense that has been incurred but not yet paid, such as rent, taxes, insurance payments, etc. (see also ACCRUAL BASIS). A *deferred liability* is one on which payment, in the form of services or goods (rather than cash), is put off; it actually is an accounting device to balance the liability side of a balance sheet with cash income received but not yet earned, as, for example, an advance against royalties, or a deposit paid on a contract not yet fulfilled.

2. In law, a required obligation or responsibility, from which a claim against an individual or business may arise. For example, the person who ultimately must pay the face amount of a negotiable instrument is said to be *liable*, that is, the possessor of the instrument may claim the money from that person. (See also LIMITED LIABILITY.) A *contingent liability* is one that may or may not materialize in the future, for example, a possible lawsuit arising from past events, or a purchase contracted for that may not be fulfilled. A landlord may be liable to claims by a tenant who has suffered injury on his property. Insurance against damage or injury of various kinds is called LIABILITY INSURANCE.

liability insurance Various forms of insurance against claims for accidental bodily injury, medical payments related to such injury, and property damage. Liability insurance is frequently part of certain PROPERTY INSURANCE policies, notably in automobile, aviation, boiler and machinery, and marine insurance. In addition, there is *personal liability insurance*, covering individuals and families against such claims as that of a letter carrier bitten by the family dog or a visitor falling down the stairs; *farmers' liability,* for accidents on the farm; *premises* and *elevator liability,* for real estate owners; *operations liability,* for contractors, manufacturers, etc.; *employers' liability* (see WORKMEN'S COMPENSATION); *product liability,* for manufacturers and merchants; *professional liability insurance,* such as the *malpractice insurance* of physicians, as well as variations of it used by architects, engineers, accountants, and other professionals (sometimes called *errors and omissions coverage*); *libel* and *slander liability*; *bailee liability,* usually part of inland marine insurance; *aviation liability,* for accidents arising from aircraft operations; and *nuclear hazard liability.* See also NO-FAULT INSURANCE.

liberalism, economic See ECONOMIC LIBERALISM.

license
1. A form of permission granted by a government or other authority to engage in some activity that is regulated by law. Licenses may be used for revenue, for obtaining records for policing or other purposes (as with *marriage licenses*), or to protect the public against unqualified practitioners of a trade, profession, or activity (*medical license, driver's license*). A license confers a privilege to which its holder has no legal right, and it is usually temporary, revocable, and renewable. Some licenses are granted freely to all applicants; others may be granted on a limited basis, so as to exclude competition from a particular field. In the United States licenses are issued by state and local governments to doctors, dentists, pharmacists, barbers, brokers, plumbers, and in other occupations; to distributors of liquor, tobacco, milk, and other goods; and to operators of hotels, restaurants, theaters, poolrooms, dance halls, taxicabs, and other public services. The Federal government requires licenses of private carriers and uses licensing to control both equipment and personnel in transport and to allocate broadcasting channels among radio and television companies. The Federal Power Commission issues licenses for private hydroelectric projects; the Atomic Energy Commission, for nuclear installations; the Federal Communications Commission, for broadcasting. See also FRANCHISE, def. 1.

2. In patent and copyright law, the authority granted by the owner to another party to make, reproduce, use, or sell the patented or copyrighted item under certain stated restrictions. Such licenses may be granted to one party or to many, and they may or may not restrict the quantity produced or sold, the market, the price, or some other condition of use. The practice of two or more patent holders mutually granting each other licenses is called *cross licensing* (see also PATENT POOL).

lien A right given to a certain kind of creditor to have debts paid out of the debtor's property, usually by selling it. A lien is always against property, as opposed to wages or other earnings (see GARNISHMENT), and usually it is against real (not personal) property. Liens come into being in several ways: resulting from a contract (such as a MORTGAGE); arising out of equity (for example, when one of two sons sharing an estate refuses to pay the taxes on his half, thus forcing his brother to pay both shares, that brother may have an *equitable lien* on the other's share as security for reimbursment of the tax payments); and legal, provided for by statute. Two common kinds of *statutory lien* are the *mechanic's lien*, whereby a contractor or worker who furnished labor and/or materials for improving land or a building and is not paid may acquire a lien on the property, which frequently takes precedence over mortgages and other liens; and a *tax lien*, for failure to pay Federal or local taxes. Other kinds include the *carrier's lien* (on shipped goods whose transport costs are not paid) and the *seller's lien* (on purchased goods not paid for); in either case the creditor may keep the goods in question. Normally a lien must be enforced through court action. See also ATTACHMENT.

lien, letter of See LETTER OF LIEN.

life annuity See under ANNUITY.

life expectancy See SERVICE LIFE.

life insurance A kind of financial protection that involves death benefits for a deceased person's survivors and/or enforced saving to build a reserve of funds, especially for old age. There are three major kinds of life insurance policy: term, straight life (including limited payment), and endowment. *Term insurance* is good for a specific period, or "term," that is, the benefit is payable only if the insured dies within that time. The term typically is 1, 5, or 10 years (occasionally as long as 20), often with an option to renew. Premiums are paid throughout this period but are generally raised upon renewal, since the policyholder, now older, presents a greater risk to the insurer. Since the premium for term policies pays only the cost of protection during the stated time, it is generally low and the policy rarely has any value if it is canceled. It thus represents purely protection for the beneficiaries, and not any form of saving. *Straight life insurance* provides protection for the policyholder's whole life at a *level premium,* that is, a fixed rate. Premiums are payable throughout the holder's lifetime, and the face of the policy is payable only at death. A *cash surrender value* builds up, however, against which the insured may borrow (see POLICY LOAN). Or, if he decides to cancel the policy, he may take the cash value as a lump-sum payment or use it to buy an annuity or some other form of retirement income (see also NONFORFEITURE). A *limited-payment life policy* also provides lifetime protection but limits the payment of premiums to a period such as 10, 20, or 30 years, or up to a certain age (usually 60, 65, or 85), according to the buyer's choice. The insured simply pays higher premiums, but for a shorter time. The higher rate endows it with greater investment value than a straight life policy, but it gives less protection in return for the same annual premium. An *endowment policy* gives still less protection to beneficiaries but offers the highest investment element. Premium payments are required for a stated period (20 to 30 years is typical), and the full face value is payable if death occurs within that

period. However, it also is payable at the end of the period if the insured is still alive, usually either as a lump-sum settlement or in the form of a guaranteed life income. Besides these three basic forms, numerous combinations of them exist. For example, *family income* or *family maintenance insurance* combines straight life and term insurance. A 20-year family income policy provides that, if the insured dies during that period, the beneficiary will receive $10 per month for each $1,000 of the basic straight life policy for the balance of the 20 years. At the end of the 20th year, the beneficiary also receives the face value of the straight life policy or its equivalent in the form of income. If the insured survives the 20-year term, he can continue the straight life portion of the policy at the rate in effect when it was first purchased. A family maintenance policy would pay monthly income for 20 years after the death of the insured (if he dies within the 20-year term) and after that, the face value of the policy.

Life insurance is sold to the American public in three principal ways. Regular life insurance companies issue *ordinary insurance,* which is the most common kind bought by individuals and families. The policies may be of any type and are usually for $1,000 or more, but there are definite limits on the amount one individual or family can buy, since companies are careful to avoid *overinsurance.* Most require a medical examination and the premiums are payable monthly, quarterly, semiannually, or annually. The same companies also sell *industrial insurance,* policies in amounts of $500 or less and payable in weekly or monthly premiums. The premiums usually are collected by insurance agents, which adds considerably to their cost. *Group life insurance* is issued by insurance companies through employers, usually for groups of 25 to 50 or more (but occasionally for fewer). No medical examination is required, and the premium charges, billed to the employer, are based on the ages and occupations of the participating employees. The employer may pay the full bill or may charge part to the employees, usually through payroll deductions. Such insurance tends to be relatively cheap (see also GROUP INSURANCE). *Savings bank life insurance,* available in only a few states, is purchased over the counter or by mail from mutual savings banks, usually in limited amounts. It permits monthly payment of premiums, and the policies may offer different cash surrender and loan value terms from those of other policies (usually a minimum waiting period is required). However, no agents are involved, meaning that no commission is paid, making this more economical than ordinary insurance. The U.S. Federal government offered life insurance to veterans of World Wars I and II and veterans of the Korean War; coverage was free during the term of service, and after discharge premium payments could be assumed by the veteran. Government insurance is the most economical of all (no private insurer charging so little could make a profit), but many veterans failed to realize it and let their policies lapse. See also ANNUITY.

LIFO Abbreviation for LAST-IN, FIRST-OUT.

Limited Also, *Ltd.* An abbreviation for LIMITED LIABILITY, used to describe a company that is legally a corporation. It is used chiefly in Great Britain and other Commonwealth countries; the terms *Incorporated* (or *Inc.*) and *Corporation* (*Corp.*) are more common in the United States.

limited liability Responsibility for the debts of a business that is restricted to the size of one's investment in it. Limited liability is a major advantage of the corporate form of business organization; see also under CORPORATION.

limited partnership See under PARTNERSHIP.

limited-payment life insurance See under LIFE INSURANCE.

limited-price store See under RETAIL.

limit order Also, *limited order, limited price order.* An order to buy or sell a given amount of a security at a specified price (or better). A limit order generally specifies also the time period during which it is to apply; it may be "good till canceled" (see OPEN ORDER, def. 1) or only for one day (see DAY ORDER).

line and staff See under ORGANIZATION, COMPANY.

linear programming A mathematical technique used to determine what combination of resources, subject to given limitations, is most likely to fulfill a particular objective, such as making Product X at the lowest possible cost or transporting Material Y in the shortest time. Like many techniques now applied to business and economic problems, linear programming was first used in military planning (it was originated by G. B. Dantzig in the 1940s). Essentially, linear programming consists of maximizing (or minimizing) some dependent variable that is a linear function of several independent variables and is subject to certain constraints. The dependent variable, for example, might be the entrepreneur's profit, and the independent variables might be the output of different products, any of which can be made with the same equipment and sold in any amount produced. However, how much of each product can be made per day is limited by existing capacity (thus the independent variables are constrained). Although it might seem fairly simple to multiply the profit made on each unit of each product by the number of units that can be produced, and to compare the results, even this process can be quite complex. A plant may be producing 24 dif-

Fig. 48. Eight assembly operations on product X (time in minutes)

Operation Number	Description	Allowed Time
1	Lift motor from overhead conveyor and place on base assembly on roller conveyor	.07
2	Insert studs to attach motor to base	.25
3	Place grommets over studs	.05
4	Fasten nuts around studs	.22
5	Run down nuts with power driver	.25
6	Place cover over motor	.18
7	Insert sheet metal screws in cover	.28
8	Tighten sheet metal screws	.30
		1.60

Source: D. S. Ammer, *Manufacturing Management and Control* (New York: Appleton-Century-Crofts, 1968), p. 158. Reprinted by permission of Prentice-Hall, Inc.

ferent items in 17 different departments, each requiring different production time in each department as well as involving different profits (owing to different materials costs), depending on the quantity produced. Similarly, a poultry farmer may be trying to decide how to provide animals with their daily quota of food at minimum cost, with each animal requiring a minimum of calories, grams of protein, etc., and the prices for feed varying from week to week. Or an advertising agency will seek to reach the largest possible audience through newspapers, magazines, radio, and television but must take into account the client's budget, required minimum audience, and differing media costs. Usually computers are called upon to deal with the many variables in linear programming problems.

linear regression See under REGRESSION ANALYSIS.

line balancing Dividing the work to be done on a product moving down an assembly line so as to get the maximum output (most work done in least time) from minimum input (fewest workers). For example, suppose Product X requires eight separate assembly operations that take a total of 1.6 minutes. Only one operation can be performed at a time. How many workers should be used to perform them? The industrial engineer will usually try several combinations, timing one, two, three, or four workers doing the job, and dividing operations among them as evenly as possible. The key factor in line balancing is the slowest operation, which necessarily limits the pace of the work. Suppose that Worker A can do his half of a job in .84 minute and that Worker B can do her half in .76 minute. Even though Worker B is faster than Worker A, she cannot do her half of the job until Worker A has completed his half. Thus, the slower worker limits the faster, and the slower time must be allowed for both. (See Figs. 48 and 49.) Today such calculations are frequently done by computer.

line of credit Also, *credit line*. The range, up to a specified maximum, within which a bank or business is willing to extend credit to a borrower or customer. Continuation of such credit is usually contingent on the borrower's maintaining the same financial status and also, frequently, on maintaining a minimum balance in a checking account to cover a portion—typically 20 per cent—of the outstanding loan. The borrower also may have to pay a commitment fee—of perhaps .5 per cent—on credit that remains available but unused.

Fig. 49. Possible line balances for product X (time in minutes)

Number of Men in Line	Job Assignment		Required Time	Allowed Time	Efficiency	Hourly Production
	Operator	*Operations*				
2	A	1,2,3,4,5	.84	.84		
	B	6,7,8	.76	.84		
			1.60	1.68	95.2%	71.4 pieces
3	A	1,2,3,4	.59	.59		
	B	5,6	.43	.59		
	C	7,8	.58	.59		
			1.60	1.77	90.4	101.7
4	A	1,2,3	.37	.47		
	B	4,5	.47	.47		
	C	6,7	.46	.47		
	D	8	.30	.47		
			1.60	1.88	85.1	127.7

Source: D. S. Ammer, *Manufacturing Management and Control* (New York: Appleton-Century-Crofts, 1968), p. 159. Reprinted by permission of Prentice-Hall, Inc.

line production A method of manufacturing involving a CONTINUOUS PROCESS on an assembly line.

liquid asset Also, *quick asset.* An ASSET that is readily convertible into cash, or that already consists of cash. Liquid assets commonly include cash on hand, readily marketable securities, or notes receivable; they differ from current assets in that they usually exclude inventories. A firm's *net liquid assets* are found by subtracting total current liabilities from total liquid assets. See also QUICK RATIO.

liquidation
1. Payment of an obligation, such as repayment of a loan. Such a loan is then said to be "liquidated."
2. Converting an asset into cash, as, for example, accounts receivable, stock, inventory, etc.
3. The dissolution of a business, estate, or other economic unit through the sale of its assets and the settlement of its liabilities. The amount that could be realized from dissolving a partnership or other business is called its *liquidation value*, which usually is quite different from its value as an ongoing business.

liquidity
1. The relative ease with which a person, firm, or organization can meet its obligations without selling fixed assets. The degree of liquidity is normally directly proportional to the amount of liquid assets (see LIQUID ASSET).
2. *international liquidity.* The sum of the world's liquid monetary reserves, that is, the total amount of gold, reserve currencies, and SPECIAL DRAWING RIGHTS (SDRs) available for financing international trade. After World War II the leading reserve currency was the U.S. dollar, but by the mid-1970s the West German Deutschmark seemed destined to become the second reserve currency. A major problem plaguing the world's chief trading countries since the late 1950s has been that liquidity has not kept up with trade expansion, that is, the quantity of gold and reserve currency simply did not grow fast enough to keep up with increasing trade. The invention in 1969 of a new international currency—the SDR—alleviated the situation some-what, but by the mid-1970s, with largely floating exchange rates, new problems concerning the valuation of SDRs had arisen. See also under EXCHANGE RATE.

liquidity preference A term originated by J. M. KEYNES to describe the preference for keeping one's savings either in cash or in some form readily convertible into cash (such as a checking account), instead of investing them so that they earn a return (as in securities). Keynes said that liquidity preference is influenced by three considerations: the *transactions motive,* meaning the desire for ready cash to carry on everyday dealings; the *precautionary motive,* the desire to keep a cash reserve for emergencies; and the *speculative motive,* the desire to keep ready cash for more lucrative future investments. Thus interest is a reward for parting with liquidity, an idea known as the *liquidity preference theory of interest* (see also ABSTINENCE THEORY OF INTEREST). According to Keynes, the MARKET RATE OF INTEREST results from the interaction of supply, represented by the quantity of money (governed by central bank policies), and demand, represented by liquidity preference. When the central bank increases the money supply (in the United States, through open-market purchases by the Federal Reserve and similar means), the interest rate tends to fall, until finally the yield of securities (stocks and bonds) is so low that they seem no more attractive to an investor than simply keeping savings under a mattress. Once the interest rate is low enough, all savers will prefer to keep their money under mattresses.

List, Friedrich A German economist (1789–1846), a forerunner of the GERMAN HISTORICAL SCHOOL, who was among the first to consider a nation's stage of economic development as basic to the principles that should guide its economic policies. List contended that nations pass through progressive economic stages: savage, pastoral, agricultural, agricultural-manufacturing, and finally, agricultural-manufacturing-commercial. Critical of the classical economists' (see CLASSICAL SCHOOL) beliefs in laissez faire, international free trade, and an underlying harmony of interests between the individual and society, List encouraged protective tariffs, wanted to limit free trade so that it existed only within national boundaries, and upheld considerable government intervention in economic affairs.

listed security   Also, *on-board security*. A SECURITY listed on an organized exchange, meaning that it has met the requirements set by the exchange.

listing   In real estate, the employment of a broker to sell or lease property. The arrangement between the broker and principal (usually the seller) may be an informal oral agreement or, as some states require, involve a written *listing contract*. Such a contract includes the names of seller and broker, a description of the property (often just a street address), the terms of sale (price, payment terms, etc.), duration of broker's employment, and commission to be paid the broker. It also includes any special agreements. Four such agreements are common. An *open listing* does not preclude the owner from selling the property himself or engaging other brokers; usually at least two are hired, unless the agreement specifies otherwise. Most informal oral agreements are open listings, and whichever broker is the first to find a ready, able, and willing buyer gets the commission. *Exclusive agency* assures the broker that no other brokers will be hired during the duration of his or her employment, but does not bar the owner from selling the property himself. *Exclusive right to sell* makes the broker the owner's sole agent and provides that the broker will get a commission no matter who sells the property (the owner, another broker, or someone else). *Multiple listing* is a means of pooling the efforts of brokers in a given area. One broker obtains an exclusive right-to-sell contract from the owner but gives a copy to all members of the pool. If a member other than the original broker sells the property, the commission is divided by the two brokers. A fifth type of agreement sometimes used is the *net listing*, whereby the broker who negotiated a sale receives, instead of the conventional percentage commission, everything above the original price set by the seller.

list price   The published or marked price for merchandise, which the final consumer (private or industrial) presumably will be asked to pay. A reduction from the list price ("off list") may be a DISCOUNT (def. 1) of one kind or another, an ALLOWANCE (def. 2), or a MARKDOWN.

living cost   See COST OF LIVING.

living trust   See under TRUST.

Lloyd's of London   See under INSURANCE.

loading
   1. See *load* or *loading charge*, under MUTUAL FUND.
   2. In insurance, an amount added to the basic rate or premium to cover the insurance company's expense in securing and maintaining the enterprise.

loan
   1. In banking and finance, a sum of money, borrowed at interest, for a specified period of time. Other property may also be lent, though if a fee is involved the terms "hire," "rent," or "lease" are similarly used; in business and finance "loan" nearly always refers to money or near money. Loans are classified according to the kind of lender or borrower, whether or not security is put up (and what kind), the time of maturity (short-, intermediate-, or long-term), conditions of repayment, and other variables.
   In terms of the type of lender or borrower, there is the *deposit loan*, in which the lender is a bank that simply credits a sum to the borrower's account or sets up a new account for this purpose; a *brokers' loan*, made by a bank to a securities broker to finance margin buying; a *participation loan*, usually involving a large sum put up jointly by several banks or lenders; a *personal loan*, usually a fairly small sum lent to an individual by a bank, FINANCE COMPANY (def. 2), or other lending institution, with or without collateral. In terms of security, there is a *collateral loan*, secured by the pledge of specific property (usually in negotiable form); a *secured loan*, secured by the pledge of personal property; an *unsecured* or *fiduciary loan*, secured only by the borrower's good name; and a *commodity loan*, secured by some *specific commodity* (sugar, cotton, etc.), usually held in a warehouse and hence also called a *warehouse receipt loan* or *field warehousing loan*. In terms of maturity, a *call*

loan, demand loan, or *sight loan* must be repaid "on call" (on demand) from the lender, although usually 24 hours' notice is allowed, whereas a *time loan* may not be repaid before a specific maturity date; a *day loan* or *morning loan* is made for one day, usually to a securities or foreign-exchange broker to help finance day-to-day operations (although interbank loans also may be overnight; see FEDERAL FUNDS MARKET); a *short-term loan* matures in less than one year; a *term loan* runs for longer than one year (frequently for about five) and usually is repayable in installments over that period. Although bonds and mortgages are, strictly speaking, long-term loans, they generally are considered in separate categories. See also BOND, def. 1; COLLATERAL; FORCED LOAN; MORTGAGE; *nonrecourse loan,* under AGRICULTURE, AID TO.

2. Also, *foreign loan, international loan.* In foreign affairs, a sum of money borrowed by one nation from another. Like other loans, these may be long- or short-term, involve high, low, or no interest, be made for specific or general purposes, and may have special conditions attached. See also SOFT LOAN; TIED LOAN.

loanable funds In economic theory, the funds available for lending, which are needed to produce or purchase capital goods. Such funds come from savings, dishoarding (the release of funds previously reserved for other purposes), and any increases in the money supply (through the creation of credit by commercial banks). The supplies of and demand for loanable funds constitute a market for credit (see MONEY MARKET; CAPITAL MARKET). Some economists, notably Alfred Marshall and his followers, and D. H. Robertson (1890–1963), hold that the supply of and demand for loanable funds determine the MARKET RATE OF INTEREST, an idea called the *loanable funds theory of interest.* The demand for loanable funds includes not just funds for investment but also demand for consumer credit and the demand for money reserves. The loanable funds theory thus assumes that the market interest rate is determined by the combined effect of all the various demands and supplies on one another. J. M. Keynes criticized this theory on the ground that it fails to take into account various levels of income, which affect both supply and demand, and substi-

tuted his LIQUIDITY PREFERENCE theory of interest. Still another theory is that of the *natural interest rate* (see under K. WICKSELL).

loan rate of interest See MARKET RATE OF INTEREST.

loan shark A person or firm lending money at excessive, illegal rates of interest, most often to those who have difficulty in obtaining loans through other channels. See also USURY.

lobby See PRESSURE GROUP.

local union See under LABOR UNION.

lockout An employer's strike, that is, the shutdown of a plant or other facility in protest against employee or union demands. In so doing, the employer hopes to force workers to accept the existing terms of employment. An early weapon against labor unions, lockouts lost much of their impact with the passing of legislation entitling locked-out workers to unemployment compensation.

logic In computers, the operation of comparing two pieces of stored data and determining whether or not they are equal.

logistics In military operations, the science of getting needed materials and equipment to the right place at the right time. The industrial counterpart of logistics is MATERIALS MANAGEMENT or physical distribution management.

long Describing a security that one has bought and actually owns. See also under SELLING SHORT.

long haul In rail transportation, the carrying of freight over long rather than short distances (called *short haul*), a largely relative distinction. However, according to a provision in the Interstate Commerce Act that is sometimes called the *long and short haul clause,* railroads may not charge more for a short haul than for a longer haul that includes the short haul. For example, the freight rate from Elizabeth to Trenton, New Jersey, may not be higher than the rate for the longer haul from Elizabeth to Philadelphia.

long-term

1. *capital gain.* A profit realized from selling an asset that has been owned six months or longer, a differentiation important because, according to U.S. Federal tax law, it is taxed at half the rate of a short-term gain (on an asset owned for less than six months).

2. *credit.* An obligation that will not become due for a year or more. All bonds represent long-term credit.

3. *forecast.* See under FORECASTING.

Lorenz curve A convenient graphic representation for measuring the spreads or inequalities of a FREQUENCY DISTRIBUTION. For example, by plotting the income distribution of a given population—that is, what per cent of the population earns what per cent of the total income—it becomes clear that income is not equitably distributed. If it were, the lowest 10 per cent of the population would receive exactly 10 per cent of the total income, the highest 40 per cent exactly 40 per cent of the total, etc., and the points plotted would form a straight 45-degree diagonal. The greater the inequality of

Fig. 50. Income distribution

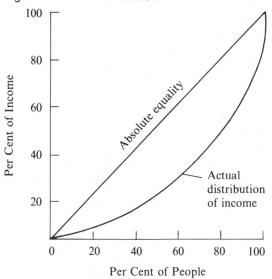

distribution, however, the deeper the curve. (See Fig. 50.) The Lorenz curve also can be used to show the distribution of sales among firms in a given industry and similar data.

loss

1. In accounting, any excess of costs over income. Loss thus is the opposite of profit, which is any income in excess of costs. Also, any unexpected, unrecoverable cost from which no future benefit can or will be derived (such as loss from fire or theft not covered by insurance).

2. In insurance, the basis of a valid claim for damages or indemnity under the terms of a given policy. In PROPERTY INSURANCE, the damage resulting from fire, for example, is the loss; in LIABILITY INSURANCE, the loss is the payment needed to settle a legal claim against the insured.

loss leader In retail merchandising, an item sold very cheaply—close to or even below cost—to attract customers to a store in the hope that they will buy more profitable items as well. In grocery stores, the advertised "special" is often a loss leader. Loss leaders are commonly used only for well-known, widely used items, such as coffee, which customers are not likely to stockpile and in which they will recognize a bona fide bargain.

loss of income insurance See under PROPERTY INSURANCE.

lot

1. In the securities and commodities trade, an amount bought or sold. See ODD LOT, def. 1; ROUND LOT.

2. In real estate, a particular tract of land.

3. Also, *batch.* In manufacturing, a definite quantity of some commodity produced under conditions that are considered uniform. Colored wool yarn, for instance, is dyed in various large quantities at one time, and each batch tends to vary slightly in color from the next. All skeins of yarn from the same dye batch are therefore marked with a lot number, so that customers will not suffer from the slight variations.

low bid See under BID, def. 1.

Lowell system   See under WALTHAM SYSTEM.

low-level language   See under PROGRAMMING.

LTL   See under FREIGHT.

Luddite   A name given to English laborers in the early 19th century who conducted a violent campaign against labor-saving machines in the belief that technological improvements were to blame for unemployment and low wages. Active in various English industrial towns from about 1811 to 1816, the Luddites are thought to have been named for Ned Lud, a workman who had destroyed textile machinery some 30 years earlier. Today the name is occasionally applied to anyone who opposes improved machinery or automation.

lump-of-labor fallacy   The idea that the total amount of work to be done is a fixed quantity, so that if workers accomplish it too fast, or if newcomers enter the labor market, or if machines take over jobs formerly done by hand, there will not be enough work for full employment. While these conditions may occasionally prevail in a particular industry for a time (particularly in instances of TECHNOLOGICAL UNEMPLOYMENT), the amount of work to be done in any economy is not in fact finite, and productivity need not be artificially restricted in order to ensure full employment. Nevertheless, as the American economist Paul SAMUELSON has pointed out, the lump-of-labor fallacy sometimes gives rise to demands for shorter work hours, restrictions on immigration, encouragement of early retirement, and restrictions on speedups and other efforts to increase output. See also MAKE-WORK.

lump-sum appropriation   See under APPROPRIATION.

lump-sum settlement   A single payment in full, rather than in several small installments; in insurance it refers to paying the total face value of a policy at once.

luxury tax   A tax imposed on goods or services considered nonessential, in order either to reduce consumption or to redistribute wealth. See also EXCISE TAX.

machine code   See under PROGRAMMING.

machine-hour rate   In cost accounting, the estimated cost of operating one machine for one hour, including both direct and indirect expenses (depreciation, power, maintenance, supplies, and a portion of factory overhead). It is used both to determine product prices or standard cost, and as a yardstick of performance.

Machinery & Allied Products Institute   See MAPI FORMULA.

machinery insurance   See PROPERTY INSURANCE.

macroeconomics   Economic analyses using aggregate data for large groups of persons or products, such as total employment, national income, or gross national product. Essentially it is based on the belief, emphasized by J. M. KEYNES and his followers, that the whole is not merely a sum of its parts, and that what is sound economic policy for each part individually may be catastrophic for the whole. For example, it is sound for each economic unit in a society to spend somewhat less than it earns, setting a little aside for "a rainy day." But the same policy applied to an entire economy or nation would be disastrous. Both income and employment would decline, and the economy collectively would be much worse off than it would have been had it never attempted to be "thrifty." (See also THRIFT, PARADOX OF.) A development of the 20th century, when the gathering and computation of large amounts of data first became feasible, macroeconomics is used in conjunction with analysis of individual sectors, called MICROECONOMICS.

macro-instructions See under PROGRAMMING.

magnetic core Also, *core memory*. In computers, a doughnut-shaped piece of magnetizable ceramic material, about .10 inch in diameter, used to store data (see also STORAGE, def. 1). By sending an electric impulse through the wires, a core can be magnetized in one direction, and it will remain so until an opposite current is sent through, which will magnetize it in the opposite direction. In a computer, cores are strung together by wires, similar to a string of beads, and each core contains one *bit* of information (see under BINARY for explanation). The time required to record or retrieve information is so short that the core is used to hold information needed for immediate computations.

magnetic disk Also, *disk memory*. In computers, a system of STORAGE (def. 1) in which data are recorded on and read from a continuously revolving disk coated with a magnetizable material, such as magnetic oxide. Such disks allow information to be removed either in sequence or at random, so that a single item can be removed for processing without

first having to "read" all the other items in the file. However, retrieving the information takes somewhat longer with disks than with a MAGNETIC CORE or MAGNETIC DRUM. Disk memories are used principally where random access to large amounts of data is needed, as, for example, in inventory control.

magnetic drum Also, *drum memory*. In computers, a cylinder of metal, covered with a magnetic material (usually magnetic oxide), that spins on its axis and on which information is recorded, stored, and retrieved. Data are recorded on the drum surface by writing heads and are "read off" by reading heads. Drum storage is slower but somewhat less expensive than MAGNETIC CORE storage. See also STORAGE, def. 1.

magnetic tape An important means of getting data into and out of a COMPUTER, as well as for temporarily storing the intermediate results of computer calculations and permanently storing large files of information. It consists of a continuous strip of plastic coated with a magnetic material (usually magnetic oxide) on which data can be recorded as a series of magnetized spots, each of which is a *bit* (see under BINARY for explanation). The recording can be kept indefinitely, or it can be automatically erased simply by recording ("writing") over a previous recording. The tape is "written on" and "read from" by means of a unit that passes the tape under its read-write head. Magnetic tape can store large quantities of data; a 2,400-foot reel of magnetic tape contains the equivalent of 200,000 PUNCHED CARDS. Tape also provides very fast, reliable computer input. Its chief disadvantages are that to obtain a single item of information all of the

Fig. 51. Magnetic tape with 7-bit alphanumeric code (using both letters and numerals)

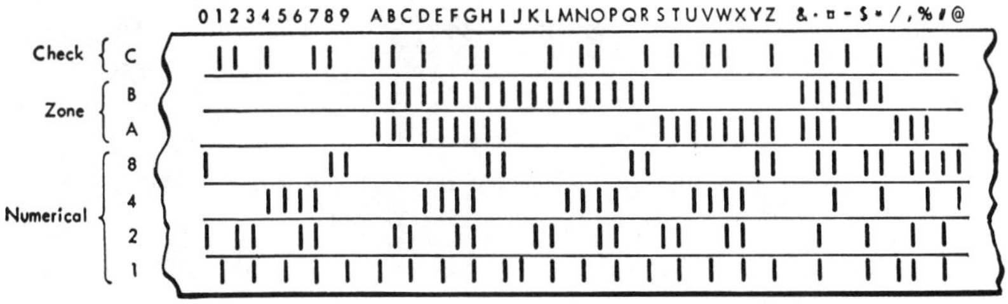

preceding tape must be searched until that item is reached, and that data on tape can be destroyed, either through physical damage or through the accidental recording of new data over old.

mail, classification of See under POSTAL SERVICE, U.S.

mailing list See under DIRECT-MAIL ADVERTISING.

mail order A form of retail selling in which customers make their selections from printed catalogs and place their orders by mail or telephone. Large mail-order houses offer a wide assortment of items within each of hundreds of merchandise lines. They usually buy direct from the manufacturer, often taking a large portion or even all of the manufacturer's output. Mail-order selling in the United States dates from the 1870s and 1880s, when improvements in rail and postal service made it possible to reach rural customers in this way. The general store, formerly the main rural source of supply, found it difficult to compete with either the prices or the variety of goods offered by the mail-order houses. The first such house, Montgomery Ward, was founded (1872) to supply the Grangers (see GRANGE). It was soon followed by the other present-day giant of the American mail-order industry, Sears, Roebuck, which began (1886) as a company selling watches, and soon branched out into other lines (by 1895 it had a 507-page catalog). With the growth of automobile travel in the 1920s, both companies added retail stores to their catalog sales; today these account for the larger share of their business, even though store prices tend to run 10 per cent higher than catalog prices. In addition to broad-market operations, there are highly specialized mail-order firms, devoted exclusively to books and/or records (all the major book clubs), electronic components, fruit and other specialty foods, imported gift or novelty items, etc. There were some 6,000 mail-order concerns in the United States in the 1970s, yet they accounted for only about 1 per cent of total retail sales.

main frame See under COMPUTER.

maintenance and repairs The processes of keeping property and/or equipment in sound working condition; also, the cost of doing so. Accountants distinguish maintenance and repairs from improvements and betterments, since the former must, for tax purposes, be regarded as operating cost and charged to current expenses. Many firms maintain an *MRO* account to cover maintenance, repairs, and operating supplies (such as oil for machinery, cleaning agents, etc.).

maintenance-of-membership clause A clause in a labor contract stipulating that all persons who are union members at the time the contract is signed must remain members for the life of the contract. Such clauses usually also offer an *escape period* of 15 to 30 days at the end of each contract period, during which any member may resign from the union and thereafter remain out of it. Very common during the 1940s, these clauses are much rarer today.

make a market In the securities trade, the regular buying and selling of stocks (including virtually simultaneous purchases and sales of the same stock) in order to regulate demand, supply, and price. On stock exchanges, making a market is the principal job of the SPECIALIST; in the OVER-THE-COUNTER MARKET, dealers frequently make a market in specific stocks.

make or buy A manufacturing company's choice of buying a fabricated product or part from another manufacturer or producing it itself. Most manufacturers purchase some needed components from other manufacturers and make or assemble the rest in their own plants. Thus they are often faced with decisions as to what to buy and what to make. Companies tend to *make* a component themselves when they can do so more cheaply than an outside supplier; when only a few suppliers are available; when the part is vital to production and requires extremely close quality control; when they already have facilities for making it and have made similar items before; and when demand for it is relatively large and stable. On the other hand, manufacturers tend to *buy* a finished part when they do not have existing facilities or skills to make it and can better invest their capital elsewhere; when patents or other legal barriers prevent them from making it; when demand for the part is either temporary or seasonal; and when the supplier can produce it more cheaply.

make-work Any job that is neither productive nor necessary but is performed solely in order to employ more workers. Labor unions, operating under the LUMP-OF-LABOR FALLACY, often try to negotiate contracts compelling an employer to use a minimum number of workers for a particular job even if fewer would do, or that limit the daily or weekly output of workers, or that specify that only members of a certain craft may do a particular job. While some authorities argue that make-work serves as a temporary relief measure in times of high unemployment, others feel it is never really necessary or even beneficial, since it leads to higher labor costs that eventually are passed on in the form of lower wages or higher prices. See also FEATHERBEDDING.

Malthus, Thomas Robert An English economist (1766–1834) remembered principally for his pessimistic theory that the human population, unless artificially limited, will increase at such a rate that it must inevitably outstrip the earth's food supply. In the first edition of his *Essay on the Principle of Population* (1798), Malthus maintained that, left unchecked, population increases in a geometric progression (1, 2, 4, 8, 16, etc.), whereas subsistence (food) increases only in an arithmetic progression (1, 2, 3, 4, 5, etc.). Therefore humankind is doomed to eventual starvation. There are two kinds of natural check on population growth: preventive checks, which reduce the birth rate (moral restraint, vice), and positive checks, which increase the death rate (disease, war, famine). Although Malthus was—and continues to be—criticized for his arithmetic, and was attacked for supposedly defending war and famine as population curbs, his doctrine was accepted by most important British economists and became a cornerstone of classical economic theory. No less important, though somewhat less known, are Malthus's ideas on the role of demand.

Unlike other economists of the CLASSICAL SCHOOL, who believed in SAY'S LAW OF MARKETS, Malthus thought that *effective* demand (which will pay both production costs and profits) cannot be taken for granted, and unless such demand is stimulated in some way, as by spending on capital goods, the market will become glutted with unwanted supplies and unemployment will rise. (In this respect Malthus was far ahead of his time, and by some is even regarded as a forerunner of J. M. KEYNES.) Malthus's thinking has again become prominent in the 20th century, when it is feared that population increases along with economic growth are responsible for the consumption of irreplaceable natural resources at an accelerated rate, hastening the day of total depletion.

managed currency Any currency whose supply is regulated by the government or a central bank, in accordance with the general price level or other economic pheonmena. Managed currency is a basic feature of modern MONETARY POLICY.

managed price See ADMINISTERED PRICE.

management

1. The job of planning, organizing, and controlling any enterprise, particularly a business firm. It may involve planning the work, staffing with competent personnel, directing the activities of subordinates and representing their views to superiors, coordinating various activities in order to meet overall goals, and controlling activities so that the results actually fit the goals. The application of scientific principles to any aspect of management is known as scientific management or MANAGEMENT SCIENCE.

2. The persons in an organization, known as managers, executives, supervisors, or bosses, who are engaged in management (see def. 1). Small organizations are run by a single manager, who may or may not also be the owner. Most organizations employing more than a dozen or so persons have more than one manager. As soon as there are two or more managers, management structure nearly always becomes hierarchical: one or several managers are subordinate to other manager(s). In such

hierarchies the highest level, sometimes called *top management*, is ultimately responsible to the owner(s) of the business. See also ORGANIZATION, COMPANY.

Management and Budget, U.S. Office of See under FEDERAL BUDGET.

management fee See under MUTUAL FUND.

management information system A SYSTEM (def. 2) whereby top management gets the information it needs to make decisions. This information consists of both physical and financial data (production figures, sales figures, number of employees, etc.) and almost always requires the help of a computer to be organized into usable form.

management science Also, *scientific management*. The application of scientific principles or techniques to any aspect of business management. They include WORK SAMPLING, OPERATIONS RESEARCH, PERT, BAYESIAN DECISION THEORY, PROBABILITY THEORY, QUEUING THEORY, LINEAR PROGRAMMING, and other sophisticated mathematical techniques, as well as older techniques such as the TIME AND MOTION STUDY. Though modern management science is said to have begun in the early 20th century with the work of F. W. TAYLOR, most of the quantitative techniques now used were developed after 1940, many having been adapted from military applications during World War II. The term "scientific management" is thought to have been coined by the American lawyer Louis D. Brandeis in 1910 at an engineers' meeting (also attended by Henry Gantt, developer of the GANTT CHART). He popularized it by using it in his brief in a famous hearing in 1910–11 before the Interstate Commerce Commission, in which Brandeis, representing shippers opposing a rail-rate increase, held that with scientific management by the railroad wages could be increased and costs could still be lowered.

Manchester school A group active in England from about 1820 to 1850 who, supported by the economic theory of the CLASSICAL SCHOOL, opposed all government interference with free trade, particularly the CORN LAWS that regulated the British grain trade. The principal leaders were Richard Cobden, founder of the Anti–Corn Law League (1839), which sought repeal of the laws, and John Bright. The Manchester school advocated complete laissez faire and opposed not only protective tariffs but also public aid to the poor, compulsory education, and factory legislation (for adults; they did approve of child-labor laws).

man-hour A unit of measure used in business and industry to estimate labor cost, productivity, the amount of supervision required, defects in products, etc. One man-hour is the equivalent of one person working at a particular job or machine for one hour; five man-hours is equivalent either to one person working for five hours, or five persons working for one hour, or an equivalent combination.

manifest A document itemizing a ship's cargo and its destination, for use by customs and other port officers.

manipulation Deliberately influencing a price that is supposedly determined by the impersonal forces of supply and demand, usually for one's personal benefit. For several kinds of stock-market manipulation, see POOL, def. 1; RIGGING; WASH SALE.

manorial system The prevailing economic system of medieval Europe, whereby land tenure, agricultural production, taxation, and justice were administered. The manorial system coincided with the age of FEUDALISM. Basically, the manorial system, which existed in many countries but took a slightly different form in various localities, consisted of the division of land into self-sufficient estates. Each estate was ruled by the lord (*seigneur*) of the manor, whose rank ranged from petty nobility to royalty. The land was tilled by peasants, who generally lived in a village attached to the estate. The lord was legal owner of the land. He lent it to the tenants who cultivated it, in return for services and dues. The lord in turn owed the tenants military protection and a livelihood; when the harvest was poor, he had to draw on his wealth to prevent mass starvation. The lord could not withdraw land from a tenant or arbitrarily increase the dues; moreover, the right to cultivate land usually passed from father to son. There were two main kinds of tenant, the *villein*, who was free, and the *serf*, who was not. In practice the distinction was less clear-cut, the terms "free" and "servile" coming to be attached to the landholding rather than to the tenant. In fact, both villein and serf were tied to the land. The land itself was divided into the lord's private land, called the *demesne*, which the tenants had to work along with their own plots; other arable land, parceled out to the tenants (see OPEN-FIELD SYSTEM); meadow or commons, for the use of all; woodlands and fish ponds, belonging to the lord but usable, at a price, for hunting, fishing, and woodcutting; and wasteland. The village usually included some small industry, producing cloth, ironware, building materials, etc. The tenants also were responsible for maintaining roads, bridges, walls, and dikes, and for the upkeep of the lord's castle. In addition to their work, the tenants paid dues, either in coin or in produce and goods, usually at specified times of year, for the use of land and such special facilities as the mill, winepress, brewery, ovens, etc. Since one lord might preside over several manors, each manor was usually administered by a special agent, who might be assisted by bailiffs and other underlings. (Occasionally one manor was owned by several lords, but the manor itself remained intact.) Justice was administered through manorial courts, presided over by the lord or his agent.

In Europe the manorial system developed with the decline of the Roman Empire. As various "barbarian" tribes attacked different places, the need for local defense and economic self-sufficiency gave rise to the manorial system. (Similar systems developed outside Europe as well, notably in Japan and India.) With the development of trade and a money economy, and the emergence of larger towns, the small economic units represented by manors gradually broke down. Once tenants were able to buy their freedom and find homes and work in towns, the system could not survive. In England the process was hastened somewhat by the ENCLOSURE movement. In Russia the system survived until the emancipation of the serfs in 1861.

Manpower Administration A branch of the U.S. Department of Labor that conducts "work-experience" and training programs (see also VOCATIONAL TRAINING), and administers the Federal-

state employment security system. The latter includes the U.S. EMPLOYMENT SERVICE, UNEMPLOYMENT COMPENSATION, apprenticeship and training programs, and a variety of "manpower development" programs to help the poor, unemployed, and underemployed.

manual labor Predominantly physical work, usually of a kind that requires little or no special skill and considerable supervision. See also BLUE-COLLAR.

manufacturers' agent See under MIDDLEMAN.

manufacturer's brand See under BRAND.

manufacturers' new orders Commitments to buy a producer's goods, most often manufactured goods, which in the aggregate are an important LEADING INDICATOR of business conditions. Since new orders generally lead to increased production, an increase usually presages increased employment and income as well. Data on new orders are so important that they are collected by numerous trade associations (usually each for its own industry) and other organizations. The U.S. Department of Commerce publishes a monthly series on new orders in manufacturing, classified further by durable and nondurable goods and by industry, as well as a separate classification for capital goods industries, where changes are particularly important to indicate the future direction of investment spending for capital goods.

manufacturers' representative See under MIDDLEMAN.

manufacturers' sales branch A wholesale establishment operated by a manufacturing firm to market its own products, eliminating the need for middlemen between the producer and the industrial user (or ultimate consumer).

manufacturing General term for the process of producing or assembling goods, by hand or machine, for sale to others. Also, any business or industry engaged in this process, or any department or division of a business directly concerned with the output of goods. Although technically a single person may manufacture a simple article by hand at home, the term today is more often associated with a number of persons employed in a place of business. (See also COTTAGE INDUSTRY; FACTORY SYSTEM; INDUSTRIAL REVOLUTION; MASS PRODUCTION.) In the United States manufacturing accounts for a higher percentage of national income, employment, and capital investment than any other industry (nonmanufacturing industries are mostly service industries).

manufacturing and trade sales   See under WHOLESALE SALES.

manufacturing overhead   Also, *factory overhead.* In accounting, costs or expenses incurred in manufacturing, usually excluding the cost of raw materials consumed and direct labor expended. They include depreciation on the machinery used, salaries of foremen and other production supervisors, and similar costs. See also OVERHEAD.

MAPI formula   A formula devised by the Machinery & Allied Products Institute (whose initials make up the name) for computing the return on a capital investment, based on the cash saving generated by the investment during the first year of its use. For example, suppose investment in a new machine will generate a cash saving of $5,000 during the first year (half of one worker's time, worth $5,000, will be freed). Net investment in the machine (its cost minus the salvage value of the machine it is replacing) is $10,000. Depreciation charges increase by $1,000 per year and the increase in income tax will be $2,000. The first-year results of the machine in terms of cash would be:

Next year operating advantage	$5,000
Less: additional depreciation	1,000
Net operating advantage	$4,000
Less: tax increase	2,000
Amount available for return on investment	$2,000

To calculate the estimated return on the machine, the amount available for return ($2,000) is divided by the actual investment ($10,000), resulting in .20, which means a 20 per cent return on investment. For another method of calculating return on investment, see DISCOUNTED CASH FLOW.

margin, buying on   Buying securities by using the broker's credit in partial payment for them. The cash put up by the broker is called the *margin.* The buyer has assured the broker that he or she is financially responsible and therefore has been allowed to open a *margin account.* A typical margin transaction might work like this: Jane Fox decides to increase her holdings by $50,000. The current margin requirement (see below for explanation) is 50 per cent, meaning that Fox must put up $25,000 in cash but may borrow $25,000 from her broker. For this loan the broker will charge her the interest he himself must pay, plus an additional $\frac{1}{2}$ to $\frac{3}{4}$ per cent for profit. (The interest on margin loans constitutes an important source of income for many brokers.) Fox's broker in all likelihood will borrow from a bank, which will extend a *broker's loan* or *call loan* (see LOAN, def. 1) at roughly the same interest rate as the PRIME RATE; the bank may demand this money back at a moment's notice (that is, on call) provided it is not supported by the required amount of collateral. The broker holds the stocks Fox now buys as security for the loan, and through the HYPOTHECATION agreement Fox must sign the broker can use them as security for his bank loan. In addition, Fox must pay brokerage commissions on any stocks bought on margin, just as for other stocks. However, once purchased, she is entitled to any dividends these stocks pay. If the dividends exceed the interest charges, as they frequently do, Fox is already profiting from her purchase. However, most buying on margin is done to realize much larger profits. If Fox's stocks rise in value, her profits from margin purchases are twice as great as they would be from outright purchases (since she has bought twice the amount of stock she could have bought with the same amount of cash). Suppose, however, that her holdings decline in price. Her broker may then make a *margin call* (or *margin maintenance call*), that is, he may demand that Fox put up more cash. If Fox cannot do so, the broker may sell her holdings, which, in view of the drop in their prices, means that Fox sustains a loss. Just how much the broker may ask Fox to put up depends entirely on the *margin maintenance rules* set by the stock exchange and by the broker's firm. Normally it is based on a minimum percentage of the current market value of the stocks, a sum that the customer must have left as equity if the stocks are sold at the current market price and the broker's loan is paid off; the New York Stock Exchange requires this to be 25 per cent, and most brokers require somewhat more (30 per cent or so).

The *margin requirement*—the minimum margin permitted on new purchases—is set by the Federal Reserve Board as well as by exchanges and individual brokers. Stated in terms of a percentage of the total value of the stock being purchased, the margin requirement has varied from 40 to 100 per cent (meaning there can be no buying on margin) since 1934, when the Federal Reserve was first empowered to control it. The requirement for stocks is usually higher than for convertible bonds (in 1974, for example, 55 per cent for stocks and 40 per cent for convertible bonds). The need for controlling credit in this way became obvious with the stock market crash of 1929, in which thousands of speculators were ruined. Prior to the 1929 crash and subsequent reforms, margin requirements had been as low as 10 per cent. In that year, after nearly a decade of feverish speculation, broker's loans reached a total of $8.5 billion. Customers were able to *pyramid* their paper profits, that is, use them to satisfy the very low margin requirements and buy still more on margin. When the market crashed, thousands of margin customers were unable to meet the margin calls, and some who had used their homes, farms, or businesses as collateral were completely wiped out. With stricter regulations that made speculation more difficult for persons lacking capital, buying on margin became far less popular. Today there are only about one-tenth as many margin accounts on the New York Stock Exchange as there were in 1929, and margin transactions account for but a small fraction of all stock exchange transactions. Margin buying, of course, tends to increase when prices are expected to rise and decrease when they decline. Both margin requirements and the total amount of margin debt thus reflect the general condition of the market at any given time.

margin account See under MARGIN, BUYING ON.

marginal cost The addition to the total cost of one extra unit of output. Owing to economy of SCALE, most manufacturing industries benefit from reductions in unit cost as their volume of output increases. However, this pattern does not continue indefinitely, and eventually marginal cost begins to rise (owing to the use of less efficient input). On a graph, therefore, the marginal cost curve is generally U-shaped (see Fig. 52).

marginal efficiency of capital See under PRODUCTIVITY.

marginalist school Also, *marginal utility school.* A group of economists whose ideas dominated Western economic thought from the 1870s to the 1930s, first replacing classical economics and then being modified by Keynesian economics (see CLASSICAL SCHOOL; J. M. KEYNES). The name comes from their emphasis on the concept of MARGINAL UTILITY, which they used to explain many economic phenomena. Unlike the classical school, the marginalists believed that demand is the primary force in determining price, and that demand in turn is based on utility; thus theirs was a *utility theory of value*, and, since utility is subjec-

Fig. 52. Marginal cost

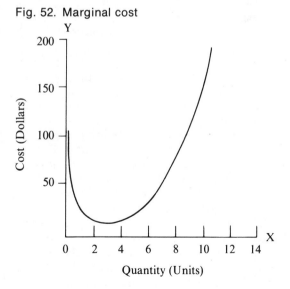

tive rather than objective—for example, one person might prefer a power lawnmower while his neighbor prefers hiring someone to cut the grass—their approach is regarded as subjective. Like the classical school, the marginalists reasoned abstractly and deductively. They hypothesized a state of pure competition, with many buyers and sellers, many homogeneous products, uniform prices, and no special influences on prices such as might be exerted by monopoly, advertising, etc. Such a market, they felt, tended toward a perfect equilibrium, so, like the classical economists, the marginalists believed that government should not interfere with markets. Finally, they assumed that economic man generally behaved rationally, minimizing pain and maximizing pleasure. The most important of the marginalists was Alfred MARSHALL. Others were W. S. JEVONS, L. WALRAS, and C. MENGER, who, working independently, arrived at the principle of marginal utility about the same time, and H. H. GOSSEN, F. von WIESER, E. BÖHM-BAWERK, J. B. CLARK, and A. C. PIGOU.

marginal physical product   Also, *extra product, marginal product*. The addition to the total physical output (of any production process) by the last unit of input. For example, suppose a particular plot of land yields 140 bushels of corn per acre. One year the farmer decides to use 10 pounds more fertilizer, and yield rises to 144 bushels per acre. The marginal physical product in this case is 4 bushels. See also MARGINAL REVENUE PRODUCT.

marginal productivity theory   A theory formulated by J. B. CLARK, who held that the distribution of social income is governed by a natural law. Social income was defined as the income of each factor of production—wages for labor, interest for capital (including rent for land), and profits for the entrepreneur. The income of each factor is determined by its marginal productivity. For wages, the worker receives what he added to the value of the product he helped produce; if he were paid less, other employers would lure him away. As more workers are hired to produce a particular product, the contribution of each worker to the value of the product diminishes (the law of diminishing returns). An employer will hire more workers only so long as their productivity—the value they add to the

product—is at least equal to the wage they receive. If a worker adds less value than his wage, obviously he is not worth the wage; if he adds more than the wage, the employer will hire additional workers, until it no longer pays to do so. Thus the wage paid tends to be equal to the value of the product contributed by the last (marginal) worker hired. Wages will rise only when the number of employees decreases, so that each contributes more value to the product, or when more highly skilled workers increase productivity (law of increasing returns). Critics of Clark's theory point out that it is based on a number of false premises: it assumes that all workers are interchangeable, having the same proficiency and the same ability to move from one employer or industry to another; it assumes full employment; it assumes a constant stock of capital that can be deployed whenever and wherever it is needed; and it assumes a market characterized by pure competition. For *marginal productivity of capital,* see under PRODUCTIVITY.

marginal propensity to consume   See PROPENSITY TO CONSUME.

marginal propensity to save   See PROPENSITY TO SAVE.

marginal revenue   The addition to the total revenue by the sale of one extra unit of output. If the price remains the same despite increased output, marginal revenue is exactly equal to the price. (If a dealer grosses $100,000 from selling 25 cars and $104,000 from 26 cars, marginal revenue is exactly $4,000, or the price of 1 car.) If the price falls when output increases, then marginal revenue is equal to the new price minus the revenue lost through lowering the price of the other units of output. If a shoe manufacturer can sell 100,000 pairs of shoes at $20 and 125,000 pairs at $18,

$$\text{marginal revenue} = \underset{\text{new revenue}}{(\$18 \times 25,000)} - \underset{\text{lost revenue}}{(\$2 \times 100,000)}$$

$$= \$250,000$$

So long as marginal revenue is equal to the extra cost of increasing output, it pays to produce more. The maximum profit any firm can make is at the point where marginal revenue and MARGINAL COST are exactly equal. The moment extra costs exceed extra revenue, it pays to cut back production.

marginal revenue product Also, *marginal value product*. The addition to the total revenue (of any business) by the last unit of input, which depends both on how much additional output is generated (see MARGINAL PHYSICAL PRODUCT) and on what price the additional output will command (see MARGINAL REVENUE). For example, suppose a firm employs nine workers for a weekly output of 90 units that sell at $10 per unit. It now hires a tenth worker. Output rises to 100 units, and the selling price remains the same. Marginal revenue product therefore is $100 (10 extra units × $10). So long as the extra worker does not receive more than $100 per week and the selling price remains constant, the firm profits from hiring extra help. If costs rise more than extra revenue, however, or if the selling price falls owing to lowered demand for the extra output, it may not pay to hire extra labor.

marginal seller A seller whose costs are just equal to revenue, so that any decrease in sales or increase in costs will force him out of business.

marginal utility The additional usefulness—positive or negative—of any unit of a good or service. For example, the marginal utility of a glass of water to a very thirsty traveler is considerable. However, the utility of a second glass of water is obviously not so great, and that of a third, fourth, fifth, or sixth glass might well be nonexistent (or even negative). The concept that utility—the ability to give satisfaction—decreases as more and more units are added is called the *law of diminishing marginal utility* or *law of satiety*. The idea that marginal utility influences demand, and therefore the prices of goods and services, was a basic premise of the MARGINALIST SCHOOL of economists. They, however, tended to ignore the fact that utility is basically subjective (what satisfies one customer won't necessarily please another) and therefore is not really measurable.

marginal utility school Another name for the MARGINALIST SCHOOL.

margin call Also, *margin maintenance call*. See under MARGIN, BUYING ON.

margin requirement See under MARGIN, BUYING ON.

marine insurance See under INSURANCE; also PROPERTY INSURANCE.

markdown A reduction in retail price, usually because an item cannot be sold at the original markup. Customers' refusal to buy the item may be due to a variety of reasons—soiling or fading, damage caused by handling, style change, too high an original markup, etc.

market
1. In general, a public place for buying and selling goods and services, either directly or through some intermediary (such as an agent or broker).
2. A retail store, particularly some kind of grocery store (for example, supermarket, meat market).
3. A place for exchanging securities, particularly a stock market, such as the New York Stock Exchange.
4. The demand for a product or service, for example, the market for wheat.
5. In economic theory, the sum of buyers and sellers of any good or service and their interaction. The goods or services exchanged may be very specific, such as automobiles, or they may comprise a large category, as in the capital market or consumer goods market. Economists classify markets in terms of their structure, that is, the number and size of buyers and sellers, the degree to which products differ from one another, and the ease with which new producers can enter a market (see also FREEDOM OF ENTRY). The structure of the market determines the amount and kind of competition that will prevail and how prices will ultimately be set. For different kinds of market structure, see MONOPOLY; DUOPOLY; IMPERFECT COMPETITION; OLIGOPOLY; PURE COMPETITION. For a market in which producers and consumers cooperate across national boundaries, see COMMON MARKET.

marketable title   Also, *merchantable title*. In real estate, a good TITLE to the property in question, free from liens, encumbrances, or defects other than those specified. The seller must convey a marketable title in most real estate contracts. See also WARRANTY DEED.

market basket   See under PRICE INDEX.

market equilibrium   See under EQUILIBRIUM.

marketing   The business activities concerned with conveying goods and services from producers to consumers, which include buying, grading, packaging, storing, and financing. Some authorities also include transportation (or physical distribution; see DISTRIBUTION, def. 1); others also include selling and promotion (which some, however, distinguish as the separate function of MERCHANDISING). Today college courses in marketing increasingly tend to treat all these areas as part of their province.

marketing agreement   In United States agriculture, a system of controlling the supply and price of certain commodities, notably vegetables, fruits, nuts, tobacco, and milk, in order to increase the producers' returns. The agreement is made between the Secretary of Agriculture and processors and distributors of farm products (whether individuals, corporations, or cooperatives). Set up by the Agricultural Marketing Agreements Act of 1937, such agreements are essentially voluntary. The same law also provides for compulsory *marketing orders,* which are agreements approved by the producers of a commodity but not necessarily by its processors and distributors, who must nevertheless abide by them.

marketing cooperative   See COOPERATIVE, def. 3.

market order   An order to buy or sell a given amount of a security at the most advantageous current price after the order reaches the floor of the exchange. Unlike a LIMIT ORDER, a market order implies that it is to be executed at once, rather than waiting for some particular price or time. Most orders placed on the New York Stock Exchange are market orders and are executed immediately by the SPECIALIST, who draws on his or her own cash or inventory if there is no other available buyer or seller. (For *marketing order*, see under MARKETING AGREEMENT.)

market-out clause   A clause in some securities underwriting contracts whereby the underwriter may withdraw from the agreement if the market should become unfavorable for selling the securities.

market price
1. In economic theory, the price determined by the interaction of supply and demand. See also PRICE.
2. The current prevailing price for a particular commodity, based on the sum of buying and selling at a given time.
3. In the securities trade, the last reported price at which a security was sold.

market rate of interest   Also, *loan rate of interest*. In economic theory, the INTEREST RATE determined by supply and demand, specifically the supply of money available for lending and the demand for credit by firms wishing to borrow for capital investment. The money supply depends on SAVING (def. 2) and the investment demand on the expected return on capital (see *productivity of capital*, under PRODUCTIVITY). Another factor, according to J. M. Keynes, is LIQUIDITY PREFERENCE, the relative preference for liquid assets (cash and the like) over investing in the hope of high future returns.

market research   Also, *marketing research*. A field concerned with studying the sale and distribution of goods and services during a given time by means of gathering, recording, and analyzing all kinds of relevant data. Principally through surveys and interviews, market researchers try to establish how many people will want a particular product or service, and how much of it, what features would make people want it more (or more of it), what sort of people are most likely to become customers, and what kind of advertising and distribution will best stimulate sales. Most large American companies have a separate commercial or market research department devoted to planning and conducting such studies. In addition, independent specialists, such as interviewing and tabulating services, as well as marketing consultants, market research firms, and the market research departments of advertising agencies, all engage in this kind of work. See also INTERVIEW; MOTIVATION RESEARCH; PANEL; SURVEY.

markets, law of See SAY'S LAW OF MARKETS.

mark sensing See under PUNCHED-CARD DATA PROCESSING.

marks of origin A mandatory indication of the country of origin on imported goods. It raises the cost of production, since the exporter must place the mark on the goods, and it alerts the buyer that the item is foreign rather than domestic, both considered import-restricting practices.

markup The percentage by which a seller increases the selling price of goods over the price he paid for them. Conventionally it is computed as a percentage of the retail selling price. Thus, if a merchant buys a hat for $10 and resells it for $15, the price is said to include a $33\frac{1}{3}$ per cent markup ($15 - $10 = $5 ÷ $15 = .333). However, the same price represents a 50 per cent markup *on cost* ($5 ÷ $10 = .50). In the retail and wholesale trades most prices are determined by using the traditional markup, which is equal to the trade or functional discount allowed by the previous seller (wholesaler to distributor, distributor to retailer; see CHAIN DISCOUNT).

Marshall, Alfred An English economist (1842–1924), leading member of the MARGINALIST SCHOOL and the most important economist of his time. His *Principles of Economics* (1890) was a standard text for several generations. Because he taught at Cambridge University, he and his followers are sometimes called the *Cambridge school*; also, because he combined elements of the CLASSICAL SCHOOL with marginalist thought, his work is sometimes described as *neoclassical*. Unlike the earlier marginalists, Marshall believed that both supply and demand (which he likened to the two blades of a pair of scissors) regulate price. In the short run, supply is fixed (only so many oranges are available at a given time or season), so consumer

demand (based on MARGINAL UTILITY) is more influential; in the long run, however, output can be increased or decreased, and supply (based on cost of production) is more important. Graphically represented, the intersection of supply and demand—one plotted on a horizontal axis and the other on a vertical axis—determine price. Similarly, the intersection of supply and demand for savings determine the price of savings, that is, the interest rate (see also LOANABLE FUNDS). Like Smith and other classical economists, Marshall believed in an underlying equilibrium of the market. Sooner or later demand and supply must meet in a "normal price," and this process is self-adjusting, requiring no outside interference to make it happen. Business cycles—the ups and downs of the overall economy—are simply temporary deviations from the ultimate norm. Although Marshall was familiar with the general equilibrium theory of Léon Walras, he devoted himself to PARTIAL EQUILIBRIUM THEORY, concentrating on a particular product or industry rather than on the economy as a whole. The "representative firm" he devised, a kind of average business—neither too old nor too new, too large nor too small—as an illustration of his theories represents a major contribution to MICROECONOMICS.

In analyzing demand, Marshall departed somewhat from earlier marginalists. Unlike them, he held that the total utility of an item was the sum of the successive marginal utilities of each unit of that item. Thus the price a consumer pays for an item never exceeds what he or she would be willing to pay rather than to do without it. Marshall called the difference between this potential price and the actual price paid a *consumer's surplus*. (Stated differently, the total benefit of any good is greater than its total monetary value, because all units of a good sell for the worth of the last unit. Therefore the consumer gets a surplus on all the previous units.) Marshall also coined the term "elasticity of demand" to describe the response of demand to small changes in price.

In analyzing supply, Marshall not only differentiated among immediate, short-run, and long-run conditions, but he recognized the operation of two kinds of cost, "prime" cost (today called "variable" or "marginal" cost) and "supplementary" cost (today called "fixed" or "nonvariable" cost). Marshall adopted RICARDO's idea that rent is a kind of surplus; since the total supply of land is fixed, the amount of rent depends on the relative fertility of the land. Marshall extended this idea to short-term returns on capital as well, saying that in the short run the supply of capital goods (such as factories) is just as fixed as the supply of land, and so returns on such goods should be considered a *quasi-rent*. Like the classical economists, Marshall believed in the QUANTITY THEORY OF MONEY, and he devised an equation to explain this relationship. The most important of Marshall's pupils were A. C. PIGOU and J. M. KEYNES.

Marshall Plan See EUROPEAN RECOVERY PROGRAM.

Marx, Karl A German theorist and radical leader (1818–83) who, with F. ENGELS, is considered the founder of communism. Though Marx had a doctorate in philosophy, he was considered too radical for a university post. He turned to journalism, and then was exiled from Germany. Moving to Paris, he published the COMMUNIST MANIFESTO (1848) and, at the request of the Prussian government, was again exiled. In 1849 he settled in London, where he remained until his death. In 1864 Marx founded the International Workingmen's Association, or *First International*, and gradually his writings, with the monetary help of Engels, became well known. In 1867 the first volume of *Das Kapital* ("Capital") appeared, the fullest exposition of his ideas. The second and third volumes were completed by Engels after Marx's death, and a fourth volume, by Karl Kautsky, entitled *Theories of Surplus Value*, appeared in three parts (1905–10). For Marx's theories, see COMMUNISM, def. 1.

Massachusetts trust Also, *business trust, common-law trust*. A form of business organization where the investors in an enterprise form a voluntary association and transfer the enterprise's property and assets to one or more persons called *trustees*, who will manage the business for them. The owners then share in the profits according to the size of their original investment. As evidence of their interest they receive *certificates of beneficial interest* (also called *trust certificates* or *shares*) in proportion to their investment, which are transfer-

able just as shares of stock are. However, unlike stockholders, the owners have no control over the trustees. A major advantage of the Massachusetts trust, so named because it was most common in that state, is that it usually confers LIMITED LIABILITY on the holders of trust certificates.

mass merchandiser A retail enterprise that combines features of the supermarket, department store, and discount house, concentrating on low prices, self-service, big sales volume, and rapid turnover. Mass merchandisers generally are set up by departments, like those of a department store. They usually have enormous floor space—the average American mass merchandiser has 60,000 square feet, or three to four times the size of a supermarket—and they frequently sell groceries, too. Most mass merchandisers are self-service operations, with checkout counters near the exit doors and virtually no sales personnel. Also, most are organized as chain stores and thus can benefit from economies of scale. Like the discount house, they settle for small profit margins, but unlike the early discounters, which concentrated on brand-name appliances and luggage, the mass merchandisers began by emphasizing soft goods and then expanded into the grocery business, in which they soon captured a notable share of sales (5 per cent in just a few years).

mass production The manufacture or processing of uniform products in large quantities, using machinery, interchangeable parts, and either a wholly automated process or a series of short, repetitive operations (division of labor). Mass production, which is said to have begun with the American inventor Eli Whitney's use of standardized, interchangeable parts in firearms manufacturing around 1800, was first used in the modern sense and on a sizable scale in the automobile factories of the early 1900s. Today some of its processes are so automated that the end-products have scarcely been touched by human hands (as with automobile ball bearings or electric light bulbs). The chief advantages of mass production are low units costs (see SCALE, ECONOMY OF) and standardization; the latter, while perhaps undesirable for such items as clothing, is extremely valuable with such products as cement or chemicals. The chief disadvantages are the huge capital investment required and the limited range of products. Also, without steady demand from a mass market and a large, reliable system of distribution, the expensive facilities may become totally useless. See also ASSEMBLY LINE.

mass storage A high-capacity storage system, usually outside of but under the control of a COMPUTER. Capable of holding enormous quantities of data, it is used to store large files, and it takes relatively long to locate and retrieve information from it. See also STORAGE, def. 1.

matched and lost In the securities trade, describing the situation of two brokers who, simultaneously offering or bidding for a stock, flip a coin to determine which of them will execute the transaction. It occurs when they bid the same price for an amount equal to (or larger than) the amount of stock offered, or when they are willing to sell at the same price an amount equal to (or larger than) the amount bid for. A customer who questions why an order was not executed even though the stock in question reached the stipulated price may be told that the broker "matched and lost," that is, either demand or supply for that stock was insufficient at the time it reached the right price.

matching grant See under GRANT-IN-AID, def. 1.

material control In manufacturing, the job of controlling the supplies of direct materials needed for production, including requisitioning, purchasing, receipt, storage, protection, and issuing of goods as needed, as well as maintenance of inventory records. It is similar to MATERIALS MANAGEMENT but is confined solely to internal control of production materials. Today much of this work is done by computer. See also PRODUCTION CONTROL.

material cost See MATERIALS COST.

material purchases See PURCHASING.

material requirements planning See INVENTORY CONTROL.

material requisition See PURCHASE REQUISITION.

materials cost Also, *material cost.* In a business, the cost of any purchased materials used in it, ranging from office supplies (paper clips, stationery, etc.) and electric light bulbs to raw materials and semifinished parts incorporated into a finished product. Cost accountants distinguish between *direct materials* (or *production parts*), which are incorporated into the firm's actual end-products, and *indirect materials* (or *nonproduction parts*), which are consumed in the course of making the end-products but do not physically become part of them. Maintenance, repairs, and operating supplies are generally considered indirect materials. Screws used to fasten the components of an end-product are direct material, but the same screws used to repair plant machinery are indirect material, and their cost would be charged to nonproduction maintenance supplies. Some examples, however, are less clear-cut. Standard packaging used for shipping a product is usually (but not always) considered indirect material. Direct materials cost and direct LABOR COST are the two major components of a manufacturing firm's DIRECT COST.

materials handling The moving, packaging, and storing of materials in every form, ranging from raw materials to finished goods, within a business firm (not including transport from place to place by common carrier). It includes the shipping, receiving, and processing of incoming items and outgoing products, returns to suppliers, scrap, and any other materials. It also involves the purchase, handling, and storage of equipment and machinery. Many kinds of special equipment and supplies facilitate materials handling, among them hand trucks, bins, fork trucks, elevators, chutes, pneumatic tubes, conveyors of various kinds, cranes, and monorails. By far the most important of these is the PALLET. In some industries, such as sand and gravel, materials handling may account for 80 per cent or more of total costs.

materials management The administering of all activities concerned with the ordering, storage, and movement of materials. In a manufacturing enterprise these include PURCHASING of raw materials, parts, and nonproduction stores (office supplies, maintenance and repair supplies, etc.); PRODUCTION CONTROL (scheduling overall production and maintaining steady supplies of needed materials); INVENTORY CONTROL (managing inventories); TRAFFIC (purchasing transportation services for both inbound and outbound shipments of goods); and physical distribution (moving finished goods from the factory to a warehouse and, eventually, to the customer). In a service industry, such as a hospital or airline, materials management includes all these functions except production control.

mathematical economics See ECONOMETRICS.

mathematical model See MODEL.

mature economy An economy that has developed to the point where both new capital investment and the rate of population growth are slowing down, and an increasing proportion of national income is being spent on consumer goods and services. Although a mature economy is characterized by a largely urban, industrial labor force that benefits from a relatively high standard of living, some economists hold that maturity inevitably will bring about stagnation and eventually also large-scale unemployment. See also SECULAR STAGNATION.

maturity The date on which a loan, bond, debenture, or other obligation falls due and is to be paid in full (*redeemed*) by the borrower. At that time, the maturity value of a bond or other security is equal to its FACE VALUE plus any interest not yet paid. Maturity may vary from periods of a few days to ten or more years. A short-term maturity represents less risk to the lender, and therefore short-term obligations are considered more liquid than long-term ones and normally command lower interest rates. See also BOND, def. 1.

maturity yield See YIELD, def. 3.

maximax See under MAXIMIN.

maximin In making decisions that involve uncertainty, choosing the course of action that will maximize the minimum possible profit, as opposed to maximizing the maximum profit (*maximax*) or minimizing the maximum loss (*minimax*).

max-min system See ORDER-POINT CONTROL.

mean Also, *arithmetic mean.* The simplest of all statistical averages, widely used in government and industry data reports, sampling, quality control, and forecasting. It is obtained by adding all the observed values together and dividing by their total number. For example, if the hourly wages of five workers are $4, $4.50, $4.50, $5, and $6, the mean wage is $24 ÷ 5 = $4.80. Other types of mean are the *geometric mean,* which applies the same process to the logarithms of the values in the series, and the *harmonic mean*, which applies it to their reciprocals. The geometric mean is used mainly to average percentages, indexes, and relatives, and to determine average per cent changes in sales, gross national product, or other business and economic series from one time period to the next. See also MEDIAN; MODE.

measured day rate See under WAGE INCENTIVE.

media See under ADVERTISING.

median In statistics, the middle value of a series that has been arranged in order of size. For example, if the annual family incomes on Hancock Street were $15,000, $17,000, $20,000, $23,000, and $62,000, the median income would be $20,000. If a sixth family built a house there and its income was $22,000, the median income would be $21,000 (halfway between the two central values, $20,000 and $22,000). Contrast this with the MEAN income, which for five families is $27,400; the total is pulled up by the much higher income of one family, distorting the overall view.

mediation The settlement of a dispute through the active intervention of a neutral third party, called the *mediator,* who clarifies issues, asks questions, and proposes solutions. A mediator has no authority over either side; each remains free to accept or reject the proposals. Mediation is used very often to settle labor disputes. The *National Mediation Board,* an independent U.S. government agency established by the Railway Labor Act of 1934, provides for the mediation of labor disputes involving rail and air carriers that cannot be settled by COLLECTIVE BARGAINING. Another U.S. agency, the *Federal Mediation and Conciliation Service,* established by the Taft-Hartley Act of 1947, assists in the settlement of management-labor disputes in industries affecting interstate commerce. See also ARBITRATION.

medical insurance See HEALTH INSURANCE.

Medicare See under SOCIAL SECURITY.

medium of exchange An item or device that serves the exchange of one good or service for another, such as MONEY, notes, checks, bank drafts, etc., eliminating the need for a direct exchange (barter).

medium-term forecast See under FORECASTING.

member bank A member of the FEDERAL RESERVE.

member firm A member of a STOCK EXCHANGE; see also under NEW YORK STOCK EXCHANGE.

memorandum check See under CHECK.

memory See STORAGE, def. 1.

Menger, Carl An Austrian economist (1840–1921), one of the principal founders of the MARGINALIST SCHOOL and an influential teacher instrumental in founding the so-called *Austrian school* (of marginalists). Like W. S. JEVONS, Menger discovered the principle of marginal utility independently and published his main work on the subject in 1871. Unlike Jevons, however, who equated exchange value with marginal utility, Menger equated exchange value with *total* utility, that is, marginal utility multiplied by the number of units available. Where Jevons held that the last unit of a consumer good had less value than the first, Menger believed the value of all units to be equal, with no one unit giving more satisfaction than any other. Menger also applied the idea of consumer demand to capital goods, such as machinery and raw materials, holding that the consumer's marginal utility for a machine tool, for example is governed by the marginal utility of the end-product made by that tool. (From this it is but one step to a

MARGINAL PRODUCTIVITY THEORY of distribution, though Menger himself never took that step.) Where Jevons criticized the British CLASSICAL SCHOOL, Menger directed his attacks against the GERMAN HISTORICAL SCHOOL and their disdain for deductive theories, and he engaged in a famous public quarrel with Gustav Schmoller. In answer to a contemptuous review of his book by Schmoller, Menger wrote a pamphlet entitled *Methodenstreit* ("Methodology Quarrel"). Schmoller retorted with a nasty letter published in a journal, and the dispute, eventually involving all their respective followers, continued for a generation.

mercantile agency See under CREDIT RATING.

mercantilism An economic and political doctrine developed between 1500 and 1775, which was at its peak in France, England, the Netherlands, Spain, and other West European countries from 1600 to 1700. The mercantilists held that gold and silver are the most important form of wealth (the doctrine of *bullionism*), and the best way to increase wealth is to import less than one exports (since presumably payment for exports is made in gold or silver). To achieve this goal, numerous regulations—and hence a strong central government to enforce them—are needed, allowing tariff-free imports of needed raw materials, imposing protective tariffs on all domestically produced raw materials and manufactured goods, and extensively encouraging domestic manufactures. Also, there must be strict control over wages, working hours, prices, and product quality. Inherent in mercantilism was *nationalism,* with each country striving for its own best interest (at the expense of all others), supported by strong armed forces and working for economic self-sufficiency. Also of great historical importance was the mercantilists' greed for colonies, which were to supply needed raw materials and provide a market for the home country's manufactured products. The mercantilists also believed in the necessity of a large laboring class willing to work hard for low wages. In effect, their policies benefited chiefly the merchant capitalists on the one hand and the king and his supporters and officials on the other.

The mercantile theorists themselves were principally businessmen. Among them were Thomas

Mun (1571–1641), an English merchant and director of the East India Company who opposed restrictions on trade but believed in the necessity of an export surplus; Gerald Maynes (died 1641), a Belgian-English merchant, government official, and author of numerous works opposing the export of bullion (on the ground that it would lead to higher prices abroad and lower prices at home) and supporting tariffs on imports and other controls; Charles Davenant (1656–1714), an English official who published several important essays on bullionism, the balance of trade, and taxes; and Jean-Baptiste COLBERT of France and Sir William PETTY of England. The protectionist views of the mercantilists were popular in the early years of the United States, which, especially after the War of 1812, enacted higher and higher protective tariffs (see under TARIFF OF ABOMINATIONS), and again in the 20th century (see NEOMERCANTILISM).

merchandise broker   See under MIDDLEMAN.

merchandising   The job of planning for the effective sale of goods, that is, deciding what is to be sold when, where, and how, to the seller's best advantage. The term usually refers to retail sales and promotion, that is, selling to ultimate consumers, and often is considered but one aspect of the larger field of MARKETING.

merchant bank   A kind of financial institution found chiefly in Europe that provides a variety of services, including investment banking, management of customers' securities portfolios, insurance, acceptance of foreign bills of exchange, dealing in bullion, etc. It originated at least as far back as the 17th century, when the rapid growth of international trade (see COMMERCIAL REVOLUTION) gave rise to the need for such services as accepting bills of exchange and trading in gold and foreign exchange. Some merchant banks have remained extremely prominent in international finance, notably the houses of the Rothschilds, Barings, Lazards, Hambros, and a few others, even though their deposits amount only to a small fraction of those of commercial banks, and their only large-scale operations involve counseling and negotiating mergers and similar affairs.

merchant guild   See under GUILD.

merchant marine   A nation's commercial vessels, including freighters, tankers, and other ships, owned either privately or by the government. In the 1970s the United States merchant fleet numbered about 54,400 vessels, with a gross tonnage of 27.4 million. Like other forms of transport, the merchant marine is strictly controlled and heavily subsidized by government. In the United States the Department of Commerce's *Maritime Administration* administers programs to help develop, promote, and operate American shipping, and it is charged with organizing and directing emergency merchant ship operations. It administers subsidy programs, helps finance shipbuilding, constructs or supervises the construction of merchant vessels for the government, and operates the U.S. Merchant Marine Academy, which trains merchant marine officers. The *Federal Maritime Commission,* established as an independent agency in 1961, regulates commercial shipping in the public interest. It approves agreements filed by common carriers, regulates their practices, accepts tariff filings, issues licenses for freight forwarding, administers regulations concerning water pollution, and generally assures that carriers comply with the law.

merchant wholesaler   A MIDDLEMAN who buys from manufacturers and sells to retailers and other merchants, and/or to industrial, professional, institutional, and commercial users, on its own account. Importers, exporters, textile converters, and industrial distributors all are considered merchant wholesalers. Usually the merchant wholesaler does not buy goods for sale to final consumers, and differs from other wholesalers—such as agents or brokers—in that it actually takes title to the goods handled. Merchant wholesalers account for about one-half of all wholesale transactions in the United States. See also DEALER, def. 1; WHOLESALE.

merger   Also, *takeover.* The union of two or more formerly independent business firms under a single ownership, accomplished by the complete *acquisition* of one company's stock by another, either for cash or for stock in the acquiring company. The acquired corporation then disappears as a separate entity, usually becoming a *subsidiary* of the acquiring company. A merger also may be effected by an outright purchase of the assets of another enterprise; the selling corporation then may survive and use its cash for some other kind of business. A merger may be horizontal, vertical, or conglomerate —that is, it may involve acquisition of a competitor in the same line, of a supplier or a customer, or of a totally unrelated business. Sometimes the term "merger" is used to designate control of another corporation based on ownership of a controlling interest in its stock (see HOLDING COMPANY). See also CONSOLIDATION.

merit rating Also, *performance evaluation.* In personnel administration, a formal system for evaluating the performance of individual employees, used to help decide such issues as promotion and individual pay rate, and sometimes to create competition among workers. Rating systems may use some version of a point method, in which the performance characteristics of each job are broken down and assigned a maximum point value. Thus, for example, employees might be given points for quantity and quality of output, cooperativeness, initiative, job knowledge, attitude toward work, etc.

microeconomics Economic analyses of a particular product, firm, industry, or individual, such as the demand for automobiles, or employment for dock workers, or average household income. Such studies, which until the early 20th century formed the basis for extensive theorizing about the economy as a whole, today are considered in conjunction with aggregates of various such data (see MACROECONOMICS). Because of its emphasis on price in the market system, microeconomics is also known as *price theory.* Early microeconomists assumed states of perfect competition or perfect monopoly. During the 1930s Joan ROBINSON of Cambridge and E. H. CHAMBERLIN of Harvard developed theories of imperfect competition and monopolistic competition. An important aspect of microeconomics is the *theory of the firm*, an attempt to account for and predict an individual company's decisions in terms of inputs (labor, materials, capital, etc.) and output (production). With the

development of sophisticated mathematical techniques such as LINEAR PROGRAMMING, the theory of the firm was adjusted to take into account more variables. Nevertheless, it remains a largely theoretical view of business behavior rather than a tool actually used by management.

middleman Any intermediary between the producer and consumer of goods, which performs such functions as storage, distribution, or transportation. There are two main kinds of middleman, the MERCHANT WHOLESALER and the *agent middleman.* The former buys goods and resells them, actually taking title to the goods in the process, and making a profit by selling at a higher price. The agent middleman acts on behalf of a buyer or seller (or both), assisting in negotiating sales or purchases (or both), not taking title to the goods and being paid a commission or fee. The principal kinds of agent middleman, active chiefly in wholesale rather than retail trade, are the broker, commission house, manufacturers' agent, selling agent, and resident buyer. A *broker* (or *merchandise broker*) represents either buyer or seller in negotiating a transaction and does not physically handle the goods involved. The broker relays offers and counteroffers until the terms of sale are satisfactory to both parties, and never sees the goods at all; the seller ships direct to the buyer. Brokers often are used in sales of seasonal products, as by small food canneries and for used machinery, real estate, and ships. A *commission house* (or *commission merchant*), most commonly used for agricultural products sold in central markets, such as livestock and grain, operates much as a broker does except that it actually handles the goods in question, completes transactions, and remits the proceeds of the sale (minus its commission) to the seller (see also FACTOR, def. 2). The *manufacturers' agent* (or *manufacturers' representative*) works for several manufacturers, handling noncompeting products, as though it were each company's salesman. Unlike a broker, which treats each transaction separately, the manufacturers' agent has a contract with each manufacturer to sell certain goods within a given territory. The agent's main job is making sales calls on wholesalers and industrial customers, frequently employing sales personnel to assist in this; the selling prices, however, are set by the manufacturer. Some manufacturers' agents also stock goods and make deliveries, but most concentrate on selling, and the producer delivers to and bills customers. Manufacturers who do not wish to maintain their own sales force use such agents, chiefly in marketing industrial goods, furniture, and hardware. The *selling agent* resembles the manufacturers' agent in having a contract but negotiates all sales of a given line of goods—or even a manufacturer's entire output—and has full authority concerning price and other terms of sale. It also may handle the competing lines of several manufacturers, in effect taking over the entire marketing function for its principal. Some selling agents also help their principals financially, providing them with working capital (see also FACTOR, def. 1). They are commonly used in highly competitive fields (textiles, coal), where marketing is more vital for a firm's survival than is production, and where special marketing expertise is required. A *resident buyer* differs from most other agent middlemen in that it represents buyers only; in effect it is a buying specialist for retailers, chiefly in such lines as furniture and clothing. Such buyers work strictly on commission and are otherwise independent of their principals; they thus differ from resident buying offices maintained by out-of-town stores in such centers as New York City, as well as from central buying offices maintained by chain stores. See also WHOLESALE.

middle management   An intermediate management position, such as that of a foreman who supervises production workers and in turn is responsible to the works manager. See also under ORGANIZATION, COMPANY.

migrant labor   Also, *migratory workers.* Workers who regularly shift from one job to another throughout the year. In the United States migrant labor is most common in agriculture, with workers following seasonal planting and harvests in various parts of the country. Among the lowest-paid and most exploited members of the labor force, they pose serious social and educational problems, both for themselves and for the communities in which they work.

Mill, John Stuart   An English philosopher and economist (1806–73), whose *Principles of Political Economy,* first published in 1848 and the most lucid exposition of the ideas of the CLASSICAL SCHOOL, remained the leading economics text for the next 50 years. Mill received a remarkable education supervised by his father, James Mill (1773–1836), a friend of Ricardo and Bentham and a leading intellectual of his time. Another important influence on his thinking was Harriet Taylor, whom he eventually married; to her Mill attributed his libertarian and humanitarian precepts, expressed in such essays as "On Liberty" (1859), "Considerations on Representative Government" (1861), and "Subjection of Women" (1869), an important early feminist tract. Mill's economics was largely that of the classical school, although he later repudiated the WAGES-FUND THEORY. The most important of his original contributions was his "law of international values." Enlarging on Ricardo's theory of comparative ADVANTAGE, Mill held that the actual terms of international trade depended on the *demand* for a product in the foreign country, as well as on efficient production. Mill also aligned himself with the social reformers, believing that the laws of production were immutable but that the laws of distribution could be adapted to the needs of society.

minimax   See under MAXIMIN.

minimum charge   Also, *minimum rate.* A price charged for a service even if it is not performed or used in full. For example, every common carrier charges a minimum freight rate, no matter how small the shipment. Railroads and trucks always charge for 100 pounds even if a shipment weighs only 20 pounds. Similarly, public utilities normally charge users a basic monthly rate for gas, electricity, or telephone service, regardless of the actual amount consumed.

minimum markup law   A law requiring retailers to mark up merchandise by some minimum amount over cost. In purpose similar to FAIR TRADE laws, minimum markup laws differ in that they apply to all merchandise, not only branded goods, and are mandatory. In the United States 34 states passed such laws during the Great Depression of the

1930s, many of which have survived into the 1970s. Most of them bar a retailer from selling an item for less than the invoice or replacement cost, whichever is lower, plus a markup designed to cover operating costs. Some specify a definite figure, such as 6 per cent. All prohibit the sale of goods below cost. Critics point out that such laws limit competition, raise prices, and protect inefficiency. In practice, however, the mandated markups are rarely very high, and many grocers in particular feel they need this form of protection against price-cutting.

minimum subsistence See SUBSISTENCE.

minimum wage The lowest hourly wage rate permitted, either by state or Federal law or by a labor contract. See also *Fair Labor Standards Act,* in Fig. 44 under LABOR LAWS.

minor Also, *infant.* In law, a person under legal age, and therefore not able to vote, enter an enforceable contract, etc. In many parts of the United States a minor is anyone under 18 years of age.

minor coin See under COIN.

mint A place where money is coined, usually under government auspices. In the United States coins are manufactured and distributed by the *U.S. Bureau of the Mint,* which has plants in several cities and also administers the depositories of bullion at Fort Knox, Kentucky, and West Point, New York. (Paper currency is manufactured by the U.S. Bureau of Engraving in Washington, D.C.) For *mint parity,* see under GOLD STANDARD; for *mint ratio,* see under BIMETALLISM.

Mises, Ludwig E. von An Austrian-born economist (1881–1973) who continued the tradition of the Austrian school and MARGINALIST SCHOOL of economic thought. Like most other marginalists, he believed that the free interaction of demand and supply, without interference, would lead to the most efficient allocation of resources, but he also developed the idea of *ordinal utility* (see UTILITY, def. 2). Mises also developed a theory of money and credit whereby he explained fluctuations in the business cycle. In his view, expanded bank credit during a boom would cause a drop in interest rates and surplus investment, which eventually would lead to a recession when the money supply was reduced. See also MONETARY THEORY.

missionary Also, *detailer, merchandising salesman.* A salesperson employed by a manufacturer to work with middlemen and their customers, developing goodwill and stimulating demand for their products. Missionaries will help middlemen train their salesmen, or help with wholesalers' and retailers' promotion efforts. Pharmaceutical manufacturers routinely employ them to call on physicians to discuss their drugs, particularly new ones, in the hope that physicians will prescribe their brands.

Mississippi Bubble See under BUBBLE.

Mitchell, Wesley Clair An American economist (1874–1948), a pupil of Thorstein VEBLEN and a member of the school of INSTITUTIONAL ECONOMICS, remembered principally for his emphasis on statistical research. A founder of the National Bureau of Economic Research and author of a classic monograph, *The Making and Use of Index Numbers* (1915), Mitchell advocated research to promote understanding of social and economic problems. He focused his efforts particularly on the recurring imbalance between production and distribution reflected in the business cycle, which he saw as a basic, inevitable characteristic of a money economy. Unlike many economists of his time, who offered what now seem to be facile explanations for the business cycle, Mitchell painstakingly amassed volumes of data that led him to emphasize the numerous and complex forces at work in the economy rather than formulating a simple theory.

mixed economy An economy with both public and private ownership of the means of production, thus combining elements of SOCIALISM and CAPITALISM. For example, the government of the United Kingdom owns and operates railroads, public utilities, airlines, the coal and steel industries, and a radio and television network, among other enterprises, whereas farming, most manufacturing, and numerous other economic ventures in Britain remain under private ownership and control. In practice just about every modern economy is mixed, for even in Communist countries there is a modicum of private ownership, and in virtually all capitalist nations there is public ownership or control of at least some public utilities.

mixing and milling regulations Rules that require the use of some specified minimum percentage of a domestic good in a product made by mixing domestic and imported goods. For example, flour milled in the United States is required to contain a minimum percentage of domestic grain. The net effect of such regulations is to restrict imports.

mode In statistics, the value in a series of data that appears most frequently. For example, if the series consists of the hourly wages of five workers—$4, $4.50, $4.50, $5, and $6—the mode is $4.50.

model Also, *economic model, mathematical model, statistical model.* A representation of an economic system (see SYSTEM, def. 3), problem, or process in mathematical form, with equations used to simulate, or represent, the behavior of the system, problem, or process under varying conditions. A major tool of ECONOMETRICS, the model is intended ultimately to show cause-effect relationships that, by inference, can be used to predict economic conditions. Models are used, for example, to forecast production or national income or investment from one year to the next year (or one decade to the next), and by government economists to forecast the results of proposed measures such as an increase or decrease in tax rates or a major change in interest rates or government spending. Among the earliest economic models is the *tableau économique* of François Quesnay, later elaborated into the vastly complex model of INPUT-OUTPUT ANALYSIS. See also STRUCTURAL EQUATION.

modular advertising The concept of providing clients with one or a few specialized advertising services, instead of a complete package of all services (market research, creating ads, styling and packaging help, media selection, etc.). Some full-service agencies that are willing to supply only those services the client desires organize so-called *service modules*, quasi-independent departments or divisions, each specializing in one area (media buying, broadcast production, new product development, product and package design, etc.). Also, there are agencies that specialize in only one or another of these services and do not offer the "full package." In either case, module or agency, the client generally pays a fixed fee for the service instead of the traditional 15 per cent commission (based on media charges). See also ADVERTISING.

momentary equilibrium See under EQUILIBRIUM.

M-1, M-2, M-3 Abbreviations for three different concepts of what constitutes the MONEY SUPPLY, used by modern economists. M-1 refers to the conventional idea of the money supply, that is, currency plus DEMAND DEPOSITS. M-2 means M-1 plus commercial bank time deposits (see TIME DEPOSIT) other than large CERTIFICATES OF DEPOSIT; M-3 means M-2 plus deposits at nonbank thrift institutions, principally savings banks and savings and loan associations. Economists distinguish among these because they are at least partly interchangeable. While the M-1 supply is the only "real" money in the sense of being instantly spendable, M-2 and M-3 can be considered almost "real" since they can be readily converted into M-1 and the central banking authorities have relatively little control over the conversion. In the early 1970s some economists, including Arthur F. Burns, then chairman of the U.S. Federal Reserve Board of Governors, went still further. Trying to defend their policies against those who felt that the Federal Reserve—the U.S. central bank—should be increasing the money supply more liberally, they pointed out as many as *eight* concepts of M (see Fig. 53). See also NEAR MONEY.

monetary bloc A group of nations that keep their primary FOREIGN EXCHANGE RESERVES in a particular currency. For an example, see STERLING AREA. Today, with flexible exchange rates, central banks increasingly tend to invest reserves in a number of foreign currencies for both greater stability and greater flexibility.

Fig. 53. Definitions of "M"

M-1	Currency + demand deposits
M-2	M-1 + time deposits (except large certificates of deposit)
*M-2′	M-2 + large certificates of deposit
M-3	M-2 + deposits in savings banks and savings and loan associations
M-4	M-3 + savings bonds and credit union shares
M-5	M-4 + large certificates of deposit
M-6	M-5 + short-term governments (Treasury bills, etc.)
M-7	M-6 + commercial paper

*Pronounced *M-2 prime*

monetary controls See under MONETARY POLICY.

monetary equations Various mathematical expressions of the effects of money expenditures on prices, which generally are based on some version of the QUANTITY THEORY OF MONEY. Such equations tend to take one of three forms. One takes into account the total volume of transactions, as well as the MONEY SUPPLY and the VELOCITY OF MONEY; for an example, see Fisher's EQUATION OF EXCHANGE. A second one takes into account the national income in terms of total physical output of goods and services and the average of their prices. The third takes into account demand for money, that is, the aggregate of cash balances that individuals and firms wish to keep on hand.

monetary policy The overall program—or any of its parts—for regulating money and credit so as to achieve certain desired goals. In most countries this program is carried out by the central bank. In the United States both formulation and implementation of monetary policy are the responsibility of the Board of Governors of the Federal Reserve System, working through the 12 Federal Reserve banks. To implement a policy, the Federal Reserve can expand or contract the reserves of commercial banks. Since reserves are the basis on which commercial banks create money by lending (see under MONEY for further explanation), their size affects how much banks can and will lend at various inter-

est rates. Changes in the money supply in turn affect the interest rate—the cost of borrowing—which in turn will influence consumers' and businesses' decisions to spend and/or invest. These in turn affect the levels of output, employment, income, and prices.

The overall objective of monetary policy usually is full employment and maximum output without inflation. There are two basic kinds of monetary policy, popularly known as *easy money* and *tight money*. An easy money policy expands commercial bank reserves and consequently the economy's MONEY SUPPLY; a tight money policy lowers reserves and reduces the money supply. Easy money encourages investment spending (more money means low interest rates and a greater demand for loans); tight money discourages investment spending. (Actually this description is an oversimplification, since some controls can be invoked to tighten credit at the same time that others operate to ease it, and other economic forces also affect the money supply simultaneously.)

The principal mechanisms whereby the Federal Reserve tightens or eases credit—that is, the total money supply—are by changing the RESERVE REQUIREMENTS, changing the DISCOUNT RATE, and engaging in OPEN-MARKET OPERATIONS. Of these, the last is by far the most important. In addition, the Federal Reserve can exert selective credit controls such as, for example, specifically limiting consumer credit or stock market credit without changing requirements for other kinds of credit, and also through MORAL SUASION. Raising or lowering the required reserve diminishes or increases the ability of commercial banks to lend money. Raising or lowering the discount rate (the interest rate charged by Federal Reserve banks to commercial banks borrowing from them) affects how much commercial banks can afford to borrow, and hence how much they can lend. Finally, the Federal Reserve can, by buying and selling government securities on the open market, raise or lower commercial banks' reserves, and hence their lending ability. In essence, then, an easy money policy might consist of reducing reserve requirements, lowering the discount rate, and buying securities on the open market, all of which would expand credit, increase the money supply, and tend to stimulate the total volume of spending. A tight money policy, on the other hand, would consist of increasing reserve requirements, increasing the discount rate, and selling government securities on the open market, all of which would reduce credit, tighten the money supply, and tend to reduce total spending.

monetary reserves The stock of bullion and government bonds that back the domestic currency. For international reserves, see FOREIGN EXCHANGE RESERVES. See also BANK RESERVES; GOLD RESERVE.

monetary theory Also, *credit theory*. Any theory that attempts to explain the BUSINESS CYCLE in terms of the supply of money or credit. There are a number of such theories, chiefly based on the view that the business cycle is an alternation of inflation (during the expansion phase) and deflation (during the contraction phase). The inflation is supported by credit expansion, that is, as the economy expands, banks are encouraged to lend money for investment. Increased demand for credit will raise its price (the interest rate), which will discourage some would-be investors. Investment therefore will begin to fall off, and a cumulative deflation will set in. Unemployment in the capital goods industries will lead to decreased demand for consumer goods, the accumulation of inventories (unsold stocks), cancellation of orders, and a further decline in investment. Finally the process halts. With reduced business activity, businesses will require fewer loans to support inventories, currency will return to the banks, liquidity will increase, and interest rates will fall back to attractively low levels. Eventually they will induce new borrowing, the banks will again expand credit, and the cycle will begin all over again.

Among the economists who subscribed to a monetary theory are Ludwig von MISES, R. G. Hawtrey, and F. A. von Hayek. Hayek's version is sometimes called the *overinvestment theory*, since he maintained that, while increased investment resulting from voluntary saving has no ill effect, investment financed by inflationary credit expansion triggers the cycle. If the banks, with ample reserves, expand credit and interest rates do *not* rise despite increased demand for loans, investment will rise beyond the limits set by voluntary saving. Wages, money incomes, and consumer-goods demand will rise, raising the demand for currency relatively more than the demand for deposit money. Thus the liquidity of commercial banks is reduced, the market rate of interest now rises, and investments contemplated at previous low interest rates must be abandoned.

A monetary theory would probably work perfectly under conditions of PURE COMPETITION and with a fixed money supply (that is, gold). In practice, a central bank can keep interest rates down at any stage of the business cycle but will most likely be forced to let them rise eventually in order to prevent runaway inflation. When high interest rates do eventually choke demand and cause the contracting phase of the cycle to begin, other restrictions may prevent costs from declining. Unemployment increases, but wage rates may decline little, if at all. To prevent further increases in unemployment, the central bank usually relaxes credit. The net effect is that the rise in the general price level that occurred during expansion is never offset by declines during the recession. Moreover, even if it were, the experience of the Great Depression of the 1930s suggests that recovery will not necessarily begin simply because interest rates are low. Businesses borrow not just because of low interest rates, but because management believes the prospects for profit are promising. In the 1930s many businesses refused to borrow at rates of 3 per cent or even lower, yet in the 1970s they were eager for credit at rates of 10 per cent or higher.

monetary unit The unit of measure for a country's money, in terms of which all of its coin and paper money are defined. Among the leading monetary units today (in terms of foreign exchange) are the U.S. dollar, French franc, West German Deutschmark, British pound sterling, Russian ruble, and Japanese yen.

monetization of the debt See DEBT MONETIZATION.

money Anything that functions as a generally accepted medium of exchange and as a standard unit of account in terms of which goods and services can be compared. There are three main kinds of money (listed in order of present-day importance): BANK MONEY, CURRENCY (coins and paper money), and COMMODITY MONEY. Today bank money, consisting largely of DEMAND DEPOSITS, accounts for more than three-fourths of the total U.S. money supply, and paper currency accounts for another one-fifth. Commodity money (gold, shells, cows, tobacco, wives, etc.) is still used in some parts of the world but not in the developed nations. Whereas commodity money may have intrinsic value (as gold coins obviously do), currency and bank money are in fact *liabilities,* that is, they are claims on the government and on banks respectively. That these claims are generally accepted as payment for physical goods represents an act of faith (see FIDUCIARY MONEY).

The value of money, as of any other commodity, stems from its scarcity relative to demand. The demand for money depends on several factors: the total volume of economic transactions, the payment habits of the economic community, and how much individuals and firms want to keep on hand for unexpected or future needs. Thus the *quantity* of money is directly related to its value. However, the value of money can be measured only in terms of what it will buy—its purchasing power—which varies inversely with the general PRICE LEVEL. Assuming a constant rate of use, if the volume of money grows more rapidly than the rate at which the output of goods and services can be increased (owing to limitations of time and physical facilities), prices will tend to rise. There will then be more money than goods to spend it on at prevailing prices. The price increase will reduce the value of money even when the monetary unit is backed by and redeemable in the soundest possible assets. If, on the other hand, the money supply does not grow as fast as the economy's current production, either prices will tend to fall or, more likely, labor, factories, and other production facilities will not be fully employed. (See also under MONEY SUPPLY.)

Many earlier economists believed that prices are in direct proportion to the money supply (see QUANTITY THEORY OF MONEY), and some modern ones cling to versions of this belief (see, for example, Irving Fisher's EQUATION OF EXCHANGE).

However, this theory fails to take into account that money may be either spent or saved. In practice, the getting and spending of money rarely coincide exactly; thus a monthly salary check must usually cover a variety of expenses, some of a daily or weekly nature (food), some monthly (rent), some quarterly (taxes, clothes), some annual (insurance). Economists distinguish between the holding of money to cover regular periodic expenses, which they call the *transactions motive* (or *transactions demand*) for money, and the holding of money against possible future contingencies—speculation that it may be worth more than other property (*speculative motive*), fear that it will be needed for some emergency (*precautionary motive*). Some economists refer to the last two motives as *liquidity demand*; see also LIQUIDITY PREFERENCE; VELOCITY OF MONEY.

The total money supply is regulated largely by the central bank (in the United States, the Federal Reserve System), but the actual process of *money creation* takes place in commercial banks. The demand liabilities (demand deposits) of commercial banks are money. These liabilities consist of customers' checking accounts. They increase when customers deposit currency and checks, and when the proceeds of loans made by the banks are credited to borrowers' accounts. In theory, banks could build up deposits endlessly just by increasing loans and investments, as long as they kept enough currency on hand to redeem whatever amounts their depositors wanted to convert into currency (by cashing checks). In practice, banks are restrained from lending by the willingness (or lack of it) of individuals, firms, and the government to borrow funds. Also, in most countries banks are further restrained from creating unlimited amounts of money through controls imposed by the central bank. In the United States these controls take the form of a prescribed legal reserve a bank must maintain on deposit with the central bank (see RESERVE REQUIREMENTS). See also COIN; CURRENCY; LEGAL TENDER; NEAR MONEY; REPRESENTATIVE MONEY; TOKEN MONEY.

money, quantity theory of See QUANTITY THEORY OF MONEY.

money-flow analysis See FLOW-OF-FUNDS ANALYSIS.

money illusion Valuing money for its face value, without any regard for what it will buy (purchasing power). Invented by the American economist Irving Fisher, the term is often used to describe the reluctance of workers to accept a pay cut even when their REAL WAGE remains the same, and their enthusiasm for a pay increase that merely brings real wages in line with rising prices.

money market The market for buying and selling short-term loanable funds, in the form of securities, loans, gold, and foreign exchange. (Long-term funds are traded in the CAPITAL MARKET.) The money market is not a single entity; it consists of numerous separate markets, each of which handles a particular kind of short-term credit: short-term promissory notes (commercial paper), collateral loans, broker's loans, bankers' acceptances, Treasury bills, etc. What these forms of credit have in common is that they generally are low in risk, are highly liquid (readily convertible into cash), and tend to offer low interest yield. As such they are principal instruments for temporary investment by business corporations, banks and other financial institutions, and the Federal government. Though these transactions typically take place in numerous financial centers, New York City is the site of the largest and most important money market in the world. London is the center of the European money market, which in Great Britain is called the *short money market* or *Lombard Street* (after the London street where many financial institutions are located). For more information on short-term credit instruments, see ACCEPTANCE, def. 2; BILL OF EXCHANGE; COLLATERAL LOAN; COMMERCIAL PAPER; TREASURY BILL.

money market fund A MUTUAL FUND specializing in short-term instruments of credit, such as Treasury bills. During periods of tight money (when interest rates are high) money market funds are able to get a much higher return with little risk than most investors could get on their own. The reason is that during such periods the Treasury, by requiring a substantial minimum purchase (some-times $10,000 or more), discourages small investors from purchasing Treasury notes in order to prevent DISINTERMEDIATION. Since few small investors can afford such sums, most must leave their money in a savings bank, earning perhaps 5 or 6 per cent interest, while Treasury bills may be yielding as much as 10 per cent. The money market fund, however, can pool the funds of many small investors and buy large quantities, taking advantage of the temporary credit squeeze.

money order An order for payment of a particular sum of money drawn on a bank, telegraph company, post office, express company, or other agency from whom the drawer purchased it. It is used primarily to make payments over a distance without mailing cash or personal checks. The payee cashes the money order at a local office of the institution on which it is drawn.

money supply The total stock of a nation's money that is available for spending, consisting of CURRENCY and DEMAND DEPOSITS held by private businesses and individuals. The distribution between these two components depends solely on public preference. When a depositor cashes a check at a commercial bank, the amount of deposits is reduced and the amount of currency in circulation is increased. Conversely, when more currency is in circulation than is needed for economic transactions, some is returned to the banks in exchange for deposits. (Although VAULT CASH held by banks is not considered a part of the stock of money available for spending by the nonbank public, some economists do consider NEAR MONEY part of the money supply; see also M-1, M-2, M-3.) The total amount of demand deposits, however, is determined by commercial banks, which in turn are regulated by the central bank (see under MONEY for an explanation of how banks create money).

The money supply has an important effect on the general PRICE LEVEL: too much money in relation to output of goods tends to raise prices; too little tends either to lower prices or to diminish output (resulting in unemployment and idle facilities). Just how much money is needed without exerting undue influence on prices depends on how intensively money is being used. Every demand deposit bal-

Fig. 54. Money market rates (per cent per annum)

Period	Prime Commercial Paper[1] 90-119 days	4 to 6 months	Finance Co. Paper Placed Directly, 3 to 6 Months[2]	Prime Bankers' Accept-ances, 90 Days[3]	Fed-eral Funds Rate[4]	U.S. Government Securities[5] 3-month bills[6] Rate on new issue	Mar-ket yield	6-month bills[6] Rate on new issue	Mar-ket yield	9-to12-month issues 1-year bill (mar-ket yield)[6]	Other[7]	3- to 5-year issues[7]
1967		5.10	4.89	4.75	4.22	4.321	4.29	4.630	4.61	4.71	4.84	5.07
1968		5.90	5.69	5.75	5.66	5.339	5.34	5.470	5.47	5.46	5.62	5.59
1969		7.83	7.16	7.61	8.21	6.677	6.67	6.853	6.86	6.79	7.06	6.85
1970		7.72	7.23	7.31	7.17	6.458	6.39	6.562	6.51	6.49	6.90	7.37
1971		5.11	4.91	4.85	4.66	4.348	4.33	4.511	4.52	4.67	4.75	5.77
1972	4.66	4.69	4.52	4.47	4.44	4.071	4.07	4.466	4.49	4.77	4.86	5.85
1973	8.20	8.15	7.40	8.08	8.74	7.041	7.03	7.178	7.20	7.01	7.30	6.92
1974	10.05	9.87	8.62	9.92	10.51	7.886	7.84	7.926	7.95	7.71	8.25	7.81
1975	6.26	6.33	6.16	6.30	5.82	5.838	5.80	6.122	6.11	6.30	6.70	7.55
1975—July	6.32	6.44	6.02	6.40	6.10	6.164	6.13	6.492	6.50	6.64	7.07	7.72
Aug	6.59	6.70	6.39	6.74	6.14	6.463	6.44	6.940	6.94	7.16	7.55	8.12
Sept	6.79	6.86	6.53	6.83	6.24	6.383	6.42	6.870	6.92	7.20	7.54	8.22
Oct	6.35	6.48	6.43	6.28	5.82	6.081	5.96	6.385	6.25	6.48	6.89	7.80
Nov	5.78	5.91	5.79	5.79	5.22	5.468	5.48	5.751	5.80	6.07	6.40	7.51
Dec	5.88	5.97	5.86	5.72	5.20	5.504	5.44	5.933	5.85	6.16	6.51	7.50
1976—Jan	5.15	5.27	5.16	5.08	4.87	4.961	4.87	5.238	5.14	5.44	5.71	7.18
Feb	5.13	5.23	5.09	4.99	4.77	4.852	4.88	5.144	5.20	5.53	5.78	7.18
Mar	5.25	5.37	5.27	5.18	4.84	5.047	5.00	5.488	5.44	5.82	6.12	7.25
Apr	5.08	5.23	r5.14	5.03	4.82	4.878	4.86	5.201	5.18	5.54	5.85	6.99
May	5.44	5.54	5.38	5.53	5.29	5.185	5.20	5.600	5.62	5.98	6.36	7.35
June	5.83	5.94	5.78	5.77	5.48	5.443	5.41	5.784	5.77	6.12	6.52	7.40
July	5.54	5.67	5.53	5.50	5.31	5.278	5.23	5.597	5.53	5.82	6.21	7.24
Week ending—												
1976—Apr 3	5.15	5.30	5.13	5.10	4.84	4.929	4.97	5.327	5.34	5.76	6.03	7.14
10	5.18	5.38	5.18	5.05	4.73	4.957	4.91	5.293	5.22	5.59	5.94	7.04
17	5.09	5.19	r5.13	5.01	4.77	4.830	4.80	5.068	5.04	5.36	5.66	6.88
24	5.00	5.13	5.13	4.94	4.78	4.763	4.78	5.089	5.11	5.47	5.76	6.92
May 1	5.03	5.15	5.13	5.07	4.93	4.909	4.88	5.230	5.24	5.61	5.90	7.04
8	5.20	5.30	5.15	5.21	5.03	4.921	4.91	5.339	5.30	5.68	5.98	7.11
15	5.30	5.43	5.30	5.39	5.02	5.072	5.11	5.426	5.51	5.89	6.21	7.28
22	5.53	5.63	5.45	5.67	5.28	5.250	5.33	5.726	5.79	6.11	6.56	7.46
29	5.73	5.83	5.63	5.87	5.50	5.495	5.47	5.908	5.89	6.26	6.68	7.56
June 5	5.88	6.00	r5.78	5.92	5.54	5.578	5.53	5.952	5.90	6.27	6.66	7.52
12	5.88	6.00	5.88	5.82	5.44	5.459	5.44	5.768	5.75	6.11	6.55	7.42
19	5.90	6.00	5.88	5.74	5.47	5.380	5.38	5.695	5.74	6.07	6.50	7.38
26	5.78	5.90	5.75	5.69	5.48	5.356	5.34	5.722	5.71	6.06	6.44	7.32
July 3	5.70	5.80	5.50	5.69	5.58	5.368	5.36	5.754	5.75	6.08	6.46	7.36
10	5.72	5.81	5.63	5.66	5.37	5.412	5.34	5.768	5.61	5.90	6.35	7.30
17	5.53	5.65	5.53	5.48	5.27	5.190	5.15	5.430	5.44	5.72	6.13	7.18
24	5.48	5.65	5.50	5.47	5.30	5.226	5.23	5.536	5.54	5.84	6.17	7.26
31	5.38	5.50	5.50	5.34	5.28	5.194	5.17	5.497	5.45	5.74	6.12	7.21

[1]Averages of the most representative daily offering rate quoted by dealers.

[2]Averages of the most representative daily offering rate published by finance companies, for varying maturities in the 90–179 day range.

[3]Beginning Aug. 15, 1974, the rate is the average of the midpoint of the range of daily dealer closing rates offered for domestic issues; prior data are averages of the most representative daily offering rate quoted by dealers.

[4]Seven-day averages of daily effective rates for week ending Wednesday. Since July 19, 1973, the daily effective Federal funds rate is an average of the rates on a given day weighted by the volume of transactions at these rates. Prior to this date, the daily effective rate was the rate considered most representative of the day's transactions, usually the one at which most transactions occurred.

[5]Except for new bill issues, yields are averages computed from daily closing bid prices.

[6]Bills quoted on bank-discount-rate basis.

[7]Selected note and bond issues.

rRevised

Source: Federal Reserve Bulletin, August 1976.

ance and every dollar bill is part of somebody's spendable funds at any given time, ready to move to other owners as transactions take place. Some owners spend money freely after they get it, thereby making it available for others to use; others tend to hold it for long periods. When some money remains idle, or *inactive*, obviously a larger total supply is needed for any given volume of transactions (see also VELOCITY OF MONEY). In sum, the money supply is determined by the actions of consumers, businesses, government, commercial banks, and the central bank (in the United States, the Federal Reserve). In the United States the total money supply has risen from $8.76 billion in 1900 to an estimated $290 billion in 1975. See also MONETARY EQUATIONS; REAL CASH BALANCE.

money wage See under REAL WAGE.

monopolistic competition Describing a market in which sellers can influence prices owing to product differentiation. Although there may be many sellers, their products differ at least slightly, or are thought to differ, from one another, a contention strongly supported by advertising. See also A. A. COURNOT; E. H. CHAMBERLIN.

monopoly, monopsony Exclusive control over a particular product or service by one seller (*monopolist*) or one buyer (*monopsonist*). The terms also apply to groups of sellers or buyers who can exert such control through mutual agreement. The monopolist's essential advantage is the absence of competitors, enabling a firm to control the supply of its commodity so as to obtain the highest possible profit. Similarly, the monopsonist, as the only buyer, can control purchases so as to obtain the lowest possible price. In practice monopoly is the more common of the two. A monopoly can be effective through control of less than 100 per cent of output. For example, the American steel industry (technically an OLIGOPOLY) has monopolistic characteristics even though the largest producer accounts for less than one-third of the market. (In Great Britain, firms controlling 33.3 per cent of the market are subject to investigation by the Monopolies Commission.) Monopoly has serious disadvantages for consumers besides high prices. It prevents resource allocation in accordance with consumer

needs or choices, supply being controlled entirely for the monopolist's benefit. It affords no protection against inferior quality, and it removes any incentive for improvements other than those that increase the monopolist's profits. Consequently, private monopolies have been at least partially regulated and restricted in the United States since the late 19th century (see ANTITRUST LEGISLATION), and competition has been strongly encouraged. Nevertheless, monopolies or near monopolies based on patents, on scarce essential items, or on the availability of huge amounts of investment capital for certain industries all have counteracted competitive forces to the point where IMPERFECT COMPETITION tends to prevail in most markets.

A *public monopoly* is an enterprise owned, operated, or strictly regulated by a government, such as a postal service, railroads, communications, lotteries, and public utilities. Some enterprises (such as telephone and postal services) can be most efficiently operated by single, large concerns, and it is obviously in the public interest that they be under some measure of government control. A public monopoly may also be a means of raising revenue (lotteries) or an effective means of controlling a product that presents social problems (as with state monopolies over liquor sales in the United States, and government monopolies over tobacco products in many other countries). In such public enterprises the inherent evils of monopoly are at least restrained, if not eliminated entirely. See also CARTEL; DUOPOLY; NATURAL MONOPOLY.

monopsony See MONOPOLY, MONOPSONY.

Monte Carlo simulation A statistical technique using RANDOM NUMBERS (as might appear on a roulette wheel; hence the name, traditionally associated with gambling) to determine whether an actual set of values is random or nonrandom. For example, in attempting to identify the cause of a production bottleneck in which a certain machine frequently creates a large backlog, and to help decide if an additional machine should be bought, past experience with the machine is analyzed to determine demand for its use. After calculating how often the machine is needed (see Fig. 19 under CUMULATIVE DISTRIBUTION) random numbers are used to *simulate* future demand for the machine (see Fig. 55). In this example, the simulation shows that the bottleneck must be nonrandom, since demand rarely exceeds capacity substantially, suggesting that some change in operations might eliminate it.

Monthly Investment Plan Also, *MIP*. A plan developed by the New York Stock Exchange whereby a small investor can buy a listed security by regularly paying a fixed monthly amount to a member broker. The chief advantage is that the investor need not wait until he or she has accumulated enough cash to buy a high-priced stock, but instead may obtain a fraction of a share of some stock each month. The chief disadvantage is that the broker charges a higher commission for such small transactions, sometimes as much as 6 per cent. The Monthly Investment Plan is a form of DOLLAR AVERAGING.

moonlighting Slang term for working at a second job, derived from the fact that such jobs often involve night work.

moral suasion A term for the efforts of the U.S. Federal Reserve to persuade—rather than coerce—banks to comply with some suggested policy, usually either to restrain credit during a time of inflation or to expand it during a time of recession.

moratorium A legally invoked period of delay during which debtors need not meet obligations when they fall due. A *bank moratorium* may be invoked by a legislature or some other public authority, in effect suspending any bank payments for a given time. See also BANK HOLIDAY, def. 2.

Morris Plan bank Also, *industrial bank*. A bank that specializes in loans to consumers rather than to business firms. It is named for Arthur J. Morris (1881–1973), an American lawyer who in 1910 formulated a plan to provide personal installment credit to wage earners based on their character and integrity, usually affirmed by cosigners to their promissory note. At that time banks tended to extend credit only to businesses, and consumers had few opportunities for borrowing. In 1917 Morris expanded the concept of consumer credit to the insurance industry and founded the Morris Plan Insurance Society, the first credit life insurance company. Today most Morris Plan banks function much as an ordinary COMMERCIAL BANK except that a greater percentage of their loans is likely to be made to consumers and small businesses rather than to large corporations.

mortality table A statistical table showing the death rate at each age, usually expressed as a given number per thousand, which is used to calculate

Fig. 55. Simulation of demand for specialized machine time

Random Number	Mean Hours of Demand	Backlog with 4 Machines		Backlog with 5 Machines	
		Hours	*Days*	*Hours*	*Days*
98	42.5	10.5	0.3	2.5	0.1
93	42.5	21.0	.7	5.0	.3
79	37.5	26.5	.8	2.5	.1
54	32.5	27.0	.8	—	—
15	12.5	14.5	.5	—	—
57	32.5	15.0	.5	—	—
80	37.5	20.5	.6	—	—
81	37.5	26.0	.8	—	—
59	32.5	26.5	.8	—	—
13	12.5	7.0	.2	—	—
43	27.5	2.5	.1	—	—
6	2.5	—	—	—	—
90	42.5	10.5	.3	2.5	.1

Source: D. S. Ammer, *Materials Management,* 3d ed. (Homewood, Ill.: Richard D. Irwin, Inc., 1974), p. 586. Reprinted by permission.

premiums in LIFE INSURANCE. Mortality tables also are constructed for plant and equipment, giving some idea of their SERVICE LIFE.

mortgage A legal agreement that creates an interest in real estate or transfers title to personal property as security for an obligation. A mortgage on personal property is called a CHATTEL MORTGAGE. A mortgage on real property—land, buildings and fixtures, or rights in land—is called a *real mortgage*; the word "mortgage" alone most often refers to a real mortgage. The person whose interest in the property is given as security—the one who "takes out" the mortgage—is the *mortgagor*; the person receiving the security is the *mortgagee*. When the obligation on which a mortgage is based is performed—that is, when the debt is paid off—the mortgage automatically terminates. If the mortgagor should fail to perform—that is, not pay the debt—the mortgagee may enforce the mortgage by FORECLOSURE. Even then, however, the mortgagor may retain the right to redeem or regain the property, in some cases even when it has been disposed of through a foreclosure sale; this is known as the *right of redemption.*

It was long believed that a mortgage gives the mortgagee some kind of legal title to the property, a view that is now disputed. In the United States most states regard the mortgagee as having merely a LIEN to secure the debt (hence they are called *lien states*), and most others take a position midway between the older title theory and the lien theory (but a few still hold the original position and so are called *title states*). The most common form of mortgage used in most states is the *regular mortgage*, a deed or conveyance of the land by borrower to lender, which includes a description of the debt and a provision that the mortgage is void when it is repaid in full. Another common form is the *deed of trust* (or *trust deed*), in which the borrower conveys to a third person, called the *trustee*, a trust to hold the property as security for the lender.

When a mortgage is viewed as a lien—that is, a claim against or right in property—the question of priority of claim may arise, for if the borrower requires additional funds the same property may be mortgaged not once but two or more times. A *first mortgage* has prior claim, though not necessarily in time; a *second mortgage* has second claim, after the first mortgage, and so is said to be *junior* to it, or *overlying,* and the first mortgage is said to be *senior* to the second, or *underlying.* In the case of default, the holder of a second mortgage generally receives no payment until the claims of the first mortgage have been satisfied.

The most common mortgage used by an individual is to purchase a house. Normally a mortgage finances the major part of the purchase price and is repayable over a specific period of time, generally 10 to 30 years. As a rule, the buyer must pay a portion of the purchase price in cash (make a *down payment*) and then receives title to the house; the buyer then uses the title as security for the unpaid balance of the purchase price; this is sometimes called a *purchase-money mortgage.* The buyer naturally looks for a mortgage offering the most favorable terms, that is, at the lowest interest rate. Most likely the mortgage obtained will be an *amortized mortgage*, that is, one in which each payment will both reduce the mortgage principal and cover interest on the amount still due. (Under a *term mortgage* the debt is payable in full at the end of the specified period, or "term.") Payments normally are made in specified amounts at regular intervals, so that early payments represent mostly interest and later ones mostly principal. If the buyer foresees a future need for funds, perhaps to add more rooms or otherwise improve the property, he or she may try to obtain an *open-end* or *open mortgage*, which permits raising the total amount of the mortgage without taking out a new one. If only a *closed mortgage*—without provisions for increases—is available, the buyer may then have to take out a second, and perhaps even a third, mortgage on the same property. Suppose, however, that instead of adding rooms, the homeowner decides to sell the house and purchase a bigger one. Most often in such cases the mortgage is paid and released in the process of sale, because an existing mortgage rarely meets the financing needs of the new buyer. However, it is possible to sell mortgaged property without providing for retirement of the old mortgage; the new buyer then simply undertakes the balance of the mortgage debt.

The conventional home mortgage calls for a fixed rate of interest. Increasingly, however, lenders are offering *floating interest rates* for home mortgages, in which the interest rate fluctuates with general MONEY MARKET conditions, much as a bank's prime rate does.

Frequently mortgagees wish to sell their mortgages (see also MORTGAGE MARKET). In selling a deed or trust, which is usually given to secure a negotiable note, the seller can simply hand the note to the buyer; if the note is payable to a specific person, the seller must endorse it to the buyer (or to bearer). In selling a regular mortgage, the seller must execute a formal ASSIGNMENT, a written record of the transaction. Though mortgages apparently date from biblical times, their extensive use in the United States dates only from about 1920 and has enormously expanded since about 1950. In the early 1970s more than two-thirds of all single-family American homes were mortgaged, and nine-tenths of those bought since 1970 involved the use of some mortgage credit. See also BLANKET MORTGAGE; MORTGAGE BOND; MORTGAGE LOAN INSURANCE; PACKAGE MORTGAGE.

mortgage bond Any BOND (def. 1) secured by a mortgage on a property whose value may or may not be equal to the value of all the mortgage bonds issued against it. A mortgage bond represents an actual claim against property. Most often the mortgage itself is held by a trustee for the benefit of the bondholders. A *general mortgage bond* is secured by a general mortgage on the property of the issuer, that is, a BLANKET MORTGAGE on all of the company's property; however, it may be outranked by one or more other mortgages. A *first mortgage bond* represents, usually, a first claim on the issuer's property, but it may be on only part of that property if it is outranked by prior bonds. A *chattel mortgage bond* is secured by a CHATTEL MORTGAGE.

mortgage loan insurance In the United States, a program for insuring mortgages and loans made by private lending institutions for the purchase, construction, rehabilitation, repair, and improvement of single-family and multifamily housing. Such insurance enables lenders to offer mortgages and housing loans for lower down payments and at lower interest rates. The program was first established by the National Housing Act of 1934 and was originally administered by the Federal Housing

Administration (FHA), which gave its name to *FHA loans*. In 1965 the FHA was absorbed by the newly created U.S. Department of Housing and Urban Development, which also administers low-rent public housing and various forms of home-ownership assistance.

mortgage market A general name for the demand for and supply of mortgages, that is, borrowers who are seeking mortgage funds and lenders who are willing to invest in mortgages. From a financial standpoint, the mortgage seeker prefers paying interest on a mortgage to investing a large amount of capital in a fixed asset (real estate)—if in fact he or she has enough capital to make such a choice. The lender, on the other hand, may find the long-term investment sufficiently profitable, particularly in view of the relatively small risk (since mortgages automatically confer on the holder a claim to the property). In the United States mortgage credit is supplied primarily by insurance companies, mutual savings banks, savings and loan associations, and commercial banks. They participate in the so-called *primary mortgage market* just described, making available funds for new mortgages. In addition, there is a *secondary mortgage market*, in which previously created mortgages are traded (with private mortgage bankers sometimes acting as intermediaries), owing to the fact that investors in mortgages may find they need funds before the mortgages mature. The U.S. Federal government has helped to promote an orderly mortgage market through both the GOVERNMENT NATIONAL MORTGAGE ASSOCIATION (Ginnie Mae) and the FEDERAL NATIONAL MORTGAGE ASSOCIATION (Fannie Mae).

moshav See under COLLECTIVE FARM.

most-favored-nation clause See under TARIFF, def. 1; also under GENERAL AGREEMENT ON TARIFFS AND TRADE.

motion study See TIME AND MOTION STUDY.

motivation research A branch of social science (particularly psychology and sociology) that seeks to discover why people behave as they do. It has been adopted in part by market researchers to find out more about the behavior of consumers—what economic and noneconomic motives dictate their choices of products and services, and how they are influenced by the buying habits of others.

moving average A series of calculations made by taking the simple average, or arithmetic MEAN, of a consecutive number of items, then discarding the first item and adding the first of the remaining items, and continuing the process, so that the number of items in the series remains constant. For example, suppose one is calculating toy sales for a 12-month period and wants to smooth out the seasonal fluctuations. Sales from June of one year to May of the following year are added and divided by 12, giving the arithmetic mean for one year. Next, June of the first year is dropped and June of the following year is added, the new total is divided by 12, yielding another arithmetic mean. The process can be repeated indefinitely. Moving averages are useful in assessing prices that fluctuate frequently (and seasonally), which is true of many raw materials as well as of toys, air conditioners, sleds, and other seasonal items. In oil refining, crude oil is customarily charged to operations on the basis of a six-months' moving average (see Fig. 56).

MRO Abbreviation for maintenance, repairs, and operating supplies; see under MAINTENANCE AND REPAIRS.

muckrakers A group of American writers of the 1890s and early 1900s who exposed corruption and dishonesty in business and politics. They included Lincoln Steffens, who concentrated on corruption in city government; Ida Tarbell, whose *History of the Standard Oil Company* revealed how that company had ruthlessly eliminated its competitors; Ray Stannard Baker, whose "Railroads on Trial" exposed corrupt management of the railroads; Thomas W. Lawson, whose "Frenzied Finance" exposed the activities of the Amalgamated Copper Company; Charles E. Russel, who attacked the meatpacking industry,; Samuel Hopkins Adams, who exposed the patent-medicine racket; and Gustavus Myers, whose *History of the Great American Fortunes* dispelled the myth that the rich are necessarily good, kind, and ethical. By arousing public interest in these and other abuses, the muckrakers' efforts eventually led to the passage of laws to correct at least some of them, such as the Pure Food and Drug Act (1906).

multi-employer agreement An agreement between a labor union and several employers, from a handful to many or even a whole industry. By combining for collective bargaining, employers—particularly small firms—are able to hire skilled lawyers to negotiate on their behalf, prevent a union from picking on one firm at a time and using agreements of other firms against it, and generally gain the benefits of collective action. On the other hand, such an agreement may reduce the independent scope of a single firm and subordinate its aims to those of the group. See also EMPLOYERS' ASSOCIATION.

multi-industry firm See CONGLOMERATE.

multilateral trade Trade among many nations, as opposed to trade between just two (bilateral trade).

multinational company Also, *international corporation.* A business firm with production facilities or other fixed assets in one or more countries other than its own and operating in a global context, particularly in terms of making major management decisions based on considerations of facilities, services, and sales in many other parts of the world. The second half of the 20th century has seen a rapid expansion in such firms, and their effect on the economies of the countries in which they operate has aroused considerable controversy.

Fig. 56. Moving average

Month	Price (in cents)	Moving Average
Jan.	10	
Feb.	11	
Mar.	12	
Apr.	11	11
May	14	12
June	14	12.75
July	16	13.75

Decisions having a significant effect on the employment and prosperity of a country's citizens may be made by foreign executives of the multinational company who are not subject to the host country's control. Also, multinationals allegedly can at times avoid taxes in one country by manipulating accounts so as to transfer profit to operations in countries with low tax rates.

multiple expansion of credit See under FRACTIONAL RESERVE BANKING.

multiple-line insurance See under CASUALTY INSURANCE.

multiple listing See under LISTING.

multiple regression See under REGRESSION ANALYSIS.

multiplier principle
   1. The idea that changes in investment spending set off a chain reaction that results in much greater (multiplied) changes in total income. Thus, if an entrepreneur builds a new factory, it increases the incomes of (1) construction workers, (2) the merchants they deal with, (3) the suppliers of those merchants, (4) the suppliers' suppliers, etc. This chain reaction is not infinite, however, since only part of each sector's new income will be spent, and the rest saved. The increase in total income therefore is calculated by inverting the fraction that is saved and multiplying it by the original investment. Thus, if 15 per cent (15/100) of each person's new income will be saved and the entrepreneur put $1.5 million into its new factory, its investment will have increased total income by $10 million (100/15 × $1.5 million = $10 million). The *multiplier* in this instance is 100/15 or 6.67, the numerical coefficient that shows the increase in income resulting from the change in investment. Originally formulated by the British economist R. F. Kahn in 1931, the multiplier principle was adopted by J. M. KEYNES, who applied it to both consumer spending and investment spending. A *decline* in investment spending causes national income and employment to decline by the multiplier. For example, a $10 billion decline in investment spending may bring

about a $30 billion decline in national income. Since the effect of a decline in investment could be so devastating in terms of unemployment, Keynes urged that government spending be used as a substitute for private investment even if it meant paying people to do completely useless work.
   2. *export multiplier, foreign trade multiplier.* The idea that an increase in exports generates an even greater increase in national income. The principle operates in the same way as an increase in domestic investment spending does (see def. 1 above), owing to the fact that increased income from exports is spent on home-produced goods. Suppose Country A experiences an increase in domestic investment that leads to even more sharply increased national income and employment. Some portion of this new income is spent on goods imported from Country B. As a result B is increasing its exports to A, and employment and new income in its export industries will rise. Some of this new income will be spent on domestically produced goods, making the overall income of Country B rise as well. Thus the economic expansion of A has been transmitted to B. See also SPREAD EFFECT.
   3. *deposit multiplier, credit multiplier.* See under FRACTIONAL RESERVE BANKING.

multiprocessing See CONCURRENT PROCESSING.

municipal bond See under BOND, def. 1.

mutual company A type of NONSTOCK CORPORATION in which profits are distributed among the members in proportion to the amount of business they do with the company. Examples include the MUTUAL INSURANCE COMPANY and mutual savings bank (see SAVINGS BANK, def. 2).

mutual fund Also, *open-end investment trust (company).* An INVESTMENT COMPANY whose capitalization is not fixed at a given number of shares but that issues shares in accordance with customer demand. Mutual funds sell their own new shares to investors, stand ready to buy back their old shares, and are not listed on organized exchanges. Mutual funds often are classified on the basis of the kinds of investment they specialize in. For example, a *common stock fund* invests only in common stocks, a *balanced fund* invests in bonds, preferred stocks, and common stocks, a *growth fund* invests in growth stocks, a MONEY MARKET FUND in short-term debt, etc. Various special-purpose funds invest their assets wholly in one industry or in one geographical area. Some mutual funds borrow money in the belief that their earnings will exceed any interest they pay (see HEDGE FUND); they are not permitted (by law) to buy on margin. A *performance fund* (or *go-go fund*, as it was called in the 1960s) diversifies its holdings among speculative stocks in the hope of making fast profits.

The price for a share of a mutual fund is determined by the trust's *net asset value per share*, that is, the total market value of all its securities, minus liabilities, divided by the number of shares it has outstanding. Naturally this figure changes constantly along with changing market values. Therefore most mutual funds compute and announce the net asset value of their shares once or twice every trading day, thereby setting the price to be charged both by dealers and by owners wishing to sell their shares.

Throughout the 1950s and 1960s, mutual funds were perhaps the fastest-growing form of investment in the United States. Between 1951 and 1961 their worth increased from $3.5 billion to $23 billion and reached a peak of $60 billion in 1972. One reason for this rapid growth was high-pressure sales methods, with thousands of fund salesmen spurred on by a very high commission rate. The buyer of most mutual fund shares normally pays a commission, called a *load* or *loading charge,* which covers both the sales commission and other costs of distribution; this fee is considerably higher than brokerage fees for trading ordinary listed securities, amounting on the average to 8 per cent (of which the salesman typically receives three-fourths). Even more lucrative for the salesman is the so-called FRONT-END LOAD FUND. There are some *no-load funds*, which employ no salesmen and charge no commission, but their shares are harder to come by; the buyer must know how to contact the fund directly. Both load and no-load funds charge each share a *management fee* of about 0.5 per cent per year, which is either fixed or varies with the performance of the fund. Despite their higher cost, mutual funds continue to attract investors who do not trust themselves to choose investments wisely and/or who wish to diversify their holdings (and hence minimize risk) more than they could through independent security purchases.

mutual insurance company An insurance firm in which each policyholder becomes a member. The policyholders are entitled to name the firm's directors or trustees who oversee its management, and they share in the company's net profit, which is returned to them in the form of either dividends or rebates on future premiums. In an *assessment mutual insurance company* policyholders may be liable for losses in excess of the company's assets; in a *legal reserve mutual insurance company* a reserve is maintained to cover such losses and policyholders are not so assessed. See also STOCK INSURANCE COMPANY.

mutualism The economic theory of Pierre Joseph Proudhon (1809–65), a Frenchman who opposed large private holdings that permit their owners to live from rent, interest, and profit, and proposed instead that voluntary workers' associations control the production and exchange of their own output. To obtain capital for this venture, Proudhon proposed a system of exchange banks issuing papers to be freely exchanged for goods and services. The amount issued would be in direct proportion to the business volume. Every worker or group of workers would be able to get interest-free credit for purchases of capital goods, and all differences between the rich and poor would disappear. Because it advocated the elimination of authority based on force, mutualism is sometimes considered a form of ANARCHISM. Proudhon actually did found a People's Bank after the Revolution of 1848, but he was arrested and tried before it went into operation.

mutual savings bank See SAVINGS BANK, def. 2.

Myrdal, Gunnar A Swedish economist and public official (1898–19) known as one of the architects of his country's extensive social welfare system and a strong advocate of foreign aid to the poor nations of the world. Highly critical of American society in his study of the American Negro (*An American Dilemma*, 1944), Myrdal went on to an equally exhaustive study of underdeveloped nations (*Rich Lands and Poor*, 1957), in which he

concluded that the widening gap between rich and poor nations could be narrowed only through systematic centralized economic planning. In 1974 he shared the Nobel Memorial Prize in Economic Science with F. A. von Hayek of the Chicago school.

narrow market See THIN MARKET.

NASA Acronym for NATIONAL AERONAUTICS AND SPACE ADMINISTRATION.

national advertising See under ADVERTISING.

National Aeronautics and Space Administration Also, *NASA*. An independent U.S. Federal agency created in 1958 to conduct research in aeronautic and space technology and its applications.

National Association of Securities Dealers An agency that represents 3,700 securities dealers (who, unlike brokers, buy and sell for themselves rather than for customers) in the United States. It is empowered by the U.S. Securities and Exchange Commission to regulate dealers' operations in the OVER-THE-COUNTER MARKET, and has the authority to censure, fine, suspend, or expel members who break its rules. It also supplies national and regional quotations for over-the-counter transactions to newspapers and other media.

national banks
   1. Today, American banks that are chartered by the Federal government, as opposed to those chartered by the various states.
   2. A system of commercial banks chartered by the U.S. Federal government, set up through the

National Banking Act of 1863 and subsequent amendments. To curb the issue of bank notes without sufficient reserve backing, a practice rampant in the absence of a central monetary authority (see under BANK OF THE UNITED STATES), a national bank was required to back its notes with U.S. government bonds. The precise reserve requirements varied depending on a bank's location: *central reserve city banks* (in New York and Chicago) had to hold a reserve of 25 per cent of deposits in vault cash; *reserve city banks* (in 47 other cities) could keep half of the required 25 per cent on deposit in central reserve city banks; and *country banks* (all other places) could hold 60 per cent of their required 15 per cent reserve in central reserve or central reserve city banks. (These distinctions were later retained by the FEDERAL RESERVE System.)

   In order to stabilize the currency further, an amendment passed in 1865 imposed a tax of 10 per cent on all bank notes issued by state banks in hopes of driving them out of the business of issuing bank notes. In practice, however, the state banks continued to prosper and grow, as checkbook deposits, which were not subject to the 10 per cent tax, increasingly replaced bank notes as money. In 1913, when the Federal Reserve Act was passed, all national banks were required to join the Federal Reserve System. At that time there were 7,473 national banks in all, holding $8.1 billion in deposits, and some 18,520 state banks, with $12 billion in deposits. In 1935 national banks were prohibited from issuing bank notes; their notes have since been replaced by Federal Reserve notes. In the mid-1970s about one-third of all commercial banks in the United States were national banks.

national brand See under BRAND.

National Bureau of Economic Research Also, *NBER*. See under STATISTICS, BUSINESS AND ECONOMIC.

National Bureau of Standards An agency of the U.S. Department of Commerce that establishes physical standards for the nation's system of measurements and conducts scientific and technological research for the government.

national debt Also, U.S. *Federal debt*. The debt of a central government. See NET NATIONAL DEBT; PUBLIC DEBT.

National Grange See GRANGE.

national income

1. Also, *national product*. The total earnings of labor and property from the production of goods and services within a nation during a given period, usually a year, consisting of all wages, salaries, and other employer's compensation (pension contributions, etc.), the income of business proprietors (business, professional, and farm), all rental income, corporate profits, and net interest. National income often is analyzed according to its point of origin, by type of industry (mining, manufacturing, communications, etc.) or by economic sector (private ownership, corporate business, household, government, etc.), and frequently is described in terms of either GROSS NATIONAL PRODUCT or NET NATIONAL PRODUCT. See also INCOME, def. 1; NATIONAL INCOME AND PRODUCT ACCOUNTS.

2. In U.S. Department of Commerce terminology, NET NATIONAL PRODUCT, including all direct

Fig. 57. U.S. national income (in billions of dollars)

Period	National Income	Compensation of Employees[1]	Proprietor's Income with Inventory Valuation and Capital Consumption Adjustments		Rental Income of Persons with Capital Consumption Adjustment	Corporate Profits with Inventory Valuation and Capital Consumption Adjustments					Net Interest
							Profits with Inventory Valuation Adjustment and without Capital Consumption Adjustment				
			Farm	*Non-farm*		*Total*	*Total*	Profits before tax	Inventory valuation adjustment	*Capital Consumption Adjustment*	
1965	566.0	396.5	12.6	44.1	17.1	77.1	73.3	75.2	−1.9	3.8	18.5
1966	622.2	439.3	13.6	46.7	18.2	82.5	78.6	80.7	−2.1	3.9	21.9
1967	655.8	471.9	12.1	48.9	19.4	79.3	75.6	77.3	−1.7	3.7	24.3
1968	714.4	519.8	12.0	51.4	18.6	85.8	82.1	85.6	−3.4	3.7	26.8
1969	767.9	571.4	13.9	52.3	18.1	81.4	77.9	83.4	−5.5	3.5	30.8
1970	798.4	609.2	13.9	51.2	18.6	67.9	66.4	71.5	−5.1	1.5	37.5
1971	858.1	650.3	14.3	53.4	20.1	77.2	76.9	82.0	−5.0	.3	42.8
1972	951.9	715.1	18.0	58.1	21.5	92.1	89.6	96.2	−6.6	2.5	47.0
1973	1,064.6	799.2	32.0	60.4	21.6	99.1	97.2	115.8	−18.6	1.9	52.3
1974	1,135.7	875.8	25.8	61.1	21.0	84.8	87.8	127.6	−39.8	−3.0	67.1
1975	1,207.6	928.8	24.9	65.3	22.4	91.6	103.1	114.5	−11.4	−11.5	74.6
1975: I	1,149.7	904.0	17.9	63.2	21.9	69.0	77.7	94.2	−16.5	−8.6	73.7
II	1,182.7	912.9	24.1	62.7	22.3	86.6	97.9	105.8	−7.8	−11.4	74.0
III	1,233.4	935.2	29.2	66.3	22.4	105.3	117.9	126.9	−9.0	−12.6	74.9
IV	1,264.6	963.1	28.3	69.0	22.9	105.6	119.1	131.3	−12.3	−13.5	75.8
1976: I	1,304.7	994.4	21.9	71.4	23.3	115.1	129.6	141.1	−11.5	−14.5	78.6
II	1,336.3	1,017.2	27.5	72.8	23.1	115.3	130.7	145.3	−14.6	−15.4	80.3

[1]Includes employer contributions for social insurance.
Source: U.S. Department of Commerce.

taxes and corporation income taxes but excluding indirect taxes (excise, sales, etc.).

national income and product accounts A statement of national earnings or output, computed for gross national product, net national product, personal income, and disposable personal income. The value of the goods and services produced are referred to as the *product* side of the account; the costs incurred and type of income earned in producing those goods and services are referred to as the *income* side of the account. The product side is divided into the major markets for the economy's output: consumer purchases, business investment, exports, and government purchases. The income side is made up of wages, salaries and other income, indirect taxes, and capital consumption allowances generated in the production process. Developed gradually since the 1930s, data for these accounts in the United States are now published on a monthly, quarterly, or annual basis and contribute to an understanding of the factors that determine national output, as well as clearly indicating its size and makeup. See also *national income and product accounts budget*, under FEDERAL BUDGET.

nationalism, economic See COLONIALISM; MERCANTILISM.

nationalization Government takeover of an enterprise formerly under private ownership or control. In some countries, nationalization has served principally as a means for eliminating foreign ownership of basic industries, particularly oil and other mineral resources (as in Chile, Venezuela, and Iran). Elsewhere it has provided a means of changing from capitalism to socialism, either suddenly (in the Soviet Union) or gradually (in Great Britain). See also DENATIONALIZATION; PUBLIC OWNERSHIP.

National Labor Relations Act Also, *Wagner Act*. See under LABOR LAWS; also UNFAIR LABOR PRACTICES.

National Labor Relations Board An independent U.S. Federal agency established by the National Labor Relations (Wagner) Act of 1935 to prevent and remedy UNFAIR LABOR PRACTICES by employers and labor unions or their agents, and to conduct secret-ballot elections to determine whether or not employees wish to be represented by a labor union.

National Mediation Board See under MEDIATION.

national product See NATIONAL INCOME; NATIONAL INCOME AND PRODUCT ACCOUNTS.

national rate See under ADVERTISING RATES.

national union See under LABOR UNION.

national wealth The value of a nation's total resources, including both reproducible tangible assets (buildings, machines, inventory) and nonreproducible assets (land, natural resources). Included are all structures (residential, institutional, farm, etc.), all equipment (producer and consumer durables), inventories, and land. The national wealth is one measure of economic growth, particularly when only the reproducible assets are taken into account. For example, U.S. national wealth in terms of reproducible assets increased from $1,024 billion in 1952 to $1,935 billion in 1968 (figures being adjusted for the rate of inflation), representing an annual increase of about 4 per cent during that period.

nation's economic budget See under FEDERAL BUDGET.

natural interest rate See under K. WICKSELL.

natural monopoly A MONOPOLY created by the nature of an enterprise, which is such that competition is self-destructive and contrary to the public interest, so that one firm can, through economy of scale, produce more at lower cost than two or more firms. Examples of natural monopoly abound in the areas of transportation, communications, and public utilities. Two or more railroads competing for the same passengers, or two telephone networks or sets of power lines serving the same area obviously are less efficient than a single one. Owing to their generally public nature, most natural monopolies have been turned into public monopolies and are regulated—if not owned—by the government.

natural order See under PHYSIOCRATS.

natural resources See LAND; also under CONSERVATION.

natural wage See under WAGE.

NC Also, *N/C*. See NUMERICAL CONTROL.

near money Assets that can readily be converted into money (see LIQUID ASSET), in contrast to common stock, houses, or other property subject to rapidly changing market conditions. Examples of near money include savings deposits and U.S. government bonds, which can readily be sold for cash but which themselves cannot be used as a medium of exchange.

negative income tax A form of welfare payment whereby all low-income individuals and families receive a direct cash subsidy from the government that is sufficient to raise them to subsistence level. The subsidy itself is the negative tax. Supporters of this idea, such as Milton FRIEDMAN, argue that it could replace all other welfare programs, along with the bureaucracy and alleged waste they engender. Critics, however, believe it would remove incentives to work, and it is similarly resisted by those who would have to pay the positive income taxes that will support the nonworkers. A version of this idea was put into practice in 1975, when all U.S. social security recipients received a supplementary check for $50, regardless of their income.

negative investment See DISINVESTMENT.

negative utility Same as DISUTILITY.

negotiable instruments Claims or rights to payment that are readily transferable from one person to another, that is, capable of being bought and sold. There are three principal kinds of negotiable instrument: the BILL OF EXCHANGE (or *draft*), CHECK, and PROMISSORY NOTE. A promissory note has two original parties, the *maker* and the *payee*; a

bill of exchange and check both have three, the *drawer, drawee,* and *payee*. In addition, a person who owns a negotiable instrument may transfer it to another person by signing his or her name on the back and delivering it to that person. The signature is called an *endorsement* (or *indorsement*), the signer the *endorser*, and the person to whom it is signed over the *endorsee*. The person in physical possession of an instrument is called the *bearer*. In the United States, according to the *Uniform Negotiable Instruments Law*, an instrument, in order to be negotiable, must be in writing and be signed by the maker or drawer, must contain an unconditional promise or order to pay a specific amount of money, must be payable on demand or at a specified future time, and must be payable to order or to bearer. If it does not meet all these requirements, an instrument is termed *nonnegotiable*. See also under CREDIT, def. 1.

negotiation
1. Dealings between buyer and seller in order to reach agreement on the price, quantity, quality, payment, and other conditions of a sale. Negotiation is an important part of PURCHASING.
2. Dealings between labor and management; see under COLLECTIVE BARGAINING.
3. The transfer of NEGOTIABLE INSTRUMENTS.

neoclassical school Also, *neoclassical synthesis*. A name sometimes used for the economic theories of Alfred MARSHALL and his followers, which combined elements of the classical school with later theory.

neoliberalism A 20th-century version of ECONOMIC LIBERALISM, which is actually a rather conservative concept. The CHICAGO SCHOOL has been called "neoliberal."

neo-Malthusianism See under POPULATION, def. 1.

neomercantilism A term sometimes used for the policies of the United States and other countries during the late 1920s and early 1930s, when, to combat unemployment and deflation, they returned to some of the old mercantilist ideas of raising tariffs on imports, subsidizing exports, imposing import quotas, and other trade restrictions in an attempt to develop an export surplus. See also MER-CANTILISM.

nepotism In business and government, favoritism toward one's family. For example, a woman who controls a company may instruct its purchasing agent to buy, whenever possible, from her brother's firm. Most American business firms frown on nepotism, and many have strict rules forbidding it, but in other parts of the world, particularly in Asia, it is considered inevitable or perhaps even desirable.

net asset See NET WORTH.

net asset value per share See under MUTUAL FUND.

net business formation An index measuring the net number of new businesses formed each month, compiled from data on firms receiving charters of incorporation (which are considerably fewer than the total number of new businesses formed but easier to track down) and data on telephone installations, *minus* the number of business failures. It is an important LEADING INDICATOR of future business conditions, anticipating the general business cycle by some months.

net cash flow See under CASH FLOW.

net change In the securities trade, the difference between the closing price of a stock on any given day and the closing price on the preceding trading day (*not* the difference between the opening and closing prices on the same day). It usually is the last figure in the stock price list appearing in the financial pages of newspapers, where, for example, $+ 1\frac{1}{2}$ means that the stock sold for $1.50 per share more than in the last sale on the previous trading day, or $-\frac{3}{8}$ means it sold for $.375 less per share. If a stock was entitled to a dividend one day but is traded EX DIVIDEND the following day, the dividend is considered in computing the net change. Thus, if the closing price on a Wednesday—the last day it was entitled to receive $1 dividend—was $36 per share and the stock closed at $35 per share on Thursday, the price would be considered un-

changed. The price of a stock selling at $60 the day before a 3-for-1 split and trading on the following day at $20 would likewise be considered unchanged.

net earnings See NET INCOME, def. 1.

net foreign investment The total acquisition of foreign assets by one country's citizens (see INTERNATIONAL INVESTMENT) *minus* the total acquisition of that country's assets by foreign residents. This concept is important in calculating a nation's balance of payments position.

net income
1. Also, *net earnings.* For a business, the difference between total sales and total costs of goods sold plus expenses over a given period, usually a year. If the difference is positive, net income reflects *net profit;* if it is negative, it represents a *net loss.* See also INCOME STATEMENT.
2. For an individual, the difference between gross income and any expenses incurred in earning that income. Such expenses are not taxable and hence may be deducted in computing one's income tax.

net investment See CAPITAL FORMATION.

net lease See under LEASE.

net national debt The sum of debts outstanding of a national government, but not including those of state or local governments or the money owed to government agencies and trust funds. See also PUBLIC DEBT.

net national product Also, *NNP.* The market value of national income, or the total money value of the flow of goods and services of a nation during a given period, usually a year, after deducting capital consumption allowances (the value of capital goods used up during production). In other words, it is GROSS NATIONAL PRODUCT (GNP, or total output) minus depreciation. Net national product is more difficult to calculate than GNP simply because capital consumption allowances are difficult to assess. See Fig. 58, page 286.

Fig. 58. Relation of gross national product, national income, and personal income and saving (in billions of dollars)

Item	1950	1955	1960	1965	1969	1970	1971	1972	1973	1974 (prel.)
Gross national product	**284.8**	**398.0**	**503.7**	**684.9**	**930.3**	**977.1**	**1,054.9**	**1,158.0**	**1,294.9**	**1,397.3**
Less: Capital consumption allowances	18.3	31.5	43.4	59.8	81.6	87.3	93.7	102.9	110.8	119.5
Equals: Net national product	**266.4**	**366.5**	**460.3**	**625.1**	**848.7**	**889.8**	**961.2**	**1,005.1**	**1,184.1**	**1,277.8**
Less: Indirect business tax and nontax liability	23.3	32.1	45.2	62.5	85.9	93.5	102.7	110.0	119.2	126.9
Business transfer payments	.8	1.2	1.9	2.7	3.8	4.0	4.3	4.6	4.9	5.2
Statistical discrepancy	1.5	2.1	−1.0	−3.1	−6.1	−6.4	−2.3	−3.8	−5.0	0
Plus: Subsidies less current surplus of govt. enterprises	.2	−.1	.2	1.3	1.0	1.7	1.1	2.3	.6	−2.9
Equals: National income	**241.1**	**331.0**	**414.5**	**564.3**	**766.0**	**800.5**	**857.7**	**946.5**	**1,065.6**	**1,142.8**
Less: Corporate profits and inventory valuation and adjustment	37.7	46.9	49.9	76.1	79.8	69.2	78.7	92.2	105.1	105.9
Contributions for social insurance	6.9	11.1	20.7	29.6	54.2	57.7	63.8	73.0	91.2	101.5
Wage accruals less disbursements	0	0	0	0	0	0	.6	0	−.1	−.5
Plus: Govt. transfer payments to persons	14.3	16.1	26.6	37.2	61.9	75.1	89.0	98.6	113.0	134.6
Interest paid by govt. (net) and by consumers	7.2	10.1	15.1	20.5	28.7	31.0	31.2	33.0	38.3	42.3
Dividends	8.8	10.5	13.4	19.8	24.3	24.7	25.0	27.3	29.6	32.7
Business transfer payments	.8	1.2	1.9	2.7	3.8	4.0	4.3	4.6	4.9	5.2
Equals: Personal income	**227.6**	**310.9**	**401.0**	**538.9**	**750.9**	**808.3**	**864.0**	**944.9**	**1,055.0**	**1,150.5**
Less: Personal tax and nontax payments	20.7	35.5	50.9	65.7	116.5	116.6	117.6	142.4	151.3	170.8
Equals: Disposable personal income	**206.9**	**275.3**	**350.0**	**473.2**	**634.4**	**691.7**	**746.4**	**802.5**	**903.7**	**979.7**
Less: Personal outlays	193.9	259.5	333.0	444.8	596.2	635.5	685.9	749.9	829.4	902.7
Equals: Personal saving	**13.1**	**15.8**	**17.0**	**28.4**	**38.2**	**56.2**	**60.5**	**52.6**	**74.4**	**77.0**

Source: U.S. Bureau of Economic Analysis.

net price

1. In business, the price actually paid. It also can be viewed as the LIST PRICE minus all discounts and other allowances.

2. In buying and selling securities in the OVER-THE-COUNTER MARKET, the price paid or charged by the dealer to the customer. In effect this is a retail price, since the dealer has presumably bought at a lower ("wholesale") price.

net product

Also, Fr. *net produit.* See under PHYSIOCRATS.

net profit

See under PROFIT, def. 1; also NET INCOME, def. 1.

net weight

For packaged goods, the weight of the items contained in the package, not including the weight of the wrapping material, container, or other packaging. (See also TARE.) For canned goods, especially foods, net weight includes all the liquid as well as the solid material contained in the can or jar.

network advertising

See under SPOT, def. 1.

net worth

In accounting, the excess of assets over liabilities. It thus represents the *equity* of the owners and is synonymous with proprietorship. With a corporation, net worth is the sum of paid-in capital (or the stated value of capital)—including both common and preferred stock—and retained earnings and appropriated surplus; it is sometimes called *stockholders' equity.*

Neumann, John von

See under GAMES THEORY.

new business

See under NET BUSINESS FORMATION.

New Deal A general term for the policies and measures of U.S. President Franklin D. Roosevelt's administration to counteract the disastrous effects of the Great Depression and bring about economic recovery. Coined by Roosevelt in a speech before the Democratic Party convention of 1932, the term embraces such short-term measures as the Emergency Banking Act of 1933 (to prevent hoarding of gold) and the Economy Act (cutting civil service wages and military pensions); various relief programs for the unemployed, ranging from an initial outright dole (Federal Emergency Relief Administration) to a large-scale public works program (Works Progress Administration, or WPA) employing 3.8 million persons in 1935; price supports to farmers; aid for industrial recovery; various forms of social insurance, culminating in the social security program; and large-scale government engineering projects, among them the Tennessee Valley Authority (TVA). Critics of the New Deal deplore the deficit financing it required (the national debt in 1935–36 was twice what it had been in 1928–29) as well as what they consider unwarranted government interference in the economy. Some economists regard the New Deal as the first widespread application of the ideas of J. M. KEYNES, particularly with regard to the use of public spending to make up for lack of private spending. Keynes himself, however, was quite critical of the New Deal, maintaining that its spending did not go far enough to assure full employment.

New Economic Policy Also, *NEP*. See under V. I. LENIN.

New Economics A term used in various ways to describe post-Keynesian economic theory. It is loosely used for the view that full employment with price stability (that is, without excessive inflation) cannot be achieved solely by aggregate fiscal and monetary policies of the kind advocated by J. M. KEYNES and his followers.

new issue See under ISSUE.

new orders See MANUFACTURERS' NEW ORDERS.

new plant and equipment expenditures The total value of private business spending for new plant, machinery, and equipment, an important barometer of general business conditions. Such spending accounts for more than half of all GROSS PRIVATE DOMESTIC INVESTMENT in the United States. The U.S. Department of Commerce compiles data on actual plant and equipment spending for the next two quarters and for the current calendar year, based on surveys of a large sample of firms. Plant and equipment spending is a LAGGING INDICATOR. Businesses tend to plan higher spending at the peak of the business cycle when they are short of capacity. However, many months—or even years—elapse before the plans are translated into real spending, so that plant and equipment spending tends to keep on rising after other business barometers have reached their peak.

New York Curb Exchange See under AMERICAN STOCK EXCHANGE.

New York Stock Exchange Also, *NYSE, Big Board, Wall Street, the Street.* The largest and oldest STOCK EXCHANGE in the United States, located on Wall Street in New York City. In the mid-1970s the securities of more than 1,500 companies were listed on it, and in an average day of trading 16 million shares, worth several hundred million dollars, might change hands. Legally the New York Stock Exchange, like most other exchanges, is a voluntary association of its members (of whom there are 1,366) and is ruled by a board of governors. The number of memberships, called *seats,* has been fixed for some years, so that anyone wishing to buy a seat must find someone else willing to sell. Most of the members are partners or officers of brokerage houses who buy and sell securities on behalf of their customers and charge a commission. A relatively small number—about 30—buy and sell on their own behalf (see FLOOR TRADER).

A typical transaction might take place in this way: Mary Smith of Denver, Colorado, decides to buy 100 shares of common stock in General Steel "at market" (at the current price). She telephones this order to her broker, the Denver office of Merrill Lynch, Pierce, Fenner, & Smith, Inc. (one of the largest American brokerage houses). The Denver office in turn either phones or wires Merrill Lynch in New York or communicates directly with a Merrill Lynch clerk at the New York Stock

Exchange, usually by teletype. The clerk in turn contacts one of the several members from Merrill Lynch who work on the *trading floor* of the exchange, a large room about two-thirds the size of a football field, ringed by booths with clerks, telephones, and teletypes. With Smith's order in hand, the member, also called *floor member* or *floor broker*, walks (running is not permitted) to one of 18 horseshoe-shaped *trading posts* on the floor, the one where General Steel is traded (along with about 74 other stocks). A price indicator at the post lists the price at which General Steel shares sold in the very last transaction (perhaps seconds earlier) as 50, meaning $50 per share. Also at the post are other brokers wanting to execute orders for General Steel. Smith's floor broker, hoping to buy more cheaply than 50, asks for offers. Another broker at the post—the SPECIALIST in that stock—may quote the highest bid so far and the lowest offer so far (the lowest for which anyone will sell), in this case $49\frac{3}{4}$ (bid) and $50\frac{1}{8}$ (offered). Smith's broker then bids 100 shares at $49\frac{7}{8}$, hoping a seller will come down to that price. If a seller suspects $50\frac{1}{8}$ is too high, he may accept the $49\frac{7}{8}$, closing the sale, or he may hold out for at least 50. In practice such decisions are made very quickly, in seconds or a few minutes at the most. As soon as a seller accepts a bid, the transaction is closed. Both buying and selling brokers record the transaction, and an exchange employee sees to it that the price indicator at the trading post is changed accordingly. Also, electronic equipment transmits the information to the TICKER, whence it is carried by wire to tickers in brokerage offices across the nation (or even the world). The actual transfer of the stock and payment for it are not concluded until after the exchange closes for the day (normal hours are 10:00 A.M. to 3:30 P.M., New York time), and then are effected through the STOCK CLEARING CORPORATION.

Although the general procedure described here is typical, stock and bond transactions vary in numerous details. Customers often present brokers with orders to buy or sell on terms other than market orders (see ORDER, def. 1; also LIMIT ORDER). To handle the more complex orders, the New York Stock Exchange specialists each deal in only a few stocks. Another specialized job is that of

the odd-lot broker, who handles small transactions; see ODD LOT, def. 1.

New York Stock Exchange Common Stock Index See under AVERAGE, def. 2.

night shift See under SHIFT, def. 1.

Nobel Memorial Prize in Economic Science An international prize established in 1968 by Riksbank, the Swedish central bank, in celebration of its 300th anniversary as a memorial to Alfred Nobel. First awarded in 1969 (jointly to Ragnar Frisch and Jan Tinbergen), the prize carries the same prestige as the other Nobel Prizes awarded for excellence in physics, chemistry, medicine, and literature and for the advancement of world peace.

no-fault insurance A form of automobile LIABILITY INSURANCE used in only a few states of the United States, which confines liability to personal injury and death and provides little or no compensation for damages to automobiles or other property. In a collision in which no one is injured, for example, the insurers of the drivers involved make no payment whatever, and each owner is responsible for the damage to his or her own car. The major advantage of no-fault insurance is much lower premiums, which, when insurance is legally required, benefits all automobile owners.

no-load fund See under MUTUAL FUND.

nominal price A price quoted for a commodity, security, currency, or other item that has not been actively traded and that therefore has no current market price. Normally a nominal price is based on the most recent market price available, or on the price for a comparable item.

nominal wage Earnings regarded in terms of their face value rather than their purchasing power; see REAL WAGE.

nominal yield See YIELD, def. 4.

nonassessable
1. For insurance, see ASSESSMENT, def. 2.

2. *nonassessable stock.* Stock that is fully paid (that is, the owner has paid the full par value for each share) and therefore cannot be assessed to pay the company's debts should it become insolvent. With the notable exception of most bank stocks, almost all American stocks are nonassessable.

nondiscretionary trust See FIXED INVESTMENT TRUST.

nondurable goods See under CONSUMER GOOD.

nonforfeiture Also, *nonforfeiture option.* A provision in most straight life insurance policies that the equity will not be forfeited if premiums are allowed to lapse. Rather than lose all coverage, as with term insurance, the insured may (1) receive the cash value of the policy, or (2) exchange it for *extended term insurance* for whatever period the paid-up premiums will allow, or (3) exchange it for a reduced PAID-UP INSURANCE policy. If the insured wishes to keep the policy in force, the company may make an *automatic premium loan*, that is, it may borrow from the policy's equity the amount of a missed premium and allow the insured to repay the loan, plus some interest, when he or she has enough cash to do so. See under LIFE INSURANCE for explanation of cash value, etc.

noninstallment credit A loan that need not be repaid in installments but can be repaid in a lump sum (see also INSTALLMENT BUYING).

noninsurable risk See under RISK, def. 3.

nonmember bank In the United States, a bank that is not a member of the FEDERAL RESERVE and hence is regulated by the law of the state in which it is chartered. Since all national banks must belong to the Federal Reserve, nonmember banks are either state or private banks. They do not join the Federal Reserve either because they do not meet the requirements for membership or because they prefer the less stringent regulations of their state, such as being allowed to keep part of their required reserves in the form of interest-bearing bonds. In the mid-1970s nonmember banks comprised about 60 per cent of all American commercial banks, but

they controlled only about 23 per cent of all commercial bank assets.

nonnegotiable instruments See under NEGOTIABLE INSTRUMENTS.

nonprice competition Any attempt by a seller to win more customers through means other than lowering prices, including product differentiation, advertising, packaging, special services, deferred payment plans, etc. See also COMPETITION.

nonproduction Another term for indirect labor or indirect materials; see under LABOR COST; MATERIALS COST.

nonprofit corporation An incorporated organization in which no stockholder or trustee shares in the profits or losses, if any, of the enterprise. Most such corporations are engaged in charitable, educational, humanitarian, or similar activities. Among them are many hospitals, colleges and universities, and foundations. In the United States nonprofit corporations are exempt from corporation income tax but must pay other taxes on any income-yielding property or enterprises they own or undertake.

nonrecourse loan See under AGRICULTURE, AID TO.

nonstock corporation A CORPORATION in which membership, with its rights and liabilities, is acquired through an agreement rather than through ownership of shares of stock. Examples of nonstock corporations include fraternal lodges, mutual companies, and some public corporations.

nonstore retailer See under RETAIL.

no-par stock A STOCK (def. 1) with no set value per share stated on the stock certificate. In practice, no-par stock has an implicit PAR VALUE when it is listed on a company's balance sheet. For example, if a company indicates that it has five million shares of no-par stock and carries it on the balance sheet as $5 million, the implicit stated value per share is $1. The stated value of a no-par stock represents an essentially arbitrary decision. However, whatever is received from the sale of common stock (either in cash or in property) must be carried either as part of the stated value of the stock or as capital surplus. For example, if a company receives $15 million from the sale of one million shares of no-par stock, it may carry the stock at $1 million, leaving $14 million for capital surplus, or it may carry the stock at only $100,000 (10 cents per share), leaving $14.9 million for capital surplus.

normal distribution Also, *normal probability distribution.* A FREQUENCY DISTRIBUTION that is widely used to estimate how often particular events will occur. Deviations from an average or MEAN value often are distributed normally. For example, it is commonly assumed that scores on intelligence tests will be normally distributed about a mean or average score of 100. Industrial processes also tend to fluctuate in a pattern that approximates a normal distribution. For example, if a gray iron casting has an average weight of 1.5 pounds, the weight of castings produced in a particular way may tend to fluctuate between 1.3 and 1.7 pounds with a frequency that is consistent with a normal distribution. In ad-

dition, when values from samples of about 30 or more castings are averaged, the frequency distribution of these sample means automatically follows a normal distribution even if the original distribution was not itself normal. This principle is widely applied in almost every procedure that involves sampling from large populations. Plotted on a graph, a normal distribution is completely symmetrical, with the mean, MEDIAN, and MODE all having the same value. See also CENTRAL LIMIT THEOREM; STANDARD DEVIATION.

no-strike clause See under LABOR CONTRACT.

notary public A licensed public officer whose principal job is attesting or certifying the validity of signatures on certain documents that require such approval. Such a document then bears the notary's signature and seal, indicating that it was signed in his or her presence (but making no claim concerning the content of the document).

note A very general term for any kind of PAPER, that is, acknowledgment of a debt and, by inference, a promise to pay. See BANK NOTE; PROMISSORY NOTE; TREASURY NOTE.

note, Treasury See TREASURY NOTE.

notes payable In accounting, the amount owed by a business to banks or other lenders in the form of short-term loans (coming due in one year or less). On the balance sheet, notes payable are classed as short-term or current liabilities. Notes payable differ from accounts payable in that they represent a written promissory note given by the borrower to the lender and usually require a specific interest payment.

notes receivable The amount owed to a business on promissory notes from customers and other debtors.

NSF check Also, *IF check; insufficient funds.* A check marked "not sufficient funds" because the bank account against which it was drawn does not contain enough cash to cover the check. (Banks do not make partial payment on a check.) A check also may be marked *NF,* or "no funds," meaning the ac-

Fig. 59. Normal distribution

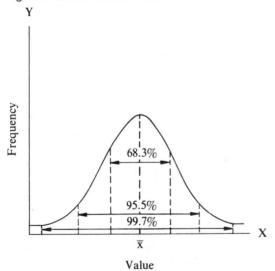

Value

Key: x̄ = mean = mode = median
68.3% = ± 1 σ (σ = standard deviation)
95.5% = ± 2 σ
99.7% = ± 3 σ

count is empty, or *NA*, "no account," meaning the drawer has no account with the bank in question. See also OVERDRAFT.

null hypothesis In statistics, a state of affairs that the analyst sets out to prove or disprove. For example, a null hypothesis might be that at least 20 per cent of all television sets were tuned in to a particular program. The analyst tests the null hypothesis by checking a sample of 1,000 sets to see if they were tuned in and discovers that 205 actually were. If the analyst accepts the null hypothesis based on this decision rule, he or she may be making a *Type II error*, or *beta error*, that is, accepting a false hypothesis. For example, if only 19 per cent of the population were actually tuned in to that program, it would be quite possible to find 205 out of a sample of 1,000 who were tuned in. On the other hand, suppose the sample includes only 150 sets that were tuned in while in fact 20 per cent of all sets in the population were tuned in. With a decision rule calling for 200, the analyst might

reject the null hypothesis; in this case he would be making a *Type I error*, or *alpha error*, that is, rejecting a true hypothesis. In QUALITY CONTROL, it is common practice to plot the probability of making Type II errors for samples and populations with various characteristics; these graphic representations are called *operating characteristic curves*, and complicated versions of them are used in industry.

number account See under ACCOUNT, def. 2.

numerical control Also, *NC, N/C*. Automatic control of production processes, particularly of machine tools such as lathes and milling machines, usually carried out by means of punched or magnetic tapes that contain a series of prerecorded signals sent to electric motors and controls. For example, in a milling operation, a piece of metal may be moved up or down or sideways under a tool, such as a rotary cutter. With numerical control, instead of a human operator controlling the movement of the workpiece, taped electronic signals that activate motors move the bed to which the piece is attached in the required directions. When the operation is completed, the tape is automatically rewound and ready for the next piece of metal to be machined.

Nurkse, Ragnar An Estonian-born economist (1907–59) who studied the problems of underdeveloped nations. Nurkse concluded that poor countries tend to remain poor because of their limited capital formation, investment lagging because real income was too low to create a lucrative market. In order to advance, such countries must turn from the exclusive production of raw materials to producing new manufactured goods, chiefly for home consumption. Also, in order to boost purchasing power, agricultural productivity should simultaneously be increased. Such *balanced growth* will break the vicious circle of poverty and begin an upward spiral of mutual advance and growth. However, in Nurkse's view, this process is not automatic, but one requiring central direction (from the government) or collective action. See also GROWTH, ECONOMIC.

Fig. 60. Null hypothesis

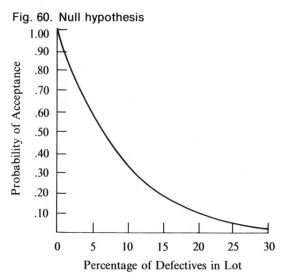

Source: D. S. Ammer, *Manufacturing Management and Control* (New York: Appleton-Century-Crofts, 1968), p. 183. Reprinted by permission of Prentice-Hall, Inc.

objectives, management by Focusing management efforts on the ultimate goals of a business enterprise. The chief goal generally is to make a profit (for private companies; for the nonprofit sector it is not running at a loss). In addition to this basic economic objective, most organizations have goals that, even if seemingly noneconomic, may be basic to their prosperity or even survival. Among them are favorable community relations, good customer service, pleasant working conditions and opportunities for advancement for employees, and technological leadership in their industry. Not only must top management decide what particular goals have priority over others, but frequently it must choose among conflicting goals. Thus, for example, continuity of supply (with no stockouts disrupting production) conflicts directly with high inventory turnover. In practical terms, management by objectives frequently involves setting specific *performance standards* for department heads and other executives directed at attaining the organization's overall goals.

obligation

1. In accounting, any kind of indebtedness.

2. In law, a duty to perform (or not perform) some act, or to pay a sum of money. The person or persons who bind themselves, or are bound, to per-

Fig. 61. Conflicting management objectives

Primary Objective	Other Objectives Adversely Affected
Low prices for purchased items	High inventory turnover, low cost of acquisition and possession, continuity of supply, consistency of quality, favorable relations with suppliers.
High inventory turnover	Low cost of acquisition and possession, low prices for materials purchased, low payroll costs, continuity of supply.
Low cost of acquisition and possession	Low prices for purchased materials, high inventory turnover, good records.
Continuity of supply	Low prices for purchased materials, consistency of quality, favorable relations with suppliers, high inventory turnover.
Consistency of quality	Low prices for purchased materials, continuity of supply, favorable relations with suppliers, low cost of acquisition and possession, high inventory turnover.
Low payroll costs	All other objectives.
Favorable relations with suppliers	Low prices for purchased materials, high inventory turnover, continuity of supply, consistency of quality.
Development of personnel	Low payroll costs.
Good records	Low cost of acquisition and possession, low payroll costs.

Source: D. S. Ammer, *Materials Management*, 3d ed. (Homewood, Ill.: Richard D. Irwin, Inc., 1974), p. 77. Reprinted by permission.

form an obligation are called the *obligor(s)*; the party in whose favor the obligation is assumed (for example, a creditor) is called the *obligee*.

obsolescence A loss in value brought about by a change in design, technology, taste, or demand, rather than by age or wear and tear (see DEPRECIATION, def. 1). See also PLANNED OBSOLESCENCE.

occupational hazard Any danger of accident or disease directly associated with performing a particular kind of work. It includes not only handling dangerous machinery or materials, but also such environmental factors as heat, light, noise, and ventilation. Sometimes the existence of occupational hazards is discovered only after the fact, as, for example, in the case of a number of poisonous and/or cancer-causing substances (asbestos, mercury, vinyl chloride, lead oxide). Sometimes, however, elimination of such a hazard may be so difficult or costly that employers simply ignore it, and occasionally they may even spend considerable sums on publicity denying the existence of the hazardous condition. This, for a long time, was the case with the black-lung disease of coal miners, and in the late 1970s still held true for the gray-lung disease of textile-mill workers. In unionized industries the labor contract frequently spells out work conditions so as to eliminate some—if not all—occupational hazards. The prevalence of such hazards in modern industry has given rise to a new branch of medicine called *industrial medicine*. The Occupational Safety and Health Act of 1970 set up an independent U.S. government agency, the Occupational Safety and Health Review Commission, to reduce occupational hazards, as well as an agency within the U.S. Department of Labor that issues regulations, oversees compliance, and has the power to penalize employers for failure to maintain adequate standards.

occupational mobility See under LABOR MOBILITY.

occupational structure The number and kind of different occupations existing or required in an economy at a given time. Analyses of occupational structure are considered important for planning vocational training programs and for evaluating and promoting general economic growth. The U.S. Bureau of the Census uses an overall classification of WHITE-COLLAR workers, BLUE-COLLAR workers, SERVICE INDUSTRY workers, and farm workers.

odd lot
1. In securities and commodity trading, any amount traded that differs from the conventional unit of trading or a multiple thereof (see ROUND LOT). In the case of stock, an odd lot usually means any number of shares other than 100 or a multiple thereof (200, 300, etc.). On some American stock exchanges trading in odd lots is executed by a special broker called the *odd-lot broker* and, since he or she renders this service to the brokerage firm's floor broker, odd-lot transactions entail both the ordinary brokerage commission plus the odd-lot broker's fee. In reality the odd-lot broker is not a broker but a dealer, who purchases stock in round lots and then makes it available in the various quantities desired. Stock exchanges normally have strict rules governing odd-lot trading. On the New York Stock Exchange the odd-lot broker must fill a MARKET ORDER for any stock at the price that prevails on the very next round-lot transaction after the odd-lot order is received. The odd-lot fee, set by the U.S. Securities and Exchange Commission, is \$.25 ($\frac{1}{4}$ point) per share on stocks sold for \$55 per share or more, and \$.125 ($\frac{1}{8}$ point) per share on stocks selling for less than \$55 per share. (The \$55 figure is called the *break point*.) Odd-lot brokers also will execute a LIMIT ORDER, but only if the price stipulated in the order is sufficient to cover the odd-lot fee. For example, on a limit order for buying at stock at $35\frac{1}{2}$, the broker will not execute the order until the price reaches $35\frac{5}{8}$, in order to get the $\frac{1}{8}$-point fee. On Canadian stock exchanges odd lots are not handled by special brokers but are subject to separate bargaining between two or more floor brokers. Normally, however, the price they reach is somewhat higher than that for round lots.
2. In business, same as BROKEN LOT.

off-board security See UNLISTED SECURITY; also OVER-THE-COUNTER MARKET.

offer
1. The terms and conditions presented in a po-

tential contract by one party, called the *offeror*, to another party, called the *offeree*. In order for the agreement to be binding, the offeree must first accept it; otherwise there is no legal contract.

2. In investment, a term sometimes used to mean the same as "ask" or "asked," that is, the price asked by the seller (see ASK, def. 2). However, it is more commonly used to describe the ISSUE of new securities, also called an *offering*.

3. For *tender offer*, see TENDER, def. 2.

officer In a corporation, any of several top management positions, as specified in the corporation's charter. Most corporations have a president, secretary, treasurer, and one or more vice-presidents. These officers normally are appointed by the board of directors, which acts for the owners (stockholders).

official exchange rate See under EXCHANGE RATE.

off-line

1. Describing a computer system that does not process input data as they are received but stores and processes them at some later time, as in BATCH PROCESSING (def. 1). See also ON-LINE, def. 1.

2. In a computer, auxiliary equipment, input-output devices, etc. that do not operate under direct control of the central processing unit; also, a piece of peripheral equipment not directly linked to a computer. See also ON-LINE, def. 2.

offshore The ocean waters and bottom within a given distance from a nation's borders, which may be leased or sold to individuals, companies, or other nations. The discovery of oil and the ability to extract it and natural gas from offshore sites have brought offshore purchases and leases to worldwide prominence. Centuries older, and just as important, are the rights to fish in offshore waters. In general, nations set a limit beyond which they lay no claim to possession of the ocean. In the 1970s the U.S. 12-mile limit was changed to 200 miles owing to the depletion of fish within those limits and widespread fishing by other nations just outside it. As a rule, the right to waters and ocean bottom belongs to the national government. In the United States, however,

such ownership, particularly the right to offshore oil wells in the Gulf of Mexico, has in part been relinquished to individual states. Since offshore drilling began, the worldwide allocation of natural resources has started to shift, in some cases drastically. The United States already had a land-based petroleum industry, but for countries such as Great Britain and Norway, which had no oil before the beginning of drilling in the North Sea, the impact was expected to be much greater. In the 1970s, offshore exploration for metals—nickel, copper, and others—was also begun.

of record Referring to stockholders as recorded on a company's books on a certain date, entitling them to a particular dividend. See RECORD DATE.

old-age pension See PENSION; SOCIAL SECURITY.

oligopoly, oligopsony Control over most of the output of a particular product or service by a small number of sellers (*oligopolists*) or buyers (*oligopsonists*). While not as restrictive of competition as either MONOPOLY or DUOPOLY, since each seller must consider the actions of all other sellers before determining price and output, oligopolies nevertheless tend to set higher prices than presumably would result from pure competition. Although in the United States antitrust legislation and other government regulation prevent collusion in price-setting, the prices in oligopolistic industries tend to be very closely matched. For example, in the American auto industry, controlled by three large firms, the prices for comparable lines of car from supposedly competing manufacturers—Ford, Chevrolet, and Plymouth—vary by only 2 or 3 per cent. Other oligopolistic American products include aluminum, steel, petroleum, computers, synthetic fibers, soap and detergents, breakfast cereals, chewing gum, and light bulbs. There may be considerable competition among the producers of consumer goods, largely in the form of product differentiation through styling, marketing, and advertising, which may be maintained even between products of the same manufacturer. For example, the General Foods Corporation markets several highly advertised, competing brands of coffee. In general, the trend in many industrialized nations, including the United States, has been toward more and more oligopoly.

Oligopsony is more common than either monopsony or duopsony; many markets are dominated by a few big buyers. Sometimes the market is made up of many small producers selling to a few big buyers (for example, small tobacco growers selling to large cigarette companies), who use their bargaining power to cut prices. In other markets a few big buyers purchase from a small group of sellers (as with sheet-steel manufacturers selling to automobile makers), in which case the two sides are more evenly matched. See also CARTEL; IMPERFECT COMPETITION.

omnibus clause A clause in LIABILITY INSURANCE policies whereby persons other than the policyholder are covered under prescribed conditions. For example, automobile liability insurance policies often contain a clause that extends coverage to another person who is driving the car with the owner's permission.

100 per cent reserve plan See under BANK RESERVES; also under I. FISHER.

on-line
1. Describing a computer system in which input data are processed as received and output data are transmitted as soon as they become available to the point where they are required. See also OFF-LINE, def. 1; REAL-TIME.
2. In a computer, auxiliary equipment, input-output devices, etc. that operate under direct control of the central processing unit (see under COMPUTER for explanation). See also OFF-LINE, def. 2.

on-the-job training Learning how to perform a given kind of work while actually employed to do it. It may involve nothing more than a departing file clerk showing his or her successor where various files are kept, or a foreman showing a new worker how to use a certain machine, or it may mean weeks or even months of study, direct supervision, and a variety of learning programs. The U.S. Department of Labor's Office of Manpower Development Programs includes a special National On-the-Job Training program whereby contracts

are made with trade associations, labor unions, and industrial corporations for training unemployed or underemployed workers.

OPEC Abbreviation for *Organization of Petroleum Exporting Countries;* see under CARTEL.

open account In accounting, an unsecured amount that is owing or owed (through buying or selling on credit).

open bid See under BID, def. 1.

open corporation A CORPORATION whose stock is available for sale to the general public, which owns substantial amounts of it. See also CLOSED CORPORATION.

open credit Credit extended by a bank or business so that a borrower or customer may make withdrawals (write checks) or purchase goods up to a certain amount, without either putting up collateral or paying cash. Sometimes the amount is determined by payments made on prior accounts; this practice is called *revolving credit.* A similar arrangement is the revolving CHARGE ACCOUNT.

open-door policy A policy designed to maintain free and equal commercial opportunities for all nations in a particular area or country. Specifically, the term refers to a policy stated by U.S. Secretary of State John Hay in 1899 with regard to the great powers trading in the Far East. After the Chinese-Japanese War of 1895, when victorious Japan annexed Formosa (now Taiwan) and made Korea a sphere of influence, France, Germany, Russia, and Great Britain, all eager to create spheres of influence of their own, demanded long-term leases on important Chinese ports. Hay requested that each nation uphold existing treaties and established interests in its sphere of influence, that no preferential or discriminatory treatment be used toward any business of any nation operating in the Far East, and that the Chinese continue to collect their own tariffs. Though no nation explicitly agreed to follow Hay's formula (based on an originally British proposal), he reaffirmed it after the Boxer Rebellion (in which Chinese nationalists rose up against foreign incursion), maintaining that the rebellion must not serve as an excuse for annexing more Chinese territory.

open-end contract A contract in which some of the terms remain unspecified, or open. Thus, a sales contract for goods might deliberately omit the quantity involved, permitting an unlimited amount to be purchased at the price stated, or a contract might call for the "price in effect at time of delivery," allowing the seller to charge the prevailing market price.

open-end investment company See MUTUAL FUND.

open-end mortgage See under MORTGAGE.

open-field system A system of farming widely used in western Europe during the Middle Ages. The arable land of each large estate, owned by a nobleman and worked by peasants, was divided into narrow strips and so apportioned that each peasant had some good land to work and some poor. Thus one man often had to cultivate widely scattered strips of land. Further, crops were rotated according to a three-field system, so that every year one-third of a field was planted in autumn, one-third in spring, and the remainder left fallow. Thus one-third of the best soil was always idle, a practical system that prevented the soil from being exhausted (fertilizer was not then used). Also, without machinery, a peasant could cultivate only a limited amount of land. See also MANORIAL SYSTEM.

opening price The price at which a security sells when trading opens for the day, which is not necessarily the same as the closing (last) price of the previous day. The SPECIALIST opens stock trading at a price where current supply and demand can match, often adding to or subtracting from his or her own inventory for this purpose. This price obviously can be different from the previous day's close.

open listing See under LISTING.

open-market operations Buying and selling government securities on the open market by a central bank in order to implement MONETARY POLICY.

In the United States this activity is carried on by the Federal Reserve banks and represents the most effective influence they have on BANK RESERVES. Federal Reserve purchasing of securities, mostly short-term Treasury bills, expands reserves (and hence the money supply); selling securities contracts reserves. For example, suppose the Federal Reserve buys $3 billion worth of Treasury bills from dealers. It pays for them by writing a check on itself to the dealer, who in turn may write a check to the banks or insurance companies from which the bills were purchased. The proceeds are deposited in a number of commercial banks, creating new deposits and thus expanding by $3 billion (less the required reserve) the amount of money those banks may now lend to borrowers. Open-market operations are controlled by the Federal Open Market Committee and are usually confined to short-term government securities—called a *bills-only policy*—which are very actively traded in the MONEY MARKET and are more like cash than any other instrument of credit (and, indeed, are widely used as operating or secondary reserves by commercial banks, insurance companies, and other lending institutions). See also REPURCHASE AGREEMENT.

open mortgage See under MORTGAGE.

open order
1. In the securities trade, a valid order to buy or sell a security that has not yet been executed.
2. In business, same as BACK ORDER.

open shop A business open on equal terms to both union and nonunion employees. Unless the union members constitute a majority of the employees, no collective bargaining takes place and no union contract is signed. If a majority want the union, the shop becomes unionized and the union becomes the workers' bargaining agent. Until the 1930s, in the United States an open shop was in effect a nonunion shop closed to union members, as defined by groups such as the National Association of Manufacturers, and consequently organized labor has remained suspicious of it.

open stock See under CLOSED STOCK.

open union See under CLOSED UNION.

operating characteristic curve See under NULL HYPOTHESIS.

operating cost Also, *operating expense*. In accounting, any expense incurred by a firm in carrying on its ordinary major activities. Nonoperating expenses, on the other hand, consist chiefly of reserve funds for paying taxes, interest on bonds, and other expenses connected with finance. The difference between its gross profit and operating costs constitutes a firm's *operating profit* (or *loss*).

operating profit Also, *operating income*. See under OPERATING COST; also PROFIT, def. 1.

operating rate Also, *capacity utilization rate*. The ratio of actual physical output to potential production, that is, the proportion of output of current operations to output at full capacity. Data on the operating rate for major manufacturing industries are useful for short-term forecasting of business conditions and, since they tend to correlate closely to profits, for estimating future profits. The chief drawback of the operating rate as an INDICATOR is the problem of defining capacity, which varies not only from industry to industry but from one firm to another. In addition, individual firms frequently find it difficult to estimate their operating rate since production often can be expanded substantially (at extra cost) through overtime and subcontracting.

operating ratio In finance, a way of measuring a company's success, derived from dividing various income-statement items by net sales, or by calculating earnings per share, or some other way. (See under INCOME STATEMENT for several examples.) Such calculations are used principally by prospective investors.

operating statement See INCOME STATEMENT.

operating system See under PROGRAMMING.

operations research Also, *operations analysis*, Brit. *operational research*. The use of quantitative techniques for solving problems related to the operating of some unit (in business, government, the armed forces, etc.). Tracing its modern-time beginnings to World War I and greatly expanded during World War II, operations research today remains a tool for decision-makers seeking to choose the best of available alternatives in a rational way. It consists chiefly of accumulating and interpreting the appropriate data, building one or more MODELS, experimenting with the models by altering any or all the possible variables, and ultimately making recommendations concerning future operations. Since its original wartime applications, it has been increasingly used in such areas of business as production and inventory control, transportation, and scheduling. Operations research traditionally involves an interdisciplinary team effort, whereby the expertise of numerous specialists is brought to bear on the problem at hand. Associated with operations research, which essentially tries to quantify the issues, is a wide variety of mathematical and engineering techniques, such as Bayesian decision theory, input-output analysis, linear programming, queuing theory, PERT, and Monte Carlo simulations. See also SYSTEMS ANALYSIS.

opportunity cost Also, *alternative cost*. The most favorable price that a factor of production (land, labor, or capital) can command. For example, if land now used to grow wheat can be subdivided for housing units that will yield more annual rent than the best year's harvest can earn, that rent is considered the land's opportunity cost, and any farmer working it is bound to "lose" money on it. In business, opportunity cost is a valuable tool for determining whether or not to invest in additional fixed assets or inventory. An investment is worthwhile provided it promises to earn at least the opportunity cost—the return available from an alternative investment. This may be as little as 5 per cent (the rate of return on short-term securities or savings bank deposits) or as much as 50 per cent or more in a company pressed for cash or with many profitable investment opportunities.

optimist See under H. C. CAREY.

optimum lot size See ECONOMIC ORDER QUANTITY.

optimum tariff See under TARIFF, def. 1.

option

1. Also, *option contract.* In business law, a binding promise to keep open a specific OFFER (def. 1) for a given period of time. If, in exchange for an option, the offeror has received consideration (payment), he or she may not revoke the offer within that period. Options are frequently combined with leases of real or personal property. For example, a tenant may rent a building for three years with an option to buy the building at a given price at the end of the rental period.

2. In investment, the right to buy or sell a specific security or commodity within a specified time at a fixed price. (See also CALL; OPTIONS EXCHANGE; PUT; STRADDLE, def. 1) Stock options are used by some employers as a form of compensation; the employee is given an option to buy the firm's stock at a fixed price—usually the market price that prevails at the time the option is granted—for a given period, for example, within the next ten years. In effect this practice is a form of PROFIT SHARING, since it is tied to the company's future development. See also RIGHTS; WARRANT, def. 1.

3. In life insurance, the choices available when required premium payments are discontinued. See under NONFORFEITURE.

optional bond   See under BOND, def. 1.

optional dividend   See under DIVIDEND, def. 1.

options exchange   An organized market for trading in stock option contracts (see OPTION, def. 2). The first such exchange in the United States was the Chicago Board Options Exchange, established in 1972. Originally dealing exclusively in calls, it expected later to begin handling puts (see CALL; PUT). By 1975 options trading also took place on the American Stock Exchange and the PBW (Philadelphia-Baltimore-Washington) Exchange. Trading in options listed on an exchange differs in some respects from open-market operations. On an exchange, both striking prices (the price at which an option is to be exercised) and expiration dates (the last date on which it may be exercised) are standardized. Expiration dates are set so that every option expires on the Saturday immediately following the third Friday of a given contract month. Further, cash dividends have no effect on striking prices, being paid (during the life of an option) only to the seller.

Here is a typical transaction: Lee Jones decides to buy a call option, called *ABC Mining April 50*, meaning that she decides to buy 100 shares of ABC Mining Corporation at $50 per share any time up to the Saturday following the third Friday of April (she hopes, of course, that the market price of ABC Mining will by then be higher than $50, so that she will get a "bargain"). The price she will have to pay for this call, the *premium*, is determined in the auction on the floor of the exchange, much as the price of stocks is determined (see under NEW YORK STOCK EXCHANGE for a description). Bids and offers for ABC Mining April 50 come to the floor, where specific registered persons, equivalent to the stock market's SPECIALIST, make markets in the options they handle. Suppose that on February 1 ABC Mining sells in the open market at $53 per share, and on March 1 it sells at $48. If Jones buys her call on February 1, she probably would have to pay more than she would a month later. Assume that she pays $600 on March 1. Suppose that the stock on the open market continues to decline, and Jones does not think it will recover by April 30. She might try to sell it to someone who thinks otherwise. The price she got would depend both on the market price of ABC and the time remaining before expiration. But even if she got only $300, her loss would be cut to $300 (if she waited until the option expired and ABC then cost $42, she might lose the entire $600). On the other hand, if ABC Mining rose, the value of her option would also rise, and she might be able to sell it for as much as $1,000, making a profit of $400 (or 66.67 per cent) in a month's time. Or, believing that the stock would rise a good deal higher still, Jones might exercise her call on the April expiration date and actually purchase the 100 shares of ABC Mining on which she had an option. See also Fig. 62.

oral agreement   See under CONTRACT.

order

1. In the securities trade, an instruction to a broker to buy or sell given securities. The two main kinds of order are the MARKET ORDER and LIMIT ORDER. See also STOP ORDER.

2. In business and trade, a request to deliver,

Fig. 62. Options quotations (partial listing)

Chicago Board

Option &	price	— Oct — Vol.	Last	— Jan — Vol.	Last	— Apr — Vol.	Last	N.Y. Close
Alcoa	... 45	4	15½	a	a	b	b	59⅞
Alcoa	... 50	3	10	5	10¾	a	a	59⅞
Alcoa	... 55	11	5½	21	7⅛	b	b	59⅞
Alcoa	60	41	1½	39	3¾	5	5	59⅞
Am Tel	..50	6	11⅝	2	11¾	b	b	61⅝
Am Tel	..55	54	6⅞	16	7¼	17	7½	61⅝
Am Tel	..60	846	1¾	218	2½	48	3¼	61⅝
Atl R	... 40	16	16¼	a	a	b	b	56
Atl R	... 45	121	11¼	56	11⅞	a	a	56
Atl R	50	185	6⅛	86	6⅞	133	8½	56
Atl R	... 60	b	b	150	1⅝	65	2½	56
Avon	35	22	14	b	b	b	b	48⅝
Avon	 40	116	9	75	9⅞	b	b	48⅝
Avon	 45	250	4⅛	80	6	24	7¼	48⅝
Avon	 50	664	⅞	619	2 15-16	134	4⅛	48⅝
BankAm	.25	2	¾	21	1⅞	41	2¼	24⅞
BankAm	.30	a	a	2	⅜	7	11-16	24⅞
Beth S	.. 35	3	7⅛	b	b	b	b	41¾
Beth S	.. 40	60	2⅜	6	3½	20	4⅜	41¾
Beth S	.. 45	35	3-16	84	1⅛	13	1½	41¾
Bruns	10	1	6¾	4	6⅞	b	b	16⅞
Bruns	... 15	129	1⅞	91	2¾	55	3⅛	16⅞
Bruns	... 20	105	1-16	71	9-16	26	1	16⅞
Burl N	.. 40	2	4⅝	10	5⅞	a	a	44¼
Burl N	.. 45	44	⅞	18	2⅝	1	3⅝	44¼
Burl N	.. 50	a	a	27	⅞	10	1⅝	44¼
Citicp	... 30	70	3	22	3¾	27	4¾	33
Citicp	... 35	348	3-16	115	1⅛	52	1 15-16	33
Citicp	... 40	20	1-16	52	¼	89	11-16	33
Delta	 35	a	a	4	6⅜	a	a	40¾
Delta	... 40	37	1⅜	2	3	15	4	40¾
Delta	... 45	69	3-16	37	1 1-16	24	1 9-16	40¾
Dow Ch	. 45	292	1 13-16	149	3⅝	2	4⅞	46
Dow Ch	. 50	212	¼	72	1 7-16	72	2⅜	46
Dow Ch	..55	a	a	85	7-16	b	b	46
Ess Kd	..90	774	3⅝	257	7⅛	32	9	91½
Eas Kd	.100	170	¼	751	2¾	103	4⅝	91½
Eas Kd	.110	8	1-16	439	¾	22	2	91½
Eas Kd	.120	50	1-16	1	¼	b	b	91½
Exxon	.. 45	10	11⅛	12	11¼	b	b	55¾
Exxon	.. 50	96	6¼	17	6⅜	12	7	55¾
Exxon	.. 55	327	1⅝	240	2 15-16	42	4	55¾

Pacific Exchange

Option &	price	— Oct — Vol.	Last	— Jan — Vol.	Last	— Apr — Vol.	Last	N.Y. Close
BankAm	.25	a	a	55	1¾	78	2 3-16	24⅞
BankAm	.30	a	a	10	¼	2	¾	24⅞
Clorox	.. 15	a	a	5	5-16	10	⅝	12¾
Cr Zel	... 40	a	a	2	2¼	a	a	40½
Cr Zel	.. 45	14	1-16	a	a	14	1¾	40½
D Sham	. 70	14	⅞	10	3½	a	a	69
D Sham	. 80	b	b	12	1	10	2	69
Disney	...45	b	b	1	7½	16	8⅝	48⅝
Disney	.. 50	40	1⅜	27	4	6	5⅝	48⅝
Disney	...60	a	a	20	15-16	3	2¼	48⅝
Levi	20	43	1⅝	14	2⅝	11	3¼	21⅜
Levi	.. 22½	76	⅜	35	1¼	1	2⅛	21⅜
Levi	25	52	⅛	51	9-16	b	b	21⅜
Merril	.. 20	54	6	18	6¾	a	a	25¾
Merril	.. 25	115	1½	5	3	6	3¾	25¾
Merril	.. 30	75	⅛	55	1 1-16	18	1 11-16	25¾
N C R	.. 30	3	5⅞	a	a	a	a	35⅞
N C R	.. 35	5	1⅝	a	a	a	a	35⅞
Polar	... 35	65	9⅛	2	9⅛	a	a	44
Polar	40	475	4⅛	72	6	14	7⅜	44
Polar	... 45	b	b	131	3	32	4⅜	44
R C A	.. 25	5	3⅜	a	a	a	a	28¼
R C A	...30	79	5-16	16	1 5-16	12	2 1-16	28¼
Sambos	..15	45	5-16	107	1 3-16	86	1⅝	14¾
Sambos	..20	20	1-16	10	3-16	34	7-16	14¾
San Fe	.. 30	18	7⅞	43	8¼	a	a	37¾
San Fe	..35	148	2¾	53	4⅜	20	5½	37¾
San Fe	.. 40	b	b	40	1¾	36	2¾	37¾
Un Oil	.. 45	80	8⅜	a	a	b	b	53⅛
Un Oil	...50	113	3⅜	21	4⅝	59	5½	53⅛
Un Oil	...60	10	1-16	15	⅝	b	b	53⅛
U S St	.. 50	5	2¼	a	a	a	a	51¾
		— Nov —		— Feb —		— May —		
A B C	... 30	a	a	1	6½	b	b	35⅛
A B C	...35	35	2	28	3¼	6	4	35⅛
A B C	...40	1	⅜	25	1⅜	3	2	35⅛
F Stor	.. 45	12	2½	2	3½	a	a	46¾
Mc D D	. 20	a	a	2	5⅝	a	a	23¾
Mc D D	25	7	¾	11	1¾	4	2¼	23¾
Scher	... 50	8	5¼	30	6¼	a	a	54¾
Scher	... 60	47	½	65	1 13-16	a	a	54¾
Travel	.. 30	a	a	6	7¾	b	b	37⅛
Travel	.. 35	a	a	4	3⅞	a	a	37⅛

American Exchange

Option &	price	— Oct — Vol.	Last	— Jan — Vol.	Last	— Apr — Vol.	Last	N.Y. Close
Aetna	... 25	58	9⅜	4	10	2	10	34⅜
Aetna	... 30	205	4½	45	5¼	19	5⅞	34⅜
Aetna	... 35	160	⅝	97	1 15-16	38	2⅞	34⅜
Am Cya	25	55	2 7-16	16	3	17	3⅝	27⅝
Am Cya	30	152	1-16	6	½	15	⅞	27⅝
Am Hom	30	2	5½	2	6	a	a	35¼
Am Hom	35	171	1	100	2¼	10	2⅞	35¼
Am Hom	40	3	1-16	103	⅝	45	1 1-16	35¼
Asarco	...15	25	1⅜	a	a	35	2⅝	16½
Asarco	...20	a	a	19	5-16	33	11-16	16½
Beat F	.. 25	43	2⅝	11	3	a	a	27¾
Beat F	..30	8	1-16	22	9-16	15	15-16	27¾
Burrgh	..90	232	5⅞	27	9	15	11¼	95
Burrgh	100	246	11-16	91	3¾	49	6	95
Burrgh	. 110	a	a	86	1	28	2¼	95
Chase	25	30	4½	13	4⅞	b	b	29½
Chase	... 30	80	7-16	86	1¼	27	1¾	29½
Chase	35	a	a	a	a	28	½	29½
C Tel	... 10	a	a	1	5⅛	3	5¼	15⅜
C Tel	15	259	¼	91	13-16	72	1⅛	15⅜
Deere	25	2	7⅛	b	b	b	b	32¼
Deere	30	48	2¾	97	4	a	a	32¼
Deere	... 35	16	3-16	141	1¼	21	1⅞	32¼
Dig Eq	150	587	12	47	19⅝	8	24½	159½
Dig Eq	160	1151	5	180	13	25	18	159½
Dig Eq	170	562	1⅜	97	8¼	33	12½	159½
Dig Eq	180	512	¼	650	4⅜	46	8½	159½

Philadelphia Exchange

Option &	price	— Oct — Vol.	Last	— Jan — Vol.	Last	— Apr — Vol.	Last	N.Y. Close
Alld C	...40	1	⅝	10	2¼	7	3⅛	39⅝
AllisC	... 25	27	2¼	21	4	13	5¼	26⅝
AllisC	... 30	60	¼	104	1½	192	2	26⅝
Branif	.. 10	8	1⅝	21	2⅛	38	2½	11½
Branif	.. 15	11	1-16	40	5-16	19	⅝	11½
Clorox	.. 10	24	2¾	a	a	19	3½	12¾
Clorox	.. 15	a	a	44	⅜	92	9-16	12¾
Comsat	..25	3	4⅝	6	5⅜	a	a	29½
Comsat	..30	24	¾	40	2 1-16	9	2⅝	29½
Cont O	.. 35	43	3⅛	6	4⅝	6	4¾	38⅛
Cont O	.. 40	158	¼	58	1⅜	6	2⅛	38⅛
Dressr	.. 40	a	a	2	5¾	a	a	43⅝
Dressr	...45	5	⅞	2	2½	2	3¾	43⅝
Engl M	..25	2	9¼	a	a	b	b	34⅛
Engl M	..35	63	⅜	8	1⅝	a	a	34⅛
G A F	...15	4	¼	5	¾	22	1⅛	14⅜
GeoPac	..35	2	½	a	a	a	a	33½
How Jn	. 10	12	1⅝	16	2⅜	2	2¾	11⅝
How Jn	. 15	22	1-16	13	⅜	40	9-16	11⅝
Scot P	...20	84	⅝	72	1½	1	2	20⅜
Scot P	.. 25	a	a	10	¼	b	b	20⅜
Teldyn	29⅛	2	47	b	b	b	b	75½
Teldyn	38⅞	4	37⅜	b	b	b	b	75½
Teldyn	...45	8	30¾	1	31	b	b	75½
Teldyn	48½	3	28	b	b	b	b	75½
Teldyn	...50	19	25¾	2	25⅛	b	b	75½
Teldyn	...60	158	16½	13	18¾	b	b	75½

Closing prices of all options. Sales unit usually is 100 shares. Security description includes exercise price. Stock close is New York Stock Exchange final price.

Source: Wall Street Journal, September 26, 1976.

sell, receive, or buy certain goods or services. The person or firm giving such an order is thereby committed to receiving the goods or services delivered as a result of the order. See also BACK ORDER; BLANKET ORDER; PURCHASE ORDER.

3. On negotiable instruments (checks, bills of exchange, etc.), an indication describing the payee, that is, the person or firm to whom payment is to be made. It usually appears as "To the order of JOHN DOE, INC.," either on the face of the instrument or in an ENDORSEMENT (def. 1).

order cost system See JOB ORDER SYSTEM.

order-point control Also, *max-min system.* Any system of inventory control in which material is ordered when stocks drop to a predetermined level, called the *order point*, which is presumably equal to the amount that will be needed until stocks can be replenished, plus a little extra for safety (the so-called SAFETY STOCK). Both the two-bin and perpetual inventory systems are of this type. The maximum (*max*) inventory occurs just after a new order

Fig. 63. Order-point control

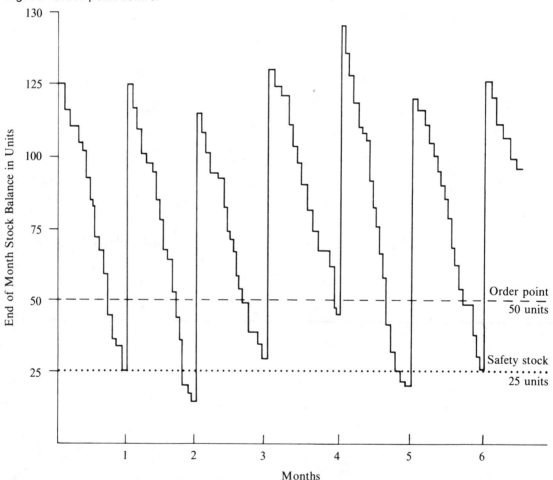

Source: D. S. Ammer, *Purchasing and Materials Management for Health Care Institutions* (Lexington, Mass.: D. C. Heath & Co., 1975), p. 96. Reprinted by permission.

of stock is received and is equal, on the average, to the order quantity plus the safety stock. The average minimum (*min*) quantity is equal to the safety stock. One problem in any such system is determining the order point. If the order point is too low, there is danger of stockouts that can delay production; if it is too high, too much capital is invested in inventories. The validity of any order-point calculation, no matter how sophisticated a statistical technique used, will depend to a large extent on how well one can predict both lead time (for replacing stock) and usage. In cases where one or both fluctuate considerably and unpredictably, PERIODIC ORDERING may be preferable. Order-point control systems are used in almost all retail and wholesale operations, as well as by most non-mass-production manufacturing firms.

order quantity The amount of any material or item being ordered, which is influenced both by its price and by the company's ordering and carrying costs. See ECONOMIC ORDER QUANTITY.

ordinal utility See under UTILITY, def. 2.

ordinary life insurance See under LIFE INSURANCE.

organization, company The apportionment of authority and responsibility among the employees of a business. There are three basic patterns of organization. In the first and oldest, called *line organization*, a single manager exercises final authority, either directly over the production workers or over several foremen or supervisors (representing *middle management*) who in turn directly supervise workers. In the second, *functional organization*, every employee who performs a particular kind of work (function) is regarded as a discrete division. Thus there is a direct line of authority from the controller to every accountant, from the electrical supervisor to every electrician, and so on. The third kind, called *line and staff organization*, is a compromise between the *centralization* of line structure and the *decentralization* of functional organization. The flow of authority proceeds mostly along fixed channels, as in line organization, but specialists in particular functions (such as purchasing, sales, accounting, etc.) are used in *staff* positions, where they advise the *line* officers, that is, those concerned with actual production (and, depending on the nature of the business, distribution). In addition to organizing so as to allocate authority, large companies—or companies producing a large variety of items—may need to decentralize in some other way, usually *by location* (with each plant to some extent running itself), or by *product* or *project* (with each division manufacturing one or a group of products being treated to some extent as a separate company), or by *stage of manufacture* (with each major stage of a production process to some extent running itself). See Fig. 64, page 302; see also SPAN OF CONTROL.

Organization of American States Also, *OAS*. An international organization made up of 24 independent nations of the western hemisphere; founded in 1948, it absorbed an earlier agency, the *Pan-American Union*. Its purposes are to maintain peace and security and provide common action against aggression, to help solve the political and economic problems of its members, and through cooperation to promote their economic, social, and cultural development. For the last purpose, three special agencies were set up, among them the *Inter-American Economic and Social Council*.

Organization for Economic Cooperation and Development Also, *OECD*. A 24-member international, intergovernmental agency founded in 1961 to promote policies leading to optimum economic growth, employment, and living standards in member countries, while maintaining financial stability and thus contributing to the development of the world economy, to economic expansion in both member and nonmember countries, and to expanded world trade. Replacing the Organization for European Economic Cooperation (OEEC) that implemented the European Recovery Program (Marshall Plan), the OECD reviews economic problems of members, conducts research, and issues publications. It also has served as a forum for discussions of international monetary problems and for promoting aid to underdeveloped countries. Its members include 19 European nations, Canada, the United States, Japan, Australia, and New

Zealand. Yugoslavia also participates in some OECD activities.

Organization for European Economic Cooperation Also, *OEEC*. See under EUROPEAN RECOVERY PROGRAM; ORGANIZATION FOR ECONOMIC COOPERATION AND DEVELOPMENT.

Organization of Petroleum Exporting Countries Also, *OPEC*. See under CARTEL.

organized labor See under LABOR UNION.

original cost
1. In inventory valuation, basing the value of

Fig. 64. Types of company organization

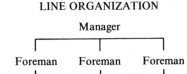
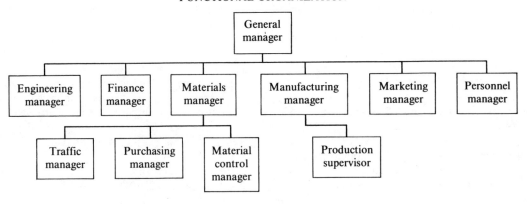
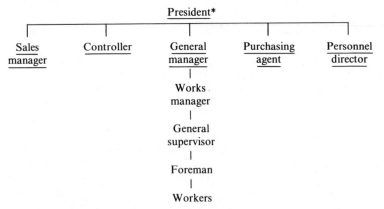

*Underscored positions are staff positions; others are line positions.

purchased items on their cost at the time of purchase. See FIRST-IN, FIRST-OUT.

2. In public utility accounting, the cost of a property at the time of its initial acquisition by the public utility, used to establish the rate to be charged in order to get a fair return on capital. This method is still widely used by telephone and electric power companies as well as by railroads.

original entry In accounting, the first recording of any transaction in what is sometimes called a *book of original entry*. See also JOURNAL.

Ottawa Agreements See under TARIFF, def. 1.

Outer Seven See under EUROPEAN FREE TRADE ASSOCIATION.

outlay An EXPENDITURE, particularly a cash expenditure, or the incurring of a liability to pay cash. Also, the transfer of property in exchange for goods or services. For capital outlay, see CAPITAL EXPENDITURE.

outlet store A retail store that specializes in selling low-priced overstocked goods, discontinued lines, obsolete merchandise, or distressed goods (inventories seized for nonpayment).

out-of-pocket cost In accounting, an expense that requires a current outlay of cash, such as wages, power bills, supplies, or taxes. See also SUNK COST.

output

1. As presented by a COMPUTER, the results of its operations.

2. Any good or service produced by a business; an end-product. Also, the total value of such goods or services, for an individual, firm, industry, nation, etc.

output per man-hour See under PRODUCTIVITY.

outside price See under INSIDE PRICE.

outstanding

1. In accounting, banking, and finance, a term meaning "uncollected" or "unpaid," applied prin-

cipally to accounts and notes receivable or payable, bank checks that have been sent but not yet cleared, and similar obligations.

2. Describing securities issued to the public and currently in public hands.

overbought

1. A term describing the market as a whole, or a particular security, in the belief that vigorous buying has driven up prices, or its price, to an unreasonably high level. See also OVERSOLD, def. 1.

2. Describing a business with too much investment in inventories.

overcapitalization The condition of a company whose total stated capital (both stocks and bonds) is so large that it cannot possibly hope to earn an adequate return on them. For example, if a firm cannot reasonably be expected to earn more than $1 million per year even under favorable conditions and it has $20 million worth of bonds outstanding with an 8 per cent coupon (interest rate), it is almost certainly overcapitalized, since it will not earn all of its bond interest, let alone a return for the owners of its common stock. The best solution in such cases usually is a RECAPITALIZATION, in which the senior security holders settle for junior securities and the holders of junior securities either are wiped out or receive a greatly reduced equity.

overcertification An overdraft (check for an amount in excess of the balance on account) made out by a broker and certified by the bank that permits the broker to buy securities, which are delivered to the bank and serve as collateral. Formerly a common practice to finance buying on margin, overcertification has been largely replaced by very short-term loans, such as morning loans (see under LOAN, def. 1).

overdraft The amount by which a check or other order for payment exceeds the funds on deposit. A check is normally returned by the bank, marked "not sufficient funds" or words to that effect. Occasionally, however, banks will cover the overdrafts of valued customers, in which case they may invoke a service charge or interest on the overdraft (see FORCED LOAN, def. 2). In British usage "overdraft" actually refers to a loan, that is, a specific amount up to which a customer may overdraw for a given period of time. Normally interest is charged only on the actual amount overdrawn, so that some businesses—chiefly those with highly fluctuating cash flows—may find overdrafts a relatively economical method of financing.

overfull employment Also, *overemployment*. A sellers' market for labor, that is, a market in which more jobs are available than there are unemployed workers to fill them. Although full employment is highly desirable, overfull employment has distinct disadvantages, notably production bottlenecks for lack of workers, excessive labor turnover (workers simply keep moving on to more desirable jobs), and high wages tending to raise prices to inflationary levels. In practice, severe general labor shortages rarely develop except in special situations, such as a war, when the government usually will impose wage and price controls to offset some of the undesirable effects.

overhead Also, *burden*. A general term for all business costs that are neither direct labor (the wages paid to production workers; see under LABOR COST) nor direct material (from which the product is made; see under MATERIALS COST). Included in overhead are all indirect labor costs (such as wages and salaries paid to inspectors, materials handlers, supervisors, etc.), as well as fringe benefits paid to all employees. In addition, overhead includes materials such as packaging, which are not incorporated directly into the end-product, as well as numerous other expenses incurred in running the business.

Overhead is calculated by adding up all costs other than direct labor and direct material incurred over some particular accounting period, usually one year. Sometimes a single calculation for an entire company is made. In most cases, however, overhead is calculated separately for each plant or division, and it often is calculated separately for individual groups of products or groups of machinery used in making products. It normally is measured in relation to direct labor. Thus, if a plant has total overhead costs of $1 million per year and expects its direct labor hours to total about 100,000 hours, then the *overhead rate* is $10 per direct labor hour. If the workers are paid $5 per hour, then the

company knows it must sell 100,000 hours' worth of direct labor at $15 per hour if it is to cover its costs. This example embraces what is normally called *manufacturing* or *factory overhead*. *Administrative* or *sales overhead* is calculated separately and normally is related to total factory costs. Accountants also distinguish between fixed and variable elements of overhead, *fixed overhead* being (theoretically, at least) independent of sales and *variable overhead*, varying directly in proportion to sales and/or production volume. See also FIXED COST; INDIRECT COST.

overinsurance The insuring of property for more than its fair or reasonable value. Overinsurance usually results from poor judgment, on the part either of whoever values the property or of the policyholder, though occasionally it represents an attempt to make dishonest claims.

overlying mortgage See under MORTGAGE.

overpopulation See under POPULATION, def. 1.

overproduction Output in excess of demand. According to SAY'S LAW OF MARKETS, overproduction can never occur except temporarily, since producers will immediately cut back, either in response to lower prices or in order to avoid unsold inventories. MALTHUS was among the first to point out that in the real world this simply does not happen. Later economists, notably J. A. HOBSON, related overproduction—or *underconsumption*, which amounts to the same thing—to the business cycle. According to this theory, excess production leads to price declines, increasing unemployment, and a general recession until the excess output has been absorbed. See also UNDERCONSUMPTION THEORY.

overproduction theory See UNDERCONSUMPTION THEORY.

oversaving, theory of See UNDERCONSUMPTION THEORY.

oversold

1. A term describing the market as a whole or a particular security, in the belief that excessive

selling activity has driven down prices in general, or an individual price, to an unreasonably low level. See also OVERBOUGHT.

2. Describing a business that has committed itself to more than it can deliver.

oversubscribed Describing a new ISSUE of securities for which there are more buyers than securities available. Usually the underwriters allocate subscriptions. For example, if an issue is 10 per cent oversubscribed, each subscriber will receive approximately 90 per cent of his subscription. The subscriber usually does not object, since an oversubscribed issue almost always sells at a premium, offering the possibility of a quick profit if one sells immediately.

over-the-counter market Also, *off-board*. In the United States, the market for securities that are not listed on an organized STOCK EXCHANGE, as well as for some listed ones that may be also traded off the exchange (see THIRD MARKET). Trading in these securities, which by far outnumber listed ones, takes place through local dealers who negotiate the transactions primarily over the telephone. Prices are listed in the financial pages of newspapers. All kinds of security—common and preferred stocks, corporate bonds, practically all U.S. government securities—are traded over the counter. Nor are stocks so traded necessarily of lower quality than listed ones. Most insurance companies and commercial banks do not bother to have their stocks and bonds listed. The chief difference is that prices in the over-the-counter market are determined by negotiation—between dealers, or between dealer and customer—rather than by auction, as on a stock exchange. The type of transaction can vary. Sometimes dealers sell directly to customers; sometimes they represent them as agents and charge a commission, just as brokers do. Though formally unregulated for many years, the over-the-counter market in the United States has regulated itself via the NATIONAL ASSOCIATION OF SECURITIES DEALERS since 1939, and since 1964 it has been more strictly supervised by the U.S. Securities and Exchange Commission as well.

overtime Any work time in excess of a given number of hours per day or per week, as defined by law, general agreement, or labor contract. The Wage and Hour Division of the Employment Standards Administration (part of the U.S. Department of Labor) defines overtime as any work in excess of 8 hours per day or 40 hours per week. Also, work on legal holidays, Saturdays, or Sundays often is agreed to constitute overtime. In industry, overtime normally commands premium pay, traditionally the *time and a half* (half again the usual wage) established by the Fair Labor Standards Act of 1938. In many businesses and professions, however, overtime commands no premium. Teachers do not get extra pay for correcting papers after school, nor do lawyers for working on briefs over weekends; in such cases the regular salary presumably covers extra work. Moreover, executives in a business firm generally do not receive overtime pay even though they may be supervising employees who are paid a premium during the very same hours.

overvalued, undervalued Terms describing the value of a nation's currency in relation to its BALANCE OF PAYMENTS position. If there is a persistent surplus in balance of payments (with export values exceeding import values), the currency is said to be *undervalued*; its exchange rate is too low in terms of other currencies. If there is a persistent deficit (import values exceed export values) the currency is *overvalued* and its exchange rate is too high. Either condition can be corrected by REVALUATION. Thus, in the 1960s West Germany, to counter its persistent surplus, appreciated the Deutschmark several times, so that it rose from $.25 to $.31, and Great Britain, which was running a persistent deficit, depreciated the pound sterling from $2.80 to $2.40.

Owen, Robert A British industrialist (1771–1858) remembered chiefly for his work in organizing cooperative communities. Owner of the New Lanark Mills in Scotland (1800–1829), Owen converted the mill town into a model community, with decent living conditions and low-priced consumer goods for workers, strict rules against child labor, schooling for young children, limited working hours, high wages, and sickness and old-age insurance. In 1825 he founded the New Harmony Colony in Indiana, where a relatively small number of persons (500 to 2,500) were to live and work, with profits distributed according to need. Within three years this community collapsed, as did another established near Glasgow, Scotland, but the idea gave rise to more than a hundred other utopian communities during the following decades. Owen also believed that goods should be sold at cost and that cost should be determined by the number of labor hours required for production. He set up a *National Equitable Labour Exchange* (1832), through which members could sell their products in exchange for notes representing hours of work, which could then be traded for other items requiring equivalent production time. The exchange failed, too, but in 1844 it gave rise to the *Rochdale Pioneers' Co-operative Society*, the first successful CONSUMER COOPERATIVE in Great Britain. See also UTOPIAN SOCIALISM.

Paasche index See under IDEAL INDEX.

package goods In the retail trade, merchandise that is bought and sold prepacked in containers (cans, bottles, jars, etc.), as opposed to bulk (pickles from a pickle barrel, beer on draught, etc.). For alcoholic beverages, the term refers to bottled liquors as opposed to those sold by the glass (hence the term "package store" for a retail liquor store).

package mortgage A MORTGAGE financing a home purchase that also covers the purchase of some equipment, such as a refrigerator, stove, washing machine, etc., that makes the property more livable. In effect it makes these articles fixtures through an agreement between mortgagor and mortgagee, even though they would ordinarily be regarded as personal property (chattels). The chief advantage of a package mortgage is that it permits appliances to be financed at the interest rate for a home mortgage, which is half that for installment buying; moreover, such a loan need not be repaid until, in many cases, long after the appliance has worn out. However, sometimes such mortgages raise legal problems, as, for example, when some of the equipment is sold during the life of the mortgage.

package pay Also, *pay package*. The joint consideration of salary or wages together with various FRINGE BENEFITS, such as pension plans, profit sharing, stock options, etc. With the increase in employer-paid fringe benefits to employees on all levels, from blue-collar worker to executive, the total "package" has become increasingly important. Thus most present-day union negotiations involve *package bargaining*, a quest for the best combination of benefits.

packaging The wrapping or enclosing of goods for purposes of protection, convenience of handling, and promotion. While packaging is obviously necessary, U.S. producers in the 1970s in sum were spending as much on packaging materials as on advertising. Occasionally package designs are misleading, sometimes deliberately so, and the great variety of such designs and sizes often makes it hard for the consumer to compare prices (at one time toothpaste was being sold in 57 different package sizes). Pressure from American consumers led to the passage of the Federal Fair Packaging and Labeling Act of 1966, which requires consumer goods to be clearly labeled and calls on both government and industry to reduce the number of package sizes. For industrial packaging, see CONTAINERIZATION.

padding Falsifying payrolls, expense accounts, and other financial records. Payrolls can be padded by adding the names of unnecessary or even nonexistent workers. Expense accounts and other bills can be padded by adding charges for goods or services not actually provided, or by inflating the prices paid.

paid circulation See under CIRCULATION.

paid-in capital See CAPITAL, def. 3.

paid-in surplus Also, *capital surplus*. Capital that is contributed by stockholders over and above the par value of the stock. The chief sources for such capital are the sale of stock at prices above its par value, and surplus resulting from RECAPITALIZATION. For example, if a company sells 100,000 shares of stock with a stated no-par value or a par value of $1 per share and receives $300,000, its balance sheet will show common stock at the par or stated value of $100,000, and the $200,000 difference between this and the cash proceeds will be credited to paid-in surplus. Paid-in surplus differs from *earned surplus*, which is generated by accumulated earnings (see RETAINED EARNINGS).

paid-up insurance A life insurance policy on which the required premiums have been paid in full. In some instances a policyholder may use the accumulated cash value of some other policy to buy such a paid-up policy.

pallet A movable platform constructed to allow the stacking of bags or boxes of goods, called *pallet* or *unit loads*, for storage or shipment. The platform often has legs to raise it from the ground, which permits the insertion of the forks of a fork truck or other mechanical lifting and carrying device. Usually made of wood, pallets are designed for access from all four sides or from opposite sides (for loading and unloading), and loaded pallets can be stacked on top of one another. Pallets were first used for military supplies during World War II and since then have revolutionized industrial MATERIALS HANDLING. Because pallet loads can be stacked and shipped entirely mechanically, they have greatly reduced the time and cost of many operations.

panel In market research, a representative group of consumers whose views are repeatedly sought through interviews, surveys, new product or advertisement testing, or some other canvassing technique. The chief advantage of canvassing a panel of the same consumers is that changes in their attitudes can be traced over a period of time.

panics, business Periods of acutely decreased confidence in the economy, usually following a period of expansion. Convinced that markets will plummet, investors rush to sell their holdings, thus precipitating the very fall in prices they fear. In addition to sharply lowered securities prices and widespread cancellation of orders, panics are characterized by liquidation of inventories and a fall in the general price level. In the United States, clearly defined panics have occurred periodically, specifically in 1819, 1837, 1857, 1873, 1884, 1893 (*Cleveland panic*, since it was the year of President Grover Cleveland's inauguration and was precipitated in part by uncertainty over his administration's policies), 1903, 1907 ("rich man's panic," largely caused by overspeculation by financiers in the large money centers), 1913, 1920, and 1929 ("Black Tuesday," October 29, 1929, the stock market crash marking the arrival of the Great Depression). A panic basically represents a particular point in the BUSINESS CYCLE, but, even though the general cycle of rising and falling activity has continued, acute panics have been largely avoided since 1929. One major fear, that of bank failure, has been laid to rest through Federal backing of many savings deposits, and regulation of stock market speculation by the Securities and Exchange Commission has limited margin buying (see MARGIN, BUYING ON) and other excesses.

paper Any form of loan, but especially one that is short-term in nature, such as a banker's acceptance, commercial paper, or Treasury bill. The name refers to the paper on which the borrower's pledge to repay a given sum of money at some particular time is printed. Most paper is negotiable, that is, it can be bought and sold as a commodity. The price at which it is traded may be measured by the effective interest the buyer collects. For example, PRIME commercial paper, payable at par 90 days hence, might sell on the basis of a 7.62 per cent interest rate on a particular day.

paper money

1. Usually, bank notes or any other CURRENCY made of paper. Paper money may be convertible, that is, redeemed into full-bodied coin or bullion, or it may be inconvertible (see FIAT MONEY). The chief kinds of U.S. paper money are bank notes and government notes, not convertible into full-bodied coin.

2. Occasionally, any kind of money made of paper, including not only CURRENCY (def. 1) but also drafts, checks, money orders, etc.

paper profit

A profit that would be realized at a given moment if the owner of a property sold it. The term is most often used for securities that are still held but whose market price has advanced over their purchase price. A profit is realized only when the security is actually sold.

paper standard

1. Another name for *floating exchange rate*. See EXCHANGE RATE.

2. Another name for FIAT MONEY, that is, currency not convertible into full-bodied coin or bullion.

par

See PAR VALUE.

paradox of thrift

See THRIFT, PARADOX OF.

paradox of value

See VALUE, PARADOX OF.

parameter

1. In statistics, a measure summarizing some characteristic of a population or universe, such as its MEAN or MEDIAN.

2. In econometrics, a constant that is assigned a value or set of values. For example, in a MODEL of national income, one parameter might be the percentage of disposable income spent by consumers (and disposable income and consumer spending would be two variables of the model).

parent company

See under SUBSIDIARY.

Paretian optimum

See under V. PARETO.

Pareto, Vilfredo

An Italian-Swiss engineer and economist (1848–1923), a colleague of Léon WALRAS, remembered chiefly for his mathematical approach to some problems of economics. Essentially a marginalist who, like Walras, worked with general equilibrium theory, Pareto helped develop the INDIFFERENCE CURVE. He also gave his name to a law of income distribution, *Pareto's law*, which states that, throughout history and in every place, the pattern of income distribution has been and will remain constant, and the only way the income of the poor can be increased is to increase overall production and income levels throughout the economy. Although Pareto's reasoning, based on data of dubious validity, has been strongly criticized, his essential point, that is, that the pattern of income distribution cannot easily be changed, has proved true despite the best efforts of welfare economics. Pareto's name is associated also with the idea that society is making the most efficient use of its resources when no individual can move into a better position without causing someone else to move to a less desirable position; this condition is called the *Paretian optimum*. An economy will have a large number of potential Paretian optima, and, without making value judgments, it is impossible to say that one Paretian optimum is preferable to another.

par exchange rate

Same as official exchange rate; see under EXCHANGE RATE.

parity price

A price paid to American farmers for numerous commodities to provide them with approximately the same purchasing power they had during 1910–14, which was considered a reasonably stable period for farmers. Purchasing power deficiencies are calculated by means of the *parity ratio* (see under PRICES PAID/RECEIVED BY FARMERS for explanation). If the parity ratio is below 100, farm prices have fallen more than other prices, an indication that farm puchasing power is reduced. The government redresses the balance by paying the farmer a certain percentage of parity (historically it has ranged from 60 to 90 per cent), specifically decided by the Secretary of Agriculture and Congress. The parity system is based on nonrecourse loans and government purchases of surplus crops as well as direct cash payments.

The practice of parity payments, long a controversial issue, is a form of price PEGGING. Supporters, including many but not all farmers, contend that farmers are subject to the vagaries of weather and crop diseases and must sell in a highly competitive market. Opponents point out that farm technology has changed drastically since 1914 and costs of production are now much lower, so that to peg relative prices on the basis of 1914 levels is absurd. Some farmers oppose parity on the ground that one farmer's revenue can become another's cost; for example, ranchers and cattle feeders benefit from low grain prices, as do poultry farmers, and so they oppose price supports for grain. In partial response to these arguments, various methods of curtailing production—chiefly *marketing quotas* and *acreage allotments*—have been imposed as conditions of price support. Moreover, numerous laws and amendments passed since the original parity price system was set up during the 1930s have, over the years, changed the commodities supported, the type of support given, etc. The Agriculture and Consumer Protection Act of 1973 set up a system of guaranteed or *target prices*, and deficiency payments for wheat, feed grains, and upland cotton, which in effect are parity prices that take into consideration recent market conditions and current production costs. When the average market price falls below the target level, the Federal government makes up the difference. See also AGRICULTURE, AID TO.

Parkinson's law As stated by Cyril Northcote Parkinson, a British historian, "Work expands so as to fill the time available for its completion." Originally part of a tongue-in-cheek critique of governmental red tape and bureaucratic inefficiency, Parkinson's law applies equally well in business and industry, where it is all too often overlooked.

par list A list of all member banks of the Federal Reserve plus all those nonmember banks that agree to take part in the clearing-house operations of their regional Federal Reserve Bank by paying all checks collected and cleared through it at par (that is, at their face value, without deducting service charges or other fees). In the 1970s more than 90 per cent of all American commercial banks were on the par list.

par of exchange Also, *mint par of exchange.* See under GOLD STANDARD.

parol contract See under CONTRACT.

partial equilibrium theory The theory that individual firms, industries, or other small economic entities can be analyzed independent of changes in the overall market or economy, which are regarded as constant (rather than variable) factors. For example, a partial equilibrium analysis might concern itself with the effect of a shortage of hides on the leather industry, or the effects of a higher retail price of milk on independent dairies, or the effects of an excise tax on the sale of furs. In such a study, the relations of prices and outputs of other goods in the market would simply be ignored. Partial equilibrium theory, which is associated particularly with the work of Alfred MARSHALL, is quite valid for limited purposes, provided it does not purport to explain larger phenomena. The total effect of a price rise in one commodity on the entire economy is not simply a sum of its effects on each individual sector or industry, and must be analyzed in terms of GENERAL EQUILIBRIUM THEORY, which takes into account the interrelationships of sectors, products, and factors of production.

partial limitation In insurance policies, a clause that provides for the payment of a total loss when that loss exceeds the amount specified in the policy. For example, with a personal property floater policy that has a $50 partial limitation clause, the loss of a watch valued at $35 would not be covered at all, but that of a ring valued at $75 would be completely covered. See also DEDUCTIBLE COVERAGE.

participating policy In insurance, a policy that calls for premiums larger than the actual anticipated cost, which are partially refunded to the policyholder as dividends if the company's experience is favorable.

participating preferred stock See under PREFERRED STOCK.

participation loan See under LOAN, def. 1.

partition A division of real property among those who own it in undivided shares, as in a JOINT TENANCY.

partnership A form of business organization in which two or more persons enter business as co-owners to share in profits and losses. A partnership is a common-law agreement, though there are statutes governing particular aspects of it. Legally, partners are jointly liable for the debts of the business, and a creditor suing to collect will sue the partners as a group. However, any one partner is wholly liable for all the debts; if two out of three partners are insolvent, the third is liable for all of the enterprise's obligations to the total extent of his or her personal assets. The advantages of a partnership are that it combines the various talents and capital of the partners, it is a simple organization, and it is relatively free from government control. Its disadvantages, besides the unlimited liability of each partner, are divided authority, the problem of compatibility of the partners, and a limited and uncertain life. A partnership is automatically dissolved whenever any of the partners wishes to withdraw. Further, usually no partner may sell his or her share to a new partner without the consent of all the remaining partners. In addition to the general partnership in which all partners have unlimited liability, the statutes of some states of the United States allow a *limited partnership*, in which certain partners, called *limited* or *special partners*, merely invest in the business, take no other part in its management, and assume LIMITED LIABILITY (and usually also limited profits) proportionate to the size of their investment. Nearly all law and public accounting firms and almost all brokerage firms in the United States are organized as partnerships. See also SILENT PARTNER.

parts A general term for components that will be incorporated into a company's end-product. Parts either may be purchased from another supplier and assembled into an end-product or they may be manufactured from raw materials in one department or division of a plant, placed in finished-parts STORES, and then reissued for assembling into a finished product.

par value The value of a stock or bond, expressed as a specific sum of money, which is printed or otherwise marked on its face. For certain bonds it is also known as the FACE VALUE. Par value at one time was supposed to represent the value of the original investment behind each share in terms of cash, goods, or services. However, after some years in operation, a company's original investment becomes irrelevant; indeed, the par value of common stocks is usually so remote from market value (what stocks could be sold for at a given time) as to be meaningless. Today many American companies issue either NO-PAR STOCK (which has no stated par value) or stock with a deliberately low par value (to minimize Federal transfer taxes and various state taxes, which are based on par value). The par value of preferred stocks and bonds, however, is significant, since it often represents the dollar value upon which dividends and interest are based. For example, a firm issuing a 3 per cent bond is promising to pay 3 per cent of the bond's par value per year. Also, the par value of preferred stocks and bonds usually (though not always) tends to be closer to their market value than does that of common stocks.

passbook Also, *bank book*. A booklet given to bank depositors in which their deposits, withdrawals, and interest earnings are recorded. American savings banks generally issue passbooks that must be presented to make a withdrawal. Passbooks are rarely issued for checking accounts.

passed dividend See under DIVIDEND, def. 1.

patent An exclusive right to make, use, or sell a particular invention (machine, device, design, process, plant variety, etc.) that is granted by a government to the inventor for a given period of time. In the United States a patent is granted for a period of 17 years and is not renewable; a patent for a design, however, is valid for only a shorter time, up to 14 years. Anyone making, using, or selling the invention during that time without permission is guilty of patent infringement and may be prosecuted. American patents, which date from the nation's first patent law, enacted in 1790, are administered, along with trademarks, by the Patent Office, part of the U.S. Department of Commerce. It examines applications for patents to ascertain whether applicants actually are entitled to patents under the law, grants patents, and keeps track of patent ownership which, like other property rights, is transferable. See also PATENT POOL.

patent medicine   See under PROPRIETARY.

patent pool   The assignment of a PATENT to a trade association or special corporation, so that a number of participants may use it. The pool may be confined to patents relating to just one product or may include numerous patents important to a given industry. Patent pools can either stimulate competition or intensify monopoly. If unrestricted licenses to the pool are given to all applicants on reasonable terms, as is the practice in the American automobile industry's patent pools, outsiders have free access to the industry's technology. By refusing to license or by charging high royalties, however, a patent pool may severely limit the number of entrants in a field and hence restrain competition. Thus, though patent pools are not illegal, they can be used in an illegal way and have often been involved in litigation.

paternalism   In business, industry, and government, an organization's extensive involvement in the welfare of its employees and citizens. In Japan, where paternalism is a long-standing tradition, the employees of a large company can expect numerous benefits, such as company-sponsored housing, education, and recreation.

patronage dividend   See under CONSUMER COOPERATIVE.

Patrons of Husbandry   See GRANGE.

pawnbroker   An individual or firm in the business of lending money for a fee, with the borrower putting up some tangible personal property as security. The property, called the *pawn*, serves as a PLEDGE that the borrower will repay the loan. In the United States pawnbrokers generally are regulated by statute in order to prevent both excessive interest charges and trafficking in stolen goods, although they usually are allowed higher interest rates than most other lenders. In most states and municipalities they must be licensed.

pay-as-you-go   A system of paying costs or expenses as they are incurred, out of current earnings. For example, the U.S. Federal income tax is paid in this fashion by most wage earners, their employers withholding some portion of their wages every payday for this purpose.

payback period   The time estimated for a capital investment to pay for itself, calculated by relating the cost of the investment to the profit it will earn. For example, suppose a manufacturer decides to replace a worker earning $5,000 per year with a machine that costs $10,000. The machine has a ten-year life, and its straight-line depreciation thus can be calculated at $1,000 per year. In addition, the firm pays a corporation income tax of 50 per cent. To calculate the payback period, first deduct $1,000 for depreciation from the $5,000 return of the first year (the wage no longer paid). This leaves $4,000 in gross profit from the machine, half of which may be taxable. The cash flow is equal to the net profit plus depreciation, or $2,000 + $1,000 = $3,000 for one year. The machine therefore should pay for itself in 3.333 years ($10,000 ÷ $3,000). For other methods of analyzing capital, see DISCOUNTED CASH FLOW and MAPI FORMULA.

paycheck   See TAKE-HOME PAY.

payee   An individual or organization to whom an obligation is paid, in money or another form. Also, the person or organization to whom a note, bill, check, or other instrument is made payable.

payload   In transportation, the revenue-yielding portion of the total load (passengers, freight, or both) transported by a carrier. See also DEADHEADING.

payments agreement   An agreement made by trading countries to settle transactions in ways that do not exhaust their FOREIGN EXCHANGE RESERVES or create serious balance of payments deficits. Bilateral payments agreements (involving just two nations) are a common form of EXCHANGE CONTROL, which has the disadvantage of restricting trade. Multilateral agreements, such as the European Monetary Agreement, whereby all parties to it settle their payments through a single clearing house, are less restrictive.

payment terms See COD; DISCOUNT, def. 1.

payroll In accounting, the total amount owed by a business to its employees for work performed during a given period (week, month, etc.). Also, a record showing the amount payable to each employee. In larger organizations numerous accounting records are required for the payroll, including time slips or time-clock cards, withholding authorizations, receipts for wages paid (or canceled paychecks), wage and salary authorizations, and individual earnings records.

payroll tax See EMPLOYMENT TAX.

peak

1. The high point of the BUSINESS CYCLE or of some particular phase of economic activity.

2. Also, *peak load*. In public utilities, the time and size of maximum demand for a service. For example, one of the peaks for electricity usage in the United States is between 5:00 and 7:00 P.M., when many households are using electric stoves, hot-water heaters, etc., to prepare the evening meal, and many factories are still operating. Public utility rate structures based on cost sometimes charge different rates for on-peak (peak-time) and off-peak use. Thus, telephone companies often charge lower rates after 5:00 P.M., when most business offices have closed and the bulk of calls made are personal ones.

peddler The earliest kind of traveling salesman, who traveled through rural regions selling whatever was light enough to carry. In the United States the earliest peddlers sold manufactured articles, many of them made in New England, and hence many peddlers were New Englanders (hence the term "Yankee peddler"). Since few customers could pay cash, they usually exchanged their wares for other goods, which they would resell. At first peddlers traveled on foot or horseback. Later, as roads were

built and improved, they drove carts and wagons. In time peddlers began to venture farther and farther from their original source of supply, and depots were established at various locations where they could restock. As rural areas became more settled, however, peddlers were replaced by retail stores, and with the coming of railroads peddling virtually disappeared.

pegging Also, *price maintenance*. Fixing or stabilizing the price of a commodity, security, or currency at some preestablished point. Security pegging, which in the United States is illegal (except under special conditions, as in floating a new issue) and is controlled by the U.S. Securities and Exchange Commission, is accomplished by heavy trading (buying and selling) at the desired price. Government price supports for agriculture are another form of pegging (see PARITY PRICE), as is the Federal Reserve's trading in Treasury notes, bills, etc. (see OPEN-MARKET OPERATIONS) in order to adjust the interest rate (the price of borrowing) to some preconceived figure. A CARTEL or POOL (def. 2) may fix the price of a good or service, frequently at whatever the traffic will bear. For pegging of foreign exchange, see under EXCHANGE CONTROLS. See also FAIR TRADE.

penny stock Any stock that sells for less than $1 per share. Most such stocks tend to be quite speculative, and the term is sometimes used pejoratively, but occasionally a penny stock develops into a valuable investment.

pension An allowance or other series of regular payments made to a retired worker by a former employer or by the government. In the United States many larger private firms have some kind of *pension plan* (or *retirement plan*). Such plans may be *contributory*, with both employer and employee adding to a *pension fund* over the years of employment, or *noncontributory*, paid entirely by the employer. Since about 1950 many labor unions have insisted on including a pension plan in their contracts, and such negotiated plans are nearly always noncontributory. A major problem with any pension plan is that of *vesting*, that is, whether or not an employee may take all or some of the pension equity along when changing jobs. In the case of pension plans that are *vested*, the employee does have that right. Vesting is encouraged by the Federal government, and the Internal Revenue Code will not permit the deduction of pension funds as a business expense under certain circumstances unless they are vested. See also SOCIAL SECURITY.

peonage A system of forced labor based on the debt of a laborer (called *peon*) to a creditor and widely practiced in Latin America from the early 19th century on. Following independence from Spain (from the 1820s on), the economy of such countries as Mexico, Guatemala, and Peru depended on large-scale cultivation of plantation crops, such as sugar, which require a steady supply of cheap labor. Through a variety of tactics—advances on wages, forcing workers to buy from company stores, and appropriation of land—plantation owners kept their agricultural laborers, most of them Indians, in a state of continual inescapable debt. So long as a peon was indebted, he could not change jobs, and prices and wages were carefully adjusted so that discharging the debt was virtually impossible. Moreover, such debts came to be considered hereditary, passing from father to son. In effect, peons were serfs, but without enjoying any of the rights of SERFDOM. Though peonage was officially outlawed in Mexico (1915) and Guatemala (1936) the practice persisted. Peonage also existed in the American Southwest (after it was acquired from Mexico), as well as in parts of the Southeast after the Civil War, binding not only Mexican-Americans and blacks but white agricultural workers as well. By 1900, however, state and Federal legislation had done away with debt peonage, though a form of it survives in SHARECROPPING. See also ENCOMIENDA; INDENTURE, def. 2; TENANT FARMING.

per capita A Latin term meaning "for each person" (literally, "by head"). Thus, *per capita income* means the amount of income per person, calculated by dividing the total income of a group by the number of individuals it comprises.

percentage depletion See under DEPLETION ALLOWANCE.

percentage lease A LEASE whereby all or part of the rent is based on a percentage of the tenant's yield from the property. For example, the rent for leased retail space within a store may be a small fixed fee per month plus a given percentage of monthly sales.

percentile In statistics, a name for the 99 values in a FREQUENCY DISTRIBUTION that divide the items into 100 equal groups. Percentiles are widely used in aptitude testing. See also DECILE; QUARTILE.

per diem A Latin term meaning "by the day," used for an allowance, payment, charge, or rental established on a daily basis. For example, a per diem expense account is a fixed amount per day allowed to a salesperson or other employee for travel or other business expenses. Similarly, a shipper who holds a railroad car for more than the maximum time prescribed by the U.S. Interstate Commerce Commission is charged a per diem rate for the car.

perfect competition
1. Usually, another name for PURE COMPETITION (and so used in this dictionary).
2. According to some writers, a market characterized by PURE COMPETITION, complete FREEDOM OF ENTRY, and no special advantages of any seller over another, along with total mobility of productive factors from one industry to another. This situation is a theoretical ideal, nonexistent in the real world.

perforated tape See PUNCHED-TAPE DATA PROCESSING.

performance fund See under MUTUAL FUND.

peril point A provision of various Federal laws, called Trade Agreement Extension acts, requiring the U.S. Tariff Commission to inform the President (who is empowered to negotiate tariff cuts) of the maximum decrease in duty that can be made without hurting domestic producers and the minimum increase needed to avoid such injury. Each of these amounts is called a "peril point." See also TARIFF, def. 1.

periodic ordering Any system of inventory control whereby material is ordered at regular intervals, with the order quantity varying according to need. For example, a purchasing agent may be authorized to buy a particular kind of casting once a month, meaning that 12 times a year the precise number of castings needed must be determined. Periodic ordering works best for items frequently ordered and costly enough to warrant tight control; for items whose use is unique or highly irregular; for items purchased in large amounts that require a substantial portion of a supplier's capacity; for many items ordered from the same supplier where joint ordering can reduce purchasing costs; when quantity discounts either are not available or when they can be applied to partial shipments. Periodic ordering is used mostly in mass-production industries by large manufacturers of a limited product line (automobiles, electric appliances). Since it is an expensive procedure, periodic ordering is used largely for a relatively small number of essential and expensive items that are considered worth the cost of such close control.

permanent consumption See under PERMANENT-INCOME HYPOTHESIS.

permanent-income hypothesis An attempt to explain the relationship of consumer spending, saving, and income in terms of long-term expectations and both permanent and transitory income. *Permanent income* is the consumer's normal earnings (and expectations of future earnings), whereas *transitory income* is some unexpected bonus or windfall. Overall spending patterns—*permanent consumption*—are determined by permanent income, but transitory income influences current spending. This distinction explains why short-term data indicate that, regardless of income changes, a family or individual tends to save and spend fairly consistent proportions of its income. Among the economists associated with the permanent-income hypothesis is M. FRIEDMAN. See also RELATIVE-INCOME HYPOTHESIS.

perpetual bond See under BOND, def. 1.

perpetual inventory system A system of inventory control in which a running record is kept of all materials, parts, subassemblies, and finished goods. A record card is maintained for each item in stock, and every transaction is posted on that card, which shows both the balance on hand and on order. Materials are automatically ordered when a particular level of stock—the order point—is reached. A periodic physical count of stock on hand verifies the records. Basically a version of the TWO-BIN SYSTEM, in which the reserve stock does not need to be segregated, a perpetual inventory system is costly owing to the extensive record-keeping required (which may now be done by computer), but its cost may be justified for valuable items subject to pilferage.

perquisite An older name for FRINGE BENEFIT.

personal check See under CHECK.

personal consumption expenditures Estimated total consumer spending for goods and services. The single largest component of GROSS NATIONAL PRODUCT in the United States, consumer expenditures account for about two-thirds of the total. It also is the component easiest to predict, because individuals consistently tend to spend a fixed proportion—90 to 94 per cent—of their disposable incomes. See also CONSUMER GOOD.

personal finance company See FINANCE COMPANY, def. 2.

personal holding company A HOLDING COMPANY organized principally for tax benefits. It is small—half the outstanding stock is owned by no more than five persons—and it must derive at least 60 per cent of its income from dividends, interest, annuities, sale of securities, and royalties, on which it may pay less income tax than would have to be paid by wealthy individuals.

personal income An individual's total income from all sources, before income taxes. It is made up of wages and salaries, proprietors' income, rental income, dividends, and interest. Since personal income is the most important determinant of consumer spending, aggregate personal income is an important INDICATOR of general business conditions. Data on personal income are published monthly by the U.S. Department of Commerce in its *Survey of Current Business*. See also DISPOSABLE INCOME.

personal loan   See under LOAN, def. 1.

personal property   Also, *chattels*. In law, any property other than real property—that is, land, buildings, and fixtures. Some authorities distinguish between *chattels real* (interests in land or real estate of limited duration, such as a lease given a tenant by a landlord) and *chattels personal*, consisting of both tangible personal property (books, furniture, automobiles) and intangible property (money claims, debt). Personal property is sold by *bill of sale*, whereas ownership of real property is transferred by means of a DEED.

personal property tax   See under PROPERTY TAX.

personnel administration   In business and government, the managing of an organization's employees. In most organizations employing more than a dozen or so persons, at least one manager—and in large firms, a whole department—is assigned the job of locating, recruiting, selecting, and sometimes also training employees, as well as helping with such employee issues as promotion, demotion, transfer, and discharge. In large firms personnel administration may also involve helping management to formulate basic personnel policies and procedures, supervising employee rating programs, preparing a JOB EVALUATION for each position in the firm, and helping set up systems of worker compensation and benefits. See also INDUSTRIAL RELATIONS.

PERT   Also, *critical path method, CPM*. A technique for scheduling and/or cost control that employs a network reflecting all of the events and activities to be accomplished by a project, and their critical interrelationships. The term is an acronym of <u>P</u>rogram <u>E</u>valuation and <u>R</u>eview <u>T</u>echnique, which was originated by the U. S. Navy to control the Polaris missile program. Today the name "critical path method" is somewhat more common in a nonmilitary context. PERT can be designed for use on various kinds of computer for large construction projects or similar jobs involving many variables

that affect one another. To construct a PERT network, each separate activity for the project is recorded, with notes as to what other activities must be completed before it can begin. Then three estimates are made of the time needed to complete each activity: an optimistic estimate (a), a realistic estimate (m), and a pessimistic estimate (b). The expected time of completion, or T_e, is then calculated, using the formula

$$T_e = \frac{a + 4m + b}{6}$$

(this is an easy substitute for a NORMAL DISTRIBUTION, which gives a result approximating that obtained with integral calculus). After calculating expected times for each operation, a PERT network is constructed. Not only will these calculations yield the expected total time required, but they will pinpoint the so-called *critical path*, the set of activities or operations that will hold up the entire project if they fall behind schedule. The critical path is the chain of events that takes the longest time to complete. In the other, noncritical paths, there is slack; they can fall somewhat behind without affecting the total time for the project. Identifying slack enables managers to hold off beginning noncritical activities until it is really necessary, with a resultant saving of resources. In Fig. 65, a very simple PERT network is drawn, with just seven events (A through G). The numbers between the events indicate the estimated number of months it will take to complete each activity. The critical path in this network is A-B-D-E-F-G ($7 + 14 + 8 + 2 + 1 = 32$); in the noncritical path A-C-E-F-G there is three months' slack ($6 + 20 + 2 + 1 = 29$; $32 - 29 = 3$). Were this a construction project, materials for events C and E

Fig. 65. A PERT network

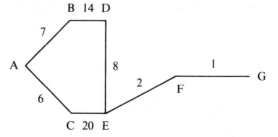

would not have to be delivered until 9 months after the start of A, and the money tied up in those materials could meanwhile be employed in some other way.

pet bank A name applied by opponents of U.S. President Andrew Jackson to any state bank used for government deposits. After Jackson vetoed renewal of the charter for the second BANK OF THE UNITED STATES (in 1832), he directed that Federal funds be removed from it (even though its charter did not expire until 1836) and placed in state banks. Those banks selected naturally benefited from the Federal deposits and might reasonably have been expected to return the favor in one way or another.

petrocurrency "Oil money," that is, money paid to purchase petroleum from its producers. The term was coined after the Arab countries quadrupled petroleum prices in 1973, thereby increasing the amount of petrocurrency so rapidly that it became a matter of great concern to international monetary experts as well as to countries being drained of foreign exchange in order to buy fuel. Petrocurrency normally is deposited in large banks (usually located in London but not necessarily British) and then lent out, primarily to countries that need it to pay for oil. Traditionally, oil prices were set in U.S. dollars, but producers often accepted payment in British pounds sterling as well. In 1975, however, petrocurrency in effect began to have its own values, as the dollar was abandoned and prices were repegged in terms of a composite bundle of currencies. See also *floating exhange rate*, under EXCHANGE RATE.

Petty, Sir William An English statistician, physician, and economist (1623–87) who embraced MERCANTILISM but also foreshadowed some of the ideas of the CLASSICAL SCHOOL. Petty favored more freedom of foreign trade; he approved tariffs on imported manufactures but opposed those on raw materials or tools. He also opposed the laws against exporting bullion, though he believed that as much money as possible should remain at home. However, he was ahead of his time in recognizing that the circulation of money—not just its quantity—was important, and in regarding rent as the surplus from land. He anticipated (by 200 years) BÖHM-BAWERK's theory of roundabout production, and he developed a LABOR THEORY OF VALUE, maintaining that the value of a bushel of corn and an ounce of silver are equal if they are produced by the same amount of labor.

petty cash In business accounting, a relatively small cash fund, either on hand or on deposit, available for minor expenditures, such as local travel, stationery, postage, etc. Most companies set a maximum amount that may be withdrawn from petty cash at any one time.

phalanx Also, *phalanstery*, Fr. *phalanstère*. See under F. M. C. FOURIER.

phantom freight A freight charge for a distance not actually traveled, as in a BASING POINT SYSTEM.

Phillips curve The graphic representation of a theory that claims a significant and calculable relationship between the level of unemployment and the percentage change of money wage rates. Advanced in 1958 by the British economist A. W. H. Phillips on the basis of a study of conditions in Great Britain from 1861 to 1957, the theory maintains that the lower the level of unemployment, the higher the rate of change in wages. In general, this relationship holds true, but economists are not able to calculate it quite as precisely as the curve would suggest. As a result, economic policymakers continue to face great difficulty in reducing inflation caused by rising wages without incurring high unemployment. (See also COST-PUSH INFLATION.)

physical distribution See DISTRIBUTION, def. 1.

physical market See SPOT MARKET.

physiocrats A group of 18th-century French thinkers led by François Quesnay who, in reaction against MERCANTILISM, developed the idea that human society was governed by a natural order, or laws of nature (the name "physiocrat" comes from Greek words meaning "rule of nature"). In an economic sense this meant that workers should enjoy the fruits of their labor without government interference except insofar as it was absolutely required to protect life and property. The physiocrats regarded land as the only source of real wealth and agriculture as the only truly productive occupation, that is, the only one that produced a surplus—which they called *net produit* (net product)—above the costs of production. Industry and commerce, though necessary and useful, were considered essentially sterile. (Despite this view, the physiocrats' doctrine of LAISSEZ FAIRE actually aided industry, which had been stifled by the over-strict government regulations of the mercantilists.) The physiocrats' most lasting contribution, however, was their overview of the entire economy and their analysis of the circular flow of wealth (see under F. QUESNAY). Other physiocrats were Pierre Samuel Dupont de Nemours (1739–1817), an ancestor of the American Dupont family, from whose book *La Physiocratie* (1767) the group took its name; the Marquis de Mirabeau (1715–89), whose son became a leader of the French Revolution; and A. R. TURGOT.

picket See under STRIKE.

pickup and delivery Door-to-door transportation service, with goods being picked up at the shipper's plant and delivered to the customer.

piecework Also, *piece rate.* A system whereby workers are paid per unit of output instead of per hour of time worked or by some other method. Dating from the days of COTTAGE INDUSTRY, when workers at home were paid for each item produced, piecework is still widely practiced in the garment and textile industries as well as in many other manufacturing industries and is incorporated into many WAGE INCENTIVE plans.

piggyback Also, *rail-trailer shipment.* A freight shipment that combines the use of truck and railroad transport. Goods are loaded into truck trailers and driven from the shipper's plant to the rail terminal. There they are driven onto rail flatcars for shipment between cities. At the terminal, each trailer is unloaded onto a truck, which then drives to the customer's plant. Piggyback shipments reduce handling expense and make for lower rates and faster service. See also FISHYBACK.

Pigou, Arthur Cecil An English economist (1877–1959) who succeeded his teacher Alfred MARSHALL at Cambridge University and also was active in various government posts. Pigou's ideas on monetary theory, employment, and national income, which were essentially those of the CLASSICAL and MARGINALIST SCHOOLS (from Adam Smith to Marshall) brought him in conflict with J. M. KEYNES. Pigou's early work on welfare, which assessed how various government policies affect the distribution and size of national output and analyzed the different effects of economic activity on entrepreneurs (marginal private net product) and on society as a whole (marginal social net product), is of lasting importance. Pigou believed that the government should maximize output by means of taxes and subsidies, but that taxes should not interfere with savings, which tend to be limited anyway by people's reluctance to postpone satisfaction. Hence he supported heavy consumption taxes but opposed property, inheritance, and progressive income taxes. Like the classical economists, he believed that an economy tended always toward full employment without government interference, a major difference between Pigou and Keynes, and that this could be achieved by cutting wages. Pigou supported his view by pointing out that a reduction in overall prices and wages will so increase the real purchasing power of liquid assets (cash) that consumption will then increase and full employment be restored. This theory is known as the *Pigou effect* or *real-balance effect.* See also REAL CASH BALANCE.

pilot A test or experiment, designed to try out a new product, production method, television series, etc.

piracy An act of robbery at sea. It differs from PRIVATEERING in that vessels of any nation may be attacked. Extremely common throughout the world from ancient times until the development of strong national navies in the 19th century, piracy in its original sense is virtually unknown today. However, the term has come to be used for various unethical or illegal activities, such as patent or copyright infringement, or the appropriation of a work of art, a piece of literature, or some other creation without permission or acknowledgment.

pit In a COMMODITY EXCHANGE, the equivalent of the trading floor of a stock exchange (see under NEW YORK STOCK EXCHANGE). It is named for the four sections of the floor of the Chicago Board of Trade, the largest American commodity exchange, each of which specializes in particular commodities. A *pit trader* is the commodity trade's counterpart of the stock exchange floor trader (who deals for his own account rather than on behalf of customers); the term is also loosely used for any commodity speculator dealing for himself. A pejorative name sometimes so used is *pit scalper*.

Pittsburgh plus pricing See under BASING POINT SYSTEM.

planned community Also, *planned unit development*. A real estate development consisting of townhouses, one-or two-family dwellings, apartments, or combinations of such residences with common open areas and sometimes also private recreational facilities. In most cases the community has a home association, a nonprofit corporation in which each homeowner is automatically a member with voting rights and through which each homesite is assessed for a proportionate share of the common expenses (common property maintenance, outdoor lighting, trash collection, etc.). A major advantage of such communities is the lowering of costs through more efficient land use and planning. In view of the low-cost objective, many such communities are located on less expensive land outside the boundaries of existing villages, towns, or cities, and the home association may undertake to provide municipal services (streets, sewer, water, etc.), at least initially.

planned economy An economy in which decisions concerning the use of economic resources are made by a central authority. Such decisions may involve not only the number and kind of goods produced and distributed—as they do in completely planned economies such as those of the So-

viet Union and People's Republic of China—but also the reduction of taxes to increase consumer purchasing power, the use of public spending or the debt to influence credit, the building of new public works to provide employment, all of them measures endemic to nations largely dedicated to free enterprise, such as Canada and the United States. In a wholly planned economy, the market mechanism—that is, the determination of price through interaction of supply and demand—is eliminated on the assumption that maximum social welfare can be achieved only through centralized goal-setting and decision-making. Not unnaturally, a planned economy, which is, after all, administered by fallible human beings, is open to disastrous error. In the 1960s a series of crop failures in the Soviet Union proved almost catastrophic. On a much lesser scale, after years of shortages of consumer goods, owing to concentration on building up heavy industry, Russian consumers began to demand different styles and quality of clothing than had been planned for, and in the early 1970s the Soviet government began to allow some decision-making by the actual producers of clothing.

planned obsolescence Incorporating easily recognizable high-fashion features into a product, to induce customers to replace it with a newer model when current fashions change. Planned obsolescence has long been a vital feature of the garment industry, but it also appears in such products as automobiles and electrical appliances.

planning, economic See PLANNED ECONOMY. See also STRATEGIC PLANNING.

plant and equipment spending See NEW PLANT AND EQUIPMENT EXPENDITURES; also CAPITAL INVESTMENT.

plantation system A system of large-scale agricultural production of one or a few crops using cheap, unskilled labor. Dependent on abundant cheap land and a large labor force, the plantation system became a basic feature of commercial agriculture in the southern United States in colonial times. The early plantations concentrated on tobacco (Virginia, North Carolina) or rice and indigo

(South Carolina, Georgia). After the Industrial Revolution cotton became the most important crop and the new nation's chief export, but tobacco, rice, sugar cane, and hemp continued to have considerable significance. The plantation system was very destructive to the soil. Tobacco, for example, exhausts the richest soil and requires continually new land. The same is true of cotton, which pushed plantations farther and farther west, eventually into Texas. (Today, most growers rotate crops and use fertilizer to counteract such depletion.) Even without the abolition of SLAVERY, the plantation system was doomed to the fate of any one-crop economy that must buy most manufactured goods with whatever profits it can muster in a fluctuating world market. Similar problems were (and are) being faced in the tropical and subtropical lands originally colonized by Europeans who took advantage of cheap land' and cheap labor in Latin America, Africa, and Southeast Asia (see also UNDERDEVELOPED NATIONS).

pledge A special BAILMENT whereby personal property is transferred to someone as security for a debt or performance of an obligation. The recipient, or *pledgee*, may keep the property until the debt or obligation is discharged and, if it is not, may sell the property. See also PAWNBROKER.

PL/1 In computer PROGRAMMING, a compiler language for computers developed to combine features of two other computer languages, COBOL and FORTRAN, for use in problems combining algebra and standard business terminology. Its name comes from Programming Language 1.

plow back To reinvest profits in a business, using the funds for expansion rather than to pay out dividends or retire loans.

point

1. In trading stocks, the unit of price. In the United States 1 point = $1, so that a stock quoted at 45, for example, costs $45 per share. Points also are quoted in fractions of one-half, one-fourth, and one-eighth; $\frac{1}{8}$ point (or $.125) normally is the smallest amount by which a stock price can change.

2. In trading bonds, see BASIS POINT.

3. In market averages, see AVERAGE, def. 2.

Point Four Program A post–World War II program of technical assistance to underdeveloped nations, so called because it was the fourth point in U.S. President Harry Truman's inaugural address of January 20, 1949. Truman proposed that both private and government investment should provide American technical skills to help underdeveloped nations help themselves, and as side benefits help stimulate world trade, check Communism, and feed the hungry. After getting United Nations approval, the program was launched with a $26.5 million appropriation; the first nations scheduled to receive aid were Iran, Liberia, and Paraguay, notably in the fields of health, agriculture, and education. The program soon ran into problems, however. Congress, influenced more and more by the military considerations of the "cold war" against Communism, was reluctant to aid nations not firmly committed to this battle. Private investors wanted the government to keep out of areas of private investment, except to help create a climate favorable for private capital; foreign governments, however, tended to view private investment as an extension of imperialism. Finally, Point Four overlapped somewhat with programs undertaken by other countries and by international organizations. In 1961 better coordination was achieved with the organization of the Agency for International Development, which took over the bulk of American FOREIGN AID programs.

point-of-purchase advertising A general term for devices used in retail stores to help identify and sell a product, such as signs, posters, display racks, models, etc. Such advertising represents an important facet of SALES PROMOTION.

Poisson distribution Also, *Poisson probability distribution, law of improbable events.* A FREQUENCY DISTRIBUTION used to estimate the likelihood of a particular event's occurrence. For example, it can be used to estimate the likelihood of running out of a certain item with a given safety stock and history of usage, or the probable number of typographical errors per printed page of a book, or the number of teacups manufactured that will have minor flaws. Named for the French statistician Simeon Poisson, who first described it in 1837, the Poisson distribution is a useful tool in operations research. On a graph it resembles a NORMAL DISTRIBUTION curve skewed to the right. See also BINOMIAL DISTRIBUTION; CUMULATIVE DISTRIBUTION.

policies and procedures Predetermined principles and practices to handle recurring situations in an organization. A *policy* is a broad overall guide to performance; a *procedure*, derived from a policy, describes a routine operation in great detail. For example, a retail merchant knows in advance that some customers will return merchandise; a production foreman almost invariably encounters absenteeism among workers; a credit department faces some overdue accounts. Policies and procedures, particularly if they are a matter of record—as in a manual—enable top managers to delegate routine decisions and to develop those standard practices that best suit overall company or department goals. Written policies and procedures sometimes are called *standard practices* or *standard operating procedures* (*SOP*).

policy
   1. An INSURANCE contract. There are many different kinds of policy, depending both on the form of insurance and on other factors. See BLANKET POLICY; PARTICIPATING POLICY; REPORTING POLICY; SCHEDULE POLICY.
   2. See POLICIES AND PROCEDURES.

policy loan A loan made by an insurance company to a policyholder, who uses the cash value of his or her life insurance policy as collateral.

political economy A common name for economics until the late 19th century, when government policies concerning finance and commerce ("politics") could at last be gradually separated from the realities of production, finance, and trade ("economics"). Thus David Ricardo's and John Stuart Mill's books (1817, 1848) still dealt with "political economy," whereas Alfred Marshall's book (1890) is entitled *Principles of Economics*. Another designation common in the 17th and 18th centuries was

political arithmetic (as in the title of Sir William Petty's book of 1690).

poll tax Also, *head tax*. A tax levied at a flat rate per person, against all persons in a particular group or category (such as all males over 21 years of age). In some countries such a tax has been used simply as a means of readily raising revenue, without requiring complicated calculations by taxpayers. In the United States it has been so used by both state and local governments. At one time required of all voters in a number of southern states, it effectively prevented the poor, especially blacks, from voting. This practice was outlawed—for Federal elections, at least—by the 24th Amendment to the Constitution (ratified in 1964).

pollution See under CONSERVATION.

pool
   1. In the securities trade, a group of investors who combine their resources to gain control of enough of a company's stock to affect its market price by buying or selling it. In the 19th-century United States it was common practice for pool operators to join forces to bid up the price of a stock, through heavy buying, and then sell it short in order to make a large speculative profit. (See also SELLING SHORT.) Pools today are illegal. However, brokers engaged in selling a new issue of stock are permitted to support the price artificially, if necessary, during the period the new security is being sold.
   2. *industrial pool*. A temporary agreement among competing companies to stop price-cutting, to combine their selling efforts, or for some similar monopolistic effort to improve their profits by reducing competition. In the second half of the 19th century American railroads frequently made such agreements, which eventually were outlawed by the Interstate Commerce Act of 1887. In other industries they can constitute violations of the Sherman Antitrust Act of 1890 (see under ANTITRUST LEGISLATION).
   3. In insurance, an association of insurers organized to share the premiums and losses of one or more specific insurances, subject to whatever conditions are determined by the group. Pools are

organized primarily to spread the risk of very large or very high-risk insurance and to help groups of small companies compete with large ones.

4. See PATENT POOL.

pool car A railroad car that combines several small shipments of different shippers who then are charged the cheaper rate applying to a full carload. If a number of commodities are being shipped in the same car, it is called a *mixed car*, and the highest rate for any of the commodities is applied to the entire shipment.

pooling of interests method In accounting, a system of treating newly merged companies as though they had always been a single company. Otherwise, if a company had been bought for more than its book value, the acquiring company would have to set up a goodwill account for the difference (between the actual price and the book value of the company) and amortize the goodwill against earnings over a period of years.

Poor Laws A series of laws enacted at various times in British history, from the 16th to the 20th centuries, which in one way or another sought to provide for the poor. Under Henry VIII, when the abolition of monasteries did away with a traditional form of charity and many tenant farmers lost their land through ENCLOSURE, the number of landless poor grew enormously. To deal with the problem, harsh laws were passed against beggars and vagabonds. These were continued under Elizabeth I, but some attempt was made at relief. The Poor Law of 1601, which remained a cornerstone of future laws for many years, directed each parish to levy taxes to care for the poor, unemployed, and orphaned. Each parish was to have workhouses where the poor would receive food, shelter, and employment. In the 18th century widespread unemployment made the workhouse system inadequate and some home relief was given. The Poor Law of 1834, however, abolished home relief except for the aged and infirm, and said that all able-bodied paupers had to earn their keep in workhouses. In essence, until the 20th century the Poor Laws all mirrored the view that poverty was brought on by the paupers themselves, a result of

the vices of idleness and shiftlessness, reflecting the middle-class work ethic carried to an unrealistic and cruel extreme (see also PROTESTANT ETHIC).

population
1. The number of persons living in a given place at a given time. The most important economic consideration of population concerns its relation to the supply of food and other necessities, the underlying fear being that, with improved medical care cutting the death rate and a lack of concomitant birth control, the human population will sooner or later outstrip the earth's resources. The most famous proponent of this view was Thomas MALTHUS, but the population explosion of the 20th century won it many new adherents, who are sometimes called *neo-Malthusians*. Population growth has accelerated at an enormous rate. In 1650 an estimated 500 million persons lived on earth, and by 1950 this number had been quintupled, to 2.5 billion. Only two decades later, in 1970, it had risen to more than 3.5 billion, a figure expected to double again by 2010. Although optimists believe that food production will continue to grow faster than population and that humankind will develop new resources to feed its growing numbers, most scientists insisted that even "zero population growth"—that is, simply maintaining the earth's population at present levels—would pose considerable problems since the planet's natural resources were already being used up faster than they could be replenished. For population movements, see IMMIGRATION.

2. In statistics, see UNIVERSE.

Populist movement A political movement active in the United States during the last third of the 19th century, which represented the agrarian and labor interests of the West and South opposed to the business and financial interests of the Northeast. In 1891 a People's (Populist) Party convention was held in Cincinnati, which nominated Presidential and Vice-Presidential candidates and wrote a platform. It demanded free and unlimited coinage of silver at 16 to 1 (see under SILVER STANDARD) and an increase in circulating currency of at least $50 per capita; a national currency issued only by the Federal government and without the use of banking corporations (see NATIONAL BANKS, def. 2); government ownership and operation of all transportation and communications facilities; a graduated income tax; a postal savings system; direct election of U.S. Senators; adoption of the secret ballot, initiative, and referendum; prohibition of alien ownership of land; a shorter working day for factory workers; and restrictions on immigration. In the 1892 election the Populists were a powerful third party, polling 1 million popular votes, 22 electoral votes, and electing several Congressmen. Though it died as a national party after the next election (in which it supported William Jennings Bryan and his free-silver policy), other leading parties adopted some of the Populist planks (notably the income tax, popular election of Senators, postal savings, and government ownership of transportation), many of which were subsequently enacted.

pork barrel A law, policy, or appropriation from the government that benefits a particular locality. The term is used particularly for nonessential projects vigorously promoted by a legislator trying to win over constituents through zealous support of their interests. The practice of legislators cooperating with one another to promote such pet projects is called *logrolling*.

portal-to-portal pay A wage based on the time spent on the employer's premises, whether or not actually performing work. A worker receiving portal-to-portal pay is paid from the moment of entering the premises until the time of leaving them. The practice originated in the coal-mining industry, where workers insisted on being paid for time spent in going from the mine entrance (called "portal") to their actual place of work, which might take as much as an hour. In some industries portal-to-portal pay is customary, and in others it may be negotiated in a labor contract.

port authority A special commission established to control the traffic of a port, whose authority may extend also to bridges, tunnels, airports, and similar approaches affecting the development, accessibility, etc., of the port.

portfolio The total holdings of securities by an individual or institution. A portfolio may include bonds, preferred stocks, common stocks, and other securities of various enterprises. A *portfolio investor* is one who plays an essentially passive role in the management of the enterprise. For *portfolio investment*, see under INTERNATIONAL INVESTMENT.

port of entry, port of exit Any place where goods and/or passengers may enter or leave a country, whether by ship, rail, air, or some other means, and where customs officials inspect incoming goods and baggage and levy duties in accordance with existing tariff laws.

Postal Service, U.S. An independent Federal agency responsible for handling the nation's mail. Originally an executive department headed by a Postmaster General of cabinet rank, the Postal Service became a separate agency in 1970. In the mid-1970s it employed 700,000 persons and handled about 90 billion pieces of mail per year; since 1900 it has been running at a steady annual deficit ranging from $5 million (in 1900) to more than $1 billion in the 1970s. The prices charged for its services, or *postal rates*, are established with the aid of another independent Federal agency, the Postal Rate Commission, and are based on a system of *mail classification*, which in turn is based on the nature of the material being mailed (size, weight, value, etc.), the speed of service desired, etc. In addition, the Postal Service provides certain other services: *special delivery* for any class of mail, which assures its immediate delivery upon arrival at the destination post office; *special handling*, which expedites delivery of third-and fourth-class mail; *priority mail*, which provides first-class airmail treatment for mail weighing more than 13 ounces; *registered mail*, for mailing of valuable items by first-class mail, which assures the sender of indemnification by the post office if the article is lost or damaged in transit; *certified mail*, which affords the sender proof of mailing and delivery (with a receipt, if requested); and *insurance*, provided for third- and fourth-class mail up to a limit of $200.

postdate To affix a date later than the existing one to a document or paper such as an invoice, granting an extension in payment terms. Sometimes a check is postdated so that it cannot be cashed before a certain time, but this practice technically turns the check into a promissory note.

Fig. 66. Classification of U.S. mail

First-class mail	Letters, postcards, and other written matter. Letters should be sealed.
Second-class mail	Newspapers, magazines, and other periodicals, when mailed by others than publishers or news agents.
Third-class mail:	
Regular	Unsealed printed material, such as advertising, merchandise, books, catalogs, etc. Also, the mailing of several identical printed letters mailed simultaneously.
Bulk	50 pounds or 200 pieces or more of identical material mailed at one time, consisting of any regular third-class material (see above). Special low rates are given to authorized nonprofit, religious, educational, scientific, philanthropic, agricultural, labor, veterans or fraternal organizations.
Fourth-class mail (Parcel post)	Merchandise, printed matter, etc. weighing 16 ounces or more. Special rates are available for books, films, etc.
Air mail (Priority mail)	Any mailable matter. Material weighing more than 9 ounces is treated as air parcel post.

postindustrial state A term used by J. K. GAL-BRAITH for an economy in the stage of development following that of direct manufacturing and production of goods, that is, one concerned chiefly with service industries, leisure activities, and education. See also MATURE ECONOMY.

posting In accounting, transferring an entry from a journal or other book of original entry, where it was first recorded, to the ledger in which it is assigned to the appropriate account.

potential gross national product Also, *full employment output*. The total monetary value of a nation's output at any given time under conditions of FULL EMPLOYMENT without inflation. Since it represents a measure of possible rather than existing conditions, potential gross national product (GNP) is at best difficult to calculate (some economists consider it impossible). Nevertheless, the idea of potential GNP has given rise to various yardsticks that allegedly show the relationship between unemployment and GNP. For example, the American economist Arthur M. Okun suggested that each extra percentage point in the unemployment rate above 4 per cent (which is traditionally considered full employment) is associated with a decrease of approximately 3 per cent in GNP. The potential GNP increases each year with growth in the quality and quantity of the labor force and as a result of increases in the stock of capital goods.

poverty Also, *disadvantaged, low-income, poor, underdeveloped*. The condition of receiving less income than the average individual or family, with little or no prospect of increasing that income. Depending on the standards used to measure income, a major part of the world's population is poor, particularly in the THIRD WORLD (see also UNDERDEVELOPED NATIONS). In the richer industrial countries, the chronically unemployed and, with increasing technological change, also the underemployed are counted among the poor. In the United States in the early 1970s, 11.9 per cent of the population was *below* what was defined as the "low income level," an index taking into account food costs and differing consumption needs based on size, composition, sex and age of family head, and farm or nonfarm residence of families. Some of the poor lived in low-income areas within or outside central cities or in metropolitan areas; others were in rural areas. Since about 1950, the existence of poverty affecting not only individuals (who are aided by various WELFARE programs) but whole areas has received increasing attention, and a number of poverty programs have been developed on the Federal level. The Economic Development Administration of the U.S. Department of Commerce, established in 1965, is chiefly concerned with the long-range economic development of *depressed* or distressed areas, that is, those with severe unemployment and low family income (such as APPALACHIA).

power of attorney　A written authorization to an AGENT to perform specific acts on behalf of the principal.

power of sale　A clause in a MORTGAGE or WILL that gives the mortgagee or executor the right to sell pledged property or part of the estate without going through special court proceedings. See also FORECLOSURE.

preemptive rights　Rights to the first opportunity to buy a new stock issue, given to existing stockholders in the charter of the corporation. Prior to a new issue, each such stockholder normally receives a *subscription warrant* indicating how many of the new shares he or she is entitled to buy, usually at a price somewhat lower than the market price. In most cases, the more shares the stockholder already owns, the more of the new issue he or she may buy. See also RIGHTS.

preferential shop　An agreement whereby an employer gives first preference in hiring to union members. See also UNION SHOP.

preferential tariff　See under TARIFF, def. 1.

preferred stock　A security that represents an ownership interest in a corporation (see also STOCK, def. 1) and gives its owner a prior claim over COMMON STOCK on the company's earnings (in the form of dividends) and on its assets should it be liquidated. Preferred stock normally is entitled to dividends at a specified rate—when declared by the firm's board of directors and before payment of a common stock dividend—depending on the terms of the issue. In the case of a *cumulative preferred stock*, if one or more dividends is omitted—a so-called *passed dividend*, which the company is unable or unwilling to pay—these payments would accumulate and must be paid before any common stock dividend is paid; most preferred stocks are of this type. On a *noncumulative preferred stock*, passed dividends do not accrue and are, as a rule, gone forever; a few older railroad preferred stocks are of this type. In the case of *participating preferred stock*, the owners may share in any extra profits a successful company might earn in prosperous years, over and above the declared dividend, by taking an additional dividend to give them a return that is at least equal to that on the common stock. Further, they may have some voting rights in company affairs. A *nonparticipating preferred stock* gives no such rights, nor any profits other than the stated declared dividend. A *convertible preferred stock* carries a provision that the owner may exchange it for a given number of shares of the firm's common stock. For this reason the market price of convertible preferred stocks tends to be more volatile than that of other preferred stocks (which are more stable than common stocks), since it is always linked to the price of the common stock into which it may be converted at the owner's discretion. Many preferred stocks carry a provision allowing the company to call in the entire issue and pay the owners at full value, plus a small premium (perhaps 5 per cent). This action would be to a firm's advantage if, for example, it believes it can replace that issue with one carrying a lower dividend. It also is a device whereby the company can force conversion if it wishes. For example, a preferred stock with a par value of $100 and callable at $105 may be convertible into two shares of common stock. If the common stock is selling at 60, the company may call the preferred stock, and the owners have no choice but to convert immediately, getting securities worth $120 per share rather than liquidating their holdings for $105 per share.

premium

1. An extra payment or bonus, in the form of cash, goods, or services. For example, an employee might receive *premium pay*, in the form of an extra wage, for working overtime. (See also WAGE INCENTIVE.) Similarly, a consumer might receive a premium in the form of a coupon toward another purchase for buying a new brand of soap, or in the form of extra merchandise (two for the price of one is a common device) or a credit on future purchases.

2. In insurance, the sum of money the policy-holder agrees to pay the insurer for an insurance policy. Also, the periodic payments of this sum. The premium is based on the insurance company's *rate*, that is, the cost of insurance per unit. For example, the rate for fire insurance might be 30 cents per $100 of insurance; insurance worth $10,000 thus would carry an annual premium of $30. The rate, and hence the premium, covers the company's estimated risk (calculated by an ACTUARY), its administrative and other operating expenses, and its profits. See also RATING, def. 3.

3. In the securities trade, a term with several meanings: (a) the amount by which the price of a stock or bond exceeds its par value or face value (see also DISCOUNT, def. 3); (b) in the case of a new security issue, the amount the market price rises above the original selling price; (c) a charge sometimes made when a stock is borrowed to make delivery on a short sale (see SELLING SHORT); (d) the redemption price of a bond or preferred stock if it is higher than the face or par value; (e) in trading stock options (see OPTION, def. 2), the price the buyer pays to the seller of an option contract.

prepaid expense Also, *deferred charge, deferred expense.* An EXPENSE (def. 2) incurred for future benefit. Examples include rent paid in advance, an advance against royalties, insurance premiums, and magazine subscriptions. On a balance sheet accountants classify such items as current assets.

prepaid medical care See under HEALTH INSURANCE.

prepayment

1. In general, the payment of an obligation before it falls due. In the case of some debts, such as installment purchases, there may be an extra charge for making full payment before the agreed time (see also INSTALLMENT BUYING).

2. The payment before maturity of a time draft (see under BILL OF EXCHANGE).

3. Paying a MORTGAGE debt before maturity. Unless the mortgage specifically states that the debt is payable *on or before* the due date, or that it is payable in monthly installments of a given sum *or*

more, or there is a specific *prepayment privilege* clause, the mortgagor cannot pay before maturity, even by offering to pay both principal and all interest up to the maturity date.

presentation A sales effort on behalf of a product, service, or idea, using various visual aids (charts, film strips, slides, etc.) and other means of demonstration.

present value method See DISCOUNTED CASH FLOW.

president In a corporation, the chief executive officer, who has final responsibility for overall policies and their execution. Like the other officers, the president usually is appointed by the board of directors, which act for the owners (stockholders).

pressure group Also, *lobby.* A group that actively tries to persuade legislators to enact laws favoring its interests and prevent possibly harmful action. In the United States most large trade associations and labor unions maintain lobbies seeking to influence both state and Federal legislators. Producers' pressure groups have succeeded in obtaining government subsidies for their industry, curbs on imports that compete with their products, and laws that protect their pricing or other policies. Unions have pressed for protective labor laws, and farm groups for price supports. Employing methods that range from personal contacts or persuasion to organized mail campaigns and testimony at Congressional hearings, lobbies have been known to spend millions of dollars and may wield influence far out of proportion to the size of the group they represent.

prevailing wage See under WAGE.

preventive maintenance Keeping property and equipment in good repair so as to minimize the need for costly major repair work or replacement. Preventive maintenance ranges from keeping simple hand tools cleaned and oiled to prevent rusting to complex procedures designed to prevent breakdowns of factory equipment.

price The exchange value of a good or service expressed in terms of money (see also VALUE). In economics the term also may be used more broadly, to describe the free-market economy (or so-called *price system*), whereby the price one must pay or can receive for goods and services is a major determinant of how and what resources will be used to produce certain goods and services (see RESOURCE ALLOCATION). Except in the dozen or so Communist nations whose economies are almost totally planned (see PLANNED ECONOMY), price is—in theory, at least—determined by the interaction of supply and demand. Since the interaction of sellers and buyers takes place in a MARKET (see def. 5), the resultant price is called a *market price*. (Also, the branch of economics that focuses on studies of the market, microeconomics, is sometimes called *price theory*.) If demand and supply are allowed to operate with complete freedom, increased demand tends to raise a price and declining demand tends to lower it; similarly, increased supply lowers a price and decreased supply raises it. (See also DEMAND CURVE; SUPPLY CURVE.) In reality both tendencies are affected not only by ELASTICITY of demand and supply (which varies with the good or service in question) but also by numerous conditions that limit PURE COMPETITION, including government price supports and price controls and the influences of limited numbers of sellers (and sometimes buyers; see IMPERFECT COMPETITION; MONOPOLY; OLIGOPOLY). See also the subsequent entries under PRICE.

price, administered See ADMINISTERED PRICE.

price control Government regulation intended to keep prices from rising inordinately. Price controls are commonly imposed on a variety of goods during wartime, to offset the scarcities of a war-oriented economy, but occasionally they are used in peacetime to counter inflation. Sometimes the prices of all goods are affected; at other times only certain goods are controlled. Large-scale price control is normally enacted and administered by the national government. If persisting over a long period, however, it generally is turned over to local control. For example, in the United States rent control, imposed by Federal law during World War II, was continued in a number of American cities for several decades after the war owing to continued housing shortages, but was eventually turned over to state or municipal control. See also FREEZE; RATIONING, def. 1.

price-cutting A systematic reduction in prices, usually undertaken to gain a larger share of the market. The danger of price-cutting is retaliation by competitors, which may lead to a *price war*—a continuing series of price reductions so drastic that each seller suffers considerable losses. Price wars were rampant among American railroads during the late 19th century, each trying to undercut the other's rates (and making up for it by charging exorbitant rates in localities where they had monopolies).

price discrimination
1. The sale of goods and services to different buyers at different prices that are not based on differences in cost (*dual pricing*), or the sale at the same price despite considerable differences in cost. Such discrimination takes many forms and has long been rampant. For example, doctors and dentists traditionally charge what they feel their patients can afford to pay. Department stores often charge less for the same goods sold in their basement stores than on their upper floors. Railroads and public utilities vary their freight and service charges. Farmers get one price for milk being made into butter or cheese and another for milk going to consumers. Manufacturers and wholesalers classify customers and charge different classes different prices (a so-called *class price*). A common means of discriminating is through shipping or freight charges (see DELIVERED PRICING). Another is through the use of various discounts (see DISCOUNT, def. 1; also FUNCTIONAL DISCOUNT). Price discrimination may be open or concealed, systematic or sporadic, permanent or temporary. However, when it is practiced in order to limit competition or to take undue advantage of a monopolistic position (as in the case of public utilities, airlines, etc.), in the United States it usually is deemed a violation of antitrust laws and is prosecuted accordingly. The Robinson-Patman Act of 1936 makes it illegal to discriminate in price among like classes of buyers for goods in interstate commerce except when the

seller is discriminating in order to meet competition. However, this law has so many loopholes that, with only a few exceptions, it has failed to serve the government as a needed tool for successful prosecution of violations.

2. In foreign trade, charging different prices for domestic and foreign markets. As in domestic price discrimination (see def. 1 above), the seller must have a degree of monopoly over its product, but in foreign trade its markets are already physically separated, making discrimination easier; moreover, there is no antitrust legislation to prevent it. However, nations often protect themselves against a seller's dumping—that is, selling goods more cheaply abroad than at home—by invoking an ANTIDUMPING TARIFF.

price-earnings ratio Also, *P-E ratio*. The current market price of a share of stock divided by the issuing company's earnings per share for a 12-month period. For example, a stock selling for $100 per share and earning $8 per share is said to be selling at a price-earnings ratio of 12½ to 1, often stated simply as 12½. The P-E ratio, which normally appears in the stock prices quoted in the financial pages of newspapers, is regarded as a yardstick of value for investors. It both measures the price of a stock against the company's profits and indicates how other investors regard the stock. A sharp drop in the P-E ratio may indicate investors' lack of confidence in a stock (unless the P-E ratios of all or most stocks are dropping at the same time). A high P-E ratio usually implies that investors anticipate that future earnings will be markedly higher than present earnings.

price fixing The setting of prices by the government or by private individuals or firms. The former is usually in the interest of avoiding wide price fluctuations for a commodity for which demand is relatively inflexible, such as the postal service. Private price fixing is practically always done to obtain huge profits, and in most instances is illegal, a major exception being the rates set by regulated utilities. See also PEGGING.

price forecasting See under FORECASTING.

price index The ratio of one price (or combination of prices) to the price of the same item (or combination of items) at a different time. This measure of changing prices is an important means of evaluating the general state of the economy. Generally a composite price is constructed by using the average price of a selected list of items, called the *market basket*, and comparing it to the average price for the same items in a preselected base year, which usually is assigned the number 100. Current prices are expressed as a percentage in relation to the base year. An index number of 123, for example, means that average prices are 23 per cent higher than in the base year; one of 93 shows prices as being 7 per cent lower. Though a price index can be constructed by using a simple average, such as the MEAN, it would then be highly misleading unless the market basket contained only one item or a group of closely related items. For example, if bread and rent were both included and rent rose by 21 per cent while bread rose by only 5 per cent, the simple average resulting—a price rise of 13 per cent—would fail to indicate that rent is a much larger budget item than bread could ever be. Consequently price indexes are generally constructed using a weighted average method, which weights items according to their relative importance. Even with weighting, price indexes fail to reflect other factors affecting purchases, such as changes in quality (usually owing to technological improvements), in preference and taste, in other prices that in turn influence spending in the area being measured, etc. See also COMMODITY PRICE INDEX; CONSUMER PRICE INDEX; IDEAL INDEX; INDEX NUMBER; WHOLESALE PRICE INDEX.

price leadership In a market characterized by imperfect competition, the role played by a single major firm in announcing price changes, which smaller firms tend to follow. In the United States this role was long played in the steel industry by U.S. Steel. See also OLIGOPOLY.

price level An average of prevailing prices at a given time. The average of all prices is called the *general price level* and, when real income is taken into account as well, constitutes a measure of economic well-being. In practice, changes in the price level are measured by means of a PRICE INDEX, which reflects both prices of items and their relative importance.

price limit The maximum price change permitted in one day's trading in a given commodity, set by the U.S. Commodity Futures Trading Commission. See also *trading limit*, under FUTURES MARKET.

price redetermination A provision for price changes in contracts for buying or selling goods. ESCALATION clauses allow for changes in labor or materials costs, or both, normally linking them to specific changes in union wage rates or raw materials prices in world markets. Price redetermination clauses tend to be still broader, permitting periodic renegotiation of prices. Such clauses are particularly useful for long-term contracts (running for several years), with a greater likelihood of price changes.

prices-paid/received-by-farmers Two indexes that measure monthly changes in the average prices paid by American farmers for both consumer goods and farm production, and in the average prices received for farm products. The base period for both indexes, which are prepared by the U.S. Bureau of Farm Economics, is 1910–14. The ratio of prices received to prices paid, called the *parity ratio*, is the basis for establishing a PARITY PRICE.

price-specie flow mechanism See under D. HUME.

price stability The maintenance of overall price levels without excessive inflation or deflation, allowing enough purchasing power for the economy to grow at a satisfactory rate, but not so much that the general PRICE LEVEL rises. Price stability is considered a major goal for any economy.

price support See PARITY PRICE; PEGGING.

price war See under PRICE-CUTTING.

pricing Any system of setting a PRICE. See AVERAGE COST, def. 2; BASING POINT SYSTEM; BREAK-EVEN ANALYSIS; COST-PLUS PRICING; DELIVERED PRICING; PRICE DISCRIMINATION.

primary boycott See under BOYCOTT.

primary offering See under ISSUE.

primary reserves See under BANK RESERVES.

prime Indicating a liability of high quality, that is, one incurred by a debtor with a very high credit rating. For example, *prime commercial paper* describes the promissory notes of firms with impeccable credit standing. See also PRIME RATE.

prime cost The cost of direct labor and direct materials incorporated into a product, excluding overhead or other costs not directly related to each individual product.

prime rate The INTEREST RATE charged by commercial banks for short-term loans to corporations whose credit standing is so high that little risk to the lender is involved. Only a small percentage of U.S. corporations qualify for the prime rate, which tends to be the lowest going interest rate and thus serves as a basis for other, higher-risk loans. Until 1971 the prime rate was simply set by bankers—in practice, by a few large New York banks—with the rest of the nation's banks following suit. In 1971, however, in response to political pressure to curb inflationary tendencies, banks began to set the prime rate according to a formula based on the open-market interest rates available from prime commercial paper or certificates of deposit. In practice bankers followed this formula when it suited them, but the prime rate was now considered a *flexible* or *floating prime rate*.

principal
1. In finance, the original amount of capital invested or lent, as distinguished from profits or interest.
2. In law, the individual being represented in a business transaction by an AGENT (def. 1) authorized to do so.

printout A printed copy of a computer's output.

priority The order of precedence in which claims may be made against a bankrupt, defaulting, or liquidated firm. In BANKRUPTCY various classes of creditor have priority over others in claims to any existing assets. With a corporation, bondholders have priority over preferred stockholders, who in turn have priority over common stockholders, with regard to both sharing the earnings (interest on bonds, dividends on stock) and, in case of liquidation, apportioning the assets. For priority of mortgages, see under MORTGAGE.

private bank An unincorporated bank, which in the United States is regulated by the state in which it operates. Some states, however, prohibit private banks entirely.

private brand See under BRAND.

private corporation See CLOSED CORPORATION.

private debt, net The total indebtedness of the private sector of the economy, that is, individuals and businesses. For individuals it consists largely of consumer credit, bank loans, and mortgages (the last accounting for about 60 per cent of total indebtedness). For corporations about half consists of short-term liabilities.

private enterprise See PRIVATE SECTOR, def. 1.

privateering Attack on and robbery of enemy merchant ships during wartime by private vessels authorized by a special government license, called a *letter of marque*. The practice was common in the 17th and 18th centuries, before national navies were powerful enough to wage war without such assistance. See also PIRACY.

private placement See DIRECT PLACEMENT.

private property Property in which one or more individuals have exclusive rights, as opposed to public property, which is owned by a local, state, or national government.

private sector
1. Also, *private enterprise*. All economic activities that are independent of government control (or outside the so-called PUBLIC SECTOR), carried on principally for profit but also including nonprofit or-

ganizations directed at satisfying private needs, such as private hospitals and private schools. Included are enterprises owned individually or by groups (such as corporations with numerous stockholders) as well as the self-employed.
2. In national income accounting, the total net value added to the economy by nongovernment producers of goods and services. This includes not only the output of profit and nonprofit private corporations, proprietorships, and partnerships, but also that of self-employed individuals such as farmers, dentists, etc. The private sector accounts for about 88 per cent of gross national product in the United States. See also PUBLIC SECTOR.

probability theory General term for a body of mathematical theory concerned with estimating the likelihood that some particular event or series of events will take place. Estimates and predictions are based on past experience and whatever relevant data are available. Probability theory is used in many areas of business and economics containing elements of uncertainty, in attempts to answer such questions as "How much of Y Output of Product X at Price Z is likely to sell in the next year?" Probability is always expressed in terms of a number between 0 and 1, that is, a fraction, ratio, decimal, or percentage. If the likelihood for an event to occur is nil (no amount of product X will be sold), the probability is 0; if an event is certain to occur, the probability is 1. If two horses of equal ability race each other, the probability that either will win is equal, or 1/2, or one out of two, or .50. See also BAYESIAN DECISION THEORY; RISK, def. 1; UNCERTAINTY.

probable life See SERVICE LIFE.

probate See under WILL.

procedure-oriented language In computer PROGRAMMING, the use of a language in which the operations and operands are described in notation designed to be convenient to the user. A program written in such a language must be translated to directly executable code, which may be accomplished by a translator program.

procedures See POLICIES AND PROCEDURES.

proceeds
1. In business, the amount realized on a transaction after deducting expenses, commissions, etc. The proceeds of a sale, for instance, is the amount received by the seller after such deductions have been made.
2. In finance, the amount received by a borrower after a promissory note or other paper has been discounted, that is, after interest has been deducted.

process capability   The ability of a machine or process to produce an item in accordance with specifications. Usually the higher the process capability, the higher the cost of production. Hence manufacturers often must choose among the operating costs of various alternative machines or processes—all of which can produce the desired item but with varying quality—relative to the cost of producing unacceptable parts. For example, a piece of cast metal may be unfinished (cheapest and least accurate process); or it may be machined with a planer or milling machine; or it may be ground (most costly and most accurate process). The engineer determines what process is needed, and the manufacturing organization then monitors this process to make sure that it is operating within its prescribed capability, a procedure called *process control.*

process control   See under PROCESS CAPABILITY.

process cost
1. The cost of a particular production process.
2. A method of cost accounting whereby costs are charged to the processes or operations of production and are averaged over the units of the product. It is used chiefly in industries where the end-product is the result of a largely continuous mass-production operation and is homogeneous, as in the canning, paper, oil refining, and chemicals industries. See also JOB ORDER SYSTEM.

processing   A kind of manufacturing in which one material is converted into another, such as sugar refining, in which cane is converted first into molasses and then into refined sugar; petroleum refining, in which crude oil is converted into oil, kerosene, and other products; and various kinds of metal production, in which minerals are converted into metals (alumina into aluminum, iron ore into steel, etc.). Generally speaking, process and product are inseparable, since the method used determines the end-product. Further, the process, consisting of a given sequence of operations, must be continuous, going through stage after stage until it is completed. These characteristics enable many processing industries to make considerable use of AUTOMATION. See also BATCH PROCESSING, def. 2; CONTINUOUS PROCESS.

procurement   See PURCHASING.

produce exchange   See COMMODITY EXCHANGE.

producer cooperative   See COOPERATIVE, def. 3.

producer goods
1. In common usage, same as capital goods (see CAPITAL, def. 1).
2. Also, *producer durable equipment.* In national income accounting, new machinery and equipment bought for business use.

product development   See RESEARCH AND DEVELOPMENT.

product differentiation   See under ADVERTISING.

production   In general, the creation or output of a good or service. Although the term can be applied equally to the service industries, it most often is used for the output of manufacturing and processing enterprises. In these, the *production department* or *division* is usually synonymous with the *manufacturing department,* that is, the areas of the business directly concerned with producing the company's end-product (as opposed to the various *service departments,* such as purchasing, traffic, accounting, personnel, etc.). Depending on the nature of the end-product, a manufacturer tends to be organized in one of two basic ways: *job order production,* in which each order is treated separately, or *line production,* which is a continuous process. In the former the end-product tends to be one of a kind; in the latter it tends to be homogeneous. See also BATCH PROCESSING, def. 2; CONTINUOUS PROCESS; JOB ORDER SYSTEM; MASS PRODUCTION; PRODUCTION CONTROL.

production, theory of A branch of economics that deals with the relations of inputs of factors of production (land, labor, capital) and outputs. See also INPUT-OUTPUT ANALYSIS; PRODUCTION FUNCTION.

production bonus See under WAGE INCENTIVE.

production control In business and industry, especially in manufacturing and processing enterprises, the control of output through planning and scheduling of workers, machinery, and materials so as to obtain maximum output with minimum input. Production control begins with a detailed forecast of product demand (in turn based on various market forecasts), followed by computing detailed requirements for parts and materials (both purchased and manufactured) from bills of material and specifications supplied by the product engineering department. This phase is called *production planning*. It continues with *scheduling* the production and/or purchase of parts and materials needed to meet overall schedules for completed end-products, which involves calculating the requirements for each item (taking into account inventory, lead time, on-order position, etc.). It proceeds with the issue of work orders to manufacturing departments and purchase requisitions to purchasing personnel to obtain parts and materials in time to meet overall schedules. This phase is also called *material control*. Production control keeps detailed records of inventory, on-order status, and potential demand for each production part and material, and makes periodic physical counts of stock to verify the accuracy of records. Finally, it maintains physical inventories of all production materials in various stages of fabrication and administers controls necessary to maximize turnover and minimize losses from spoilage, obsolescence, or pilferage. This phase is called *inventory control*. Today many elements of production control, particularly in larger firms, are handled by computer.

production factors See FACTORS OF PRODUCTION.

production function A mathematical equation that expresses how size of output is related to the input of the FACTORS OF PRODUCTION. A highly simplified example might be:

$$\frac{1{,}000 \text{ hats}}{\text{per week}} = 20 \text{ workers} + 1{,}000 \text{ units materials}$$
$$+ \, 10 \text{ machines} + 1 \text{ workshop}$$

Naturally each of these items has a price, which is the figure the producer is most interested in. Filling in prices, the equation might now be:

$$\underset{\text{(cost)}}{\$20{,}000} = \underset{\text{(wages)}}{\$10{,}000} + \underset{\text{(materials)}}{\$8{,}000}$$

$$+ \underset{\substack{\text{(interest,}\\ \text{depreciation,}\\ \text{etc.)}}}{\$1{,}800} + \underset{\text{(rent)}}{\$200}$$

The purpose of such an equation is to find the best possible combination, yielding the highest output with the lowest input (or the greatest profit at the least cost). This is accomplished by varying the factors until the optimum is found. The elements of the production function are far more variable than might first appear. The level of skill of workers (as compared with their pay), the quality and price of materials used, the type of machine, and the ability of management are but some of the variables that affect output. Moreover, the same output often can be achieved by more than one combination. The production function is useful not only for individual firms but for assessing the economy as a whole. See also COBB-DOUGLAS PRODUCTION FUNCTION; INPUT-OUTPUT ANALYSIS; RETURNS TO SCALE.

production index see INDUSTRIAL PRODUCTION INDEX.

production method Also, *service-output method, unit of product method*. A method of calculating the depreciation of a fixed asset during each accounting period over its life. It is particularly helpful for assets whose usage varies considerably. Usage generally is expressed in such terms as hours of operation or number of units produced. First the cost of an asset (minus salvage value) is divided by the total number of hours or product units estimated for its entire service life; then depreciation for any one accounting period is found by multiplying the actual hours of use or units of product in that period by depreciation per hour or unit. For example, a truck costing $15,000 will, it is estimated, be driven 100,000 miles during its service life, and its salvage value is $1,000. The depreciation per mile then will be ($15,000 − $1,000)/100,000 = $.14. If the truck is driven 20,000 miles during the first year, depreciation will be 20,000 × $.14 = $2,800.

production planning See under PRODUCTION CONTROL. See also PRODUCT PLANNING.

production-possibility curve See TRANSFORMATION CURVE.

productivity In economic theory, the output of any factor of production—land, labor, or capital—per unit of input. Productivity can be measured in various ways. The productivity of land may be measured, for example, in terms of output per acre. The productivity of labor is more likely to be measured in terms of output per working hour (see also MARGINAL PRODUCTIVITY THEORY). The *productivity of capital* cannot be measured quite as easily, since it involves comparing physical output to the current real value of the capital invested in an enterprise and thus depends on such factors as level of technology, organization and management, and the type of capital employed (plant, machinery, etc.). It normally is expressed as a percentage per year, which represents the annual yield of that particular capital investment. Since capital goods tend to decline in value and eventually wear out, most economists distinguish between *gross capital productivity* (total yield) and *net capital productivity*, which discounts depreciation. The British economist J. M. Keynes called the latter *marginal efficiency of capital* (the expected yield of the last additional unit of capital; see also under KEYNES), the term used by many present-day economists, although some prefer *marginal productivity of capital*; the American economist Irving Fisher called it *rate of return over cost*. The concept is essentially the same, however, and it is important because of its close relation to the INTEREST RATE. Net capital productivity (or marginal efficiency) is the annual percentage yield earned by the capital, which is equivalent to the market rate of interest at which it would just pay to undertake a given investment. For example, if the market rate of interest is 8 per cent, it obviously would not pay to invest in a project that yields only $7\frac{1}{2}$ per cent. The net productivity of capital itself influences the long-term interest rate. Like other economic phenomena, yield on capital is subject to the law of DIMINISHING RETURNS; when high-yield investments are exhausted, capital is used for lower-yield projects, and its net productivity will decline (described as *declining marginal efficiency*). The market rate of interest then will fall, encouraging more investors to undertake projects that previously were not profitable. See also *natural interest rate*, under K. WICKSELL.

productivity clause See ANNUAL IMPROVEMENT FACTOR.

product mix The various products sold by any one firm. In some cases they may be closely related, but in others they may be as disparate as fertilizer and breakfast cereal.

product planning Deciding what products to sell and in what amounts, designing new products or redesigning existing ones (*product design*), and determining their quality standards and price ranges. Closely associated with these areas is market research to determine what products are likely to sell, and technical research and development in both products and processes. In some industries, notably drugs and cosmetics, a substantial percentage of earnings is devoted to product planning.

profession Any occupation that requires considerable education and specialized training, as opposed to purely technical or manual skills. Law, medicine, dentistry, architecture, science, engineering, accounting, teaching, social work, religion, writing, art, and entertainment are the principal professions recognized by the U.S. Bureau of the Census.

profit
1. In accounting, any excess of revenues over the costs incurred in obtaining revenues. *Gross profit* is the amount received from sales *minus* the cost of the goods or services sold; other expenses, such as sales, advertising, salaries, or rent, have not been deducted. *Net profit*, on the other hand, is the

amount received from sales *minus* all the expenses of business operations (see also NET INCOME, def. 1). *Operating profit* (or *operating income*) represents earnings from regular business operations and does not include revenues from other sources, such as return on investments in other businesses, interest on loans, etc. See also INCOME STATEMENT.

2. In economic theory, a surplus earned above the normal return on investment of capital in a business, created when the prices received for goods sold exceed the cost of producing them. Whereas economists of the CLASSICAL SCHOOL described profit as the entrepreneur's reward for risk-taking, many 19th-century economists, including Alfred MARSHALL, regarded profit as a kind of wage for able management. The American economist Frank Hyneman Knight, in his *Risk, Uncertainty, and Profit* (1921), returned to the earlier idea, distinguishing between insurable risk (whose insurance premiums then become part of the cost of production) and uninsurable uncertainty. Profit then becomes a reward for guessing right on unpredictable changes in future demand and selling prices, and so is related not only to risk-taking but to the rate of economic change and the entrepreneur's business acumen. Still another view is that profit is a QUASI-RENT, that is, a return resulting from scarcity. From this standpoint, such advantages as higher managerial skill or better location relative to markets and/or suppliers, which enable lower-cost production, are regarded as scarcities that earn a high return.

profit-and-loss statement See INCOME STATEMENT.

profit center A department, division, or other unit of a firm that is regarded as a separate entity in terms of operating at a profit. A profit center may be as large as the Chevrolet Division of General Motors Corporation or as small as the lingerie department of a single local department store. In either case the overall manager of the division is responsible for achieving the profit goals set by top management.

profiteering Reaping excessive profits from a business operation, particularly by taking advantage of a shortage caused by war or some natural disaster and charging exorbitant prices.

profit margin Also, *gross margin.* Gross profit (see PROFIT, def. 1) expressed as a percentage of net sales, used chiefly in retail and wholesale accounting. It is calculated by subtracting the total cost of goods sold from net sales income. For example, suppose a druggist pays $10,000 for inventories (total costs) over a six-month period and sells these goods for $18,000 (gross sales). From that the druggist might deduct $1,000 for returns and allowances, making for net sales of $17,000. The gross margin then is $7,000 ($17,000 − $10,000) or 41 per cent of net sales. However, the *net margin* (after deducting expenses connected with operating the store) might be less than 5 per cent. For operating margin of profit, see under INCOME STATEMENT.

profit sharing The practice of distributing some of a business firm's profits to some or all of its employees as a kind of bonus, in addition to regular wages and salaries. The bonus may be in cash, stock, an option to buy stock, or some other form. It may be distributed at intervals of one year or less, or deposited in a trust and credited to the accounts of individual employees, who then receive it only when they leave the company (through termination, retirement, or death).

profit squeeze A colloquial term describing the plight of the producer whose profits are diminishing because costs are rising faster than selling prices. For example, a farmer is caught in a profit squeeze when the prices for fertilizer, seed, and tractor fuel continue to rise while the prices for crops remain stable or even decline.

pro forma A Latin term, meaning "as a matter of form," used for a financial statement that treats hypothetical events as though they had actually taken place and hence includes, in whole or in part, fictitious data. For example, a pro forma balance sheet might show the effect of not yet completed financing, or a pro forma income statement might treat two companies that had not yet merged as a single entity.

program, computer See under PROGRAMMING.

program flow chart See FLOW CHART, def. 2.

programming The process of producing a sequence of instructions, called a *program* or *routine*, which when carried out on a computer results in specific arithmetic or data-processing operations. Every instruction consists of two elements, an *operation code* that initiates the actual operation (add, move, write, etc.) and an *operand* that designates the *address* (location in the memory) of information or a device (such as a card reader or tape drive) to which the operation applies. For example, if the operation is "add," the operand is the addresses of the data to be added; if it is "print out," the operand would designate the memory address from which the data are to be printed. More than one operand may be needed. If the operation were "move," a second operand could indicate the address *to* which the data should be moved. Instructions generally are one of three kinds: (1) those involving data, consisting of an operation code (add, move, compare, etc.) and one or more addresses to be operated on; (2) those involving equipment, consisting of an operation code (read, write, punch, etc.) and the designation of the equipment that is to carry out the operation (tape drive, card punch, etc.); (3) those involving *branching*, consisting of an operation code and an operand to which the computer is to "branch" (begin executing a different series of instructions, or a *subroutine*). Complicated programs can involve numerous subroutines (sometimes called "miniprograms").

The writing of programs is done in a hierarchy of "languages" that are ultimately converted into *machine language* or *machine code*, that is, the instructions that control the computer itself. Owing to the nature of computer machinery (see COMPUTER for further explanation), a machine code must use the *binary number system*, based on 2, instead of the conventional decimal system, based on 10 (see BINARY). In the early days of computers, programmers had to write instructions directly in machine language, requiring them to memorize many specific addresses. With the development of *assembler programs*, the programmer could use mnemonics—a readily memorized *symbolic language*, using "SUB" for "subtract," "DIV" for

"divide," etc.—for operation codes and assign symbolic names to variables, which were then assigned proper machine addresses by the assembler program. The assembler thus translated the symbols from the *source program* (original program) into machine code (or *object code*), which the computer used as the actual program to be run. The process was extended with the development, somewhat later, of *macro-instructions* or *macros*, a predefined sequence of instructions that could be inserted into an assembler program by reference (in assembler language) to the macro name. Macros require *arguments*, the values or names of variables to be used in their execution. With assembler language, also known as *low-level language*, each statement usually represents but a single machine instruction; with macros a single statement is "expanded" into a series of instructions. *Compiler languages* (or *high-level languages*) carry this even further, so that a single statement can represent several series of instructions. Compilers are language translators making it possible for a program to be written in notation and syntax closely resembling the ordinary tools of the particular application. Among the compiler languages most used are FORTRAN, which resembles algebraic notation, and COBOL, which uses syntax resembling business English. (See also ALGOL; APT; PL/1). Compilers produce object language from source language; typically this object code consists of a series of "calls" to the subroutines required for performing the particular operation desired. Another kind of high-level language is represented by the interpretive languages that are not translated into machine code for subsequent execution, but, instead are "interpreted" for immediate execution. BASIC is the most widely used interpretive language.

By no means all programs are "written to order" for a given problem or task. Computer manufacturers supply prefabricated programs to perform the most frequently needed tasks and computations; such programs are called "utility programs" or *software* (to distinguish them from the machinery itself, called *hardware*). In general, whether done by manufacturer or user, there are two principal kinds of programming. One, called *applications programming*, is concerned with solving specific problems (payrolls, numerical analyses, statistical computations, etc.). The other, called *systems programming*, is concerned with writing and maintaining *operating systems*, that is, series of programs that control the operations of the computer itself (such as the order in which it handles input and output).

Programming Language 1 See PL/1.

progressive tax Also, *equitable tax*. A tax that takes a larger proportion of high incomes than of low, as opposed to a *regressive* tax, which takes a larger proportion of low incomes than of high. In the United States, the Federal taxes on personal income, inherited estates (death tax), and gifts are progressive in nature, while state sales taxes (based on a fixed percentage of each dollar spent) and excise taxes (on cigarettes, liquor, etc.) are regressive. The effects of some taxes are mixed, depending both on income group and on other factors. For example, payroll (employment) taxes tend to be progressive for families with very low incomes, since much of their income (such as welfare payments) is not subject to these taxes; for middle- and high-income families payroll taxes often are regressive, since they are levied at a flat rate up to a maximum amount of annual earnings. Further, the corporation income tax, if borne by stockholders and other property owners, is highly progressive; but if at least half that tax is shifted to consumers (in the form of higher prices paid by all consumers, regardless of income), it becomes regressive. See also DEGRESSIVE TAX.

proletariat A name for the working class. In ancient Rome it meant citizens who, having neither property nor a definite income, frequently joined the army; they were considered a source of discontent and political instability. During the French Revolution the name was used for the urban working class, as opposed to the BOURGEOISIE, or middle class. In Marxist doctrine, the proletariat is described as a propertyless class originally made up of landless peasants and retainers left from the breakup of feudal estates. In the capitalist society that replaced feudalism, they were forced to sell their labor for wages in the new industrial centers. Eventually, said Marx, they would rise up against their capitalist employers and set up a dictatorship of their own—the dictatorship of the proletariat—but

in time their class, along with all other classes, would be eliminated, and society would become classless. See also under COMMUNISM, def. 1.

promissory note An unconditional written promise to pay a given amount to a particular person (or to the bearer) at a given time and place. Interest may or may not be involved, the note may or may not be secured, and it may be payable on demand (*demand note*). Some (but not all) notes are negotiable, that is, transferable to another person by endorsement. Promissory notes are commonly used for consumer installment purchases and for transactions between individuals.

promoter
1. A person who helps organize or launch a business; an ENTREPRENEUR.
2. In sports and certain other industries, a person who organizes a particular performance, event, series of events, or tour, bringing together the participants and arranging for a time and place, publicity, etc., in exchange for a percentage of the profits.

promotion
1. The overall activity of furthering or advancing a business, particularly through increasing the sales of its services or products. In many firms promotion is considered a branch of MARKETING. See also ADVERTISING; PUBLIC RELATIONS.
2. A special merchandising effort, usually sponsored by the manufacturer but sometimes undertaken by the retailer on its own initiative. The promotion usually features a price cut on the merchandise during a given period, but it may consist simply of novel packaging or other features designed to attract customers during the period of the promotion "event." See also SALES PROMOTION.
3. Appointment to a position of higher rank or a job with more responsibility or requiring more skill. It usually (but not always) is awarded in conjunction with a raise in salary.

propensity to consume The tendency to spend a certain portion of one's income. The British economist J. M. KEYNES pointed out that not only does everyone spend part of his income (for food and shelter, if nothing else) but that there is a fairly fixed relationship between the proportion of spending and the amount of income, which varies with the level of income. Thus the $100-per-week clerk might spend all of his or her income, and the $1,000-per-week executive only half, saving the rest. This proportion will tend to remain quite stable. A graph or table showing the relation between consumption and income is called a *consumption schedule*. Economists generally are interested in the *average propensity to consume (APC)*, that is, a consumption schedule for an entire nation, and in the *marginal propensity to consume (MPC)*, that is, the *extra* amount that will be spent on consumption for every extra dollar of income. It usually is expressed as a ratio of the change in consumption and the change in income:

$$MPC = \frac{\text{change in consumption}}{\text{change in income}}$$

Graphically it is shown by the slope of the consumption schedule, a steep slope indicating a high MPC and a flat one a low MPC. For example, suppose disposable income increases from $10,000 to $12,000 per year, or by $2,000, and consumption

increases from $9,000 to $10,500, or by $1,500. The extra consumption is 1,500/2,000 = .75 of the extra income, with $.25 of each extra dollar going to savings. The MPC therefore is .75 between $10,000 and $12,000. See also ENGEL'S LAW; PROPENSITY TO SAVE.

propensity to import The value of imports as a percentage of income. Though it might be considered on an individual basis—for example, what proportion of individual disposable income is spent on imported goods such as wines and cheeses—economists tend to be more interested in *average propensity to import*, that is, the value of imports as a percentage of national income, and *marginal propensity to import*, that is, the increase in imports generated by increases in national income. Depending on a variety of conditions, such as whether luxuries or basic necessities constitute imports, increased national income may lead to either an increase or a decrease in imports. The relation of the two—average propensity to marginal propensity to import—is called the *income elasticity of demand for imports* and is expressed as:

$$\text{income elasticity of import demand} = \frac{\text{marginal propensity to import}}{\text{average propensity to import}}$$

Income elasticity of import demand is a way of assessing the effect of economic fluctuations (national income and employment levels) in one country on the countries with which it trades and on the balance of international payments. Propensity to import becomes of major concern when one country expands its national income more rapidly than its trading partners do. It then automatically attracts more imports, but its exports do not grow because its trading partners are not expanding their incomes at the same rate. As a result, the expanding country is soon faced with balance of payments problems, that is, its exports are not sufficient to pay for its rising level of imports.

propensity to invest The ratio of new CAPITAL FORMATION (net capital investment) to total NATIONAL INCOME. Investment is, along with consumption, a vital component of national income. According to J. M. Keynes, who first used the term "propensity" for this concept, the propensity to in-

Fig. 67. Consumption schedule

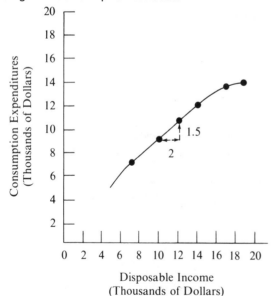

Disposable Income
(Thousands of Dollars)

The curve represents the consumption schedule. Its slope, measured by drawing a triangle and relating altitude to base, is the marginal propensity to consume.

vest is, under conditions of equilibrium, exactly equal to the PROPENSITY TO SAVE. Under different conditions, however, either may exceed the other: if savings exceed investment, national income is reduced; if investment exceeds savings, income rises. The propensity to invest depends on both the interest rate and the expected return on capital. See also under J. M. KEYNES.

propensity to save The tendency to postpone spending a certain portion of disposable personal income. The relation of saving to income is expressed in a graph or table called a *saving schedule*. The lower the income, the lower the proportion that is saved, since most (if not all) of it must presumably be spent on necessities. Indeed, on the lowest income levels, spending often exceeds income and *dissaving* occurs, either by using up previously accumulated savings or by going into debt. Such dissaving appears on the saving schedule as a negative quantity. Economists are interested principally in the *average propensity to save (APS)*, that is, a saving schedule for an entire nation, and in the *marginal propensity to save (MPS)*, that is, the *extra* saving generated by each extra dollar of income. It usually is expressed as a ratio:

$$\text{MPS} = \frac{\text{change in saving}}{\text{change in income}}$$

Fig. 68. Saving schedule

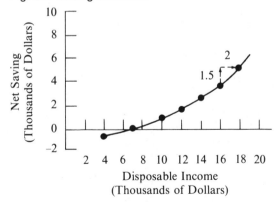

The curve represents the saving schedule; note the negative net saving, or dissaving, when disposable income is under $7,000. The slope of the curve, measured by drawing a triangle and relating altitude to base, is the marginal propensity to save.

Graphically this relationship is indicated by the slope of the saving schedule. The propensity to save is closely connected to the PROPENSITY TO CONSUME, since every dollar of income that is not saved is used for consumption. Saving plus consumption equals disposable income. The same holds true for *marginal saving* and *marginal consumption*, so that $\text{MPS} = 1 - \text{MPC}$ (every portion of each extra dollar that is not consumed is saved). Since MPC tends to decline as income increases, saving necessarily increases as well.

property insurance Any INSURANCE that protects against loss of or damage to property. Property may be a home and its contents, an automobile, freighter, factory, the contents of a truck or rail car, machinery, crop, etc., and damage or loss may occur as a result of fire, wind, hail, smoke, explosion, riot, motor vehicles, aircraft, heating system malfunctions, water, vandalism, theft and other crimes, freezing, collapse, etc. The most common kinds of property insurance are *fire insurance*, which generally is required for all mortgaged property and often includes *extended coverage* against other disasters (hail, smoke, explosion, etc.; see Fig. 69); *crop insurance* (see under AGRICULTURE, AID TO); *marine* and *aviation insurance*, for vessels, aircraft, and their cargo; *inland marine insurance*, a broad category embracing goods in transit in a variety of ways (see also FLOATER); *boiler* and *machinery insurance; automobile insurance* (both family and commercial); *dishonesty insurance* (against burglary, robbery, theft, etc.); and various kinds of *package insurance*, such as HOMEOWNERS INSURANCE, which combine insurance for various properties or against various hazards. Property insurance may be *all-risk comprehensive insurance*, which covers any loss or damage to property with certain named exceptions, or it may insure only against *named* hazards; for example, comprehensive automobile insurance might cover any loss or damage to a car except that caused by collision or upset. In many cases property insurance is combined with some form of LIABILITY INSURANCE (against claims for damages or injury sustained in accidents, etc.); in the case of auto insurance liability insurance may be required by law.

Just exactly what an insurance policy will pay when damage or loss occurs varies widely. In cases

Fig. 69. Three kinds of property insurance

Hazard	Fire and Extended Coverage	Fire, Extended Coverage, and Additional Extended Coverage	Fire, Extended Coverage, and "All-Risk" Comprehensive
Windstorm	x	x	x
Hail	x	x	x
Smoke	x	x	x (broad)
Riot	x	x	x
Explosion	x	x	x
Vehicle	x	x (broad)	x (broad)
Aircraft	x	x	x
Heating system		x	x
Water damage		x (limited)	x (broad)
Vandalism		x	x
Glass breakage		x	x
Fall of trees		x (limited)	x (broad)
Freezing		x	x
Collapse		x	x
Landslide			x
Earthquake			x
Rain			x
Ice, snow, sleet			x
Dust storm			x
Virtually any cause of damage other than specific exceptions named			x

of total loss, as when a building burns to the ground, it may pay a cash value specified at the time the policy was taken out (this is sometimes called a *valued policy*). In some cases it may pay the *replacement cost*, that is, the insurer will repair or replace the damaged property (usually a building) without making any allowance for depreciation; this is called *replacement insurance*. Occasionally property insurance includes provisions to compensate policyholders for their *loss of income* when property damage occurs. For example, the owner of an apartment building that burns down loses not only the building itself but also the rental income it yielded; similarly, the loss of a warehouse filled with goods entails loss not only of the goods but of the profit expected to be made in their sale. Loss-of-income coverage generally is available only for commercial enterprises and sometimes is called *business-interruption insurance*.

property tax A tax levied on various kinds of property—personal (jewelry, automobiles, furniture, etc.) and real (land and buildings). In the United States property taxes account for a large proportion—up to one-half—of the total revenue of state and local governments, the bulk coming from real estate taxes. Most real estate taxes are based on an annual rate set by the locality, such as 6 per cent of the assessed valuation of a building or tract of land. However, assessed valuations often do not reflect the current market value of the property (which usually is substantially higher), and the high cost and political unpopularity of reassessment militate against such revaluations. As a result, property taxes tend to be inflexible. In the case of rented property, moreover, property taxes tend to be shifted, at least in part, through the simple expedient of raising the rent. A similar shift takes place with taxes on business property, which are considered a cost (like other business costs) and hence are passed on in the form of higher prices. For a proposal that a tax on land be the only tax levied, see under H. GEORGE.

proportional tax   A tax whose rate remains constant, regardless of the size of the base, and which usually is stated as a flat percentage of the base. For example, a real estate tax of $60 per $1,000 of assessed valuation represents a proportional tax of 6 per cent on the assessed valuation of the property (house, land, etc.).

proprietary   Pertaining to exclusive ownership, or to a private or patented design, formula, method of manufacture, etc. A *proprietary drug* (or *patent medicine*) is one that, either through secret formulation or simply through brand identification, cannot be readily duplicated by a competitor.

proprietary lease   See under COOPERATIVE, def. 5.

proprietorship   Also, *single (sole) proprietorship*. A form of business organization in which an individual owns and manages the entire enterprise. The oldest kind of business, proprietorships still account for the majority of firms in the United States and other advanced countries, as well as in the poorer nations. Most proprietorships tend to be small. Expansion usually would require more capital than an individual possesses or can borrow. The chief advantages of a proprietorship are its simplicity, freedom from government control and business income tax, minimum legal restrictions, and individual accountability. Its drawbacks are that its life and success depend heavily on one individual, who is personally liable for all business debts and who may have trouble raising capital needed to expand.

pro rate
   1. In accounting, to assign a portion of a cost to an account according to some given procedure. For example, the cost of a material used in Products A, B, and C may be charged to the accounts for each of them on the basis of the amount used, a unit cost being then derived from total cost and total quantity.

   2. In insurance, the distribution of the total amount of insurance in one policy among several objects or places covered in proportion to their value. Also, the distribution of liability among several insurers who have policies on a single risk.

prospectus   See under ISSUE.

prosperity   A prolonged period of increasingly expanded business activity in which production increases, prices and wages usually rise, there is little unemployment, many new businesses are formed, capital investment increases, and credit expands. One threat to prosperity is inflation, that is, prices may rise at an accelerating rate. Demand for credit then pushes up interest rates rapidly, making it more difficult for business to continue to expand production and employment. See also BUSINESS CYCLE.

protective tariff   See under TARIFF, def. 1.

Protestant ethic   Also, *work ethic*. The idea that austere living, thrift, and devotion to hard work and money-making are a valid and desirable way of life. Some economists, notably Max WEBER, have claimed that the Protestant ethic was a basic force in the early development of capitalism. However, a similar ethic has been found in countries where Protestantism is at most a minority religion, notably Japan and China.

Proudhon, Pierre Joseph   See under MUTUALISM.

proxy   A written authorization from a shareholder to some other person to represent him or her and vote for his or her shares at a stockholders' meeting. In the United States, before such representatives may solicit proxies from shareholders, the U.S. Securities and Exchange Commission requires them to issue a *proxy statement* giving shareholders certain essential information. Proxies frequently are solicited by a corporation's own management, but occasionally they are sought by an opposition that hopes to muster enough votes to oust them. A battle for such votes is called a *proxy fight*.

prudent-man rule An investment standard for certain institutions and fiduciaries used by several states in the United States. According to this rule, a trustee may invest in a security only if it is one that a "prudent man" of discretion and intelligence, seeking reasonable income and preservation of capital, would buy. See also LEGAL LIST.

psychic income Intangible satisfaction derived from goods or services or some form of economic activity. For example, the gratification a factory worker may derive from free coffee provided by the employer may be far in excess of the coffee's cost; a business executive may get great satisfaction out of defeating a competitor in bidding on a contract even if the contract itself is not exceptionally advantageous; a consumer may enjoy saving $1 per week by shopping at three different stores instead of one, despite the extra time involved. The concept of psychic income is recognized particularly by consumer advertising, which often tries to promote a product's image in ways calculated to boost the buyer's self-esteem.

psychological theory See under BUSINESS CYCLE.

public accountant An accountant who offers professional services to the public and who may be wholly competent, but who has not been certified by a state examining body (see CERTIFIED PUBLIC ACCOUNTANT).

public assistance See WELFARE.

public corporation A corporation formed for purposes of government and the administration of public affairs. In the United States a city, for example, is a public corporation acting under the authority granted it by the state. A *private corporation*, on the other hand, is one established by private individuals, whether for charitable purposes or for profit. See also QUASI-PUBLIC CORPORATION.

public debt In a given country, the sum of debts outstanding of local, state, and national governments, that of the national government alone being called the *national public debt* or *national debt*. When revenues fall short of expenditures, govern-ments borrow; such borrowing is the source of the public debt. Interest on the loans must be paid by the taxpayers, and when long-term obligations such as bonds mature, they must be either repaid or refinanced through more borrowing. These payments are sometimes referred to as the *burden of the public debt*. In effect the public debt is a precise measure of the extent to which government expenditures are financed by borrowing rather than taxation. To what extent borrowing constitutes a wise fiscal policy has long been a matter of controversy. In the past a large public debt was generally considered disastrous, an omen of national bankruptcy and an intolerable burden for future generations. Today most economists agree that only a large *external* debt—one owed to foreigners—creates serious problems. An internal debt—borrowed and repaid by citizens of the same country—merely makes for shifts in income, without any direct loss of goods or services. Further, a government can always raise taxes or increase the money supply, ruling out the possibility of bankruptcy. On the other hand, interest payments on the public debt, raised through extra taxes, do represent funds that might otherwise be more productively employed.

Since World War II, the costs of which increased the United States public debt from $49 billion to $269 billion, the Federal debt has been steadily increasing in absolute terms but decreasing in relation to gross national product (or GNP, the nation's total output), from nearly 100 per cent of GNP just after the war to less than 40 per cent in 1975. The U.S. government's creditors are various financial institutions, individuals, and state and local governments, the biggest holders of Federal obligations being commercial banks (12.7 per cent), Federal Reserve banks (16 per cent), various U.S. government accounts (26.7 per cent), and private individuals (16.4 per cent). The obligations themselves range from 90-day Treasury bills to bonds not maturing for 20 or more years. A major problem in *managing the public debt*, which is the job of the U.S. Department of the Treasury's *Bureau of Public Debt*, is to prevent its average length—the average period for all securities before they fall due—from getting shorter and shorter. As old issues expire they usually must be replaced by new ones. However, unlike a private corporation, which merely seeks the lowest-cost financing, the government must consider the effect of its debt-management policies on the economy as a whole. If it sought purely to minimize interest costs, it would issue large quantities of long-term bonds when interest rates are low (at the bottom of a recession) and short-term notes when they are high (during a boom). But such a course might accentuate economic instability. Between about 1965 and 1975 almost all Federal borrowing was short-term, so that the Treasury and Federal Reserve had to work in tandem to coordinate their policies of debt management and monetary policy (see also DEBT MONETIZATION).

public domain

1. Also, *public lands.* Land owned by the government. During the first half of the 19th century acquisitions of land by the U.S. government increased its holdings from 200 million acres in 1802 to 1.2 billion in 1850. During the next 75 years, however, more than 1 billion acres of Federal land were disposed of, either sold or given away to private individuals and to state governments. At first the sale of lands provided revenue. After passage of the Homestead Act of 1862, however, emphasis shifted to promoting western settlement, and private individuals were able to acquire land under increasingly generous terms (see HOMESTEAD). By the turn of the century the growing conservation movement gained more and more support for the view that public lands should be reserved for public use and administered by the government. As a result, from a low of 413 million acres in 1946, public holdings gradually increased again, totaling more than 760 million acres by 1973. Of this, 353 million acres lay in Alaska and most of the rest in 11 western states. In the 1970s the principal concern with Federal lands was conservation of natural resources. Extractive industries (oil, gas, other minerals), grazing, and recreational use were permitted though strictly controlled. The U.S. Forest Service managed 187 million acres of forests and grazing lands in 41 states and Puerto Rico, some of which was leased for grazing and timber harvesting. Most of the remaining public lands were administered by various bureaus within the Department of the Interior: the Fish and Wildlife Service (wildlife refuges, fish hatcheries); National Park Service (parks, historic sites, recreational areas); Bureau of Indian Affairs (trustee for more than 50,000 acres of Indian lands); Bureau of Reclamation (irrigation and other reclamation projects; collects rent for water use); Bureau of Land Management (144 million of grazing and timber land and 310 million acres of submerged land with mineral rights). See also CONSERVATION.

2. The legal condition of a publication, product, or process that is not protected by copyright or patent.

public finance The area of economics concerned with the revenue-getting and expenditure activities of government. It focuses particularly on the effects of the budget on economic affairs (see FEDERAL BUDGET), as well as taxation (see TAX), PUBLIC SPENDING, and management of the PUBLIC DEBT. An important branch of public finance, FISCAL POLICY, concentrates on the short-term effects of government budgets, spending, and taxation on employment and price levels.

public housing In the United States, low-rent housing provided for low-income families by local housing authorities with Federal assistance. First instituted through the Housing Act of 1937, public housing today is administered by the U.S. Department of Housing and Urban Development. It gives loans and direct subsidies to local housing authorities, which provide public housing through new construction, rehabilitation of existing structures, purchases from private builders or developers, and leasing from private owners. Special provisions allow for purchase of such housing by low-income families.

publicity Any news or information about a product, service, individual, or organization that is printed or broadcast free of charge (as opposed to ADVERTISING, which is always paid). Obtaining favorable publicity is a major objective of PUBLIC RELATIONS, but in some cases even unfavorable publicity is considered desirable simply because it stimulates public interest. Public relations departments and specialists, sometimes called *press agents,* issue *news releases* or *press releases* to newspapers, television stations, and other outlets to inform the public about particular activities or events. The media treat these in the same way as they do ordinary news items, although on product publicity they sometimes tend to favor advertisers.

public lands See PUBLIC DOMAIN, def. 1.

public ownership Ownership and operation of an economic enterprise by the central government. If its acquisition involves the displacement of a private owner, the process is called NATIONALIZATION. In public ownership the government assumes the role of the private capitalist, supplying capital, controlling management, and setting prices for the output, assuming all risks and reaping whatever benefits may accrue in the form of profits. Supporters of public ownership claim that it is economically more efficient, making for better overall planning and control, and that it is socially more equitable (than a system in which wealth is concentrated in the hands of private individuals). Critics feel it promotes red tape, bureaucracy, and waste. Public ownership of the means of production is basic to both SOCIALISM and COMMUNISM, but it is by no means confined to countries embracing those systems. Numerous enterprises, such as the postal service and armed forces, have for centuries been publicly owned in most countries, and various kinds of transportation, public utilities and communications networks are among the earliest examples of public ownership in largely capitalist nations, such as France, West Germany, Canada, and the United States.

public power project A power facility owned and operated by the government. The United States government began producing and selling electricity on a sizable scale in the 1930s, an outgrowth of earlier government efforts to control the flow of water in river valleys by means of dams. The earliest large-scale American public power project was the *Tenessee Valley Authority* (*TVA*), created in 1933, a huge multipurpose development with 29 dams, used for flood control, irrigation, a navigation channel, recreational facilities, and other valley development projects as well as for supplying power. Similar facilities were built in the basins of the Colorado, Columbia, Missouri, and St. Lawrence rivers. Most new public power projects use generators fueled by coal or nuclear reactors since most good water-power sites are already in use.

public relations The job of maintaining good relations between the general public and a particular individual, company, product, or organization. It usually involves disseminating information about the person's or group's activities (in the form of PUBLICITY) and answering legitimate requests for information. In large companies the public relations department may undertake community programs to foster friendly relations and promote a favorable image for the company, such as building a community playground or swimming pool, or heavily underwriting some other local project.

public sector

1. In general usage, all economic activities—mostly services—that are carried out directly by government agencies (or outside the PRIVATE SECTOR), largely for the public benefit rather than for profit. Included is the entire machinery of government offices and agencies on the local, state, and national levels, and all the various enterprises they support (police and fire protection, military payrolls, highway maintenance, public education, etc.).

2. In national income accounting, the value added to the economy by government agencies and other publicly owned bodies, consisting primarily of services performed by government employees. In the United States, with but few exceptions (such as ships built in navy yards and guns made in army arsenals) the goods used in the public sector are produced in the PRIVATE SECTOR. For example, a bomber used by the air force or a municipal fire truck represent output of the private sector even though they are used in the public sector. For this reason, the contribution of the public sector to national output—about 12 per cent of gross national product—is less than government purchases of goods and services (about 22 per cent), which includes both government payrolls and purchases from private contractors. See also PUBLIC SPENDING.

public service commission Also, *public utility commission.* In the United States, a semi-independent state agency that regulates the public utilities in the state, including their rates and the quantity and quality of their services. Though they vary from state to state, most public service commissions control the railroads, motor carriers, water, electricity, gas, and telephone service within their states, and often also street railways, taxicabs, and gas pipelines. Interstate transportation and utility services are controlled by five Federal regulatory commissions: the INTERSTATE COMMERCE COMMISSION, FEDERAL COMMUNICATIONS COMMISSION, FEDERAL POWER COMMISSION, CIVIL AERONAUTICS BOARD, and SECURITIES AND EXCHANGE COMMISSION.

public spending The sum of local, state, and central government expenditures. There are two main kinds of public spending: (1) for goods and services, principally purchased from the PRIVATE SECTOR; (2) transfer payments, involving a redistribution of income without the production of goods or services (for example, pensions; see also TRANSFER PAYMENT). The increasing or decreasing of government spending is a prime instrument of FISCAL POLICY. See also PUBLIC SECTOR; PUBLIC WORKS; PUMP PRIMING.

public utility A private industry whose services are considered of such public value that it is given special status by the government, usually that of a government-regulated monopoly. The most important public utilities are those supplying water, electric power, gas, telephone and telegraph service, and local transportation (subways, buses, etc.). Some authorities also include common carriers, which similarly operate under government franchise and are strictly regulated. In the United States the rates of public utilities are regulated in two ways: control of the rate level and of the rate structure. The former is concerned with obtaining a *fair rate of return* on investment in a public utility company, neither so high that it exploits customers nor so low that it cannot attract capital. The *rate structure* concerns various rates paid for different units of service by different classes of customer. Public utilities generally discriminate among customers, but at least in theory, they may not do so unfairly. Differences in rates are partly based on differences in cost; it may cost less to serve some customers than others or to sell in large rather than

small quantities. More often, however, such differences tend to be based on differences in demand, rates being set low where demand is elastic and high where it is inelastic. By and large the regulating agencies tend to accept such discrimination, stepping in only when rate differences appear to favor certain customers over their competitors. In the United States most public utilities are regulated by state commissions (see PUBLIC SERVICE COMMISSION) although in a few states control is entrusted to local governments. Since passage of the Public Utility Act of 1935 and the Natural Gas Act of 1938, electricity and gas companies have also fallen under the jurisdiction of the Federal Power Commission and the U.S. Securities and Exchange Commission (the latter to control holding companies); in the case of telephone and telegraph service the Federal Communications Commission regulates interstate service.

public warehouse See under WAREHOUSE.

public welfare See WELFARE.

public works A general term for government-sponsored construction projects such as highways, dams, bridges, conservation projects, slum clearance, rural electrification, atomic energy facilities, and the like, but also including expenditures for military and civil defense. In the United States such projects are frequently undertaken to offset downturns of the business cycle. During the Great Depression of the 1930s many public works were initiated to provide employment (see WORKS PROGRESS ADMINISTRATION). Since World War II this policy has been continued in an attempt to provide greater economic stability. Ideally public works consist of projects that are needed but would not be undertaken by the private sector, and they represent one of the few ways—aside from tax cuts—in which government fiscal policy can directly affect employment. However, some economists question the validity of public works and their role in stimulating the economy (see PUMP PRIMING) on a number of grounds. Some point to inefficiency and waste, which often result when the main goal is spending money rather than carrying out useful work. Further, there is a time lag between the identification of need for spending and its execution.

Also, pump priming directly benefits a very special part of the economy, not necessarily that which most needs relief from unemployment. Nevertheless, the Federal government continues to increase spending for public works, both directly and through grants and loans in aid of construction by state and local governments. Between 1960 and 1973 its spending nearly doubled, from $6.8 billion to $12.7 billion. Since passage of the Public Works and Economic Development Act of 1965, Federal involvement in public works has been handled by the Department of Commerce's Economic Development Administration.

pump priming   Large-scale government spending with the express purpose of stimulating the economy by increasing employment and general purchasing power. (See also under PUBLIC WORKS.) In effect such spending serves as a substitute for the investment spending private business is not willing to undertake. The first big pump priming program in the United States was undertaken by the NEW DEAL, when government spending rose from $10 billion in 1933 to $15 billion in 1936. National income and consumption similarly rose by 50 per cent during this period, but large-scale unemployment persisted, largely because business, instead of being stimulated by the Federal program, regarded it as a threat to private enterprise and hesitated to embark on new investment. See also DEFICIT FINANCE.

punched-card data processing   A system of information processing in which a card stores information in the form of holes that represent characters, digits, punctuation marks, etc. This information is punched onto the card, which is then fed into special equipment designed to handle the card and interpret the information it contains. Punched-card equipment can be used to classify information automatically, perform arithmetic operations on numerical data, and print out the information on a sheet of paper or transmit it into a computer for further processing. The standard card contains 80 columns and 12 rows, and can hold 80 pieces of information (numbers, letters, characters such as $ or %, etc.). These are represented on the card by means

of the *Hollerith Code*, numbers being represented by one punch in the appropriate row and letters by two punches, consisting of 1 of 3 zone punches (indicating what part of the alphabet) and a numerical punch (where in that part). Information for any given set of cards must appear in the same place on each card, since the machines identify data only by location.

Four different kinds of equipment (sometimes called *unit-record* equipment) are required for punched-card data processing: recording equipment, classifying equipment, calculating equipment, and accounting equipment. Recording equipment includes the *key punch, verifier,* and *reproducer*. The first operation is key punching (punching holes into the cards), accomplished by means of an operator's depressing keys or a keyboard much like a typewriter's. A second operator then uses the verifier, which looks almost exactly like a key punch, to check the key puncher's accuracy; the operator depresses the verifier keys while reading from the same source data, and the machine compares the key depressed with the hole already punched in the card. In case of a difference the machine stops, indicating a possible error. The reproducer can punch all or part of the information on one deck of cards into another deck. It also can perform *gang punching*, that is, the automatic copying of punched information from one card into one or more succeeding cards, and can be used for *mark sensing*, whereby information recorded in the form of magnetic pencil marks on cards is automatically transcribed as punched holes on the same cards. Finally, some machines can be attached by a cable to an accounting machine to do *summary punching*, that is, produce a summary card whenever the accounting machine produces a total or subtotal. Classifying equipment includes the *sorter, collator,* and *interpreter*. The first machine arranges cards in the desired alphabetical or numerical order; it also can group cards and select desired cards from a deck, merge card decks that are already in sequence, compare two decks to find matching cards, and merge the matching cards in a single file. The interpreter "reads" the information punched into a card and prints it at the top of the card. The *calculating machine* is just that, varying

Fig. 70. An 80-column card

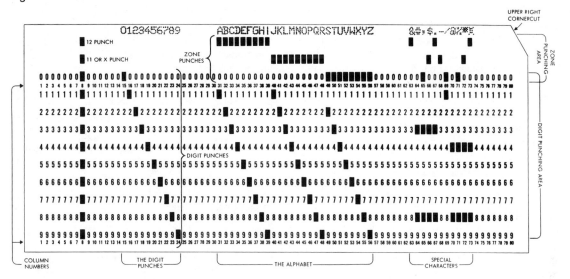

in the complexity of arithmetic operations it can perform. The *accounting machine* prints alphabetical and numerical data from punched cards onto paper and totals data by some desired classification.

Today punched-card systems are widely used in accounting, and also, to a lesser extent, in inventory control, production control, and sales analyses. Punched cards themselves are a basic method of transcribing information from a source document into a form acceptable to a COMPUTER. Even for machines that use magnetic tape primarily, the data often are first punched into cards and then transferred to tape. See also PUNCHED-TAPE DATA PROCESSING.

punched-tape data processing Also, *perforated-tape data processing, paper-tape processing.* A system of information processing resembling PUNCHED-CARD DATA PROCESSING except that, instead of separate cards, a continuous roll of paper, metal foil, plastic, or some other material is perforated with holes that represent characters, digits, punctuation marks, etc. Like punched cards, punched tape is then fed into special equipment, sometimes linked to a computer designed to interpret (or further process) the information on it.

purchased materials index An important LEADING INDICATOR of business conditions. The index measures the percentage of firms reporting higher inventories. It tends to reach a peak some months before the business cycle, when 65 to 70 per cent of the participating firms are boosting their inventories, and reaches a trough at about the same time a business slump is ending, with only 30 to 40 per cent of firms increasing inventories. Developed by the National Bureau of Economic Research, the purchased materials index is published monthly in *Business Conditions Digest.*

purchase group See SYNDICATE, def. 2.

purchase order In business and industry, a written authorization to an outside supplier or seller to supply certain goods or services in a given amount, at a given price, and at a certain time and place. When accepted by the seller (or if representing the acceptance of terms stated by the seller), the purchase order legally becomes a CONTRACT, called a *purchase contract.* A purchase order normally is issued by an employee of a business who is specifically assigned this duty, and it is legally binding on the company (see also under PURCHASING). Each quotation (or bid)—verbal or written—by a supplier is an OFFER (def. 1) to sell; every purchase order is either an ACCEPTANCE (def. 4) of such an offer, or, if its terms differ from the quotation, a *counteroffer*. Counteroffers must be accepted before the contract is binding. The terms of purchase orders specify price and payment (see COD; COST-PLUS CONTRACT; ESCALATION; FIXED-PRICE CONTRACT; INCENTIVE CONTRACT); delivery (see C.I.F.; F.A.S.; F.O.B.); acceptable quality (see SPECIFICATIONS); and, for important purchases, provision for cancellation. See also INDENT.

purchase requisition Also, *material requisition*. In business and industry, an authorized request from the department needing an item that the item be ordered and purchased. A purchase requisition thus provides the authority to issue a PURCHASE ORDER to a supplier.

purchasing Also, *buying, procurement*. In business and industry, the acquisition of goods (materials, parts, supplies, equipment) required to carry on the enterprise. In a small business or shop this work might be done by the owner-manager; in most firms with 100 or more employees it is done by a *purchasing agent*. The purchasing agent may be simply a clerk who buys the less important items needed, processes requisition forms from the production departments, and perhaps keeps track of the supply storeroom. In a large organization, however, he or she may play an important part in deciding what is purchased, when, and from whom. Such a purchasing agent usually heads an entire department, which buys materials in amounts authorized by requisitions from the production control and stores departments. The chief activities of a purchasing department are (1) selecting suppliers, negotiating the most advantageous purchase terms, and issuing purchase orders; (2) expediting delivery of purchased items and negotiating any changes in purchase schedules required; (3) acting as liaison between suppliers and other company departments (engineering, quality control, production control, manufacturing, finance) on all problems involving purchased materials; (4) seeking out new products, materials, and suppliers, and keeping track of market conditions and other factors that can affect company operations. The purchasing agent is legally an AGENT for the company; if he or she agrees to buy a ton of sheet steel from a supplier, for example, the agent's employer is legally obligated to buy that steel. The company is liable for the agent's actions, whether or not they were specifically approved by top management. For retail purchasing, see BUYER.

purchasing agent See under PURCHASING; also, BUYER.

purchasing power The ability to buy, particularly as distinguished from the possession of money. Purchasing power depends on the general PRICE LEVEL; if prices are high, the same amount of money will buy less, that is, it has less purchasing power, than when prices are low.

purchasing power parity theory The idea that exchange rates reflect the ratios of the domestic purchasing power of the various national currencies. Suppose, for example, that Switzerland and the United States are at equilibrium at an exchange rate of $.40 per Swiss franc. According to the purchasing power parity theory, this means that $.40 will buy the same goods in America as 1 franc will buy in Switzerland. If this were not true—if either the U.S. dollar or Swiss franc had greater purchasing power—it would pay to convert to that currency and buy in that country. This change in demand would change price levels, and eventually the exchange rate would be adjusted so that parity would be reestablished. The theory, propounded principally by the Swedish economist Gustav Cassel in an attempt to explain monetary affairs in the period following World War I, has little practical validity, since numerous factors other than purchasing power determine exchange rates, and it is difficult to compare purchasing power among countries because goods actually purchased in different places vary widely.

pure competition Also, *free competition, perfect competition*; sometimes *atomism, atomistic competition*. A market characterized by a large number of sellers of identical goods and services and readily entered by still more sellers. In this situation no single seller can significantly influence either the price or the supply of goods, and buyers are assured of a wide supply at the lowest possible price. In practice pure competition rarely exists today. In the United States and other industrialized nations only a few agricultural products are sold under these conditions, the greater part of goods sold being subject to IMPERFECT COMPETITION.

purposive sampling In statistics, selecting a sample on the basis of its resemblance to the universe as a whole. For example, because its past voting performance in U.S. Presidential elections has a close correlation to the entire nation's pattern, New Hampshire is often selected as a sample for polling voters in order to predict the outcome of elections. Naturally the possibility for sampling error in this process is almost limitless.

put An option to sell a given amount of a particular stock at a specified price (called the *striking price*) within a certain time. (An option to buy stock is a CALL.) A put is bought by a person who thinks the stock will decline in price and therefore wants an option to sell it at the current, higher price. It gives the holder the right to sell the stock, and obligates the seller of the option contract, called the *writer* or *maker*, to take delivery of the stock within that time and pay for it at that price. If the stock does not go down as anticipated, the buyer has the option of not exercising the put. Puts—and calls—tend to have contracts for 35 days, 95 days, or 6 months and 10 days (occasionally longer periods are involved). Typically the striking price is determined by the market price at the time the option contract is written. The cost of the put usually varies with both the stock's price and the dealer's estimate of how much that price is likely to change. Puts and calls formerly were traded by giving an order to one's regular stock broker, who passed it on to a *put-and-call dealer*; if the options were exercised, they were handled by the broker, who charged a standard commission. However, options became such a popular form of speculation that in 1972 the first formal market for them was opened. See also OPTION, def. 2; OPTIONS EXCHANGE.

putting-out system See COTTAGE INDUSTRY.

pyramid
1. *of credit*. See under FRACTIONAL RESERVE BANKING.
2. In investment, the practice of using the paper profits of a margin account (SEE MARGIN, BUYING ON) to support purchases of additional stock without investing more cash. A very common practice when margin requirements were low—as low as 10 or 20 per cent in the 1920s—pyramiding became less feasible when margin requirements were set at 50 per cent or higher. Nevertheless, some pyramiding is still carried on. For example, suppose one buys 200 shares of a $10 stock on margin, putting up a required 50 per cent ($1,000) in cash. If the stock rises to $12, one still owes $1,000 on the margin account but one has an equity 20 per cent greater, $1,200 worth. As a result, one can buy $200 worth more stock without putting up more cash.
3. Control of businesses through a series of holding companies. See under HOLDING COMPANY.

quality control In business and industry, the system of methods, procedures, and policies used to maintain acceptable and dependable levels of quality in a company's output of goods and services, as well as in its purchases. Quality control activities include *receiving inspection* (inspecting purchased goods when they are delivered and checking them against SPECIFICATIONS), checking production processes and methods, INSPECTION of finished products, and review of usage to provide for possible revision of specifications. For inspection in particular, quality control frequently relies on samples rather than inspecting every single item; since the selection of samples uses one or another mathematical formula, such procedures are sometimes referred to as *statistical quality control*. In industrial organizations quality control is usually part of the manufacturing division. See also ACCEPTABLE QUALITY LEVEL; ACCEPTANCE SAMPLING; FREQUENCY DISTRIBUTION.

quantitative trade restriction See EXPORT QUOTA; IMPORT QUOTA.

quantity discount See under DISCOUNT, def. 1.

quantity equation of exchange See EQUATION OF EXCHANGE.

quantity theory of money The idea that the level of spending and prices is directly proportional to the amount of money in circulation, so that an increase in circulating money will raise prices and a decrease will lower prices. Stated as early as the 17th century (by HUME, among others), this theory was generally accepted by economists, from the CLASSICAL SCHOOL through Alfred MARSHALL. In its simple form, it assumes that prices always are proportional to total spending, and that total spending always is proportional to the total money supply. (Marshall devised an equation, sometimes called the *Cambridge equation*, expressing this relationship: $N = Y/K$, where N is the total number of monetary units, Y is the level of money income, and K is the sum of consumer goods and services.) However, neither basic assumption is valid. Sometimes more efficient production increases the total output and prices need not rise much (or at all) for the producer to increase profits; in that case prices clearly are not proportional to total spending. Further, the total money supply is not a simple constant, and total spending represents a flow of income over time; the quantity theory fails to take into account the rate of that flow (the so-called velocity of circulation of money). Nevertheless, variations of the theory, popularized in the United States by Irving FISHER, continue to be propounded by some economists, notably Milton FRIEDMAN; for Fisher's version, see EQUATION OF EXCHANGE.

quartile In statistics, a name for the three values in a FREQUENCY DISTRIBUTION that divide the items into four equal groups, that is, the first quarter from the second, the second from the third, and the third from the fourth. The second quartile is identical to the middle value, or MEDIAN. See also DECILE; PERCENTILE.

quasi-public corporation Also, *public service corporation, public utility*. A CORPORATION established by private interests to furnish services on which the public is highly dependent. Examples include companies that operate railroads, bridges, tunnels, and canals, as well as enterprises supplying gas, electric power, and water. Most quasi-public corporations receive special franchises and powers, notably the right of EMINENT DOMAIN. See also PUBLIC UTILITY.

quasi-rent Also, *economic rent.* A return on capital or labor whose supply is temporarily or permanently fixed, so called to distinguish it from a *real rent*, the return on land (whose supply is always fixed). The first producer of a unique product (such as a patented toy) may temporarily enjoy a quasi-rent by commanding higher prices, until competitors enter the field (with similar toys) and drive prices down to levels that yield only normal profits. A more permanent quasi-rent can be earned by producers of proprietary products with real or alleged unique properties. For example, most of the unusually high profits earned by "genuine" Bayer aspirin, Polaroid cameras, and similar branded items are quasi-rents. Similarly, the high income earned by outstandingly talented performers—musicians, actors, athletes—is largely quasi-rent. Babe Ruth, had he been unable to play baseball, might have had to work as a truck driver. In fact, had he no other choice, he undoubtedly would have been willing to play baseball for a trucker's wages. The difference between this and his actual earnings was quasi-rent. The term "quasi-rent" was coined by Alfred Marshall.

Quesnay, François A French thinker (1694–1774), founder of the PHYSIOCRATS. A physician to Louis XV and Madame de Pompadour, Quesnay likened the circulation of wealth in the economy to the circulation of blood in the body. He devised a *Tableau économique* ("Economic Table," 1758, revised 1766) that showed the circular flow of goods and money under conditions of free competition. In Quesnay's scheme, only farmers create a surplus, part of which they keep for subsistence and to carry on their work. The rest is paid to landowners in the form of rent, which finances the consumption of agricultural products by them and by others engaged in nonfarming pursuits. Later economists, among them Adam Smith, Marx, and Keynes, credited Quesnay with making the first attempt at national INCOME ANALYSIS.

queuing theory A mathematical analysis concerned with minimizing the costs of waiting in line. For example, how many checkout stations and clerks should a supermarket have in operation in order to serve customers adequately without wasting time or labor during slack periods? Similarly, how many landing strips are needed for aircraft? How much service personnel to repair machinery? How many stock clerks at a spare-parts center? In some cases, both arrivals and services follow a given time schedule with random variations (as with scheduled aircraft arriving at an airport); in other cases arrivals occur at random from an infinite universe—that is, practically anywhere—as with theatergoers at a box office. Simple queuing problems sometimes can be solved by MONTE CARLO SIMULATION, but complex ones require the use of sophisticated mathematical formulas. Queuing theory was invented by A. K. Erland, a Danish mathematician who in 1917 published a paper on dealing with the fluctuating demand for telephone facilities and its effect on automatic dialing equipment. It was not until the 1940s, however, that Erland's work was extended to other problems involving waiting lines.

quick asset See LIQUID ASSET.

quick ratio Also, *acid test, acid-test ratio.* In analyzing a balance sheet, the proportion of quick assets, or LIQUID ASSETS, to current liabilities. (Quick assets consist of those that are readily converted into cash, usually current assets minus inventories.) A quick ratio of 1 to 1 is normally considered satisfactory. Note that it is lower than an acceptable CURRENT RATIO, which includes less liquid assets.

quitclaim deed A DEED that purports to convey the grantor's present interest in land, if any, rather than the land itself. It does not imply that the grantor has good title, or any title at all, and in no way obligates the grantor. If, however, the grantor should have complete ownership of the property at the time the deed is executed, the deed is sufficient to transfer such ownership. See also WARRANTY DEED.

quota See EXPORT QUOTA; IMPORT QUOTA. For *immigration quota*, see under IMMIGRATION. For *marketing quota*, see under AGRICULTURE, AID TO.

quota sampling In statistics, a method of sampling in which a scheme of proportionate samples is set up, with the numbers to be interviewed in each class embodying the traits of the overall population. For example, if 10 per cent of the total population is gray-haired and more than 55 years of age, 10 per cent of the sample must share these characteristics. The individuals in the sample, however, are selected by the interviewer, who is likely to choose the most accessible respondents (all from one neighborhood, for example) and hence produce somewhat biased results.

quotation See BID, defs. 1 and 2.

race discrimination See DISCRIMINATION, def. 1; also AFFIRMATIVE ACTION; CLOSED UNION; POLL TAX; RESTRICTIVE COVENANT.

racketeering

1. In business, carrying on a dishonest or illegal scheme in order to make money. (Such an enterprise is called a *racket*.) It ranges from transporting liquor across state lines to avoid excise taxes to bribing a jockey in a horse race.

2. In organized labor, collusion between union officials and employers in writing contracts, coercion of employers to accept union terms, appropriation of pension and strike funds for private gain by union officials, and similar practices. In 1957 the AFL-CIO expelled several unions for unethical behavior, and the Landrum-Griffin Act of 1959 instituted a number of measures to safeguard union members against corrupt officials (see under LABOR LAWS).

rack jobber See under WHOLESALE.

raid See *bear raid*, under BEAR.

Railroad Retirement Board A United States government agency created by the Railroad Retirement Act of 1935 to administer retirement insurance for railroad employees. The Railroad Unemployment Insurance Act of 1938 also authorized it to administer unemployment and health insurance. The board maintains a free employment service for railroad employees.

rail-trailer shipment See PIGGYBACK.

rally Also, *upswing, upturn, uptrend*. Beginning to rise again, describing security or commodity prices, or the market or economy as a whole. See also RECOVERY.

R and D See RESEARCH AND DEVELOPMENT.

random access In computers, the technique of retrieving any piece of recorded information without first scanning other data. The most common random access device is the MAGNETIC DISK; another is the MAGNETIC DRUM. Usually the advantage of random access is at least partly offset by the disadvantage of longer access time (more time needed for retrieval).

random numbers A series of numbers that is statistically random and therefore can be used in sampling. Such a series can be generated by a computer, by using a mechanical device such as a squirrel cage, or simply by blindly drawing numbers from a container, as was done in the World War II draft lottery.

random sampling In statistical sampling, the process of selecting sample units in such a way that all units under consideration have the same probability of being selected. By using such means as a table of RANDOM NUMBERS and a large enough number of sample units, the results will approximate those of the parent population within a measurable margin of error (the SAMPLING ERROR). In cases where the statistical units already are arranged into classes or strata (villages by size, contributors by amount contributed, etc.), random numbers can be used to take samples of each of the classes, a procedure called *stratified random sampling*.

random variable In statistics, a variable whose value is unknown until an event occurs but for which the probability can be calculated. For example, the possible number of times "heads" will come up when flipping a coin ten times, or the outcomes from throwing a pair of dice, or the number of backpacks that will be sold from a stock of K backpacks all are random variables. See also PROBABILITY THEORY.

random walk hypothesis The idea that over a period of time anyone can make money by investing in a group of common stocks chosen at random, and that on the average the yield from such investment will exceed returns on any other form of investment. It is based on an exhaustive study of the prices of 1,715 common stocks listed on the New York Stock Exchange from 1926 through 1960, which indicated that the average rate of return, assuming reinvestment of all dividends and deduction of all commissions, was 9 per cent per year compounded annually. Profit is inevitable (although not spectacularly large) if a diversified group of stocks is selected by this method and is held for a sufficient period of time.

range In statistics, the difference between the highest and lowest values in a FREQUENCY DISTRIBUTION. It sometimes is used in quality control as an approximation of a STANDARD DEVIATION.

rank and file The ordinary members of a labor union, as distinguished from the officials who run it.

rate base In a public utility, the total investment on which the company seeks a return. The amount of this investment depends on the method of calculation used, that is, what values are assigned to tangible property, which items are included and which left out, whether value is based on original cost or reproduction cost, how much is allowed for land, how one assesses intangible assets, etc. The total value is sometimes called *fair value*, and the return on investment is termed *fair return*. See also PUBLIC UTILITY.

rate bureau Also, *tariff bureau*. A regional office for trucking companies that publishes trucking rate schedules for its area. The rate schedules are not mandatory but rather provide guidelines for both the truckers and their customers.

rate-making See under FREIGHT; PUBLIC UTILITY; RATE BUREAU; for insurance rate-making, see RATING, def. 3.

rate of exchange See EXCHANGE RATE.

rate of interest See INTEREST RATE.

rate of return
  1. For investment, see RETURN, def. 1; YIELD.
  2. For public utilities, see under PUBLIC UTILITY; RATE BASE.

rating
  1. See CREDIT RATING.
  2. In the television industry, a system of ranking national programs according to the number of persons who watch them, based on telephone surveys and similar market research. It is used primarily to estimate the size of the audience a show's sponsor will reach. Ratings usually are supplied by a firm that sells its services to advertising agencies and advertisers.
  3. Also, *rate-making*. Setting the rates for insurance, which in turn determine the premiums to be paid for various kinds of protection. Rates are based on statistics, probability theory, mortality tables, and other mathematical analyses, on past experience with various kinds of risk, on intuition and personal judgment, etc. Though there are many variations, there are three basic systems of rating.

One involves arriving at a *class rate*, one that applies to each of many homogeneous clients in the class. Another is a *schedule system*, where, beginning with a base figure, the precise rate is determined by the positive and negative attributes of the insured (for example, in the case of fire insurance, presence or absence of a sprinkling system). The third is *experience rating*, which reflects the loss experience of the insured (how many automobile accidents a car owner had in the past decade) rather than current good or bad features.

ratio chart   In presenting statistics, a graph that shows relative rather than absolute variations, that is, percentage changes rather than absolute changes. Mostly commonly, it is plotted on semilogarithm paper which, instead of the equally spaced squares on ordinary graph paper, shows logarithmic divisions (ratios) on the Y-axis (vertical axis) and arithmetic divisions (1, 2, 3) on the X-axis (horizontal axis). Ratio charts are used to depict percentage changes in sales, gross national product, or similar statistics.

ratio-delay study   See WORK SAMPLING.

rationing
   1. A system of allocating goods that are in scarce supply owing to war or some other emergency, enacted to prevent prices from soaring to unreasonable heights and to ensure equitable distribution. During World War II the United States government administered a rationing system based on points and coupons for numerous scarce consumer goods (butter, meat, coffee, sugar, gasoline, etc.).
   2. *of foreign exchange.* See under EXCHANGE CONTROLS.

ratio-to-moving-average method   In statistics, a method of computing cyclical and seasonal fluctuations, so as to get a clear picture of a trend in sales, output, or some other time series. First a preliminary trend is determined by taking a 12-month MOVING AVERAGE of the original data. Then ratios are obtained by dividing the original data by the preliminary trend cycle to obtain a specific seasonal index. The seasonal indexes then are smoothed out by removing irregular fluctuations. See also EXPONENTIAL SMOOTHING.

raw material   A natural or semifinished good that is used in manufacturing or processing to make some other good. Bauxite is the raw material (ore) from which aluminum is made; aluminum in turn can be the raw material from which household utensils are manufactured.

reacquired stock   See TREASURY STOCK.

readership   See under CIRCULATION.

real
   1. In economics, describing data that have been adjusted to take into account purchasing power or the foreign exchange rate. For example, REAL WAGE means earnings adjusted to changes in consumer prices.
   2. In accounting, physical or tangible, as opposed to intangible. A firm's real assets include its plant and equipment, but not customer goodwill, patents, etc.
   3. In business law, a term for certain property; see REAL PROPERTY.

real account   See under ACCOUNT, def. 1.

real-balance effect   See under A. C. PIGOU. See also REAL CASH BALANCE.

real-bills doctrine   Also, *commercial loan theory of banking.* The theory held by the BANKING SCHOOL of economists that, were commercial bank loans confined to "real bills"—that is, short-term obligations growing out of actual business transactions—the money supply would automatically expand and contract in accordance with business activity. The Federal Reserve Act of 1913 was to a large extent based on this theory, which still survives in the provision that Reserve banks may discount (or rediscount) only short-term, self-liquidating paper. (See also *bills-only policy*, under OPEN-MARKET OPERATIONS.) However, this theory fails to take into account that the supply of commercial paper is not necessarily an indication of legitimate demand for money, and that commercial banks do not necessarily regard such paper as their most liquid asset, since its liquidity depends in part on the salability of the goods in process or inventories involved, which may decline in times of recession. In practice most Federal Reserve loans today take the form of advances (see ADVANCE, def. 3), for which a variety of assets may be used as collateral.

real cash balance The total quantity of money, in the form of currency in circulation and demand deposits, at any given time, adjusted for changes in price levels. This indicator is considered important by some economists who feel that the *nominal money stock*—the money supply considered apart from price level—is misleading for judging economic growth. If the nominal money supply increases but at a lower rate than prices increase, there is a decline in growth, with unemployment increasing while prices fail to decline significantly. This situation occurred in the United States off and on from the mid-1960s to the early 1970s. Classical economists such as Pigou had seen the importance of considering money in relation to purchasing power but used their analysis quite differently, predicting that it would lead to employment and growth (see A. C. PIGOU). Today most economists reason that when the money supply increases, people have extra cash and therefore spend more on goods, services, and financial assets (investments). The extra spending results in a perpetually higher demand for goods and services than the supply at given price levels. If there are abundant idle resources, output will expand to meet the new demand, which in turn will generate more income, and supply and demand will balance. But if the economy is already operating at full capacity, output (and therefore real income) cannot expand, so, with demand exceeding supply, prices will rise. The resulting inflation will decrease the real money value (purchasing power) until real cash balances drop to original levels.

real cost
1. The cost of an item viewed in terms of alternative uses of the same funds. See OPPORTUNITY COST.
2. The cost of an item expressed in terms of some physical measurement (bushels, tons, miles, man-hours).
3. The cost of an item adjusted for changes in purchasing power. For example, the real cost of air travel has declined since 1950, even though it costs more to travel from one city to another, because the price of airline tickets has risen much more slowly than prices for other items during this period.

real-dollar value See CONSTANT-DOLLAR VALUE.

real estate Land and any objects more or less permanently attached to it, such as buildings or fences. See also REAL PROPERTY.

real estate financing Obtaining funds for the purchase or construction of real estate. Borrowers include individuals and families who wish to buy homes, as well as promoters of commercial and industrial ventures who hope to obtain a higher yield than the interest they will have to pay for borrowed funds. Lenders are chiefly commercial banks, mutual savings banks, savings and loan associations, life insurance companies, pension funds, private individuals, and, in the United States, the Federal government (chiefly through loan guarantees by the Veterans Administration and Department of Housing and Urban Development, and more direct participation by quasi-government agencies such as the Federal National Mortgage Association). The principal form of housing loan is the MORTGAGE, for which the housing itself serves as collateral.

real estate investment trust Also, *REIT*. A real estate lending organization set up much like a MUTUAL FUND, selling shares to investors and using the funds to invest in real estate holdings. Most such trusts fall into one of two categories: *equity trusts*, which invest in income-producing properties, and *mortgage trusts*, which lend funds for construction and development projects (mostly for a short term, such as one to three years, but sometimes for longer terms). Provided they distribute at least 90 per cent of annual earnings among shareholders and meet certain other requirements, the trusts are not subject to Federal corporation income tax (though individual shareholders must still pay income tax on their dividends). This feature made them very attractive to American investors in the 1960s, when they expanded greatly. By the mid-1970s, however, many found themselves in financial difficulties owing to the high interest rates of the early 1970s, which squeezed builders and forced many of them to default on their loans.

real estate tax See PROPERTY TAX.

real income The purchasing power of the income of an individual, group, or nation, computed by adjusting money income to price changes. A comparison between incomes earned during 1950 and 1970, for example, would be pointless unless 1950 and 1970 price levels were identical. Using a price index showing, for example, that average consumer prices increased by 50 per cent between those years, it becomes clear that $1,000 in 1970 buys what $667 bought in 1950. Thus, even if total income actually doubled, real income would double only if prices remained constant.

realization
1. The conversion of any asset into cash.
2. The earning of a return, either through selling goods or services or profiting from an investment.

real national income See REAL INCOME.

real property An interest in land, buildings, and fixtures, as opposed to PERSONAL PROPERTY, such as furnishings, automobiles, clothes, etc. An interest in real property is transferred from one person to another by means of a DEED. See also REAL ESTATE.

real-time In computer terminology, describing an environment in which information is gathered, processed, and made available sufficiently fast to control an ongoing process. Typical real-time computer applications involve gathering data to control machinery or other devices. Real-time environments often are referred to as *on-line* (see ON-LINE, def. 1), which is not always accurate, since a real-time system may operate slowly enough to process control data in batch mode (see BATCH PROCESSING, def. 1) and still be timely enough for the given purpose.

realtor An active member of a local real estate board affiliated with the National Association of Real Estate Boards. See also BROKER, def. 3.

real wage The amount of a worker's earnings (the so-called *money wage*) adjusted to take purchasing power into account. Real wages depend on the general PRICE LEVEL, since purchasing power increases with low prices and declines with high prices. Thus a real wage can change while the money wage remains the same. A real wage is calculated by dividing an index number of general prices into the money wage,

$$R = \frac{M}{p\,(.01)}$$

where R is the real wage, M the money wage, and p the price index number (usually based on 100, hence multiplied here). For example, if the money wage remained constant between 1967 and 1972 at $10,000, but the consumer price index advanced from 100 to 125.3, the real 1972 wage in 1967 dollars would be

$$R = \frac{\$10,000}{1.253} = \$7,980$$

or more than 20 per cent lower than in 1967. In practice, therefore, if prices rise faster than money wages, the real wage declines; if money wages decline more slowly than prices (as during a business slump), real wages rise.

rebate The return of part of a payment, representing a deduction from the full amount previously charged and paid. It differs from a DISCOUNT (def. 1) in that it is paid back rather than deducted in advance, and it usually is differentiated from a REFUND in that it does not result from an overpayment. See also DRAWBACK.

rebuilt Also, *reconditioned.* Describing a piece of machinery or other manufactured item that has been taken apart and put back together, cleaned, with the worn or defective parts replaced, and given a general refurbishing. Typewriters, bicycles, sewing machines, vacuum cleaners, and musical instruments are among the consumer goods often available rebuilt, at considerably lower prices than new ones.

recapitalization Changing the capital structure of a corporation by readjusting the securities outstanding. Existing stock may be called in and reissued in a new amount, or common stock may be partly replaced by preferred stock, or debentures might be replaced with some other kind of bond. Sometimes recapitalization is a result of BANK-

RUPTCY. If a company goes bankrupt, the bond-holders may receive common stock in the subsequent reorganization while the stockholders are simply wiped out. Recapitalization also may reflect the company's desire either to reduce its tax liability or to improve its credit rating. For the former, an American company may exchange bonds for its preferred stocks, since bond interest may be deducted before corporation income taxes are calculated, while preferred stock dividends are paid after taxes. Or a company might issue $1,000 long-term bonds with a 10 per cent coupon in place of $1,500 long-term bonds with a 5 per cent coupon. In this case the bondholders accept the exchange because it gives them higher income, and the company is willing to pay higher interest because it has reduced the indebtedness shown on its balance sheet and therefore can borrow more.

receipt

1. A written acknowledgment that money or something else of value has been physically received. See also VOUCHER; for *warehouse receipt,* see WAREHOUSE.

2. Also, *receipts.* Any asset(s), in cash or some other form, that have been acquired.

receivable   See ACCOUNTS RECEIVABLE; NOTES RECEIVABLE.

receiver   An impartial person appointed by a court of law to administer property or funds that are disputed. The receiver takes possession of (but not title to) the property or funds, receives their rents, profits, or other issue, and uses them as directed by the court. The proceeding of appointing a receiver is called *receivership,* and a business administered by a receiver is said to be "in receivership." See also BANKRUPTCY.

receiving   In business and industry, accepting delivery of goods at a shop, plant, warehouse, etc. Most shipments contain a packing slip and/or other documents (bill of lading, freight invoice, etc.) to identify the contents. The receiving clerk checks these against a file of unfilled purchase orders to make certain the goods were actually ordered by the company, and then physically checks the ship-

ment to see that it conforms to both packing slip and purchase order. The receiving clerk then fills out a receiving report describing the shipment, copies of which are sent to the purchasing, accounting, and using departments. The shipment is inspected (*receiving inspection*) to make sure the quality of the incoming goods conforms to specifications or blueprints (see also QUALITY CONTROL). If the shipment passes inspection, the clerk may prepare a "move" ticket indicating to what area of the plant or warehouse the material is to be transferred. If it goes into STORES, as most routine purchases do, the material becomes part of the company's inventory and is carried on the balance sheet as an asset until it is actually used up.

recession   A broad downward movement of the economy, that is, an extended, substantial, and widespread decline in aggregate economic activity. The National Bureau of Economic Research has never labeled an American recession as such until it was practically over, which is prudent over the long term but creates problems for policy-makers in government and business who are concerned with stabilizing the economy. Some economists have suggested specific criteria for defining a recession in terms of (1) duration, (2) depth, and (3) diffusion. For example, one set of criteria might be (1) an economic decline lasting nine months or longer as measured by a decline in employment in all sectors except agriculture; (2) a decline of at least 1.5 per cent in gross national product that extends over at least two quarters (six months) and a rise in the unemployment rate of more than two points and to a level above 6 per cent; (3) declines in employment lasting six months or longer in 75 per cent of all industries. See also BUSINESS CYCLE.

reciprocal exchange   See under INSURANCE.

reciprocity

1. In business and industry, the practice of deliberately buying from one's customers. For example, an oil company may buy all its pipe from steel producers that purchase its industrial lubricants, or a chemical concern may sell one raw material to another chemical company and in turn buy a second material from it. Though reciprocity is not necessarily illegal, it often is uneconomic—one

frequently could do better by buying from another supplier—and it generally is considered unfair.

2. In international trade, any mutual international agreement providing for the exchange of goods or services on special advantageous terms. Included are the reciprocal trade agreements allowed under the U.S. Reciprocal Trade Agreements Act (originally enacted in 1934 and since renewed; see Fig. 83, under TARIFF OF ABOMINATIONS), as well as bilateral trade and payments agreements (see under EXCHANGE CONTROLS), customs unions, free trade areas, and the multilateral policies agreed on under the GENERAL AGREEMENT ON TARIFFS AND TRADE.

reclamation
1. In banking, the correction of a mistake made in recording the face value of a check or other commercial paper in the clearing house.
2. The restoration of a natural resource, such as land, to productive use. It includes reclaiming deserts through irrigation, eroded fields and hillsides through proper cultivation and replanting, etc. In the United States the *Bureau of Reclamation* of the Department of the Interior is charged with administering major reclamation projects, which provide for irrigation, municipal and industrial water supply, hydroelectric power generation and transmission, flood control, navigation, and similar benefits of water resource projects. See also under CONSERVATION.

reconciliation In accounting, bringing into agreement two or more accounts or statements that show a discrepancy. For example, if a firm's bank statement does not agree with its own cash account record, its accountant may prepare a new statement listing all deposits and checks.

reconditioned
1. In manufacturing, describing a piece that was defective but has been repaired.
2. See REBUILT.

record
1. In computers, a collection of information representing one of many similar events or items to be stored or processed. Records contain *fields* of information in a fixed order, or *record structure*; ex-

amples of fields would be name, social security number, date of birth, address, etc. Records generally are grouped into *files*; thus, a group of personnel records constitutes a personnel file.
2. In accounting, any of several books used to keep track of transactions. Also, to enter a transaction in such a book.

record date The date on which the buyer of a stock must be registered in the company's books in order to receive a declared dividend or voting rights. See also EX-DIVIDEND.

recoup To recover a loss or an outlay through sale or use, or by charging it to profit and loss.

recourse In finance, the right to collect from the endorser or other guarantor of a loan in the event that the borrower fails to meet the obligation. However, a negotiable instrument such as a promissory note may be sold *without recourse*, meaning that the seller or endorser is not liable or otherwise responsible for its payment. For *nonrecourse loan*, see under AGRICULTURE, AID TO.

recovery An upturn in business activity following a recession (see BUSINESS CYCLE). The economy returns to its former level and perhaps even expands. See also RALLY.

recruitment Seeking out prospective new employees. Recruitment is undertaken by employment agencies to augment their files of jobseekers, as well as by businesses themselves, usually through their personnel departments. The chief sources tapped are private and public employment agencies, educational institutions (colleges, universities, technical schools, etc.), and labor unions. Also, some firms deliberately try to hire employees away from their competitors, luring them with offers of higher pay, stock options, and other benefits.

red, in the See IN THE RED.

redeemable bond See under BOND, def. 1.

redemption
1. In finance, the repurchase of a note, currency, stock, bond, or other form of indebtedness

by the corporation, bank, or government that issued it, usually in return for cash (but sometimes for bullion or some other valuable that is specified).

2. In real estate, the freeing of a mortgaged property of the mortgage lien after default. In many states the right of redemption may be exercised within a certain period following foreclosure and sale, but usually only by a person whose interests are affected by foreclosure. See also MORTGAGE.

red herring   See under ISSUE.

red ink   See IN THE RED.

rediscounting   Discounting again, that is, selling or discounting a negotiable instrument, such as commercial paper, that has already been discounted once (see DISCOUNT, def. 2). For example, in the United States a member bank may sell a discounted obligation it has purchased to its Federal Reserve Bank, which deducts a second discount (the rediscount) from the purchase price. (That is why the percentage of interest charged by the Federal Reserve—the DISCOUNT RATE—is also called the *rediscount rate*.) However, a bank need not sell to the Federal Reserve but can sell to some other bank, which may charge less for the service.

redistribution
  1. *Of land*; see LAND REFORM.
  2. *Of income*; see INCOME DISTRIBUTION.

redistribution multiplier   The chain reaction set off by government attempts to redistribute national income by taxing the rich and paying benefits to the poor (see also MULTIPLIER, def. 1). During the Great Depression of the 1930s such a policy was proposed as a means of stimulating the economy through increasing the spending ability of low-income groups (by giving them more to spend). Thus, perhaps $.50 of each $1 might have been saved had it not been taxed away from the rich, but perhaps only $.05 (or less) would have been saved if the same $1 were redistributed to the poor, giving a distribution multiplier of 10 in this instance.

redlining   A practice whereby banks and other institutional lenders arbitrarily exclude certain class-es of borrower. A "red line" is drawn around certain neighborhoods on a city map—usually both poor and largely black neighborhoods—and the banks either refuse to lend to residents or do so only on premium terms. Originally applied to real estate loans, the term is now used for almost any kind of investment policy in which certain categories are systematically excluded.

reduced form equation   In econometrics, a set of equations in which each of the ENDOGENOUS VARIABLES of a MODEL is expressed as a function of all of the exogenous variables of the model. In a simple model of the corn market (see under STRUCTURAL EQUATION), the reduced form would consist of three equations expressing the price of corn, the quantity demanded, and the quantity supplied, each as a function of rainfall and consumer income only.

re-export   The exporting of previously imported goods without additional processing or alteration. If they remain at a FREE PORT or bonded warehouse, such goods usually are not subject to duty.

referee in bankruptcy   See under BANKRUPTCY.

refinancing   See REFUNDING.

reflation   The deliberate and planned termination of a disinflationary program, in the expectation that the rate of inflation will begin to increase once again. It is accomplished by fiscal and monetary policies that put more money into the hands of consumers and business: tax cuts, increased government spending, and low interest rates. Reflation is undertaken usually because the government or central bank fears that DISINFLATION will cause excessive unemployment or other distress. It also may be undertaken because a nation's exchange rate has become too high relative to other nations—that is, its goods are too cheap—in order to bring its prices more in line with those of its trading partners.

refund   The return of part or all of a payment, owing to overpayment. A *cash refund* is just that; a *merchandise refund* stipulates that the refund be spent on other merchandise offered by the same seller. See also REBATE.

refunding Also, *refinancing*. In investment, floating a new issue of securities to obtain funds to retire existing securities. The object may be to save interest costs, to extend the maturity of the loan, or both.

regional stock exchange In the United States, a STOCK EXCHANGE outside New York City.

register

1. In accounting, a book in which transactions are recorded. It may or may not be a JOURNAL. See also under VOUCHER, def. 2.

2. A book maintained by a corporation that lists all of its shareholders. Such a book may be kept by the company itself or by a TRANSFER AGENT.

3. *of ships.* A list of ships—their names, owners, and general descriptions—kept by a port officer or by an insurance agency. See also REGISTRY, MARINE.

registered bond See under BOND, def. 1.

registered coupon bond See under BOND, def. 1.

registered check See under CHECK.

registered representative Also, *account executive, customer's man, customer's broker*. An employee of a brokerage firm who takes orders from customers and passes them on to the firm's floor broker, who executes tham on the STOCK EXCHANGE floor. The name comes from the fact that this person represents the floor broker in taking an order and is licensed by the U.S. Securities and Exchange Commission and approved by the stock exchange as being of good character and qualified to work in the securities trade. On the New York Stock Exchange a registered representative must pass an examination before being approved.

registered trader See FLOOR TRADER.

register of deeds See under DEED.

registrar A person charged with the responsibility of blocking the issue of unauthorized stock by a company. A registrar frequently is employed by a trust company or bank.

registration The submission of a statement to the U.S. Securities and Exchange Commission, which is required before securities may be offered to the public in interstate commerce or through the mails, either by the issuing corporation or by controlling stockholders. The registration statement contains information about the company's operations, securities, management, and the purpose of the issue in question, in the detail required by the Securities Act of 1933. Further, according to the Securities Exchange Act of 1934, any security to be listed on a national exchange must be registered with the exchange in question and with the Securities and Exchange Commission, which requires similar information. See also under ISSUE.

registry, marine The practice of listing a vessel under the name of the particular nation whose flag it flies. Since each nation has different maritime laws, shipowners are inclined to register under the most favorable. For example, the Republic of Panama has exceptionally lax regulations concerning equipment, crew, etc., and therefore many merchant vessels, regardless of the owners' nationality, are registered under Panama's maritime laws and fly the Panamanian flag. See also REGISTER, def. 3.

regression analysis In statistics and econometrics, a method for predicting the value of a dependent variable from known values of independent variables. For example, it might be used to predict the output of certain production workers (dependent variable) based on the results of testing them for mechanical aptitude (independent variable). *Simple regression analysis* involves just one independent variable; *multiple regression analysis* involves several independent variables. In the example above, if mechanical aptitude were the only variable, simple analysis would suffice, but if other factors, such as work experience, age, educational level, and intelligence quotient also appeared to affect output, multiple regression analysis would be required. A *scatter chart* or *scatter diagram* frequently is used to develop an equation for the dependent variable. It consists simply of a graph on which the dependent variable (above, output) is

Fig. 71. Scatter chart

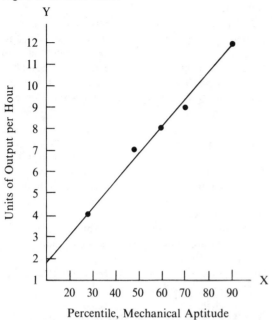

Percentile, Mechanical Aptitude

and output, and the latter could be precisely predicted on the basis of the former. In fact, however, some points fall off the line; they are close enough to the line to indicate a relationship, but nevertheless some of the variation in output is not explained by the test scores, indicating some uncertainty or error. Were there many dots outside the line—so-called *scatter*—there would be an even greater proportion of unexplained variation, and were it great enough it might indicate that test scores had absolutely no connection with output. Measuring the closeness of this relationship is a statistical process called *correlation analysis*, which determines first the *coefficient of determination* (the proportion of explained variations to total variations) and then its square root, called the *correlation coefficient*. A correlation coefficient of zero indicates there is no relationship between the variables; a coefficient of 1 would indicate a very direct positive relationship; and −1 would mean a direct negative relationship.

regressive tax See under PROGRESSIVE TAX.

regular dividend See under DIVIDEND, def. 1.

Regulation Q A rule, first instituted in the Banking Act of 1933, whereby the Federal Reserve Board of Governors can control the interest rate on time and savings deposits of member banks. Although relatively stable for a long time, in the 1960s and early 1970s the interest rate was manipulated by the Federal Reserve as part of its efforts to control the availability of credit and to prevent, or at least limit, DISINTERMEDIATION. In 1973 a Financial Institutions bill, whereby ceilings on time deposit interest rates would gradually be eliminated, was introduced in Congress, but it met considerable opposition.

reinstatement In insurance, restoration of a policy to its original amount after the payment of a claim, which in many instances will have reduced the policy by the amount of the claim. Depending on the terms of the policy, reinstatement may or may not require payment of an additional premium, and it may occur automatically or only at the policyholder's request.

plotted on the Y-axis (vertical axis) and the independent variable (test scores) is plotted on the X-axis (horizontal axis). Fig. 71 shows the test scores of five employees, expressed as percentile of mechanical aptitude (90th, 80th, 70th, etc.), and their output in terms of units per hour (ranging from 4 to 12 units). A glance at the chart shows higher test scores are associated with higher output. The average path of the points is a straight line (called a *regression line*), so the equation expressing the relationship of X and Y will be a linear one (*linear regression*). Though one can simply draw a freehand line that will pass through most of the points plotted, a more accurate estimate can be made by means of the *least-squares method*, a mathematical formula that minimizes the sum of the squares of the vertical deviations above or below the line, so that the equation indeed expresses the values closest to the line. The fact that not all of the points plotted in the scatter chart fall on the line (see Fig. 71) is extremely important. If they all did fall on the line, the prediction of output would be totally accurate, provided the sample were large enough to rule out accidental coincidence. There would clearly be a direct relationship between mechanical aptitude

reinsurance The assumption by one insurance firm of all or part of a risk originally undertaken by another insurer. The company buying the reinsurance is the *reinsured*; the one selling it is the *reinsurer*. Reinsurance generally is bought to reduce liability, to provide financial support to the primary insurer, or to gain underwriting capacity. Reinsurance is a worldwide enterprise, with numerous companies, especially in Europe, devoted entirely to this activity.

relative-income hypothesis An attempt to explain the relationship of consumer spending, saving, and income in terms of a consumer's relative position within his or her income class or community. This idea, largely developed by the American economist James S. Duesenberry, helps explain why farmers, small-town dwellers, and blacks tend to save more at any given level of income than white urban consumers. For example, a small-town physician with an annual income of $30,000 may be closer to the top of his or her income class than a big-city surgeon earning $80,000 per year, and consequently may save a larger proportion of annual income. See also PERMANENT-INCOME HYPOTHESIS.

relative price differences Same as *comparative advantage*; see under ADVANTAGE.

release In law, the giving up of some right or benefit or claim to a person against whom the right is to be enforced or the claim exercised. See also WAIVER.

reliability In quality control, the ability of an item to perform a required function under stated conditions for a stated time—in other words, dependability of performance.

relief Also, *unemployment relief, work relief.* The creation of jobs, by government, in order to relieve widespread unemployment. Among the principal relief programs enacted by the United States during the Great Depression were the Civilian Conservation Corps (CCC) and the WORKS PROGRESS ADMINISTRATION (WPA). See also WELFARE.

remainder
1. In publishing, an overstock of new books for which there is little or no demand. Also, to sell such books at reduced prices.
2. In real estate law, a future interest in real property for a person other than the original grantor. For example, Smith may give a parcel of land to his sister, to keep until her death (a life estate); after her death Smith's son is to have the land. Smith's son's interest in the land is called a *remainder*. See also REVERSION.

remittance A sum of money sent from one person to another, usually as a payment for goods or services. The remittance may be in cash or in the form of a check or other negotiable instrument.

remote device Any of several devices for providing input to or receiving output from a COMPUTER that are not located in the same room as the computer. They may be only a few yards or hundreds of miles away. See also TERMINAL, COMPUTER.

removal bond A bond that must be posted on removal of imported goods from a bonded warehouse, for processing for re-export or a similar purpose, so as to cover any customs duties or other charges that would be incurred if the goods were retained for domestic sale. See also under WAREHOUSE.

rendu price The delivered price for an imported good, that is, including all freight, tariff, insurance, and other shipping charges.

renewal In insurance, the reinstatement of a policy that is about to expire, made by issuing either a new policy or a renewal receipt under the same conditions. For *renewable term insurance*, see under LIFE INSURANCE.

rent
1. Also, *real rent.* In classic economic theory, the return earned by LAND, one of the three factors of production (along with capital and labor). Unlike most commodities, land has a relatively inelastic supply that will not respond to changes in price. For *economic rent*, see under D. RICARDO. See also QUASI-RENT.
2. In general usage, a payment made for the use of a property—a building, land tract, special equip-

ment, musical instrument, etc.—over a period of time. In the case of land or buildings, the property's owner is the *landlord* and the renter is a *tenant*. The written agreement between landlord and tenant, which sets forth the terms of rental, is called a LEASE. Rent may be paid in money, services, chattels, or crops. Ordinarily, landlord and tenant may specify whatever rent they agree to, but in special instances the government may impose limitations on rent, called *rent control* (see under PRICE CONTROL). The lease usually fixes the time of payment of rent (weekly, monthly, annually, etc.); when it does not, rent usually is due at the end of the term (and always so when it is paid in crops).

rent control   See under PRICE CONTROL.

rentier   A French word (it comes from a kind of French government bond called *rente*) for a person who derives most of his or her income from fixed investments in the form of interest or annuity payments. Since the rentier's income depends on past economic activity and is independent of current productivity and growth, his best interest lies in maintaining the status quo, particularly with regard to purchasing power. In France after World War I, the rentiers were politically allied with small industrialists and shopkeepers against big business and banking interests. Whereas the latter believed in a strong central government and opposed every form of economic radicalism, the rentiers wanted only security and cared not at all about economic growth.

reorganization bond   See under BOND, def. 1.

repairs   See MAINTENANCE AND REPAIRS.

reparations   See under WAR, FINANCING OF.

repartimiento   See under ENCOMIENDA.

repayment of loans   See FOREIGN AID; PREPAYMENT; SOFT LOAN; WAR, FINANCING OF.

replacement insurance   See under PROPERTY INSURANCE.

replacement method   A method of calculating the depreciation of a fixed asset by considering its current replacement cost in addition to its original cost, thus taking into account changes in price levels. The depreciation normally is calculated by the STRAIGHT-LINE METHOD, but to it is added a percentage of the increase in replacement cost. Thus, if a $14,000 truck with a seven-year service life will probably cost $17,500 to replace, straight-line depreciation of $2,000 per year might be augmented by 1/7 of the $3,500 extra cost of replacement, making total annual depreciation $2,500 per year. See also REPRODUCTION COST.

report, annual   See ANNUAL REPORT.

reporting pay   Also, *call-in pay*. Wages paid to workers who report on a regular working day but find there is no work for them. Most union contracts call for reporting pay, usually two to four hours' pay. Few payments are actually made under such clauses, however, for the potential penalty tends to make employers careful to notify workers in good time.

reporting policy   In property insurance, a policy covering goods whose value fluctuates and therefore must periodically be reported to the insurer, who then adjusts the premium accordingly. In marine insurance, for example, a policy may cover the freight carried by certain vessels traveling between certain ports. Since the value of each shipment varies, the shipper must report it to the insurer, who then sets the premium for that voyage.

repossession   See under INSTALLMENT BUYING.

representation, exclusive   See under LABOR UNION.

representative money   Paper money backed by a precious metal (gold or silver), which it "represents" or "stands for."

repressed inflation   See SUPPRESSED INFLATION.

reproducer   See under PUNCHED-CARD DATA PROCESSING.

reproduction cost   Also, *current reproduction cost*. In accounting, valuing a fixed asset in terms of how much its replacement would cost in the current market. See also ORIGINAL COST, def. 1; REPLACEMENT METHOD.

repurchase agreement The sale of securities on a temporary basis, involving the seller's agreement to buy them back from the buyer after a specified time. Repurchase agreements are used by the Federal Reserve to expand credit when it temporarily becomes tight. The Federal Reserve buys securities, chiefly Treasury bills, from dealers, who deposit the proceeds of the sale in their checking accounts, thereby adding to bank reserves. After a specified time (usually a few days), with credit presumably expanded, the dealers repurchase the securities. Such agreements can also work in reverse. The Federal Reserve absorbs temporary excess liquidity by selling Treasury bills to dealers (who finance the purchases with loans from commercial banks), agreeing to buy the bills back a few days later. See also OPEN-MARKET OPERATIONS.

required reserve See RESERVE REQUIREMENTS.

requisition A formal, written request for materials, supplies, delivery of goods or property, etc. See also PURCHASE REQUISITION.

resale
1. In business, buying goods from a supplier and reselling them without further processing or other changes. Some sales contracts specify that goods may *not* be resold in this manner. For the setting of resale prices, see FAIR TRADE.
2. Selling to another customer goods for which the original customer has not paid or on which he has defaulted in some other way. The right to resell goods in this way may be spelled out or restricted by the provisions of the original sales contract.

resale price maintenance See FAIR TRADE.

rescission The termination of a contract, which is then said to be *rescinded*. It may be done by mutual agreement of the parties involved, in which case the contract is simply annulled, or it may be accomplished by one party, usually when the other party does not or cannot carry out his part of the agreement. In either case, the effect of rescission is to revest in the original parties any title that was transferred and to return any payment made under the contract.

research and development Also, *R and D.* Basic and applied research directed toward the discovery, invention, design, or development of new products and processes. It may be undertaken by private companies, whole industries, nonprofit organizations, or governments. It can be carried out within a company, as in the development of a new product, or through an outside consultant or contractor. While research and development have been important ever since the beginning of industrialization, they did not in themselves constitute a large-scale industry until after World War II. By the early 1970s about $20 billion per year was being spent in the United States on R and D. Many of the companies devoted exclusively to these activities are almost entirely dependent on government contracts, particularly defense contracts.

reserve army of the unemployed A term used by Karl Marx to describe the large labor reserve that employers could use to intimidate their workers and keep wages down to a bare subsistence level.

reserve balance See under BANK RESERVES.

Reserve bank credit See FEDERAL RESERVE BANK CREDIT.

reserve city bank See under NATIONAL BANKS, def. 2.

reserve currency A currency in which nations keep their foreign exchange reserves in addition to or instead of gold and/or SPECIAL DRAWING RIGHTS (SDRs). Such a currency must have a relatively stable exchange rate, be involved in a significant amount of world trade, and be readily CONVERTIBLE (def. 2) in the FOREIGN EXCHANGE MARKET. Since World War II the U.S. dollar has been the leading reserve currency and every major trading nation except Switzerland has carried a substantial (and in many cases a major) part of its reserves in U.S. dollars.

reserve plan, 100 per cent See under BANK RESERVES; also under I. FISHER.

reserve ratio The ratio of a commercial bank's required deposit in a central bank to the total demand deposits it holds. See also RESERVE REQUIREMENTS.

reserve requirements The portion of their deposits that United States commercial banks must, by law, set aside as BANK RESERVES. For state banks this amount is determined by state law; for members of the FEDERAL RESERVE it is established by the Federal Reserve Board of Governors, on the basis of a bank's location and size. (The Federal Reserve Act of 1913 followed the classification of banks used by the National Banking system but from 1961 on changes were made in these categories; see under NATIONAL BANKS, def. 2.) In the mid-1970s the *required reserve*, or *reserve ratio*, ranged from $12\frac{1}{2}$ per cent to 22 per cent for demand deposits, and 3 per cent to 10 per cent for savings and time deposits. Reserves could be in the form of vault cash or deposits at a Federal Reserve Bank. (In practice the major part of member banks' reserves are in the latter form, with vault cash accounting for a relatively small percentage.) The purpose of reserve requirements is to protect depositors and, in the case of Federal Reserve member banks, to give the monetary authority a means of controlling the money supply (see MONETARY POLICY). See also EXCESS RESERVES; FRACTIONAL RESERVE BANKING; PRIMARY RESERVES.

reserves

1. In finance, a stock of assets from which debts can be paid. Such assets serve as security for currency in circulation (*monetary reserves*) or security for bank deposits (BANK RESERVES) or security for foreign debts (FOREIGN EXCHANGE RESERVES). See also GOLD RESERVE; LIQUIDITY, INTERNATIONAL; RESERVE CURRENCY.

2. Also, *allowance*. In accounting, funds set aside from profits and transferred to a special liability account in order to meet either anticipated or unforeseen future needs. Among these are reserves from which to redeem long-term debts (see also SINKING FUND), to pay taxes, to meet operating expenses certain to occur but not identifiable in advance, to replace assets that are depleted (see also DEPLETION ALLOWANCE), to replace fixed assets that are expected to wear out, and to provide for changes in the value of a firm's assets (called a *valuation reserve*; see DEPRECIATION RESERVE).

3. In insurance, funds set aside by the insurer to meet policy claims and other obligations. In the United States most companies that issue PROPERTY and LIABILITY INSURANCE must maintain not only *loss reserves* (to pay claims for losses) but also *unearned premium reserves*. (The insured pays a premium at the beginning of each period of insurance, while protection is given only as time elapses during the period; the unearned premium is that part of the premium which the company has not yet had time to earn.) By law the insurer must show as a reserve the unused portion of the premiums of all policies on the books.

residence A more or less permanent dwelling place. See also DOMICILE.

resource allocation The assignment of a society's resources—land, labor, capital—to produce the goods and services it needs. Were the supply of resources unlimited, there would be no need for allocation (see SCARCITY). Since this is not the case, every economy faces the problem of precisely how resources will be employed and what will be produced. Today most nations of the world fall somewhere between the two extremes of a totally PLANNED ECONOMY, in which resource allocation is almost wholly determined by a central agency, and a totally free market economy, where demand and supply channel resources to the most profitable uses. A free market economy can work perfectly only under pure competition, where neither buyers nor sellers have any special advantages, so that the price people are willing to pay determines realistic production priorities. In practice, however, external factors nearly always influence the market, so that even in free market economies government must interfere to some extent to provide checks and balances. Allocation of resources can also be considered in terms of individual firms (should a company manufacture cars or tractors, refrigerators or air conditioners, or both? etc.), farms (plant wheat, corn, or soy beans, and how much of each?), and other enterprises. For a graphic approach to the problem, see TRANSFORMATION CURVE.

restraint of trade Any attempt to restrict competition by combining, for example, to create a monopoly, to maintain or increase prices, or to apportion the available business. In the United States contracts in restraint of trade are illegal on the ground that they are contrary to the public interest. See also ANTITRUST LEGISLATION; COMBINATION; MONOPOLY.

restrictive covenant A clause in a contract that denies the buyer or lessor full rights to the property in question. For example, a landlord may stipulate in a lease that a tenant may not paint an apartment unless the colors are first approved by the landlord, or the purchaser of a lot may be required to obtain the seller's approval of the style of house he proposes to build there—a right that would otherwise be unqualifiedly his as the new owner of the land. At one time, restrictive covenants were common in real estate transactions to prevent members of minority groups from purchasing or renting homes in choice residential neighborhoods.

restrictive endorsement See under ENDORSEMENT, def. 1.

retail Describing a business engaged chiefly in selling goods directly for final consumption rather than for processing or resale. The chief customers of retail sellers, or *retailers*, are individuals and households. The chief methods of selling at retail are MAIL ORDER, DOOR-TO-DOOR SELLING, VENDING MACHINES (for candy, cigarettes, etc.), and the many different kinds of *retail store*; the first three are called *nonstore retailers*. Since retailers sell to the ultimate consumer, they tend to be located near their customers, at least in the case of stores, and hence retail establishments are more numerous than wholesalers or manufacturers. In the United States there are about 6.5 retailers for every wholesaler (more than 1.5 million retail firms in all). However, retail sales total only some $310 billion per year, compared to more than $459 billion annual wholesale sales. Also, though retailing is essentially composed of many small firms, the larger re-

tail stores, principally big department stores and supermarkets, which comprise only some 3 per cent of all retail stores, account for more than 44 per cent of sales.

By far the most common kind of retail store is the *independent store*, which in the United States evolved from the frontier trading post and country *general store*. A few general stores still exist in rural areas, carrying mostly food but also some clothing, notions, farm supplies, and gasoline. Independent stores range from quite small to quite large; their essential feature is that they are individually owned and/or managed. Since the small independent store often must compete with large retail chains, supermarkets, and department stores, and generally buys from wholesalers rather than producers (and therefore must charge higher prices), it usually must offer its customers some compensating convenience—personalized service, good location, longer hours, free delivery, credit, etc. Most independent shops are *single-line* or *limited-line* stores, specializing in one or a few kinds of goods, such as dry goods, clothing, furniture, drugs and cosmetics, or groceries. Some specialize not only in a single line (such as food) but a single class of item (such as meat or baked goods). The *specialty shop* is a limited-line store that aims for a carefully defined market by offering a unique assortment of products, knowledgeable sales help, and good service; a common example is the *boutique* offering a particular kind of fashionable apparel. The *variety store*, on the other hand, offers a large selection of items. It may be a *limited-price store* as well, such as a *five-and-ten* (or "dime store"), which tends to stock relatively low-priced goods, and often it is a *self-service store*, with customers helping themselves to the goods on display and paying at a central cash register. Though a few American variety stores remain independent, most today are part of a chain (see CHAIN STORE). Historically the variety store, also an offshoot of the rural general store, became first a large chain and then expanded still further, combining some elements of both the large DISCOUNT HOUSE (see def. 1) and SUPERMARKET to become a MASS MERCHANDISER. See also DEPARTMENT STORE.

retail inventory method A method of inventory accounting widely used by retail businesses, whereby goods in stock are valued at their intended selling prices. If the item eventually is sold for a lower price, the difference is accounted for in the store's markdown account.

retail sales The dollar value of goods sold directly to the consumer by retail stores, an important CO-INCIDENT INDICATOR of business conditions. Data on retail sales are compiled weekly and monthly for a variety of establishments by the U.S. Department of Commerce and are published in the *Survey of Current Business* (and elsewhere).

retained earnings Also, *earned surplus, retained income, undistributed profits.* The income left to a company after taxes and dividends have been paid. Retained earnings are a major source of funds for a firm's expansion without increasing its long-term obligations or further diluting its ownership (by issuing more bonds or stocks).

retainer A fee paid for professional services, or a contract providing for such a fee. Normally such a contract stipulates that the person engaged will not do similar work, or work for a competitor, during the period covered. A *general retainer* covers any work over a specified time; a *special retainer* covers a particular job or project.

retaliatory tariff See under TARIFF, def. 1.

retire
1. To stop working, more or less permanently, usually but not necessarily on account of old age or ill health. Some organizations allow voluntary retirement at a given age, whereas others insist on mandatory retirement after a certain age. For a long time the traditional retirement age in the United States was 65, but today it tends to vary widely. Many organizations have a *retirement plan* whereby an employee may draw a PENSION after retiring.
2. To withdraw a security from circulation, or, in the case of an obligation, to redeem it by paying off the principal and any accumulated interest. A stock, bond, bill of exchange, etc. is said to be retired in this way.

retirement and survivors' insurance See under SOCIAL SECURITY.

retirement plan See under PENSION.

return
1. The rate of profit earned in relation to the value of the capital investment required. This concept is used in business to calculate the profitability of various capital investments, and also in investment, where "return" is usually called YIELD.
2. *of merchandise.* A purchased item returned by a customer for a refund, in exchange for another item, or for credit toward a future purchase. Most retailers have specific policies concerning merchandise returns, such as offering a cash refund only if goods are returned within three days of purchase, or refusing returns on items marked "final sale." To determine net sales, returns must be deducted from gross sales. In industrial purchasing the contract normally defines the terms, if any, under which goods may be returned; in such cases returns are almost always based on quality failure.
3. *tax return.* A detailed report of income earned, expenses and other deductions and exemptions claimed, and taxes due, which all taxpayers are required to send to the government along with their tax payments. See also JOINT RETURN.

returns to scale The increases in output resulting from increases in input of all FACTORS OF PRODUCTION required to produce a particular item. For example, suppose a broom manufacturer produces 200,000 brooms a year in a factory employing 20 workers, 1 foreman, 20 units of machinery, and using 500 units of materials. It then acquires a partner who puts up enough money to employ twice the number of workers and machines and materials. Input of factors of production has exactly doubled; what will happen to output? If output doubles too, to 400,000 brooms, returns to scale are said to be *constant*; if output increases somewhat less, to 350,000 brooms, returns to scale are termed *decreasing*; if output increases more, to 450,000 brooms, returns to scale are *increasing*. Unlike economy of SCALE, the concept of returns to scale refers to physical output rather than to cost. The chief use of calculating returns to scale is for analyzing different technological conditions. See also PRODUCTION FUNCTION.

revaluation The change in value of a nation's currency relative to other currencies. An increase in value is called *appreciation*; a decrease is called *depreciation* (see also EXCHANGE DEPRECIATION). In the past revaluation was always the result of individual government action (since governments set exchange rates), but since World War II the chief trading countries, as well as many lesser ones, have tended to work more cooperatively. Members of the INTERNATIONAL MONETARY FUND are supposed to obtain that body's approval before revaluing their currency, and in practice they generally do. See also DEVALUATION.

revenue
1. The total income of a unit of government —local, state, or central. The chief source of revenue is taxes. In the United States the principal sources of Federal revenue are personal and corporation income taxes, which make up well over half of all government receipts. The remainder comes from social insurance taxes and contributions (social security, payroll and employment taxes, accounting for about one-fourth of the total), excise taxes, customs duties, estate and gift taxes, and miscellaneous sources. The Federal government regularly shares some of its revenue with the individual states, which in turn share their revenues with local governments, a practice called *revenue sharing*. See also *revenue bond*, under BOND, def. 1; *revenue tariff*, under TARIFF, def. 1.
2. In accounting, a term used variously to mean the total income of a business or government (see INCOME, def. 2), income generated by the sale of goods only, or income generated only from sources other than sales. In the case of a utility, transportation facility, or other service enterprise, what would be called "net sales" in a manufacturing company is called "operating revenues." See also INCOME STATEMENT.
3. See MARGINAL REVENUE.

revenue bond See under BOND, def. 1.

revenue stamp See under EXCISE TAX; TRANSFER TAX.

revenue tariff See under TARIFF, def. 1.

revenue ton-mile See under TON-MILE.

reverse cost method In cost accounting, a way of determining the cost of producing by-products in which the net yield from a by-product is deducted from total costs. It is used principally to determine the price a producer can pay for raw materials and still make a profit or to determine what price should be charged for by-products. For example, in flour milling, the chief product is standard-grade flour, and the smaller amounts of high-grade and low-grade flour produced are considered by-products. The accountant now works backward ("in reverse"), that is, milling costs—both variable and fixed—are deducted from the total value of products obtainable from 100 bushels of wheat, which depend on the yield of the various flours. The resulting figure is the price the miller can pay for wheat without losing money.

reverse split See under SPLIT.

reversion The residue of a fee simple (complete ownership of real property) remaining to a grantor, or the state of a landlord during the existence of a leasehold. For example, Jones may deed a lot to Smith with the provision that Smith may not sell or use alcoholic beverages on the lot, and in case of violation ownership will revert to Jones. Smith dies and his daughter erects a liquor store on the lot. Jones sues, and the court returns the lot to him. Or, if Green rents a house to Black, Black's interest in the house is called a leasehold but Green's is a reversion; possession reverts to Green when the lease expires. See also REMAINDER, def. 2.

revisionism See under E. BERNSTEIN; FABIAN SOCIALISM.

revocation The withdrawal by the offeror of an OFFER, which is then said to be revoked.

revolving charge account See under CHARGE ACCOUNT.

revolving fund A fund that is continually replenished as it is spent, often through income generated by the fund itself. For example, in many states revenues from motor vehicle taxes and licenses automatically are channeled into a fund for road construction and maintenance.

Rhode Island system A system of factory organization used by Samuel Slater, who built a textile mill in 1790 at Pawtucket, Rhode Island. His mill, where machine-made cotton warp was spun into thread, is considered the birthplace of the factory system in America. Slater eventually built other mills in Rhode Island, mostly near villages, where whole families would be employed to work the machines and where workers often lived in company-owned housing. His operations were much smaller, however, than those established a few years later by Francis Lowell and his associates (see WALTHAM SYSTEM).

Ricardo, David An English economist (1772–1823), prominent member of the CLASSICAL SCHOOL. A successful businessman, Ricardo retired at 42 and devoted the last nine years of his life to writing on economics, an occupation begun in 1809 with an unsigned newspaper article pointing out the need for a gold standard to back currency. A firm believer in free trade and the COST OF PRODUCTION THEORY OF VALUE (that value depends on cost of production, in terms of wages and profits), Ricardo summarized his ideas in *The Principles of Political Economy* (1817). They included his theory of rent, or *economic rent*, which, Ricardo held, represents the difference in quality (depending on fertility and location) of two tracts of land. Rent results from the higher productivity of good land, with no rent being paid for marginal land. (This idea of marginal utility was later greatly expanded by Alfred MARSHALL.) Rent does not influence prices; on the contrary, prices of goods influence rent. As the population grows, the increased demand for food raises food prices. Then poorer land will be cultivated and better land worked harder, and rents will rise. Since wages also must rise (to pay for higher-priced food), profits will decrease. Ultimately, therefore, landlords will benefit at the expense of capitalists (rents rise while profits fall). This tendency could be partly offset by improvements in agriculture, raising the productivity of poorer land, and by imports of cheap grain. For this reason Ricardo strongly opposed Britain's import-restricting CORN LAWS. Ricardo also believed in the IRON LAW OF WAGES. See also QUASI-RENT.

rich man's panic See under PANICS, BUSINESS.

rider In insurance, a form adding special provisions to a policy. See also ENDORSEMENT, def. 3.

rigging Driving a security's price sharply up or down through heavy buying or selling. Freely practiced in the United States until the 1920s, rigging today is largely prevented by the strict regulations of the Securities and Exchange Commission (but is perfectly legal when a new issue is marketed).

right of way See under EASEMENT.

rights Also, *stock rights*. The privilege of buying new securities at a price somewhat lower than the market price, called the *subscription price*. This privilege normally is given to stockholders in proportion to the amount of stock they own. However, rights usually are transferable, and because of the price advantage they acquire a market value of their own and are actively traded. In most cases rights must be exercised within a relatively short time; failure to exercise or sell them within that time may result in actual loss to the holder. (However, see also WARRANT, def. 1.) While issuing rights is a way for a corporation to raise money from its own stockholders, it may be more costly than floating an issue through ordinary channels (see UNDERWRITING). Also, should the open market price for existing stock drop below the subscription price, the entire issue will be ruined, since it then becomes cheaper to buy at market price than to exercise the rights. See also PREEMPTIVE RIGHTS.

right-to-work law A law that forbids any requirement of union membership for getting or holding a job, thereby effectively outlawing the UNION SHOP in all its versions. Encouraged by Section 14b of the Taft-Hartley Act of 1947, such laws were passed in about 20 states, mostly in southern and midwestern agricultural states, but rarely have been enforced. In some cases they were enacted less to hurt unions than to attract new industry to an area, and at least one major corporation publicly stated that it preferred to set up new plants in states with right-to-work laws.

ringing out Also, *ringing up*. In the FUTURES MARKET, the practice of settling or clearing outstanding futures contracts among brokers and dealers, by exchanging futures among themselves before they become due for delivery. The outstanding feature of futures trading is that most of it is done not by producers or consumers of the commodities being traded but by speculators. Therefore brokers and dealers find it to their advantage to clear transactions among themselves rather than finding a buyer who actually wants the commodity when a contract matures.

risk
1. In economics, the chance that a particular decision or action can give rise to a variety of outcomes for which one can calculate the mathematical probability. See under UNCERTAINTY.
2. In investment, the probability of losing money or making a profit on one's investments. In the case of obligations, such as bonds, a company may default on interest or even on principal. In the case of equity, such as stocks, the company may simply not have enough earnings to give stockholders much of a share, and the price of the stock may fall appreciably. In addition to the risks involved owing to the fortunes of the company and its ability to pay dividends, investors must face the risk that overall market prices may decline, or that inflation will reduce purchasing power so that even seemingly good profits become comparatively worthless.
3. In insurance, a general term for any possibility of loss. Also, the person or property covered by an insurance policy. A risk for which the probability cannot be calculated generally is considered too great for insurance and hence is termed *noninsurable*. Sometimes, however, such a risk must be protected to comply with the law. The insurance then may be handled through a pool of insurers and is assigned to different companies in turn; this is called an *assigned risk*.

risk capital Also, *venture capital*. In corporate finance, funds invested in an enterprise with a large element of risk for the owners or shareholders.

Robinson, Joan Violet A British economist (1903–) who published an analysis of imperfect competition (1933) similar in many ways to that of E. H. CHAMBERLIN (who called it "monopolistic competition"). Like Chamberlin, Robinson concluded that most firms try to establish a monopoly on their products by persuading customers of their unique properties, even though competing firms produce virtually the same goods or very close substitutes. A pupil of Alfred MARSHALL and colleague of John M. Keynes at Cambridge University, Robinson also wrote a critique of Marxism, a study on accumulation of capital (1956), essays on economic growth, and a study of the effectiveness of government economic controls. A socialist, Robinson believed that profit is based on the constant battle among society's classes and hence has no real economic justification, and income distribution should therefore be altered to favor the weak and the poor.

Robinson-Patman Act See under ANTITRUST LEGISLATION; also under CHAIN STORE.

Rochdale Plan See under CONSUMER COOPERATIVE.

rolling stock In railroad terminology, any property on wheels, including all railroad cars and locomotives, as well as wheeled carts, cranes, etc. By extension, any wheeled vehicle.

rollover A method of issuing a new government security by subscribing for it in terms of a maturing bond or other obligation. The new issue is paid for simply by turning in holdings of the old one.

Roscher, Wilhelm A German economist (1817–94), one of the founders of the GERMAN HISTORICAL SCHOOL. He is remembered both for emphasizing the study of history as a key to understanding economics and for his grasp of the interrelatedness of all human institutions—language, art, religion, and law, as well as politics and economics.

rotating shift See under SHIFT, def. 1.

roundabout production A term used by E. BÖHM-BAWERK to describe the complexity of modern production methods, which delay the capitalist's return on investment. Often the investment itself is in machinery or other equipment used only indirectly to make an end-product, as in machine tools that make the machinery that make automobile parts, which eventually are incorporated in cars and trucks. In the long run, of course, roundabout production is more efficient than simpler, more direct methods.

round lot The conventional unit of trading in stocks, bonds, or commodities, and any multiple thereof. The round lot for stocks traded on the New York Stock Exchange (and many other American exchanges) is 100 shares (though in some inactive stocks it may be 10 shares), and for bonds it is a par value of $1,000. In commodity trading it varies with the commodity, as, for example, 5,000 bushels of wheat or 36,000 pounds of frozen pork bellies per contract. In Canada the unit of trading depends both on the kind of stock (that is, the business the issuing corporation is in) and its price. For example, on the Toronto Stock Exchange, the trading unit for industrial stocks selling at $25 to $100 per share is 25 shares, and for those selling for more than $100 it is 10 shares. For oil and mining stocks selling for less than $1 per share (a *penny stock*) the unit is 500 shares. These various units are called *board lots*. See also ODD LOT, def. 1.

round turn Also, *round transaction, round trip.* In the securities and commodities trade, a transaction involving the purchase and resale of the same lot of stock or commodities. Since a commission must be paid for both buying and selling the lot, the speculator usually waits until the price is high enough to cover both commissions and yield a profit as well.

routine A computer program or part of a program. See PROGRAMMING.

routing Establishing the precise route that a shipment of goods is to follow. For example, a shipment from Portland, Maine, to Greensboro, North Carolina, could be sent via a number of routes (such as Boston & Maine Railroad to Hartford, Connecticut; New York, New Haven & Hartford Railroad to New York City; Penn Central Railroad to Washington, D.C.; Southern Railroad to Greensboro). The best route from the shipper's standpoint may not be the best from the carrier's; carriers get maximum revenue from their own lines, which may not be the fastest or cheapest route for a given shipment.

royalty A payment made in return for some privilege or right, as to an author by a publisher for publishing and selling his or her works, to the holder of a patent for the privilege of using it, or to a landowner by a mine operator holding a mineral lease. Such privileges originally were granted by the crown, which also received the payments for them, and hence the name.

rubber check Colloquial term for a bad check, that is, one returned by the bank owing to lack of funds in the account against which it is drawn. Such a check is said to "bounce" (be refused); hence, "rubber." See also NSF CHECK; OVERDRAFT.

rule of reason See under ANTITRUST LEGISLATION.

run
1. The operation of a single computer program or of several programs in sequence (see PROGRAMMING).
2. See BANK RUN.

runaway industry An industry that transfers some or all of its operations elsewhere to take advantage of cheaper labor, lower taxes, special subsidies, or other cost-lowering advantages. In effect this practice represents an application of the principle of *comparative advantage* (see under ADVANTAGE), and naturally it is vigorously opposed by labor unions, who see their hard-won gains lost to workers in underdeveloped areas. (See also RUNAWAY SHOP.) Among the first runaway industries were American textile firms that escaped the high wages and taxes of New England by moving their plants to the South. In the two decades after World War II, first Japan and then Hong Kong, Taiwan,

Mexico, Singapore, the Philippines, South Korea, Pakistan, and India all saw the influx of foreign firms, especially American ones, which made use of their much cheaper local labor in numerous kinds of manufacturing enterprise. (By 1970 Japan no longer offered such an advantage, its labor costs by then rivaling those of the United States.) The practice spread so rapidly in the 1960s that in 1971 the United States, whose balance of payments had suffered considerably as a result, imposed a 10 per cent tax on imports (goods produced by American firms abroad being considered "imports"), but it seemed to have little or no deterrent effect, at least not on those American companies firmly entrenched in foreign operations. Runaway industries are of little benefit to the host country's economy. They tend to call for relatively unskilled labor (chiefly for assembling components, so that they sometimes are called "screwdriver" industries), and apart from wages, some local purchases, and taxes (if and when they are imposed), the economy has little to gain. Thus the chief benefits are to the company itself, which through cost-cutting presumably increases its profits, and to the consumer, should the company choose to lower its prices.

runaway inflation Also, *galloping inflation*, *hyperinflation*. A rapid, seemingly limitless rise in the general PRICE LEVEL. As a result, purchasing power declines so rapidly that the currency soon is practically worthless, and eventually the monetary system breaks down entirely. Runaway inflation tends to feed on itself, becoming more and more severe. Prices rise so fast that consumers become convinced they will rise still more and try to buy as much as possible today to beat tomorrow's higher price; businesses behave similarly in capital expenditures. Further, businesses begin to hoard their output, waiting in hopes of receiving still higher prices. Creditors avoid repayment of loans in the current cheap money, and money ceases to function as a proper medium of exchange. The end result usually is monetary collapse, depression, and often also social and political upheaval. Runaway inflation frequently comes in the aftermath of a war, as it did in Germany after World War I and in Greece, Hungary, and China after World War II. (In Hungary in 1946, 828 octillion pengös—828 followed by 27 zeros—equaled the purchasing power of 1 prewar pengö.) See also WAR, FINANCING OF.

A few nations, notably Brazil, have prospered despite an annual inflation rate of 20 per cent or more for years on end. Their (partial, at least) solution is *indexation* or *indexing*, whereby escalators tie prices, wages, interest rates, and other transactions to changes in price indexes. For example, money invested in a Brazilian savings and loan association earns not only the guaranteed interest of 6 per cent per year but also a "monetary correction" roughly equal to the increase in the cost of living. In 1974 Brazil's inflation rate was 34 per cent, so savings and loan accounts yielded 40 per cent. At the same time, mortgage rates were increased by a similar amount. so the savings and loan institutions did not lose, either.

sabbatical An extended vacation with pay, usually lasting several months to a year. Sabbaticals are a traditional fringe benefit of the teaching profession, intended to provide time for research and intellectual renewal. In 1968 the American steelworkers' union negotiated an agreement with 11 firms whereby employees on the top half of each plant's seniority list receive 13 weeks' paid vacation for every 5 years and those in the lower half of the list receive 3 weeks every fifth year in addition to their regular vacation. The union's underlying purpose, however, was to create more jobs, since presumably replacements would be hired for workers on sabbatical leave. See also LUMP-OF-LABOR FALLACY.

sabotage Any of several illegal tactics used by workers during labor disputes, such as wilfully damaging machinery or other property of the employer, wasting or destroying materials, and obstructing or interfering with normal business operations.

safe deposit A place of safekeeping for valuables, rented out by a bank, trust company, or other institution. A *safe deposit company* specializes in the business of maintaining vaults for this purpose.

safety factor The ratio of the total interest on funded debt (outstanding long-term obligations, such as bonds) to net income after such interest has been paid. It is an important determinant of a company's credit rating and its ability to borrow additional funds.

safety stock An extra amount of inventory kept on hand to protect a company against delivery failures or an unforeseen increase in LEAD TIME or USAGE. A company should carry just enough safety stock of any item to give it the degree of protection against stockouts it is willing to pay for. Excess safety stock boosts inventory investment; too little safety stock falls short of desired protection. Though many companies determine their safety stocks on a trial-and-error basis, various formulas have been developed based on past usage, lead time, etc., including some that apply PROBABILITY THEORY.

Saint-Simon, Claude Henri de Rouvroy, Comte de A French nobleman and thinker (1760–1825) who proposed an ideal new society based on work and industry. Since an industrial society was inevitable, said Saint-Simon, the government should function as a central planning agency. The parliament would consist of three chambers: one of artists and engineers, who would plan public works; one of scientists, to examine their projects and control education; and one of industrial leaders, to carry out the projects and control the budget. Saint-Simon himself did not oppose private property, but some of his followers urged collective ownership, and long after Saint-Simon's death their enthusiasm for large-scale enterprise helped inspire numerous large undertakings in France, among them banks, railways, and the Suez Canal.

salary In economics, the same as WAGE. In business usage, the earnings of professional, executive, and clerical personnel, paid on a weekly, monthly, or longer basis, the term "wage" being reserved for earnings of production workers paid by the hour or day or by unit of production.

sale
1. In business law, a transfer of title to goods or

tangible personal property in consideration of a payment of money, called the *price*. (If the consideration is other property or services, the transaction is termed an *exchange* or *barter*, not a sale.) The parties to a sale are the owner of the property, called *seller* or *vendor*, and the person to whom title is transferred, the *buyer* or *vendee*. A sale generally is considered a contractual agreement and so is subject to the law of contracts, particularly as it relates to fraud. One can sell only goods or tangible personal property, but one can enter a *contract to sell* nonexistent or future goods, a distinction important when goods are damaged or destroyed and someone must bear the loss. A sale differs from a BAILMENT in that it involves a transfer of title and is considered final. See also CONDITIONAL SALE; CONSIGNMENT; FORCED SALE; LEASEBACK; SALES; TERMS OF SALE.

2. An opportunity to buy goods at reduced prices. Such goods are then said to be "on sale." See also BARGAIN, def. 1; CLEARANCE SALE.

sale and leaseback See LEASEBACK.

sales In business accounting, the total income derived from goods and services sold. This income may be assigned to either the accounting period when it is earned or the period when it is received (see ACCRUAL BASIS; CASH BASIS). *Gross sales* refers to total sales without any deductions for allowances, discounts, or returned goods; *net sales* is total sales minus returns, allowances, and discounts. The concept of the *sales dollar* is used by management to show how each $1 of sales (usually gross but sometimes net) is allocated among costs, expenses, and profit. See also INCOME STATEMENT; SALE, def. 1.

sales and administrative expense In accounting, a group of OVERHEAD costs that are allocated among a firm's end-products. Sales expense includes salespersons' salaries and commissions, advertising and promotion, travel, and entertainment. (Note that it differs from COST OF SALES.) Administrative expense includes clerical and executive salaries, office supplies, telephone, office rent, accounting, etc. See also under INCOME STATEMENT.

sales dollar See under SALES.

sales finance company See FINANCE COMPANY, def. 3.

sales forecast A prediction of the expected volume of sales of a company or product during a given future time. The period may consist of weeks, months, or years. Long-range forecasts (such as five years) tend to be fairly general; short-range ones (for two or three months) might be quite specific for each item sold. Forecasts, which often are vital in planning a firm's operations, are based on past experience and data and estimates from a variety of sources—government, economic bureaus, market research, sales personnel, customers, etc. Methods of calculation range from simple averages to highly complex statistical analyses.

sales manager In business and industry, the person responsible for organizing, planning, and controlling the sales of a company's end-products. The sales manager heads a department that may be organized by geographic territory, by product, or by customer, depending on the nature of the end-products. His or her work includes making SALES FORECASTS, establishing territories for each person or group in the sales force, establishing SALES QUOTAS, routing and scheduling the sales force, planning advertising and promotion, and checking on all sales operations to make sure they satisfy the firm's needs and goals.

sales promotion Any of several specific activities that attract customers to a particular product or service, such as store signs and displays, booklets and leaflets, premium offers, and catalogs. Such efforts tend to be custom-tailored to particular selling situations, and complement large-scale general advertising and personal selling. In some companies sales promotion is a function of the sales department; in others it is considered a separate facet of marketing. See also POINT-OF-PURCHASE ADVERTISING.

sales quota The volume or value of sales that a salesperson or sales department is expected to achieve in a given time. Such quotas are based on past experience, the overall sales forecast, general sales policies, the competition in a sales territory, and similar considerations.

sales tax A tax levied on the sale of goods, usually involving a fixed percentage of the price. A *retail sales tax* is one based on the retail price and is paid by the consumer. A *gross sales* or *turnover tax* is based on the wholesaler's or retail merchant's total sales and is paid by the wholesaler or retailer (though it often is passed on to the consumer in the form of higher prices). A *general sales tax* affects all goods sold; more often a sales tax exempts some items, notably food or other necessities. Sales taxes are regressive in that, being paid by all consumers, they take a larger proportion of small incomes than of large ones. In the United States sales taxes (most often retail sales taxes) constitute a major source of revenue for many state and some local governments. The Federal government levies no sales taxes but does use the EXCISE TAX.

salvage

1. In cost accounting, the value an item possesses for some use other than that to which it has been devoted, or for resale. *Net salvage value* is an item's gross salvage value minus the cost of removing it. See also SCRAP.

2. In insurance, the value of property after it has been partly destroyed or damaged by fire, storm, or some other hazard.

sample

1. In statistics, a group of units selected from a larger collection of units, or universe, for the purpose of drawing conclusions about the universe, a process called *statistical inference*. Though there are many kinds of statistical sample, all can be classified either as *random* or *probability samples,* so constructed that SAMPLING ERROR can be calculated, or as *judgment samples* or *convenience samples,* which are based on qualities of personal judgment or the existence of a small, accessible group and are open to bias that cannot be isolated and measured. See also AREA SAMPLE; PURPOSIVE SAMPLE; QUOTA SAMPLING; RANDOM SAMPLING; SYSTEMATIC SAMPLING.

2. Also, *free sample, giveaway.* In merchandising, a small quantity of a product, often packaged specially for this purpose, that is given away to encourage prospective customers to buy the product.

sampling error In statistics, an error arising from the fact that the sample used does not correspond closely enough to the population from which it is selected. In effect, it arises from the very fact that a sample—rather than the entire population—was used. Hence, as the size of a sample increases, the likelihood of sampling error decreases. Sampling error differs from other kinds of statistical error in that it occurs at random and is unbiased. Nonsampling error, on the other hand, is error that can be attributed to mistakes in data collection or tabulation or analysis, etc. See also STANDARD ERROR.

Samuelson, Paul A. An American economist (1915–), author of the general economics textbook most widely used in American colleges and universities since its original publication in 1948, who has made numerous contributions to general equilibrium theory and consumer behavior theory. He devised the theory of *revealed preference* to explain consumer behavior, and the *factor price equalization theorem* to show that free trade led not only to a similarity of commodity prices in different countries but also to a similarity in factor prices, particularly income (the price of labor). In macroeconomics he was the first to build a model showing the interaction of the ACCELERATION PRINCIPLE and the MULTIPLIER PRINCIPLE (def. 1), and he also contributed to the theory of LINEAR PROGRAMMING. He was awarded the Nobel Memorial Prize in Economic Science in 1970.

sanction, economic A measure taken against a country's economy, usually by some international organization, to make its government obey international law or conform to some collective international decision. The United Nations and the Organization of American States (OAS) both have provisions for imposing economic sanctions, which include a boycott of a country's exports, selective trade restrictions, various kinds of EMBARGO (def. 1), blocking of a nation's bank deposits abroad, and the like. In the 1960s and the 1970s Rhodesia was the object of economic sanctions by the United States, the United Kingdom, and other nations because of the highly restrictive policies its white ruling minority exercised over the black majority.

satisfaction

1. Carrying out the terms of an agreement, such as fulfilling an obligation (repaying a loan, paying off a mortgage).

2. Carrying out the judgment of a court.

saturation

In marketing and in advertising, using every available means to reach every possible part of a potential market, so that all conceivable demand for goods, services, or information will be satisfied.

saving

1. Also, *personal saving*. The postponement of using some part of disposable personal income on consumption. Any personal income that is not spent is saved. Personal savings usually are kept in the form of cash, bank deposits, or securities (the last is popularly called "investment" but in economic terms it is a form of saving). Most personal saving is done to provide future income (in old age, for illness, or to improve one's living standard) or for future expenditures (saving for a house, automobile, college tuition, etc.). The amount saved depends principally on the size of income. The poor have little or no spare income to save, whereas the rich can save relatively large amounts if they wish. See also PROPENSITY TO SAVE.

2. Also, *aggregate saving*. A shift in factors of production from goods and services for immediate consumption to producer goods that are not consumed but are used, directly or indirectly, in production. In effect, the total saving of individuals and businesses is what finances capital formation. The desire of individuals to save and the willingness of businesses to invest are brought in line with one another by changes in national income, the equilibrium level of national income occurring when saving and investment are equal. (See under J. M. KEYNES for further explanation.) If saving tends to exceed investment greatly, demand for products will shrink and unsold inventories will pile up. In time, firms will cut back production and lay off workers, until income has declined enough to make individuals reduce their savings. Government can offset the tendency toward excess saving by increasing its spending and/or by giving businesses greater incentive to spend more on capital goods (as through a tax cut).

savings and loan association

An institution that provides both a safe form of investment and funds for financing, primarily of home mortgages. It may be organized either as a cooperative or as a corporation. In the United States a cooperative association is usually Federally chartered and supervised by the Federal Home Loan Bank Board and is known as a *Federal savings and loan association;* it must then belong to the Federal Savings and Loan Insurance Corporation. Such a cooperative association is owned by its members, who, when they deposit money, are actually buying stock in the association; in withdrawing money they in effect are asking the association to buy back their shares (which it must do). In return for keeping their money deposited, they are paid dividends, that is, their share of the association's net earnings. The corporate form of savings and loan association, which usually is chartered and regulated by the state in which it operates, is also known by such names as *cooperative bank, homestead-aid benefit association, benefit society, building society* (the British name for any savings and loan association), and *mutual loan association.*

Whatever their form, savings and loan associations invest almost exclusively in home mortgages, and tend, of course, to favor loans to their own members or shareholders. Experiencing a rapid spurt of growth from about 1960 on, these institutions accounted for almost half the mortgage debt held by private financial institutions in the United States in the mid-1970s, with the state-chartered corporate associations, especially strong in California, dominating the field.

Deposits in savings and loan associations are technically TIME DEPOSITS and are not especially liquid (convertible into cash), since the money is invested in mortgages (mortgages may be sold for cash but in times of financial stress they do not necessarily command their par value). Though savings and loan associations have the right to make a depositor wait before authorizing withdrawals, in practice they rarely do so. Instead, when pressed for funds, they may (whether corporate or cooperative) borrow from the Federal Home Loan Bank, using their home mortgages as collateral; the Home Loan Bank in turn borrows from the general public.

savings bank

1. An institution that functions chiefly to accept interest-bearing TIME DEPOSITS and invests its funds primarily in mortgages but also in high-grade securities.

2. *mutual savings bank.* The most common kind of savings bank in the United States today. It is owned by the depositors, who share its net earnings, but it is run by a self-perpetuating board of directors (that is, they elect their own successors without interference from the legal "owners"). Practically all such banks are chartered by the states in which they operate, which also regulate the amount of interest they may pay on deposits, how they invest their funds, and how they insure deposits.

3. *stock savings bank.* A savings bank that is set up as a profit-making corporation, with capital stock and stockholders. The stockholders receive dividends in addition to the interest paid on ordinary time deposits. Though they accept principally time deposits, many stock savings banks also accept demand deposits and may lend money, making them indistinguishable from a state-chartered COMMERCIAL BANK.

savings bond A United States government bond that is not traded in any market but can be bought only from the government and sold back to the government at a set price. Since such a bond by definition cannot suffer from market fluctuations, it is about as low-risk an investment as can be found; however, it yields less interest than most other bonds. There are two series of such bonds. *Series E,* first issued in 1941, is sold at a discount (75 per cent of face value), accumulates interest while it is held, and is redeemed at face value. *Series H,* first issued in 1952, is sold at full face value, with semiannual interest payments, and matures in nine to ten years. The smallest denomination of E bond is $25, whereas the smallest H bond is $500. Savings bonds may be bought at most banks, and no commission is charged for their sale.

savings ratio The proportion of savings to income. See under PROPENSITY TO SAVE.

Say's law of markets A principle formulated by the French economist Jean Baptiste Say (1767–1832), who held that supply creates its own demand and therefore neither overproduction nor underemployment can develop. When goods are produced, the factors of production (land, labor, capital) receive payment for their services (rent, wages, interest). With this payment the persons controlling the factors (landlords, workers, capitalists) are able to purchase the very goods they helped produce. If a particular product—black riding boots, for example—is produced in such quantities that the price it commands will not cover its total cost of production, the factors of production either will earn less or will be shifted to some more profitable product. Though Say's idea that the economy will automatically regulate itself, bringing demand and supply into balance, is clearly fallacious—it rules out recessions and unemployment, which, of course, can and do occur—it was accepted by most economists of the CLASSICAL SCHOOL and their followers for a century or more after its original formulation, in 1803. Among the first to refute Say was Thomas Malthus, who pointed out that capitalists do not necessarily reinvest their profits in the economy but tend to hoard them. It remained for J. M. Keynes to relegate Say's law to the very minor position it now holds in economic theory.

scab Slang for an employee who refuses to join a strike of his fellow workers but instead continues to work. Also, a worker who will accept lower than union wages.

scale, economy of A decrease in the unit cost of a product or service owing to large-scale production. The decrease may result from volume purchases of raw materials or parts at a lower price or special discount, more efficient machinery that can be afforded only when total output is large, sizable generation of by-products that yield new profits, or greater bargaining power with labor unions, banks or other lenders, etc. Frequently an economy of scale results simply from the fact that a certain factor of production is *indivisible*, that is, it cannot be divided into smaller units. (The economist J. A. Schumpeter termed this condition "lumpage.") A large machine, for example, can be used with maximum efficiency only when output is large; if output is small and the machine operates at half capacity, unit costs clearly will be higher than if it operated at full capacity.

One can distinguish between *internal* economies of scale, which involve a change in operations within a firm, and *external* ones, which are industrywide. Increased output that enables a firm to hire more specialized (and therefore more efficient) workers is considered an internal economy of scale; an industrywide public relations campaign, in which most or all firms in the industry participate, is an external economy.

An increase in unit cost is called a *diseconomy of scale*. Such diseconomies may occur when, as a firm grows larger, management becomes less efficient, raw materials costs rise because local supplies are exhausted, or for similar reasons. Avoiding diseconomy of scale is a major purpose of the decentralization policies of some very large corporations, such as General Electric or International Telephone & Telegraph (ITT), which have set up separate, virtually independent divisions for different products.

scale locus　See under ISOCOST CURVE.

scalper　A speculator who buys and sells principally to make quick profits. A *ticket scalper* buys tickets for theatrical performances, concerts, sporting events, and similar activities and makes a profit by reselling them at prices far above their face value. In the securities and commodities trade the term is sometimes used for traders who deal for their own accounts rather than for customers. See also under FLOOR TRADER; PIT.

Scanlon Plan　See under WAGE INCENTIVE.

scarce currency clause　A clause of the INTERNATIONAL MONETARY FUND (IMF), based on the belief that a nation with a BALANCE OF PAYMENTS

surplus is as much responsible for international payments imbalances as a nation with a deficit and therefore should act to adjust the situation. It is so called because a payments surplus nearly always means that demand for the nation's currency in the foreign exchange market exceeds the supply that its central bank is willing to make available. Also, one nation's payments surplus is automatically another's deficit, so in a sense both debtor and creditor are at fault. Throughout the 1960s West Germany, with a surplus, abided by this provision by revaluing its currency, thereby increasing export prices and lowering import prices. Naturally, such actions benefit the deficit nations more than the surplus nation, at least in the short run.

scarcity　In economic theory, a shortage of a good or service relative to potential demand for it, so that it can command a price. Defined in this way, practically all goods and services are scarce, except for a very few so-called *free goods* abundantly provided by nature, such as air (see also under GOODS). In cases where the demand for a good is exceptionally high—or, put differently, when the supply is exceptionally small—its price will also be exceptionally high, and it will be said to have *scarcity value*. Some goods always have scarcity value, for example, great works of art, antiques, large gemstones. Other goods may acquire scarcity value owing to special circumstances, for example, vaccine during an epidemic, boats in time of flood, or water in a drought. Some scarcities, such as a beautiful singing voice, are natural; others, such as a one-of-a-kind, custom-designed dress, are contrived, that is, the producer deliberately limits the supply in order to keep the price high. Some economists call the extra earnings resulting from scarcity *profit*. See also QUASI-RENT.

scatter chart　See under REGRESSION ANALYSIS.

schedule policy　An insurance policy that covers, under separate agreements, several hazards normally covered under separate policies. It differs from a *comprehensive* policy, however, in that it covers only those hazards named in the policy.

Schmoller, Gustav　A German economist (1838–1917), leader of the "younger" GERMAN

HISTORICAL SCHOOL, who during a long academic career influenced generations of students and public officials. Dedicated to inductive historical study and opposed to deductive theories, including those of the Austrian marginalists, he engaged in a famous public dispute with MENGER. Schmoller also felt that the "older" historical school, represented by Roscher and others, was too quick to apply the lessons of history, which he felt required more study and analysis to serve as a valid basis for national economic policy. Like others of the historical school, however, Schmoller believed in social reform aimed at a more equitable distribution of income.

Schuman Plan See under EUROPEAN COAL AND STEEL COMMUNITY.

Schumpeter, Joseph Alois An Austrian-born American economist (1883–1950) remembered for his belief that effective economic change comes about through the "entrepreneur-innovator." Economic *innovation*, said Schumpeter, consists of introducing new products or production methods, opening new markets, acquiring new sources of raw material or finished goods, or applying a new invention to industry. Economic life essentially is a static, circular flow; without innovation it would be unchanging. Profit and interest would not exist, since profit is the innovator's reward and interest is possible only where there is profit. Innovators also are responsible for the business cycle, which Schumpeter regarded as natural and inevitable. Historically innovations have not come singly but in clusters. Each great new innovation brings a wave of prosperity, with expanded credit and rising prices and incomes. But eventually higher prices deter investment, competition with new products leads to losses for some firms, and a period of contraction ensues, followed by deflation. Educated at the University of Vienna, where he studied under two leading Austrian economists, Böhm-Bawerk and F. von Wieser, Schumpeter departed from them in emphasizing the dynamic, changing aspects of economics. He strongly opposed the theories of J. M. Keynes, however, deploring government interference in economic affairs. Ultimately, Schumpeter believed capitalism was already declining, and eventually it would stagnate completely.

scrap Capital equipment or inventories that no longer have any value other than that of the salvageable materials they contain, such as the value of metals in machinery damaged beyond repair, or metal shavings and pieces left over after milling. Their value is called *scrap value.*

scrip A written claim issued in place of money or shares of stock, for which the scrip will later be redeemable. Scrip was used by the United States armed forces in occupied areas after World War II to prevent a black market in dollars. Service personnel could spend scrip directly in post exchanges and other service facilities, or they could exchange it for local currency, but they were not permitted to exchange or spend dollar currency directly.

SDRs Abbreviation for SPECIAL DRAWING RIGHTS.

sealed bid See under BID, def. 1.

seasonal unemployment Unemployment that occurs periodically owing to SEASONAL VARIATION in particular industries. It is particularly evident in jobs affected by weather, either in terms of the ability to perform any work at all (construction, agriculture) or in terms of consumer demand for the end-product (Christmas ornaments, air conditioners, summer and winter resorts).

seasonal variation A regularly recurring pattern of change that occurs in nearly all business and economic activities owing to periodic climate changes, holidays, vacations, etc. For example, retail sales of clothing in the United States tend to peak just before Christmas and Easter and slump in January and the summer months, whereas auto sales peak in May or June, again in October, and slump from November through March. The output of printers declines in August, when many firms shut down for several weeks' vacation, while farm income is highest in fall, owing to sales of summer crops. Some changes occur weekly; retail sales are heaviest on Friday and Saturday. In analyzing economic data, such seasonal variation can so distort or obscure the overall trend of an economic activity that it needs to be discounted through statistical procedures, a process called *seasonal adjustment.*

Numerous methods are used, one of the most satisfactory being the RATIO-TO-MOVING-AVERAGE METHOD.

seat A membership on a STOCK EXCHANGE; see also under NEW YORK STOCK EXCHANGE.

seat-mile The movement of one passenger seat of a scheduled airline for one mile, a measure used to compare the capacity of different airlines.

second In consumer goods, describing an item with a flaw that may affect its appearance and/or durability and that generally makes the seller reduce its price. For example, a "second" piece of furniture may have a damaged frame, the fabric of drapes may have a hole, or a dish may be cracked. See also IRREGULAR.

secondary boycott See under BOYCOTT.

secondary offering See under ISSUE.

secondary reserves See under BANK RESERVES.

secondhand Used merchandise offered for sale. The degree of use varies from not at all (in some states, goods still in their original packing but sold for a second time are legally considered secondhand) to badly worn, and the general rule for such purchases, in which the seller offers no warranty, is CAVEAT EMPTOR.

second mortgage See under MORTGAGE.

sector, economic In national income accounting, an area of the economy that is considered in terms of the goods and services and capital that flow between it and other areas of the economy. The U.S. Department of Commerce divides the American economy into four economic sectors: business, government (public sector), personal, and rest-of-the-world (meaning all transactions involving other nations). See also PRIVATE SECTOR; PUBLIC SECTOR.

secular stagnation The idea, originated by the British economist J. M. Keynes and developed by the American economist Alvin Hansen (1887–

1975), that in a mature industrial economy unemployment is the normal, long-term result of the maturation process. In 1938, no doubt influenced by the disastrous Great Depression of the 1930s, Hansen proposed that each of the three major bases for investment—population growth, new frontiers, and technological development—had declined, or, in the case of the last, had so changed that it no longer provided sufficient investment opportunities relative to the total volume of SAVING (def. 2). Though technology continued to advance, most innovations now were capital-saving, that is, eliminating the need for capital- and labor-intensive investment. For example, the newer oxygen-charge steel-making process permits one furnace to produce more than twice as much steel per day as it did with older processes; similarly the "supertanker" reduces both the labor and capital needed to transport a given amount of crude oil. With saving exceeding investment, national income will decline, or at best remain at a standstill, and economic growth will stagnate. Though during World War II full employment resumed, seemingly contradicting the inevitability of secular stagnation, some economists continued to view each subsequent business recession with gloom, believing their worst fears would soon be confirmed.

secular trend In statistical analysis, a long-term trend in any TIME SERIES, considerably longer than any business cycle. For example, there is an upward secular trend in the use of aluminum of perhaps 4 to 5 per cent per year. However, because of cyclical factors, aluminum usage may increase by as much as 10 per cent during prosperous years and actually decline during years when the business cycle is moving to a cyclical low point. In most business and economic series, the secular trend tends to be positive or upward, indicating growth. Steepness of slope thus indicates the rate of growth. There are various ways of estimating secular trend in a time series, the preferred one being the *least-squares method* (see under REGRESSION ANALYSIS), although for very quick analysis a straight line can simply be drawn through the graph-plotted information at what appears to be the midpoint of each high and low. Secular trends are used chiefly in forecasting the growth rate of various industries and estimating the value of output over a projected

Fig. 72. Secular trend of sales

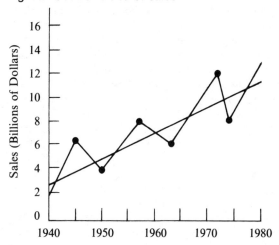

period. However, unexpected changes may occur in a secular trend if its underlying causes are not wholly understood.

secured bond   See under BOND, def. 1.

Securities and Exchange Commission   Also, *SEC*. An independent U.S. Federal regulatory agency, created by the Securities Exchange Act of 1934, which administers statutes designed to provide the fullest possible disclosure to the investing public and to protect the interest of both the general public and investors against malpractice in the securities and financial markets. It supervises all national securities exchanges and associations, registers all issues of securities offered in interstate commerce or through the mails (see under ISSUE), registers brokers and dealers who engage in OVER-THE-COUNTER trading, and regulates MUTUAL FUNDS and other investment companies, investment counselors and advisers, and practically all other individuals and firms engaged in the investment business. It enforces a number of Federal laws, including the Securities Act of 1933, Securities and Exchange Act of 1934, Public Utility Holding Company Act of 1935, Trust Indenture Act of 1939, Investment Advisers Act of 1940, and Investment Company Act of 1940.

security
   1. A written instrument showing evidence of the indebtedness or equity ownership of a business, government, or other enterprise. In the United States there are numerous definitions of "security" that differ from one another somewhat, among them those of the Uniform Commercial Code, the Securities Act of 1933 (and subsequent amendments to it), the Internal Revenue Service, and the various individual states. A security may be payable to the bearer (for example, a note) or registered in the owner's name (certificate of ownership). Some securities commonly are traded, either on formally organized exchanges (*listed* securities) or in informal markets (*unlisted* or off-board securities), and are considered a form of investment; chief among these are corporate stocks and bonds. Some securities are *convertible* into other securities; some are *redeemable* (can be cashed in). Some bear *interest* (bonds) and some pay *dividends* (stocks); these profits may be taxable or tax-exempt. See also BOND, def. 1; DEBENTURE; EQUIPMENT TRUST CERTIFICATE; FACE VALUE; ISSUE; MATURITY; OPTION, def. 2; PAR VALUE; STOCK, def. 1; WARRANT; YIELD.

   2. A pledge or property given to a lender as assurance that a loan will be repaid. The term is broader than COLLATERAL since it also includes a promise (pledge) to repay, and is not just an object with monetary value.

seigniorage   See under COIN.

selective inventory control   See ABC CONTROL.

self-employed   Describing individuals who work more or less regularly but usually do so in their own homes or offices and are not normally listed on anyone's payroll. They may employ assistants, but these are usually few in number, and most of the VALUE ADDED is contributed by the self-employed person. The self-employed include many farmers, professionals (doctors, lawyers, dentists, architects, consultants), writers, artists, musicians, and others who work on a FREE-LANCE, assignment basis. In the 1970s more than seven million Americans were self-employed.

self insurance   See under INSURANCE.

self-interest   In economic affairs, seeking maximum personal gain. For producers, it usually takes the form of charging the highest possible price; for consumers, it means obtaining what they want at the lowest price. Self-interest thus is a basic motive for the market mechanism. See also ECONOMIC MAN; HARMONY OF INTERESTS.

self-liquidating Describing an investment or loan that will pay for itself within a reasonable time.

self-service store See under RETAIL.

self-sufficiency In economic affairs, the ability of a given area—city, state, nation, region—to produce all the goods and services it requires without relying on imports. The chief advantage of self-sufficency is that it eliminates dependence on what may be (or become) monopolistic, high-priced producers of basic necessitiies; thus the crisis precipitated by the Arab oil producers' quadrupling of oil prices in 1973 aroused a strong desire for self-sufficiency in petroleum production on the part of the United States and other nations. The chief disadvantage of self-sufficiency is that it tends to encourage and protect less efficient producers of various commodities. See also *comparative advantage,* under ADVANTAGE.

sellers' market A market in which demand is greater than supply, that is, one with far more potential customers than there are goods for sale. Sellers therefore have a strong influence on the prices charged, which tend to be high or rising. See also BUYERS' MARKET.

seller's surplus The difference between the actual price a seller receives and the lowest price he should have accepted.

selling against the box See under SELLING SHORT.

selling short Selling securities, commodities, or foreign exchange that one does not actually own, in the belief that their price will go down and the seller will be able to *cover* the sale—that is, actually buy the security or other item in question—more cheaply and thereby make a profit. Such a transaction is called a *short sale.* In the case of stocks, the short seller borrows the security from the broker,

who in turn obtains the stock from margin accounts (see HYPOTHECATION) or borrows it from another broker or stockholder. In the case of commodities and foreign exchange, the sale involves a promise to deliver at some future date, and in most cases short sellers cover before that date. Dealers frequently sell short to accommodate customers wishing to buy stock the dealer currently does not have. Selling short also is practiced by short-term traders who hope for a quick profit, as well as by investors who wish to protect their profit in a longer-term investment. For example, suppose an investor's 100 shares of stock in XYZ Company has appreciated in value by several thousand dollars. (These shares were *bought long*, that is, are actually owned.) It is now November, however, and the owner wants to put off paying taxes on the profit until the following year. However, by January XYZ stock, which is quite volatile, may have declined again. The owner therefore instructs a broker to sell short 100 shares of XYZ. If XYZ does go down, the owner can cover by buying 100 shares at the new lower price, which will just about offset the loss in market value of the stock retained. If XYZ goes up, the owner can cover with the 100 shares already owned, which will offset the loss on the short sale. This kind of *hedging*, which works only when one is both short and long an equal number of shares in a given stock, is called *selling against the box.*

In the United States short sales are regulated both by the Federal Reserve Board of Governors and by exchanges in essentially the same way as margin buying. The margin requirements for short sales tend to be even a little higher, because the seller is liable also for any dividends that the stock may accrue during the course of the transaction. See also MARGIN, BUYING ON.

semiaverage method A method of calculating long-term trends by means of graphically connecting the average for the first half of the data with the average for the second half. For example, suppose that sales of Preparation X have been charted for the first 20 years of the product's existence. Sales for Years 1 through 10 average $7,745,000 per year; sales for Years 11 through 20 average $14,551,000 per year. The difference between these two figures, $6,806,000, represents ten years' growth or increment. The annual increment therefore is one-tenth of that, or $680,600. See also MOVING AVERAGE METHOD.

semidurable goods See under CONSUMER GOOD.

semiskilled labor Work that requires some degree of skill and training, though not as much as SKILLED LABOR. Also, workers engaged in such jobs.

semivariable cost Also, *semifixed cost*. A business cost that varies somewhat with the volume of production but not in direct proportion to it. For example, a factory may need two foremen on the night shift when it is working at full capacity but only one when it is at half capacity. Or a hospital's electric power bill may go down by 10 per cent when only two-thirds of the beds are occupied.

Senior, Nassau William An English economist (1790–1864) of the CLASSICAL SCHOOL who became the first professor of political economy at Oxford University (1825). Senior rejected Adam Smith's LABOR THEORY OF VALUE and instead adopted Ricardo's COST OF PRODUCTION THEORY OF VALUE, which he enlarged to include the productivity of capital. In order to accumulate investment capital, the capitalist must forgo some consumption; the profits and interest then paid the capitalist are a reward for this abstinence (see ABSTINENCE THEORY OF INTEREST). Thus Senior believed that the principal factors of production are labor and abstinence. In effect, he sought to preserve classical theory but also to explain profits and interest, which his predecessors had not done satisfactorily. Senior also held a number of government posts in which he championed free trade and strongly opposed the trade union movement.

seniority In employment, ranking by length of service, used as a basis for promotion, layoffs, vacations, and other practices. Union contracts frequently contain provisions concerning seniority, usually requiring that the most recently hired workers be the first laid off, and that those with the most seniority be the first to be recalled. In highly unstable industries, seniority provides a measure of

security for employees (though at the expense of those most recently hired). Some employers feel that the practice interferes with efficiency in that a newer worker may be superior to an older one, and that workers with seniority may become lazy and complacent. Others argue that there tends to be a high correlation between long experience and efficiency, that seniority will make companies more careful in their initial hiring and placement, and that seniority gives old-time employees a greater stake in the company. See also BUMPING; SUPERSENIORITY; TENURE, def. 1.

separation rate Also, *layoff rate*. The total number of employees who quit their jobs, are laid off, discharged, and retired during a given period of time. The U.S. Department of Labor, which compiles monthly statistics on layoffs, generally expresses them as a percentage of total employment. The separation rate in manufacturing industries is an important LEADING INDICATOR of future business conditions, moving exactly opposite to the direction of the business cycle. When layoffs increase, business is declining; when they decrease, business is expanding. See also UNEMPLOYMENT.

serfdom A kind of hereditary bondage under which nearly all peasant labor operated in feudal times (see also MANORIAL SYSTEM). It differed from outright SLAVERY in that serfs, unlike slaves, had certain inviolable rights, chief among them attachment to their land. While serfs could not voluntarily leave their land, neither could they be deprived of it, though they might—and generally did—have to pay for the privilege of farming it. In the Middle Ages serfdom was first practiced in western Europe (England, France, Italy, Spain) and then spread through Germany to the Slavic countries. The status of serfs on a manor was strictly regulated by local custom, which governed the kind and amount of labor they owed the lord as well as the fixed dues they had to pay. Serfdom disappeared in England well before the end of the Middle Ages but lingered on in parts of the Hapsburg empire and France until it was ended (officially) in 1781 by Joseph II and the French Revolution, respectively; in Prussia it was abolished by Frederick William III in 1807. In Russia, where serfdom began only in the 16th century, the serfs originally were bound to the land, as elsewhere, but under Peter the Great they were bound to the landowner, making them indistinguishable from slaves. Because of pressure by small Russian landowners, whose economic survival depended on the system, serfdom was not abolished until 1861 (by Alexander II). Outside Europe, varieties of serfdom were found wherever feudal arrangements existed, as in China, Japan, India, pre-Columbian Mexico, and elsewhere. See also PEONAGE.

serial bond See under BOND, def. 1; for *series* bonds, see SAVINGS BOND.

service charge In business, an extra fee added to a price in exchange for some special service, such as the extension of credit. A bank, finance company, or other credit insitution may invoke a service charge for handling a special CHECKING ACCOUNT with no minimum balance, processing a loan, etc.

service department In industry, a company department concerned with activities other than those that directly generate income (known as *production departments*), as, for example, accounting, personnel, legal, and public relations.

service industry An industry that produces services rather than goods. The chief service industries are transportation; retail trade; insurance and real estate; banking and finance; entertainment and recreation; hotels and other lodgings; laundries and other cleaning establishments; barber and beauty shops; legal, engineering, and miscellaneous professional services; government; wholesale trade; medical and health services; domestic service; private education; business services; automobile and other repair services; welfare, religious, and charitable organizations. In an advanced economy, the service industries tend to take on increasing importance. As the standard of living rises, businesses and consumers demand more services; further, as the production of goods becomes increasingly automated, the service industries account for a larger and larger share of employment. In the 1970s about 40 per cent of all personal spending in the United States was devoted to various services, and more than half the work force was employed in service industries.

service life Also, *economic life, life expectancy, probable life, productive life.* The period of time a fixed asset can be used by its owner in the production or sale of other assets or services. Service life need not be the same as *potential life.* A dictating machine may have a potential life of 15 years, but if maintenance or other costs indicate that it would pay to trade in old machines for new ones every 5 years, the machine's service life (in that particular firm) is 5 years. The cost of new machines, less their trade-in value, is then charged to DEPRECIATION (def. 1) expense over a 5-year period. In order to allocate depreciation over time, total service life must be estimated when a fixed asset is purchased. Numerous factors must be considered in such an estimate, among them wear and tear, the effect of elements, adequacy of capacity (for example, whether a machine is large enough to handle needed output), and obsolescence. Experience, engineering studies, and judgment enter into such estimates. The U.S. Internal Revenue Service publishes a booklet, *Bulletin F,* which lists the estimated service life of hundreds of assets.

set-up cost Also, *starting-load cost.* In cost accounting, the labor cost of beginning production whether for a new product, with a new method, or with a new or newly reopened department or plant. It normally is separated from ordinary operating labor costs and is charged to the total number of units of end-product made. Set-up cost varies widely, ranging, for example, from a few minutes needed for a machine adjustment to accommodate a different size of lumber to several hundred hours needed to install new dies for metal moldings.

severance pay Also, *dismissal pay.* Compensation, usually in the form of a lump-sum cash payment, paid by employers to workers who are laid off through no fault of their own. Union contracts may include a provision for severance pay. See also LAYOFF.

sex discrimination See AFFIRMATIVE ACTION; DISCRIMINATION, def. 1; also under LABOR FORCE.

shallow organization See under SPAN OF CONTROL.

share

1. A portion of interest in a business. Also, the smallest unit of ownership in a business, usually referred to as a share of STOCK (def. 1). See also FRACTIONAL SHARE.

2. In British terminology, any stock, the word "stock" being reserved for various kinds of BOND (def. 1).

sharecropping A system of TENANT FARMING whereby a landowner rents land, tools, seed, and animals, and advances living expenses, in return for a portion (often half or more) of the crop raised. Since the owner takes a LIEN on a future crop, sharecropping is also called a *crop-lien system.* Sharecropping, along with tenant farming for cash, became widespread in the American South after the Civil War, when there was a large supply of unskilled labor (the freed slaves) and a scarcity of cash among plantation owners to pay wages. Sharecropping generally is detrimental to the land as well as inhumane. It tends to perpetuate a one-crop system (in the South, it was cotton) and crude and wasteful farming methods, and also keeps the sharecropper in perpetual debt to the landlord.

shaving a note

1. In finance, discounting a promissory note or other paper at a higher rate than the legal or prevailing market rate. This generally happens in the case of a low-grade note (when the borrower's credit rating is poor) or when government regulations or usage have established an interest rate lower than what lenders will accept.

2. In the securities trade, charging a premium for extending the time to deliver a security or pay a note.

shift

1. A fixed period of working time. Also, a collective term for the employees working during that period. Many factories operate around the clock, usually on three eight-hour shifts per day, as do many service industries (hospitals, fire departments, police departments). The *day shift* may be the period from 8:00 A.M. to 4:00 P.M.; the next

shift, from 4:00 P.M. to midnight, is called the *swing shift,* a term formerly used for a schedule in which hours and days of work varied weekly in factories operating seven days per week (in nursing and other service activities it is sometimes called the *relief shift*); the last shift, from midnight to 8:00 A.M., is called *night shift* or *graveyard shift.* Some employers use a *split shift,* in which an employee works part of the day on one shift and the rest on another. Still others use a *rotating shift* system whereby, for example, every worker must work on the night shift every third week.

2. In taxation, changing the tax burden so that someone other than the person or firm on whom the tax is levied pays part or all of it. See under TAX.

shipping

1. Specifically, the transport of goods or passengers over water. Also, a collective term for the vessels used in commercial transportation.

2. In business, a general term for the transportation of goods, whether by land, air, or water. Also, the department of a firm concerned with the physical dispatch of goods, and often also the acceptance of delivered goods (called *shipping and receiving*). See also RECEIVING.

shop

1. A retail store; see RETAIL.

2. Any establishment in which services are sold, such as a barber shop or beauty shop.

3. Any manufacturing enterprise or division of a firm in which mechanical work is done, such as a machine shop (where metal is machined with various machine tools).

4. Any place of employment; see CLOSED SHOP; OPEN SHOP; UNION SHOP.

shopping center A group of retail stores planned, developed, owned, and managed as a unit. Normally off-street parking is provided on the property, which frequently is located in a suburb or outlying community. Shopping centers range in size from a small *neighborhood center,* serving as few as 7,500 persons, to the *community center,* occupying 10 to 30 acres and serving more than 100,000, and the huge *regional center,* serving 150,000 within a five-to-six-mile radius. Whereas the neighborhood center might include only a supermarket and perhaps a dozen other small stores, the community center usually will have a variety or small department store, and the regional center, with 50 or more stores, will almost certainly have 1 or 2 large department stores. Indeed, some of the early shopping centers were built by the owners of large urban department stores who set up a suburban branch and wanted to provide a full range of small shops and services to attract more customers.

shopping goods Retail merchandise for which customers tend to compare the price and quality of various brands, visit several stores, study performance evaluations, read advertisements, and otherwise consider carefully before buying. Examples include furniture, automobiles, large household appliances, and some clothing. See also CONVENIENCE GOODS.

shop steward An appointed or elected representative of the labor union within a shop, division, or department of a company. He or she normally is a regular employee of the company but is allowed time off from work to handle union business, chiefly grievances. This time may be paid for by the company, the union, or both, depending on the labor contract in force.

shortage
1. In business and commerce, a deficiency in weight, number of items, or some other measurable dimension of a shipment or stock of goods.
2. In accounting and finance, a deficiency of funds in an account.
3. In general, a widespread lack of supply of some material on a local, regional, or national level, such as a gasoline shortage.

short haul See under LONG HAUL.

short interest Also, *short position*. The total stocks sold short and not covered as of a particular date (see SELLING SHORT). On the New York Stock Exchange, a tabulation is issued a few days after the middle of each month listing all issues on the exchange in which there is a short interest at the mid-month settlement date of 5,000 or more shares, and issues in which the short position has changed

by 2,000 or more shares in the preceding month. A sizable short interest usually is thought to indicate a strong market; covering short sales will necessarily involve buying, which will at least stabilize prices and perhaps drive them upward. The term "short interest" also is used to indicate the short sales of an individual speculator that are not covered.

short position See SHORT INTEREST.

short sale See SELLING SHORT.

short-term
1. *capital gain*. A profit realized from selling an asset that has been owned for less than six months. Such profits are not regarded as capital gains by the U.S. Internal Revenue Code but are treated—and taxed—as ordinary income.
2. *capital movements*. See FLIGHT OF CAPITAL.
3. *credit*. Liabilities whose maturities range from a single day (as in the case of Federal funds) to several months (usually 30, 60, or 90 days), as in the case of time loans, up to 1 year (Treasury bills). Loans maturing in more than 1 year are regarded as long-term credit.
4. *forecast*. See under FORECASTING.

shrinkage A decrease in the amount, weight, size, or some other measurable physical quality of an asset. In this sense shrinkage is the same as depletion. However, the former term also is used for a decrease in inventories owing to theft, loss, or clerical error.

sick leave Authorized time off from work for reasons of illness or accident, without loss of seniority or reemployment. The time off may be given with full or partial pay, or without pay, or it may be compensated through disability insurance.

sight bill Also, *sight draft*. See under BILL OF EXCHANGE.

sigma A Greek letter commonly used in statistics. The capital form, Σ, signifies "sum of"; the lower-case form, σ, signifies STANDARD DEVIATION.

silent partner Also, *sleeping partner*. An individual who invests funds in a PARTNERSHIP but takes no other part in the business. Like the other partners, the silent partner is fully liable for the firm's debts. Silent partners are sometimes used to spread business profits among different members of a family in order to minimize income tax liability.

silver certificate See under SILVER STANDARD.

silver standard A system whereby a country defines its monetary unit in terms of a given amount of silver, which is equivalent to establishing an official price per ounce of silver. It thus becomes the central bank's job to buy and sell silver in such a way as to maintain the official price, which may, of course, be either higher or lower than the world market price. A silver standard used to be considered logical for a country that produces a great deal of silver and not much gold, as was once the case with China.

When the United States first became a nation, it used a combined silver and gold standard (see BIMETALLISM), with the ratio of silver to gold established at 15 to 1. In the 1830s this ratio was changed to 16 to 1, the gold dollar then containing 23.22 grains of pure gold and the silver dollar 371.25 grains of pure silver. Since this actually represented an overvaluation of gold, silver gradually disappeared—it could be sold abroad at a higher price—and gold came into wider circulation (see GRESHAM'S LAW for further explanation). By 1873 the silver dollar was worth $1.02 in gold and was no longer profitable to coin, and Congress discontinued the minting of new silver dollars in that year (this move was called the *demonetization of silver*, and later, by its opponents, "the Crime of '73"). However, in the next few years the situation was reversed. Several European countries adopted the GOLD STANDARD and limited the coinage of silver, and large silver deposits were found in Nevada, which threw still more silver on the market, sharply reducing its market price. By 1876 a silver dollar was worth only $.90, with the prospect of further decline. American silver-mining interests had a strong lobby, which promoted the passage of the Bland-Allison Act of 1878, whereby the coining of silver was resumed. Further, the U.S.

Treasury began to issue *silver certificates* in exchange for silver coin (and, from 1886 on, for one-, two-, and five-dollar bills). Despite these measures silver prices continued to decline, along with other prices, and silver did not drive out gold (according to Gresham's law) because the rapidly expanding American economy easily absorbed more and more currency. Nevertheless, the country's silver interests remained politically powerful and by then had been joined by farmers and laborers who wanted to inflate the money supply and raise prices. They helped pass the Sherman Silver Purchase Act of 1890, which required the Treasury to buy still more silver—by now just about the entire output of U.S. silver mines. By 1893 the market price had fallen to $.60 and, alarmed by the flood of cheap money so created, bankers and other business interests of the Northeast rose up in opposition to the western and southern mining and labor interests. The latter were represented by William Jennings Bryan and the Democratic Party, which was defeated with the election of President McKinley in 1896. (It was in this campaign that Bryan made his famous *Cross of Gold* speech, saying that his opponents "shall not crucify mankind upon a cross of gold.")

Government silver purchases were now halted, not to be resumed until 1934, although silver certificates continued to be issued. The Silver Purchase Act of 1934 authorized both silver purchases and the issue of silver certificates, and made the Treasury add all domestic stocks of silver to the nation's reserves, in the mistaken belief that this move would stimulate a rise in the greatly lowered price levels of the Great Depression. In the early 1960s silver certificates still were the second most important form of American currency (after Federal Reserve notes), but by the mid-1960s the Silver Purchase Act of 1934 had been repealed and silver certificates were gradually being phased out of circulation, replaced by Federal Reserve notes.

simple interest An interest charge computed by applying the percentage rate of interest to the principal of the loan only, and not to previous interest charges. Simple interest ordinarily is paid at the end of the period in which it is earned, but even if it is accumulated it does not, like COMPOUND INTEREST, itself earn interest. See Fig. 73, page 386.

Fig. 73. Simple interest table (interest on $100 at various rates)

Time Period	Interest Rate					
	3%	4%	5%	6%	7%	8%
1 day	0.8¢	1.1¢	1.3¢	1.6¢	1.9¢	2.2¢
2 days	1.6¢	2.2¢	2.7¢	3.2¢	3.8¢	4.4¢
4 days	3.3¢	4.5¢	5.3¢	6.6¢	7.7¢	8.9¢
6 days	4.9¢	6.7¢	8.3¢	11¢	11.6¢	13.3¢
1 month	25.0¢	33.4¢	41.6¢	50¢	58.3¢	66.7¢
3 months	75.0¢	$1.00	$1.25	$1.50	$1.75	$2.00
6 months	$1.50	$2.00	$2.50	$3.00	$3.50	$4.00
12 months	$3.00	$4.00	$5.00	$6.00	$7.00	$8.00

simulation An artificial MODEL of a potential or real-life situation, set up in order to test an outcome with different variables. It has become a popular technique of business management for attempting to determine the results of an action before it is actually executed. Most often the appropriate information is loaded into a computer, which performs the numerous calculations needed much faster than manual manipulation could. Simulation has been used most frequently for waiting lines (see QUEUING THEORY) and in various problems of inventory control. See also GAMES THEORY; MONTE CARLO SIMULATION.

sinecure A job or office without regular duties but with regular pay. The term was first used for the medieval practice of giving lucrative church appointments to men who did not have to perform the offices normally attached to them. Today it is used for the job of a SILENT PARTNER, or for that of an elderly employee not yet ready to be pensioned off who is retained on the payroll, or similar circumstances.

single entry A system of BOOKKEEPING in which every transaction is recorded only once instead of twice (see DOUBLE ENTRY). Generally only cash transactions and personal accounts are maintained in this way. Only two books are needed, a journal in which every transaction is recorded and a ledger for making final entries. Single-entry bookkeeping today is considered suitable only for personal finances and for small businesses whose transactions are either infrequent or of a limited nature.

single tax See under H. GEORGE.

sinking fund Funds regularly set aside by a company or other institution to redeem its bonds, debentures, or preferred stock periodically, as specified in the indenture or charter. The money frequently is very conservatively invested, as in U.S. government bonds, whose income is added to the fund. In the case of certain long-term obligations, particularly bonds, the issue itself may specify that a sinking fund be established to assure redemption at maturity; this is called a *sinking-fund bond*. Usually the borrower meets sinking fund requirements by purchasing bonds on the open market. If the bond is selling at a discount from par, this practice can save money. For example, a requirement for a $1 million addition to the sinking fund can be met by an expenditure of only $500,000 if the bonds sell at 50.

Sismondi, Jean Charles Leonardo Simonde de A Swiss historian and economist (1773–1842) who was one of the earliest critics of the CLASSICAL SCHOOL, particularly of the doctrine of laissez faire and of Say's law of markets. Sismondi maintained that unchecked free enterprise inevitably leads to unemployment and misery for the working classes, since it perpetuates the business cycle with its periodic economic crises. When wages are low (at subsistence level), more capital is available for investment in machines. Then the output of manufactures increases, but demand for consumer goods drops. With overproduction, manufacturers must seek foreign markets to sell their goods, which results in imperialism and wars. Only government intervention that guarantees workers decent wages and some social security will offset these trends. Employment in public works will help draw workers from overproducing industries where they cannot earn enough to live, and thus will also discourage manufacturers from overproducing.

sitdown strike See STRIKE.

sit-in strike

1. In labor disputes, same as sitdown STRIKE.
2. A device used in civil rights protests and similar demonstrations in which protesters occupy the premises of an individual or organization in order to gain acceptance of (or at least publicity for) their demands.

skewness In statistics, the lack of symmetry of the values in a FREQUENCY DISTRIBUTION. A normal distribution is completely symmetrical, as can be seen from the curve depicting it (see Fig. 59), with the MEAN, MEDIAN, and MODE all having the same value. With *positive skewness*, the frequencies in the distribution are spread over a greater range of values on the high-value end of the distribution, so that the right side of the curve is flatter; with *negative skewness* they are spread over a greater range on the low-value side of the curve. The relative flatness or peakedness of a curve is called its *kurtosis*; a curve closely resembling the normal curve is called *mesokurtic*, one more peaked than the normal curve is *leptokurtic*, and one that is flatter than the normal curve is *platykurtic*.

skilled labor Work that requires considerable skill, relatively long training, and usually also considerable judgment on the worker's part. Also, workers engaged in such jobs.

slavery The practice of using human beings as a form of property, usually for the purpose of obtaining their labor. Slavery has been practiced since ancient times in practically all societies, and it still exists today, although on a relatively small scale. In the Western world it is confined almost entirely to penal institutions or colonies, where prisoners are compelled to work but are not bought and sold. Viewed purely from an economic standpoint, slavery made possible some large-scale achievements that, at the time, probably could not have been realized in any other way. It is doubtful that free labor alone could ever have built the Egyptian pyra-

mids or manned Roman galleys, at least not to the extent that was required. Indeed, though in Western Europe slavery had largely vanished by the late Middle Ages, slaves continued to be used on galleys for several centuries. On the other hand, slavery also has economic disadvantages. Slave labor is generally rendered reluctantly, requires constant supervision, and is essentially unskilled. As a result it tends to be inefficient.

The modern African slave trade began in the 15th century, when the Portuguese brought the first blacks from Africa, and for the next four centuries that trade was among the world's most profitable businesses. From the 17th through the 19th century slaves made possible a plantation economy in much of the western hemisphere, from Brazil northward to the American South. In the United States the number of slaves grew from 700,000 in 1790 to nearly 4 million in 1860. Though the British slave trade was made illegal in 1807, trade in human beings continued long after, and indeed British slavery in the West Indies did not end until 1833. Exactly 30 years later U.S. President Lincoln's Emancipation Proclamation took effect (January 1, 1863), freeing American slaves. In Brazil slaves were not free until 1888. The African slave trade continued well into the 20th century, with African blacks being sold mostly to Moslems in North Africa and to other black African tribes. Slavery still is practiced on a small scale in the Arab countries and the Far East, as well as among some of the primitive peoples of the Pacific islands. See also ENCOMIENDA; INDENTURE, def. 2; PEONAGE; SERFDOM.

sleeper Slang for an item for which there is unanticipated heavy demand or for a stock whose value unexpectedly appreciates.

sleeping partner See SILENT PARTNER.

slide error In accounting, a figure recorded in the wrong decimal column, so that, for example, $1.00 is recorded as $.100 or $10.00.

sliding scale A set of rates that vary according to some mathematical formula. For example, a sliding scale tariff may charge a smaller percentage of the purchase price of inexpensive items, and a higher percentage of costly ones, according to some set formula. The U.S. Federal income tax is based on a sliding scale of income, with different percentages being charged for different income brackets.

slowdown A deliberate slowing of the normal work pace in order to reduce output and force an employer to give in to some particular demand.

slump Same as RECESSION; see also BUSINESS CYCLE.

Slutsky theorem A principle relating to consumer reactions to price changes, formulated by the Russian economist Eugen Slutsky (1880–1948). In calculating such reactions, which in effect are changes in demand, Slutsky tried to differentiate between changes that stem from a change in consumer income and those based purely on price change. He also took into account the SUBSTITUTION EFFECT, allowing for the fact that a decline in the price of one good would lead to some substitution of that good for similar goods whose prices had not dropped. Slutsky's underlying assumption was that utility and value are not absolute concepts but a matter of relative preferences.

small business In general, any business firm that operates on a small scale. The U.S. Small Business Administration (SBA), an independent Federal agency created in 1953 for the purpose of helping small businesses survive in competition against large rich corporations, defines a small business as "one which is independently owned and operated and which is not dominant in its field of operations." However, it adds numerous specific definitions—in terms of number of employees, dollar volume of business, etc.—for the various industries and for different purposes of definition, as for extending SBA loans, awarding government leases, naming government subcontractors, etc., and these definitions are changed from time to time. American small businesses also are aided by such government programs as *ACE* (*Active Corps of Executives*), which provides on a volunteer basis the counsel of top executives to small businesses, and the *Office of Minority Business Enterprise* of the Department of Commerce, which helps enterprises owned by members of minority groups.

small business investment company A private firm whose sole function is to provide venture capital, in the form of equity financing, long-term loan funds, and management services, to SMALL BUSINESS concerns. Set up under the Small Business Investment Act of 1958, such companies are licensed, regulated, and financially aided by the U.S. Small Business Administration. They are, however, free to choose what companies they will assist, and naturally tend to select those they consider potentially most profitable.

small-loan company See FINANCE COMPANY, def. 2.

Smith, Adam A British economist and philosopher (1723–90), considered the founder of the CLASSICAL SCHOOL. He wrote one of the most famous books on economics of all time, *An Inquiry into the Nature and Causes of the Wealth of Nations* (1776), often referred to simply as *The Wealth of Nations*. Smith was essentially concerned with how wealth is created but, unlike his predecessors, he argued that it arose not from a favorable trade balance (see MERCANTILISM) or from land (see PHYSIOCRATS) but from human labor. The division of labor, which renders production more efficient, increases wealth. Moreover, the more an economy is allowed to run itself, without government interference, the more wealth will be created. Smith believed that the satisfaction of individual self-interest, limited naturally by the self-interest of other individuals, will yield the greatest benefit for the greatest number. Hence he supported free, unregulated trade. Nevertheless, he recognized that some government interference is required to prevent injustice and oppression, to advance education, protect public health, and maintain those necessary enterprises that would not be established by private capital. Smith's ideas, welcomed particularly by the newly important industrialists of his time who chafed under the old mercantilist controls, had a strong influence on British economic policy for the next century or more. See also INVISIBLE HAND; VALUE, PARADOX OF.

smuggling The practice of secretly importing goods, either to avoid paying customs duties or to obtain goods that may not legally be imported, such as narcotics.

snake in the tunnel Also, *joint float*. A practice devised by the European COMMON MARKET nations in the 1970s to enable them to maintain relatively stable relationships among their currencies (for example, the German Deutschmark relative to the Dutch guilder). Each of the member nations' central banks was committed to buy and sell its own currency in sufficient amounts to keep it within narrow limits of the relative prices of other Common Market currencies. The "snake" they followed was the German Deutschmark, by far the strongest European currency, and the "tunnel" represented the range of fluctuation permitted by a particular central bank relative to the Deutschmark. Although not members of the Common Market, Switzerland, Austria, Sweden, and Norway also kept within the tunnel because of their considerable trade with Common Market members. For example, the Austrian central bank might try to hold the Austrian Schilling's value to about 0.14 Deutschmark. If the Deutschmark rose in price relative to the U.S. dollar (which was not part of the tunnel), then the Austrian central bank would be required to sell dollars for Schillings in order to preserve the same relationship. Various Common Market members were forced to drop out of the "snake" for extended periods when their currency weakened and had to be devalued. See also under EXCHANGE RATE.

social capital Also, *social overhead capital*; see under INFRASTRUCTURE.

social Darwinism An economic doctrine that applies Charles Darwin's idea that evolution took place through a struggle for existence in which the fittest survive to social and economic human affairs. The social Darwinists, most notably Herbert Spencer (1820–1903) of England and William Graham Sumner (1840–1910) of the United States, believed that completely unrestricted competition would eliminate the inefficient and reward the economically fittest. Therefore government should refrain from interfering with economic affairs; indeed, Spencer, whose influence was stronger in America than in England, even opposed compulsory public education. Social Darwinism was thought to give the doctrines of the CLASSICAL SCHOOL a new "scientific" basis (that is, the precepts of biology).

social insurance Any form of INSURANCE made available through government agencies to all citizens or to certain classes of citizen. In the United States the major social insurance programs undertaken by the Federal government include WORKMEN'S COMPENSATION, SOCIAL SECURITY, crop insurance (see under AGRICULTURE, AID TO), and, together with the states, UNEMPLOYMENT COMPENSATION. In most other industrialized countries the government also provides HEALTH INSURANCE.

socialism

1. Today, an economic doctrine often defined as a "middle way" between CAPITALISM and COMMUNISM and characterized by state ownership of the means of production, centralized economic planning, and the redistribution of income through taxation and social welfare programs. Under Western socialism, the state owns most of the critical industries—rails, coal mines, steel mills, etc.—but agriculture, services, and less critical manufacturing industries continue to be largely in the private sector. While socialism has manifested itself in many different forms and today exists to varying degrees in many countries (Great Britain, Sweden, Norway, Denmark, Australia, and New Zealand, among others), it tended to evolve gradually and peacefully by means of legislation and reform rather than by revolution or upheaval. In Great Britain it came about after World World War II when the Labour Party came to power, beginning with the extension of social welfare programs and heavy taxation of income and estates and the NATIONALIZATION of the coal, electric power, and rail industries. See also E. BERNSTEIN; L. BLANC; CHRISTIAN SOCIALISM; FABIAN SOCIALISM; GUILD SOCIALISM; UTOPIAN SOCIALISM; WELFARE STATE. For systems that contain elements of socialism even though they want to do away with the machinery of the state entirely, see ANARCHISM; MUTUALISM; SYNDICALISM.

2. In the mid-19th century, a term used for what is today generally called COMMUNISM (def. 1); in Marxist theory, the historical state of economic development following capitalism and preceding a classless society.

socialized medicine A general term for public health care, that is, professional medical care provided to the public and paid for by the government. Under such a system, private medical care may or may not be available to those who want it (it is not in the Soviet Union or People's Republic of China; it is in Great Britain). By the mid-1970s the United States was one of the few advanced countries of the world that did not yet have some form of socialized medicine. However, numerous proposals for some kind of national health care were under serious consideration, with the rapidly rising costs of health care finally overcoming the resistance of physicians and others who feared it would promote inefficiency, bureaucratic red tape, and poorer quality of care.

social overhead capital Also, *social capital*; see under INFRASTRUCTURE.

social security A broad system of contributory social insurance sponsored by the U.S. Federal government whereby employees, employers, and the self-employed all pay contributions that are pooled in special trust funds. When an individual's earnings cease or are reduced owing to retirement, death, or disability, they are replaced at least in part by social security payments. The principal kinds of insurance included are *retirement and survivors insurance* and *disability insurance*. Part of the contributions go into a separate insurance trust fund, so that when workers and their dependents reach the age of 65 they can be helped to pay possible hospital bills. They also may elect to receive help with doctor bills and other medical expenses by paying one-half of supplementary medical insurance premiums, the Federal government then paying the balance. Together these latter two programs are known as *Medicare*. Since 1974 the Social Security Administration, a branch of the Department of Health, Education, and Welfare, has also administered a program of supplemental security income (SSI) for the aged, blind, and disabled.

Originally established by the Social Security Act of 1935, the American social security program was intended to protect wage earners against loss of income and originally was also responsible for developing state unemployment compensation. Practically all industrial nations have some program of this kind, in some cases narrower and in others much broader than that of the United States.

social-welfare principle The idea that tax assessments should reflect the overall purpose of taxes, which is to redistribute income more equitably, with the rich paying practically all taxes and the poor almost none.

social workshop See under L. BLANC.

socioeconomic Describing social as well as economic status or relationships. Thus "socioeconomic class" takes into account level of education, cultural interests, and other social factors, as well as wealth and earnings.

soft goods
1. Same as nondurable goods; see under CONSUMER GOOD.
2. Consumer goods that are "soft" to the touch, usually textiles (bedding, clothes, carpeting, etc.).

soft loan In international trade, a loan that may be repaid in the borrower's currency, as opposed to a *hard loan*, which must be repaid in the lender's currency or in gold or a reserve currency. A soft loan almost always is a disguised gift. The country that is repaid in "soft" currency cannot, in practice, spend it without disrupting the borrowing country's economy. However, the fiction of a loan helps the borrower save face and also may alleviate fears of extravagance among voters in the donor country. See also GRANT-IN-AID, def. 2.

soft market A market in which supply is increasing faster than demand, and therefore prices are declining. It differs from a *firm market*, where there is sufficient demand to balance supply and hence prices tend to fluctuate relatively little.

software See under PROGRAMMING.

soil conservation See under CONSERVATION.

sole proprietorship See PROPRIETORSHIP.

solvency In business, the ability to meet one's debts and obligations without liquidating any fixed assets. Hence, an excess of relatively liquid assets over short-term liabilities.

Sombart, Werner A German economist (1863–1941), the last of the GERMAN HISTORICAL SCHOOL, who is remembered for assigning to Judaism the role that Max WEBER had given to Calvinism. Capitalism, Sombart held, depended on entrepreneurs (of whom the most successful were, in his view, Jews), the mechanism of the modern state, and industrial technology. He discerned three stages of capitalism—early (1400–1760), high (1760–1914), and later (after 1914)—with the last period marked by decline. Capitalism would endure, but it would continue to change. A follower of Marxist thought early in his career, Sombart later rejected it and became an ardent Nazi.

sorter See under PUNCHED-CARD DATA PROCESSING.

source and application of funds statement Also, *flow of funds statement, funds statement.* A summary of changes in a business firm's cash position during a particular accounting period. The *funds* referred to mean working capital, that is, current assets minus current liabilities; they move in a circular flow, with cash being used to buy merchandise, which is sold and converted into accounts receivable, which in turn are collected and turned back into cash, used to buy more merchandise, and so on. The *sources* of a company's funds are transactions that increase its working capital, such as funds from operations (earnings), from long-term loans, from depreciation of plant and equipment, from the sale of fixed assets, and from the sale of stock. *Application* of funds refers to any outgo of funds other than for acquiring current assets or paying current liabilities, such as purchases of plant, equipment, or other capital assets, payment of long-term debts, and payment of dividends.

source document In automatic or electronic data processing, such as a punched card system or computer, the original information that is to be fed into and processed by the system, before it is converted into "machine-readable" form.

source program See under PROGRAMMING.

South Sea Bubble See under BUBBLE.

space salesperson See under ADVERTISING.

span of control Also, *chain of command.* In business and industry, the number of subordinates a person supervises. For example, suppose a department of 50 has 1 manager and 49 workers; the manager's span of control is 49 and the department's organization is said to be *flat* or *shallow*, consisting of only two levels, boss and workers. Suppose, however, there are 1 manager, 3 assistant

Fig. 74. Change during an accounting period

Sources of Cash	Applications of Cash
Borrowing	Repayment of debt
Sale of securities	Stock dividends and bond inter.
Decrease in inventories	Increase in inventories
Decrease in accounts receivable	Increase in accounts receivable
Increase in accounts payable	Decrease in accounts payable
Decrease in securities held	Increase in investments
Increase in accrued expenses	Decrease in accrued expenses
Net income after taxes	Deficit
Depreciation	

Fig. 75. Spans of control

FLAT ORGANIZATION, BROAD SPAN OF CONTROL

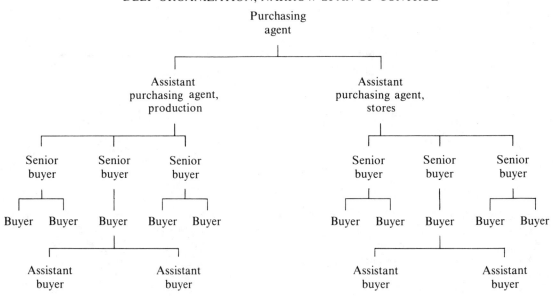

DEEP ORGANIZATION, NARROW SPAN OF CONTROL

managers, 6 supervisors, 12 assistant supervisors, and 28 production workers. The department would now have five different levels, a rather *deep* organization (considering the small number of employees involved), and the manager's span of control would be quite *narrow*. In practice span of control tends to narrow near the top of an organization and broaden at the bottom; a production foreman may readily supervise 20 or 30 workers, whereas a company vice-president may have only 3 or 4 high-level managers reporting directly to him or her.

special assessment A charge made by a local government for the cost of an improvement or service, such as installing sewers or pavements, widening streets, etc., usually levied on those whom it will benefit most directly. Since the total cost of the work may not be collected for some years but usually must be paid out sooner, localities frequently issue a *special assessment bond* to finance such work. Interest and principal payments on the bond then are included in taxes paid by those who benefit from the improvement.

special deposit

1. A deposit of cash or other property in a bank for safekeeping, with the understanding that the bank will not use it as security, to make loans, or in other ways. Unlike demand and time deposits, a special deposit does not become the bank's property but always remains the owner's.

2. A method of controlling the British money supply that was introduced by the Bank of England about 1960, whereby commercial banks were

required to increase their deposits at the central bank by a given percentage. These special deposits earned interest but served to reduce the amount of money banks had available for lending.

Special Drawing Rights Also, *SDRs.* A kind of international money created in 1969 by the International Monetary Fund (IMF) to replace gold as the principal means for clearing international financial transactions (and so sometimes called "paper gold"). Each nation can pay off its balance of payments deficits with SDRs as well as with gold or some other currency. SDRs were created to alleviate the relative shortages of gold and reserve currencies in relation to world trade. Gold supplies (from mining) were growing at a rate of less than 2 per cent per year, and the reserve currencies, chiefly the U.S. dollar and British pound sterling, could not be expanded more rapidly to take up the slack. In fact, severe balance of payments deficits in both countries, accompanied by deteriorating balances of trade, were already causing other nations to lose confidence in their currencies. In the past (until 1971) the United States had always stood ready to support its currency with gold at $35 per ounce, but the American gold supply had declined so precipitously that it was obvious this policy could not be continued. In 1970, therefore,

Fig. 76. "Standard basket" of SDRs, June 28, 1974

1 SDR=	0.40	Dollar (United States)
	0.38	Deutschmark (West Germany)
	0.045	Pound sterling (Great Britain)
	0.44	Franc (France)
	26.00	Yen (Japan)
	0.071	Dollar (Canada)
	47.00	Lira (Italy)
	0.14	Guilder (Netherlands)
	1.6	Franc (Belgium)
	0.13	Krona (Sweden)
	0.012	Dollar (Australia)
	0.11	Krone (Denmark)
	0.099	Krone (Norway)
	1.1	Peseta (Spain)
	0.22	Schilling (Austria)
	0.0082	Rand (South Africa)

SDR values fluctuate daily, along with other foreign exchange rates.

SDRs began to be issued every year as a substitute for gold or a gold-backed dollar. Within limits, each participating nation could exchange its own currency at the IMF for SDRs, which, in turn, became the reserve that it used to support its own currency and to draw on in case of an international payments deficit. Note that SDRs are used exclusively to make settlements between central banks and the IMF; they do not exist physically (there are no SDR "bills") and there is no symbol for them (such as $ for "dollar").

Until mid-1974 SDRs themselves were valued in terms of gold. Recognizing that such valuation was unrealistic but reluctant to substitute the then weakening U.S. dollar, the world's major trading nations decided to set SDR values in terms of a group of currencies, those of the leading trading countries. Accordingly, 16 were selected, with each weighted according to the country's share of world exports (see Fig. 76). As a result, SDRs became considerably more stable than individual currencies and their use expanded a great deal.

specialist A member of a STOCK EXCHANGE who confines his or her activities to a very few stocks (or even a single one) sold at one location of a stock exchange trading post. The specialist has two principal functions: (1) to maintain an orderly market, buying and selling for his or her own account in order to prevent large price fluctuations; (2) to help floor brokers execute limit orders (see LIMIT ORDER) when the floor broker cannot wait at the trading post to execute an order. For example, if a broker has an order to buy at 35 a stock currently selling at 42, it might take hours or days of waiting at the post until the stock sells at that level. Consequently, the broker turns the order over to the specialist in that stock who executes it when the market declines to the desired point (and in exchange receives a portion of the broker's commission on the transaction). The specialist must always execute such orders in the order they are received and may never put his or her own interests first. Orders are written down in the *specialist's book*, one book being kept for each stock dealt in.

No broker may work as a specialist without the permission of the exchange, which also has strict regulations concerning their operations. Most specialists are persons with considerable capital of their own, since they must be able to buy a sizable portion—on the New York Stock Exchange, 2,000 shares—of every stock in which they specialize. If a broker bidding for a stock can find no seller at the trading post, the specialist frequently offers it for sale; such buying and selling by specialists accounts for about 15 per cent of all exchange transactions. In their role as stabilizers, specialists see to it that prices rarely fluctuate more than one-fourth of a point ($.25) between transactions, and that there is (usually) no more than one-fourth or one-half of a point's gap between prices bid and prices offered. To offset wide differences, they are expected to buy and sell for their own accounts. Their profits come largely from selling from their inventory when prices rise temporarily and by adding to their inventory when prices decline.

specialization

1. In business, narrowing the scope of output or of job responsibility. A company may begin by manufacturing various electrical components and gradually concentrate on producing only those items—or a single item—with which it is most successful. (See also DIVERSIFICATION, def. 1.) Similarly, a firm may be so organized that each employee concentrates solely on his or her own particular job, a pattern called *functional organization* (see also under ORGANIZATION, COMPANY). Further, in mass-production industries each operation may be broken down into smaller and smaller components, with the result that a worker's entire job may, for example, consist simply of placing three screws into a subassembly, over and over again.

2. *regional specialization, national specialization.* The practice of specializing in producing those goods and services in which a region or nation has the greatest *comparative advantage* (see under ADVANTAGE).

special offering

1. See under ISSUE.

2. An already existing option to buy stock offered by a dealer from his or her own inventory.

special partnership

A partnership formed for a single transaction, such as the purchase or sale of a piece of real estate. However, the term "special partner" sometimes is used in the meaning of "limited partner"; see under PARTNERSHIP.

specialty shop

See under RETAIL.

specie

Coins of precious metal, usually gold or silver, which at one time were considered superior to coins of base metal or paper currency. For *price-specie-flow mechanism*, see under D. HUME.

specifications

A detailed description, frequently accompanied by drawings or diagrams, of a manufactured item to be bought or made. Buyers use specifications to check the quality of purchased items. Generally, such specifications fall into three basic categories: technical, performance, and brand name. *Technical specifications* spell out standards of materials that can be measured by instruments and gauges. Buyers of most raw materials can refer to available industry or professional standards. Thus, the Society of Automotive Engineers (SAE) has set standards for hundreds of items, so that a buyer can simply order one-inch bar stock made of SAE 4320 steel, for example, which will pass various SAE tests. Moreover, if the steel is to be used in the manufacture of parts, the buyer's blueprints can further specify the exact dimensions, with permitted tolerances. *Performance specifications* are used mainly in purchases of finished products designed and made by a supplier. In such instances the buyer is less interested in the raw materials used than in how well the product performs. Finally, buyers often rely on *brand name*, a specification developed by testing several brands over time and keeping records of breakdowns, repairs, user preference, and the like. While brand-name buying gives less assurance of quality than the other types of specification, it is nevertheless widely used, partly because even large firms do not bother to develop specifications for nonproduction equipment and supplies, and small ones often cannot afford to develop them even for vital production items.

specific tariff

See under AD VALOREM.

speculation

The purchase of some kind of property for the purpose of resale at a profit, usually within a fairly short time. The difference between speculation and INVESTMENT (def. 1) tends to be one of degree. In general, speculators want to make a quick profit and are willing to assume a greater risk than investors, who are more interested in a reasonable and regular return. However, although some speculators buy and sell on the same day, others (or even the same individuals) may speculate in enterprises that are not expected to yield a profit for months or even years and represent a fairly high risk. From a conservative viewpoint, only such securities as government and municipal bonds and the bonds of highly reputable, first-class corporations are considered investments, all other securities being regarded as somewhat speculative. In the United States speculation is sometimes aided by favorable tax laws, as some speculative profits are taxed at a lower rate. (In most countries, such gains are not taxed at all.) In commodities sales and foreign exchange, practically all buyers are speculators (except for the few that actually need the commodity or foreign currency they are buying). Since they pay no interest or dividends, there is no reason to buy commodities or foreign exchange other than the expectation of gain through changes in price.

speedup The practice of gradually increasing the work pace as employees gain experience and dexterity. In some cases the employer offers premium pay for a fast work pace, and then, once this pace is established, "restudies" the job and forces employees to work at the same rapid pace without premium pay. Needless to say, what is considered a "fair day's work" by an employer may well be regarded as a "speedup" by an employee.

spendable average weekly earnings See TAKE-HOME PAY.

spinoff The transfer of one corporation's stock to the stockholders of another corporation. Such a transfer may result from an antitrust decree requiring a large corporation to break up by spinning off one or more subsidiaries. A spinoff may create additional market value for a stock if the company spun off is in an industry currently favored by investors. For example, the shareholders of Olin Corporation were getting stocks with higher market value (but identical intrinsic worth) when they received a spinoff of shares of Squibb-Beechnut; the latter was considered more "glamorous" by investors because it produced such visible, branded items as proprietary drugs, chewing gum, and baby food, whereas Olin is primarily a producer of chemicals unknown to most consumers. See also SPLIT-OFF; SPLITUP, def. 2.

split Also, *stock split* (*splitup*). The division of the outstanding shares of a company's stock into a larger number of shares. For example, a 3-for-1 split by a company with 1 million shares outstanding results in 3 million shares outstanding. Each holder of 100 shares before the split would then have 300 shares, although his or her proportionate equity in the company would remain exactly the same. Ordinary stock splits normally are voted by the company's board of directors and must be approved by the shareholders. When a stock is split, initially its market price is divided in the same proportion; in the example above, if the stock had sold for $60 per share, it would sell for $20 immediately after the 3-for-1 split. However, splits sometimes attract new investors, and shortly after a split the price of the stock may rise (owing to increased demand), partly because most investors prefer stocks selling at $20 to $30 or so. If a stock sells at a much lower price, it may undergo a *reverse split* to reduce the number of shares outstanding. For example, a stock selling for $5 may be reverse split 1-to-4 so that it will sell for $20.

splitoff The transfer of some of a corporation's assets to another corporation in exchange for its stock, which it then distributes to stockholders in exchange for some of its own stock. Most often the corporations so involved are a parent organization and a newly established subsidiary. See also SPINOFF; SPLITUP, def. 2.

split shift See under SHIFT, def. 1.

splitup
1. See SPLIT.
2. The replacement of a single corporation by two or more new corporations. The original firm's

stockholders then own the stock of the new firms, and its assets are divided among them.

spoilage A decrease in the value of assets owing to natural or man-imposed physical deterioration. Workers can spoil material or parts through ignorance, inexperience, or simply human error. Also, many materials are to some extent perishable and spoil when stored too long.

sponsor See under ADVERTISING.

spot
1. In advertising, any radio or television activity (announcement, identification, participation, or program) sponsored by a national or regional advertiser and selected and bought on a station-to-station basis. It includes commercials run between both network and nonnetwork programs, as well as complete programs, but not commercials sponsored by local retailers, which are designated *local advertising*. Each spot commercial, however, originates locally. In contrast, in *network advertising* both commercials and programs originate centrally and are bought on a full-network basis.
2. In business, describing a transaction involving immediate cash payment and delivery, as opposed to future terms. See also SPOT MARKET.

spot market Also, *actual market, cash market, physical market*. A market for buying and selling commodities for immediate (as opposed to future) delivery and for cash payment. The price for such commodities is called the *spot price* or *cash price*. Local spot markets exist in areas where the commodity is produced. For example, every medium-sized town in a major farm state like Iowa or Illinois has a grain elevator whose operator buys corn, soybeans, and other grains for cash from producers. The local operator in turn usually sells to dealers or through brokers in the major market areas, such as Kansas City for wheat; Memphis for cotton; Chicago for corn, soybeans, and eggs; and Minneapolis for flax and barley. These dealers in turn both trade in futures contracts and sell to manufacturers and exporters of the commodities. See also FUTURES MARKET.

spread
1. The difference between two prices, usually a buying price and a selling price. For merchandise, it is identical to a MARKUP. For securities, it may mean (a) the difference between a broker's or dealer's buying and selling price, which constitute his profit; (b) the difference between an underwriter's buying and selling price for a new issue, also called *gross spread*; (c) the difference between the ask and bid (prices) in any transaction; (d) a substantial difference in the price of a security in two different markets at the same time (a minimal difference being called *back spread*; see also ARBITRAGE, def. 1); (e) another term for STRADDLE (def. 1).
For currencies, all but definition (b) for securities apply.
2. In publishing, the facing pages of a newspaper, magazine, or book. In advertising, an advertisement occupying facing pages.

spread effect The beneficial effect of international trade on the domestic economies of the trading nations. As export values rise, there is a general increase in demand for all of the economy's goods, which in turn has a multiplier effect on per capita income, with essentially the same short-run effect as an increase in domestic investment spending might have (see also MULTIPLIER PRINCIPLE, def. 2). The spread effect tends to be greater in industrial, developed nations than in underdeveloped nations, where, some economists claim, it usually is more than offset by unfavorable effects (the so-called *backwash*). Thus, instead of increased exports resulting in growth, they allegedly represent a diversion of capital that instead should have been invested in domestic manufactures and industrial development. In practice, however, such capital might just as readily have been spent on consumption or deposited by the wealthy in bank accounts in Switzerland or the United States.

stability A condition of economic well-being without severe fluctuations of the BUSINESS CYCLE, characterized by increasing production, growing employment, and constant price levels. See also BUILT-IN STABILIZER; PRICE STABILITY.

stabilization funds See under EXCHANGE CONTROLS.

staff and line See under ORGANIZATION, COMPANY.

stagflation A term coined in the late 1960s to describe the state of the economy at that time, that is, rising prices (inflation) accompanied by insufficient economic expansion (stagnation) and consequently increasing unemployment. See also COST-PUSH INFLATION.

stagnation A less than satisfactory annual rate of growth or an actual decline in per capita real income. In the 1970s a 3 per cent annual growth rate was considered "normal" for the United States. A number of economists have predicted that stagnation is the inevitable end of every capitalist economy. David Ricardo and others of the CLASSICAL SCHOOL believed that, as investment grew, the rate of profits would gradually decrease (law of diminishing returns) to the point where it would no longer pay to invest, and so net capital formation would come to a halt. For a more recent pessimistic view, see SECULAR STAGNATION.

stamp tax Same as *revenue stamp*; see under EXCISE TAX; TRANSFER TAX.

Standard & Poor's Composite Index See under AVERAGE, def. 2.

standard cost A forecast of what costs should be incurred in producing a good or service under normal operating conditions. Made on the basis of engineering and accounting studies, it is useful for comparing the costs actually incurred when the product or service is produced. The differences between standard cost and actual cost are charged to variance accounts (see VARIANCE, def. 2).

standard deviation In statistics, a measure of the tendency of individual values to differ from the MEAN. It is computed by taking the square root of the *variance*, which is the sum of the squares of the deviations from the mean in a series of values, divided by the sample size:

$$\sigma = \sqrt{\frac{\Sigma(x - \bar{x})^2}{n - 1}}$$

where σ is a standard deviation, Σ stands for "sum of," $(x - \bar{x})^2$ means deviations from the mean squared, and n stands for the size of the sample. For example, in the following series of observations of 9 workers assembling part A, the mean number of parts assembled per hour is $270 \div 9 = 30$.

Worker	No. Parts Assembled	Deviation from Mean	Deviation Squared
1	28	−2	4
2	29	−1	1
3	29	−1	1
4	30	0	0
5	30	0	0
6	30	0	0
7	31	+1	1
8	31	+1	1
9	32	+2	4
	270		12

The variance is $12 \div (9 - 1) = 1.50$, and the standard deviation is $\sqrt{1.50} = 1.22$. In a normal distribution, 68.3 per cent of the individual values will differ from the mean by less than 1 standard deviation, 95.5 per cent by less than 2 standard deviations, and 99.7 per cent by less than 3 standard deviations. (See also Fig. 59.)

The standard deviation is the most important measure of DISPERSION used in statistics and is involved in practically all work with PROBABILITY THEORY. In business and industry it is particularly useful in QUALITY CONTROL and process control (see PROCESS CAPABILITY; STATISTICAL CONTROL).

standard error Also, *standard error of the mean.* In statistics, a measurement of dispersion of a population of sample means. If the sample is large enough, the distribution is always normal (see NORMAL DISTRIBUTION), and as a result probabilities can be precisely calculated even if the underlying process is highly erratic. For example, a manufacturer of fasteners might periodically check lots of 30 fasteners for some characteristic, such as tensile strength. The average value from this sample and others would be distributed normally around the mean of the process. From this it would be possible to determine the probability that the process was "in control" and functioning satisfactorily. Numerically, the standard error of the mean is equal to the STANDARD DEVIATION of the process divided by the square root of the sample size. A table of the normal curve can then be used to indicate the probability of a given occurrence or range of occurrences.

standard forecast   The tendency of most economists to make essentially the same year-ahead forecast for the economy, reflecting the fact that they are trained to interpret the same data in just about the same way. See also FORECASTING.

standardization   In business, industry, and commerce, the use of a set of measurable values, concerning thickness, size, weight, alloy content, etc., whereby products can be compared. Such standardization is also used to *grade* or rank some goods, such as agricultural products (milk, eggs, meat, etc.).

standard of living   A broad economic concept concerning the amount and kind of goods and services that the average individual or family, in a given area at a given time, considers essential. A major variable is the level of income. For example, in the 1970s the average American family with two children and an annual income of $20,000 would probably consider a telephone and automobile essential possessions, whereas a family with only $7,500 might confine itself to basic items (food, clothing, shelter). Though frequently difficult to measure in terms of money value, the idea of a minimum living standard underlies many quite specific statistical analyses. See also COST OF LIVING.

standard operating procedure   Also, *SOP*. See POLICIES AND PROCEDURES.

Standards, Bureau of   See NATIONAL BUREAU OF STANDARDS.

standby cost   See FIXED COST.

standing order   See BLANKET ORDER.

staple   General term for a basic commodity, such as wheat, corn, or cotton.

state bank   In the United States, a commercial bank that receives its charter from the state in which it is located, as opposed to NATIONAL BANKS chartered by the Federal government. A state bank may belong to both the Federal Reserve System and the Federal Deposit Insurance Corporation, provided it conforms to the appropriate regulations; in practice only the largest state banks belong to the former, but most belong to the latter. Although about three-fifths of all American commercial banks today are state banks, their deposits amount to only about two-fifths of the total, since many of them are quite small. Historically, it was the opposition of the state banks that prevented the renewal of the charters of the first and second BANK OF THE UNITED STATES, and it also accounts for the regional character of the Federal Reserve and the absence of the kind of genuine central bank found in most other developed countries.

state farm   See under COLLECTIVE FARM.

state income tax   See under INCOME TAX.

statement   Also, *financial statement.* In accounting, a formal report of the status of accounts at a particular time or at the end of a given period, prepared to show their financial condition, the operating results of a firm, etc. Such statements, derived from accounting records, include the BALANCE SHEET, INCOME STATEMENT, and STATEMENT OF ACCOUNT.

statement of account   An account that summarizes the transactions between a buyer and seller, or a creditor and debtor, over a given period, usually a month. For example, a monthly bill from a retail store to a customer would include the balance, if any, carried over from the previous month, the amounts charged during the specified month, payments received, and any unpaid balance. A statement of account alone does not signify a request for payment but may be accompanied by such a request. See also BANK STATEMENT.

state ownership   See PUBLIC OWNERSHIP.

state trading   A system of conducting all or some international trade through a government agency. State trade monopolizes the foreign trade of the Soviet Union, People's Republic of China, and other Communist nations, but it is also used on a smaller scale by many other countries. It nearly always involves negotiating trade agreements and long-term contracts with foreign governments or private firms. Such dealings are basically restrictive, binding each party to a deal with the other and thus limiting the market. For example, Great Britain after World War II used a bulk-purchase program for importing raw materials and foodstuffs, whereby it made agreements, mostly with STERLING AREA nations or others with "soft" currency, to buy all their exportable surpluses of certain commodities. Thus Britain agreed to buy all of Australia's surplus beef, lamb, and mutton over a given period of time.

statics   See COMPARATIVE STATICS.

stationary state   See STAGNATION.

statistical control   Control of any industrial process by statistical methods, so that variations from the quality desired, beyond the permitted ones, can be attributed to chance or random causes. Most quality control engineers and inspectors use control limits of three standard deviations (or three sigmas; see STANDARD DEVIATION). If the process has a normal distribution, 99.72 per cent of all occurrences will fall within three standard deviations of the mean, and the process will be assumed to be in control so long as it operates within this range.

statistical model   See MODEL.

statistical quality control   See QUALITY CONTROL; also STATISTICAL CONTROL.

statistics   A branch of mathematics concerned with collecting, organizing, analyzing, and interpreting numerical data. Also, a term for the data themselves. Statistics is used in two principal ways: to *describe* the numerical characteristics of some group, organization, nation, firm, etc., or to *infer*, from a sample of a whole or from past events, either the probable characteristics of the whole or the probable events of the future. For example, a census, such as the nationwide count undertaken by the United States government every ten years, yields data that describe virtually every member of the entire population. An opinion poll of a sample group of voters or the test marketing of a product in a single city yields information from which statisticians draw inferences about all voters or consumers in all cities. In business and economics, statistical techniques, greatly aided by the use of computers, are used increasingly in such areas as production control, inventory control, quality control, and sales forecasting, as well as in analyses and predictions of larger economic pheonomena (demand, supply, income distribution, the business cycle, etc.). See also STATISTICS, BUSINESS AND ECONOMIC.

statistics, business and economic   The gathering of data concerning business and economic affairs. (See also STATISTICS.) In the United States on a nationwide basis most of this work is supervised by the Social and Economic Statistics Administration of the Department of Commerce, which includes both the Bureau of the CENSUS and the Office of Economic Analysis. The latter (formerly called Office of Business Economics) collects, processes, and analyzes a variety of data concerning the economy. It maintains the national economic accounts, summarized by the GROSS NATIONAL PRODUCT, and serves as the central economic research organization for the U.S. government. Among numerous private agencies the most important is the *National Bureau of Economic Research*, a nonprofit organization founded in 1920 that has developed many basic economic measures and indexes now widely used. In the 1970s its studies focused on business cycles, financial institutions and processes, economic growth, national income, consumption, and capital formation, as well as on international economic relations.

statute of limitations   Any of numerous laws that limit the period of time over which certain rights are legally enforceable. These laws vary, not only from state to state but also depending on the type of right involved.

statutory law The body of laws enacted by legislatures on various levels of government, from local to central. It tends to change with some frequency, since statutes can be passed and repealed with relative ease. Statutory law is subordinate to constitutional law—that is, it cannot run counter to the constitution of a state or country—but in many cases it represents simply a codification of COMMON LAW.

sterilization, gold See GOLD STERILIZATION.

sterling area Also, *sterling bloc*. A group of nations whose primary FOREIGN EXCHANGE RESERVES were kept in pounds sterling (deposited in British banks) rather than in U.S. dollars or gold. When Great Britain abandoned the gold standard in 1931, a group of countries with which it had close financial, political, and economic ties decided to stabilize their foreign exchange in terms of sterling. To do this their governments (or central banks) bought and sold sterling in unlimited quantities at a fixed price in terms of their domestic currency. As a result, transactions among these countries were kept relatively stable, even when the pound sterling fluctuated in relation to the dollar and other currencies, because their rates of exchange remained stable. Until Britain's financial crises of the 1970s, the sterling area included most of the Commonwealth countries (Canada was a major exception) and even some big oil producers, notably Kuwait.

steward See SHOP STEWARD.

sticky Describing a price that is slow to respond to a change in market conditions, usually owing to monopolistic forces. For example, in an industry dominated by a few large producers that exercise considerable control over the price of their commodity (as with steel or automobiles), the firms may be reluctant to lower prices (or increase output) even when demand is sharply increased, fearing that in the long run it would not pay to do so. Thus, the American steel industry in effect created a steel shortage after World War II because it failed to adjust prices and output to rising demand. Stock prices are sticky when they fail to rise in response to higher corporate profits or to decline in response to lower profits or dividends.

stochastic equation In econometrics, a formula that describes the relationship between two or more variables and that is tested with actual data, making statistical allowance for error. In a simple MODEL of the corn market, for example, the equations explaining the demand and supply for corn are stochastic equations, since the precise form of these relations is determined by employing actual data. The equation stating that the quantity demanded equals the quantity supplied is not a stochastic equation, since it is assumed to be true and hence no attempt is made to verify it with the help of data.

stock
   1. A share in the ownership or equity of a corporate business. The sum total of capital invested in the business, as represented by shares of stock in the form of *stock certificates*, is called its *capital stock*. Possessing stock in a business gives the owner, called *stockholder* or *shareholder*, certain privileges and rights, depending on the kind of stock it is. There are two chief kinds, *common stock* and *preferred stock*. Usually the owners of common stock are the last to be paid if the firm goes out of business (after preferred stockholders, who are paid after bondholders) and thus they assume the greatest risk. However, they usually have the most control over a company's operations, since they are entitled to vote at its annual meeting, and they also stand to gain greater rewards in both dividends and capital appreciation. See also COMMON STOCK; CORPORATION; ISSUE; OPTION, def. 2; PREFERRED STOCK; SECURITY.
   2. In business, originally a term for merchandise or finished goods ready for sale. Today, the term is sometimes used for all goods in a company's possession that will go into its finished product, including raw materials, parts, work in process, and finished goods.
   3. See CLOSED STOCK.

stockbroker See under BROKER, def. 1.

stock certificate Written evidence of stock ownership, issued to each stockholder and indicating the number and kind of shares held. The paper used for stock certificates is usually watermarked and finely engraved with delicate markings to discour-

Fig. 77. A stock certificate

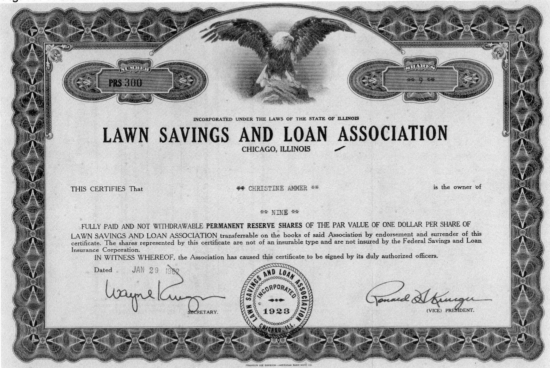

INCORPORATED UNDER THE LAWS OF THE STATE OF ILLINOIS

LAWN SAVINGS AND LOAN ASSOCIATION
CHICAGO, ILLINOIS

PRS 300

** 9 **

THIS CERTIFIES That ** CHRISTINE AMMER ** is the owner of

** NINE **

FULLY PAID AND NOT WITHDRAWABLE **PERMANENT RESERVE SHARES** OF THE PAR VALUE OF ONE DOLLAR PER SHARE OF LAWN SAVINGS AND LOAN ASSOCIATION transferrable on the books of said Association by endorsement and surrender of this certificate. The shares represented by this certificate are not of an insurable type and are not insured by the Federal Savings and Loan Insurance Corporation.

IN WITNESS WHEREOF, the Association has caused this certificate to be signed by its duly authorized officers.

Dated JAN 29 1962

SECRETARY.   (VICE) PRESIDENT.

age forgery. A stock certificate is a NEGOTIABLE INSTRUMENT; its loss can cause considerable inconvenience, even financial loss.

Stock Clearing Corporation A subsidiary of the New York Stock Exchange that acts as a central agency for clearing transactions made on the exchange and providing for their settlement, that is, physical delivery of securities and money payments. One of its departments, the Central Certificate Service, effects security deliveries between brokerage firms by means of computerized bookkeeping entries that eliminate—or at least reduce —the physical movement of stock certificates.

stock dividend A DIVIDEND paid in the form of stock rather than cash. Such payment may be preferred by stockholders wishing to avoid taxes on cash dividends, and by corporations wishing to conserve cash for investment in capital equipment or other future outlays. The stock paid out may consist of additional shares of the issuing company or

shares of another company (usually a subsidiary) held by the issuing company.

stock exchange Also, *securities exchange*. An organized market where traders buy and sell securities, either for themselves or for their customers. In the United States there are 16 stock exchanges, 13 of them registered with the Securities and Exchange Commission (SEC); the other 3 are quite small. The New York Stock Exchange is by far the largest, in the 1970s handling more than 80 per cent of all shares traded over exchanges; the second largest is the American Stock Exchange, also in New York City, which accounted for 6 per cent or so. All American exchanges are regulated by the SEC as to their manner of operation, the securities they list, and the brokers and dealers who trade on them.

A company wishing to have its shares listed must meet the standards set by the particular exchange. In 1974 the New York Stock Exchange, which has always had the strictest regulations, required that a company earn at least $2.5 million before Federal income tax during the previous year and at least $2 million per year in the two preceding years; have net tangible assets of at least $16 million; a total of at least $16 million in market value of publicly held stock; at least 1 million shares of common stock held publicly; and 2,000 holders of 100 shares or more. Moreover, once a firm is listed it must continue to meet the requirements or it can be either suspended or dropped ("delisted"). Listed firms must publish quarterly reports on their financial condition (as certified by independent accountants), and they may not issue additional shares without exchange approval.

The companies listed have no control over the exchange's operations. Rather, it is regulated by its own board of governors, and the actual trading is conducted by the brokers and dealers, who must, in most cases, be *members* of the exchange (in Canada some may be agents of members). Normally brokerage firms purchase one or more memberships, called *seats*, on the exchange, for use by their partners or voting stockholders; some seats, however, belong to individual dealers who buy and sell for themselves exclusively (see FLOOR TRADER). The cost of a seat is determined by supply and demand since the total number is fixed and anyone who wants a seat must buy it from someone who is relinquishing one. On the New York Stock Exchange the cost of a seat in this century has

Fig. 78. Leading North American exchanges

United States

American Stock Exchange	New York, N.Y.
Boston Stock Exchange	Boston, Mass.
Chicago Board of Trade[1]	Chicago, Ill.
Chicago Board Options Exchange	Chicago, Ill.
Cincinnati Stock Exchange	Cincinnati, Ohio
Colorado Springs Exchange[2]	Colorado Springs, Colo.
Detroit Stock Exchange	Detroit, Mich.
Honolulu Stock Exchange	Honolulu, Hawaii
Intermountain Stock Exchange[2]	Salt Lake City, Utah
Midwest Stock Exchange	Chicago, Ill.
National Stock Exchange	New York, N.Y.
New York Stock Exchange	New York, N.Y.
Pacific Stock Exchange	Los Angeles, Calif.
(2 divisions)	San Francisco, Calif.
PBW (Philadelphia-Baltimore-Washington) Stock Exchange	Philadelphia, Pa.
Pittsburgh Stock Exchange[2]	Pittsburgh, Pa.
Richmond Stock Exchange[2]	Richmond, Va.
Spokane Stock Exchange	Spokane, Wash.
Wheeling Stock Exchange[2]	Wheeling, West Va.

Canada

Calgary Stock Exchange	Calgary, Alta.
Canadian Stock Exchange	Montreal, Que.
Montreal Stock Exchange	Montreal, Que.
Toronto Stock Exchange[3]	Toronto, Ont.
Vancouver Stock Exchange	Vancouver, B.C.
Winnipeg Stock Exchange	Winnipeg, Man.

[1] Leading commodity market in the United States.
[2] Too small to be registered with the Securities and Exchange Commission.
[3] Largest Canadian exchange, handling about 80 per cent of the volume and 67 per cent of the dollar value of all trade.

varied from a high of $625,000 in 1929 to a low of $17,000 in 1942.

An institution that grew from a handful of 18th-century British merchants meeting daily in coffeehouses to trade securities, the stock exchange first came into being under that name in London in 1773. The New York Stock Exchange was founded in 1792 on Wall Street. Today there is a stock exchange is in almost every major city in the world. The stock exchange is one of the few markets that claims to have practically PURE COMPETITION, with prices determined almost wholly by demand and supply. (However, numerous strict regulations prevent prices from fluctuating drastically or suddenly, so that many feel this claim to be unsubstantiated.) On most exchanges buyers and sellers must orally bid for and offer quantities of securities at particular prices where all other potential buyers and sellers can hear them, as in an *auction*. Though a broker may simultaneously have orders to buy and sell the same security, he or she must conclude the transaction openly through the exchange, that is, the broker is required to send all buy and sell orders to the exchange floor, rather than simply effecting a transfer of stock between two customers. (However, large blocks of listed stock may be traded simultaneously outside the exchange by dealers in the so-called THIRD MARKET.)

Prices of stocks listed on principal stock exchanges are printed daily in the financial sections of leading newspapers. Prices are quoted in *points* and fractions of points. In the United States 1 point = $1, and the fractions used are confined to eighths, quarters, and halves. (A stock listed at $45\frac{1}{2}$ sells for $45.50 per share; if it goes up one-eighth of a point, to $45\frac{5}{8}$, it sells for $45.625 per share.) For an example of a stock exchange transaction, see under NEW YORK STOCK EXCHANGE; see also AMERICAN STOCK EXCHANGE; COMMODITY EXCHANGE; OPTIONS EXCHANGE; OVER-THE-COUNTER MARKET; SECURITY; STOCK CLEARING CORPORATION.

stockholders' equity   See EQUITY, def. 2.

Stockholm school   A name sometimes used for the Swedish economists WICKSELL, CASSEL, and MYRDAL, and their respective followers.

stock insurance company   A CORPORATION whose chief business is insuring others against various hazards. Like other corporations, it raises funds by issuing shares, whose buyers become the owners and elect a board of directors. About 70 per cent of all property and liability insurance firms in the United States are stock companies. See also under INSURANCE; MUTUAL INSURANCE COMPANY.

stock market
1. An organized market where stocks are traded; see STOCK EXCHANGE.
2. A broad term for the trading of all securities and commodities, including futures, options, warrants, etc.

stockout   Running out of a needed item. Preventing stockouts without overinvesting in inventories is a major goal in inventory control. To protect against stockout of critical items, most companies maintain a SAFETY STOCK.

stockpile   See STRATEGIC MATERIALS.

stock rights   See RIGHTS.

stock split   See SPLIT.

stop order   In the securities trade, an order to buy or sell a given quantity of a security when the market price in relation to a stated price called the *stop price* is either at that price or higher (for buying) or lower (for selling). For example, suppose Jane Doe buys General Steel at 35 and it rises to 45. However, the market then begins to drop. In order to protect her profit, she tells her broker to sell her shares if the stock declines to $42\frac{1}{2}$. If it actually falls to $42\frac{1}{2}$ (or perhaps even skips down to $42\frac{1}{4}$ or $42\frac{3}{8}$) her stop order becomes a market order, to be executed at once at the most favorable current price. Similarly, if Doe wants to buy more General Steel when the price drops, the same procedure is used. See also LIMIT ORDER.

stop payment   A depositor's order to his or her bank that the bank refuse to honor a particular check written by the depositor. It is used to invalidate a check that has been lost or stolen or when the goods or services being paid for by that check are unsatisfactory.

storage

1. Also, *store*. In a COMPUTER, any device used to retain information or data. Such devices include punch cards, MAGNETIC DISKS (also called *random access devices* or *remote storage*), MAGNETIC TAPES, data cells, and MAGNETIC CORES. The last are used in the internal computer *memory* or *core memory,* the level of storage that is most expensive and most readily accessible for processing by the computer. (In fact, no information may be processed by a computer unless it is retained in memory storage.) The various kinds of storage vary in terms of cost (usually expressed as *bits* or *bytes* per cent; see BINARY for explanation) and of *access time,* the time required to make information held in a given storage medium available for computation. For internal (memory) storage, access time is the fastest, measured in microseconds or nanoseconds (millionths or billionths of seconds); for disk storage it is measured in milliseconds (thousandths of seconds), and for magnetic tapes or punched cards it is measured in minutes.

The requirement that information be retained in internal storage for computer processing had been a restricting factor in the size and design of computer programs. However, the development of *virtual storage* has made the information stored on magnetic disks available for processing without the need for specific instructions first to read that information into the memory. With virtual storage the computer operating system monitors the data addresses (locations of stored data) generated by a program while it is being executed. When an address is encountered that is beyond the boundaries of data located in internal storage, the address of the data on disk is calculated and the "block" of data containing the required address is "read" into "core" for processing. Virtual storage thus enables a programmer to design programs without regard for the amount of core available to hold the needed data.

2. The holding of goods in a safe place for future use or sale. Storage within a business concern normally involves either raw materials or parts awaiting incorporation into an end-product, or finished goods awaiting shipment to customers. (See also STORES.) For large quantities of supplies, however, businesses that do not have any or enough warehouses may, like individual consumers, rent space in a public WAREHOUSE. Goods that are expected to remain in storage for a long time are put into relatively inaccessible places, so-called *dead storage,* whereas goods to which the owner needs ready access are put in *live storage,* which tends to be much costlier than dead storage.

store See under RETAIL; also STORAGE, def. 1.

stores In general, the goods or supplie held in a warehouse or other place of storage until they are used. In particular, materials and supplies that will be used by a business for its operations rather than simply being resold to customers (the latter are sometimes called *stock*; see STOCK, def. 2).

straddle

1. Also, *double option, spread*. In the securities trade, a PUT and CALL held at the same time on the same stock. A straddle permits the speculator to protect a holding whether the stock's price goes up or down.

2. SELLING SHORT a security that is equivalent to another security being purchased. For example, suppose Corporation ABC has an agreement to merge with Corporation XYZ that calls for an exchange of two shares of ABC for one share of XYZ. In the market, however, ABC shares are selling for 25 and XYZ shares for 40. The speculator therefore sells short 200 ABC shares and buys 100 shares of XYZ long. If the merger actually takes place, the speculator is certain to make a profit, regardless of what happens to the market price of either security.

straight life insurance See under LIFE INSURANCE.

straight-line method In accounting, a method of calculating the depreciation of a fixed asset so that the asset is considered to lose the same proportion of its total value during each year of its service life. For example, suppose a $15,000 truck has an estimated service life of seven years and a salvage value of $1,000. After deducting salvage value, it is valued at $12,000 after one year, $10,000 after two years, and so on. This method is the simplest way to allocate depreciation and is very widely used. For a variation of it, see under DECLINING BALANCE METHOD.

straight time The normal number of hours or days worked, paid for on the basis of time spent (in dollars per hour) rather than output (see PIECEWORK). See also OVERTIME.

strategic materials Also, *strategic stockpile*. Materials considered essential for national defense. The United States government maintains a stockpile of about 100 materials, including metals, minerals, and agricultural commodities. In time of war, it is believed, many of these materials would not be available on world markets, and in some instances they are never available on the open market, at least not without special arrangements. The strategic stockpile is maintained by the Federal Supply Service of the U.S. General Services Administration.

strategic planning, corporate The process of determining how a business may make the best possible use of its resources in the future. Whereas conventional planning concentrates on making the best use of current resources (employees, capital, customers), strategic planning focuses on ways in which these resources can gradually be changed in order to permit the enterprise to become more successful in the future.

stratified sampling See under RANDOM SAMPLING.

straw boss A slang term for FOREMAN, especially in construction or on a production line. In the past such supervisors often wore straw hats, hence the name.

street name Describing a customer's security (stock, bond) being held by a broker, either for safekeeping or as collateral for margin purchases (see MARGIN, BUYING ON). Such a security then is said to be "carried in a street name."

strike Also, *walkout*. A work stoppage by employees acting together in an attempt to bring pressure on management to give in to their demands concerning wages, working conditions, union recognition, or some other issue. Today the majority of strikes taking place in the United States are called by unions when negotiations for new labor contracts break down. A *wildcat strike*, on the other hand, is one that breaks out during the life of a contract and in violation of a *no-strike clause*, or one that is called by disgruntled workers without the approval of their union leaders (also known as *unauthorized strike*). A *sympathy strike* is one called by a union in support of another union already on strike, rather than because of any disputes of its own. A *jurisdictional strike* occurs when there is a conflict between two unions over the assignment of jobs to members of one or the other. In the United States both sympathy and jurisdictional strikes were outlawed by the Taft-Hartley Act of 1947. In a *sitdown* or *sit-in strike* the workers remain in the plant to prevent management from replacing them; these were common in the 1930s when, in view of mass unemployment during the Great Depression, workers could easily have been replaced.

In 1972 in the United States, 5,010 strikes were called, lasting an average of 24 days and involving 1.7 million workers (about 2.3 per cent of the labor force). The major issue by far was wages. Other issues involved disputes about plant administration, union organization and security, job security, and a variety of contractual matters. Today, strikes tend to be peaceful and orderly. When a union's contract expires and no agreement is reached on a new one, its members may vote to walk out. According to the Taft-Hartley Act, they must notify the employer 60 days before expiration of the contract (a compulsory *cooling-off period*) before they can actually stop work. Usually they will not only leave work but set up a *picket line*, consisting of a group of persons (called *pickets*) who walk up and down in front of the employer's premises carrying signs that publicize their complaint, denounce the employer, and/or try to gain public support; they often are aided by a sound truck broadcasting this information. Pickets may try to prevent customers or employees from entering the premises, either by intimidation or by physical action; such *mass picketing* is usually illegal. While the strike is under way, union and management representatives may con-

Fig. 79 Notable U.S. strikes

Great Railroad Strike	1877	Originally against wage cuts by Baltimore & Ohio. Extended from east coast to Mississippi, involving 60,000 rail workers. Violence at Pittsburgh and Martinsburg, W. Va. Federal troops called in.
Chicago General Strike	1886	General strike for an 8-hour work day, led by Knights of Labor. Unsuccessful.
Homestead Massacre	1892	Strike against Carnegie Steel Co. at Homestead, Pa. Strikers fought Pinkerton detectives, were defeated when state militia was called in.
Pullman Strike	1894	Strike by Eugene V. Debs's American Railway Union (independent) with a boycott on Pullman cars, tying up all midwestern railroads. 3,400 special deputies sworn in and sent to run railroads. Violence quelled by Federal troops. Debs jailed. Strike failed.
Anthracite Coal Strike	1902	Strike by United Mine Workers under John Mitchell against mine owners who refused arbitration. Pres. T. Roosevelt appointed mediators who awarded miners wage increase but refused to recognize union.
Steel Strike	1919	AFL strike against U.S. Steel; abandoned after 3½ months.
Little Steel Strike	1937	Steelworkers' strike against Bethlehem, Inland, Republic, and Youngstown Sheet & Tube. Strikers demonstrating against Republic in South Chicago fired on by police ("Memorial Day Massacre"). Strike unsuccessful.
Bituminous Coal Strike	1946	United Mine Workers strike against mine operators. Pres. Truman seized mines. Union fined.
Steel Strike	1959	Steelworkers strike for 116 days.
New York Newspaper Strike	1962–6	Citywide strike shut down all New York papers from Dec. 8 to March 31.
General Motors Strike	1970	Auto workers shut down General Motors for more than 3 months.

tinue negotiating in an attempt to settle their differences; if they cannot and the strike drags on, they may resort to MEDIATION or ARBITRATION. The striking workers meanwhile live on savings, credit, and from stipends of the union's *strike fund* (if it has one), accumulated from union dues. Clearly the resumption of work is both to their best interest and to management's.

Strikes in the United States date back to the late 18th century, but the great era of violent strikes did not begin until the development of strong national unions, after the Civil War. Among the earliest were the Railroad Strikes of 1877, the first against the Baltimore & Ohio Railroad to protest wage cuts and then spreading to numerous other lines. Mobs tore up tracks, Federal troops were sent into ten states, and many persons were killed. Both management and strikers contributed to the violence and bloodshed. Employers hired detectives and armed guards to break up union meetings and picket lines. Strikers countered with armed groups of their own; the most notorious of these were the *Molly Maguires*, a secret miners' group in eastern Pennsylvania that enforced its demands by murdering some of the employers. (See also Fig. 79.)

Today there is much less propensity to call a strike than in the early days of unionization. Some major industries now have an established tradition of successful collective bargaining, and in others increased automation and less reliance on human labor have reduced the effectiveness of strikes. Also, union leaders have tended to become more conservative, particularly in the upper echelons of national unions, and hence are less prone to call a strike that might ultimately threaten their own position. See also BOYCOTT; GENERAL STRIKE; LABOR UNION.

strikebreaker

1. An employee hired to replace a worker out on strike. See FINK; SCAB.

2. A person hired to disrupt union meetings, break up picket lines, and otherwise interfere with a strike. See also GOON.

structural equation In econometrics, a mathematical representation of a causal relationship among statistical variables. For example, the quantity of fresh corn that consumers will buy (or demand) is likely to depend on the price they must pay and on their income. The quantity that farmers will produce (or supply) will probably depend on the price they will receive and on the amount of rainfall. And the quantity demanded will in the end be equal to the quantity supplied. These three relationships, expressed as equations, constitute the structural equations of a simple MODEL of the corn market. See also ENDOGENOUS VARIABLE; REDUCED FORM EQUATION.

structural unemployment Unemployment resulting from changes in the overall economy, principally changes in population, government policies, technology (see also TECHNOLOGICAL UNEMPLOYMENT), and consumer tastes, but not from the ups and downs of the business cycle (which can cause CYCLICAL UNEMPLOYMENT). For example, a declining birth rate in the 1970s resulted in increasing unemployment among teachers; reduced government spending for defense caused massive unemployment in defense-related industries; and the fashion for longer hair among men and boys led to many unemployed or underemployed barbers. See also FRICTIONAL UNEMPLOYMENT.

stuffer A piece of advertising literature enclosed in an envelope containing other material already being mailed. Department stores often include such ads with their customers' monthly bills.

subcontract See under CONTRACTOR.

subdivision A piece of land that is divided into a number of parcels or lots for purposes of sale and/or development. In many communities the subdivision of land is subject to strict local regulations, particularly with regard to utilities, streets, curbs, gutters, sidewalks, sewers, etc.

sublease Also, *sublet*. See under LEASE.

subpoena A legal order or writ commanding an individual to appear and testify in legal proceedings.

subrogation The substitution of one person for another with respect to a lawful claim or right. For example, suppose a debtor defaults on a promissory note, and the creditor, after trying all possible means to collect, collects the debt from a guarantor (see SURETY BOND for further explanation). Under subrogation the guarantor may now sue the debtor to recover his loss. Similarly, if Brown claims fire insurance from XYZ Company because her house burned down and her neighbor, White, was responsible for setting the fire, XYZ Company may sue White to recover the loss he caused Brown.

subroutine See under PROGRAMMING.

subscription

1. An agreement to purchase a periodical, a series of theater or concert tickets, or some other item to be used over a period of time. Since payment in full usually must accompany the subscription order, subscriptions are a form of advance financing.

2. An agreement to buy a security. Since the buyer provides capital in exchange for the stock, the money paid for the stock is called *subscription capital*. Similarly, RIGHTS to buy a new issue are sometimes called *subscription rights*.

subsidiary A business firm that is controlled by another company, called the *parent company*, which owns most or all of its stock (in the case of all the stock, it is termed a *wholly owned subsidiary*). Unlike a company branch or division, a subsidiary is itself a corporation, with its own charter, tax liabilities, etc. It is formed either when the parent company acquires a controlling interest in an existing firm (see MERGER) or when a new corporation is formed, with the parent company owning a controlling interest (see CONSOLIDATION).

subsidiary coin   See under COIN.

subsidy   Government support of an individual, company, or industry, allegedly to encourage the development of productive activities that are inadequately supported but considered essential or desirable. Some subsidies do fulfill this purpose, but others serve chiefly to confer favors on politically powerful or other groups at the expense of the rest of the community. Subsidies may be *direct*, in the form of outright gifts (such as grants of public lands, Treasury payments, or price supports), but more often they are *indirect*, in the form of tax rebates or exemptions or reductions, free services, government buying or selling of goods or services at highly advantageous (to business) prices, cheap credit, protective tariffs and other shelters from competition, etc. Direct subsidies are financed by taxpayers; indirect subsidies often are financed by the consumer, who as a result pays higher prices. In some cases subsidies are essential for the maintenance of an undertaking (though critics point out that such an enterprise still may not be worth the cost); among them, in the United States, are crop insurance, local airlines, and shipbuilding. In other cases subsidies may not be essential for an industry's survival (though they may have been at one time), but powerful lobbies continue to pressure legislators in their favor; among these (in the United States) are petroleum (see DEPLETION ALLOWANCE), trucking (subsidized through highway construction), and rural electric systems. Still other subsidies constitute a form of social WELFARE payment; among these are school lunch programs, FOOD STAMPS, aid to veterans, and Medicare. The term "subsidy" occasionally is used for payments made by the central government to state governments (and the state to local governments) but this kind of support is more often called revenue sharing or a GRANT-IN-AID (def. 1). See also AGRICULTURE, AID TO; PARITY PRICE; PRESSURE GROUP.

subsistence   The minimum food, clothing, and shelter a person or family needs for survival. In farming, a *subsistence crop* is just sufficient to feed the farmer and his family, as opposed to a *cash crop*, which exceeds such needs (and can be sold for cash). For the *subsistence theory of wages*, see IRON LAW OF WAGES.

substitutes   See COMPLEMENTS AND SUBSTITUTES.

substitution, law of   Also, *law of diminishing substitution*. The principle that the scarcer a good, the greater its substitution value. For example, suppose a boy has a clothing allowance earmarked for shirts and pants. He doesn't care whether he divides the money equally between shirts and pants (three shirts, three pants) or unequally (four shirts, two pants or two shirts, four pants). Suppose, however, he buys five shirts and one pair of pants. Pants now are a scarce item in his wardrobe. He might no longer be willing to trade pants for a shirt. He might possibly agree to trade his only pair of pants for two shirts or, more likely, for three of four shirts. The substitution value of the scarce good (pants) has now risen, from one to three or four. See also INDIFFERENCE CURVE.

substitution effect   The effect on the overall demand for a product of a price change that results in users' substituting a cheaper product for it. Thus, if the price of coffee rises substantially and other prices remain constant, many coffee drinkers may switch to tea, thereby changing the total demand for coffee. Similarly, if a factory owner substitutes a machine tool that operates automatically for one that requires 3 high-salaried operators to run it 24 hours a day, sooner or later cost of production will decrease owing to this substitution, and the owner will either make a bigger profit or pass on the saving to customers through lower prices (or both). See also INCOME EFFECT.

suggestion box   A system whereby an organization invites criticism of its operations and suggestions for improvement from employees, customers, and others with whom it deals. Some firms actually use a box in which written anonymous comments can be placed.

summons   See under ACTION.

sum-of-digits method Also, *sum-of-the-years digits method.* A method of calculating the depreciation of a fixed asset so that the highest depreciation is charged to the early years of its life. It resembles the DECLINING BALANCE METHOD, except that it eventually reduces the asset's value to zero. The amount of annual depreciation is calculated by assigning a numerical value to each year of the asset's expected service life. For a $15,000 truck with an expected use of seven years and a salvage value of $1,000, the first year is given the digit 7, the second year 6, and so on. The digit for each year is then divided by the sum of all the digits for the truck's life ($7 + 6 + 5 + 4 + 3 + 2 + 1 = 28$) to determine the proportion of its total value by which it has depreciated during that year. In the first year depreciation will be 7/28 of the total value ($15,000 − $1,000 × 7/28 = $3,500), in the second year 6/28, or $3,000, and so on.

sunk cost In accounting, a cost that grows out of a past, irrevocable decision. A typical example is a fixed asset, such as a machine, that has become obsolete and whose book value therefore cannot be recovered. See also OUT-OF-POCKET COST.

sunspot-weather theory An attempt to attribute the ups and downs of the business cycle to the sunspot cycle, which allegedly influences weather, which in turn influences crops. When sunspots are at a maximum, weather is poor and crops fail; when they are at a minimum, bumper crops lower food prices, which leaves surplus income to be spent on other goods, thus stimulating industrial production. Another explanation is that sunspots produce alternating waves of optimism and pessimism in the business community, which overinvests and underinvests accordingly. The best-known proponent of the sunspot theory was W. S. JEVONS.

supermarket A large grocery store, independent or part of a chain, that sells chiefly food and grocery items at relatively low prices in large volume, mostly on a self-service basis. Begun in the 1930s by independent American food retailers, supermarkets soon were being built by the leading grocery chains, which still dominate the grocery business in the United States (see CHAIN STORE). By the 1960s they were beginning to stock nu-

merous nonfood products, chiefly drugs, household utensils, hardware items, and garden supplies, all of which command a higher profit margin than the average 1 per cent after-tax net profit on groceries. In the early 1970s there were more than 28,000 supermarkets in the United States, accounting for about 14 per cent of all grocery stores and handling 66.7 per cent of all grocery sales. Because they need high sales volume in order to make a profit at all, most supermarkets require large floor space to display their wares and adequate storage space for reserve stock. Most supermarkets also provide parking areas and check-cashing facilities. In that both of them offer low prices, a wide variety of goods, self-service, and well-known brand items, the supermarket and large DISCOUNT HOUSE (def. 1) have much in common. In fact, the very similarity has led some discount houses to add grocery departments. See also MASS MERCHANDISER.

supernumerary income See DISCRETIONARY INCOME.

superseniority The device of giving union officials and shop stewards top seniority in their jobs for layoff purposes regardless of length of employment. The chief purpose is to prevent the undermining of a union's strength through layoffs of union leaders with low SENIORITY, which otherwise might even be deliberately arranged by an employer who wishes to weaken the union.

supervisor In business and industry, a person who oversees the work of others (called *subordinates*) and has the authority to direct it. Depending on the supervisor's own rank in the organization, he or she may be empowered to hire, promote, discipline, or dismiss subordinates, or to recommend such action to higher-level supervisors.

supplemental unemployment benefits Also, *SUB.* See GUARANTEED ANNUAL WAGE; also under LAYOFF.

supplementary cost In accounting, any cost of a product other than direct labor and direct materials, such as allocated OVERHEAD. See also PRIME COST, def. 1.

supplier Also, *vendor.* In business and industry, a person or firm that regularly sells its goods or services to another. In the retail business a supplier is also called a *resource* or *source.*

supply In economic theory, the willingness of producers to sell a given amount of goods or services for a particular price at a particular time. The relationship of amounts of goods that will be sold at various prices can be charted in the form of a *supply schedule* (see Fig. 80) or it can be depicted on a graph (see Fig. 81). As a rule, the higher the price, the more producers wish to sell, and the lower the price, the more reluctant they are to sell. However, the supply of some goods simply cannot be increased over the short term, no matter how high the price rises, although, given enough time, the supply of even very scarce commodities (such as gold and platinum) can usually be increased if the price is high enough. The degree to which supply responds to price changes is called its ELASTICITY (see def. 2). See also DEMAND.

supply curve A graphic representation of the prices commanded by some commodity at various quantities of supply. For example, to show the supply of soybeans, prices are indicated on the Y-axis (vertical axis) and quantities supplied on the X-axis (horizontal axis). The supply curve normally slopes upward and to the right, showing a definite relationship between price and supply: the higher the price, the more producers will supply. In a competitive market, which exists for many agricultural products, the intersection of the supply curve with the DEMAND CURVE is the point of market EQUILIBRIUM and, in theory at least, indicates the market price.

Fig. 80. Supply schedule for soybeans

Price per Bushel	Quantity Sellers Will Supply per Month
$1	0
2	7,500,000
3	12,500,000
4	17,500,000
5	20,000,000
6	22,500,000

supported price A price that is artifically kept high; see under PARITY PRICE; PEGGING.

suppressed inflation Also, *repressed inflation.* The suppression of an increase in the general price level through price control and rationing. During World War II, the United States economy was at full employment and real income rose substantially, but the supply of consumer goods was limited owing to war production priorities. Left unrestricted, prices of scarce goods would have risen sky-high, but the government imposed both price controls and rationing to ensure fair distribution of what goods were available. As soon as controls and rationing were stopped, prices of many goods did rise, indicating that inflation had indeed been suppressed.

surety bond A kind of insurance that a loan will be repaid in which a third person, called the *surety,*

Fig. 81. Supply curve

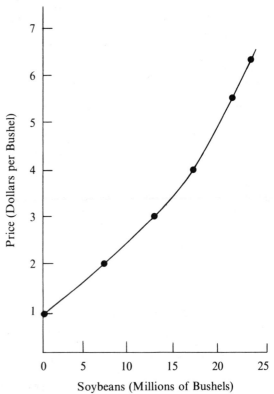

Price (Dollars per Bushel) / Soybeans (Millions of Bushels)

promises that it will. If the debtor defaults, the surety is primarily liable for the debt. A surety bond thus differs somewhat from a GUARANTY, in which the third person (called *guarantor*) also backs a debt but is only secondarily liable; if the debtor defaults, the creditor first must try to collect from the principal, bringing suit if necessary. Only if after all possible effort the debt is still unpaid may the creditor demand payment from or sue the guarantor. A messenger who carries valuables, for example, may be protected by means of a surety bond (and then is said to be *bonded*). See also FIDELITY BOND.

surplus

1. Also, *surplus value*. In economic theory, any earnings of one of the FACTORS OF PRODUCTION in excess of what was needed to draw it into production. See also *consumer's surplus*, under A. MARSHALL; SELLERS' SURPLUS.

2. In Marxist theory, the SURPLUS LABOR AND VALUE THEORY.

3. In accounting and finance, the equity of shareholders in a corporation in excess of the par value or stated value of the shares of capital stock. It includes both earned surplus (or RETAINED EARNINGS) and PAID-IN SURPLUS.

4. An excess of revenues over expenditures, such as a balance of payments surplus or a budget surplus.

surplus labor and value theory Also, *doctrine of surplus value*. Karl Marx's version of the LABOR THEORY OF VALUE. According to Marx, the absolute value of a commodity is created by the amount of average labor that goes into producing it. Therefore any rewards other than actual wages, such as profits, interest, or rents, constitute *surplus value*, and the difference between wages and surplus value represents the measure of exploitation of workers by the owners of capital.

surtax An extra tax, levied in addition to a normal tax. It may be applied to incomes at the top of the scale in order to make an income tax more PROGRESSIVE. In the United States the personal income tax used to be based on a fixed percentage of all incomes, with a surtax imposed on higher incomes; today the surtax is incorporated into the general tax rate. The excess profits tax periodically levied on corporations similarly is a surtax.

survey A series of questions designed to elicit the respondent's views about an issue, product, company, business outlook, political candidate, etc. Surveys customarily are distributed to a sample of persons considered representative of a given group, and the answers, when tabulated, presumably supply information about the views of that group. Surveys are used principally in various kinds of research, such as market research. See also PANEL.

suspense account An account in which items are carried temporarily. For example, a claim against an insurance company might be carried in a suspense account pending its final disposition.

sustainable growth A steady rate of growth in per capita real income or per capita real gross national product that can continue over a long term. In the 1970s such a rate was thought to be about 2.7 per cent per year for the United States, since at this rate increased employment would more than keep pace with population growth. See also GROWTH, ECONOMIC; STAGNATION.

swap agreement See CURRENCY SWAP.

sweatshop A factory or other shop where employees are paid a very low wage, usually on a PIECEWORK basis, and work under crowded, unhealthful conditions. Sweatshops were particularly prevalent in the garment industry until they were eliminated by stringent labor laws.

sweetheart agreement A labor contract negotiated by a dishonest union official in collusion with the employer, so that its terms are weighted in the employer's favor.

swing credits Margins within which the parties to a payments agreement may incur a deficit without having to settle their account. Bilateral payments agreements (see under EXCHANGE CONTROLS) include a provision for swing credits to allow for temporary imbalances in trading.

swing shift   See under SHIFT, def. 1.

switch order   Also, *contingent order.* In the securities trade, an order to buy (or sell) one stock and sell (or buy) another at a stipulated difference between their prices.

symbolic language   See under PROGRAMMING.

sympathy strike   See under STRIKE.

syndicalism   A doctrine that advocates the abolition of private property and the state, and the reorganization of society into associations of producers, called *syndicates.* Each industry would have its syndicate, run by the workers of that industry and governing its members in all their activities as producers. Social reorganization would be accomplished by direct action on the part of workers, taking the form of general strikes and of sabotage against capitalist employers. The chief proponent of syndicalism, which combines features of both ANARCHISM and SOCIALISM, was Georges Sorel (1847–1922), a French social philosopher. The doctrine flourished chiefly in Europe's Latin countries, especially France, from about 1900 to 1920, losing most of its impact after World War I. In the United States the INDUSTRIAL WORKERS OF THE WORLD (organized 1905) was a syndicalist union.

syndicate
1. A group of individuals or companies that join together for some business enterprise, usually of a financial nature.
2. Also, *purchase group, underwriting syndicate.* An organization of investment bankers formed to market a new issue of securities or a large block of an outstanding issue. This practice is very common, since often too much capital is required for a single investment banker to handle the issue alone. Syndicates may be incorporated, in which case they legally resemble any other corporation; when not incorporated, they usually take the form of a PARTNERSHIP.

system
1. In a COMPUTER, the executive or operating system that controls its operating environment, that is, scheduling of programs, resource allocation, dynamic memory swapping, and similar activities.
2. Also, *information system.* A set of computer programs designed and written to carry out a specific process or procedure, such as payroll or sales accounting. See also MANAGEMENT INFORMATION SYSTEM.
3. In business management, an organized collection of parts, or *subsystems,* that are united by regular interaction. For example, the various production departments of a manufacturing firm can be said to make up a production system. See also SYSTEMS ANALYSIS.

systematic sampling   In statistics, a method of sampling in which a fixed sampling interval is chosen and used, beginning with a unit drawn at random. For example, a quality control inspector might decide to check every tenth unit of a batch of parts, beginning with one drawn at random. Systematic sampling is widely used, both because it is economical and because it often is more feasible than RANDOM SAMPLING.

systems analysis   Any analytic study of a very broad and complex problem that calls for deciding on a preferred course of action among many alternatives. (See also SYSTEM, def. 3.) Systems analysis in effect is a broader and less purely quantitative version of OPERATIONS RESEARCH. Whereas the latter deals with such problems as how many delivery trucks taking what routes would best serve a company, systems analysis considers such questions as how national resources should be allocated for space exploration, or what program can be developed to relieve poverty and urban blight simultaneously. Systems analysts use the MODEL and simulation to test various alternatives.

Since about 1960 the so-called *systems approach* has become popular in business management. It involves viewing a business firm as a system in terms of input and output, an approach intended to put decision-making on a more objective and quantitative basis. Each department or project becomes a subsystem related to the main system. Instead of the traditional organization with largely static

Fig. 82. A materials subsystem for a given product

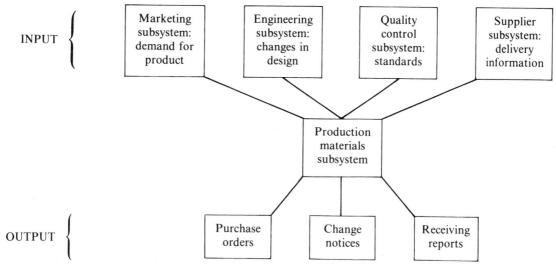

departments, each of which functions independently, the systems approach is essentially dynamic, taking into account the interaction of the various activities. Since such fluidity often requires prompt reaction, the systems approach is almost impossible to apply without the aid of a computer, which can process and transmit needed information very fast. Fig. 82 shows a materials subsystem for a given product, indicating the input from other subsystems and its own output.

systems approach See under SYSTEMS ANALYSIS.

systems programming See under PROGRAMMING.

T

Tableau économique   See under F. QUESNAY.

T-account   See under ACCOUNT, def. 1.

Taft-Hartley Act   See under LABOR LAWS; also under UNFAIR LABOR PRACTICES.

take-home pay   Also, *paycheck.* The portion of an employee's earnings actually paid in cash, after the deduction of withholding tax, social security, union dues, and similar fees. Take-home pay, particularly for high-salaried employees, may amount to no more than about two-thirds of the total salary, or *gross pay.* The closest statistical estimate of take-home pay in the United States, compiled monthly by the Bureau of Labor Statistics, computes the *spendable average weekly earnings* of two classes of manufacturing production worker, those with no dependents and those with three dependents. However, it actually is an overestimate, since it is based on gross pay minus Federal income tax and social security and does not allow for other deductions (union dues, pension contribution, insurance, etc.).

takeoff period   In theories of economic growth, a period characterized by accelerated investment, the development of manufacturing, and the gradual emergence of an INFRASTRUCTURE to support rapid economic expansion. The American economist Walt W. Rostow cited as takeoff periods the years 1850–75 in Germany, 1876–1900 in Japan, 1950–60 in India and China, 1783–1803 in Great Britain, and 1835–60 in France and the United States. In effect the takeoff period establishes the climate for rapid economic progress.

takeover   See MERGER.

414

tangible asset   See under ASSET.

tape   See MAGNETIC TAPE; PUNCHED TAPE. For ticker tape, see under TICKER.

tare   The weight of the packaging, wrapping, container, or other material used in shipping goods. Tare weight plus NET WEIGHT make up gross weight.

tariff

1. A tax levied by a national government on goods that are imported or, less often, exported across its borders. The amount collected is called the *duty* or *customs duty.* There are two principal reasons for imposing a tariff: (1) to raise revenue (*revenue tariff*); (2) to discourage imports in order to protect a nation's domestic industry or favor its balance of international payments (*protective tariff*). At one time all tariffs were revenue tariffs, originating as they did in the tolls collected by feudal lords and sovereigns on goods that moved into or through their domain. After the development of strong national states, however, tariffs tended to be principally protective. The imposition of protective and preferential tariffs was a fundamental policy of MERCANTILISM and was opposed by the economists of the CLASSICAL SCHOOL, who claimed that interfering with the market mechanism by protecting domestic industries promoted inefficiency and was detrimental to general economic welfare. Advocates of protectionism argue that exactly the right tariff—a so-called *optimum tariff*—can benefit a country's trading position and balance of payments, and protect a new enterprise ("infant industry") until it can compete on its own.

   Though protectionism in one form or another was the rule from the 17th to the mid-20th century, its drawbacks were also recognized. Internal trade barriers had existed in France until the French Revolution (though COLBERT, during his ministry, had tried to abolish them a century earlier). The German states, too, suffered from innumerable trade barriers, a situation corrected during the 19th century (1818–71) through the ZOLLVEREIN (customs union) movement. Only since World War II, however, has there been strong international sentiment against high tariffs and for freer trade. In 1948 some agreement began to be reached at Geneva concerning fair policies governing trade barriers (see GENERAL AGREEMENT ON TARIFFS AND TRADE, or GATT), and in the postwar period a number of free-trade organizations came into being, among them Benelux, the Common Market, and the European Free Trade Association. (See also CUSTOMS UNION; FREE TRADE AREA.)

There has been some return to revenue tariffs in the form of the *export tariff*; Canada, for example, has taxed crude oil exported to the United States, Jamaica has levied a tariff on the export of alumina, etc. Agreements such as GATT notwithstanding, tariffs still are used to discriminate against some nations (*retaliatory tariff*) and favor others (*preferential tariff*), or to offset an export bounty paid by the exporting country (*countervailing tariff*). Examples of the first include the notorious "chicken war" of the 1960s, when the Common Market nations raised chicken tariffs to deter American poultry exports to Germany and to favor Dutch, German, and French chicken farmers. The United States responded by raising tariffs on three specialized items: potato starch, a Dutch export; the Volkswagen Microbus, a German car; and cognac, made only in France. An important preferential tariff agreement was the Empire preference system set up by the *Ottawa Agreements* of 1932, involving Great Britain and the self-governing members of the Commonwealth in a system of mutually favorable tariffs. Though this and other colonial preference systems were abolished or greatly modified when the nations in question entered the Common Market, preferential tariffs still exist. One such method is use of the *most-favored nation clause,* which binds two nations signing a commercial treaty to confer on one another any favorable trade concession (such as tariff cuts) they may in the future grant to some

other nation. In the United States the U.S. Tariff Commission, an independent Federal agency created in 1916, serves in an advisory and fact-finding capacity on foreign trade, particularly concerning imports that pose a potential threat to domestic producers. For more on American tariff policies, see TARIFF OF ABOMINATIONS. See also AD VALOREM; ANTIDUMPING TARIFF; CUSTOMS BROKER; FREE LIST; FREE PORT; SMUGGLING.

2. A schedule of rates or charges, particularly transportation rates. For freight rates, see under FREIGHT.

Tariff of Abominations An American tariff enacted in 1828 that was the most extreme of the protective tariffs enacted from 1816 on (prior tariffs had been chiefly for revenue; see TARIFF, def. 1). It called for an AD VALOREM duty of 50 per cent as well as a specific duty of 4 cents per pound on raw wool, a 45 per cent ad valorem duty on most woolen goods, and a sharp increase in duties on pig and bar iron and on hemp. By 1828 dispute over tariffs had become sharply sectional, with the South generally opposing protection and the rest of the states favoring it. Henry Clay was the most important advocate of protection. In addition to shielding America's "infant industries" from foreign competition, Clay believed that, with the loss of European markets during the Napoleonic wars, American farmers needed larger industrial centers at home to market their output, a program he called the *American System.* The largely agricultural South, however, wanted cheap manufactured imports. Actually, though the Tariff of 1828 was proposed by protectionists, it was supported also by other politicians who considered it so extreme that they were sure it would be defeated. To their surprise it was passed, but it remained so unpopular that it was awarded its nickname. In 1832 a new bill was passed that abrogated most of its provisions and in effect restored tariffs to the levels set in 1842. The new law still was protective, and in November 1832 South Carolina passed its Nullification Ordinance, declaring the tariffs of 1828 *and* 1832 "null and void." President Andrew Jackson took an uncompromising stand on national unity, however, and Clay introduced a compromise tariff to which both sides agreed in 1833. U.S. tariffs from 1789 to 1962 are listed in Fig. 83, page 416.

Fig. 83. U.S. tariffs, 1789–1962

Enacted	Name	Provisions
1789		Specific duties on 30 commodities, including molasses, hemp, steel, and nails; ad valorem duties (average rate, 8½%) on listed articles; 5% duty on all other goods (raised to 7½% in 1792); 10% reduction on duty if imported in U.S.-built or U.S.-owned ship.
1812		Ad valorem level rose to 12½%.
1814		Ad valorem level rose to about 25%.
1816		Ad valorem duties of 30% on paper, leather, hats, and other manufactures; 25% on most woolen, cotton and iron products; 25 cents per yard on cheap cottons; 15% on all other commodities.
1818		Higher rates on iron manufactures; 25% on woolens and cotton extended to 1826.
1824		Higher rates on iron, lead, glass, hemp, cotton bagging; 25% minimum on cotton and woolens raised to 33⅓%; raw wool rates raised by 15%.
1828	Tariff of Abominations	Ad valorem duty of 50% plus 4 cents per lb. on raw wool; 45% ad valorem on most woolens; higher rates on iron, hemp, sailcloth, molasses.
1832		No duties on cheap raw wool and flax; higher rate on woolen goods.
1833	Compromise Tariff	No duty on worsted goods and linens; gradual reduction of all rates higher than 20% to 20% by 1842.
1842		Return to 1832 tariffs, rates averaging between 23% and 35%.
1846	Walker Tariff	Change from specific to ad valorem duties; general lowering of rates, some items duty-free; classed all items A, B, C, D (A, luxury, 100% tax; B, semi-luxury, 40%; C and D, commercial, 5%–30%); introduced warehouse storage of goods until duty paid.
1857		General average reduced to 20%; enlarged duty-free list.
1861	Morrill Tariff	Change from ad valorem to specific duties; most duties raised by 5% to 10%; with later revisions (by 1869) raised most items to average rate of 47%.
1870		130 new duty-free articles (most raw materials) and some rates reduced.
1872		Reduced by 10% rates on manufactures (but most restored by 1875).
1883		Lowered rates by 5%.
1890	McKinley Tariff	Raised average rate to 49.5%.
1894	Wilson-Gorman Tariff	Removed duties on wool, copper, lumber; lowered average rate to 39.9%.
1897	Dingley Tariff	Raised average rate to 57%; raised duties on raw and manufactured wool; restored duty on hides.
1909	Payne-Aldrich Tariff	Lowered rates to average of about 38%.

Fig. 83. U.S. tariffs, 1789–1962 (*continued*)

Enacted	Name	Provisions
1913	Underwood Tariff	Lowered general rate to about 30%; removed duties on more than 100 items, including iron, steel, raw wool, and (in 1916) sugar.
1921	Emergency Tariff	Raised rates on most agricultural products.
1922	Fordney-McCumber Tariff	Exceeded 1909 rates on manufactured goods by up to 25%, raising average rate to 52%; raised rates on agricultural products.
1931	Hawley-Smoot Tariff	Raised agricultural raw material rates from 38% to 49%, other commodities from 31% to 34%; special protection to sugar and textiles.
1934	Reciprocal Trade Agreements Act	Authorized U.S. President to negotiate tariff reductions up to 50%.
1962	Trade Expansion Act	Further extended President's discretionary powers, to point of waiving tariffs in certain cases.

tax A compulsory payment to a local, state, or central government, usually made on a regular basis (annually, quarterly, or other). Taxes constitute the chief source of government revenue. In the United States in the 1970s about one-fourth of the average family's income was paid in taxes. Half the Federal government's tax revenues came from the personal INCOME TAX and another one-fourth from the CORPORATION INCOME TAX, whereas almost half the revenues of local and state governments came from the PROPERTY TAX. Other important kinds of tax are the DEATH TAX, EMPLOYMENT TAX, EXCISE TAX, SALES TAX, customs duties (see TARIFF, def. 1), and HIGHWAY USER TAX.

Every tax is made up of two elements, a *base*, consisting of the object to be taxed (personal income, tobacco, land, etc.), and a *rate structure*, indicating how the base is to be taxed. A base may be taxed at a *flat rate* (so much per $1,000 of property valuation, so much per sales dollar, etc.), or it may involve a complicated graduated structure (as with progressive income taxes).

Taxation has a profound effect on the economy as a whole and hence is a critical element of FISCAL POLICY. By decreasing or increasing taxes, the central government can either increase or decrease spendable income. However, the precise effect of a tax varies, depending largely on who ultimately pays it. Some taxes are *direct*, their *burden* falling largely on the person on whom the tax is levied—that is, he or she pays the tax—rather than being passed on to someone else. The personal income tax is direct, being paid by the earner of income and no one else. Other taxes are *indirect*, that is, they can readily be *shifted* to someone else; an excise tax on liquor levied against producers and distributors is generally passed on to consumers in the form of higher prices. The final effect of a tax, sometimes called its *incidence*, governs how the tax redistributes (*shifts*) income—from wage earner to central government, from property owner to local government, from consumer to manufacturer, etc. In establishing any tax system, therefore, incidence is a primary consideration, with *fairness* often being the ultimate goal. Since the time of Adam Smith, who set forth *canons* (rules) *of taxation* (in *Wealth of Nations*, 1776), economists have proposed various principles on which tax systems should be based. Smith suggested the ABILITY-TO-PAY PRINCIPLE; two other such principles are the BENEFITS-RECEIVED PRINCIPLE and the SOCIAL WELFARE PRINCIPLE.

tax accounting A branch of accounting concerned with keeping records for tax purposes, setting up accounts for paying taxes, computing Federal, state, and local taxes for individuals and businesses, and preparing tax returns. Tax accountants are most often employed to advise businesses concerning the probable effect on tax liability of a variety of business decisions and how to minimize that liability.

tax anticipation bill Any of several kinds of short-term, interest-bearing credit instrument sold by the United States Treasury and by some state and local governments, principally to business firms, which may use them to pay their taxes. Treasury tax anticipation bills are sold at auction, at a discount, and mature when taxes are due. For the buyer they have the advantage of earning interest; for the seller they in effect bring in tax revenues at regular intervals and in a more even flow.

tax base See under TAX.

tax bond See under BOND, def. 1.

tax burden See under TAX.

Tax Court, United States Formerly, *U.S. Board of Tax Appeals*. A special court that tries and adjudicates tax disputes between individuals or firms and the Internal Revenue Service. Its decisions are subject to review by the U.S. Court of Appeals for the District of Columbia, and thereafter by the Supreme Court.

tax credit An expenditure that may be deducted from an American taxpayer's tax liability, that is, from the total amount owed to the government. It thus differs from other kinds of TAX DEDUCTION, which are subtracted from taxable income *before* the tax liability is calculated. For example, tax credits are allowed for any foreign tax an individual has paid on income from abroad. Also, from time to time Congress has passed laws allowing an *investment tax credit*, whereby businesses are allowed to deduct a given percentage of the cost of additional investment in plant and equipment from their tax liability. For example, if a company spent $1 million on additional equipment, it might be able to deduct 7 per cent, or $70,000, from its taxes.

tax deduction An expenditure that may legally be deducted from taxable income by taxpayers. See under INCOME TAX; also TAX CREDIT.

tax equalization Any attempt by a local unit of government, such as a county or state, to apportion property assessments equitably among its tax districts. In the case of property taxes, the most important single source of local revenues, some districts may try to undervalue property in order to reduce the share of tax revenues they must pay to the country or state. To prevent this, the central unit may appoint a board of equalization to determine the total valuation for each taxing district, whose assessment then is brought in line with those of other districts.

tax equity The fairness of any tax system, necessary both to enlist voluntary compliance on the part of taxpayers and to attempt a reasonable distribution of the tax burden. For horizontal equity, see under ABILITY-TO-PAY PRINCIPLE.

tax evasion Illegal avoidance of tax payments. It differs from *tax avoidance,* which simply means manipulating finances in order to take advantages of tax loopholes, in that it may involve falsifying accounts, failing to declare taxable income, or other forms of deceit. See also DELINQUENT TAX.

tax exemption
1. A specific sum that an American taxpayer may deduct from taxable income for him- or herself and for each dependent, the precise amount being determined by tax law. See under INCOME TAX.
2. Also, *tax-exempt*. Certain kinds of income not subject to income tax. Included for American taxpayers are income from state and municipal bonds, social security payments, workmen's compensation, gifts and dividends up to specified sums, and veterans' pensions.

tax-exempt security An interest-bearing SECURITY wholly or partly exempt from U.S. Federal income tax. The most important are municipal, state, and other kinds of government bond.

tax haven Any locality or nation that levies very low taxes, or none at all on foreigners. For example, because Liechtenstein and Andorra, two tiny European nations, have no income tax or other taxes, many wealthy foreign businesses and individuals have made them their legal residence, thus avoiding taxes. Foreigners also sometimes deposit illegally made profits in Swiss banks, which are not required to disclose their clients' assets.

tax incidence   See under TAX.

tax lien   A government claim on property for which taxes have not been paid when due. In the United States such claims are governed by various state laws, in some cases taking effect immediately and in others only after a prescribed interval. In extreme cases the property reverts to the government. See also LIEN.

tax loophole   A legal provision that can be used to reduce one's tax liability. Such provisions may be unintentional discrepancies in the law, or they may be intended to benefit one or another industry or group (as, for example, the oil DEPLETION ALLOWANCE). Loopholes include various devices whereby capital gains (which command a lower tax rate than other forms of income) can be maximized and other income minimized, the formation of holding companies to create more deductions, and the creation of trusts for members of a family. See also TAX EVASION; also, under INCOME TAX.

tax-loss carryback   Also, *tax-loss carryforward.* A legal provision allowing businesses to apply operating losses to previous or future years showing a profit. The time period for which losses can be so transferred has varied with changes in U.S. tax laws; in 1970, for example, it was three years for carrybacks and five years for carryforwards.

taxpayer
   1. In real estate, a property (such as a parking lot) used so as to produce enough income to pay the property taxes on the land it occupies.
   2. Any person or firm that pays taxes, particularly INCOME TAX.

tax rebate   A partial refund to taxpayers of taxes already paid, usually part of a program of tax reduction to counter a business recession.

tax sharing   The practice of a state or central government levying a tax and sharing its proceeds with a local government (county, town), often in proportion to the origin of tax receipts. Thus, if 20 per cent of the total tax receipts came from County A and the state planned to share revenue on a 50-50 basis, County A would receive 10 per cent of the total.

tax shelter   A device whereby a taxpayer may reinvest earnings on capital without paying income tax on them. Examples include company and individual pension plans, contributions to which are not considered income until they are paid out after retirement, and life insurance policies, where the interest earned on each policy is allowed to accrue without being considered taxable income.

Taylor, Frederick W.   An American management engineer (1856–1915) considered the founder of MANAGEMENT SCIENCE, which for a time was also called "Taylorism." Taylor began his working career in a Philadelphia machine shop, where he rose to foreman, and then worked in the steel industry. One of the earliest conductors of time studies (see TIME AND MOTION STUDY), Taylor also advocated standardization of tools and work movements, a differential rate for piecework (to motivate workers), the use of routing systems for work-in-process, and careful cost estimating. He also believed that optimum efficiency could be attained only with friendly cooperation between management and workers, and he devised a system of graduated staff supervision whereby the lines of communication would be kept open.

tear sheet   A page torn from a periodical (newspaper, magazine, etc.), used as proof to advertisers that a particular advertisement actually appeared.

technical aid   See under FOREIGN AID.

technically strong   Describing a market where prices are steadily rising and the volume of sales is heavy while they rise and light when they temporarily decline. Conversely, the term *technically weak* refers to a market where prices are steadily declining and sales volume is heavy on the down side and light when prices temporarily rise. For another measure of market strength, see SHORT INTEREST.

technocracy Control of society and the economy by scientists and industrial engineers, a concept that became prominent in the early 1930s. Its supporters, called *technocrats,* held that the benefits of improved technology were not being passed on to consumers, and that the increasing complexity of modern society called for control by those who had helped to create that complexity.

technological unemployment Unemployment resulting from changes in technology, usually but not always involving the substitution of machinery for some human labor and requiring more highly skilled personnel. For example, the development of gypsum wall board in the American housing industry in the 1930s completely eliminated the need for lathers, a job that had employed thousands of workers in the 1920s. Similarly, the diesel locomotive eliminated the need for firemen. Improved technology affects both the number (fewer) and the kind (more highly trained) of workers needed, and tends to involve principally unskilled and semiskilled labor. Moreover, it not only may result in short-term unemployment (until at least some of the unemployed acquire needed new skills) but some of the jobless will remain so for a long time, either because they cannot be retrained or because fewer workers are needed in the industry affected. However, over the long term the new technology presumably will increase productivity and eventually will reduce prices; reduced prices then will raise demand in some industries, which will consequently expand and need more labor. In the meantime, government aid may be needed. In the United States the Manpower Administration of the Department of Labor operates numerous programs—including on-the-job training, apprenticeships, and concentrated employment (for areas hard hit by unemployment)—to give job skills to the unskilled unemployed as well as to workers endangered by changing technology. See also UNEMPLOYMENT.

technology The body of knowledge concerned with applying science to the production of goods and services. It deals with the development of new materials and products and of machinery and processes that improve production, as well as use of the scientific method in solving technical problems. Considered the backbone of the Industrial Revolution, modern technology has also given rise to special problems (see TECHNOLOGICAL UNEMPLOYMENT). See also AUTOMATION.

technostructure A term invented by the American economist J. K. GALBRAITH to describe the bureaucratic complex that runs but does not own the huge corporations that dominate the private sector of the American economy. The technostructure is made up not only of scientists, engineers, and technicians, but of sales and marketing specialists, executives and coordinators, public relations experts, lobbyists, and lawyers—the entire management of a large corporation such as General Motors or International Telephone & Telegraph—or, in Galbraith's words, "all who bring specialized knowledge, talent, or experience to group decision-making." As managers rather than owners, its members are at least as concerned with perpetuating themselves and augmenting their power as they are with corporate profit. Thus sheer growth often becomes the major goal.

Telecommunications, Office of See under FEDERAL COMMUNICATIONS COMMISSION.

teller A bank employee or officer who actually handles money, receiving deposits and paying out withdrawals. In large banks there may be separate tellers for different transactions, such as paying, receiving, collecting notes, etc. The literal meaning of the word is "one who counts," and it sometimes is still used in this sense for a person who counts votes at business or political meetings.

Ten, Group of See GROUP OF TEN.

tenancy Occupying or holding land or other real estate on a rental basis, with or without a written LEASE. In the United States, most states require that a lease for more than one year be in writing, but rentals for shorter periods may be less formally arranged, and often they are not even definite as to the length of time in question. The most common sort is the *month-to-month tenancy,* with the tenant simply paying rent every month. Normally either tenant or landlord must give the other notice if the tenancy is to end, usually 30 days. A *year-to-year tenancy* may develop when a lease has expired, and landlord and tenant simply continue their previous contract without benefit of a formal agreement. A *tenancy at will* is one that can be ended by either landlord or tenant whenever they wish. A *tenancy at sufferance* is one where the tenant stays on wrongfully, without the landlord's consent, and therefore may be dispossessed. For *tenancy in common* and *tenancy by entirety*, see under JOINT TENANCY.

tenant The recipient of a lease, or lessee. See LEASE.

tenant farming A system whereby a landowner rents all or portions of his or her land to one or more farmers who work it, in exchange for payments of cash or, more often, a portion of the crop (see also SHARECROPPING). Tenant farming became common in the American South after the Civil War, when plantation owners, deprived of slave labor, could not afford to continue their enterprises under a wage system. Many of them therefore broke up their holdings into small farms, usually of 20 to 50 acres, and rented them to the newly emancipated slaves. About 75 per cent of such tenancies were arranged under a sharecropping system. After 1890, when the westward movement had effectively ended and land became scarcer and higher-priced, tenant farming began to increase among white farmers as well, particularly in places where land rose rapidly in value and crops required expensive machinery. Since World War II, with greatly increased mechanization of agriculture and consequently reduced need for farm labor, American tenant farming has waned considerably.

tender
1. In law, an offer to perform, which may or may not mean paying a debt. A *valid tender* is an unconditional offer of the exact sum due at the time it is due, and in the form of lawful money (see also LEGAL TENDER).
2. Also, *tender offer*. In corporate finance, a method of taking over a corporation by asking its stockholders to sell their shares at a fixed price by a set date. For example, suppose Firm A wants to buy Firm B against the wishes of B's management. Firm A advertises its willingness to buy B's stock at a price well above its current market value (although often below its book value). If enough of B's stockholders are willing to sell, A can take over the company.

10-K report A version of an ANNUAL REPORT that all U.S. corporations are required to file with the Securities and Exchange Commission (SEC). It frequently contains more information than the annual report distributed to stockholders (which may even be deliberately misleading). Since 1974 the SEC has required corporations with listed stock to make their 10-K reports available to interested stockholders.

Tennessee Valley Authority Also, *TVA*. See under PUBLIC POWER PROJECT.

tenor A name for the period of time between the start of an obligation (date of issue of a bond or note, date of acceptance of a bill of exchange, etc.) and its maturity (date of maturity of a bond, date of payment of a bill).

tenure
1. In employment, the period of time or the condition under which an office or job is held. Some positions (notably in teaching and the civil service) carry *permanent tenure*, that is, subject to certain conditions they may be held until death or retirement, unless the holder is found guilty of a serious offense.
2. In real estate, the manner in which an interest in land is held; see ESTATE, def. 2.

terminal, computer A device connected to a COMPUTER for sending and/or receiving data. Most terminals are single-user oriented (for example, a teletypewriter) as opposed to card readers or line printers, which are usually intrinsic to the computer's own input/output section. Remote terminals can be used by business executives, scientists, and others in their homes or offices. See also TIME SHARING.

termination
1. Also, *separation*. The process of leaving a job,

either voluntarily (in cases of resignation or retirement) or involuntarily (see LAYOFF).

2. In law, the ending of a CONTRACT. Normally contracts are terminated when their terms have been carried out. However, they also may be terminated by specific agreement (see also RESCISSION), by impossibility (when their terms cannot be carried out, owing to acts beyond the parties' control), by BREACH OF CONTRACT, or by some operation of the law (for example, when a new statute makes part of the contract illegal, or the statute of limitations applies, or one party becomes bankrupt).

3. *of a lease.* See under LEASE.

term insurance   See under LIFE INSURANCE.

terms of sale

1. The conditions of a sale, usually as laid down in a written sales contract. They spell out the time, place, and manner of delivery, the quantity delivered, whether it is to be delivered in full or in installments, the buyer's acceptance of the goods, the terms of payment (see def. 2, below), and liability for damage or destruction.

2. The *terms of payment* for a sale, particularly regarding the time of payment and any discount to be allowed for prompt or early payment. *Cash terms of sale* call for payment on or before delivery (sometimes at the same time the order is placed). *Net terms of sale* call for payment in full within a certain time, usually with a discount allowed for paying sooner; for example, "1% 10 days, net 30 days" means payment in full must be made within 30 days after submission of the invoice, but if payment is made within 10 days the buyer may take a 1 per cent discount.

terms of trade   The final exchange ratio of exports and imports, that is, the relationship of export and import prices. When only two commodities are traded—if, for example, Brazil exports coffee to the United States in exchange for American steel—the terms of trade consist simply of the ratio of their prices. If one unit of coffee is worth $.75 and one comparable unit of steel $7.50, the terms of trade are 1 steel = 10 coffee; or for Brazil, each unit of export exchanges for 0.1 units of import, and for the United States, each unit of export exchanges

for 10 units of import. Clearly this differential will affect each nation's BALANCE OF PAYMENTS. Since commodity prices depend on such factors as cost of production as well as supply and demand, the terms of trade reflect these factors, along with the presence or absence of a comparative ADVANTAGE in producing any commodity. A nation's terms of trade are said to improve if export prices exceed import prices, and to deteriorate if the opposite is true. One problem faced by underdeveloped nations is that they tend to export raw materials and import manufactured goods, which has brought them increasingly less favorable terms of trade. Prices of the crude products they sell are set in relatively free markets by supply and demand, whereas prices of the manufactured goods they buy are "administered" by giant corporations and are more monopolistic in character.

testimonial   In advertising, a personal endorsement of a product or service by a satisfied customer.

test piece   In manufacturing, a part or product fabricated from a sample or manufactured from a specimen, for the purpose of testing a production process, quality, etc.

T. F.   Abbreviation for TILL FORBID.

theft insurance   See under PROPERTY INSURANCE.

theory of games   See GAMES THEORY.

thin market   Also, *inactive market, narrow market.* In the securities and commodities trade, a market in which trading is light and price fluctuations relative to volume tend to be much greater than when trading is very active (see HEAVY MARKET). A market in a particular stock is said to be "thin" if the price drops by a point or two between 100-share trades for no apparent reason. This situation may indicate either lack of interest in the issue or a limited availability of stock.

third market   A term for outside trading of stocks listed on the New York Stock Exchange (the first and second markets being the STOCK EXCHANGE and the OVER-THE-COUNTER MARKET). The third market began to develop in the 1960s because large institutional investors (bank trust departments, mutual funds, etc.) were buying and selling the stocks of major corporations in such large blocks that specialists could not handle the transactions easily or cheaply. As a result, individual brokers who were not members of the exchange began "positioning" these blocks by acting as middlemen or brokers working directly with buyers and sellers. For example, suppose the Morgan Guaranty Trust Company wanted to sell 100,000 shares of General Motors stock from one of its pension funds. A third-market broker, also called a *block trader,* would then telephone a number of other banks, mutual funds, or other large institutional investors to see if any were interested in buying these 100,000 shares. The price would then be negotiated, either at the price at which General Motors was currently being traded on the stock exchange or, in weak markets, at a slighlty lower rate.

Third World Today, another name for UNDERDEVELOPED NATIONS. It came into use in the 1950s, when it was applied to those countries committed neither to Communism nor to a Western system of government; consequently, they were actively wooed by both the Soviet Union and the United States as potential allies in their "cold war."

thrift, paradox of The seeming contradiction that excessive saving results in lower real savings when an economy is operating at less than full employment. In this situation, the excess savings are in effect pulled out of the economy, making for a drop in overall national income and output and eventually bringing real savings back into balance with a reduced level of investment. Conversely, if savings are spent and channeled into the economy, investment and real wealth are increased. Stated by J. M. KEYNES, this principle was first applied to the depressed economy of the 1930s with its massive unemployment. In a booming economy at full employment, excess saving may be beneficial; if the savings were spent, the extra demand generated could not bring about extra output since capacity has temporarily reached its limit. Rather, it would simply push up prices, bringing about an increase in

national income in terms of money but not in terms of physical output.

through freight The transportation rate for a shipment from its point of origin to its final destination. Occasionally a railroad will permit a shipper to stop a shipment en route for processing, storage, or some other reason, and to continue to its final destination at some later time, and still charge only the through rate. This practice, also called *transit privilege,* is particularly important in the flour-milling industry, where it is also known as *milling in transit.*

throwaway A small printed advertisement, designed to be handed out on the street to passers-by or distributed from door to door, in the hope that it will be read before being thrown away.

ticker A device that prints the prices and volume of securities traded in cities and towns throughout the United States and Canada within minutes after each transaction is completed. The traditional ticker is a kind of typewriter that prints the code letters for the various securities, along with quantities and prices traded, on a continuous paper or cellophane tape. The tape may be read directly or be projected onto a screen in a broker's office (see BOARD ROOM) or at a stock exchange. A newer system involves a ticker screen that uses no tape. Instead, transactions pass through a computer and then are projected on a screen. Though reported in normal sequence for reading (from left to right), the figures do not move across the screen, as with the tape, but are constantly replaced by new figures flashed onto the screen.

tickler A filing system or similar device that serves as a daily reminder for correspondence or other business that should be taken care of on that day. One such system consists of 31 numbered file folders, 1 for each day of the month. Letters calling for an answer by a certain time, unpaid invoices, and similar items are placed in the folder for the appropriate day, and the tickler is checked daily for its contents.

tied loan In international trade, a loan carrying the condition that goods and services purchased with its proceeds must be bought from the lending country. Credit extended by the U.S. EXPORT-IM-PORT BANK nearly always takes this form. Tied loans naturally are trade-restrictive, limiting certain transactions to two countries.

tie-in sale See TYING RESTRICTIONS.

tight money See under MONETARY POLICY.

till forbid Also, *T.F.* In advertising, an indication that a particular ad is to be run in every issue of a periodical until the advertiser or agency issues instructions to the contrary.

till money Same as VAULT CASH, def. 1.

time and motion study A detailed analysis of any industrial operation in terms of the precise performance time for the entire job and each of its elements, as well as every hand and body movement used in its performance. Time and motion studies usually are made by industrial engineers for the purpose of setting work standards and wage rates, improving machines and methods, and other means of obtaining maximum efficiency at minimum cost. For their observations, engineers use stopwatches calibrated in hundreths of a minute; they may observe workers in person or use motion-picture film or closed-circuit television. Often a very simple change in method can greatly boost efficiency; for example, moving a bin from a worker's right side to the left may make it possible to feed material into a machine without involving the (right) hand that is operating it.

Time and motion studies were pioneered by F. W. TAYLOR, who in 1903 reported that he had been able to increase the handling of raw materials at the Bethlehem Steel Company from 16 tons per day per man to 57 tons. Taylor's system was threefold: (1) select the right method (tools, movements, etc.) to do the job; (2) measure the time an experienced worker needs to do it, using the right method, and use this result as a work standard; (3) give a worker extra pay if the standard is exceeded. In companies too small to warrant an elaborate (and expensive) time-motion study of their own, or for jobs that are essentially unique, work standards or cost estimates can be set according to *predetermined*

times. In such cases a job is broken down into its various components, for each of which a standard time is available, and from this an overall standard is calculated. Although less accurate than an individual study, predetermined times are much less expensive to obtain and often may be just as useful. See also WORK SAMPLING.

time bill Also, *time draft*. See under BILL OF EXCHANGE.

time deposit A deposit in a bank account that must remain for a given period of time or that cannot be withdrawn without advance notice (usually 30 to 60 days). In practice, banks rarely require notice for withdrawals from individual time deposits, but nearly always do from accounts of large firms. In the United States a time deposit, which normally earns interest, can be held by either a commercial bank or a mutual savings bank; in the latter case it is commonly called a *savings deposit*. Time deposits are subject to RESERVE REQUIREMENTS invoked by the Federal Reserve for member banks and by state law for nonmember banks. However, the required reserve is much lower than for demand deposits; in the mid-1970s it usually ranged from 3 to 6 per cent.

time loan See under LOAN, def. 1.

time preference theory of interest The idea that interest is a price paid by the borrower for immediate consumption (made possible by funds borrowed). The lender, on the other hand, must postpone using those funds for consumption. The stronger the preference for immediate consumption, the higher the interest rate will be. See also ABSTINENCE THEORY OF INTEREST; LIQUIDITY PREFERENCE.

time series A record of a set of variables—sales, production, prices, investment, etc.—observed over a period of time. Observations are recorded at regular intervals, such as weekly, monthly, or yearly. *Time-series analysis* is an important forecasting tool. Many time series are used to construct indexes (see INDEX NUMBER). See also FORECAST-

ING; INDICATOR; INVERTED ECONOMIC SERIES; SEASONAL VARIATION; SECULAR TREND.

time sharing A system of computer utilization whereby a number of customers at scattered locations can use the same computer, each paying for its proportionate share of computer time. Developed because of the inefficiencies of BATCH PROCESSING (def. 1), time sharing can take several forms. A common system is to have each user provided with a TERMINAL (a device with a keyboard, similar to a typewriter) linked to a computer over an ordinary telephone line. The user types the problem on the terminal, the problem is transmitted to the computation center, and solutions (or notices of errors in the program) are typed out immediately on the terminal. The terminals generally are connected not to the main computer but to a communications processor (see FRONT-END PROCESSOR), which transfers the problem to the main computer after it has been completely typed out. (The typing usually takes a few minutes, and the computation only hundredths of seconds or less; therefore the main computer need not be tied up during the typing.) Though it operates very fast, the central processing unit (see under COMPUTER) can only handle one problem at a time. To avoid conflicts, it is generally programmed to work with some kind of scheduling formula, such as a simple round robin, whereby each user is assigned a brief spell of computing time. Moreover, most computers have a large enough STORAGE capacity so that users may, if they wish, have their programs stored for future use, or they may select a program from a "library" of standard programs that solve a variety of frequently encountered problems.

time study See TIME AND MOTION STUDY.

time wage rate A system of wage payment based on the number of hours or other time period spent working. See also PIECEWORK.

tip
   1. Inside information that will presumably profit the securities investor, business executive, real estate speculator, or other individuals able to act on it. The U.S. Securities and Exchange Commission has strict regulations governing the behavior of business executives who are privy to such information.
   2. Also, *gratuity.* An extra payment given for a service by the customer, as to a cabdriver, waitress, porter, barber, etc.

tithe A tax to support the church. Originally, in Europe one-tenth of the profits from farming was paid to support the parish priest. A British law passed in 1836 made all tithes in England and Wales payable in money (instead of crops), and a century later the Tithes Act separated tithe payments from the Church of England, replacing them with a kind of government annuity. In the United States, where church and state are constitutionally separate, tithes have never been exacted by the government, but they are common among some religious sects, such as the Church of Jesus Christ of Latter-Day Saints (Mormon Church).

title In law, evidence of ownership of real or personal property. Title to property may be acquired and transferred to others in a variety of ways—by gift, inheritance, occupancy, purchase, tax sale, etc. For goods sold by one party to another, the exact time when title passes is particularly important, since it ordinarily is the owner who bears the loss if goods are destroyed, damaged, or stolen. For real property (land and buildings), title often is a matter of public record. Before a sale of real estate takes place, the buyer generally undertakes a *title search* to make sure that no one except the seller has a valid claim to the property. (See also ABSTRACT OF TITLE; DEED.) Some states in the United States have adopted a plan for registering and securing official declarations of title, issuing a *certificate of title* to the owner who has proved ownership of a certain property to the satisfaction of a court or court officer. See also MARKETABLE TITLE; QUITCLAIM DEED; SALE, def. 1; TITLE INSURANCE; TORRENS SYSTEM; WARRANTY DEED.

title insurance Insurance against any defects in TITLE to real property, that is, ownership of real estate. Such insurance can be bought from a *title company,* an organization authorized by law to examine and insure titles in exchange for a fee or premium.

The amount of the premium usually is based on the value of the property to which title is being insured and is paid in one payment (unlike most other insurance premiums). The company makes a careful *title search* (tracing the history of the title). If it finds no defects, it insures against loss. Should there be a loss due to forgery or some other defect, the title company pays the loss.

token money   Money whose face value is greater than the value of the material from which it is made. All modern coins are token money, as opposed to the full-bodied gold and silver coins of former times (as recently as 1933 for the silver dollar).

tolerance   The deviation from a given standard of size, quality, or some other measurable characteristic allowed in the SPECIFICATIONS for a product.

toll

1. A tax levied on users of some public facility, such as a bridge, tunnel, or highway.
2. A charge for long-distance telephone calls, often called *toll calls*.
3. A charge levied by a manufacturer for processing material to which it theoretically does not take title. For example, a smelter may refine copper on a toll basis, charging the copper company a fee of so many cents per pound.

ton-mile   The movement of 1 ton of goods over 1 mile, a common way of measuring the value of various kinds of transportation. The total of ton-miles is the sum of distances each ton of freight is carried; thus, if 10 tons of gravel are carried 100 miles, the total movement is 1,000 ton-miles. In terms of ton-miles, railways are by far the most important freight carrier in the United States, chiefly because they tend to be used for heavy material shipped in bulk. (See also FREIGHT.) A *revenue ton-mile* represents the average receipts per mile for every ton of freight, computed by dividing the total ton-miles into total freight revenues for a given period.

tonnage   The number of tons of cargo a vessel can carry, which can be measured in several ways. *Dead weight tonnage* is the amount of cargo, stores, and fuel a vessel can carry, calculated as the difference in long tons (2,240 pounds = 1 ton) of water displaced when it is empty and when it is loaded to its load (or plimsoll) line; *gross tonnage* is the number of cubic feet a vessel encloses, whether or not all that space is for cargo, divided by 100; *net tonnage* is gross tonnage minus the area taken up by machinery, fuel, stores, crew, etc., that is, the space presumably available for passengers and/or cargo.

tontine   A kind of fund to which a large number of persons contribute and which, after a specified time, is distributed among those of them who survive. A common form of distribution is an annuity paid to each survivor, which increases in value as the original contributors die off. Although insurance policies based on such a plan, with surviving policyholders sharing the dividends of an entire class of policy, are illegal in the United States, the tontine feature is retained in many company profit-sharing and pension plans, where the contributions of those who leave the company before retirement are divided among those who remain.

Torrens system   A system of land registration introduced in Australia in the 19th century by Sir Robert Torrens, whereby titles are permanently registered and there is an assurance fund from which losses arising out of title defects are paid. The system has been adopted in the United States by a number of states but has not, for the most part, eliminated the need for title searches. See also TITLE.

tort   In law, an actionable injury or wrong committed to the person or property of another person.

trackage   The privilege of running the trains of one railroad on the tracks of another.

trade

1. See INTERNATIONAL TRADE.
2. *securities trade.* The exchange of various kinds of SECURITY, taking place both on organized exchanges (see STOCK EXCHANGE) and informally (see OVER-THE-COUNTER MARKET).
3. *commodity trade.* The exchange of various

kinds of goods, mostly but not entirely raw materials, which takes place principally on organized exchanges (see COMMODITY EXCHANGE).

4. See RETAIL.

5. See WHOLESALE.

trade acceptance See under BILL OF EXCHANGE.

trade association An organization formed by companies in a particular industry or field, for the purpose of promoting their mutual interests. It frequently acts as a central public relations agency for the industry, collecting and publishing industry statistics, and it sometimes serves as an industry consultant, advising members on technological, management, or other problems. Though some American trade associations in the early 20th century were formed for the purpose of fighting labor unions and to work toward industry monopolies, today their chief purpose is industrial cooperation. Among the larger well-known American trade associations are the American Iron & Steel Institute, the National Association of Manufacturers, and the Pharmaceutical Manufacturers Association. See also CHAMBER OF COMMERCE.

trade barrier Any restriction on the international exchange of goods, such as a tariff, import quota, import license, import embargo, government-purchasing preference, exchange controls, subsidy to domestic producers, required marks of origin on goods, or similar restriction. Though tariffs originally were intended purely as a source of revenue, their chief function in modern times, like that of other trade barriers, has been to protect home industry or otherwise improve a nation's trading position. Since trade barriers nearly always provoke retaliation by the country against which they are raised, their net effect is to reduce the total volume of trade, protect less efficient producers, and raise prices. See also FREE TRADE; TARIFF, def. 1.

trade deficit See under BALANCE OF TRADE.

trade discount See under DISCOUNT, def. 1.

trade fair See under FAIR.

trade-in The use of a piece of used merchandise as partial payment for the purchase of a new item. Trade-ins are commonly used by American consumers in purchasing automobiles, the buyer "turning in" his or her old car and receiving in exchange a *trade-in allowance,* or discount from the price of the new car.

trademark A distinctive mark or symbol, or a word or letter in a distinctive script or style, that serves to identify a product, service, or company, and that is or can be protected by registration with the U.S. Patent Office. (See also *brand name,* under BRAND.) Until 1946, when the Lanham Act was passed, trademarks were protected from competition under common law and later under various state statutes. The new law, with subsequent amendments, provides for a Principal Register at the Patent Office for trademarks as well as several other classifications, defined as: *trademarks,* used to distinguish a single seller of goods; *service marks,* distinguishing a single seller of services; *certification marks,* covering the goods or services of several sellers; and *collective marks,* identifying the members of an association, such as a cooperative. The law also provides for a Supplemental Register for names descriptive of goods and places (in effect, brand names), which, however, are not given exclusive rights in the United States but can be used to obtain rights abroad. Once registered and maintained, a trademark is the exclusive property of its owner. (Registry is not essential to its validity but provides prima facie evidence of ownership.) A product may be protected by both a PATENT and a trademark. The patent eventually will expire, but the monopoly it has conferred on the product may be perpetuated by the trademark. The validity of trademarks is upheld by their owners through successfully bringing suit against infringements. Trademark owners themselves are sometimes sued when they use a mark to violate antitrust laws. In theory and in practice, the purpose of a trademark is to limit (or even eliminate) competition by establishing strong consumer preference for a product or company. Under present laws there is a large gray area between legal and illegal restraints of competition, but in many cases the courts have enjoined monopolistic practices involving trademarks.

trade publication A periodical—magazine, journal, or newspaper—devoted to subjects of interest in one or more specific businesses, trades, industries, or professions, and circulated primarily among members of those groups. For example, *Purchasing Magazine* is addressed principally to purchasing agents, *Iron Age* to manufacturers of metal products, and the *Journal of Ophthalmology* to eye specialists.

trader In general, a person who buys or sells goods, commodities, or securities. In the securities industry a trader is the same as a DEALER (def. 2), buying and selling for his or her own account rather than as an agent for customers (see BROKER, def. 1), and is often associated with dealing for short-term profit. See also FLOOR TRADER.

trade relations See RECIPROCITY, def. 1.

trade school Also, *vocational school.* A school that provides instruction in various trades, ranging from home economics and office skills to specialized industrial trades and agriculture. Widely known in Europe since the 19th century, trade schools were slower to develop in the United States, although Federal funds for this purpose have been available since the passage of the Smith-Hughes Act, in 1917. Between 1953 and 1973, however, both student enrollment and Federal aid to various vocational programs, including elementary, secondary, and adult training, trebled. It was believed this growth would continue, since a complex industrial society increasingly needs fewer unskilled workers and more better-trained ones. See also VOCATIONAL TRAINING.

trade union See under LABOR UNION.

trade-weighted dollar The percentage change in the market exchange rate of the U.S. dollar weighted for the volume of American trade. The change is calculated relative to some base period (such as December 1971, when fixed exchange rates were replaced by a floating rate; see under EXCHANGE RATE). The change is considered important because it is a measure of the effective change in international purchasing power, which can be

Fig. 84. Trade-weighted dollar

New York—Morgan Guaranty Trust Co. reported the dollar's percentage change in market value, weighted for volume of trade with the U.S., against 15 other currencies, as of noon Eastern time, from the following dates:

	5/29/70[a]	12/18/71[b]	2/15/73[c]
9/24/76	−12.28	−2.82	+3.06
Preceding day	−12.26	−2.79	+3.09
Week ago	−12.33	−2.87	+3.00
Year ago	−11.87	−1.35	+4.49

[a] Parities prior to Canadian dollar float.
[b] Smithsonian agreement central rates.
[c] Market rates following dollar devaluation.
Source: *Wall Street Journal*, September 27, 1976.

calculated by taking into account the amount of trade affected when exchange rates change. For example, if the market rate of the Canadian dollar rises from U.S. $1 to U.S. $1.01, and 10 per cent of the United States' total trade is with Canada, this 1 per cent revaluation of Canadian currency would decrease the value of the trade-weighted dollar by 10 per cent of 1 per cent, or 0.1 per cent. In the mid-1970s the trade-weighted dollar was calculated in terms of trade volume with the 15 or so countries that constituted the United States' major trading partners.

trading floor See under NEW YORK STOCK EXCHANGE.

trading limit See under FUTURES MARKET.

trading post See under NEW YORK STOCK EXCHANGE.

trading stamp A kind of coupon, used as a promotional device by retailers to attract customers. The customers receive trading stamps in amounts proportionate to their purchases (usually 2 to 3 per cent of their value) and, when they have accumulated enough stamps, exchange them for merchandise offered by the stamp company. The retailer either sets up its own plan or buys stamps from trading-stamp companies, which advertise the merchandise available at premiums and, in the case of larger companies, operate showrooms where customers can select and pick up merchandise. Consumers presumably are convinced they are getting "free" merchandise, since they would be making the same grocery and other retail purchases even if stamps were not offered. In reality, retailers who offer trading stamps nearly always raise their prices 2 to 3 per cent to cover the cost of the stamps. However, the retailer usually pays much less for the trading stamps than their equivalent value in merchandise, because the stamp company knows from experience that many stamps will in fact never be redeemed. Further, merchandise offered is always at list price and frequently would be available from conventional dealers at a lower price. Trading stamps were used as early as the 1890s. Exceedingly popular in the United States in the 1950s and the 1960s, they were offered by most large supermarket chains. During the next decade, however, many retailers stopped using them, in part because of price competition from discount stores.

traffic A general term for commerce and more particularly for the transportation of goods and/or passengers. In a business enterprise the *traffic department* is responsible for shipments of goods, both within and to and from the company. This work includes the selection of carriers and routes for shipments, tracing inbound (and sometimes outbound) shipments, auditing carriers' invoices, filing claims (for damages, loss, excess charges), and trying to reduce transportation cost through negotiation with carriers, analysis of rates, special studies of plant location, etc. (See also under FREIGHT.) The typical traffic department also handles travel reservations for company personnel and household moves for company employees, and it may be responsible for all company-owned vehicles. In most manufacturing companies transportation services are the third biggest expenditure, after purchased materials and labor, and in some cases represent one-fourth or more of the sales dollar, so that traffic management has considerable economic importance.

training See ON-THE-JOB-TRAINING; VOCATIONAL TRAINING.

tramp steamer A merchant ship with no regular route, whose itinerary depends on where it can pick up cargo and on the cargo's destination.

transaction equation See EQUATION OF EXCHANGE.

transactions demand Also, *transactions motive.* See under MONEY; also, LIQUIDITY PREFERENCE.

transfer, stock
1. The delivery of a stock certificate from the seller's broker to the buyer's broker and legal change of ownership, normally accomplished within a few days of the transaction.
2. The recording of the change of ownership of stock on the books of the issuing corporation by the TRANSFER AGENT.

transfer agent An individual responsible for keeping records of the shareholders of a corporation, with names, addresses, and number of shares owned, as well as for cancellation of the stock certificates that are sold and for the issuing of new certificates to the new owners. Transfer agents may be employees of the corporation, but more often they work for a bank, trust company, or other agency that performs this service for a corporation.

transfer payment A payment that represents a redistribution of national wealth rather than compensation for goods produced or services rendered. Transfer payments made by the United States Federal government include social security benefits, veterans pensions, and similar welfare payments, and interest on the public debt (bonds and other government obligations); transfer payments by businesses include bad debts, contributions to charity, and contest prizes. A transfer payment represents spendable income to a payee who, however, has not produced either a good or service in return. For this reason transfer payments are not considered part of NET NATIONAL PRODUCT. Between 1950 and 1975 Federal transfer payments increased more than sevenfold, from $15.6 billion to more than $107 billion (or more than 37 per cent of total Federal spending).

transfer tax A tax on the transfer of documents such as land titles, securities, licenses, etc. It frequently is collected through the sale of *revenue stamps* which must be attached to the document in question. Transfer taxes often are levied by local and state governments.

transformation curve Also, *production-possibility curve*. A graphic representation of various possible outputs of two goods with a fixed supply of resources that are fully employed. It is useful for either an entire economy (for example, to show various combinations of defense and nondefense production) or an individual enterprise (to show how many cars and how many tractors it should produce). The curve is always concave owing to the operation of the law of DIMINISHING RETURNS. When all available resources are concentrated on one of the two goods under consideration, some of them tend to be better suited to producing the other good. For example, while using the same factory workers to make tractors rather than textiles, it will become clear that some of them are better at making textiles; if they must now make tractors, their productivity will decline. Conversely, a shift to textiles can be expected to result in a lower output from those used to making tractors. The transformation curve traces a pattern based on a given set of circumstances, which involve full employment of all possible resources (in the case of the economy, full employment of the work force) and a given level of technology. Improved machines or methods that enable greater output of one of the two goods considered will, of course, change the curve.

transit number In the United States, an identification number printed on the face of a bank's checks to speed their routing and collection. Usually appearing in the upper right-hand corner, it consists of three numbers, arranged $\frac{1-2}{3}$; 1 refers to the bank's location, 2 to its name, and 3 to its Federal Reserve district and the area within that district.

transitory income See under PERMANENT-INCOME HYPOTHESIS.

transloading In rail transportation, a means of delivering parts of an original carload shipment to two or more destinations. The goods first are moved to a single point that is closest to the various final destinations, and the railroad then reloads portions of the shipment into other cars for the remaining distance. This practice enables shippers to pay the premium less-than-carload rate for small shipments over only a minimum distance.

transshipment
1. Movement of goods from one carrier to another, as in TRANSLOADING.
2. In business, goods shipped from one dealer to another who is outside the first dealer's territory. The first dealer may have accepted more than it could sell in order to obtain a quantity discount, or simply may be getting rid of overstock.

traveler's check A special kind of CHECK sold by banks and some large travel agencies to travelers who do not wish to carry cash or negotiable instruments. The check is signed by the buyer at the time of purchase, and again when it is used to make a payment, in the presence of the payee. It thus can be used only by the original purchaser.

traveler's letter of credit See under LETTER OF CREDIT.

treasurer The officer of a business firm or other organization who is charged with the receipt, cus-

Fig. 85. Transformation curve

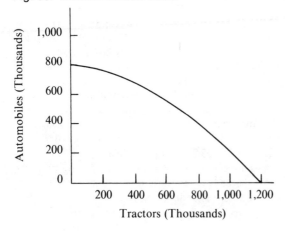

tody, and disbursement of its funds. In some organizations the job of treasurer and CONTROLLER are one and the same, and in others not. A corporation may be required by law to have a treasurer but not a controller.

Treasury, Department of the The division of the U.S. Federal government that manages the nation's finances. Its principal functions are formulating and recommending financial, tax, and fiscal policies, serving as the government's financial agent, manufacturing coins and currency, and Federal law enforcement. It includes among its branches the U.S. Customs Service, Bureau of the Mint, Bureau of Engraving and Printing, U.S. Secret Service, and Internal Revenue Service.

Treasury bill A short-term obligation of the central government, in effect a promissory note that bears no interest but is sold at a discount. Carrying little risk (owing to the government's secure credit standing), Treasury bills are considered an attractive short-term investment, especially by banks (including foreign central banks) and by businesses wanting to earn a return on temporarily idle capital. At the same time, they give the government a relatively cheap means of borrowing. United States Treasury bills are the shortest-term government security issued, usually maturing in 91 days or 182 days (though some kinds mature in 1 year). They are offered to the public at weekly auctions. Treasury bills are the principal security bought and sold by the Federal Reserve as part of its efforts to stabilize the economy. If there is a sudden shortage of funds, the Federal Reserve buys a few billion dollars' worth of Treasury bills from dealers, who either sell them out of inventory or in turn buy them from banks, insurance companies, and similar traditional sources (see also OPEN-MARKET OPERATIONS). The British government issues similar short-term obligations of the same name.

treasury bond

1. A corporate BOND (def. 1) that has been bought back by the issuing corporation and is held in its treasury, sometimes for resale at a later date but usually to avoid paying further interest on it until maturity or to use for SINKING FUND requirements. See also TREASURY STOCK.

2. Also, *Treasury bond.* Any bond issued by the U.S. government. See BOND, def. 1.

Treasury certificate A short-term obligation of the U.S. Federal government, usually maturing in one year and bearing interest paid by coupon. Corporations sometimes buy Treasury certificates to establish a reserve from which to pay taxes.

Treasury note An intermediate-term obligation of the United States government, maturing in one to five years and bearing interest paid by coupon.

treasury stock Also, *reacquired stock.* Stock issued by a company and later bought back by it. It may be held by the company indefinitely, or it may be retired, or it may later be resold to the public on the open market. It earns dividends and carries no vote while held by the company. See also TREASURY BOND, def. 1.

trial balance See under DOUBLE ENTRY.

triangular trade A system of trade that developed in the 17th century between the northern American colonies (New England and the Middle Atlantic colonies) and England. Because some of the colonies' staple products were kept out of England by high tariffs while at the same time the colonies needed to import manufactured goods from England, other markets for those staples (chiefly fish, grain, and other food products) had to be found. The chief such outlet was the West Indies, which the colonies supplied with fish, grain, lumber, and meat. In return the colonies received molasses (made into rum for the fishing fleet, slave trade, or domestic use), along with cash and some commodities that could be exported to England. The rum for the slave trade went to Africa, which in turn sent slaves to the West Indies (until 1776 nearly all Africans were sent to the Indies first, and then a portion of them would go to the American mainland). A similar triangle existed with southern Europe to which the colonies sent goods in exchange for fruit and wine, in turn sold to England for manufactured goods. See Fig. 86, page 432.

trough The lowest point of the BUSINESS CYCLE, or some single phase of economic activity.

Fig. 86. Triangular trade

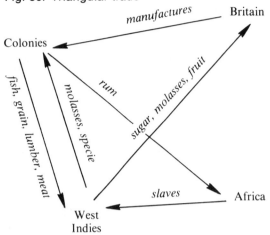

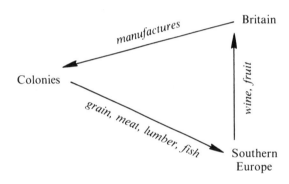

truck wholesaler See under WHOLESALE.

trust

1. In law, a transfer of property from one person, called the *settlor* or *donor*, to another person, called the *trustee*, who is to hold the property for the benefit or use of a third person, called the *beneficiary*. Property so held is also known as the *trust corpus, trust res, trust fund,* or *trust estate*, and a distinction is made between it, the principal, and whatever income is earned from it. If the trust takes effect while the settlor is still living, it is a *living trust*; if it is provided for in the settlor's will, it is a *testamentary trust*. If the beneficiary is one or more private individuals, the trust is a *private trust*; if it is for the benefit of the public (or some portion of the public) it is a *charitable trust*. The effect of a trust is to divide property so that legal title to it is retained by the trustee but beneficial interest passes to the

beneficiary. Normally a trustee must invest the trust money or property in income-yielding enterprises and (unless specifically forbidden by the settlor) has the power to sell, mortgage, or lease trust property as the need arises. Trusts are established for a variety of reasons, including the reduction of tax liability. See also TRUST COMPANY. For *trustee in bankruptcy*, see under BANKRUPTCY; for *deed of trust* (or *trust deed*), see under MORTGAGE.

2. In business, a large corporation or combination of corporations that has a monopoly or near monopoly on the production or distribution of a particular good or service. The name comes from the practice of transferring all or most of the voting stock of a group of corporations to a board of trustees, which would use the votes in the interest of the entire group (*voting trust*). Though later monopolies were not necessarily set up in this way, the name "trust" persisted. In the United States such trusts are illegal. See also ANTITRUST LEGISLATION; MASSACHUSETTS TRUST. For *investment trust*, see INVESTMENT COMPANY.

3. See TRUST COMPANY.

trustbusting Any activity directed against business monopolies (see TRUST, def. 2). The term is associated particularly with the active role of the U.S. Department of Justice under President Theodore Roosevelt in prosecuting violations of ANTITRUST LEGISLATION.

trust company A financial organization whose chief function is to act as trustee, fiduciary, or agent for individuals or firms in a variety of capacities, such as administering trust funds (including their investment), executing wills, acting as custodian for property held in trust, etc. Many trust companies also perform other banking functions, such as accepting deposits and making loans. In the United States trust companies are regulated by state law. See also TRUST, def. 1.

trustee See under TRUST, def. 1.

trust receipt A means of financing business transactions in which a dealer obtains goods to sell by having a bank or finance company buy them in exchange for a receipt stating that the dealer (or a warehouse) holds the property. The dealer then sells the goods to customers and repays the lender. Title to the goods passes either directly from the financer to the ultimate customer or from the financer first to the dealer and thence to the customer.

Truth-in-Lending Act See under CONSUMER PROTECTION LAWS.

Turgot, Anne Robert Jacques A French statesman and economist (1727–81), one of the PHYSIOCRATS and controller of finance under Louis XVI (1774–76). Like the other physiocrats, Turgot, who for years served as administrator of the Limoges district (1761–74), believed that agriculture was the only truly productive activity. As controller, he tried to remedy the country's desperate financial situation by abolishing the then prevalent system of unpaid labor, by suppressing internal taxes and tolls on various agricultural items that prevented free internal trade, and by abolishing the trade guilds, which he believed were raising commodity prices too high. Turgot's program met great opposition, however, and he was dismissed, his reforms abandoned until they were reinstated after the French Revolution. In his *Reflections on the Formation and Distribution of Wealth* (1766), Turgot anticipated some of the ideas of the CLASSICAL SCHOOL, notably that competition among workers lowers wages to the subsistence level (see IRON LAW OF WAGES). He also understood the law of diminishing returns and its application to agriculture, a principle ignored by Adam Smith but later applied to rents by Ricardo and other classical economists.

turning point A change in the general direction of business and economic activity, from up to down, or vice versa. See BUSINESS CYCLE.

turnover

1. In general, the number of times a cycle is completed in a given period of time. Particularly, how often a stock of merchandise, raw materials, capital, accounts receivable, or some other asset is used in a year or other time period. It usually is expressed as a ratio. Thus, *annual merchandise turnover* in a retail store is equal to the ratio of total annual sales volume to average inventory on hand; *raw material turnover* is the ratio of goods being processed during a period, divided by the average raw material inventory; *accounts receivable turnover* is the ratio of credit sales during a period to the average amount of accounts receivable outstanding; *capital turnover* is the ratio of sales during a period to the average capital invested (bonds plus net worth); and so on.

2. The number of workers hired to replace those terminated in an individual firm or industry, in relation to the total number of workers employed during the same period.

3. In British terminology, sales. A firm with annual sales of £1 million is said to have a turnover of that amount.

turnover tax See under SALES TAX.

turnpike Originally, a TOLL (def. 1) road; today, any large highway.

twisting In insurance, the practice of persuading a policyholder to cancel one life insurance policy in order to replace it with another, so that the agent may get the high initial commission. In many places twisting is illegal.

two-bin system The oldest and simplest system of inventory control. One bin holds a reserve of material equal to the amount that will normally be consumed during the lead time (the time needed to replace it); a second bin holds the balance of the inventory. When stock in the second bin is used up, the order point (time to order more material) has been reached; while the order is being filled, the company draws on the first bin. When the order is delivered, the reserve in the first bin is restored to its former level and the balance is put in the second bin for immediate needs. The two-bin system eliminates the need for further record-keeping, and sometimes even the need for two bins. The only requirement is that the reserve supply be physically separated from the rest of the stock. While useful for items of low value, fairly consistent usage, and short lead time, such as office and maintenance supplies, the two-bin system is rarely suitable for production materials because it is not responsive to changes in demand and lead time and does not provide any record of stock on hand. See also PERPETUAL INVENTORY SYSTEM.

two-dollar broker A member of a STOCK EX-CHANGE handling a transaction for another broker, who is either too busy to handle the order or temporarily absent from the exchange floor. The name comes from the fact that for many years the fee for this service was $2 per 100 shares traded. Today, however, the fee varies with the price of the stock, but usually is higher than $2.

two-name paper Any commercial paper for whose payment two or more persons are liable, either as its drawers or as its endorsers.

two-tier system A system set up in the 1960s whereby the major industrial nations agreed not to buy or sell gold except to one another at the official pegged price (see PEGGING, def. 1), originally $35 per ounce (by 1973, $42.22). So long as the market price was significantly higher than the pegged price, they also agreed not to buy gold for more than the official price from South Africa and other gold-producing countries, which would then have to sell gold on the free market and thus drive down the price. Set up to prevent excess speculation in gold, the two-tier system was intended to relieve pressure on international GOLD RESERVES.

tying restrictions Also, *exclusive dealership, full-line forcing, tie-in sale.* Conditions attached to the sale of goods or services requiring the buyer to purchase additional goods or services, whether or not they are actually needed. For example, a seller of office equipment may require a buyer to purchase a service contract for maintaining and repairing the equipment, or a motion picture distributor may require theaters to show a number of films they do not necessarily want in order to obtain those they do want (also called *block booking*). In cases where the additional good or service is actually necessary, as when a machine will operate only with certain lubricants, or a camera with certain film, tying restrictions are legal in the United States, but if an equally effective product or service is available they are considered a violation of the Clayton Antitrust Act.

Type I, Type II errors See under NULL HYPOTHESIS.

uncertainty Inability to predict the outcome of an event in advance. Almost all business and economic decisions involve some uncertainty. For example, the U.S. Federal Reserve Board of Governors can never predict the exact results of a particular monetary policy, nor can a business executive ever be wholly certain that a particular new product will be successful. Uncertainty differs from *risk* in that the probability of an event's occurrence cannot be calculated. For example, making a bet on whether a coin will come up heads or tails involves a risk (but not an uncertainty); the probability of one or the other outcome is exactly 50 per cent. On the other hand, betting that the next vehicle one passes on the road will be green and have a 4 on its license plate involves uncertainty as well as risk. The differentiation between risk and uncertainty was first made by the American economist Frank H. Knight, who in his *Risk, Uncertainty and Profit* (1921) pointed out that uncertainty helps give rise to profit, which is the entrepreneur's reward for guessing right.

under bond Also, *in bond.* Describing goods being stored in a bonded WAREHOUSE.

underconsumption theory Also, *overproduction theory, oversaving theory.* The idea that the business cycle is the result of underconsumption. According to this reasoning, the rich cannot spend all the money they have and consequently save too much. These savings, when invested, lead to OVERPRODUCTION, since the poor don't have enough money to buy up all the additional goods being produced. As a result, with too large a supply, prices drop, unemployment increases, and a depression ensues, which lasts until the surplus of goods has been absorbed. Versions of the underconsumption theory were developed by Thomas MALTHUS and Karl Marx, and it was most fully stated by J. A. HOBSON. One of its chief failings is that it does not explain the upturns and booms of the business cycle. However, as J. M. KEYNES pointed out, if investment lags behind saving, unemployment will result, so the government should take up whatever slack is left by private investment.

underdeveloped nation Any country where per capita real income is much lower than in the industrial nations of the world, and where national income is too low to allow savings needed for investment, which in turn is needed for economic development. Most underdeveloped nations share several of the following characteristics: heavy dependence on agriculture (engaging more than half the labor force), producing one or a few key products for export; relatively primitive farming methods and low agricultural productivity; little industry; little opportunity for employment outside farming; scarcity of natural resources or, in case of relative abundance (of oil, minerals, etc.), the plentiful resources are those requiring heavy capital investment and/or advanced technology for extraction, causing dependency on outsiders to exploit them; relatively recent independent status (in Asia and Africa) and/or plagued with continual or frequent political instability since independence (Latin America); widespread corruption in government; density of population; rapid population growth, with a high birth rate offsetting what progress is made; inequitable income distribution, with a small rich class and a huge, desperately poor one. In the mid-1970s most of the nations of Asia, Africa, and Latin America—sometimes called the *Third World* —were still underdeveloped, and the gap between them and the so-called advanced nations was widening despite increased efforts through FOREIGN

AID from individual governments, United Nations agencies, and other international bodies. One major problem was the steadily deteriorating trading position of the underdeveloped nations. They tend to export raw materials, whose prices fluctuate widely and which continue to be in less demand (owing to technological improvements providing substitutes or simply less need for materials) than the high-priced goods they must import. As a result they receive less money than they must spend. To reduce this gap, they frequently restrict imports through a quota system. A rising population needs more food imports; therefore, the cutbacks are made in imports essential to development (capital goods). Foreign loans and grants have narrowed this gap in the past, but economists remain undecided over what policies would best aid long-term development.

underemployment Also, *disguised unemployment*. The situation where workers put in less than the desired or standard hours of work per week (normally 35 to 40) and/or are forced to work at jobs for which they are overqualified (such as teachers becoming teaching aides and/or working part-time instead of full-time).

underinvestment Too little investment relative to saving; see PROPENSITY TO INVEST; also under J. M. KEYNES.

undervalued See OVERVALUED, UNDERVALUED.

underwriting The assumption of a risk, particularly in investment and insurance. In the former it means the purchase of an entire new issue of a security from the corporation issuing it and selling it to the general public, either directly or through dealers. In effect the underwriter for a fee, usually a commission, guarantees that the issuing corporation will receive a given amount of money for the issue and assumes the risk that it may have to sell it for less than that amount. (See also INVESTMENT BANKING.) In insurance, a person or company undertakes all or part of the risk against theft, fire, death, or whatever the policy stipulates, in exchange for a payment called a premium.

undistributed profits See RETAINED EARNINGS.

unearned income
1. Income from sources other than work performed, such as dividends, interest, rent, etc.
2. Same as DEFERRED INCOME.

unearned increment An increase in the value of land or other property that results from some external cause rather than from the owner's efforts. For example, construction of a new highway can increase (or decrease) the value of the adjacent land.

uneconomic Also, *uneconomical*. The opposite of ECONOMIC, def. 2.

unemployment The nonavailability of jobs for persons able and willing to work at the prevailing wage rate. Unemployment is an important measure of the economic health, since FULL EMPLOYMENT is generally considered a highly desirable goal. The U.S. Department of Commerce, which regularly compiles statistics on unemployment, defines *unemployed persons* as any civilians over 16 years of age who, during a given week, had no employment but were available for work, and (1) had been actively seeking a job (through an employment office, interviews, etc.) within the past 4 weeks; or (2) were waiting to return to a job from which they had been laid off; or (3) were waiting to report to a new paid job within 30 days. Unemployment statistics, which are reported monthly, are adjusted to account for seasonal variation. An unemployment rate of 4 per cent (of the total labor force) is considered normal and indeed is defined as "full employment"; a rate of 6 per cent or higher is usually considered an indication of a RECESSION. See also CHRONIC UNEMPLOYMENT; CYCLICAL UNEMPLOYMENT; SEASONAL UNEMPLOYMENT; SEPARATION RATE; STRUCTURAL UNEMPLOYMENT; TECHNOLOGICAL UNEMPLOYMENT; UNDEREMPLOYMENT.

unemployment compensation A system of insurance whereby those who lose their jobs receive periodic payments from an unemployment compensation fund for a period of time presumably long enough to allow them to find new jobs. Originally set up in the United States by the Social Security Act of 1937, unemployment compensation is organized by the individual states at the instigation of the Federal government. Payments are made into a reserve fund obtained through a tax on employers. Then, if a worker is laid off and meets certain basic requirements (for example, having worked a minimum number of weeks prior to layoff), he or she may apply for weekly unemployment compensation checks. The amount paid and the length of payment vary considerably from state to state. Payments are rarely generous, and supplemental benefits may be paid by employers under union contracts (see also GUARANTEED ANNUAL WAGE). The number of persons collecting unemployment compensation at any one time is directly related to the general state of the economy, and the number of *initial* claims for unemployment insurance per week is considered an important LEADING INDICATOR of the business cycle. Moreover, since the reserve fund grows during a period of prosperity (when few unemployed workers draw on it) and helps sustain consumption during a time of recession, it acts as a BUILT-IN STABILIZER for the economy.

unfair competition As defined in Federal ANTITRUST LEGISLATION of the United States, any acts designed to mislead and confuse the public and to incur deceptive substitution of one product for another, in the interests of obtaining an unfair advantage over one's competitors. Practically all such activities are illegal. See also CUTTHROAT COMPETITION.

unfair labor practices Certain practices of employers that were, in the United States, outlawed by the National Labor Relations (Wagner) Act of 1935 (see also under LABOR LAWS), chiefly on the ground that they curtail or deny employees the right of collective bargaining. The law singled out five such practices: (1) interfering with, restraining, or coercing employees in bargaining collectively through representatives of their own choosing; (2) dominating or interfering with the formation or administration of any labor organization, or contributing to its support (this provision effectively outlawed the COMPANY UNION); (3) discriminating between union and nonunion employees; (4) discriminating against anyone who filed charges under this law; (5) refusing to recognize and bargain with representatives selected by the employees.

The Taft-Hartley Act of 1947 upheld these provisions of the Wagner Act but extended the concept of unfair labor practices to unions as well. Accordingly, it held it unfair for labor unions to (1) restrain or coerce an employer in selecting its representatives for collective bargaining or grievance adjustment; (2) engage in or support a strike or boycott to push an employer into an employers' association, which would then bargain for it; (3) coerce employees in their selection of a bargaining representative (that is, in choosing one union over another); (4) try to make an employer discriminate between union and nonunion workers (except under a union security clause); (5) strike in order to force an employer to recognize one union when another is already duly certified.

unfavorable balance of trade   See under BAL-
ANCE OF TRADE.

unfilled orders   Orders received by producers (usually manufacturers) that have not yet passed through their sales accounts. The sum of unfilled orders in durable goods industries at any given time is an important COINCIDENT INDICATOR of the business cycle. Order backlogs begin to decline just as the business cycle reaches a peak and tend to rise about the time the general business cycle bottoms out.

unfunded debt   See FLOATING DEBT.

unified bond   See under BOND, def. 1.

Uniform Commercial Code   In the United States, a coordinated code of laws governing the most important legal aspects of business and financial transactions. Prepared over a period of years by the American Law Institute and the National Conference of Commissioners on Uniform State Laws, by 1975 the code had been accepted in every state except Louisiana. It covers such topics as sales, commercial paper, bank deposits and collections, letters of credit, bulk transfers, warehouse receipts and other documents of title, investment securities, secured transactions, sales of accounts, contract rights, and chattel paper. The Uniform Commercial Code includes many formerly separate "uniform" laws, such as the Uniform Sales Act and the Uniform Warehouse Receipts Act. As of 1975, however, it still did not include the Uniform Partnership Act, even though that law had been adopted in most states.

uniform delivered price   See DELIVERED PRIC-
ING.

unilateral transfer   See under BALANCE OF PAY-
MENTS.

union   See LABOR UNION.

union label   A label marking the output of union members. It frequently is used during a BOYCOTT, when a particular union seeks to induce members of other unions and the general public to refuse to buy goods not bearing that label. For example, American West Coast unions fighting fruit and vegetable growers who refuse to hire union help have conducted a nationwide campaign to persuade consumers to buy only union-picked produce.

union shop   An agreement whereby an employer may hire either union members or nonmembers, but the latter then must join the union within 30 days of hiring. Union shops are common in mass-production industries, where there are many kinds of job within each firm and employment is on a relatively long-term basis. In effect it represents a form of CLOSED SHOP with the provision of a 30-day waiting period. (The Taft-Hartley Act of 1947 originally also required a majority vote by employees for a union shop, but this provision was rescinded in 1951.) Some states, however, have outlawed union shops by means of RIGHT-TO-WORK LAWS. A variation on the union shop is the *agency shop*, which may employ nonunion members who, however, must pay regular union dues and fees. In effect these payments are charges by the union for its bargaining power, which from the union's viewpoint prevents nonmembers from benefiting at the expense of others. See also OPEN SHOP.

unitary elasticity   See under ELASTICITY, def. 1.

unit banking A system whereby banks operate a single office rather than several branches (see BRANCH BANKING). The American banking system was long based on the principle of unit banking (in order to avoid concentration of economic power) but in the second half of the 20th century slowly began to succumb to branch banking, despite stringent state regulations.

unit cost In cost accounting, the cost of a selected quantity of output. *Average unit cost* is calculated by dividing the total number of units produced into total costs. (See also AVERAGE COST, def. 1.) Costing units may consist of units of measure (cost per ton, gallon, yard, square foot, etc.), of time spent (cost per man-hour or machine-hour), or of some arbitrary unit set up with a weighted-average method or some other mathematical formula. Unit cost generally is used only in industries were a largely homogeneous product is produced in a reasonably continuous process. See also under PROCESS COST.

United Nations Economic and Social Council See ECONOMIC AND SOCIAL COUNCIL, UNITED NATIONS.

United States, Bank of the See BANK OF THE UNITED STATES.

United States government For government agencies, such as the Bureau of the Budget or the Department of the Treasury, see under the subject component of the title (e.g., Budget, Bureau of the; Treasury, Department of the).

unit investment trust A specialized kind of FRONT-END LOAD PLAN consisting of a package of bonds, either corporate or municipal. The investor buys not individual bonds but units of approximately $1,000 each and in return receives a certificate attesting to ownership of so many units. The trusts are self-liquidating over a period of time. As the various bonds mature and as each comes due, the investor in the unit trust gets back a proportionate part of the investment, and throughout also receives monthly checks representing interest payments. Most unit investment trusts are put together by brokerage houses, which frequently also partici-

pate in the original underwriting of the bonds in the trust. In these cases the trust serves as a vehicle for marketing the issue.

unit-record equipment See under PUNCHED-CARD DATA PROCESSING.

universe Also, *population*. In statistics, the totality of the set of items or units under consideration. For example, in a U.S. Presidential election, the universe used by the Gallup poll would include all registered voters, and statistical inference from a SAMPLE (def. 1) of these voters would be applied to predict their actual choices.

unlisted security A SECURITY not listed on an organized exchange and therefore traded only in the OVER-THE-COUNTER MARKET.

unsecured loan See under LOAN, def. 1.

upswing Also, *upturn*. See RALLY.

up tick In trading stocks, describing a stock price above that of the preceding transaction. Also called a *plus tick*, it is designated by a plus sign (+) before the price displayed at the STOCK EXCHANGE trading post at which the stock is traded. A *zero-plus tick* means a price unchanged from the preceding transaction but higher than the preceding different price. In the United States short sales may take place only on an up tick or zero-plus tick (see SELLING SHORT). See also DOWN TICK.

urbanization The growth of cities, brought about by a population shift from rural areas and small communities to large ones, and the change from a largely agricultural economy to an industrial one. In the United States a great shift in population from rural to urban areas began in the late 19th century, and it has continued to this day. In 1860 only 16.1 per cent of the American population lived in cities; by 1900 this figure had risen to 32.9 per cent, in 1950 it was 64 per cent, and in 1970, 73.5 per cent. One of the obvious conclusions that may be drawn is that fewer and fewer farmers were needed to feed the nation, even though the total population increased from fewer than 76 million in 1900 to more than 203 million in 1970.

Urban Mass Transportation Administration A division of the U.S. Department of Transportation concerned with developing improved mass transport facilities, especially in large urban areas, and helping state and local governments finance such systems.

urban renewal In the United States, any of various programs undertaken by government and private business (usually in cooperation) to redevelop and improve portions of cities. These measures include slum clearance, rehabilitation of specific neighborhoods, interim assistance for blighted areas, concentrated enforcement of building codes, and demolition of inadequate structures. The U.S. Department of Housing and Urban Development provides loans and grants for such projects, which in some states also are helped by state agencies and funds.

usage In inventory control, the amount of a given material or part used in a given period of time. Usage of production items usually depends directly on the demand for the firm's end-products. If usage is steady, forecasting the need for materials normally presents no problem. If, as happens more often, usage fluctuates, a number of factors may be responsible, such as secular change (changes in need or taste), cyclical variation (the state of the business cycle), seasonal variation, or simply random events.

user cost A way of calculating depreciation on capital equipment that takes into account its estimated future earnings. Instead of depreciation being calculated simply as a percentage cost over the years of the equipment's usefulness (whether the equipment is actually being used or not), user cost represents the amount by which the discounted future earnings of a piece of equipment have been reduced by use. This approach is an outgrowth of the Keynesian concept of the marginal efficiency of capital, which J. M. KEYNES regarded as a major inducement for capital investment (for an explanation of *marginal efficiency of capital* see under PRODUCTIVITY).

use tax A tax levied on the use of particular goods or services rather than on their sale. In the United States, states having a SALES TAX may levy a use tax to prevent residents from buying goods in neighboring states to avoid payment of the sales tax.

usury The crime of charging borrowers a higher rate of interest than legally allowed. In the United States interest rates are regulated by state laws setting forth a *maximum contract rate of interest* as the highest legal annual rate. Some economists believe that interest rates on personal loans should not be regulated at all but be geared to demand for and supply of loanable funds. In practice, however, this market—like most—is characterized by IMPERFECT COMPETITION. Further, many individuals seeking loans (particularly consumers seeking personal loans) are ignorant of the true interest rate they are being charged. Despite enactment of a strong Truth-in-Lending Law (see under CONSUMER PROTECTION LAWS) whereby lenders must indicate interest clearly, usurious lending practices have not been completely eliminated.

utilitarianism See under J. BENTHAM.

utility
   1. See PUBLIC UTILITY.
   2. In economic theory, the usefulness of a good or service, or the satisfaction it yields. Utility is a subjective phenomenon, varying from person to person and frequently depending on various external factors, so that it cannot be objectively measured. The concept of utility lies at the heart of classical economics, especially the concept of MARGINAL UTILITY, which it uses to explain consumer demand (see also MARGINALIST SCHOOL). Later theorists, among them J. R. Hicks and L. E. von Mises, suggested that while utility could not be expressed in absolute terms, it could be described in relative terms, and that consumer preference for—or indifference to—various goods, shown by ranking them in order of preference, would constitute a valid measure of utility. This concept is sometimes called the *theory of ordinal utility*. See also VALUE.

utility theory of value See under MARGINALIST SCHOOL.

utopian socialism A very diverse movement based on the idea that free enterprise and competition promote injustice, and that the social and economic evils of the world can be eliminated in some kind of ideal ("utopian") cooperative community. The utopians reached the peak of their strength during the first half of the 19th century, with such leaders as Louis BLANC, FOURIER, and OWEN. Others, while not specifically interested in cooperative communities, had similar ideas, notably SAINT-SIMON and Simonde de SISMONDI. See also SOCIALISM.

valuation See ASSESSMENT, def. 1.

value Also, *exchange value, market value, value in exchange*. The worth or usefulness of a good or service expressed in terms of either a specific sum of money (called its *price*) or a certain quantity of some other good or service. See also BOOK VALUE; CAPITALIZED VALUE; DENOMINATIONAL VALUE; PAR VALUE; UTILITY, def. 2; VALUE ADDED. For *scarcity value*, see under SCARCITY. For economic theories of value, see COST OF PRODUCTION THEORY OF VALUE; LABOR THEORY OF VALUE; utility theory of value, under MARGINALIST SCHOOL; SURPLUS LABOR AND VALUE THEORY.

value, paradox of A famous question put by the 18th-century economist Adam Smith, who asked, "Why is water, which is essential to life, so much cheaper than diamonds, which are quite unnecessary?" Smith explained this paradox simply by saying that the "value in use" of a good—that is, its utility—was different from its "value in exchange," or market value. Smith concluded that the difference in value between diamonds and water is based on the amount of labor required to obtain them (see LABOR THEORY OF VALUE), whereas most modern theorists would state it as a difference of supply relative to demand: water is plentiful (despite huge demand for it) but diamonds are scarce.

value added Also, *value added by manufacture*. The difference between the price of purchased raw materials, semifinished and finished parts, and services that are used to make a product and that product's final selling price. In other words, value added is the increase in price of these purchased elements created by a firm's production processes. Thus a company with total annual sales of $1 million and purchases of $600,000 per year would have value added—either by manufacture or by distribution—of $400,000. Calculating value added is a far more accurate way of determining an industry's contribution to the overall economy than simply calculating gross sales, since it indicates just how much value has been contributed by the manufacturing process. The concept is sometimes also extended to productive services, such as those rendered by professionals. See also VALUE-ADDED TAX.

value-added tax A tax on business income, based on the value added by the operations of the business, which is defined as the total value of output minus the value of purchased materials input. In effect, the value added is thus equal to the sum of profits, interest, depreciation, and total labor costs. Proposed as an alternative to the U.S. Federal tax on corporation income, the value-added tax is widely used in Europe.

value analysis A cost-reduction technique whereby the relationship of design, function, and cost of any material or service is examined with the object of reducing costs through modifying a design or material specification, using a more efficient manufacturing process, finding a better source of supply, eliminating a part entirely, or some other means. The object of value analysis is to get more value from an item in terms of its function. For example, if a die-cast nut made of zinc can be substituted for a brass nut turned out on a screw machine, the cost of nuts may be reduced by more than half. While the absolute saving might amount to only a few dollars per thousand, a company using hundreds of millions of nuts per year may achieve a substantial saving. The usefulness of value analysis is by no means confined to business and industry. The consumer who decides that a supermarket house brand of bleach costing half as much as a nationally advertised brand is equally effective is practicing value analysis.

variable annuity See under ANNUITY.

variable cost Also, *variable expense.* A business cost that varies in direct proportion to the volume of output. Thus a variable cost by definition cannot be incurred when output is at a standstill. The principal variable costs of any manufacturing enterprise are direct labor and direct materials. Other examples are certain factory supplies, sales commissions, and (usually) power used for production (but not for running accounting machines, lighting administrative offices, etc.). See also DIRECT COST; FIXED COST; SEMIVARIABLE COST.

variable overhead See under OVERHEAD.

variable proportions, law of See DIMINISHING RETURNS, LAW OF.

variables, inspection by See under INSPECTION.

variance
1. In statistics, the sum of the squares of the deviations from the mean (see also under STANDARD DEVIATION). *Analysis of variance* involves determining whether a particular item or value comes from a population. For example, if a drill press equipped with a .750 drill actually drills a hole with a diameter of .800, the statistician can determine the probability that this event could occur, given that the process is supposed to produce .750 holes.
2. In accounting, the difference between standard or anticipated costs and actual costs of production. Normally such costs are divided into direct labor, materials, and overhead for each department. A separate *variance account* is set up for each category to record the appropriate cost differences. If variances are positive, the company can expect its costs to be lower and its profits probably higher than originally anticipated; if variances are negative, management must make some change to prevent a decline in profit. Variance accounts also can be used to measure the performance of the manager responsible for the costs.

variety store See under RETAIL.

vault cash
1. Also, *till money.* General term for the currency a bank keeps on hand for cash transactions, such as cashing checks.
2. The total currency held by all banks as part of their reserves. It is not considered part of the MONEY SUPPLY because banks require some minimum cash inventory simply to operate, and this cash does not really circulate.

Veblen, Thorstein An American economist (1857–1929), founder of INSTITUTIONAL ECONOMICS and remembered principally for his idea that the institution of private property tends to make people seek property and power for their own sake rather than to work for a sense of satisfaction or to improve the quality of life. Veblen's first and most famous book, *The Theory of the Leisure Class* (1899), postulated that society is ruled by a leisure class that is, in effect, predatory, and those who accumulate wealth want to display their acquisitions (or, as Veblen put it, indulge in *conspicuous consumption*). Poorer people, who must work merely to subsist, still imitate the values of their "betters" (Veblen called this "pecuniary emulation"). Social institutions, said Veblen, evolve through a process of natural selection similar to that of biological evolution. The leisure class, however, has been so sheltered from economic forces that it resists natural change. Essentially a pessimist, Veblen criticized the entire system of profit-making as wasteful but proposed no viable reforms or alternatives.

velocity of money Also, *velocity of circulation of money.* The rate at which money circulates within the economy, viewed in terms of either spending (*transactions velocity*) or income (*income velocity*). The transactions velocity of money is measured by how many times during a year (or some other period) the same dollar (or other monetary unit) is spent, which is calculated by dividing total sales volume by the total money supply in circulation. If individuals and businesses are holding on to money, the transactions velocity slows down, indicating declining business activity; if they spend it soon after they receive it, it tends to rise, indicating expanding business activity. The income velocity of money is measured by how many times during a year (or other period) the same dollar (or other monetary unit) becomes someone else's income, calculated by dividing GROSS NATIONAL PRODUCT by the total money supply (currency plus demand deposits). Both transactions and income velocity nearly always exceed 1, meaning that the same money changes hands more than once a year. The precise velocity, however, varies. To some extent it is influenced by the prevailing INTEREST RATE, which reflects the availability of bank credit to would-be borrowers. When interest rates are low, people are willing to hold on to more cash; when they are high, they hope to benefit from interest payments and therefore are willing to hold less cash (see also LIQUIDITY PREFERENCE).

vending machine Also, *automatic selling.* A coin-operated machine selling goods or services, notably cigarettes, candy, and beverages, as well as laundering, drying, and dry-cleaning services. The earliest vending machines in the United States date from the 1880s, when the Tutti Frutti Company installed chewing-gum machines at elevated railroad stations. Today 20 per cent of all candy bars, 25 per cent of all bottled soft drinks, and 16 per cent of all cigarettes in the United States are sold by such machines. Nevertheless, automatic selling accounts for only about 2 per cent of all retail sales. The major drawback is high operating costs, including the high cost of the machines themselves as well as the labor required to stock and maintain them in working order.

vendor
1. In general, any seller.
2. In business and industry, same as SUPPLIER.
3. In business law, the owner of a property whose title is being transferred to another party, called the buyer or *vendee.*

vendor performance index An index of the percentage of American purchasing agents who report slower deliveries from suppliers, an important LEADING INDICATOR of business conditions. It reaches a peak six months to a year ahead of the general business cycle, with 70 per cent or more of respondents reporting slower deliveries (showing suppliers cannot keep up with demand), and generally touches bottom a few months ahead of the cycle, with 25 per cent or fewer reporting slow deliveries. Developed by the National Bureau of Economic Research, the vendor performance index is published regularly in *Business Conditions Digest.*

venture capital See RISK CAPITAL.

verbal agreement See under CONTRACT.

verifier See under PUNCHED-CARD DATA PROCESSING.

vertical equity See under ABILITY-TO-PAY PRINCIPLE.

vertical integration Also, *vertical expansion.* The expansion of a business through the acquisition of more divisions or other firms engaged in earlier or later stages of production of its commodity. For example, an auto manufacturer might first build its own steel mill and then develop mines for the coal, limestone, and iron ore needed to make the steel. This is "backward" vertical integration. "Forward" vertical integration would occur when the manufacturer began to sell directly to automobile buyers (consumers) instead of through independent dealers.

vested interest

1. A legal claim or right to the present or future enjoyment of some property or activity. For example, employees have a vested interest in a company pension fund to which they have contributed and from which they expect to receive benefits upon retirement.

2. A loosely used term for wealthy property owners as a class, who have well-established interests.

Veterans Administration

Also, *VA*. An independent Federal agency established in 1930 to administer laws covering a wide range of benefits for former members of the U.S. armed forces and their dependents and beneficiaries. Among the benefits are special compensations and pensions, education, rehabilitation of disabled veterans, guaranty of housing loans, and life insurance. The Veterans Administration also operates hundreds of hospitals, clinics, and nursing homes that provide medical care for veterans.

virtual storage

See under STORAGE, def. 1.

visible item

See under INVISIBLE ITEM.

visual display

Also, *graphic*. The results of a computer's operations presented in the form of drawings, figures, graphs, or characters, usually via a cathode-ray tube. For an example, see under TICKER.

vocational training

Learning how to perform a given kind of work for a business or trade, at a vocational or trade school, in an APPRENTICE program, or on the job. In the United States the Federal government has assisted state and local vocational training programs since passage of the Smith-Hughes Act of 1917. After World War II, rapid technological change led to major *retraining* programs for employees whose jobs were phased out in various industries, in some cases administered by the individual firms (particularly large corpora-

tions). In the 1960s and 1970s several Federal laws were passed to provide funds for helping unemployed or underemployed workers develop new skills and to train the chronically unemployed and disadvantaged. In addition, several states established training and retraining programs for the unemployed, and some labor unions have tried (with mixed success) to incorporate provisions for retraining laid-off workers in their labor contracts.

void

See under CONTRACT.

volume of money

Same as MONEY SUPPLY.

volume of trade

In the securities market, the total number of shares that change hands in a day's trading on an organized exchange. The term is also sometimes used for trade in a single stock.

voluntary bankruptcy

See under BANKRUPTCY.

voluntary chain

See under CHAIN STORE.

voluntary export quota

See EXPORT QUOTA, def. 2.

von Wieser, Friedrich

See under WIESER.

voting right

The stockholder's right to vote in the affairs of the issuing corporation. Most shares of common stock carry one vote each. Preferred stock normally carries the right to vote only when dividends are in default for a specified period. A stockholder's right to vote may be delegated to another person by means of a PROXY.

voting trust

See under TRUST, def. 2.

voucher

1. Any written document that serves as proof that money has been paid or received, such as a canceled check, petty cash receipt, receipted bill, etc. See also RECEIPT, def. 1.

2. *voucher system*. An accounting system of internal control for cash outlays based on the use of vouchers as evidence of all cash payments. Every purchase or disbursement is recorded in voucher form. A typical voucher includes the voucher number, date, name of payee, description of items or services covered, price, discount, net amount, and approval for payment; relevant invoices and other papers are attached to it. The voucher may further show the accounts to be debited for the transaction, the amount to be credited to the vouchers payable account, due date for payment, actual date of payment, and the number of the check used for payment. Each voucher is entered into the *voucher register*, a separate book kept for this pur-pose; from it the transactions periodically are entered into the ledger under the appropriate accounts. A voucher system lends itself readily to electronic data processing, the whole process then being handled by computer.

voucher check A CHECK that shows other particulars of the transaction for which it is used, such as a discount or other deductions, invoice number, description of goods or services being paid for, or other information about the nature of the payment.

wage Also, *wages*. In economics, any regular payment to an employee of a business for his or her labor by the hour, week, month, or some other period, or by units of output. (For a more restricted definition, see under SALARY.) To the employee a wage is income; to the business it is part of the cost of production, specifically labor cost. The role of wages in a business depends largely on the relationship of its labor costs to its total costs: if labor represents a sizable percentage of total cost, a relatively small change in wages can have a substantial effect on the business as a whole; if it represents but a small fraction, even a considerable change may have little effect. Wages, like other costs in a capitalist economy, are at least partly determined by supply and demand (in socialist countries they are established by the government). Other factors include the mobility (or lack of it) of workers, the influence of labor unions, company policy, legislative controls, product market competition, and numerous irrational considerations (for example, employers' reluctance to cut wages or workers' refusal to accept lower wages or to move to another location where wages are higher). As a result, *wage structure*—the various rates of pay within a given firm—varies widely from company to company, and *wage differentials*—differences in pay for essentially the same work—are even wider from industry to industry. For example, a secretary in one small manufacturing firm may be paid 50 per cent more than a secretary in a competing firm, or a truck driver in the textile industry may receive as much as 50 per cent less than a driver for a steel company. Wages also vary with geographic location (in the United States, wage rates in the South have long been lower than in the Midwest), and according to sex and race (women often earn less than men, blacks less than whites). Within a company the overall *wage scale* (how much is paid to whom) is determined largely through a combination of JOB EVALUATION, the *prevailing wage* (or *going rate*) for given jobs in the particular area at that time, and, in unionized industries, collective bargaining.

Since the time of Adam SMITH and even earlier, economists have formulated theories concerning wages. Smith himself, along with others of the CLASSICAL SCHOOL, believed in a *natural wage*, determined solely by supply and demand. The minimum wage must be a *subsistence* wage (sufficient for survival), but when demand for labor rose, wages would rise above this minimum. Less optimistic theorists, such as David Ricardo, believed that wages always tend to remain at the bare subsistence level (see IRON LAW OF WAGES). John Stuart Mill and others saw wages as determined by the number of workers who must share a fixed quantity of capital set aside by entrepreneurs (see WAGES-FUND THEORY). The marginalists devised the MARGINAL PRODUCTIVITY THEORY of wages, linking wages to workers' productivity. The *bargaining theory of wages*, developed when labor unions grew more powerful, holds that wages are never higher than the capitalist's break-even point or lower than the worker's subsistence level, but exactly where between those two points they fall depends on the relative bargaining power of capitalists and of workers. Most present-day economists would agree that the broad, overall level of wages is determined by productivity, but that specific wages are determined by a complex interplay of many forces, which in turn influence the supply of and demand for labor.

wage control   See under COST-PUSH INFLATION.

wage differential   See under WAGE.

wage incentive   A system of wage payments that are tied directly to standards of productivity of individuals or groups of workers and/or the profitability of the organization. Wage incentives represent financial inducements to motivate employees to perform better than they presumably would at their regular basic wage rate. (In most cases wage incentives are additions to a basic wage rate, or *base pay*; among the exceptions are real estate firms, which ordinarily pay sales personnel on a straight commission basis.) There are four main kinds of wage incentive plan: individual incentive plans; group incentive plans; plantwide productivity plans; and PROFIT-SHARING plans. Except for profit-sharing, most incentive plans apply to production workers and only rarely to white-collar jobs other than sales positions. However, a high percentage of sales jobs are on a wage incentive plan (usually a sales commission).

Incentive plans for production workers, individuals or groups, tend to be one of two types: (1) *piece-rate plans*, which provide for wage payments based on the number of units produced; (2) *production bonus plans*, with payments based on unit produc-

tion in excess of standard output in standard time (standards being set by time and motion studies or other industrial engineering techniques). Piece-rate plans are the more common of the two. Among the many production bonus plans are the *Bedaux point system*, in which an employee receives a premium of 75 per cent of the points in excess of 60 per hour, each point representing one minute of productive work at normal speed; the *Emerson efficiency plan*, whereby the employee receives a base rate for standard output plus an *accelerating premium* for any work in excess of two-thirds of standard output (the more output, the higher the premium); the *Gantt premium plan*, whereby an employee receives base pay for standard output and a standard piece rate plus a percentage premium on work in excess of standard output; and variations on these plans known as the *Barth plan, Halsey premium plan, Rowan premium plan,* and *Taylor differential piece rate*. Still other incentive plans are *sales-pay plans*, with commissions or bonuses based on the dollar volume or number of items sold, and the *measured day-rate plan*, whereby employees are rated periodically on productivity, quality of output, reliability, etc., and are paid a premium according to their current rating. (In the auto industry, however, the latter term refers to a predetermined minimum daily output, based on time studies and required of all workers.)

Plantwide productivity plans aim to increase production efficiency and reduce labor costs through worker participation on committees to develop constructive suggestions about machines, methods, plant layout, materials, and so on. Cost reductions then are measured in some way, and all or part of the savings are passed on to the employees in the form of a wage premium. One of the best-known such plans is the *Scanlon plan*, originated about 1950 by William Scanlon. In similar plans individual workers receive a bonus as a reward for cost-cutting suggestions.

wage-price spiral   See COST-PUSH INFLATION.

wage push   See COST-PUSH INFLATION.

wages, theories of   See under WAGE.

wage scale   See under WAGE.

wages-fund theory The idea held by John Stuart Mill and some other 19th-century economists that wages are determined by a fixed amount of capital set aside by entrepreneurs, which is divided by the total number of workers in the labor force. Thus the only way to increase wages is to cut the number of workers sharing the fixed sum (or "fund"), or to increase capitalists' profits (through higher prices) so that they can set aside more capital for the "fund." However, since industrial employers can pay wages from current production or even from borrowed funds, there is no need for such a fixed fund. Mill himself retracted the theory in later writings. The wages-fund theory replaced the IRON LAW OF WAGES theory and was itself superseded by the MARGINAL PRODUCTIVITY THEORY.

wage structure See under WAGE.

Wagner Act See under LABOR LAWS; also UNFAIR LABOR PRACTICES.

wagon jobber See under WHOLESALE.

waiting period Same as *cooling-off period*; see under STRIKE.

waiver In law, renouncing, abandoning, or surrendering some right, claim, or privilege. See also RELEASE.

walking delegate An older name for BUSINESS AGENT.

walkout See STRIKE.

Walras, Léon A French economist (1834–1910), one of the founders of the MARGINALIST SCHOOL and an important innovator in the application of mathematical techniques to economic analysis. After trying his hand at various fields of endeavor, Walras in 1870 became a professor of political economy at the University of Lausanne, Switzerland, where most of his important work in economics was to be done. Like JEVONS and MENGER, Walras independently arrived at the idea that marginal utility (in French, *rareté*) was the essence of value, and that buyers and sellers alike try to maximize it for themselves. A more original contribution was his GENERAL EQUILIBRIUM THEORY, which for the first time recognized the interrelation of price and output both for commodities produced and for factors of production. Walras's analysis involved a system of equations that showed the effect of a change in one item on all the others.

Waltham system The consolidation of all processes of textile manufacture in a single factory. It is named for the town of Waltham, Massachusetts, where in 1814 Francis Cabot Lowell, a Boston merchant, installed a new set of spinning machinery and a power loom in his factory. Other features of the system were large capital investment, the recruitment of farm girls (who were housed in dormitories) to work in the factory, and the standardization of production. In 1822 Lowell's brother-in-law, Patrick Tracy Jackson, founded the town of Lowell and built a textile mill there using the same methods and principles, though on an even larger scale. Therefore the Waltham system is also known as the *Lowell system*. See also RHODE ISLAND SYSTEM.

want A need or desire for a good or service, not necessarily accompanied by the means (money, opportunity, ability, etc.) for satisfying it. See also DEMAND.

want ad See under CLASSIFIED ADVERTISING.

war, financing of The special problems created by the tremendous demand for goods and services that every participant in a war must somehow finance. So long as a nation produces all its own munitions, the financing of the war theoretically creates no problems. Higher taxes will enable the government to buy all the arms it needs and will leave the private economy with so little money to spend that production of civilian goods will have to be cut back for lack of demand, thereby also making available more capacity for munitions production. In practice, however, governments never have raised taxes high enough to make wars self-financing. Instead, they issue bonds, bought by the general public and by banks. In the former case they work just as a tax would, except that after the war income tends to be further redistributed, with a stream of interest payments (on the bonds) going to the "savers" and being taxed from the "spenders" who did not buy them. Most bonds end up being bought by banks, simply because private buyers cannot or will not save enough. These bonds sooner or later become primary reserves in the banking system, leading to an expansion of the money supply and, ultimately, inflation, which also works as a tax to reduce civilian purchasing power. Price inflation has been experienced by every major participant in every major war.

War financing generates even more complications when munitions are imported and cannot be financed by exports or by liquidating investments. As a result, the belligerent nations are left with a *war debt* on which interest and principal payments have to be met for many years after the end of hostilities. The debtor must be willing to divert a part of its production to payment of interest and principal (and also to *reparations* if the debtor was on the losing side). This allocation of resources leaves its population with fewer goods and services. For example, for many years after World War II a major part of Finnish industrial production was shipped directly to the Soviet Union as part of the reparations demanded for Finnish "aggression" against Russia. (Finland, a small, weak neighbor of the Soviet Union, had no choice but to comply.)

Unfortunately, many creditor nations are not willing or able to accept repayment in the form of exports, lest their balance of trade become unfavorable and the extra imports have an adverse effect on their own employment and production. This was the case with the United States after World War I. Both Great Britain and France had generated huge debts by purchasing American munitions, and all participants borrowed even more early in the postwar period. However, the United States maintained high tariffs, a barrier to payment of the debt in the form of goods (which therefore could not compete with domestically produced items), and continued to enjoy a favorable balance of trade after the war. Consequently, interest and principal on the European war debt could be financed only by additional debt. In the end, the entire system collapsed with the Great Depression of the 1930s. Almost all of the debt was eventually repudiated, but only after an economic shock that not only reverberated throughout the entire world but also, in the opinion of many, became a major cause of World War II.

war debt See under WAR, FINANCING OF.

warehouse A building or other structure used for storing goods of various kinds. A *public warehouse* is one in which businesses and individuals can rent space for storing property (merchandise, household goods, cars, etc.) for varying periods of time. The operators of such warehouses, called *warehousemen*, usually also provide such services as receiving, packing, and crating. A *bonded warehouse* is one licensed and bonded by the government to insure against loss of customs duties or taxes. Goods subject to customs duty or to tax (imported goods, alcoholic beverages, etc.) may be stored there without paying either duty or tax; such goods are said to be *under bond*. In the case of imports they may then be re-exported (without payment of duty); in the case of taxable items the tax need not be paid until they are withdrawn from the warehouse.

When goods are placed in a warehouse, the warehouseman issues to the owner a *warehouse receipt*, which may be a NEGOTIABLE INSTRUMENT (if it states the goods will be delivered to the bearer, or to the order of any person named in the receipt, it is negotiable). Negotiable warehouse receipts often are used as collateral for loans, especially by businesses that periodically accumulate large inventories of either raw materials or finished goods. By storing these inventories in a warehouse, they can use the warehouse receipt to borrow working capital. This use has led to the practice of *field warehousing*, in which the goods may actually be kept on the owner's premises but a warehouser takes charge of the actual place of storage, enabling the owner to receive a negotiable warehouse receipt. Through this device the goods need not be transported, saving both shipping and storage costs.

warrant

1. Also, *option warrant, stock-purchase warrant.* A certificate that gives the holder the right to buy shares of stock at a given price within a specified

time or in perpetuity. A warrant may be either separate or attached to a bond, short-term note, or certificate of preferred stock. Warrants so attached often serve as inducements to buy the obligation or stock. Unattached warrants or those that can be detached from such issues are traded on the open market just as securities are. (Nondetachable warrants cannot be bought or sold separately from the security.) However, they tend to be quite speculative since, unlike stock rights (which they resemble), they tend to involve a longer time period, during which both overall prices and specific prices are apt to change more than over a short term. See also RIGHTS.

2. *subscription warrant.* See under PREEMPTIVE RIGHTS.

warranty In selling a commodity, an undertaking of responsibility by the seller for the quality or suitability of the product. An *express warranty* is a specific statement by the seller that the quality, capacity, or some other characteristic of the merchandise is adequate (for example, that a paint is suitable for outdoor use, or that a fabric is 100 per cent cotton). An *implied warranty* is one not made directly by the seller but implied by law (for example, that the seller has title to the goods and hence may sell them, or that a product sold as food is fit for human comsumption). In general a seller is liable for damages for *breach of warranty* (violation of an express or implied warranty) to the immediate purchaser. However, in many cases the courts tend to hold manufacturers and processors liable to the ultimate consumer for such damages. Thus, for example, if defective wiring in a household appliance causes a fire, the consumer might sue not only the dealer from which the appliance was purchased but also the distributor or manufacturer. See also GUARANTY.

warranty deed Also, *general warranty deed.* In real estate law, a document containing certain assurances or guarantees that a DEED conveys a good and unencumbered title. These guarantees, also known as *convenants of title,* vary with local practice but usually hold that the deed's grantor has good title to the property conveyed, that there are no ENCUMBRANCES on it except as stated in the deed, and that the deed's grantee will not be evicted by someone holding a better title or LIEN. See also QUITCLAIM DEED.

wash sale The simultaneous buying and selling of large blocks of a stock, in order to create the illusion of great activity in trading it. If persuaded, the public generally reacts by increasing its purchases of the stock, driving up the price. The market manipulators then frequently begin selling it short, bringing down the price sharply, and then buy it back to make a huge profit. In the United States wash sales are basically illegal, but even if they were not, they would be difficult to effect because the Securities and Exchange Commission allows SELLING SHORT only on an UP TICK (that is, a gain over the previous trading price).

waste In the processing and manufacuring industries, the loss of material, often unavoidable. For example, any cutting operation generates some bits and pieces; such process SCRAP often has some resale value.

wasting assets corporation A CORPORATION engaged in a business that deliberately exhuasts its assets. The most common examples are the various extractive industries, such as coal, iron, oil, and other minerals. A wasting assets corporation also may be formed specifically to buy and liquidate a given stock of merchandise, such as the assets of a company in bankruptcy. Unlike other corporations, which may pay stockholders dividends only from earned surplus, a wasting assets corporation may pay out almost its entire cash flow as dividends—not only earnings but also depletion and depreciation allowances—gradually exhausting all of its assets.

watered stock A stock issued with an inflated value. For example, a buyer might pay only $1 million for a company and then issue $2 million worth of stock in it. The owner then would either sell all the stock and pocket the extra $1 million, or sell only half and keep the other half, retaining half ownership in the company at zero cost. The term "watered" comes from the practice of first feeding cattle salt and then letting them drink freely on the way to market, temporarily increasing their weight to bring up their price.

waybill A document issued by a carrier that contains the same information as a BILL OF LADING (origin of goods, destination, consignor, consignee, description of shipment) but, unlike the latter, does not represent a contract between the shipper and the carrier or a document of title to the goods.

wealth

1. In economic theory, the sum of tangible assets of an individual, called *personal wealth*, or of a nation, called NATIONAL WEALTH. Some economists include all property, but many exclude securities, deeds, mortgages, and similar assets because they regard them more as claims on property than as actual property. Similarly, many economists do not regard money as wealth but simply as a medium of exchange, with which wealth (assets) can be acquired.

2. In business practice and general usage, the sum of a person's or firm's assets, both tangible (real estate, clothing, factories, machinery, stocks, bonds, bank accounts, etc.) and intangible (good health, professional skill, etc.).

Webb, Beatrice Potter and Sidney See under FABIAN SOCIALISM.

Weber, Max A German lawyer and economist (1864–1920), member of the GERMAN HISTORICAL SCHOOL, who is remembered principally for his thesis that Protestantism—particularly Calvinism—created the necessary environment for the rise of CAPITALISM. Applying the historical method to his study of successful businessmen in both Protestant and Roman Catholic nations, Weber found that virtually all of them were Calvinists and concluded that Calvinism itself, with its emphasis on hard work and achievement, was responsible for the self-interest and profit motives that characterize successful entrepreneurs. Weber's critics point out that economic and social changes themselves had created the climate for Calvinism, and, further, that history is too complex to single out one factor as being responsible for change. Weber stated his thesis in his most famous book, *The Protestant Ethic and the Rise of Capitalism,* but in other works he stressed such factors as the role of central government and the rise of industrial technology,

implying that he had never considered religion the sole cause of such complex phenomena.

weighted average An average of items in which some or all of them are increased, or "weighted," by given values, called "weights." An item that is assigned a triple weight, for instance, would be multiplied by 3. In computing the average, the sum of the items is divided by the sum of the weights (instead of by the total number of items, as for an arithmetic MEAN). For example, suppose the items and weights are as follows:

Weight	Item	Weighted item
2.0	12	24
1.5	14	21
2.5	16	40
6.0	42	85

To compute the mean, one would divide the total values of the items, 42, by the number of items, 3, and arrive at 14. To take a weighted average, one would divide the total of weighted items, 85, by the sum of the weights, 6, arriving at 14.6667. The purpose of weighted averages is to adjust the actual values in a series so as to reflect their relative importance, so that, for example, in averaging a family's expenditures one can take into account the fact that rent represents a more important outlay than a club membership. Consequently, weighted averages are often used in constructing various kinds of index (see also INDEX NUMBER).

welfare Also, *public assistance, public welfare.* Any of various programs undertaken by government to provide financial assistance to persons in need, among them the old, the blind, the disabled, and dependent children. In the United States the *Social and Rehabilitation Service* of the Department of Health, Education, and Welfare administers most Federal programs providing technical and financial aid for this purpose to states, local communities, other organizations, and individuals. Chief among its programs are the *Aid to Families with Dependent Children (AFDC)* and the associated *Work Incentive (WIN)* program designed to help AFDC recipients become self-supporting. It also administers medical and social-service assistance, principally through grants to state agencies, as well as state-Federal programs of vocational rehabilitation for the disabled and those with developmental disabilities (mental retardation, etc.). See also POVERTY.

welfare capitalism The concept that workers will be discouraged from joining labor unions if employers create sufficiently favorable conditions. This approach, taken by some American firms in the 1920s included such tactics as supplying cafeterias, recreation facilities, and comfortable washrooms, and sponsoring intramural athletic contests, publishing company magazines, and other features designed to boost worker morale. Some companies even sold stock to employees, while others concentrated on forming a COMPANY UNION.

welfare economics A branch of economics concerned with attaining various goals of social welfare through specific economic policies. These goals generally include the highest possible living standard for all individuals, a more equitable distribution of income (eliminating the extremes of rich and poor), and maximum freedom of economic choice. Welfare economists simply assume that these ends are universally desirable. Policies to achieve them might include heavy taxation of the rich, a special dole for the poor, and the elimination of monopolies. An economy that concentrates on the provision of social services to eliminate income differences is sometimes called a WELFARE STATE. One of the earliest proponents of welfare economics, which has as many opponents as supporters, was A. C. PIGOU.

welfare state An economic system combining CAPITALISM with elements of SOCIALISM, in that private ownership of property and business enterprise is retained, but at the same time the government enacts far-reaching social programs that seek to provide every individual with adequate education, medical care, employment, housing, pensions, etc. Attempts to assure employment and a decent living standard tend to involve increased government control of the business cycle and of total economic output, chiefly through adjusting government spending and fiscal policy. In the United States

movement toward a welfare state has been gradual, with social services greatly increased under President Franklin D. Roosevelt's "New Deal" and continuing with President Truman's "Fair Deal," Kennedy's "New Frontier," and L. B. Johnson's "War on Poverty." The only Republican President during this 36-year span (1932–68), Dwight D. Eisenhower, characterized these changes as "creeping socialism." The Full Employment Act of 1946 was the first Federal law acknowledging that the government felt responsible for providing full employment. The Economic Opportunity Act of 1964 continued the trend, providing programs for aiding needy high school and college students, loans to low-income farmers and business, education and job training, and Federal aid to various community, educational, and development projects. By the mid-1970s Federal health-care assistance through Medicare and Medicaid were widely believed to be inadequate, and a comprehensive national health program was under serious consideration. Other countries, notably the United Kingdom and Sweden, had long since gone much further, providing "cradle-to-grave" benefits programs for all their citizens.

wetback A pejorative term for Mexican MIGRANT LABOR in the United States, which comes from the fact that many such workers enter the country illegally by crossing the Rio Grande. The U.S. Department of Labor has imposed numerous restrictions on the employment of wetbacks, with employers subject to fines and workers to deportation. Nevertheless, thousands of wetbacks continue to enter the country and find employment, frequently being exploited by employers who pay them substandard wages.

when issued A basis for trading in new stocks and bonds shortly after they are announced and registered but before they actually exist. For example, if a company splits its stock 3-for-1, trading may begin immediately in the new stock on a when-issued basis, with the price of the new stock being roughly (but rarely exactly) one-third that of the old. While one may buy or sell on a when-issued basis, the actual settlement of the transaction cannot take place until after the security has been formally issued.

white-collar Describing workers who do predominantly nonphysical work, ranging from unskilled to semiskilled and highly skilled jobs. The term comes from the fact that, unlike manual labor (see BLUE-COLLAR), such work usually requires no special attire other than ordinary street clothes, traditionally a suit and white-collared shirt for men. Among those classified as white-collar workers by the U.S Bureau of the Census are professional and technical workers (including health-care professionals and teachers), managers and administrators (both salaried and self-employed), sales workers and clerical workers. The proportion of white-collar workers in the American labor force has been growing steadily, particularly since about 1950 (from 37.5 per cent then to 48.8 per cent in 1974), a trend considered likely to continue. See also GRAY-COLLAR.

wholesale Describing the buying and reselling of merchandise to retailers and other merchants, and to industrial, institutional, and commercial users, but not (or rarely) to ultimate consumers. A WHOLESALER thus is a middleman between producer and consumer and, like all middlemen, either takes title to the goods it buys and resells (see MERCHANT WHOLESALER) or acts as an agent on behalf of someone else (or an *agent middleman*; see under MIDDLEMAN). Wholesale trade is classified according to the range of merchandise an enterprise handles, or according to its method of operation. *General merchandise wholesalers* carry two or more unrelated kinds of goods (dry goods, hardware, furniture, sporting goods, etc.), while *general-line wholesalers* (or *single-line wholesalers*) restrict themselves to one line or closely related lines (groceries or hardware, for example); a *specialty wholesaler* deals only in a narrow line (automotive items or health foods, for example). Some wholesalers perform most or all of the functions and services associated with the wholesale trade; known as *full-service* or *service wholesalers*, they engage in selling and merchandising, buying and assembling, storage, transportation, risk-bearing, marketing, financing, and gathering market information. In contrast, *truck wholesalers* (or *wagon jobbers*) combine selling, delivery, and collection, selling their stock (chiefly perishable) direct from their trucks or wagons. A *rack jobber* takes care of stocking supermarkets and other grocery stores with nonfood items (toiletries, hardware, housewares, etc.), frequently providing the display racks and other merchandising materials needed. A *drop-shipment wholesaler* (or *drop-shipper* or *desk-jobber*) obtains orders for goods, usually large bulky items, from retailers, other wholesalers, or industrial buyers, and passes them on to producers who ship directly to the customer; the wholesaler takes title to and technically owns the goods in question but does not physically handle, stock, or deliver them. Its chief function is getting orders, but it also may locate supplies, arrange transport, finance purchases, and assume some of the risk of taking title to the goods. A *cash-and-carry wholesaler* acts as a kind of "discount store" for retailers too small to have full-service wholesalers solicit their business. Instead of salespersons coming to retailers, giving them credit, and delivering orders, retailers go to the wholesale warehouse, pick up their orders, pay cash, and "carry" them home. *Mail-order wholesalers* operate like MAIL ORDER retailers, selling by mail through their catalogs; they are used mainly for staple consumer items such as hardware, jewelry, and sporting goods. Sometimes producers combine to perform their own wholesale functions, forming a *producer cooperative*. Used mainly for agricultural products such as citrus fruits, they distribute their members' products much as full-service wholesalers do (see COOPERATIVE, def. 3).

wholesale price index A PRICE INDEX constructed monthly by the U.S. Bureau of Labor Statistics from the prices of more than 2,300 representative commodities, ranging from raw materials (crude rubber, cotton, etc.) to manufactured products. Like most price indexes, the wholesale price index weights products by their importance (in terms of the dollar value of shipments) and compares prices to those of a given base year, expressing current prices as a percentage of prices in that year. In addition to the all-commodities index, component indexes are constructed by stage of processing, durability of product, and industry groups and subgroups. A major deficiency of the wholesale price index, the oldest continuously published price index in the United States, is the accuracy of the prices on which it is based. Current prices are ob-

Fig. 87. Relative importance of commodities included in the wholesale price index, December 1969

By Industry

Farm products	10.7
Processed foods and feeds	16.5
Textile products and apparel	7.1
Hides, skins, leather, and related products	1.3
Fuels and related products, and power	6.8
Chemicals and allied products	5.9
Rubber and plastic products	2.4
Lumber and wood products	2.7
Pulp, paper, and allied products	4.8
Metals and metal products	13.4
Machinery and equipment	12.3
Furniture and household durables	3.5
Nonmetallic mineral products	3.1
Transportation equipment	7.2
Miscellaneous products	2.5
Total	100.0

By Stage of Processing

Crude materials for further processing	11.3	
Foodstuffs and feedstuffs		7.5
Nonfood materials except fuel		2.9
Crude fuel		0.8
Intermediate materials, supplies, and components	44.8	
Materials and components for manufacturing		24.8
Materials and components for construction		9.3
Processed fuels and lubricants		2.6
Containers		1.6
Supplies		6.5
Finished goods (including raw foods and fuel)	43.9	
Consumer goods		33.8
Producer finished goods		10.1
Total	100.0	

Source: W. H. Wallace, *Measuring Price Changes*, 2d ed. (Federal Reserve Bank of Richmond, 1972).

tained monthly by questionnaire, but frequently the prices quoted are list or spot prices quoted by manufacturers or trade associations rather than contract prices at which the commodities are actually traded.

wholesale sales The dollar value of goods sold to retailers, jobbers, and business firms (rather than to consumers), an important COINCIDENT INDICATOR of economic activity at an intermediate stage of distribution. Wholesale data frequently are combined with manufacturing and retail sales data (together called *manufacturing and trade sales*) in order to give a meaningful picture of total sales volume for given periods, but this may create problems of overlap, with the same figures being counted twice. Thus wholesale sales must exclude transactions by manufacturers' sales offices, for example, because these already are included in manufacturing sales. Data on wholesale sales are compiled

Fig. 88. Business sales and inventories (seasonally adjusted rates; in millions of dollars)

Period	Total Business[1] Sales[2]	Total Business[1] Inventories[3]	Wholesale Sales[2]	Wholesale Inventories[3]	Retail Sales[2] Total	Retail Sales[2] Durable goods stores	Retail Sales[2] Non-durable goods stores	Retail Inventories[3] Total	Retail Inventories[3] Durable goods stores	Retail Inventories[3] Non-durable goods stores	Inventory-Sales Ratio[4] Total business[1]	Inventory-Sales Ratio[4] Retail
1970	104,736	175,561	20,583	27,290	31,294	9,524	21,770	46,626	20,345	26,281	1.64	1.47
1971	112,315	184,711	22,327	29,695	34,071	10,985	23,086	52,571	23,864	28,707	1.61	1.47
1972	124,289	197,692	24,862	32,817	37,365	12,472	24,893	57,156	26,056	31,100	1.53	1.46
1973	143,823	224,401	30,400	38,302	41,943	14,190	27,754	65,229	29,593	35,636	1.46	1.46
1974	163,991	271,050	37,344	46,564	44,815	13,943	30,872	74,082	34,649	39,433	1.50	1.54
1975	168,009	264,770	36,583	45,115	48,702	15,060	33,642	73,081	33,592	39,489	1.59	1.49
1975: June	165,877	263,749	36,186	44,850	48,652	15,006	33,646	70,840	31,909	38,931	1.59	1.46
July	169,007	263,345	36,567	44,653	49,411	15,372	34,039	71,503	32,270	39,233	1.56	1.45
Aug	172,150	264,662	37,166	45,501	49,774	15,410	34,364	72,578	33,324	39,254	1.54	1.46
Sept	173,448	265,087	37,604	45,625	49,644	15,417	34,227	73,049	33,471	39,578	1.53	1.47
Oct	174,847	266,867	37,449	45,715	49,995	15,772	34,223	74,642	33,813	40,829	1.53	1.49
Nov	174,085	266,064	37,018	45,554	50,552	15,904	34,648	73,839	33,712	40,127	1.53	1.46
Dec	176,259	264,770	37,360	45,115	51,283	16,239	35,044	73,081	33,592	39,489	1.50	1.43
1976: Jan	179,027	266,285	38,159	45,645	51,592	16,730	34,862	73,610	33,510	40,100	1.49	1.43
Feb	182,329	267,979	38,816	46,307	52,601	17,397	35,204	74,344	33,490	40,854	1.47	1.41
Mar	185,488	269,637	39,094	46,398	53,344	17,403	35,941	75,089	33,920	41,169	1.45	1.41
Apr	187,074	270,599	39,530	46,826	53,696	18,046	35,650	75,652	33,994	41,658	1.45	1.41
May	186,341	272,548	39,386	47,799	52,868	17,419	35,449	75,710	33,936	41,774	1.46	1.43
June	188,944	275,999	40,853	48,417	53,847	17,751	36,096	76,671	34,150	42,521	1.46	1.42
July					53,205	17,435	35,770					

[1]The term "business" also includes manufacturing.
[2]Monthly average for year and total for month.
[3]Book value, end of period, seasonally adjusted.
[4]For annual periods, ratio of weighted average inventories to average monthly sales; for monthly data, ratio of inventories at end of month to sales for month.
Source: U.S. Department of Commerce.

monthly by the U.S. Bureau of the Census on the basis of a survey of wholesalers, which includes only MERCHANT WHOLESALERS in the sample.

Wicksell, Knut A Swedish economist (1851–1926) who is remembered chiefly for his work in monetary theory, his views on the business cycle, and his theory of interest. Considering the question of why prices rise or fall, Wicksell concluded that when the central bank sets too low a market rate of interest, saving is discouraged (not enough interest can be earned), spending increases, and therefore overall prices rise. Conversely, when the interest rate is too high, people will save more and spend less, and prices will fall. Only when the interest rate is equal to the marginal productivity of capital—which Wicksell called the *natural interest rate*—will saving and investment be balanced (for marginal productivity of capital, see explanation

under PRODUCTIVITY). Then prices will remain stable, and the violent ups and downs of the business cycle will end. In his stress of the important role of overall saving and investment and the cumulative process of business expansion and contraction, Wicksell is considered a forerunner of J. M. KEYNES.

Wiener, Norbert See under CYBERNETICS.

Wieser, Friedrich von An Austrian economist (1851–1926), disciple and successor of Carl Menger at the University of Vienna, and member of the MARGINALIST SCHOOL. The first to use the term "marginal utility" (in German, *Grenznutzen*) for Menger's concept, Wieser contrasted "natural value," which is based on the marginal utility of goods, with "exchange value," which is based on both marginal utility and purchasing power. Not content with considering value a subjective concept, Wieser regarded cost of production as a subjective factor as well, formulating his OPPORTUNITY COST principle (sometimes called *Wieser's law of costs*). Whenever an entrepreneur incurs cost in order to produce a given item, said Wieser, he is giving up the opportunity to use capital and raw materials to make some other, alternative item. For example, in the long run the cost of producing more houses may be producing fewer tractors, just as buying a steak dinner today may mean giving up next week's trip to the circus.

wildcat bank   In the 19th-century United States, a bank that issued far more bank notes than it could redeem. The bank usually was part of a branch banking system in which each branch could make or collect a loan but only the so-called main office would redeem notes in specie. That main office was in some backwoods location populated by wildcats and other wild life (hence the name); in other words, it did not in fact exist, and the notes were unredeemable. Common in such states as Michigan and Wisconsin, wildcat banking was effectively eliminated by the National Banking Act of 1863, which set up reserve requirements (see NATIONAL BANKS).

wildcat strike   See under STRIKE.

will   A written document that provides for the distribution of the writer's property after his or her death. The writer is called a *testator* (or *testatrix*); a gift of personal property by will is a *legacy* or *bequest*, and the recipient is a *beneficiary* or *legatee*; a gift of real property by will is a *devise*, and the recipient a *devisee*. A will transfers no interest in property until the testator's death, and it may be revoked by the testator at any time. In the United States each state has different laws concerning how wills must be drawn up in order to be valid, what and how real and personal property may be distributed, and what becomes of property if the owner dies *intestate* (without making a will). The acceptance of a will as valid by the proper authority is called *probate*, and until a will is probated it has no legal force.

windfall   An unanticipated sizable profit or other gain, such as an unexpected inheritance, rise in stock prices, etc.

wire house   A member firm of a STOCK EXCHANGE that maintains a communications network linking its own branch offices, the offices of correspondent firms, or a combination of such offices, both with one another and with the exchange.

withdrawal   The removal of money or valuables from a bank or other place of deposit; the opposite of DEPOSIT, def. 1.

withholding tax   A system of collecting the U.S. Federal INCOME TAX whereby money is periodically deducted from an employee's paycheck and forwarded to the Treasury. At the end of the year, the taxpayer files the withholding tax receipts with his or her income tax statement, and in case of overpayment, can ask for a cash refund or apply the amount involved to future taxes. Self-employed and professional persons usually estimate their total taxable income for the coming year and pay it in quarterly installments. Begun during World War II, the withholding tax system makes the Federal government a preferred creditor (over other creditors), reduces the possibility of tax evasion, and simplifies tax collection. For the taxpayer, it represents a kind of pay-as-you-go or installment plan of taxation, so that taxes are more or less paid by year's end even if all other income has been spent.

Wobblies   See INDUSTRIAL WORKERS OF THE WORLD.

womanpower   The female LABOR FORCE.

Women's Bureau   An agency within the Employment Standards Administration of the U.S. Department of Labor concerned with promoting the welfare of wage-earning women, improving their work conditions, increasing their efficiency, advancing their professional employment opportunities, and similar efforts.

word   In a COMPUTER, a unit of information made up of a predetermined number of bits that may be processed as a whole unit in arithmetic operations (see under BINARY for explanation of *bit*). Computers generally process single-word and double-word (or "double-precision") operations.

work ethic See PROTESTANT ETHIC.

working capital Also, *net current assets, net working capital*. In finance and accounting, the excess of a company's current assets over its current liabilities—that is, cash plus accounts receivable plus inventory minus the sum of accounts payable plus accrued liabilities and short-term loans. The ability of a company to meet its obligations, expand its volume, and take advantage of favorable opportunities is at least partly determined by the amount of working capital it has available. See also under BALANCE SHEET.

working class A very general term used for unskilled or semiskilled laborers who work for a wage. See BLUE-COLLAR; GRAY-COLLAR; PROLETARIAT.

working control In theory, ownership of 51 per cent of a corporation's voting stock. In practice, however, effective control sometimes can be achieved—especially in large corporations—by ownership of much less than half the voting stock, either individually or by a group acting together.

working papers
 1. An official statement required by a minor in some states of the United States in order to be allowed to work. It normally includes a statement by parents or guardian and by school authorities to the effect that the child has permission to work.
 2. In accounting, the notes, memoranda, schedules, and other detailed data prepared by an auditor while examining books of account, to be used as a basis of the final audit report.

work in process Also, *goods in process, in-process inventory*. The partly finished products of a manufacturing or processing concern. Cost accountants normally include in such inventories the cost of direct materials and direct labor, plus a portion of indirect costs. In some cases, however, work in process is valued at either cost or market, whichever is lower.

workmen's compensation Payment by employers to workers or their families for work-related injuries or disease. American employers usually buy insurance to cover their liability in this regard (in some states such insurance is compulsory). Workmen's compensation is administered by state laws and thus varies from state to state as to the extent of coverage and other details. By establishing employer liability, however, such laws have led to significant improvements in the safety of working conditions (the first workmen's compensation law was passed in 1902 by Maryland, a law subsequently declared unconstitutional). Owing in large measure to the influence of President Theodore Roosevelt, who was instrumental in the enactment of workmen's compensation for Federal employees in 1908, workmen's compensation laws were passed in 30 states between 1910 and 1915 (and were upheld as constitutional by the Supreme Court in 1917), and in time they were passed by all other states as well.

work rules Minimum standards of conduct or performance that are required of all employees in an enterprise. Such rules may pertain to beginning and stopping work, rest periods, timekeeping, insubordination, smoking in hazardous areas, reporting injuries, etc. Employees are expected to obey work rules and may be penalized or disciplined for infractions, with penalties ranging from warnings to dismissal. Work rules often are incorporated in labor contracts.

work sampling Also, *ratio-delay study*. A detailed analysis of a job that does not lend itself to a TIME AND MOTION STUDY but for which some performance standards are desired. In work sampling, the job is broken up into its components and is observed at random intervals, for example, once every hour, with the precise minute of the hour selected from a table of random numbers. From this one can calculate just how much time is being spent on what element of the job. The accuracy of the results depends on the number of observations made; several thousand will give a more accurate

Fig. 89. Ratio-delay study of secretaries' performance

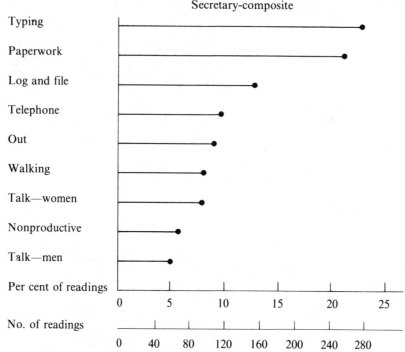

Results of work sampling of ten buyers' secretaries enable comparison of individual secretary with the average.

Source: D. S. Ammer, *Materials Management,* 3d ed. (Homewood, Ill.: Richard D. Irwin, Inc., 1974), p. 637. Reprinted by permission.

result than a few hundred. The accuracy of the data can be measured using the formula

$$\sigma = \sqrt{\frac{p\,(1-p)}{n}}$$

where σ stands for the STANDARD DEVIATION for an event that occurred p per cent (expressed as a decimal) of n number of observations. Suppose, for example, a buyer was found attending a meeting 1,000 times out of 10,000 observations. Here $p = 10$ per cent, or .10, and

$$\sigma = \sqrt{\frac{.10\,(1 - .10)}{10,000}} = \sqrt{\frac{.09}{10,000}} = .003 = 0.3\%$$

Since 3 standard deviations embrace 99.72 per cent of a NORMAL DISTRIBUTION, it is more than 99 per cent certain that the buyer spends at least 9.1 per cent of the time $[10\% - (3 \times 0.3\%)]$ and not more

than 10.9 per cent of the time $[10\% + (3 \times 0.3\%)]$ attending meetings. Work sampling is particularly useful for clerical and other nonrepetitive jobs that require but a modicum of skill. It is less practical for jobs where the most efficient person may be one who appears to be doing nothing much of the time, because he or she has completed the routine, observable aspects of the job with dispatch and spends more time thinking (about cost-cutting measures, product improvements, new markets, etc.).

Works Progress Administration Also, *WPA, Works Projects Administration.* A Federal public works program enacted by law in 1935 to provide work for Americans who needed it and which, during the next seven years, employed a total of about 8.5 million persons. Among their accomplishments were the construction of thousands of public buildings and bridges, several hundred airports, and thousands of miles of new roads and sewers, as well as parks, playgrounds, reservoirs, and other construction. Critics maintained that the program was wasteful and inefficient ($10.5 billion was spent in all), was politically motivated, and did not do away with unemployment. Supporters said it saved the self-respect of unemployed workers who, because of it, did not have to accept charity, and that it accomplished considerable needed work.

World Bank See INTERNATIONAL BANK FOR RECONSTRUCTION AND DEVELOPMENT.

world trade See INTERNATIONAL TRADE.

write-down In accounting, to reduce the recorded value of an asset in order to allow for depreciation, or to adjust to the current market, or for some other reason. In practice, a portion of an asset account is transferred to an expense account or to profit and loss. For example, if a company produces an inventory of yo-yos at a cost of 50 cents each, it would write these down to 35 cents if yo-yos could be sold for only 35 cents, charging the

15-cent loss either to retained earnings or to current profits.

write-off In accounting, removal of a bad debt or worthless asset by reducing its value to zero. Usually the records are balanced by adding the amount of the loss to an account set up for bad debts, or by deducting the loss from earnings during the current accounting period or previous periods (by deducting it from retained earnings).

write-up In accounting, an increase in the recorded value of an asset. Write-ups often are made to make a company's financial position appear more favorable.

W-2 form The annual wage and tax statement all American employers must furnish to their employees, indicating the amounts of Federal income tax, compensation, contributions to social security or other insurance, and state tax (if any) withheld. A copy of this statement must be attached to the employee's Federal and state income tax returns.

yardstick The rates charged by one business used as a measure for setting other rates. In the 1930s in the United States, the rates charged by public power projects often were set forth as a yardstick to measure the propriety of private rates. Critics of this policy point out that public and private projects are not really comparable in terms of cost and other factors, but for many years the rates set by the Tennessee Valley Authority (TVA; see under PUBLIC POWER PROJECT) were in fact used in this way.

year-end dividend An EXTRA DIVIDEND paid at the end of the fiscal year. Some companies pay such dividends only rarely, after an exceptionally profit-

able year; others do so regularly, paying deliberately small regular dividends in order to allow for a year-end dividend.

yellow-dog contract An agreement to the effect that a new employee would refrain from joining a union, which employers fighting unionization forced workers to sign. The Norris–La Guardia Act of 1932 made such contracts unenforceable.

yield
  1. Also, *return.* The rate of return on any investment, expressed as a percentage. For example, a stock bought for $100 that pays a dividend of $5 per year is said to yield—or have a dividend

yield—of 5 per cent per year (5 ÷ 100). It makes no difference if the stock sells for $80 or $120 at the end of that year; so long as the $5 dividend is paid it still represents a yield of 5 per cent to the original purchaser. If the dividend goes up to $5.75, however, the stock will yield $5\frac{3}{4}$ per cent. Similarly, a bond bought for $10,000 that pays interest of $50 per year is said to yield 5 per cent.

2. *current yield.* The dollar amount of interest per year divided by the current market price of the the investment. For example, if a $1,000 bond paying 6 per cent interest per year has a market value of $950, current yield is $60 ÷ $95 = 6.31 per cent. See also RETURN, def. 1.

3. *maturity yield, yield to maturity.* The rate of return on a long-term investment, such as a bond, taking into consideration its purchase price and redemption value, the total of annual interest payments, and the time period until maturity. Suppose an investor pays $900 for a $1,000 bond with a $7\frac{7}{8}$ coupon that matures in 20 years. The current yield (see def. 2 above) is $8\frac{3}{4}$ per cent (7.875 ÷ 9). In addition, the investor will receive $100 more when the bond matures (because its face value is $1,000). If the discounted value of this $100 is added to the current yield, a *bond yield table* will show that maturity yield of this bond is 8.95 per cent. Bond yield tables are available at most banks and brokerage offices, and also are printed in financial sources relating to the bond market.

4. *nominal yield.* The rate of return stated on the face of an obligation. For example, a promissory note that promises to repay $100 at the end of a year with 6 per cent interest has a nominal yield of 6 per cent.

yield to maturity See YIELD, def. 3.

York-Antwerp rules An international set of regulations governing maritime shipping, designed to eliminate or help settle disputes arising from losses. They often are incorporated in shipping contracts.

zero defects A QUALITY CONTROL program that aims for absolutely perfect quality, with no allowance for failures. Originally developed to boost the quality of components used in missiles and spacecraft, the concept of zero defects is based on the idea that a product's quality depends on the motivation of those who make it. If suppliers know that inspectors are willing to accept a defect rate of 4 or 5 per cent, they probably will deliver at least that many defective items, and in all likelihood even more. If the goal is a defect rate of zero and management works hard to make suppliers adhere to this high standard, the defect rate may not be zero but probably will tend to be lower than otherwise.

zero population growth See under POPULATION, def. 1.

Zollverein The German word for CUSTOMS UNION, specifically referring to a series of customs unions established among various German states in the 19th century. In 1818 Prussia abolished internal tariffs and began the formation of a North German Zollverein. In 1828 two similar organizations were formed, the South German Zollverein (Bavaria and Württemberg) and the Central German Trade Union (Hesse-Darmstadt). In 1833 all three merged into the German Zollverein, which eliminated tariffs among its members, instituted a common, uniform tariff against nonmembers, and collected joint customs at the frontiers. The following year a rival body, the Steuerverein of central Germany, was organized, but by 1854 it had joined the German Zollverein, which by then included Luxembourg and all the German states except Mecklenburg and the Hanseatic towns. During this period uniform currency and weights and measures were instituted, effecting a large degree of economic unification among the members.

zone pricing See under DELIVERED PRICING.

zoning The establishment of districts in which manufacturing enterprises, warehouses, retail establishments, and various kinds of residence (highrise, one-family, two-family, etc.) may be located. As a result, the various kinds of building and business may be erected and operated only in specifically zoned areas. Zoning normally is the province of local government authorities (in the United States, a town planning board, city zoning commission, etc.) and is intended to provide optimum convenience, beauty, etc. for residents and protect property values.

Selected Bibliography

BARAN, PAUL A. *The Political Economy of Growth.* New York: Monthly Review Press, 1957.

BERLE, A. A., JR. *Twentieth Century Capitalist Revolution.* New York: Harcourt, Brace, 1954.

———, and C. GARDNER MEANS. *The Modern Corporation and Private Property.* New York: Macmillan, 1933.

BEVERIDGE, WILLIAM L. *Full Employment in a Free Society.* New York: W. W. Norton, 1945.

BENTHAM, JEREMY. *An Introduction to the Principles of Morals and Legislation.* New York: Hafner, 1948 (orig. pub. 1780).

BERNSTEIN, EDUARD. *Evolutionary Socialism.* Trans. E. C. Harvey. New York: Huebsch, 1909.

BLANC, LOUIS. *Organization of Work,* Trans. M. P. Dickoré. Cincinnati: University of Cincinnati Press, 1911 (orig. pub. 1839).

BÖHM-BAWERK, EUGEN VON. *The Positive Theory of Capital.* Trans. W. Smart. London: Macmillan, 1891 (orig. pub. 1888).

CANTILLON, RICHARD. *Essai sur la nature du commerce en général.* London: Macmillan, 1931 (orig. pub. 1755; in French and English).

CAREY, HENRY C. *Principles of Social Science.* 3 vols. Philadelphia: Lippincott, 1888 (orig. pub. 1858).

CASSEL, GUSTAV. *The Theory of Social Economy.* Trans. S. L. Barron. Rev. ed. New York: Harcourt, Brace, 1932.

CHAMBERLIN, EDWIN H. *The Theory of Monopolistic Competition.* 8th ed. Cambridge, Mass.: Harvard University Press, 1957.

CLARK, JOHN BATES. *The Distribution of Wealth.* New York: Macmillan, 1899.

CLARK, JOHN MAURICE. *Alternative to Serfdom.* New York: Knopf, 1948.

———. *Studies in the Economics of Overhead Costs.* Chicago: University of Chicago Press, 1923.

COMMONS, JOHN R. *Institutional Economics.* New York: Macmillan, 1934.

———, ed. *History of Labor in the United States.* 2 vols. New York: Macmillan, 1918.

——— et al. *A Documentary History of American Industrial Society.* 10 vols. Cleveland, 1910.

COURNOT, AUGUSTIN. *Researches into the Mathematical Principles of the Theory of Wealth.* Trans. N. T. Bacon. New York: Macmillan, 1927 (orig. pub. 1838).

EDGEWORTH, FRANCIS Y. *Mathematical Psychics.* London: Kegan Paul, 1881.

FISHER, IRVING. *The Money Illusion.* New York: Adelphi, 1928.

———. *The Theory of Interest.* New York: Macmillan, 1930.

FOURIER, CHARLES. *Theory of Social Organization.* New York: Somerby, 1876 (orig. pub. 1822).

FRIEDMAN, MILTON. *Capitalism and Freedom.* Chicago: University of Chicago Press, 1962.

———. *Optimum Quantity of Money and Other Essays.* Chicago: Aldine, 1969.

GALBRAITH, JOHN KENNETH. *American Capitalism, The Concept of Countervailing Power.* Boston: Houghton Mifflin, 1952.

———. *The Affluent Society.* Boston: Houghton Mifflin, 1958.

GEORGE, HENRY. *Progress and Poverty.* New York: Schalkenbach Foundation, 1942 (orig. pub. 1879).

GODWIN, WILLIAM. *An Enquiry Concerning Political Justice and Its Influence on General Virtue and Happiness.* 2 vols. New York: Knopf, 1926 (orig. pub. 1793).

HABERLER, GOTTFRIED. *Prosperity and Depression.* Geneva: League of Nations, 1941.

———. *Theory of International Trade.* New York: Macmillan, 1937.

HAMILTON, ALEXANDER. *Papers on Public Credit, Commerce, and Finance.* Ed. S. McKee, Jr. New York: Columbia University Press, 1934.

HANSEN, ALVIN H. *Fiscal Policy and Business Cycles.* New York: W. W. Norton, 1941.

HAWTREY, RALPH GEORGE. *Currency and Credit.* London: Longmans Green, 1919.

HAYEK, FRIEDRICH A. *Monetary Theory and the Trade Cycle.* London: Harcourt, Brace, 1932.

———. *Road to Serfdom.* Chicago: University of Chicago Press, 1944.

HOBSON, J. A. *The Economics of Unemployment.* 2d ed. New York: Macmillan, 1931.

———. *Imperialism.* 3d ed. London: Allen & Unwin, 1938 (orig. pub. 1902).

———. *The Industrial System.* 2d ed. New York: Scribner's, 1910.

JEVONS, WILLIAM STANLEY. *The Theory of Political Economy.* 4th ed. London: Macmillan, 1911 (orig. pub. 1871).

KEYNES, JOHN MAYNARD. *Essays in Biography.* New York: Horizon, 1951.

———. *The General Theory of Employment, Interest and Money.* London: Macmillan, 1936.

———. *A Treatise on Money.* 2 vols. London: Macmillan, 1930.

KNIGHT, FRANK H. *Risk, Uncertainty and Profit.* London: London School of Economics, Reprints of Scarce Tracts, No. 16, 1933 (orig. pub. 1921).

LEONTIEFF, W. W. *The Structure of American Economy, 1919–1939.* 2d ed. New York: Oxford University Press, 1951.

LIST, FRIEDRICH. *National System of Political Economy.* Trans. G. A. Matile. Philadelphia: Lippincott, 1856 (orig. pub. 1841).

MAISEL, SHERMAN J. *Fluctuations, Growth and Forecasting.* New York: John Wiley, 1957.

MALTHUS, THOMAS. *An Essay on the Principle of Population.* London, 1798.

———. *Principles of Political Economy.* New York: Kelley, 1951 (orig. pub. 1820).

MARSHALL, ALFRED. *Principles of Economics.* 8th ed. London: Macmillan, 1920 (orig. pub. 1890).

MARX, KARL. *Capital.* 3 vols. Trans. S. Moore, E. Aveling, E. Untermann. Chicago: Kerr, 1906–9 (orig. pub. 1867–95).

MENGER, CARL. *Principles of Economics.* Trans. J. Dingwall, B. F. Hoselitz. New York: Free Press, 1950 (orig. pub. 1871).

MILL, JOHN STUART. *Autobiography.* London, 1873.

———. *Principles of Political Economy.* London: Longmans Green, 1920 (orig. pub. 1848).

MITCHELL, WESLEY C. *The Backward Art of Spending Money, and Other Essays.* New York: Kelley, 1950 (orig. pub. 1912–36).

———. *Business Cycles: The Problem and Its Setting.* New York: National Bureau of Economic Research, 1927.

MUN, THOMAS. *England's Treasure by Forraign Trade.* New York: Macmillan, 1895 (orig. pub. c. 1630).

MURRAY, PHILIP, AND M. L. COOKE. *Organized Labor and Production.* New York: Harper, 1940.

MYRDAL, GUNNAR. *Beyond the Welfare State.* New Haven: Yale University Press, 1960.

———. *Rich Lands and Poor.* New York: Harper, 1957.

NEUMANN, JOHN VON, and OSKAR MORGENSTERN. *Theory of Games and Economic Behavior.* Princeton: Princeton University Press, 1944.

NORTH, DUDLEY. *Discourses upon Trade.* Baltimore: Johns Hopkins Press, 1907 (orig. pub. 1691).

NURKSE, RAGNAR. *Problems of Capital Formation in Underdeveloped Countries.* New York: Oxford University Press, 1953.

OWEN, ROBERT. *A New View of Society and Other Writings.* London: Dent, 1927 (written 1813–21).

PETTY, WILLIAM. *Economic Writings.* 2 vols. Cambridge: At the University Press, 1899.

PIGOU, A. C. *The Economics of Welfare.* 4th ed. London: Macmillan, 1932 (orig. pub. 1920).

PROUDHON, PIERRE-JOSEPH. *General Idea of the Revolution in the Nineteenth Century.* Trans. J. B. Robinson. London: Freedom Press, 1923 (orig. pub. 1851).

———. *What Is Property?* Trans. B. R. Tucker. London: Reeves, n.d. (orig. pub. 1840).

RICARDO, DAVID. *Works and Correspondence.* 10 vols. Ed. Piero Sraffa, Cambridge: At the University Press, 1951–55.

ROBERTSON, DENNIS H. *Essays in Monetary Theory.* London: Staples Press, 1948.

——. *Money.* 6th ed. New York: Pitman, 1948.

ROBINSON, JOAN. *The Economics of Imperfect Competition.* London: Macmillan, 1933.

ROSCHER, WILLIAM. *Principles of Political Economy,* 2 vols. Trans. J. J. Lalor. New York: Holt, 1878 (orig. pub. 1854).

ROSTOW, WALT W. *The Stages of Economic Growth.* Cambridge: At the University Press, 1960.

SAINT-SIMON, COMTE DE. *Selected Writings.* Ed. F. M. H. Markham. Oxford: Blackwell, 1952.

SAY, JEAN BAPTISTE. *A Treatise on Political Economy.* 2 vols. Trans. C. R. Prinsep. Boston: Wells & Lilly, 1821 (orig. pub. 1803).

SCHUMPETER, JOSEPH A. *Capitalism, Socialism, and Democracy.* 3d ed. New York: Harper, 1950.

——. *Ten Great Economists.* New York: Oxford University Press, 1951.

——. *The Theory of Economic Development.* Trans. R. Opie. New York: Oxford University Press, 1961 (orig. pub. 1911).

SENIOR, NASSAU. *An Outline of the Science of Political Economy.* New York: Kelley, 1951 (orig. pub. 1836).

SISMONDI, SIMONDE DE. *Political Economy and the Philosophy of Government.* New York: Chapman, 1847 (orig. pub. 1826–37).

SLICHTER, SUMNER H. *The Challenge of Industrial Relations.* Ithaca: Cornell University Press, 1947.

SMITH, ADAM. *An Inquiry into the Nature and Causes of the Wealth of Nations.* New York: Random House, Modern Library, 1937 (orig. pub. 1776).

SOMBART, WERNER. *The Jews and Modern Capitalism.* Trans. M. Epstein. New York: Free Press, 1951 (orig. pub. 1911).

STIGLER, GEORGE J. *Production and Distribution Theories.* New York: Macmillan, 1941.

TAUSSIG, F. W. *Some Aspects of the Tariff Question.* Rev. ed. Cambridge: Harvard University Press, 1931.

TAWNEY, R. H. *Religion and the Rise of Capitalism.* New York: Harcourt, Brace, 1926.

TURGOT, ANNE ROBERT JACQUES. *Reflections on the Formation and Distribution of Riches.* New York: Macmillan, 1898 (orig. pub. 1766).

VEBLEN, THORSTEIN. *The Engineers and the Price System.* New York: Viking, 1947 (orig. pub. 1921).

——. *The Instinct of Workmanship.* New York: Huebsch, 1918 (orig. pub. 1914).

——. *The Theory of Business Enterprise.* New York: Scribner, 1904.

——. *The Theory of the Leisure Class.* New York: Random House, Modern Library, 1934 (orig. pub. 1899).

WALRAS, LÉON. *Elements of Pure Economics.* Trans. W. Jaffé. Homewood Ill.: Irwin, 1954 (orig. pub. 1874, 1877).

WEBB, SIDNEY, and BEATRICE WEBB. *The Decay of Capitalist Civilization.* New York: Harcourt, Brace, 1923.

WEBER, MAX. *The Protestant Ethic and the Spirit of Capitalism.* Trans. T. Parsons. London: Allen & Unwin, 1930 (orig. pub. 1904–5).

WICKSELL, KURT. *Lectures on Political Economy.* 2 vols. Trans. E. Classen. London: Routledge, 1934–35 (orig. pub. 1901, 1906).

WIENER, NORBERT. *The Human Use of Human Beings.* New York: Cambridge University Press, 1950.

WIESER, FRIEDRICH VON. *Natural Value.* Trans. C. A. Malloch. London: Macmillan, 1893 (orig. pub. 1889).

——. *Social Economics.* Trans. A. F. Hinrichs. New York: Adelphi, 1917 (orig. pub. 1914).